World Religions

AN INTRODUCTION FOR STUDENTS

The Sussex Library of Religious Beliefs and Practices

<u>Published</u>

Sikhism   W. Owen Cole and Piara Sing Sambhi

Hinduism   Jeaneane Fowler

The Jews   Alan Unterman

<u>Forthcoming</u>

Buddhism   *Christian Theology*   *The Diversity of Christianity Today*

Bhagavad Gita (a student's commentary)   *Confucianism*   *Humanism*

The Ancient Egyptians   *Islam*   *Jainism*   *Taoism*   *Zen*

Zoroastrianism

This series is intended for students of religion, social sciences and history, and for the interested layperson. It is concerned with the beliefs and practices of religions in their social, cultural and historical setting.

<u>Other religious titles of interest</u>

Confucianism and Christianity: A Comparative Study of Jen and Agape   Xinzhong Yao

The Bible as Theatre
Theatre and Holy Spirit   Shimon Levy

Jainism: The World of Conquerors (2 volumes)   Natubhai Shah

The Supreme Doctrine: Psychological Studies in Zen Thought   Hubert Benoit, with Forewords by Aldous Huxley and Tim Barrett

Hinduism: Perspectives of Reality   Jeaneane Fowler

Glimpses of the Divine: A Spiritual Anthology for Use on Every Day of the Year
Cyril Bulley

World Religions

AN INTRODUCTION FOR STUDENTS

Jeaneane Fowler, Merv Fowler,
David Norcliffe, Nora Hill,
and Diane Watkins

sussex
ACADEMIC
PRESS

2 4 6 8 10 9 7 5 3 1

First published 1997 in Great Britain by
SUSSEX ACADEMIC PRESS
Box 2950
Brighton BN2 5SP

and in the United States of America by
SUSSEX ACADEMIC PRESS
c/o International Specialized Book Services, Inc.
5804 N.E. Hassalo St.
Portland, Oregon 97213–3644

British Library Cataloguing in Publication Data

A CIP catalogue record for this book is available from the British Library.

Library of Congress Cataloging-in-Publication Data

World religions : an introduction for students / Jeaneane Fowler . . .
[et al.]
p.   cm.
Includes bibliographical references (p.   ) and index.
ISBN 1–898723–48–6 (hc : alk. paper)
ISBN 1–898723–49–4 (pbk)
1. Religions.   I. Fowler, Jeaneane D.
BL80.2.W656   1997
291—dc21   97–34865
CIP

Printed and bound in Great Britain by
Bookcraft (Bath) Ltd., Midsomer Norton, Somerset

Contents

Foreword

The first principle that has to be adopted by anyone asked to write a foreword for a book is: do I respect the academic integrity of its authors, and, in this case, do I recogise their professional expertise in writing for the audience for which it is intended. My answer in both cases is yes. That is why I am now writing this piece, which should act as a guarantee of the value of the substance and guidance of the book as a whole.

The approach taken is interesting and to be valued. The study of religion has come a long way from its beginnings. Originally understood as largely or even wholly as a scriptural investigation it has blossomed into the study of people, groups and communities who still unite under the banner of specific traditions. We might say that originally we began by studying "other" texts from a western perspective (understanding that term as having colonial and patronising connotations). We now recognise that in the diversity of world views (and world views within world views) we have to be more humble in our attitudes, we have much to learn.

Also there is the question of what we are actually studying. This understanding has shifted significantly from the recognition of the written word to the importance of the meaning of faith in the lives of believers. Even as I write I recognise the contestability of my latter assertion by some who are the subjects of study. Thus we come to recognise the fluidity of such an enquiry and the shifting ground on which we walk.

Given this there is a need to establish some appropriate framework for enquiry for those embarking on the perilous adventure of engaging with those who attempt to live out their faith. This study does just that, never by engaging in simplification to the point of erroneous stereotyping, nor by providing a plethora of information that cannot be cohered to establish a recognised identity.

What should be understood as the aim of such a book? In my view it is simple and succinct: that after reading, wrestling with and imbibing these accounts you are competent to meet with those who represent religious groups and properly engage in conversation to mutual benefit, both as individuals and to the betterment of society.

This book fulfils that role and deserves to be returned to as understanding grows.

With regard to the expressed purpose, in the introduction, of serving future teachers of our next generation, we need to be clear as to professional responsibilities. In a recent period in which teachers have, to say the least, not been supported, and in which religious education has been inadequately resourced, we must be assertive and knowledgeable about our social responsibilities. Religious education is not just about the delivery of information but the engagement of minds, those of young people in our charge, those of believers in religious communities represented in our nation(s) and we must also engage with our own mind in both the cognitive and affective sense. There is a need for a change of attitudes amongst the majority of our population toward the minorities in our population. This book serves that cause, and I hope it will be widely read and digested by those engaged in the study of religions, religious education and beyond.

Clive Erricker
Head of the School of Religion and Theology,
University College of Chichester

Preface and Acknowledgments

Religious Education has not, in the past, enjoyed an honored position in the post-modern educational curriculum, other than in a few, rare, establishments. The confessional approach to its delivery, the solely scriptural basis to its content, and the lack of diverse application in terms of pupil and student learning outcomes, contributed to make the study of religion a generally unexciting one for many students. But times have changed radically and *Religious Studies* – the study of religion – is becoming a very dynamic subject, exploring a multiplicity of dimensions under the broad gamut of the term *religion*. It is in the light of these changes that this book has been written. The study of world religions has lent a vibrancy to the subject area and has created a need for foundational material particularly to encourage and support those approaching the subject for the first time. These readers will be students, as well as those teachers who, given the wider curricular expectations of the subject, need some understanding of the religions presented here – Judaism, Christianity, Islam, Hinduism, Buddhism and Sikhism. There are also many students who, while specializing in one or two of these religions in the past, find themselves ignorant of others – a position in which many of the students embarking on Religious Studies courses in our own University find themselves. While the approach of many books to a particular religion is often a wholly historical one, this is not our purpose here, for this book is, in the main, concerned with living religion, examining the beliefs and practices of the adherents of the religions.

The authors have worked together at the University of Wales College, Newport in the department of Philosophy and Religious Studies for a number of years. The team has extensive experience in teaching world religions to those students training for teaching, to serving teachers, to undergraduate students who are interested in the study of religion as a non-vocational, academic subject, as well as to post-graduate students, with some students engaged in doctoral research. But at the same time, all the authors are qualified teachers with experience of teaching all ages from infants to mature undergraduates and postgraduates. This book thus represents a team project which will inform both our own teaching and facilitate that in other educational establishments.

In recent years we have gained many friends in the religious communities of South Wales, and some of these are featured on the front cover of this book. Regrettably, one dear friend, Eze Nathan, who, with his wife Nina, has been responsible for welcoming hundreds of students in the past to the Orthodox Jewish synagogue in Newport, has died. The term "learning outcomes" is particularly apt when one considers the magnificent art work, craft, written accounts and displays which school children produced at their visits to the synagogue. The authors are grateful to Nina for her outstanding warmth and continued support to our students. In the absence of Eze, it is Eze's family which represents Judaism in the photograph on the front cover of the book, but it is to Eze and his memory that this book is dedicated.

Gurnam Bhogal is an accomplished Sikh *ragi* (musician). For many years he has taught our students at the University about the significance and intricacies of various *rags*. The workshop sessions invite the students to participate and have been an invaluable experience for staff and students – along with practice in the noble art of tying a turban! Gurnam is a member of the Pearl Street *Gurdwara,* Cardiff, where he and his fellow Sikhs have welcomed students for a decade or more at the Sunday service of *diwan*, as well as warmly inviting the sometimes large groups of students to share *langar*.

Brian Gay is both friend and neighbor of two of the authors and is pictured in traditional meditation, *zazen*, of Soto Zen, and wearing the *rakkhusu* of the lay minister. Brian is affiliated to Throssel Hole Buddhist Abbey and is the Abbey's representative on the Network of Buddhist Organizations in the United Kingdom, and on the European Buddhist Union. As a university lecturer for many years, Brian is an excellent speaker and has a rare rapport with students. His talks on Soto Zen Buddhism, and the Order of Buddhist Contemplatives of which he is a very dedicated member, have been greatly appreciated.

Roma Choudhuri is a Hindu and a very accomplished woman. She is a graduate in Indian music and specializes in *Rabindra Sangeet*, the singing of the poems of Rabindranath Tagore. She has written a book in Bengali about his songs, and their particular notation, which has become standard for those studying the songs. She has also contributed to books written in English, on the subject of Hinduism. Her workshops on *alpana*, Indian floor paintings constructed in rice powder, are well known and the television production of *A Day in the Life of Roma Choudhuri*, encapsulates the many dimensions of this remarkable Hindu woman. But above all, she is an excellent teacher, visiting schools, colleges and universities to talk about Hinduism.

Visits to the mosque of the SouthWales Islamic Centre at Cardiff have been well appreciated by staff and students for many years.

Sheikh Said Ismail, as his photograph on the cover suggests, is a scholar and a very erudite speaker, as those who have heard him on radio and television will agree. He has always welcomed students warmly and is a particularly gifted teacher, handling contentious issues with ease and openness and stimulating reflective knowledge amongst the students.

The photograph of the Christian Church-in-Wales minister is of a long-standing friend, the Reverend Christopher Blanchard. Originally Head of Modern Languages in a comprehensive school, he left teaching to become ordained, but has never lost his contact with students and has welcomed them at the beautiful old pre-Reformation church in the picturesque scenery of Patriciou. This is a church remarkable enough to be visited by people from all over the world and Christopher's enthusiasm for his new vocation is combined well with an excellent teaching ability.

The authors would like to express their thanks to these people and the many other friends and communities to whom we owe our gratitude for helpful discussion and valuable contact through the years. We would also like to encourage the readers of this book to explore the possibilities of new friends and acquaintances amongst the different religious communities in their own localities. The authors would also like to acknowledge their debt to the many students whose enthusiasm for world religions make such a book as this a necessity, as well as those students who did such a good job of proof reading in current lectures. Tony Grahame at Sussex Academic Press has been, as always, thoroughly supportive, hardworking, constructively helpful and readily available for advice at all stages of the preparation of this book. Every effort has been made to ensure that there are no errors in the text, but for any which remain, the authors take full responsibility.

University of Wales College, Newport, September 1997

Introduction

To understand the dimensions of religion it is necessary to look beyond the confines of one's immediate culture to the beliefs, practices and rituals of other religions in the world. Only by such an investigation can one hope to gain some impression of what this word religion really means. In approaching religions beyond one's immediate culture it is necessary to be open-minded and tolerant. As Owen Cole once said,[1] when approaching another person's religion you should take off your shoes because the ground on which you are venturing will be holy! The North American Indians have a similar saying: when you first meet someone, you should walk a mile in that person's mocassins before speaking to him or her. This is an apt way of saying that when studying another religion we are dealing with people's dreams and their deepest and most sensitive aspirations and beliefs about life: we need to tread this path with sympathy and empathy.

Religion is conveyed partially by its scriptures. The scriptures of an individual's own culture are more familiar and this often means offensive, strange, or nonsensical incidents are taken for granted; when similar incidents are recounted from other cultures, it can sometimes be hard to reconcile them, let alone approve of them. For example, in the Judeo-Christian scriptures there are elements in the *Old Testament* such as the sacrifice of Jephthah's daughter or the slaughter of thousands of men, women and children in the conquest of Canaan by Joshua which may seem offensive to those of non-Jewish, non-Christian cultures. Similarly, the fratricidal war of the Hindu scriptures, the *Mahabharat* and the *Bhagavad Gita*, may to some also appear offensive. Then, there are aspects which may stretch the bounds of the imagination too far, such as the story of Jonah inside the whale in the Judeo-Christian tradition, the virgin birth of Jesus in the Christian tradition, the birth of the Buddha from his mother's side, and the monkey general Hanuman, increasing so much in size that he is able to leap across the sea from the tip of India to the island of (Sri) Lanka, in the Hindu scripture the *Ramayan*. Most religions have this kind of mythological content and when we meet such elements in other cultures than our own we need to do so without prejudice. Very often such elements have an underlying symbolism or theological point which is far more important than the outward event or myth. In order to understand other world religions we have to learn to see, to interpret and to understand this symbolism.

In all religions there are periods of great spiritual achievement in thought and practice but there are also periods of lower ethical practice. There are times of great humanitarianism but also times when one can point to religion for its total disregard for human life. There are members of some religions that we can admire – the ordinary person as much as the well known – but there are also those who are poor advertisements for their faiths. Such is life. But our purpose here in this book is to understand something of the *essence* of the religions and the way in which those religions affect the life of the individual in the midst of the vicissitudes of life.

Religion is a universal phenomenon: it relates to the way people live their lives *now*, though it has its roots in the past and these are reflected in its scriptures. But essentially religion is about the *living* faith of individuals. The purpose of this book is to examine this living nature of religion, and we shall do so with an open mind. If we want to understand human beings we need to understand their beliefs, their purposes, their ideals, and the important aspects of religion which inform their daily life. And even where an individual is not a practising member of a particular faith, there will be festivals, life-cycle rites and general principles held about life which have a great deal to do with religion. When religion is studied from a multi-faith viewpoint we are able to see how other people have answered, or attempted to answer, the basic problems concerning human existence and its purpose, and we are, to a certain extent, able to share the perspective others have of life. True understanding of *what* people do in religion and *why* they do it, goes a long way to dispelling intolerance and prejudice. Studying other religions, therefore, involves an attempt to *share*, in some measure, the experience of other human beings.

One of the most fascinating aspects of the dimension of religion is its diversity. A child who is asked the question "What is a Christian?" might be forgiven for answering that it is a person who dresses in a navy blue uniform with a strange hat and who plays a brass instrument in the centre of town and sings hymns. If the only experience a person has of a Christian is of a member of the Salvation Army, then he or she might be forgiven for thinking that all Christians are the same! But not only is religion itself diverse, there is often immense diversity within each individual faith, so much so that in some cases total ignorance of someone else's beliefs in the same faith often obtains.

Nevertheless there is today a considerable interest in world religions. We live in a more cosmopolitan world than ever before, in which people from other cultural and religious traditions are educated together, work together or live in the same environment. Sadly, the mutual understanding of cultures does not always occur but the educational scene in some countries is changing in order to take on board the wider perspectives of the dimension of religion. In Britain, for example, the 1988 Education Act required schools to study the principal religious traditions represented in Great Britain and by this it did not mean *Christian* religious traditions but specifically traditions of the major faiths which now inform British society. The six religions presented in this book are generally regarded as those which constitute the principal religions which now need to be taught. Thus, religions such as Jainism, Taoism, and the non-religious stance of Humanism have been excluded for the present, though separate publications here are forthcoming.

It is in the light of such changes in the educational approach to the teaching of Religious Education that this book was written. We have therefore aimed to provide basic information on six major world faiths for those with little or no previous knowledge of each religion, with the purpose of assisting teachers who need the background material to inform their Religious Education curriculum, as well as students who are approaching Religious Studies' courses. It is not meant to be a comparative study of the religions and each religion has therefore been explored discretely. It is also as far as possible a study of *living* religion, what it means to be a Jew, a Christian, Muslim, Hindu, Buddhist and Sikh in the world of today.

While there are many different approaches to the teaching of world religions the format of this book will allow a teacher to approach religion from a thematic angle as well as from the more discrete approach of an individual religion. Themes such as festivals, life-cycle rites, marriage, birth, worship, scriptures and many more can be structured from the relevant sections of each of the religons presented. A theme of *Symbols*, for example, could be informed by a study of Jewish *tefillin*, *tallit*, *mezuzah*, star of David and *menorah*, alongside the symbols found in the Christian churches, the symbols epitomized in the figure of the Buddha, the Hindu *Aum* and *svastika*, the Sikh Five Ks and the Muslim Five Pillars.

The emphasis on *living* religion broadens the horizons of the subject, and can make it colourful and exciting in the context of teaching. Indeed, the historically, scripture-based teaching of the past has given way to an educational approach which is very visual and experiential. Teaching world faiths from the perspective of living religion means that there is a wealth of artefacts which can be the means to allow a more experiential learning situation. In just one area such as religious dress, for example, to be able to examine Jewish *tefillin*, *tallit* and *kippah*, or to discover just how to put on a *sari*, to see and handle the Sikh Five Ks, or to have a Christian minister show pupils or students the varied vestments of the established Church, adds a very different perspective to the study of religion. And the same is the case for other thematic topics, for example, sacred buildings, food, festivals, symbols, famous people, and so on. Then, too, there is the opportunity to visit religious communities. To sit, for example, in a Sikh *gurdwara* listening to the hymns of the Gurus being sung by the *ragis* and to join the Sikhs for *langar* after the main worship, is an experiential way of learning about Sikhism, particularly if it is informed by basic groundwork such as the nature of the *gurdwara*, the Sikh form of worship, the symbols of Sikhism and Sikh dress, and related areas. This book is designed to make such visits to religious communities a more meaningful experience. Indeed, having explored the material in each chapter, the reader should be well equipped to undertake such visits and gain from them a more practical awareness of other faiths through participation rather than mere observation. And most religious communites are only too pleased to extend a very warm welcome to those who take the time to enquire about their faith and worship. Today, too, there is a vast amount of video material to support a "living" religion approach to Religious Education.

The approach taken for each religion is slightly different, but each chapter attempts to convey what is *living* religion as much as possible. The *dimensions* of religion are examined with the expectation that this book will play a part in breaking down barriers of ignorance about belief and practice between one religion and another. The approach taken is mainly a phenomenological one, infused with some historical perspective. A suggested further reading list is given at the end of the book, in addition to a substantial *Glossary* listing the important terms in each of the religions. Also supplied is a comprehensive, though selective, bibliography.

The book is divided into six chapters, each devoted to a specific religion. It begins with Merv Fowler's treatment of *Judaism*. Here, while the diversity of Jewish belief is emphasized, the content concentrates in the main on Orthodox belief and practice since this has been the foundation of most expressions of Judaism. The chapter exemplifies how religion and culture can be synonymous; it does not attempt a detailed historical development of Judaism, which has been almost exclusively the approach applied to this religion in the past. The emphasis is on *living* religion – what it is to be a Jew in the world of today.

The chapter on *Christianity*, written by Nora Hill and Diane Watkins, adopts a more historical approach because it is specifically the historical development of Christianity which highlights its diversity and the means by which this came about. In this religion there is more of a division in terms of religion and culture for many Christians, but this division is less obvious in the case of some of the newer sects in Christianity. The diversity of the Christian religion has led to considerable ignorance of its many strands. Jehovah's Witnesses, for example, may be frequent visitors to our doors, but few could claim to know anything about them. The exploration of the Christian dimension of religion therefore seeks to examine not only "mainstream" denominations, but some of the Christian sects which inform our present society. Those denominations included here exemplify the diversity of the Christian faith. The chapter begins with a historical approach, set out systematically by Nora Hill, who also examines the beliefs and practices of some of the mainstream aspects of Christian denominations today. Diane Watkins then examines some of the lesser well known areas of Christianity – the Eastern Orthodox Churches, Quakers, Jehovah's Witnesses, the Church of Jesus Christ of the Latter-day Saints (the Mormons), and the Church of Christ, Scientist.

David Norcliffe's chapter on Islam emphasizes the central belief of Islam that there is only one God who is an unfathomable Creator beyond human comprehension yet who is revealed to humankind through his prophets and particularly through the medium of the sacred scripture of the *Qur'an*. It is noted, however, that although Muslims try to conform to the injunctions of the *Qur'an*, which are both social and religious in nature (indeed Muslims argue that there is no distinction between these two areas), there is nevertheless considerable diversity between Muslim cultures. The cultural expression of Islam to be found in Indonesia, for example, differs greatly from its expression in the Gulf States, and both of them differ from the way in which Muslims in the West live their lives. Underlying this diversity, however, is belief in the one God and the revelation given through the medium of his prophet, Muhammad, and this lends to Islamic cultural diversity an essential religious unity in the concept of the unity of God and a communal unity in the *ummah*. David Norcliffe presents a view of an essentially *active* religion and one in which everything done in life is an act of worship. The approach taken to the religion is partially historical in its presentation of the life of Muhammad but also phenomenological in its treatment of the aspects of daily life and practice.

Unity underlies most aspects of Hinduism and the chapter on *Hinduism* by Jeaneane Fowler seeks to emphasize this point whilst at the same time demonstrating the immense diversity which is characteristic of the concepts of the divine in its manifested aspects. The chapter concentrates intitially on an examination of the way in which an unmanifest, unified Source can produce the diversity of the concept of the divine in Hinduism which is evident today, then moves on to an examination of the concept of the self, and then to the way in which diverse concepts of the divine inform the wealth of beliefs and practices that are pertinent to Hinduism today. A different approach was adopted in the earlier work (Jeaneane Fowler's *Hinduism: Beliefs and Practices* [Brighton: Sussex Academic Press 1997]); material from this work has been included in this chapter. Accommodation is the norm for Hindu beliefs and practices, and the multiplicity of dimensions to this religion are emphasized. But at the same time the unity of all things which stem from the same Source as an unmanifest Ground of all being is stressed.

The chapter on *Buddhism,* written by Jeaneane Fowler, examines the life and basic teachings of the Buddha, and then the character of Theravada and Mahayana Buddhism. The diversity of belief and practice in the latter is emphasized in an examination of some of the major expressions of Mahayana Buddhism in the Far East and in Tibet. Historical material is largely overlooked here in a desire to concentrate on the diversity of beliefs and practices to be found in the many expressions of Buddhism today. Rather than examine Buddhism country by country, the characteristics which inform Zen, Nichiren Shoshu and Nichiren Daishonin Buddhism, Shingon, Pure Land and Tibetan Buddhism are detailed.

The chapter *Sikhism,* written by Merv Fowler, combines both a historical approach and a phenomenological one. The historical aspect looks at the life of the founder of Sikhism, Guru Nanak and then chronologically deals with the lives of the nine Gurus who followed him, and with their particular contributions to Sikhism. But it is the dynamism of Sikhism today which forms the emphasis of the chapter.

The six religions presented here are designed as an *introduction* for students and teachers who are approaching the subject of Religious Studies for the first time. The authors have not assumed any prior knowledge in presenting the material for each of the religions. The book is thus suitable for introductory courses on world religions at level one in higher education establishments and is particularly intended as a basis of knowledge for student teachers who intend to specialize in Religious Education at primary and secondary levels, as well as practising teachers of Religious Education and world religions. A secondary purpose is to inspire further study and to enable readers to take up more detailed analysis of independent religions in the future.

1

Judaism

Merv Fowler

The Lord bless you and keep you.
The Lord make his face to shine upon you
and be gracious to you.
The Lord lift up his countenance upon you
And give you peace. *Numbers*

When we think of the terms "Christian", "Hindu", "Muslim" and so on, we think of a person who belongs to a particular religious grouping – Christians, Hindus, Muslims – all characterized by the common religious beliefs and practices of the respective religion. The designation "Jew", however, is different, for to think of a Jew or Judaism simply in terms of religion is incorrect (indeed, the words *Judaism* and *religion* do not exist in Hebrew). This is mainly because whereas, for example, a Christian is baptized into Christianity, a Jew is *born* into Judaism and will be a Jew whether or not he or she follows the religious precepts of Judaism. This seems to suggest that to be Jewish is to belong to a particular *race*. Yet this, too, is incorrect, for right from its beginnings Judaism has always been composed of a variety of races, and today there are black Jews, yellow Jews, Nordic Jews and so on. Even to say that Jews are a *people* is misleading, because they are not always a people on their own soil, with their own language. Jews, indeed, are of mixed race, but are held together purely by the fact of being born a Jew, for a Jew is the child of a Jewish mother.[1]

For many Jews there is very much a sense of *belongingness*, a sense of belonging to *Bet Yisrael*, the house of Israel. So being born a Jew usually gives the individual a sense of belonging to the *family* of Jews who are linked together by the bond of Jewishness, no matter where they may be, no matter what language they speak, and no matter what their particular beliefs are.

While many Jews may not be religious at all, for some there is little, if any, separation between religion and culture, particularly within the more orthodox strands of Judaism. This is to say that the daily life of the Jew is also a daily *religious* life. This is seen in terms of what the Jew will or will not eat, what is worn, the many celebrations and festivals, and the special nature of the days between festivals. There is no time, in fact, when the Orthodox Jew, for example, is not practising his or her religion: religion and culture are one. The important linking factor between all practising Jews is the *covenant* which was made between God and his people in the very beginnings of Jewish history. We shall look at this concept of covenant in more detail below, but it is important to note in this context that the covenant binds the Jewish people together now, in the present, just as much as it did so in the past. For this reason the many celebrations and festivals in Judaism provide a powerful bond with past traditions, so powerful in fact, that a Jew does not so much simply remember past events as *reenact* them, and live them again as if he or she had been there in the past. This we shall see when we examine Jewish festivals.

JEWISH SECTS

Before examining the life stance of the Jew, it is important to realize that in the "family" of Judaism there are a number of different sects. Arguably, the most interesting Jewish sect to study is Orthodox Judaism, because of the richness in practice and celebration. Since Orthodox Judaism lies at the root of all the other sects, it is mainly Orthodoxy with which we shall be concerned. However, we need to be aware at the outset of the variety of sects within Judaism, but while there are such divergences, Judaism remains one: marriages between the different sects are, indeed, common. In Israel itself, however, differences in culture and outlook have presented some difficulties, particularly between Eastern and Western Jews whose places of origin are very different indeed. These difficulties will become apparent as we examine the different branches of Judaism.

Sephardic **and** *Ashkenazic* **Jewry** For many centuries Jews have settled in diverse parts of the world, being exposed to diverse cultures and social orders. In the period of the Roman Empire they migrated from Palestine to countries such as France, Spain, Germany, Poland and Russia. This resulted in the emergence of two major cultural streams, the *Sephardic* tradition which included mainly Mediterranean Jews and which owes its name to the medieval Hebrew word for the Iberian Peninsula, *Sefarad*, and the *Ashkenazic* tradition (*Ashkenaz* was the medieval Hebrew for northern France and Germany) which embraced the Jews of northern and eastern Europe.[2] The pronunciation of Hebrew by these two divisions is slightly different, but the Hebrew spoken in Israel follows the *Sephardic* pronunciation.[3]

Orthodox Judaism The term Orthodox is not a designation used by devotees of this form of Judaism when speaking of themselves. Rather, they prefer to describe themselves as "observant" Jews, perhaps because the origins of the word *Orthodox* in Judaism were pejorative. Strictly Orthodox Judaism considers the first five books of the *Bible*, called the *Torah*, to be the divine words of God, and therefore they must be obeyed to the letter. Many Orthodox Jews believe that they should remain separate from the outside world and resist entirely its modernity and challenges to change. They feel that obeying the commandments (*mitzvot*) of the *Torah* has helped them through the many periods of violent persecution in the past. Indeed, the greater the persecution, the more Orthodox Jews immersed themselves in *Torah*, and though such persecution is, mercifully, not so conspicuous today, the practice of immersion in *Torah* is deeply ingrained. Orthodoxy regards itself as the true Judaism, and non-orthodox Jews as sinful Jews (but still Jews nevertheless). For Orthodox Jews, the Law, the *Torah*, affects everything in life – food, dress, work, sex, marriage, family life, inheritance laws and a host of practices in daily life. In fact, Orthodoxy is the official religion of the State of Israel, and such observances as marriage, divorce, family and inheritance laws in Israel, as well as observance of the Sabbath, still come under the jurisdiction of these religious laws; this can lead to serious problems, as we shall see.

It is in Eastern Europe where Orthodox Judaism was, and still is, very firmly rooted. Even those Eastern Orthodox Jews who have migrated to other lands continue to resist any kind of modernity and change. The Eastern Orthodox Jews avoid any secular studies. They wear the same style of clothes that their ancestors wore and seem very out of place in modern cities, where they tend to live together in close communities. Coming mainly from Russia and Poland, these Jews tended to favour settlement in Israel, though some felt that it would not be right to leave their homes for Israel until the awaited Messiah comes to lead all Jews from the corners of the earth back to the Promised Land. Those Eastern Jews who did settle in Israel or in America found their lifestyles very different indeed from that of their counterparts in Western Jewry. So today, we still recognize Polish Eastern Orthodox Jews by their black *caftans*, the old fashioned black coats, accompanied with black stockings, and sometimes characteristic fur hats in the shape of a car tyre, like the ones worn by their ancestors in the colder Eastern European climate. In *Leviticus* 19:27 it says that "You shall not round the corners of your head; neither shall you mar the corners of the beard", and Eastern Orthodox Jews have taken this to mean that they are commanded in the *Torah* not to cut the sideburns of their hair or of their beards. These Jews, then, are easily recognizable in any country by their ringlets as sideburns, as well as their unusual black dress:

> Thus a strange looking Jew emerged in self-styled uniqueness He was forcefully secluded, and, by his actions, removed himself even further.[4]

Hasidic **Judaism**   *Hasidic* Judaism is an offshoot of Orthodoxy, which has become very popular.[5] *Hasid* means "the pious one", but the word "pious" here is meant in a very mystical sense, for *Hasidism* emphasizes direct mystical experience of God. Such mystical experience is brought about by fasting, meditation and separation from the world. Mystical experience can be given only to those initiated into the sect by "special transference", which in Hebrew is termed *kabalah*. Here, there is much more emphasis on asceticism and withdrawal from the world, along with the spiritual passion for God often associated with mystical religion. The mystical emphasis encouraged a mystical interpretation of the scriptures with much allegory and symbolism, particularly numerical symbolism.

Hasidic Jews believe that all the words of the *Torah* are realignments of the Divine Name YHWH which the true *Hasid* could fathom and become a "Master of the Name", a *Baal Shem*. There is much emphasis on evil and good spirits and demons, and the power of the Divine Name to control these. All the ideas associated with this sect of Judaism are contained in an ancient book called the *Zohar*, the "Book of Radiance", the central idea of which is that of God as the centre of the universe and as Infinite. The soul of man has to find its way to this Infinite Being through the many layers of gross existence. Union with God is symbolized in the act of sex, when all dualities are lost and the individual glimpses perfect union with the Divine.

Although this seems rather metaphysical, it was exactly what inspired many European Jews in times of immense persecution, when life seemed hopeless. It provided a way of emphasizing the inner, spiritual life of the soul, when the outer, physical life of the body was so severely persecuted. The *Hasidic* Jew is very intense in his worship. He prays with his whole body, swaying backwards and forwards with fervour in prayer, bending the knee whenever he mentions the Divine Name, YHWH, and often joining together with other men to dance in an equally fervent way. Many of the Jews from Eastern Europe are *Hasidic* in belief.

Neo Orthodox Judaism   In contrast to the Orthodox Judaism that characterized Eastern Europe in the main, Western Jewry was much more exposed to the kind of influences that were more liberating and which encouraged Jews to immerse themselves more in the culture of the country in which they lived. Neo-Orthodoxy was a response to this. Neo-Orthodoxy attempted to retain its distinct Orthodox Jewishness but at the same time integrate fully and contribute fully to life in society. Some *Hasidic* rabbis fit into this Neo-Orthodoxy, the recently deceased Lubavitcher Rebbe in New York, being perhaps the most well-known. Neo-Orthodoxy is, therefore, more outgoing, and one of its main beliefs is that it is the Jew's religious duty to be an example to the world, and he can hardly be this if he is totally segregated from it. Having said this, although it is important for the Jew to adjust to the modern world, observance of the *Torah* is never sacrificed.

Reform Judaism In Reform Judaism there is much more of a turning away from the strict interpretation of the *Torah*, and a more obvious adaptation to the outside world. It was a movement which appealed to Jews in the West particularly, because it stressed that Judaism needed to adapt its laws in tune with the rapid progress of society. Reform Judaism gave more individuality to the Jew, suggesting that observance of commandments was much more a matter of individual choice than a question of obeying the whole *Torah* interpreted literally. This enabled Jews to take account of scientific theories, to modernize their views, to integrate into society in a much more positive way, and to cast off what they felt to be some of the older taboos in Judaism such as the commandments concerning food. Reform Jews today ignore many of the food laws strictly observed by Orthodox Judaism, which are found in *Leviticus*, chapter 11. There is no longer a need to see the *Bible* as written by the hand of God, but rather as written by many human authors, perhaps inspired by God. Ultimately the individual is the judge of what he or she wishes to accept. Reform Judaism is therefore much less strict in its observances of religious practice. Parts of the Jewish Prayer Book have been altered or deleted in order to bring Jewish thought into line with modern thinking. For example, the *Mussaf*, the prayer for the restoration of animal sacrifice in the Temple, has been dropped entirely by Reform Judaism since most Western Jews would find the idea of animal sacrifice repulsive in this day and age. The *Mussaf* is, however, retained in the Orthodox worship.

Conservative Judaism Conservative Judaism arose out of a reaction to Reform, which seemed to many Jews to have gone too far in departing from traditional Judaism. While it accepts that all humankind must progress and that the biblical laws are more valid for society if they are ever-changing and evolutionary in character, it was felt that there should be more unanimity of decision about what should be followed. Thus Conservatism is traditional yet ever-changing, a synthesis of the two. It allowed Jews in America, for example, to involve themselves in American life, yet at the same time retain their specific Jewish traditions and historical roots. By making the Jewish people themselves the focus of the Law, each generation could add its changing and more advanced views to amend that Law so that Judaism itself would continue to evolve. Yet it does not advocate lightly the changing of the traditional laws of Judaism but rather prefers a stretching of the laws to accommodate modern life.

Reconstructionist Judaism Reconstructionism emphasizes even more than Conservatism the idea of the peoplehood of Judaism, the collective nature of the Jewish people even though they are dispersed throughout the entire world. This collective entity of a people is connected to the impersonal God, and all the laws of the *Torah* are symbols which need much reinterpretation in order to help the people collectively to strive towards that impersonal force. Jewish laws are only felt to be valid if they have some purposeful use for humankind, and for the collective Jewish people. If they do not have such purposefulness, then it is permissible to discard them. Laws are thus reconstructed in the light of the collective experience of all Jews. In many ways Reconstructionist Judaism is very humanistic, emphasizing what it calls the ethical nationhood of the Jewish people and the necessity of working for an improved world and a better humanity. Its roots were in America and it has the kind of broad vision we associate with American thinking. It allowed Jews in America to be both American and to be Jewish, retaining all that was most valuable in their ancient traditions.

JEWISH BELIEFS

The Covenant Jews believe that they are bound to God by a covenant, called a *b'rit*. The account of how the covenant or agreement came into being is told in the first five books of the *Bible*, which are called the *Torah* – its nearest equivalent meaning in English being "Law" or, better, "Instruction". The *Torah* tells the Jews what this covenant entails. It lays down certain laws or commandments, called *mitzvot* in Hebrew, which must be kept in order for the covenant to be maintained. All the commandments together represent the *Halakhah*, the Jewish religious law.

The covenant between God and Israel is epitomized in the revered words of what is called the *Shema*. These are the injunctions of *Deuteronomy* 6:4–9, the first word of which is *Shema* in Hebrew ("Hear!"), which appropriately gives its name to the whole statement:

> Hear O Israel: The Lord our God, the Lord is One; and you shall love the Lord your God with all your heart, and with all your soul, and with all your might. And these words which I command you this day shall be upon your heart; and you shall teach them diligently to your children, and shall talk of them when you sit in your house, and when you walk by the way, and when you lie down, and when you rise. And you shall bind them as a sign upon your hand, and they shall be as frontlets between your eyes. And you shall write them on the doorposts of your house and on your gates.

These words depict the essence of Judaism. The first statement is, indeed, a summation of the Jewish belief in the absolute oneness of God, and the insistence that God cannot be divided into parts: there could be no concept of a divine trinity in Judaism. So when Jews recite the *Shema*, they close their eyes and traditionally stretch out the word "one", *ehad*, so that they can meditate on God's absolute oneness while doing so. The following verses of the passage bind the Jews to the absolute God through the covenant, and the commandments imposed on them by God in the Law, the *Torah*. An Orthodox Jew maintains all the laws of the *Torah* so that his whole way of life is lived according to the *mitzvot*. In Judaism, therefore, religion and culture are mainly one and the same thing. This is expressed in dress, food, ceremonies, festivals and the many aspects of life which are part of the Jewish way of life. Most male Jews undertake to accept and observe the *mitzvot* at the important ceremony of *Bar Mitzvah*.

Bar Mitzvah   This means "Son of the Commandment", and a boy of thirteen and one day becomes a "son of the commandment" at the vitally important ceremony of *Bar Mitzvah*. At this point in his life he is expected to observe all the commandments and religious rites, and will have been well prepared for the occasion, having learned to read Hebrew and having being given thorough instruction in the Jewish religion. He would also understand the importance of the religious dress which he wears at his *Bar Mitzvah*.

The *Bar Mitzvah* takes place on the Sabbath nearest to the boy's thirteenth birthday. In Jerusalem the ceremony is held on Monday mornings at the Western Wall: this is in order not to break the Sabbath law concerning travel. It is every boy's dream to have his *Bar Mitzvah* in Jerusalem, and families travel from far and near to the Western Wall of Herod's Temple. The scene is one of immense joy (and some trepidation for the reader) as boy after boy is brought into the sacred area with the *Torah* scroll by the male relatives of his family. Amid tears and laughter, female relatives lean on the surrounding courtyard wall, wailing in loud voices and throwing sweets.

Away from Jerusalem and the Western Wall, after the morning service in the synagogue, the boy's name is called in Hebrew, and he climbs onto a platform called a *bimah* on which has been placed a reading desk. On the reading desk is the *Sefer Torah*, the Scroll of the Law, which has been taken out of its cupboard called an Ark. The boy chants portions from the *Sefer Torah* and, if he has studied well, he may also be asked to read from the books of the *Prophets*. During his *Bar Mitzvah*, the boy wears a prayer shawl called a *tallit* and an embroidered silk skullcap called a *kippah*. Once his *Bar Mitzvah* is over, and the boy passes into adulthood, he will be able to wear the *tallit* when praying, like all Orthodox Jews, and he will also be able to wear the *tefillin*. The *tallith* and *tefillin* are both symbols of the covenant between God and the Jewish people. At his *Bar Mitzvah,* the boy puts on the *tefillin* (Hebrew) or *phylacteries* (Greek) for the first time. They are bound on his forehead and on his left arm, and this he will continue to do during his morning prayers each day whether at home or in the synagogue. The *tefillin* are two small square boxes containing handwritten passages from the *Torah*.

After the boy has chanted the passages from the *Torah*, the rabbi preaches a sermon, telling the boy that he must now take on all the religious responsibilities of an adult Jew. Finally, he gives the boy the blessing:

> The Lord bless you and keep you.
> The Lord make his face to shine upon you
> and be gracious to you.
> The Lord lift up his countenance upon you
> And give you peace.

After his *Bar Mitzvah*, the boy becomes a member of the community and an adult. He can now join in synagogue worship since he can be included in the *minyan*, the number of males necessary to form a synagogue. The *minyan* is a quorum of ten males; traditionally, worship cannot take place without this minimum number. In Orthodox Judaism only men are included in a *minyan*, whereas in Conservative Judaism women can be included at the discretion of the individual congregation. In Reform Judaism, no *minyan* at all is required for worship, though it is desirable. Women have equal status here with men and there are a number of women rabbis in Reform Judaism; the first was ordained in 1972. A *minyan* forms a synagogue or "gathering", so a synagogue does not have to be a building; it is anywhere where ten or more male Jews meet for worship.

On the Sunday after the Sabbath (the Sabbath lasts from sunset on Friday until sunset on Saturday), a party is held for the boy, and many friends and relatives are invited. These parties, which are often lavish affairs, illustrate the importance of the *Bene Mitzvah* (plural, i.e. "sons of the commandment") in Jewish life. Liberal and Reform Jews also have a *Bat Mitzvah* for girls at the age of twelve. Orthodox Jews, however, do not accept this practice.

Despite the importance of the *Bar Mitzvah*, really speaking no rite of initiation is necessary for the transition from childhood to responsibility for *mitzvot*; the transition is automatic at thirteen years and one day. But for most Jews, *Bar Mitzvah* is one of the most important occasions in a Jew's life, regardless of the sect of Judaism to which he belongs. This is the time when the boy positively identifies with his people, and the preparation for *Bar Mitzvah* encourages the boy to know as much as possible about his people, about ritual, ceremonies, traditions, history, destiny and ethical conduct. *Bar Mitzvah* is thus a personal declaration of faith in all Jewish sects.

RELIGIOUS DRESS

The *Tallit* The *tallit* was once a square cloak, similar to the striped blanket worn by the Bedouin in the desert. When the Israelites were brought out of Egypt by Moses, they were given many commandments which held the structure of their society together during their wanderings in the Wilderness, before they had a land of their own. It is to this time that the *tallit* is related. Moses was commanded to:

> Speak to the people of Israel, and bid them to make tassels on the corners of their garments throughout their generations, and to put upon the tassel of each corner a cord of blue; and it shall be to you a tassel to look upon and remember all the commandments of the Lord, to do them, not to follow after your own heart and your own eyes, which you are inclined to go after wantonly. So you shall remember and do all my commandments, and be holy to your God. (*Numbers* 15: 37–40)

This, then, is the purpose of the *tallit*. Eventually this tasselled garment became the prayer shawl worn by Orthodox male Jews. Today, the tassels are at the two ends of the shawl and the strands and knots represent the 613 laws of the *Torah*. A *tallit* can be of any colour, size or material but it must have two white tassels called *tzitzit* on each corner. The *tzitzit* has four long strands which are looped through a hole in the corner of the garment. In older times, one strand of the *tzitzit* had to be hyacinth blue, the blue symbolizing God's heaven, and the white of the *tallit* purity. These, too, are the colours used on the Israeli flag. Blue is also an indication of royalty. In ancient times, only princes were allowed to wear blue, so the blue colour in the *tzitzit,* and today in the blue stripe of the *tallit* itself, confers royalty on its wearer. Sometimes the *tallit* has black stripes which remind the Jew of the Fall of the Temple in Jerusalem in 70 CE. The band on the shawl is the *attarah*, which must always be on the top and the outside when worn, but is removed when the owner dies; one strand of the *tzitzit* is cut to make the garment *patul* or unacceptable to God. It can then be wrapped around the dead person.

The worshipper wraps the *tallit* around himself while reciting a blessing to show that the commandments are wrapped around him. The *tallit* is worn during morning prayer either at home or at the synagogue, but is not worn on the Sabbath. Orthodox Jews also wear an undergarment called a *tallith katan* or *anarba kanfot*, which is a small *tallit* with *tzitzit*. Reform Jews no longer wear a *tallit*. Women are not permitted to wear a *tallit* at all in Orthodox Judaism though there is no real scriptural evidence to suggest why they should not:[6] indeed one ancient rabbi sewed *tzitzit* on his wife's apron. Women are generally freed from having to obey *mitzvot* which are linked to special times of the day, because this would cause difficulties for them when rearing children.

Tefillin   The *tefillin* or *phylacteries* are worn because of the commandment in the *Shema* that some of the most important precepts should be in the heart of every Jew. *Tefillin* are an important part of worship and prayer. Indeed, the word comes from a Hebrew root *palal* meaning "prayer" or "meditation". Orthodox Jews believe that even God himself wears *tefillin*. The *tefillin* are worn at the weekday morning prayer by all Orthodox Jewish males. One is placed on the left upper arm (of a right-handed male) facing the heart with the strap wound around the arm seven times right down to the wrist onto the hand and two fingers. The other is strapped onto the forehead. When the strap is being wound around the middle fingers of the left hand, a special prayer is said:

> I will betroth thee unto Me forever
> I will betroth thee unto Me in righteousness
> and in judgement and in loving kindness and in mercy . . .
> and in faithfulness and thou shalt know the Lord.

This indicates that the *tefillin* are symbolic of the devotion and affection between Israel and her God. They are a wedding bond, as the above words show, between God and the Jewish people, and are a symbol of the covenant and the mutual responsibility of the two partners in the covenant, just like the mutual responsibility which should exist between husband and wife. Within this covenant relationship, God undertakes the care of his people, but certain obligations are necessary on the part of the Jews. These obligations are evident in this special prayer:

1. Righteousness: Heb. *sedaqa*
2. Justice: Heb. *mispat*
3. Loving kindness: Heb. *hesed*
4. Faithfulness: Heb. *emet*

Each Jew is expected to live by these principles, displaying them not only in relation to God, but in relation to his fellow Jew. This is because God showed such qualities in bringing Israel out of bondage in the Land of Egypt, so Jews must also show such qualities in their daily living. The *tefillin* on the left hand opposite the heart reminds Jews that it is their duty to subject the designs of their hearts and their feelings to God; the one on the forehead reminds them to concentrate their thoughts on God's service and teachings. Each of the cubes is called a *bayit,* which means "house". On one is the Hebrew letter *shin* and on the other side the same letter with an extra stroke ש . This cube is placed on the head and tightened by the special knot at the back. The knot is also indicative of a Hebrew letter, the letter *daleth* – ד – both upright and upside down ⌐ . The straps then fall over each shoulder to the front. Inside the *bayit* there are four separate compartments each containing a scroll.

The other *bayit* has only one compartment, and the words on the four scrolls are written on one scroll. The strap has a loop on one side which is tied by a knot in the shape of a letter *yodh*. The significance of the letters on the *tefillin* is debated. Some consider the *shin-daleth* and *yodh – sh-d-y* to represent *Shadday,* one of the names of the Hebrew God. The significance of the four-pronged *shin* is more mysterious and mystical and some consider it to be symbolic of the complete knowledge of God and the true meaning of *Torah.* Some believe it to correspond to the four letters of the Divine Name YHWH, a name never spoken by Jews. *Tefillin* are worn only on weekdays, not on *Shabbat* (Sabbath)or holy days.

Inside the *tefillin* are four particular passages from the Jewish *Torah,* the first five books of the *Bible* representing the law of Moses:

1. *Deuteronomy* 6:4–9   This is the centrally important Hebrew *Shema,* which we noted above.

2. *Deuteronomy* 11:13–21   This passage tells the Jews that God will send the rains in their seasons so that the grain and wine and oil will be plentiful, also the grass for their cattle so that they will not hunger, on condition that the Jews worship no other Gods. Again, this is followed by the same words as *Deuteronomy* 6:6–9, "And these words which I command you this day shall be upon your heart . . ."

3. *Exodus* 13:1–10   This passage is concerned with the Festival of Unleavened Bread. When the Hebrews came out of Egypt, they left so quickly that they had no time to leaven their bread, or at least to wait for the bread to rise, and so had to eat it unleavened. The passage commands the Israelites to keep the Feast in order to remember the great act of God in bringing them out of Egypt:

> And you shall tell your son on that day, "it is because of what the Lord did for me when I came out of Egypt." And it shall be to you as a sign on your hand and as a memorial between your eyes, that the law of the Lord be in your mouth; for with a strong hand the Lord has brought you out of Egypt. You shall therefore keep this ordinance at its appointed time from year to year. (*Exodus* 13: 8–10)

4. *Exodus* 13:11–16   This passage states that the Hebrews, on entering the Promised Land after wandering in the Wilderness, should dedicate all first-born males of cattle and men to God. When the Hebrews were in slavery in Egypt, Pharaoh stubbornly refused to release them despite being afflicted with nine plagues. It was only the final tenth plague, the death of all the first-born men and cattle in Egypt, which caused Pharaoh to change his mind. The passage ends with the words:

> It shall be as a mark on your hand or frontlets between your eyes; for by a strong hand the Lord brought us out of Egypt.

The *kippah* or *kappel* (Yiddish *yarmulka*)   This is the skullcap worn during prayer in the home or in the synagogue. Some Jews wear it permanently. It is worn to show reverence for God, and to remind the Jew that there is always someone (God) more important than he is. Sometimes the caps are plain, but frequently they are made in many different colours and designs. A white one, however, is usually preferred for important holy days since white is a symbol of purity.

**THE
MEZUZAH**

Deuteronomy 6:9 states that not only should the laws be bound on the hand and before the eyes, but also:

> you shall write them on the doorposts of your house and on your gates.

When entering a Jewish home, therefore, a small case made of metal, glass or olive wood will be seen on the doorpost. It is called a *mezuzah* and is another symbol of the covenant. Seeing it reminds the Jews once again of their religious laws. Inside the *mezuzah* is parchment, just as in the *tefillin,* and on it is written the *Shema,* and the injunctions found in *Deuteronomy* 6:9 and 11:20.

> The mezuzah is the guardian of the home in a twofold sense. It ensures that our home is more than just a physical residence and gives a spiritual dimension to our immediate physical environment.[7]

The *mezuzah* makes each room in the house into a sanctuary, though it may have originated as a protective amulet and even today is a symbolic protection against evil. The same letters which are featured on the *tefillin* are also found on the *mezuzah* – sh-d-y (*Shadday*), the name of God. On the outside of the scroll on the bottom are the letters:

> *kwzw bmwksz kwzw.*

This is nonsensical, but when each letter is replaced with the previous letter of the Hebrew alphabet it reads:

> *yhwh alhynu yhwh/Adonai Elohenu Adonai*
> 'The Lord our God is the Lord'.

Whenever a Jewish family moves to a new home, they buy a new *mezuzah* from a Jewish bookseller. When the new *mezuzah* is fixed to the front doorpost, a short ceremony takes place. The *mezuzot* (plural) are always fixed so that they can be touched easily, and some Jews touch the *mezuzah* on the way in or out of the house, possibly kissing their fingers after they have touched it. Some Jews even place *mezuzot* on the doorposts of their living rooms and bedrooms. The *mezuzah* should be fixed to the doors (but not bathroom, toilet, storeroom or cupboard doors) within the first thirty days after moving into a house. Traditionally, inside a Jewish home, a *mezuzah* should be fixed only to the doorpost of living rooms. Seeking a definition of what constitutes a living room, Jews concluded that this must be a room wherein food is partaken. Originally, this restricted its location to the dining room, but today so many Jewish homes have television in several rooms, where the viewers take sandwiches, and children love to eat biscuits in their bedrooms, that the location of the *mezuzot* within the home is far more widespread.

Jews do not take a *mezuzah* with them, it is always left in place when they move. The *mezuzah* is put on the front right-hand doorpost with the top of it pointing inside the house, so that it lies on a diagonal. According to tradition, the *mezuzah* is slanted out of respect for two great rabbis, Hillel and Shammai. One said it should be positioned vertically and the other said it should be horizontal – so the Jews compromised by positioning it in between the two. As it is being put into position the following words are said:

> *Barukh . . . vetzivanu likboa mezuzah*
> Blessed are You . . . He, who has commanded us to affix the mezuzah.[8]

A famous rabbi called Eliezer ben Jacob said:

> He who wears Tefillin on his head and Tefillin on his arms, who carries Tzitzit on his garment and has placed a mezuzah on his door, is sheltered. He will not fall into sin, as we are told: A threefold cord will not easily break. (*Menahot* 436, *cf. Ecclesiastes* 4:12)

The *Torah* In reading about the *Bar Mitzvah,* we noted the importance of keeping the commandments of the *Torah,* the most important of the Jewish scriptures. These are the first five books of the *Bible*. *Torah* is not an easy word to interpret. It really means "Instruction", though it is usually translated as "Law"; essentially it provides God's "instruction" to his people. It is this instruction which has been translated into the *mitzvot* that bind the Jews to the God of the covenant. Although it may seem as if the *Torah* is a law or instruction rooted in the past, to many Jews it is seen as an expression of the covenant, and therefore something which is renewed each day, something which is a vibrant part of daily life, a living Law.

It is through the *Torah* that God is felt to speak directly to the Jewish people. For some Jews this means that God's words must be obeyed implicitly, and for other Jews it means that they are words which need to be interpreted by humans in an attempt to understand the message which God imparts. Naturally, such interpretation of the word of God will vary in time and will be affected by circumstances. Even in the

JEWISH SCRIPTURES

biblical history of the Jews, the prophets found it necessary to rein-
terpret the scriptures in times of difficulty or, indeed, in times of ease.
But this does not mean to say that anyone could interpret the words
of God. This function was left to the rabbis who, being experts in the
Law, were able to apply it to the many situations of life which evolved
in the centuries following the giving of the Law to Moses at Sinai. So,
generally, the *Torah* is not static but dynamic. Having said this, it is
generally believed in Judaism that the older traditions of the rabbis are
far more authentic than the later ones, simply because they are nearer
to the Sinaitic Law in time: the earlier rabbis are therefore given the
greatest respect, and their interpretations of the Law are regarded as
part of the Law itself. Even when these great rabbis disagreed with
each other, they were all felt to be right, and somehow a compromise
had to be made between the different opinions so that they were all
accommodated: thus, the *mezuzah* is placed in a slanting position on
doors, as noted above, to accommodate the different views of two
great rabbis.

The importance of the *Torah* in Judaism is shown in the reverence
with which the scriptures are treated in the synagogues. To be called
up to read the *Torah* is a great honour, and one in Orthodox Judaism
which is accorded only to men. When the *Torah* is brought out of the
Ark and carried around the synagogue, many will touch it with the
tzitzit of their prayer shawls in reverence. The actual word *Torah*
therefore can mean three things. It can mean the words of the first five
books of the *Bible*, it can mean the scroll on which those words are
written, and it can also mean the Law in the sense of all the later interpretations of the original *Torah*. Leo Trepp sums up the importance
of *Torah* rather well when he says:

> Torah in the fullest meaning of the term thus is synonymous with
> "Jewish Heritage". It is important to remember it. Torah contains
> laws, but it is not simply law; it is instruction. The meaning of the
> word Torah changes with the context in which it is used. It stands
> for "Spirit of Judaism"; it is the essence of Judaism. Jews are the
> people of Torah, but they are not a legalistic people.[9]

When visiting any synagogue the focus of attention is always the
Ark, the cupboard which contains the sacred scroll or scrolls of the
Torah. Usually a community of Jews has a number of such scrolls,
often handed down from neighbouring former synagogues, so that the
Ark, when opened, is full. The word "scroll" suggests straight away
that the *Torah* of the synagogue is not in book form. It is found on a
large scroll which is unwound by means of two poles, one at each end.
The words of the Law are considered to be so precious that the scroll
is clothed in a velvet or silk cover, often beautifully embroidered by
members of the community. The special nature of the scrolls is usually

depicted by a crown placed on top, and sometimes they have a breast-plate hung on them. The breastplate usually has a little window in it in which a tablet (usually silver, but never gold) can be put. This tells people to which part of the Law the scroll is set. This is helpful when different texts have to be read in the synagogue: it is much easier to open a book and find the right place than to unwind a lengthy scroll.[10]

Because the scroll is holy, its text is never changed, and every letter, word and paragraph is counted to make sure that the text is accurate and that there are no errors in it. This task is done by a specially qual-ified person called a *sofer,* whose sole occupation is working on such scrolls. The text is considered so sacred that it is never touched, and a special pointer called a *yad* is used in order to point to the text while it is being read.[11] This pointer has a little hand on the end with a finger pointing forward to indicate the text; *yad* in Hebrew (pronounced *yod* in *Ashkenazic, yarth* in *Sephardic*) thus means "hand'. The script on the scrolls "sits" on the parchment. That is to say it does not soak into the parchment but just lies on the top and so can be easily chipped off. Once this happens, the whole scroll is *patul,* unacceptable to God, and unusable. The *yad,* then, ensures that the text does not become *patul.* All the decorations on the scrolls are usually in silver. Any other material may be used except for gold. This is because the Hebrews were once tempted to make and worship a golden calf, just at the time when Moses was on Mount Sinai receiving the *Torah* from God. (*Exodus* 32)

When a scroll is used it is taken from the Ark, the cupboard in which the scrolls are secured, and is carried solemnly to the reading desk in the synagogue where the text is read. The community follows the reading in their own printed books. If the day comes when the scroll is no longer able to be used in worship because it has been damaged and has become *patul,* then it is buried in a Jewish cemetery in a clay container. Some very special people are honoured by having a *Torah* scroll buried with them.

Navi'im   Apart from the *Torah,* the books of the *Prophets* contained in the *Hebrew Bible* (what Christians call the *Old Testament*) are also part of the Jewish scriptures. The word for "prophets" in Hebrew is *navi'im.* It was the prophets who ensured the survival of Judaism by striving to bring the Hebrews, Israelites or Jews back to the terms of the covenant each time they strayed from it, and also for ensuring their survival in the difficult years of exile.

Ketubim   These are the Collected Writings which are part of the *Hebrew Bible – Psalms, Proverbs, Job, Song of Songs, Ruth, Lamentations, Ecclesiastes, Esther, Daniel, Ezra* and *Nehemiah* and *Chronicles I* and *II.* Of these books, *Psalms* is particularly important in Jewish worship. In all other books, God speaks to man; in *Psalms,* humans speak to God and it is here, in this book, that humankind can express their grievances and the many emotions that are part and parcel of daily life. So worship begins and ends in Judaism with *Psalms*. The Sabbath is praised with *Psalms*, and holy days are marked with a special recital from *Psalms* called the *Hallel* (*Psalms* 113–118).

If we take the first letters of the three sections of Scripture, we find *Torah, Navi'im* and *Ketubim*, T, N and K. So the entire Hebrew scriptures are called the *Tenakh*, the *Hebrew Bible*.

The *Mishnah* We have said that, apart from the *Torah* itself, there were also its various interpretations by the rabbis which became known as the *Oral Torah*. These are believed to have been handed down from generation to generation in a continuous stream of oral tradition. In 170 CE, a famous rabbi, Judah the Prince, came to think that the numerous interpretations of the Law had reached such proportion that it would be difficult for anyone to remember them in their entirety. Moreover, in times of persecution some of these masters of the *Torah* did not survive, and there was a danger that the oral tradition would be lost. So Rabbi Judah recorded the basics of the *Oral Torah*, taking care to include all the views of the opposing schools of rabbis.

This work became the *Mishnah*. It set down all the rules and regulations of Judaism which are known as the "fence" around the Law; the oral laws provided an extra set of laws which made sure that the inner core of *mitzvot* would never be transgressed – hence the "fence" around the Law. A tractate known as *Pirke Arvot* (Sayings of the Fathers), which was added to the *Mishnah* in about 250 CE, exempilifies the belief in this continuous stream of oral tradition:

> Moses received the Torah on Sinai, and handed it down to Joshua; Joshua to the elders; the elders to the prophets; and the prophets handed it down to the Men of the Great Assembly. They said three things: Be deliberate in judgment; raise up many disciples; and make a fence round the Torah . . .

This provided Judaism with the *Halakhah*, the "walk" in life, the *Haggadah*, "preaching" about how to conduct life, and a commentary on scripture known as *Midrash*.[12] There are six sections in the *Mishnah*:

Zeraim	Seeds	deals with agriculture
Moed	Appointed days	deals with *Shabbat* and festivals
Nashim	Women	deals with marriage and divorce
Nezikin	Damages	deals with criminal law
Kadashim	Holy things	deals with Temple sacrifice and dietary rules
Taharot	Purifications	deals with ritual purity

The *Talmud* Eventually, the *Mishnah* needed new interpretations, and it was out of this need that another great work emerged, the *Talmud*. The *Talmud* is in fact a compilation of two works, the *Mishnah* and the *Gemara*. The word *Gemara* means "completion" and it records all the discussions of the rabbis on the text of the *Mishnah*. The rabbis met together twice a year with prepared interpretations of sections of the *Mishnah* and debated and argued with each other about the interpretations of the text. Every word of their debate was taken down, no matter how verbose and rambling their discussion may have been at times. And it is this which has become the *Talmud*. Obviously, it is no easy text to read! Its contents cover almost every aspect of human life. Since it was compiled by rabbis of the Babylonian Jewish community it is sometimes referred to as the *Babylonian Talmud*.

Rabbis The forerunners of the rabbis were the scribes, who were not a religious body but, as their name suggests, writers (Heb. *soferim*) or copyists, who dutifully recorded the words of the *Torah*. The scribes were essentially members of a profession rather than a religious group, but a growing familiarity with the teachings of the *Torah* placed them in the enviable position of being qualified to prepare documents, advising society on its conduct in the light of the sacred word. In time, this accumulated knowledge accorded the scribes increasing respect, and they became Teachers of the Law, commanding the title Master (Heb. *Rabbi*), a title they accepted with no little pride. Indeed, in the Christian *New Testament* they are sometimes termed "lawyers", e.g. in *Luke* 10:25. The period following the two wars with Rome found the rabbis transmitting a cultivated Oral Tradition to writing, in the forms of the *Mishnah* and the *Talmud*.

When we read the text of the *New Testament* we become familiar with the Pharisees, a group of Jewish teachers who were despised by Jesus of Nazareth. However, had it not been for the Pharisees, it is doubtful whether the Jews would ever have survived the overthrow of Jerusalem and the fall of the Temple in 70 CE. The Pharisees were both rich and poor, but were close to the people. Collectively, at least immediately before and for a century and a half after the destruction of the Jerusalem Temple in 70 CE, they were known as *tannaim*, a word derived from the Aramaic *teni* (to repeat),[13] but each individual was known and addressed as "teacher", *rabbi*. Although they were part of a religious group they were not professionals and most had other occupations. But it was this tradition of rabbis which formulated the Jewish literature that we have reviewed. In many ways, the Pharisees were the builders of Judaism. We should not be biased against Pharisees because of the picture built up of them in the *New Testament*. Some of them, like the famous Rabbi Hillel, were great humanists, and though remarkably poor, left an unforgettable legacy to Judaism, shaping its destiny. There are, however, some justifications for criticism of a minority of Pharisees, known in Judaism as "the painted ones": it may have been to such that Jesus referred in the Gospels. They were called "the painted ones" because their piety was painted on – in other words, they were hypocrites. But they were certainly in the minority.

Apart from the very important ceremony of *Bar Mitzvah*, other major Jewish ceremonies not connected with the calendar are the rites of circumcision, marriage and death.

CEREMONIES **Circumcision** When eight days old, every male Jewish baby is circumcised. The ceremony usually takes place in the home, and is carried out by a *mohel* in the presence of ten males (a *minyan*). The act of circumcision fulfils the requirements of the Jewish Law, so it is a *mitzvah*. It is the sign of the covenant between God and man, and was instituted in the time of Abraham. God had told Abraham to leave his own country and to go to a place which he would show him. He promised Abraham a land, and a multitude of descendants, and Abraham's part of the bargain was to "walk before me and be blameless" (*Genesis* 17: 1). It was as a sign of this covenant that circumcision was introduced as an outward physical act, representing an inward relationship with God. Today it also links Jews together in a special way. At his circumcision, the boy is given his religious name which will be used at his *Bar Mitzvah*, on his wedding certificate, and on his gravestone. However, if a Jew is not circumcised he is still a Jew, though a sinful one because he has disobeyed a *mitzvah*.

Circumcision is such a special event that it must be properly performed. Some Jewish parents have their male babies circumcised on about the third day after birth by the physician in the hospital, but strictly speaking this is not acceptable under Jewish Law and would certainly not be accepted by Orthodox Jews. So important is circumcision on the eighth day that even if it falls on the Sabbath or on the high holy day of the festival of *Yom Kippur*, it is still performed.

It is a Jewish father's duty to ensure that his son is circumcised at the correct time: indeed, he could carry out the ceremony himself if he wished, though few fathers do. It is a very patriarchal affair, for the mother is not required to attend, though today it is usually an occasion for celebration by the whole family as well as other guests. Interestingly, as Trepp points out, the baby has godparents, and the word for godfather is *sandek*, a word derived from the Greek *syntekhos* "he who accompanies the child", which is the name given to the godfather in Greek Orthodox Christianity.[14] This is therefore suggestive of a Christian origin for the use of godparents in Judaism. It is the *sandek* who has the honour of holding the baby during the operation.

B'rit milah, the seal of the covenant, is thus a very important cere-mony. The house is decorated with flowers and candles, and a special meal follows at which *hallah* loaves are used. These are the two loaves of bread which are always used on the Sabbath. They are easily recog-nized by their plaited tops. They symbolize the *manna* which the Hebrews ate in the desert, when they first left Egypt to journey to the Promised Land. Wine is also important, and the child may be given a special goblet which he will use at special times in life. The goblet is filled with wine symbolizing a cup of joy. When this cup is raised by the *mohel*, the boy is given his Hebrew name for the first time.

When the ceremony takes place, the godmother brings in the baby and passes him to the *sandek*, then she returns to stay with the mother. Two chairs will be placed either side of the *mohel*. On the left sits the *sandek* and on the right is the chair of the prophet Elijah, the guardian of Israel who is always a feature of important occasions. The *sandek* hands the baby to his father, who passes him to the *mohel*, and the *mohel* places the baby on Elijah's chair and asks for Elijah's blessing. Then the child is placed on the *sandek's* lap for the operation. No cere-monies are necessary for girls, though Reform Judaism has adapted the words of the *B'rit* into a special ceremony for them called "The Covenant for Life".

Marriage The Hebrew word for marriage is *kiddushin*, meaning "to be holy", "sanctification", or "to be set aside." It is a holy covenant entered into by the two concerned, so it is a very sacred relationship, but is not a sacrament, as it is in some denominations of Christianity. It used to be unusual for a Jew to marry a Gentile, but in more recent times such a mixed marriage has become much more common. Since it is a *mitzvah* to have children, celibacy would be frowned on in Judaism: a Jew without a wife is homeless. Traditionally, the Jew obtains the girl's consent to marriage, and then asks the parents for their consent.

Weddings usually take place in the synagogue, though some may occur in the bride's house or in the open air. The wedding can take place on any day except the Sabbath or a festival day but must not take place at twilight in case the day changes in the middle of the cere-mony. Traditionally, a wife was acquired in three ways, by a legal contract, by payment of money or by sexual intercourse. Today, these three things are combined. The wedding ring represents the money paid for the bride, the marriage document or *ketubah* is the legal contract and *yihud*, being alone with each other, is the consummation.

On the eve of the wedding, the bride and groom exchange gifts, the bride very often giving the groom a new *tallit*. On the day of the wedding, they both fast, and in Judaism the groom is expected to look at the bride before the ceremony to check that he has the right one, unlike Jacob in the story of Jacob and Rachel in *Genesis* 29:16–26! So the bride wears white and wears a veil, but need not cover her face. Just before the ceremony, the marriage document is signed by the bridegroom. This document is the *ketubah* and it contains the following pledge:

> I faithfully promise that I will be a true husband unto thee. I will honour and cherish thee, I will work for thee, I will protect and support thee.

After the *ketubah* has been signed by the bridegroom and the witnesses, the groom and his father stand underneath a *huppah*. This is an embroidered cloth supported by four poles and forming a canopy. Everyone in the brightly lit synagogue faces the entrance of the synagogue to watch the bride and her father walk up the aisle. Following behind them are the mothers of the bride and groom, the bridesmaids, and the best man. As this takes place, a cantor sings in Hebrew. The cantor in the synagogue is no ordinary singer, but usually has a magnificent voice, and sings blessings for the couple. The bride and groom stand underneath the canopy which represents their future home. They will be expected to regard their home as a sanctuary.

The couple is addressed by the rabbi, and the cantor then recites blessings of betrothal over a goblet of wine from which the couple sip, symbolically sharing the wine as they will share their future home and the cup of life. Then the groom puts a ring on the forefinger of the right hand of the bride saying:

> Behold, thou art consecrated unto me by this ring according to the Law of Moses and Israel.

Once the ring is accepted by the bride, she becomes the man's wife. The *ketubah* is read aloud and is then given to the wife to keep. Seven blessings are then given, for example:

> Blessed art Thou O Lord our God, King of the Universe, who has created joy and gladness, bridegroom and bride . . . pleasures and delight . . . brotherhood, peace and fellowship.

Once again, the couple drink from the blessed goblet and finally the groom breaks a glass with his foot. Although the whole marriage ceremony is a joyous occasion, this act serves to illustrate that even such happy occasions should be balanced by some serious thoughts. The breaking of the glass is also a reminder of the time when the Temple in Jerusalem was destroyed by the Romans in 70 CE. Additionally, it is probably an ancient custom undertaken to expel evil spirits. Following the ceremony is the *yihud*, the period when the marriage is consummated, the couple being led to a quiet room. The traditional wedding feast then takes place.

Strictly speaking, inter-faith marriage is frowned on in Judaism because it is believed that such a marriage would threaten the very foundations of Jewish life. Jews find it difficult to envisage how two people of different faiths can have a common bond in the home. In fact, Orthodox, Conservative and Reconstructionist rabbis would refuse to marry a couple if both were not Jews. Even in Reform Judaism, it would be rare to find a rabbi who would undertake the ceremony, though a few feel that for the sake of any future children of the couple who might be lost to the Jewish faith they should be prepared to perform the ceremony:

> But accommodation merely disguises the realities. Christians are married "in the name of the Father, the Son, and the Holy Spirit", Jews are married "in accordance with the law of Moses and Israel". Whether or not these words are used, they are the foundation of the marriage bond. The marriage may be valid under the laws of the state; the religious ceremony, however, will rest on a self-deception.[15]

Divorce   Divorce in Reform Judaism is becoming more frequent, its procedure conforming to the usual regulations of the country, and is open to both men and women. Divorce in Orthodox Judaism is less frequent. Religious customs here have a stabilizing and unifying effect on the home. The family and the home are of immense importance in Jewish life, and divorce, therefore, is seen as a tragedy. It is said in Judaism that the altar cries when divorce happens, though the word altar here is symbolic as Jews have had no altar since the destruction of the Temple in 70 CE.

Although outside Israel a Jewish couple must have a civil divorce in accordance with the law of the country, for the religious divorce, the process is very easy. The husband hands his wife a document called a *get*. This is written on parchment in Aramaic in a very exact legal form, and is signed by two witnesses. On this *get* it states that the woman is freed from her marriage obligations to her husband. No reason is required other than that the husband no longer finds that his wife pleases him. This process is quite straightforward, but there is a religious court called the *bet din* which controls the issuing of the *get*, and this court may order the couple to try a reconciliation. The court may then deliberately take a long time to issue the *get* so that the couple have time to change their minds. In addition, a wife can reject a *get* unless she has seriously misbehaved in some way. In Orthodox Judaism only the man can obtain a *get*, and if the woman does not have a *get*, she cannot re-marry. Here, if a woman has grounds for divorce she can take her case to the *bet din* which may order her husband to issue a *get*, but there is little she can do if her husband still refuses to issue one. The *bet din* may also make some decision concerning alimony.

The *get* is specially prepared by a *sofer*, a trained scribe, for there must not be one mistake in the document. Once the woman takes the *get* into her hands she is divorced, but today it is given back to the *bet din* to keep, and the divorced couple are each given a certificate of divorce, to show that a *get* has been issued. Without the *get*, even if a civil divorce has been granted, a woman is still regarded as married according to both Orthodox and Conservative Jewish law. Even if a woman's husband is missing and presumed dead, without the *get* she can never remarry.

Death   With the emphasis on religious ritual, festivals, the joy of the Sabbath and the importance of family life and children, it could be said that Judaism concentrates more on this life than on the next one after death. It is believed that God sets a limit to each person's life and if one's name is there to encounter *Malak Hamavet*, the Angel of Death, then one must die. But, according to an old custom, the Angel of Death can be cheated. In the rite of *shinui ha-shem*, when a person is close to death it is possible to change his/her name and personality. The scriptures are opened at random and read until the first personal name occurs. This then becomes the person's new name which, if he or she survives, is retained. The Angel of Death arrives to find the person he wanted is not there! Judaism believes in resurrection into the hereafter. Orthodox Judaism also accepts a state of purgatory for one year after death, with relief for the sufferers in purgatory each Sabbath day. Resurrection means bodily resurrection, that is to say it is the physical self which is resurrected not just the soul.

There is in Jewish communities what is called a *Hevrah Kadishah*, a Holy Fellowship. It is an organisation which assists relatives at the last stage of someone's life and after the person's death. If the dying person is conscious, members will encourage him or her to bless their children, confess their sins, commit themselves to God and die reciting the *Shema*; if the patient is not conscious, they do these things for him or her. Once death has occurred, each person present makes a small tear in his or her clothing saying "Blessed are you, the True Judge". The *Hevrah Kadishah* then carry out all necessary preparations of the body, cleaning and dressing the body. Coffins are rough and simple and if the deceased is a male, a *tallit* with one *tzitzit* cut off to make it *patul*, "unacceptable", is placed over the shroud, so that when the body is laid in the coffin the *tallit* is wrapped around it. Earth from Israel is sprinkled over the body before the lid is sealed: this symbolizes burial in the Holy Land. Nothing else may be put in the coffin, though anything with the deceased at the time of death remains.

Funerals are simple; mourners all dress alike to show that death is the common denominator: in countries where coffins are used these are of unpolished wood for the same reason. There are no flowers, and ostentation is against the Jewish traditions. The funeral takes place quickly, within twenty-four hours if possible, though the law of the particular country may not permit this. Because of the belief in bodily resurrection, a postmortem is particularly distressing to families of the deceased. Jews believe that the body must return to dust and decompose as quickly as possible, hence the flimsy coffin. In some countries, such as Israel, the law does not require the deceased to be contained in a coffin, and the body is simply wrapped and buried in a *tallit*.

It is a *mitzvah* to accompany the coffin to the cemetery, and it will be friends who will carry the coffin. When the coffin is laid in the grave the relatives again perform *keriah*, the tearing of a piece of their clothing. The tear is about a hand's breadth long: the *keriah* for parents must never be repaired, though for others it can be after the period of mourning. Conservative Jews attach a ribbon to their clothes so that this can be used for *keriah*. The clothing showing *keriah* is then worn throughout the period of mourning. Reform Jews, however, no longer observe this law. Even children are encouraged to attend the cemetery: they are the first to throw earth in the grave, followed by the relatives. Then the grave is filled in by those assembled there, and the traditional prayers are said.

Following the funeral is a period of seven days deep mourning called *shivah*. Mirrors are covered so that mourners need not see how dreadful they look, though the custom is ancient and originally had more to do with warding off evil sprits.[16] The male does not wear leather, sits on a low stool, does not shave or cut his beard or hair, does not engage in religious ritual and does not study the *Torah*. Others will conduct services for him morning and evening, in the home. Then there is a period of *sheloshim*, thirty days to complete the mourning before returning to normal life, though mourning for parents continues partially for a whole year.

Jewish cemeteries are very simple. Flowers are not encouraged, though wild ones are: the grave should blend in with its surroundings. Whatever inscription appears on the tombstone there will usually be an abbreviation for "Here is buried" at the top, and "May his/her soul be bound up in the bond of life" at the bottom, both in Hebrew letters. The stone is set at the end of the period of mourning when the mourners are allowed to visit the grave for the first time. On certain festival days it is customary to visit the graves, as well as on the *Yahrzeit*, the anniversary of the death. Traditionally, the mourner leaves a pebble or stone on the tombstone after each visit. This used to keep a mound over the grave well maintained in older times.

Medical ethics   Euthanasia in Judaism is strictly against religious law, and is regarded as murder. As far as life-prolonging devices are concerned, Judaism is divided in its attitudes. Strictly speaking, Jewish tradition holds a person to be dead when the heart and lungs cease to function, not the brain, so a person may be declared to be brain-dead on a life-supporting machine, but would not be dead at all from the Jewish point of view. Reform Judaism has no problem here and accepts that life-supporting equipment can be withdrawn if someone is brain dead. But Orthodox and Conservative Judaism do not seem to have agreed decisively on any solution. Generally, rabbis vary in their advice, but while it is considered that it is not advisable to use life-prolonging devices in the first place, it is inadvisable to remove them after they have been used. Suicide is totally forbidden in Judaism for the supreme commandment is to live, and to preserve the self. Donations of organs at death are permissible to help others, though Orthodox Judaism is less likely to accept this. Autopsy, often required by law, is also problematic to Orthodox Jews and any dissected parts of the body must be buried with the body in the coffin.

FAMILY LIFE The home and the synagogue are the focal points of Jewish life:

> Our home is our school of life. It exists in space and should be a holy enclave in space, but it earns its title of honour through the Jewish spirit that rests in it and is renewed constantly by those who dwell in it. It acquires its distinction by the way the members of the Jewish home shape their times together. The Jewish home makes time live and permits us to live in time that has meaning.[17]

The whole Jewish year is studded with special days, from the weekly Sabbaths to the many festivals: it is the home which is the focal point for maintaining these traditions. The home is seen as a sanctuary, and the duty of the Jewish male is to sustain it and work for it, while the duty of the woman is to maintain its traditions.

It has always been considered particularly meritorious in Judaism to have a large family. This is because it was God's command in the *Torah* to have children, but it is also important in the preservation of Judaism. Judaism is a somewhat paternalistic religion, and the birth of a boy in some sects is perhaps the occasion of greater joy than that of a girl. But because procreation is a *mitzvah*, children, whichever sex they may be, are a blessing: there is no concept in Judaism that the celibate are holier than the married. Children begin at a very early age to understand the Jewish traditions. Traditionally it was a father's duty to teach his children to read and write, while the mother taught the children the blessings and some of the prayers. Judaism does not encourage parents to leave the education of their children to the schools, they themselves should also teach.

Women The status of women varies considerably in Judaism. In Eastern Orthodox Judaism, for example, the women's status seems wholly subservient to the male, while at the other end of the spectrum, a woman in Reform Judaism fares no differently than any other

Western woman. Generally, few Jewish women give the impression of being in any way subservient or unequal to their male counterpart, yet there is a difference in the respective roles of the male and female. The woman's role is generally concerned with the home, but when one considers the importance of the home as one of the two focal points in Judaism, this is not viewed as an inferior role: it is the woman who is the upholder of the Jewish culture. Reform Judaism has gone the furthest to promote equality between the sexes, accepting women rabbis,[18] and having mixed male and female congregations, unlike the traditional separation of women from men familiar to other Jewish sects.

Talmudic laws state that a husband should regard his wife as his equal, honour her, never hurt her, and support her, but although the woman's role in the home is traditional, her influence barely extends to anything outside the home. In fact, while there is respect for women on the one hand, there is intense criticism of them in Talmudic tracts on the other. Much of the blame for the inequality of women in religion and in society at large is placed on the second story of creation where woman is made from the rib of Adam, and because of her disobedience in eating the forbidden fruit. In the first account of Creation in *Genesis* 1, man and woman are created equally and contemporaneously. In commenting on this in the *Mishnah*, the rabbis explained that Adam must have had two wives, the "first Eve" who was called Lilith, and the second one the Eve of *Genesis 2*. Lilith, the Jewish commentary tells us, irritated God by insisting on absolute equality with her husband because she had been created in the same way at the same time. She committed the sin of uttering God's name and was changed to a demon to haunt humankind, striving to reduce man through the power of woman. She inspired the serpent to tempt Eve in the garden of Eden. Eve, though created from man, was superior to him. It was she who had initiative, but God punished her for her presumptuousness and took her power and position away from her, making man her ruler.

Although women in the *Hebrew Bible* are presented favourably, Judaism subsequently reviewed its women with some contempt. In the *Mishnah* we find the rabbis saying that they are gluttons, eavesdroppers, lazy and spiteful. They are depicted as excitable, talkative, thieving, run-abouts, fond of making themselves up and ornamenting themselves and craving fun and jewellery; even one of the blessings in Judaism states, "Blessed are you, God, . . . who has not made me a woman"! Although women were once released from those *mitzvot* which required them to undertake religious actions at certain times – a sympathetic concession in consideration of pregnancy, nursing or bringing up children – eventually they were prohibited from such *mitzvot*.

All sorts of prohibitions still obtain in Orthodox Judaism. Women are not permitted to worship alongside men, and in synagogue worship are confined to a women's gallery behind a *mehitzah* or screen. Orthodox women do not wear *tefillin* or *tallit*, or read and study the *Torah* or *Talmud*, and they would never be called to read the *Torah* in the synagogue. Additionally, Orthodox Jewish women cannot form a *minyan*. Non-Orthodox Judaism has changed much of this with its acceptance of women rabbis (though Conservative Judaism has very few), the abolition of the women's gallery, and the acceptance of women being called up to read the *Torah*. Women may also wear *tallit* and *tefillin*, and be counted with men in a *minyan*, become a *shohet*, or a *mohel*, or even a rabbi.

Sex and sexuality   In the family in Judaism, there has rarely been a lasting adverse attitude to sex. Sexuality in Judaism is something to enjoy, though the *mitzvot* to have children should never be forgotten. *Hasidic* Judaism, in fact, sees the sex act as a reflection of the mystical union between God and his people. Its importance is seen in the fact that it is permissible on the Sabbath and on most of the festival days, with the exception of *Yom Kippur*, the Day of Atonement. There is a time, however, when intercourse is not permitted, and this involves the laws of *niddah*. *Naddah* means "she who is separated", and its laws are fairly strictly practised throughout Judaism with the exception of Reform Judaism. When a woman is menstruating she is unclean for seven days, and everything she comes into contact with is unclean during this time, including her husband. During the days of her period and for seven days afterwards, husband and wife do not sleep in the same bed; the wife remains separated from her husband for at least twelve days. At the end of this time her body has to be purified in *mayim hayim*, the waters of life, traditionally a stream or the ocean, today a *mikvah*. The *mikvah* is a special pool, because the water must be combined with rainwater from a cistern, or the groundwater of a stream. The *mikvah* is deep enough to stand in immersed. In order to end her uncleanness, the woman removes all her jewellery, and bandages and anything which blocks access of the water to her skin. She would have already bathed, brushed her hair and cleaned her nails before reaching the *mikvah*. There are usually steps leading down into the *mikvah* and hot water is added to make the temperature more comfortable. The woman walks into the water until the last strand of her hair is immersed. This she does twice, saying a blessing between each immersion. An attendant watches to ensure that the practice is done correctly.

Judaism regards the law of *niddah* as important in maintaining the purity of the family. The law gives women a certain amount of independence and dignity, when the woman belongs to God and cannot be subject to any whim of her husband. Additionally, the wife returns to her husband's bed at the time when she is most likely to conceive, and the 12–14 days' abstinence renews their sexual interest in each other. The law also tends to prevent Jewish men from engaging in extramarital sex, since they would have no idea whether or not another woman would be in *niddah*.

In strict Orthodox Judaism, contact between the sexes is minimal, and an Eastern Orthodox Jew, for example, never looks at a woman, who is regarded as a temptress and indecent. He would not walk with a woman, be alone with a woman, sit next to one and would not even talk too much to his wife! Hence women, here, tend to be much more subservient, with procreation being their main function in life as well as the maintaining of their Jewish home.

Contraception   The use of contraceptives in marriage varies. Contraception was permitted by the rabbis in special circumstances, such as the prevention of conception too soon after a woman had given birth, but the norm was to regard having a large number of children as a *mitzvah*. The *mitzvah* actually says that every man is commanded to bring into the world at least a son and a daughter. So Conservative Judaism accepts the use of contraception if this commandment has been fulfilled. Reform Judaism allows unrestricted use of contraceptives, but Orthodox Judaism believes that a couple should have as many children as God would grant them. Any contraception which is permitted by the rabbis can only be the use of the pill since this does not interfere with natural insemination. Surgical appliances are generally not accepted in Judaism.

With the emphasis on having children what, we may ask, happens in the case of couples who fail to have any children? Adoption is perfectly acceptable in Judaism, the adopted child being considered as if the mother had given birth to it herself. *In vitro* insemination to produce a child is acceptable because both sperm and egg have been taken from the married Jewish couple; it would be unacceptable if the sperm came from another donor.

Judaism in general is opposed to abortion for convenience. But abortion is mandatory in Judaism if the mother's life is in danger. The fetus is regarded as potential life and sacred, but not as life itself, until after birth. Interestingly, the *Talmud* actually describes present-day abortion techniques when it states:

> If a woman has grave hardship in giving birth, we are to dissect the child in her womb and bring it out piece-by-piece, for her life takes precedence over its life. Has the greater part [of the child] emerged, we may not touch it, for we may not take one life for another life. (*Olahot* 7:6)

An Abortion Law was passed in Israel in 1977 which rejected abortion for convenience but permitted abortion in the case of minors, rape, incest, deformity of the fetus and the like; the law was strongly opposed by Orthodox Jews but even today there is no consensus in Judaism as to the nature or origin of the *halakhic* prohibition on abortion.[19]

Illegitimacy does not exist in Judaism. A child born to an unmarried woman is totally legitimate even if the father is married to someone else. But there is a special term for children born to women who commit adultery or incest. This term is *mamzer*, and a *mamzer* is an outcaste in Judaism, not being permitted to join in any religious ceremonies or to practise the religion in any way. A *mamzer* can only marry outside Judaism or another *mamzer*. Reform Judaism does not recognize the *mitzvot* concerning *mamzerot* at all, and Conservative Judaism has relaxed its attitude in the last decade, but Orthodoxy applies it strictly. The mother of a *mamzer*, however, retains her Jewish identity; she is just regarded as a sinful Jew.

Kashrut: **dietary laws**   The term *kashrut* is a wide one denoting the observance of laws in the correct tradition and manner. It comes from the same root, *k-sh-r,* "to be fit, proper" as the word *kosher* with which many non-Jews are familiar. Nevertheless, *kashrut* has become associated with the dietary laws in Judaism. These are maintained strictly by Orthodox Jews and by most Conservative Jews but are not binding on Reform Jews:

> It is a bond, linking us to the generations of the past;
> it is a distinguishing mark, linking Jew to Jew in the present;
> it creates a Jewish style of life;
> it is an act of discipline, strengthening character;
> it is an affirmation of the Jewish people and its will to survive;
> it is a bond between Diaspora Jewry and Israel;
> it has hygienic value, preserving health;
> it is an affirmation of the covenant, a law of God.[20]

The dietary laws in Jewish religion are very important. Each Jewish housewife prepares and cooks her meals according to special rules. In the traditional Jewish home, every meal is a religious rite because it has to be prepared according to the commandments of God in the *Torah*. It has to be *kosher* "fit", "proper" or "legitimate". Everything that a Jew does in life is tied up with religion. There is, in fact, no word for "religion" in Judaism since each person's identity and activity constitute what we would call religion. Since all meals are religious occasions Jews are reminded of their Jewish identity and relationship with God every few hours. Similarly, Jewish people are always reminded that God is the source of their food and lives, through the practice of giving a blessing over the food they are eating.

According to Jewish law, in *Leviticus* 11:3 meat may be eaten from any animal which "parts the hoof and is cloven-footed and chews the cud", but not if it has died of natural causes, or has been killed by another animal. *Leviticus* tells us the camel, which chews the cud, and the rock badger and the hare which also chew the cud, are still unfit for food because they have not got a parted hoof. Similarly, the pig parts the hoof so is cloven footed, but it does not chew the cud so is unfit for food. This is why Jews will not eat pork. *Deuteronomy* 14:4–5 gives a list of animals fit for human consumption, such as "the ox, the sheep, the goat, the hart, the gazelle, the roebuck, the wild goat, the ibex, the antelope, and the mountain sheep". To be *kosher*, meat must always be slaughtered in a special way called *shehitah* by a *shohet* or professional slaughterer.

It was particularly prohibited for Israelites to eat blood, for blood is life and belongs to God, and the Jewish method of slaughtering ensures that much of the blood is drained away. The *shohet* must cut both the arteries of the neck and the windpipe in a single, quick stroke. This causes a rapid gush of blood from the animal's brain to prevent any sensation of pain. It is claimed that this is the most humane way of killing an animal. The *shohet* examines the animal carefully after slaughter to make sure that it is not diseased in any way and then it is passed to the butcher for the arteries and sinews to be removed. A Jewish butcher thus has to be a religious, practising Jew. The butcher may then extract the blood, or this may be done in the home. The sinew of the thigh in particular must not be eaten because Jacob's thigh was dislocated by the angel of God in *Genesis* 32:33. Before the meat is cooked it is soaked in cold water for about half an hour. Then it is rinsed and salted and put on a perforated board which is tilted, to allow further blood to drain off. After another hour, it is washed again, and then cooked.

In the *Torah* it also states, "you shall not boil a kid in its mother's milk" (*Deuteronomy* 14:12). This is taken to mean that meat and milk cannot be eaten at the same meal, and in an Orthodox and Conservative Jewish kitchen, separate sets of red and blue cooking utensils are used for the preparation of milk (blue) and meat (red) dishes, and some families even have two dishwashers. Strict Jews will not eat any dairy food after a meal with meat; coffee with milk or After Eight Mints would not be acceptable. Even separate crockery, for meat and dairy food, is used in some Jewish homes. The rule seems fairly easy to follow, but even basic things such as frying meat in butter or having a sandwich with butter and meat would not be *kosher*. The same rule applies to the eating of fowl and milk, but combining fish and milk is permitted. The time which one should wait before eating milk or meat varies considerably from half an hour to as long as six hours.

Only fish which have fins and scales may be eaten, so shrimps, prawns, whelks, cockles, mussels, eels, crabs, etc., are unacceptable. Fowl can be eaten if it is a domesticated bird like chicken, duck, goose, turkey, etc. Birds of prey are unfit, and *Deuteronomy* 14:12–18 gives a long list of birds which are not acceptable; these are all birds which would not, in any case, be eaten by many Gentiles. Insects, reptiles and the like may not be eaten. Additionally, there are other items containing non-*kosher* materials which cannot be used. Many soaps, for example, contain animal fats and some tinned foods contain non-*kosher* ingredients. A bold **K** for *kosher* stamped on a product usually indicates to the buyer that the food is fit to eat. Orthodox Jews will not eat hard cheese, though some Conservative Jews will. Even milk can only be drunk if it comes from *kosher* animals, so many Orthodox Jews will only drink milk which has the *kosher* seal on it, and will not eat milk chocolate. Orthodox Jews will also only drink *kosher* wine.

Grace after meals is a very important Jewish Tradition. The *Torah* requires that God should be thanked for the sustenance he sends, for the land which he gave, for Jerusalem his holy city and for goodness. The set grace is fairly long, and it includes a song. It is designed to give the meal a sacred character.

Special foods [21]   At festival times, in particular, special foods will be prepared. The bread baked for the weekly Sabbath is called *hallah*. These are several plaited loaves which are very light and tasty. Two of the loaves are blessed at the Sabbath meal. At the New Year Festival of *Rosh Hashanah*, all members of the family eat apple dipped in honey. The act is symbolic of the hope for a sweet and fruitful year for which the family prays. At the festival of *Hanukah* it is traditional to eat dairy foods and foods cooked in oil. The dairy foods remind the Jews of the story of Judith, who fed the Syrian general Holofernes great quantities of cheese in order to bring about his death; the oil commemorates the miracle of the burning lamp in the story.[22] In eastern Europe potato pancakes, *latkes*, are eaten. These consist of cooked potato mixed with grated onion, flour, eggs, salt and pepper. Tablespoons of the mixture are fried in oil until brown on both sides. In Israel fried doughnuts called *sufganiyot* are eaten.[23]

On the fifteenth day of *Shevat*, about February, when everything is green in Israel, the New Year for Trees Festival takes place. On this day, Jewish people try to plant trees or eat different kinds of fruit. In Israel, the people often eat the seven different kinds of food which the *Torah* says grow in the Land of Promise:

> For the Lord your God is bringing you into a good land, a land of brooks of water, of fountains and springs, flowing forth in valleys and hills, a land of wheat and barley, of vines and fig trees and pomegranates, a land of olive trees and honey. (*Deuteronomy* 8: 7–8)

All sorts of food are associated with the Festival of Passover. *Matzoth* or unleavened wafers are eaten, made from flour and water and baked without yeast. This reminds the Jews that they had to leave

Egypt so quickly that they had no time to leaven their bread. A roasted shank-bone represents the Passover lamb and is left uneaten. Nor is the egg eaten. The egg reminds the family of spring, new life, and the hope of resurrection. It looks dead, but inside there is life. Parsley is dipped in salt water or vinegar, reminding the Jews of the tears they shed in bondage in Egypt, while bitter herbs are a reminder of the bitterness of slavery. *Haroseth*, which is a mixture of apples, nuts, cinnamon and wine, is eaten with the herbs and is symbolic of the mortar used by the slaves in building for the Egyptian Pharaoh, and is also symbolic of the concept of bondage.

Thus food – such an integral part of daily life – is frequently given religious and symbolic significance in Judaism. The recurring nature of this religious symbolism will be particularly evident when we come to look at the weekly celebration of the Sabbath.

Judaism is rich in symbols We have already discussed the important symbols of the covenant, the *tallit*, *tefillin*, and *mezuzah*. Additionally, many of the festivals, particularly Passover, include important symbols which link present-day activities to the traditions of the past. Other well-known symbols are the following:

JEWISH SYMBOLS

The *menorah*

The *menorah* is the oldest symbol of Judaism, and is a seven-branched candelabrum. A detailed account of the first *menorah* is found in *Exodus* 25:31–40 and 27:20–21. It was made by a craftsman called Bezalel at the time when the Hebrews were wandering in the Wilderness before they entered the Promised Land. At this time they had a sanctuary which could be moved with their wandering – a tent, or tabernacle. All the items which belonged in the tabernacle were carefully made according to the commandments which Moses gave to the craftsmen, and this special *menorah* was always kept alight. When the Israelites settled in their own land, and a permanent sanctuary, the Temple, was built, the *menorah* was housed in it. When the Temple finally ceased to exist in 70 CE, the custom of burning a light in the place of worship was retained in the synagogues. So every synagogue has a *ner* (light) *tamid* (eternal) in front of the Ark which contains the

JUDAISM

scrolls of the *Torah*. These lamps are always kept burning, symbolizing that the light of *Torah* will never be extinguished. The *menorah* is frequently found in Jewish life; it is a feature of the festival of *Hanukah* for example, and a huge bronze *menorah* stands near the *Knesset*, the Israeli Parliament, in Jerusalem. It is now the symbol of the State of Israel.

The Star of David

The Star of David consists of two interlaced triangles. The Hebrew term for this symbol, *magen dawid*, actually means "shield of David". It is uncertain how the symbol originated. Some suggest that the star represents the shield which David used. Others consider the shape to be the Hebrew letter *daleth* in its early form which was a triangle. This would represent the first letter of King David's name. Others suggest that the six-sided inner figure represents the Sabbath, and the outer six points the six working days. The sign was found on old Jewish buildings in Israel and other countries, as well as on tombstones. It is often found embroidered on synagogue coverings and vestments. The Jewish mystics, the *Kabbalists* used the symbol, also Christian mystics, and present-day Freemasons. It began to appear on tombstones in the late 1700s. In the 18th century, it was adopted by Jews in Europe as a sign of identification. Later still, the Nazis used a yellow star to identify Jews.

The *shofar*

The *shofar* is the ram's horn trumpet. It is a reminder of the ram offered as a sacrifice by Abraham as a substitute for his son Isaac in *Genesis* 22:13. It is a famous Jewish ritual instrument, and by far the most frequently mentioned biblical musical instrument. It sounded all signals in war and peace; it was sounded at the new moon, at the beginning of the Sabbath, at the death of some well-known person, at the approach of danger, when someone was excommunicated, when someone was healed by magic, and at an exorcism. It is believed to carry the voices of the people to God. Since it has few notes, it makes more of a noise than music, and perhaps this was why it survived in Israelite religion when other musical instruments were banished after the destruction of the Temple in 70 CE. Today, it is still associated with religious ritual. For example, at the Jewish New Year, *Rosh Hashanah*, the *shofar* is blown each day during the month before, at the festival itself, and ten days later at *Yom Kippur*.

The Temple   Some of the earliest man-made structures were temples or shrines, which represented the "house" in which a god or gods lived, like the Tower of Babel in the *Hebrew Bible*. When the Hebrews settled in the land of Canaan, a Temple was eventually built by King Solomon. The site of this Temple is on the eastern side of the Old City of Jerusalem, and although it is difficult to be precise, it is believed that the Muslim Dome of the Rock covers the place where the innermost sacred sanctuary or altar of burnt offering would have been. Nothing has been found of the remains of Solomon's Temple which was eventually destroyed by the Babylonian King, Nebuchadrezzar, in 587 BCE.

BUILDINGS

When Nebuchadrezzar was overthrown by the Persians, the Persian King, Cyrus, allowed all those people[24] who had been transported to Babylon to return to Judea, and even authorized the rebuilding of the Temple in 537 BCE. This Temple stood for 500 years, until King Herod extended it into a magnificent structure of cream stone and gold. This work was begun in 19 BCE, and completed in 64 CE. However, it had scarcely been finished before it was destroyed by the Romans in 70 CE.

Throughout the *Hebrew Bible* we see a gradual concentration of worship at the Temple in Jerusalem. It became the only place at which sacrifice could take place, and three times a year everyone was expected to attend the major festivals centred at the Temple. Thus the Temple became a focal point in Jewish worship and, though it was destroyed in 70 CE, the tiny part of it which still remains, the Western Wall, holds immense importance for most Jews, and is a focal point for Jews in Israel.

The synagogue   When the Israelites were taken into Babylon as exiles from the years 587 to 538 BCE they had no means of worshipping since they no longer had access to their Temple which, in any case, had been destroyed. However, the people were encouraged by the prophet Jeremiah, who was not deported from Judea, and who wrote to the exiles from a ruined Jerusalem. He told them to settle down in Babylon. This is what they did, and when the Jews were eventually allowed to return to Israel, not all of them were prepared or wanted to do so. Without the Temple, Jews met in gatherings, the Greek word for "to gather together" being *synagein*. This may be how synagogues began, although they would not have had this name until the later Hellenistic period. "Gathering" or "assembly" in Hebrew is *knesset*, which would probably pre-date the term "synagogue". Today, the synagogue may also be called a *Bet Ha-Knesset* "House of Assembly", a *Bet Ha-Midrash* "House of Study" or a *Bet Am* "House of the People." Reform Jews refer to it as a temple.

A long time elapsed between the end of what Christians call the *Old Testament* period and the beginning of the *New Testament*, and by the latter period, synagogues were everywhere. But strictly speaking, a synagogue can be formed as long as there are ten adult males in the gathering. In the early part of the *New Testament* period the Temple was also standing, but the synagogues had become so important in Jewish worship that the loss of the Temple was not as catastrophic for Jewish worship as might have been expected. Today, Jewish religious life focuses on two points, the home and the synagogue.

The modern synagogue Most synagogues follow the structural design of the Jerusalem Temple with three main parts: the auditorium, the Holy Ark and the *bimah*. The building is usually rectangular, with seats facing inwards on three sides. The auditorium is the place where the people sit, which corresponds to the courts where the people gathered in the Jerusalem Temple. On the fourth side is a recess in which is a double door, and this is covered with a curtain. The double doors are those of the Holy Ark, the box or cupboard in which the scrolls of the *Torah* are placed. This corresponds to the Holy of Holies in the old Temple, the holiest part of the Temple hidden by a great curtain; most present-day synagogues have a curtain in front of the Holy Ark also. This fourth wall is normally the Eastern wall, thus facing the direction of Jerusalem. On either side of the Ark, or above it, the Ten Commandments are written in Hebrew on two plaques, representing the two tablets on which Moses originally received the Law (*Exodus* 31). Often only the first two words of each commandment are given. At the side of the Ark is a *menorah* and in front of the Ark is the lamp which burns continually, indicating the continual presence of God, like the light which burnt in the Temple. Each scroll is on two rollers with a velvet cover, which is often very elaborate and expensively encased. When the scrolls are taken out during services, the congregation stands respectfully. The curtain in front of the Ark is also very beautifully embroidered. It is called a *parohet* and is embroidered by the women of the synagogue.

In the centre of the synagogue is a *bimah* or a raised platform on which worship is conducted and the scrolls are read, although some synagogues have a pulpit on one side of the Ark; this is a recent development. The *bimah* of the synagogue corresponds to the Sanctuary of the old Temple. Normally, men sit on the ground floor and women in an upstairs gallery. Non-Orthodox Jews allow men and women to sit together and also have less orthodox buildings. Orthodox Jews conduct their worship in Hebrew, and Reform Jews in a combination of Hebrew and English.

A special feature of the synagogue service is the *Hazzan* or Cantor who sings Jewish prayers according to the old traditional Jewish music; it is a very sensitive religious art. The liturgical music which the cantor sings is very exact and the cantor has to know all the arrangements by heart, so it is often a tradition which is handed down from generation to generation. There were many instruments used for music in the time of the Temple, but when it was destroyed instrumental music was not permitted in Orthodox worship, and women's voices have always been forbidden here. However, today even some Orthodox synagogues use wind or string instruments during weekday services, but not on *Shabbat* or festivals. A rabbi as a religious leader and teacher interprets Jewish scripture and Law, but does not necessarily lead the services in the synagogue: this can be done by any adult male.

A synagogue does not have to take place in a building; a synagogue occurs whenever ten males gather together for worship, providing a *minyan*. The fact that a *minyan* is necessary stresses the communal nature of Judaism: Jews are a people of the covenant so the whole community, the whole people is important. Individualism is not stressed in Judaism, and even before personal prayer, a Jew prays for all the Jewish people. Communal worship in the synagogue is therefore very important, and the congregation should meet three times a day, in the morning *(Shaharit)*, in the afternoon *(Minhah)* and at nightfall *(Maariv)*. Communal prayer is regarded as more valuable than individual prayer, for it unites the people in the covenant before God. The synagogue is not only a place of worship, but is also a community centre, the place where Hebrew is taught and has always been connected with education. It is also a "house of law" a *bet din*, even a bakery for unleavened bread at times.

Visiting a synagogue during a service is a remarkable experience since there almost seems to be a lack of decorum. People come and go as they wish, chat to each other when they wish, and children may play around the adults. In Orthodox Judaism dancing is an important part of worship in some festivals such as *Simhat Torah*. But men may only dance with men. The only time they are allowed to dance with women is at weddings though here, because men and women are not allowed to touch each other, they each hold the corner of a handkerchief while they dance. Synagogues are usually very light because windows are an important feature, as in the ancient Temple. Light does not only pour in, but the light of the *Torah* pours out into the world. The old Temple was high up so that it could be seen by everyone, and the rabbis said that synagogues too should be higher than all other buildings. This, however, proved impossible to fulfil, particularly in times of persecution, so some place a pole with the Star of David on top on the roofs of their synagogues to symbolize such height.

Despite the relaxed and seemingly noisy atmosphere at times in the synagogue, the worship and prayer is very structured and communal. Worship takes place three times a day, because in the *Torah*, Abraham worshipped in the morning (*Genesis* 19:27), Isaac worshipped in the evening (*Genesis* 24:63) – this would be what non-Jews would call the afternoon because the Jewish day ends at sunset – and Jacob worshipped at night (*Genesis* 28:11). It was King David who set specific times for worship in the morning, at noon, and at night and these have been retained by Orthodox Jewry, though Conservative Judaism has combined the noon and night services into one. Reform no longer follows these traditions.

FESTIVALS

The Jewish Sabbath   The Jewish Sabbath lasts from sunset on Friday until sunset on Saturday. Days begin at sunset because in the *Genesis* account of Creation we have the expressions, "it was evening and it was morning, the first day, it was evening and it was morning, the second day", and so on. Hebrew *sabbat* means "rest", and the Sabbath day is one on which no unnecessary or creative work is done. In the fourth of the Ten Commandments the Jews are commanded to observe the Sabbath Day and keep it holy, and to remember that God brought them out of slavery in Egypt. The Sabbath, then, is a day of rest, a holy day, and a day of joy because God released them from slavery. It is a day when *all* Jews rest, equally, no matter what their situation in life. In the past, even a servant was required to rest on *Shabbat*, and however poor an individual was, it was possible to look forward to one day in the week when cares could be forgotten. Even mourning is suspended on *Shabbat:*

> The Sabbath was appointed that we might learn the meaning and the sanctity of time, experiencing time without exploiting it for work but simply as a holy gift out of the hand of God. No work may be done. With this sanctification of time, all relationships, between man and man and between man and nature, are transformed. Sabbath observance is, therefore, equivalent to observance of Torah as a whole.[25]

The Jewish Sabbath is also an expression of the covenant between God and his Chosen People. This is made clear in *Exodus* 31: 16,17

> Therefore the people of Israel shall keep the sabbath throughout their generations, as a perpetual covenant. It is a sign for ever between me and the people of Israel that in six days the Lord made heaven and earth, and on the seventh day he rested, and was refreshed.

Orthodox Judaism, therefore, refrains from any kind of work on *Shabbat* which would break this covenant relationship. Conservative Jewry also tends to observe Sabbath regulations quite strictly. It is only Reform Judaism which no longer does so.

Although the commandment to do no work on the Sabbath seems very simple, the oral tradition of the rabbis laid down very clearly what was and was not permitted. This led to a wealth of regulations covering the minutest of actions. For example, nothing may be carried on *Shabbat* outside the home, though it is permitted to carry a baby. But even the carrying of a *tallit* in a bag in order to take it to the synagogue is not allowed, it can only be worn there. Sometimes, the rabbis got over this problem by declaring a whole city to be a home if it had a wall or wire fence around it. Jerusalem is a city like this, the old city having a wall right round it and thus anything may be carried inside the city/home on *Shabbat*. A limit is set how far one can walk on *Shabbat* (1,200 metres or 1,300 yards); fire cannot be lit and this includes turning on electricity, a cooker, heat, lights, the television, radio or the engine of a car. Conservative Jews, however, do use cars to get to a synagogue on *Shabbat* if there is no other way of reaching it, and radios and televisions may be used for religious programmes.

Shelter cannot be provided on *Shabbat*, so you cannot put up an umbrella; you can read a letter if it is already opened, but you cannot open one, and any business letters must not be read at all; cooking is prohibited though if a timer-switch is used on a cooker this is acceptable, or food can be kept simmering during *Shabbat* if it can be arranged before *Shabbat* starts. Sometimes a *Shabbes Goy* helps out, a non-Jew who is able to cook food, turn the light off or, for farmers, milk the cows. Having said all this, if life is in danger on *Shabbat* any of the rules may be broken. The rabbis ruled that, since it says in *Exodus*, "You shall keep the sabbath, because it is holy for you" (*Exodus* 31: 14) the Sabbath is given to man, not man to the Sabbath.

The Sabbath is welcomed by a set ritual. Just before the sun sets on Friday, the mother of the Jewish household lights two or more Sabbath candles. As the light spreads through the room, this is symbolic of the spread of the happiness and peace of the Sabbath. The mother is always the person to welcome the Sabbath with this ritual. After she has lit the candles, she shields her eyes with her hands to avoid looking at the Sabbath light until after she has said the blessing.

Traditionally, the men attend the synagogue on the Sabbath eve, the Friday evening, though women may attend also. This service welcomes the Sabbath like the arrival of a bride. *Psalms* 115–119, which are psalms of praise, are sung, followed by a hymn which welcomes the Sabbath as a bride, and biblical readings related to the Sabbath. On leaving the synagogue at the end of the service, everyone shakes hands and kisses, and wishes each other *Shabbat Shalom* (Hebrew) "Peaceful Sabbath" or *Gut Shabbes* (Yiddish) "Good Sabbath". On returning home from the synagogue, the father blesses his children with the words:

> The Lord bless you and keep you
> The Lord make His face shine upon you and be gracious unto you.
> The Lord lift up His face upon you and give you peace.

After the blessing the father reads from the *Book of Proverbs*, saying some well-known verses in praise of his wife such as:

> A woman of worth who can find her?
> For her price is far above rubies.

> Many women have done admirable things but you surpass them all.

The extracts chosen describe the ideal woman and pay tribute to Jewish wives and mothers. The Jewish woman is very much the centre of her family and is greatly respected in this role.

The Sabbath meal [26]   The family then gathers around the table which is spread with a white cloth and has on it the candles, bread and wine. A special prayer is said, describing the holiness of the Sabbath. It is called the *Kiddush* and also reminds the Jews of God's care for the world and the escape of the slaves from Egypt. The bread on the table is the *hallah*. *Hallah*, in fact, was the portion of bread given as food to the priests in the time of the Temple and it had to be eaten ritually by them (*Numbers* 17–21). Since the Temple no longer exists and this cannot be done, a little piece of dough is taken by the baker and burnt, to symbolize the *hallah*, the portion for the priests.

The *hallah* loaves are specially baked for the Sabbath and also remind Jews of the *manna* they ate in the Wilderness when they left Egypt (*Exodus* 16). The loaves are wrapped in a very special white cloth usually beautifully embroidered with religious designs. It is a *mitzvah* to surround *Shabbat* with everything that is beautiful, so the very best in crockery, tablecloths, wine goblets, candlesticks and so on, are used. The father blesses the bread and thanks God for it. Following the blessing of the bread, the father pours some wine into a silver goblet and everyone present drinks a little. Because the Sabbath is a joyful day, it is a religious obligation to drink wine and to eat tasty foods. The Sabbath meal which follows usually contains special dishes because it is a festive occasion. Many Jewish families sing songs called *zemirot* at their meal. The meal ends with grace, thanking God for providing all that is necessary.

On the Sabbath morning, people go to the synagogue for the Sabbath service. It is at this time that a *Bar* or *Bat Mitzvah* may be celebrated, and when the family return home they share a meal together again, accompanied by wine, *hallah* loaves and songs, as on the Friday evening. After the meal, the afternoon is a relaxing time, the traditional after-meal nap being specially observed. Some families may go out for a walk together or meet friends for a chat. Then comes the afternoon service in the synagogue followed by the third and final meal of *Shabbat*.

A special prayer marks the end of the Sabbath. It is called the *havdalah* which means "distinction", "separation". The father lights a special twisted candle and says a blessing over it. Then a spice box is passed around so that each member of the family can smell its fragrance. This, like the welcoming in of the Sabbath, represents symbolically the hope that the fragrance of the Sabbath will linger on through the whole of the following week. A cup of wine is also filled so that it overflows onto a plate, a wish that blessings too may be brimming over during the week. *Havdalah* thus separates the holy Sabbath from the rest of the week. The Sabbath candles are extinguished in the wine that has spilt over and *Shabbat* is over. Everyone wishes each other *Shavua Tob* or in Yiddish *Gute Voch*, "a good week". Tradition states that this last meal of *Shabbat* goes back to the time of David who knew that he would die on *Shabbat*, but not on which one. As *Shabbat* ended each week, therefore, he gave thanks for the extra week of life given to him by God.

The Sabbath is at the heart of Jewish ritual observance, for it maintains the religion in the home, keeping family life very close. It is the best day of the week so the house is cleaned thoroughly before sunset, and the best crockery and linen are used. It is the only Jewish day which has a name, such is its uniqueness – the following day being called the First day of the week, the next being the Second day of the week, and so on. It is a day of rest and the idea of the weekend is a Jewish legacy to the Western world.

The New Year Festival: *Rosh Hashanah* The Jewish calendar consists of twelve lunar months with an extra month added every two or three years to make the adjustment to the solar year of 365 days. The *Torah* makes clear that it is the spring month of *Nisan* which is to be the "beginning of months". God makes this plain to Moses and Aaron when he gives his instructions for the celebration of the first Passover in Egypt (*Exodus* 12). Traditionally, however, the Jewish New Year begins in the autumn, seven months after *Nisan* on the first of *Tishri*. It is called *Rosh Hashanah*, or the "Head of the Year". Originally a one-day festival, it is now celebrated over two days with the last day of the previous month, *Elul*, also called *Rosh Hashanah*.[27]

It is said that this was the day when Adam was created out of clay; it is the birthday of Abraham, Isaac and Jacob; the day when Joseph was set free from prison; and the day when Moses came before Pharaoh. It is also said that on *Rosh Hashanah* the heavenly Book of Life is opened and the deeds, both good and evil, of each Jew are recounted. This shows the fate of everyone for the coming year. On all Jewish New Year cards is written, in Hebrew, the wish, "May you be inscribed for a good year".

The Jewish New Year is the time for the asking of forgiveness. Prayers of repentance are said. This is the "Day of the sounding of the Ram's Horn", and the *shofar* is blown in the synagogues during the morning service. The notes and long blasts of this instrument urge the people to return to God, mend their ways and be forgiven. After the morning service of *Rosh Hashanah* the family gathers for a meal at which bread and apples are dipped in honey in the hope that the coming year will be sweet. *Rosh Hashanah* ends ten days later with *Yom Kippur*, the solemn Day of Atonement.

Yom Kippur   The Day of Atonement, *Yom Kippur*, is considered to be the holiest day in the Jewish religious year. Atonement implies being "at one" with the heavenly Creator. This is a fast day for all except the sick and children under the age of thirteen. The fast begins at sunset on the eve of the Day of Atonement and ends at nightfall the following day. The Day of Atonement is devoted to worship and prayer. From early morning until evening there are services in the synagogue at which prayers of confession are made. The Ark and the reading desk in the synagogue have white coverings and drapings: the rabbi and many members of the synagogue wear white robes as a sign of purity. The additional service in the synagogue on this awe-inspiring day recalls vividly that during its celebration at the time of the Temple, the High Priest, wearing simple white garments during the service, pronounced confession of sin for himself and the priests and the people of Israel in the Holy of Holies (*Leviticus* 16: 17). According to an ancient tradition, as they heard the High Priest pronounce the divine name, the priests and the people in the forecourt of the Temple prostrated themselves, and so in the synagogue the rabbis, readers and members of the congregation prostrate themselves when this historic passage about the High Priest's atonement is chanted.

The opening prayer on the eve of the fast asks God to forgive people who, through forgetfulness or in error, have failed to keep the promises they made to him. The constant theme of the services during this time is that of repentance (or return to God) and charity (loving kindness to others). In the afternoon the *Book of Jonah* is read for it tells of God's forgiveness to those who sincerely repent: Ninevah, a great city of ancient Assyria, was warned by Jonah, God's messenger, that it was in danger because of its wickedness. The king and the people fasted and prayed to God. God then spared them because of their sincere repentance.

The service which ends the Day of Atonement begins at sunset. The Ark remains open throughout the service during which many of the congregation stand. As the service ends, the congregation repeats the words of the *Shema*. The sound of the *shofar* rings in the ears of the congregation at the end of the Day of Atonement in order to remind the people that repentance and good deeds should continue throughout the coming year. *Yom Kippur* is the last day of the "ten days of penitence" which begin with *Rosh Hashanah*.[28]

Sukkot This harvest festival, which is also known as "Tabernacles", begins five days after *Yom Kippur*. It lasts for seven days, beginning and ending with a day of rest. Like Passover and Pentecost, *Sukkot* was once one of three "foot" or "pilgrimage" festivals whereupon righteous Jews would journey annually to Jerusalem at the seasonal harvests. In *Leviticus* 23: 39–44 the Hebrews are told to build together a bouquet consisting of the product of the *hadar* trees, branches of palm trees, boughs of leafy trees and willows of the brook as an offering of thanks. They should also build booths in which they must live for seven days, so "that your generations may know that I made the people of Israel dwell in booths when I brought them out of the land of Egypt" (*Leviticus* 23: 43). These booths are called *sukkot*.

For the festive bouquet, the *arba minim* of the offering of thanks, they use if possible the four species mentioned in *Leviticus*. The product of the *hadar* tree is the *etrog*, a citrus fruit (but not a lemon). The branch of the date palm is the *lulav*; usually this should be green and is kept in water to preserve the greenness and to make it pliable. Boughs of leafy trees or *hadassim* come from a special kind of myrtle and the willows of the brook are *aravot*. The plants are a thanksgiving offering for the harvest.

Although some devout Jews actually spend seven days in the *sukkot*, many Jews only inhabit them for meals, and only if the weather is good. The sides of the *sukkah* (singular) can be of any material, but the roof is special, it must be made of inedible plants in their natural state and must not be attached to the ground (so that a tree, or the like, could not be used for the roof). The roof must be just thick enough to make the *sukkah* more shady than sunny by day, and by night just thin enough to see the stars. The inside of the *sukkah* is always decorated, and traditionally the names of special guests whom each Jew will meet one day are hung inside. These guests are Abraham, Isaac, Jacob, Joseph, Moses, Aaron and David.

When the Hebrews were brought out of Egypt by Moses, during their long period of wandering in the desert they had no permanent homes and their eyes at night were directed to the heavens, as they lived in their temporary homes. Like the seven special guests, all Jews may perhaps be homeless for some period during their lives, so the festival is not only a memorial of the past, but an expression of a hope for God's protection in the future.

Sukkot, like many Hebrew festivals, is a joyous festival. In fact, the Hebrew term for "festival" is *Yom Tov* "A Good Day". The last day of the festival is called *Simhat Torah* "joy in *Torah*". On this day, the cycle of readings of the *Torah* ends and an immediate new cycle of readings begins for the following year. The day is a very joyous one and on some occasions women are allowed to mix with the men in the synagogues instead of being separated. Each person takes it in turn to carry one of the scrolls of the *Torah* in the synagogue and children follow in a procession with flags. Sometimes there is dancing, and sweets and biscuits are given to the children.

Hanukah   The eight-day festival of *Hanukah* begins some two months after the end of *Sukkot* on the 25th day of the Hebrew month of *Kislev*. It is a joyous holiday, a festival of light celebrating a miracle wrought by God recounted in the *Talmud*, a time (*c.* 165 BCE) when the Jews of Palestine were dominated by the rule of Antiochus IV, a Syrian-Greek emperor who demanded that everyone in his empire follow his ways of worship. Attempting to enforce his pagan ways, he seized the Jews' Temple in Jerusalem, erected therein a statue of the Greek God Zeus, and then ordered the Jews to abandon their faith on pain of death. Also the Jews were forbidden to observe the Sabbath and their holy days. The sacred scrolls were destroyed and the Jews were ordered to worship idols which were placed in the Temple.

However, the Jews refused to give up their faith in the One God. This outstanding story of human courage and sacrifice to preserve faith is vividly described in the *Book of Maccabees* in the *Apocrypha*. The revolt against the pagan tyranny began in the small town of Modin inspired by an old priest name Mattathias. The Jews followed their leader into the hills where Judah Maccabee, one of Mattathias' five sons, organized them into an army. Judah received the name "Maccabee", which means "hammer" because of the blows he struck for freedom. After three years of battle against vastly superior numbers, Judah was finally successful against the Syrian-Greeks.

When Judah Maccabee finally let his victorious troops back to Jerusalem, the Jews cleansed and purified the Temple of every pagan object and made it once again a house for the worship of God. However, it is the Talmudic account, not that in Maccabees, which tells that when Judah's men were cleaning out the Temple, they found just a single jar of the Holy oil, only enough to keep the Eternal Light before the Ark burning for one day. Miraculously, this one jar burned for eight days and eight nights, allowing the priests of the Temple enough time to prepare a sufficient supply of oil so that the *menorah* could remain lit without interruption. It is the Talmudic account which is accepted by traditional Judaism, and which accounts for the burning of lights for eight days.[29]

Judah Maccabee then proclaimed an eight-day holiday to celebrate the re-dedication of the Temple to God. Thus the festival received its name, for *Hanukah* mean "dedication". In this celebration of *Hanukah*, both in the synagogue and at home, one light is lit on the *menorah* on the first evening, and an additional one is lit on of each of the following evenings so that eight lights are lit by the eighth evening. This special *menorah* has nine candles and is called a *Hanukkiyah*.

Today, children love this holiday, not only because it has become a time for the giving of small gifts, but also because *Hanukah* is the traditional time for playing the *dreidle* game. The *dreidle* is a small four-sided wooden or metal top which has four Hebrew letters inscribed on the sides. Players depend on the spin of the *dreidle* for their spoils of the kitty, a pot containing a number of nuts, raisins, sweets or coins. In the days of Antiochus Epiphanes, before the Maccabees revolt, Jews studied the *Torah* on pain of death. Tradition has it that practising Jews always had a *dreidle* at the ready, which could be produced instantly on hearing approaching soldiers' footsteps.[30] It is also traditional to serve *latkes*, a kind of potato pancake, at *Hanukah* parties. The entire family sings together the many songs of the holiday. The *Maoz Tsur* (Rock of Ages) is a favourite.[31]

Over the centuries, the *Hanukah* candles have taken on a deep meaning for the Jews. They symbolize the light of religious freedom that Judah Maccabee and his followers kept alive. In the glow of the candles, many Jews rededicate themselves to the ideals of their faith. It strengthens the belief that religious freedom is the right of every people and that God desires man to worship him in freedom. For secularist Jews in the State of Israel, the great lesson of *Hanukah* is not belief in a divine miracle, but that a small group of people with tremendous courage were successful against apparently insurmountable odds. This event has long been a source of inspiration to the weak and small in number who fight for freedom and justice against stronger and tyrannical foes.

Purim   The festival of *Purim* falls on the 14th day of *Adar*, the most joyous month of the Jewish year.[32] The origin of the festival of *Purim* is to be found in the biblical *Book of Esther*. The story takes place in the time of the exile in Babylon when Babylon and Palestine were under Persian rule. The Persian King Ahasverus cast out his queen Vashti and held a contest at which all young girls were required to attend. A Jewish girl, ward of a wise Jew called Mordechai, was chosen as Queen Esther; when she moved to the palace, Mordechai spent his time at the palace gates. While there he overheard two of the King's servants plotting to kill their monarch; Mordechai reported the plot to Esther who, in turn, warned the King.

Ahasverus elected as viceroy of the Empire the vicious Haman whose character was such that he ordered all to prostrate themselves before him. Mordechai refused to do so and Haman, despising the Jews, secured permission from Ahasverus to exterminate all of them. Haman cast lots, to determine on which date the Jews would be killed.

It is from this act that the festival takes its name; the Hebrew name for "lots" is *purim*. On 13th *Nisan* the edict for the destruction of the Jews was announced, and the date for the destruction was to be 13th *Adar*.

Mordechai contacted Esther in the palace with this news and begged her to intercede. However, Esther could, only on pain of death, gain an audience with the King without being summoned. She sent word to Mordechai that all Jews should fast for three days, while she also would fast, and on the third day she would confront the King. "And if I perish, I perish", she said (*Esther* 4:16). Esther's great beauty won the heart of the King, however. Not only did he forgive the intrusion, but he granted his Queen a wish. Esther consequently invited both Ahasverus and Haman to her private party, where she repeated her invitation for the following evening.

The King, meanwhile, had learned how Mordechai had saved his life, and he turned to Haman for advice on how to reward someone whom his majesty held in high esteem. Haman thought the object of attention was himself, and he proudly told the King that such a person deserved to be paraded through the streets with his praises loudly sung. To his utter astonishment, Haman was then commanded to do precisely that for Mordechai! For his pains, the advisor was hanged from the very pole he had constructed in order to execute Mordechai, just as soon as the King learned of his evil intent against the Jews, of whom his Queen was one. The end of the story is a happy one, if not for Haman, and Mordechai and Esther ordered the Jews to celebrate the occasion forever with feasting and happiness. So the 14th and 15th of *Adar* are celebrated as the days of *Purim* each year.

Purim is a joyful feast, but is preceded by a fast. At the entrance to the synagogue, two plates are found, one for a (half-shekel) silver coin and the other for free-will offerings for the poor, fulfilling the words of the *Book of Esther* that *Purim* should be celebrated,

> as the days on which the Jews got relief from their enemies, and as the month that had been turned for them from sorrow into gladness and from mourning into a holiday; that they should make them days of feasting and gladness, days for sending choice portions to one another and gifts to the poor. (*Esther* 9:22)

After the evening prayer is read in the synagogue, a handwritten scroll *(megillah)* of the *Book of Esther* is read. Children take to the synagogue all sorts of noisy rattles, etc. so that every time the name Haman is read out in the story they create as much noise as possible and stamp their feet in order to drown the name of Haman with noise, symbolic of the casting out of the evil enemy.

At *Purim*, *Hamantaschen* (Haman's ears) are eaten; these are three-cornered biscuits usually filled with fruit or poppy seeds. They represent the three-cornered hat of Haman. The word for poppy seed in Yiddish is *mon* and the word for "the" is *ha* so "poppy seed" is *hamon,* a pun on Haman. This is typical of the fun which character-izes *Purim,* the most secular of Jewish festivals. Gifts of food are often exchanged as are at least two gifts between friends, and any number given to the poor. In Israel, the children join in a parade in the after-noon, dressing up in costumes and masks, and throughout the world such dressing up, dances, and puppet-plays usually precede the festival. In the afternoon there is a family banquet, at which each person is expected to get so drunk that he no longer can distinguish between the words "Haman be cursed" and "Mordechai be blessed" (*Megillah* 7).

Passover Passover (Heb. *Pesah*) is celebrated in the spring. It is a memorial of the time when God "passed over" the houses of the Hebrews and spared their firstborn when they were captives in Egypt (*Exodus* 12). This, the last of the ten plagues, persuaded Pharaoh to release the Hebrews from slavery. Passover is therefore a festival of freedom:

> This day shall be for you a memorial day, and you shall keep it as a feast to the Lord; throughout your generations you shall observe it as an ordi-nance forever. (*Exodus* 12:14)

Although originally two distinct festivals, Passover today is also called "The Feast of Unleavened Bread" as only bread without yeast may be eaten during the festival. The Children of Israel left Egypt in haste and did not have time to make bread that rose in the usual way.

The Passover Festival lasts for eight days. It is very much a family meal though it may be celebrated outside the family circle. No leav-ened bread or anything containing yeast (Heb. *hametz*) is allowed in the home during Passover, which lasts from the 15th to the 21st of the Jewish month of *Nisan.* Thus on the eve of Passover the mother puts little pieces of leavened bread around the house. The father and the children search for it by candlelight and collect it on a wooden spoon, so as not to affront the injunctions of *Exodus* 12:19:

> For seven days no leaven shall be found in your houses; for if anyone eats what is leavened, that person shall be cut off from the congreation of Israel.

By the time Passover begins at sunset, no *hametz* must remain in the house. Some will have been burned earlier on a bonfire. Even special crockery and cutlery will be used just for Passover to make sure that everything is *hametz* free.

On the first night of the Passover there is a special meal called the *Seder.* The *Seder* table is spread with a white cloth and lighted candles.

The word *Seder* means "order" and it is important that the table is arranged in the correct manner. Also there are four goblets of wine which everyone must drink in their proper order. A goblet is set aside for the biblical prophet Elijah, as it is believed that he will return before the Messiah comes to bring peace to the world. The four goblets of wine are drunk during the service. One reason for drinking the four goblets of wine is that it serves as a reminder of the four ways in which God promised Moses he would redeem the Children of Israel:

> I will bring you out from under the burdens of the Egyptians, and I will deliver you from their bondage, and I will redeem you with an outstretched arm and with great acts of judgement, and I will take you for my people, and I will be your God . . . (*Exodus* 6:6–7)

The proceedings for the Passover ritual are set down in a book called the *Haggadah*. Everyone present has a copy. The *Seder* starts with the father reciting the *Kiddush* over the wine. The father then washes his hands and passes everyone parsley or lettuce dipped in salt water. Lettuce, parsley or celery are eaten as symbols of the poor food the Hebrews ate in Egyptian bondage. These are dipped in salt water which stands for the tears that were shed at the time.

In front of the father on a tray or three-tiered *Seder* Plate, are three loaves of unleavened bread made of wheat flour and water. These loaves are called *matzoth*. Two of the pieces are the double portions for Sabbaths and the Holydays, and the third is known as the "the bread of affliction". The three pieces also represent the priest, the Levite (priest's helper), and the Children of Israel. The middle piece of unleavened bread is broken in two by the father. One piece is to be eaten during the meal, and the other, the *aphikoman* (dessert) is to be eaten at the end of the meal. With the *matzoth* on the *Seder* table there are: a baked egg which is a symbol of the free-will offering made when the lamb was sacrificed in the Temple; a roasted shankbone which cannot be eaten, it represents the Passover lamb; bitter herbs which are usually horseradish, standing as a symbol of the bitterness of slavery experienced by the Hebrews in Egypt; *haroseth* which is a paste of apples, almonds, cinnamon and wine, a symbol of the mortar made by the Hebrews while in bondage. The father points to the unleavened bread, and everyone looks at it. The father then reads the *Haggadah* which means "telling". The *Haggadah* is one of the oldest books in Judaism. The order of the *Seder* is given in this book:

> This is the bread of affliction that our ancestors ate in the land of Egypt. All who are hungry – let them come and eat: all who are needy – let them come and celebrate the Passover.

Then the youngest member of the family has to ask four questions:

(i) "Why is this night different from all other nights?"

Answer: It differs for on all other nights we may eat leavened or unleavened bread, but on this night only unleavened.

(ii) "And what is the second difference?"

Answer: On all other nights we may eat other kinds of herbs, but on this night only bitter herbs.

(iii) "And what is the third difference between this night and all other nights?"

Answer: On all other nights we need not dip our herbs even once but on this night we do so twice. (Already the herbs will have been dipped in salt water, but later the bitter herbs will be dipped in *Haroseth*).

(iv) "And what is the fourth difference?"

Answer: On all other nights we eat either sitting or reclining, while on this night we all recline. (As slaves they had eaten their meals hurriedly while sitting on the floor).

The father and others present reply to the questions.

References are made to Jewish history, to Abraham, Isaac and Jacob, the Hebrew patriarchs, telling how their descendants came to Egypt, and of their subsequent life of misery and slavery. This, indeed, is the important reliving of the Exodus from Egypt, an act of God which transformed a group of Hebrew slaves into a nation. The name of Moses is, however, nowhere mentioned; all the praise is given to God instead.

Glasses of wine are raised and the following passage is recited:

> It is our duty therefore to thank, praise . . . and adore him . . . He led us out of slavery into freedom from anguish to joy out of darkness into light: out of bondage into redemption. Let us sing to Him a new song, Hallelujah.

There follows the first two psalms of *Hallel, Psalms* 113–114, which refer to the Hebrews leaving Egypt. The father blesses the second cup of wine, and then everyone washes their hands, and the upper and middle portions of the unleavened bread are blessed and handed round. After another blessing, the bitter herb is dipped in the *Haroseth*. Then the father breaks the third piece of unleavened bread, and the real meal begins with another blessing. Each person eats a piece of unleavened bread like a sandwich with the bitter herb inside.

When the meal is over, the father gives everyone a piece of the half of the middle *matzah*, which is called the *aphikoman* (dessert). This is hidden for the children to find. Grace is said and the third cup of wine is drunk. The door is then opened for Elijah to enter. Elijah is considered to be the guardian of the covenant who will arrive with the Messiah. The second half of the *Seder* service includes the remainder of the *Hallel* from *Psalms* 115–118 and 131. Poetry, ditties and stories are also included. The fourth cup of wine is drunk.

Shavuot   Seven weeks after Passover, the Jews celebrate the Feast of Weeks, "the season of the giving of our Law". It commemorates the giving of the Ten Commandments at Mount Sinai. In this way it completes the story of Passover. The Feast of Weeks is one of the three pilgrim festivals. It is also called Pentecost. Its name "Feast of Weeks" is associated with the harvests of the Holy Land. It was the beginning of the barley harvest in Israel and on the second day a measure of barley was brought into the Temple. Fruit was also offered – olives, dates, figs and grapes. Today, the synagogues are decorated with beautiful flowers and plants. The floral decorations of the synagogues help to express gratitude to God for his kindness to humankind.

Devout Jews devote the whole of the first night of the festival to reading from the scriptures and the *Talmud*, a custom derived from God's command that no one should touch the borders of Mount Sinai for three days before Moses received the Ten Commandments. The Book of Ruth is read during the festival because it describes the ancient harvest practice in Israel of inviting the poor and the stranger to glean in the fields, and because Ruth accepted the teachings of Judaism, which were foreign to her, with loving devotion. At home, the festival meal takes place after the morning service in the synagogue. There are two loaves of round bread decorated with a ladder, a reminder of Moses going up to Mount Sinai.

Judaism is a festival conscious religion. The rich symbolism, ritual practices and prayers, special foods and customs of the Jewish holidays remind the Jews of their historical roots. It is through the celebration of festivals that they re-live the past in the present, as Jews everywhere reaffirm their Jewishness, and confirm their identity with the Children of Israel.

CONCLUSION

To the non-Jew, Judaism in general may appear very legalistic and, at times, somewhat antiquated in customs and practices. However, it is a miracle that Judaism and world Jewry have survived, and that survival owes itself mainly to the preservation of traditions and customs throughout generations of persecution and even genocide. A fascinating extract from Leo Trepp's book, *A History of the Jewish Experience*, is worth quoting here. Writing of the fall of Jerusalem in 70 CE, he states:

> On the ninth day of the Jewish month of Ab, in spite of heroic defense, Jerusalem falls; the Temple goes up in flames. Titus, the conquering hero, returns to Rome in triumph. An arch is erected in his honor. On it can be seen to this day the holy candelabrum carried in triumph to Rome, followed by Jewish prisoners in chains. Rome strikes a coin, bearing the

inscription "Judaea Capta". It shows the "widow" of Judah dejectedly weeping her fate under a tree whose fruits she will no more enjoy. A conquering Roman soldier watches proudly. But Judah cannot be captured. In 1958, the Israeli government struck another medal in celebration of the new state's tenth anniversary. On one side it shows the replica of the Roman coin. On the reverse, under the caption "Israel Liberata", it presents a mother proudly holding her child to the rays of the sun of freedom. She is standing under the fruit tree, which has grown tall and sturdy. At her side is her husband, kneeling, planting a new seedling to grow to health and strength with the child and the land.[33]

After all is said and done, perhaps the never to be forgotten words of G. K. Chesterson are the most fitting to close our look at Judaism, for it was he who reminded us that, despite centuries of persecution, often with a fanaticism beyond the bounds of credibility, the reality of the situation is that *a Jew will always stand at the grave of his persecutor.*

2

Christianity

Nora Hill and Diane Watkins

> For God so loved the world that he gave his only Son, that
> whoever believes in him should not perish but have eternal life.
> *John* 3:16

THE FAITH   The word Christianity is derived from the name given to those who
follow the teachings of one Jesus Christ, in Greek *Christos*, "the
anointed one". However it seems they were not originally known by
this name. Robert J. Krieg gives an account of the events:

> Initially, after Jesus' death and Resurrection, his followers called them-
> selves the "brethren" (Acts 1:16), "disciples" (Acts 11:26), "believers"
> (Acts 2:44), and "those of the Way." But within ten years or so, the name
> "Christian" was applied to the disciples by people who did not belong
> to their communities.[1]

The basic tenets of the faith are that there is but one God who created
all that there is out of love, and that God sent Jesus Christ to point the
way forward with his teachings, and that salvation will follow if these
teachings are kept. God therefore has been revealed in Jesus Christ,
and his death and resurrection are a pattern for all his followers:

> The Christian hope is grounded in the conviction that Jesus Christ, the
> incarnate Son of God, died on the cross for our sins and rose again. In
> his death he paid the penalty for humanity's sin and in his resurrection
> he overcame the powers of death.[2]

The "Church" is the name given to both the community of believers
and the building where they come together for worship. The word
itself comes from the Greek *kyriake* and *ekklesia,* meaning "belonging
to the Lord" and "assembly". The Church may sometimes be called
"the body of Christ", and this may further be defined as being both
local and universal. It signifies how the Church is united in and to Jesus

Christ, and is meant to show the interdependence of each to the other, expressed in an extract from the book of the Church's holy scriptures, known as the *Bible*.

> This is the Spirit of truth, whom the world cannot receive, because it neither sees him nor knows him. You know him because he abides with you, and he will be in you. (John 14:17)

The Christian faith has survived for two thousand years, and investigation into it has never ceased. No other faith has subjected itself to such close and prolonged scrutiny and yet survived in its basic urge to be united spiritually with its founder.

Different schools of theology existed very early in the church, and this has continued to be the case throughout its history. Christian theology today is very diverse, and further complicated by profound distinctions between the official teachings of each denomination and the opinions that exist within them. Despite this diversity, it has remained essentially united in the fundamentals of the faith, at the heart of which lie the common elements of Baptism, Eucharist, Scripture, and the expectation of the coming of the Kingdom of God, though there is a freedom of thought and interpretation within these.

Christianity is a missionary faith and has always existed to evangelize to the world at large, bringing the word and mission of Jesus Christ to all who will listen, following his instruction to make disciples in all nations. In this sense it is a people-centered faith and finds its reason for being in the service of others. The Church is active in all parts of the world, working within a variety of social and political structures, endeavouring to reach out and to reflect the will of God for humankind. It has to bear witness to its scriptures and demonstrate how belief in them will bring new life and hope to all, especially in the practice of forgiveness, the reality of God's grace, and the benefits of servanthood. Christians engage with each other and the rest of the world through the "gifts of the spirit" which proceed directly from God, given to empower Christians in undertaking these tasks.

Essential doctrines   Two essential doctrines of the Church are those of the Creation and Fall, and the Trinity. Many people today wish to "prove" the creation of the world through scientific thought and speculation, but for Christians creation is an expression of God's relationship with the world. It assumes a God that is not dependent on the world but a world that is dependent on God, a God that created the world out of nothing but love. Alister McGrath posits the major implications of the doctrine of creation as:

1   Distinction must be drawn between God and the creation.

2   Creation implies God's authority over the world.
3   The doctrine of God as creator implies the goodness of creation.
4   Creation implies that human beings are created in the image of God.[3]

The message of the Fall is that the world, as it appears today with all its problems and the imperfections of humankind, is not of God's creation but has been caused by the wilfulness and obstinacy of humanity in not accepting the sovereignty of God.

> The imagery of "the Fall" derives from Genesis 3, and expresses the idea that human nature has "fallen" from its original pristine state. The present state of human nature is thus not what it is intended to be by God. The created order no longer directly corresponds to the "goodness" of its original integrity. It has lapsed." [4]

However, the world will remain ordered and secure because of the redemption given by the saviour of the world Jesus Christ upon the cross.

The doctrine of the Trinity is highly complex and there are, of course, different interpretations. Basically it denotes that one God exists as three Persons, Father, Son and Holy Spirit, but also as one substance. God has three modes of existence yet remains one. Its purpose is to perceive the presence of God in the world throughout history, in the form of Jesus Christ and the Holy Spirit. The words "Father, Son and Holy Spirit" represent both God's transcendence and immanence, and whilst God is infinite and therefore unable to be fully disclosed to humanity which is finite, the actions of God may be discernible, in the study of past events.

> The basic feature of this doctrine is that there are three persons within the Godhead – Father, Son, and Holy Spirit – and that these are to be regarded as equally divine and of equal status.[5]

In reality the exercise of Christian worship, doctrine and practice takes a variety of forms and articulation, and therefore it would be impossible to give a comprehensive synopsis of all that is Christian in one chapter. The approach adopted here is to identify commonly held beliefs, history and disciplines, and the way in which these features are expressed in the mainstream Christian groups, while at the same time contrasting and thereby examining some of the less well known branches of Christianity. What may be said of "The Church", then, is that various Christian communities unite under the verse from its Holy Scriptures, "one Lord, one faith, one baptism" (*Ephesians* 4:5) but may differ in how they bear witness to it.

Christianity is a monotheistic faith, that is, having a belief in the existence of only one God who is the creator and foundation of all that there is. This is the same God of the Jewish scriptures, one who is all powerful and all seeing. So for these reasons Christianity claims a connection with Judaism through these scriptures, known by Christians as the *Old Testament*, and seen by them as looking forward to the coming of Jesus. These books form a basis for the *New Testament*, which is believed to be a compilation of letters and accounts of the life and ministry of Jesus Christ, written by people who either witnessed the events or were very close to those who did. Together the *Old* and *New Testaments* are identified as the *Bible*, the foundation on which Christian teaching rests. McGrath details the four senses in which the scriptures may be understood:

THE BIBLE

1   The *literal* sense of Scripture, in which the text could be taken at face value.
2   The *allegorical* sense, which interpreted certain passages of Scripture to produce statements of doctrine. Those passages either tended to be obscure, or to have a literal meaning which was unacceptable, for theological reasons, to readers.
3   The *tropological* or *moral* sense, which interpreted such passages to produce ethical guidance for Christian conduct.
4   The *anagogical* sense, which interpreted passages to indicate the grounds of Christian hope, pointing towards the future fulfillment of the divine promises in the New Jerusalem.[6]

The Gospels   The first part of the *New Testament* provides the principal sources for the life of Jesus and are known as the Gospels. These comprise the books of *Matthew, Mark, Luke and John,* and were written to give the gospel or "good news" of the ministry and teachings of their subject Jesus Christ. The message is that Jesus was revealed as God's son, who through his death and Resurrection can bring salvation to all who believe. Three of the Gospels are parallel attempts to interpret the meaning of his life and death, and are known as the Synoptic Gospels. These are the books of *Matthew, Mark and Luke*, and most contemporary scholars accept that *Mark* was the first book to be written, with this information being used later in the compiling of *Matthew* and *Luke*. *Matthew* and *Luke* have also used what appears to be a collection of the sayings of Jesus known as *Q* or *Quelle*, plus some other separate sources. The fourth Gospel, the one according to John, has much more information in it and so must have had more sources to draw on than the first three.

It is thought that *Mark* was written around 65 AD and consists of a variety of short stories, with seemingly no chronological order. What this author presents is a lively and enthusiastic series of pictures which produce a dramatic account of the ministry of Jesus. Mark records very strongly who he thought Jesus was. This man is "Jesus Christ the Son of God'. It may have been written to encourage the early Christians who were being persecuted severely by the Romans for their beliefs and would have been in dire need of emotional sustenance. Some of the details in the book appear to be those of an eyewitness and it is thought that Peter, one of the disciples of Jesus, was this character.

Matthew was written about ten years after *Mark* and there are in it a number of quotations used from the *Old Testament*. Christianity is presented as the "New Israel', the Church having taken over from the original "Chosen People', the Jews. *Luke,* written about 85 CE, is by far the most polished of the first three gospels and is full of joy and praise. Luke perhaps may be seen as the first pluralist, taking the "good news" out to all people regardless of nationality, status or religion, commending Christianity to everyone. Luke's Jesus becomes the "Universal Saviour" and in reaching this analysis aligns himself with Paul the author of what are called "The Letters" in the *New Testament.*

Paul's letters   Between the Gospels and the *Letters* of Paul is the next volume from Luke, the *Acts of the Apostles.* It provides for background reading to Paul, giving a theological basis for the "good news" and concentrates on events of the "Spirit'. The *Letters,* or "Epistles" which follow *Acts* are mostly attributed to Paul, and are amongst the earliest writings of the *New Testament.* They were clearly written for a time and place, to new groups of Christians throughout the then known world who were experiencing great difficulties and traumas in the practice of their faith. Paul's copious correspondence to the Churches in Cyprus, Asia Minor, Macedonia and Greece, accounts for one-third of the *New Testament* and are letters by someone who clearly sees himself in authority. He was a man who always seemed to be in a hurry and yet could not resist entering into theological arguments. It could well be argued that Paul was the first to see the potential of the Christian faith in the world, travelling many thousands of miles by land and sea in times of great hardship and deprivation. It was certainly his enthusiasm to promote the "good news" that appears to have been the decisive factor in making Christianity the world-wide religion it became.

Other letters   There are eight other letters written by the early Church leaders in the *New Testament,* not seemingly written to specific groups but to the Church in general. There is the *Epistle of James,* its author, thought to have been the head of the Church community in Jerusalem, which is followed by the *First Letter of Peter,* which is thought by some scholars to have originally been for use at baptism. There is a *Second Letter of Peter,* but this is thought to have been compiled long after Peter's death and so would not have been by the hand of the same author. Next come the three letters of John thought to be by the same author as the fourth Gospel. The second and third of these letters were warnings of the dangers of thinking that in understanding God one somehow became God-like oneself, whilst the first letter expounds the traditional teaching of the Incarnation which had united Christians to God. The short following letter of Jude was written for the Churches in Asia Minor about the year 80 AD.

Revelation   The last book in the *Bible* is that of *Revelation* and is quite different from all the others. It seems to be written in some sort of code and its message is one of "Apocalypse", or the end of history, presented as if in visions. This style of writing ran from 200 BC to 100 AD and claimed to give the already determined signs of these "end times". Jesus is seen as gaining a victory over evil, an assurance that the Church will be victorious in times of trial and tribulation. The early readers of this document would have equated their problems with the evils expressed in *Revelation*, and indeed it may well be that in different stages of history successive generations of Christians have seen themselves interpreting the book in their own particular circumstances. Ralph Martin applies his reasoning:

> we may state that its primary purpose is that of the encouragement and strengthening of the afflicted principle of God as they undergo trial and persecution. This conclusion is borne out by an inspection of individual verses (e.g. 2: 10; 13: 10; 14: 12) and thus it becomes a principle which helps us to interpret the message of the whole book.[7]

There would be Christians today who would see the symbolism in the narrative as having some significance for this last century, one that has been full of wars, natural disasters and injustice on a global scale.

Significance   The *Bible* is a book of authority for the Christian, and as such most denominations of the Church will use both *Old* and *New Testaments* of the *Bible* in their services. They are also used as vehicles of prayer and personal development, and small groups within Christian communities will hold *Bible* study groups to gain extra insight into them. What has to be realized is that it is a collection of sixty-six books, compiled by a variety of people at different times and with different perspectives of situations. Due to the passage of time there may have been alterations made, not just in content but in the very nature of translation, the earliest ones having been first written in Aramaic. Others would have been compiled in Greek but all would have suffered in the translation into Latin and then into English, losing something of the original meaning. What most Christians will say is that it is "inspired", and that the message of God is somehow conveyed through it. To some this will imply the *Bible* contains complete truths, that the writers wrote what God told them to regardless of meaning. To others examination must take place in the light of new knowledge of early Middle Eastern cultures, history and language, thus allowing for its message to be relevant today.

What is known about the period from which Christianity emerged comes from these writings of followers of Jesus who recorded his actions and teachings. As records date from as early as fifty years after his death they are deemed to have been written by those who either witnessed the events or had them passed down to them orally. What they record are miracles and signs said to have been worked by Jesus, and given in answer to faith and conversion. Christians would say this proves he was in a special relationship with God. He himself is said to have referred to God as Father.

At the same time the scriptures convey that all Christians are said to have a very personal and loving relationship with God and this relationship is expressed through the phrase "God the Father", and the use of the pronoun "He", when referring to God. This is not to give any picture or image to God, for Christian theologians have always acknowledged that God may never be expressed, only addressed. For Christians, then, God exists and is still active in the world, is considered worthy of praise and adulation, and is infinite and not flawed. Monotheism, the belief in one God, is also the basis of Judaism, but where Judaism and Christianity diverge is in the doctrine of the "Incarnation". This doctrine is central to the Christian belief, and posits that Jesus of Nazareth, later to be known as the "Christ', was the "Incarnation", or actual presence of God in the world. That is, that without in any way ceasing to be, God was revealed in human form in the world, for the salvation of the world.

JESUS OF NAZARETH

Birth of the Messiah Jesus as a specific character very definitely lived. He was born in an area known then as Judea, which today is the country of Israel, in the small town of Bethlehem. From the writings of people of the period it seems that his physical arrival into the world was not particularly grand or dignified. Traditionally it is said he was born in the stable of an inn where his mother Mary was taken in the last throes of labour by her husband Joseph:

> And she gave birth to her firstborn son and wrapped him in bands of cloth and laid him in a manger because there was no room for them at the inn. (*Luke* 2:7)

This apparently was the only available place to rest in a very crowded town, the place where many had gathered to register for a census in compliance with the orders of the Roman Governor of the time, one Caesar Augustus. Joseph and Mary had been made to travel a long way from their home in Nazareth for the census because they were of the line of the House of David, and Bethlehem was the place that all the descendants of that line were to be recorded. That Jesus is placed in the House of David is significant, because in the *Old Testament* there are indications that it would be a descendant of David that would arise to redeem the people, a "Messiah', or "Anointed One'. Bethlehem as the place of the birth is also important, for the book of *Micah* in the *Old Testament* reads:

> But you, O Bethlehem of Ephrathah, who are one of the little clans of Judah, from you shall come forth for me one who is to rule in Israel, whose origin is from old, from ancient days. (*Micah* 5:2)

All the signs, then, were seen to be pointing to this particular birth.

The concept of the "Messiah" held by the people of that time and place, was of someone who would deliver them from the oppression of the Romans, and throughout their history they had looked and longed for this coming event. In this sense they were expecting a political leader, a king behind whom they would unite in freedom, and so the time was ripe with anticipation. However, the baby onto whom a certain group of Jews, who later became known as Christians, laid the mantle of the "Anointed" could not have been further from this idea. Tradition has it that very soon after his birth shepherds were directed to the stable by angels who told them that this child was to be the saviour for whom they had waited so long:

> In that region there were shepherds living in the fields, keeping watch over their flock by night. Then an angel of the Lord stood before them, and the glory of the Lord shone around them, and they were terrified. But the angel said to them, "Do not be afraid; for see — I am bringing you good news of great joy for all the people: to you is born this day in the city of David a Savior, who is the Messiah, the Lord. This will be a sign for you: you will find a child wrapped in bands of cloth and lying in a manger. (*Luke* 2:8–12)

That wise men, or kings from the east, were also guided to the spot by a bright star has also become established within the tradition, and after paying homage to the child, "they offered him gifts of gold, frankincense, and myrrh" (*Matthew* 2:11) These scenes are re-enacted every year around December 25, the period of Christmas, the festival kept to remember the birth of Jesus. Christian children in schools and churches throughout the world perform these short plays which are known as the "nativity" plays.

A central doctrine of Christianity is that this was no ordinary birth, for Jesus is understood not to have been conceived in the normal way but by the miraculous intervention of God. As the Christian creed dictates, Jesus was "conceived by the Holy Spirit and born of the Virgin Mary".[8] Mary then was selected by God for the task of giving birth to this miracle after being visited by the angel Gabriel:

> The angel said to her, "Do not be afraid, Mary, for you have found favour with God. And now You will conceive in your womb and bear a son, and you will name him Jesus. He will be great, and will be called the Son of the Most High, and the Lord will give to him the throne of his ancestor David. He will reign over the house of Jacob forever, and of his kingdom there will be no end." (*Luke* 1:30–33)

Mary is said to have consciously agreed:

> Then Mary said, "Here I am, the servant of the Lord; let it be with me according to your word". (*Luke* 1:38)

So in some way God intervened in history, and this action was interpreted as being for the salvation of humankind.

Mary, the mother of Jesus was Jewish, as was Joseph her husband, and so Jesus would have been brought up in that tradition, observing all the festivals, and customs as required. His childhood was spent in a place called Nazareth, in an area known as Galilee, in the north of the country, and as Joseph was believed to have been a carpenter, he would have followed that profession.

Jesus' ministry   Jesus' ministry is introduced in the *Bible* through the activities of one John the Baptist, a man of wild appearance who proclaimed to all who would listen, the imminent arrival of the long expected Messiah.

> This is the one of whom the prophet Isaiah spoke when he said, "The voice of one crying in the wilderness: "Prepare the way of the Lord make his paths straight." (*Matthew* 3:3)

John was baptizing in the River Jordan, the practice of immersion in water thereby marking a spiritual re-birth, when Jesus stepped out of the crowd and asked to be baptized. John knew Jesus as the already "Anointed" by God, and this is confirmed in the *Bible:*
And when Jesus had been baptized, just as he came up from the water, suddenly the heavens were opened to him and he saw the Spirit of God descending like a dove, and a voice from heaven said, "This is my Son, the Beloved, with whom I am well pleased" (*Matthew* 3:16–17).

After his baptism Jesus began his ministry and gathered a group of twelve men around him who became known as the disciples. He was to become a charismatic figure in the area, renowned for his authoritative teachings and his healing, even to the extent of bringing the dead to life. There were to be many such miracles recorded, amazing things which could not be explained by logic. He often taught in what are called parables, a story that has some meaning which has to be searched for, stories that would teach through personal experiences. He associated with those who were outside the margins of Jewish society and continually tried to re-interpret the Law of the Jews, engaging with their leaders in ethical debates on the meaning behind the legalities. His central message was of the nearness of the "Kingdom of God', that God and divine salvation were near, a climax was coming that would bring about the reign of God. To the Romans this would have meant the arrival of a new ruler behind whom the Jews might rally, but the meaning to Christianity is more fluid. The "Kingdom of God" refers to the reign of God, or the sovereignty of God. It is a way of speaking about the power and the strength of God, and so in the prayer that all Christians pray, the "Lord's Prayer", are the words, "your kingdom come" and "your will be done". The focus is not on the kingdom but on God. It was clear though that its arrival was thought to be imminent, and it can be reasoned that at some stage these viewpoints were going to bring Jesus into conflict with both the Jewish and the ruling Roman authorities; the Jewish leaders because he was questioning their religious powers, and the Roman hierarchy because he was seen to be an agitator of the masses, expressing opinions and views that were not consistent with the tight political control of the mighty Roman Empire.

Tensions in Palestine at the time were already at breaking point, the Roman authorities needed no excuse to put down potential uprisings, and the Jewish Elders were going to use this Roman nervousness to their own advantage. Many of the ordinary people had also become disillusioned with Jesus, for he was not helping them to put their misery behind them; indeed, those who had been baptized and were trying to adhere to his teachings were finding their new faith was giving them considerable problems with their relatives and friends who had not converted. The climax to all these circumstances began at the time of the Jewish feast of Passover, a time when Jerusalem was thronged with people anxious to perform their sacrifice at the Temple. Jesus and his disciples were also going to Jerusalem at this time, but it seems as if he had knowledge of much greater happenings. He told his followers that the time had come for him to leave them and to prepare themselves for the future without him:

> See, we are going up to Jerusalem, and the Son of Man will be handed over to the chief Priests and scribes and they will condemn him to death; then they will hand him over to the Gentiles to be mocked and flogged and crucified; and on the third day he will be raised. (*Matthew* 20:18–19)

The *Bible* reveals that the disciples were astounded.

Jesus' death   Jesus sent the disciples to fetch a donkey on which he would ride through Jerusalem, and this fulfilled a prophecy given in the *Old Testament,* that the Messiah would come seated on a donkey. Large crowds waving palms came out to meet him as he entered the city, their expectations raised that this time he would deliver them out of the hands of their persecutors. He made for the Temple and was appalled to see the courtyard full of moneychangers and those buying and selling animals and birds for sacrifice inside. He showed his anger by overturning their merchandise and throwing the money away: he said to them, "It is written, "My house shall be called a house of prayer"; but you are making it a den of robbers" (*Matthew* 21:13) The High Priest together with the chief priests and others in authority were keen to have Jesus accused of something for which they could hand him over to the Romans for execution, and so they made it sound as if he was going to set himself up as King of the Jews. The Romans soon heard of this and demanded to know where he could be found. The religious leaders did not want to be implicated in his arrest in case the people became alarmed, and so the help offered to them by the disciple Judas Iscariot was accepted. Judas was to identify Jesus to the Roman soldiers by kissing him on the cheek, and in exchange, the scriptures say, he was given thirty pieces of silver. Recent theology raises the pertinent question as to how far the actions of Judas Iscariot may have been pre-ordained, in that, if one believes a master plan had already been put into action by God, the life, death and resurrection of Jesus were central to it, and Judas was merely playing out his part in it. There is also the theory that early Christians were looking for a scape-goat for the death of Jesus, and imposed the story of the betrayal upon Judas, in order to implicate Jews in general, and for them to be seen as evil and cruel.

The Roman Governor at the time, Pontius Pilate, is said to have felt some compassion for Jesus, in that he could not in all conscience find him actually guilty on the evidence before him. In an effort to please the Jewish authorities and to absolve himself of any miscarriage of justice, he gave the choice of what to do with Jesus to the people. It had become the custom to release a prisoner at Passover time, and so the choice was given, the life of Jesus or of a notorious convict Barabbas. The crowd, whipped into a frenzy by priests, chose Barabbas:

> So when Pilate saw that he could do nothing, but rather that a riot was beginning, he took some water and washed his hands before the crowd, saying, "I am innocent of this man's blood; see to it yourselves." Then the people as a whole answered, "His blood be on us and on our children!" So he released Barabbas for them; and after flogging Jesus handed him over to be crucified. (*Matthew* 27:24–26)

Nothing can be certain about the life of Jesus, but the Christian view is that it was an offer of salvation for a world not living in accordance with the will of God. Jesus called for repentance time and time again:

> The time is fulfilled, and the kingdom of God has come near; repent, and believe in the good news. (*Mark* 1:15)

He is deemed to have accepted responsibility in full by his subsequent violent death upon the cross, for the reluctance or inability of humankind to respond to the call. The Nicene Creed, instituted in 325 AD, and said at all mainstream Christian acts of worship, states as a central part of Christian doctrine:

> I believe in one God the Father Almighty, maker of heaven and earth, ... And in one Lord Jesus Christ, the only-begotten Son of God ... who for us men, and for our salvation came down from heaven, ... and was crucified also for us under Pontius Pilot. He suffered and was buried.[8]

However it goes on:

> and on the third day he rose again ... and ascended into heaven and is seated at the right hand of the Father.[9]

It is this last confession that signals to the Christian the absolute authority of the man Jesus.

For the closest of his followers his death seemed to have spelt defeat for their hopes and ideals. They were devastated and as we read in *Luke*, it is said a man by the name of Joseph of Arimathea, a member of the Jewish council which had sought the help of the Romans in killing Jesus, was allowed to take the body from the cross and place it in a tomb: "Then he took it down, wrapped it in a linen cloth , and laid it in a rock-hewn tomb where no one had ever been laid." (*Luke* 23:53) One can almost touch the sadness and desperation that must have been felt by those who only a few days earlier had experienced the triumphal entrance into Jerusalem. However, within three days, as the Gospels re-count, all this was to change. Some of the women followers of Jesus were the first to go to the tomb after the crucifixion, and to their amazement found the heavy stone which guarded the entrance rolled away. There was no body inside to anoint, as was the custom, and so they rushed to report this sensational news to the disciples. Their excitement is captured in *Matthew*: "So they left the tomb quickly with fear and great joy, and ran to tell his disciples" (*Matthew* 28:8)

The Resurrection
When the disciples themselves turned up to investigate it is said that

all they found were the burial wrappings from the body. From this moment then the cross was to become, for the Christian, a symbol that God had power over death. The Gospels insist that Jesus did not die naturally as others do, but that the whole scenario was part of God's master plan to restore the world to wholeness. It may be said that Christianity hangs or falls on the belief in the Resurrection of Jesus, and whilst the Gospel accounts vary in their descriptions of what happened, it is these differences that seem to make them more plausible. For if it had been a story concocted for the time surely more care would have been taken in the collusion in case its authors were found out? Likewise it seems that the Jewish authorities were never able to give a satisfactory answer to the phenomenon of the missing corpse. There are no reports of a body being found, and one would expect in the circumstances that a very thorough search would have been instigated. Likewise the Roman authorities of the time would have wanted the matter cleared up in a sensible and logical way to avoid the continuing nuisance of the early Christians.

What is also recorded in the Gospels is that Jesus made himself known to several of his immediate followers very soon after his resurrection, thus indicating to them his triumph over death, and giving them encouragement to go forward in proclaiming his mission to the early Church. These appearances were the vital link in making Jesus the focal point for the disciples' teaching and evangelism. He was the Messiah, the *Christos*, a Greek term for the Hebrew/Aramaic Messiah. Jesus is said to have continued to be seen after his death for a period of forty days:

> he appeared to Cephas, then to the twelve. Then he appeared to more than five hundred brothers and sisters at one time, most of whom are still alive, though some have died. Then he appeared to James, then to all the apostles. (*1 Corinthians* 15:5–7)

Paul records seeing Jesus in a vision on the road to Damascus, as does John on the island of Patmos. Many people have recorded their encounters with the "Risen Christ" across the centuries, and these moments in history add further conviction to the Christian belief that Jesus is still involved with them. They believe that "He is risen" and it is this cry that goes up at their Easter services, the time when the whole calendar of events of the last week in the life of Jesus Christ are remembered.

Holy week

This commemoration of the last week of Jesus' life is known in the Church as "Holy Week". It begins with remembering the ride into Jerusalem on the donkey and this day is referred to as Palm Sunday. In many churches palm leaves in the shape of a cross are distributed on this Sunday, recalling how the crowds welcomed Jesus into the city by tearing down palms from the trees, and laying them on the road for the donkey to walk over. Monday, Tuesday and Wednesday call to mind Jesus teaching in the Temple that week, and most churches on these days will hold some services and informal teaching sessions. Thursday begins the most solemn period of the week, and looks back on the final meal that Jesus and his followers were to take together; this is spoken of as "The Last Supper', an event that sees his washing the feet of the disciples as if to suggest he was their servant. Through the symbolism of the meal Jesus makes himself the offering of salvation.

> While they were eating, Jesus took a loaf of bread, and after blessing it he broke it, gave it to the disciples, and said, "Take, eat; this is my body." Then he took the cup, and after giving thanks he gave it to them, saying, "Drink from it, all of you; for this is my blood of the covenant, which is poured out for many for the forgiveness of sins." (*Matthew* 26:26–28)

It is this offering in particular which forms the major commitment for Christians, with the "Eucharist" or act of "thanksgiving" having been incorporated into their worship and symbolized by the receiving of bread and wine by members of the church. Thursday of Holy Week is also the day of the week deemed to be the day Jesus was betrayed by Judas Iscariot, the one who led the Roman soldiers to him so they could arrest him and begin his trial. In many churches all–night vigils are held through Thursday night to try to reflect on what actually took place. Altars are stripped of any cloths or candles and the mood of the congregation becomes very sombre. This day is called Maundy Thursday.

This solemn period continues on to the Friday, known as Good Friday. This day is for remembering the death of Jesus upon the cross, and how this provides for the mystery of salvation. For Christians this is a very important day, and many communities will take part in processions behind huge wooden crosses, to indicate to others the importance of the cross in their lives. Crucifixion represents a most barbaric style of execution and the suffering to which Christians believe Jesus must have willingly subjected himself is evident in both the actions and the words of worship that they take part in on this day. Saturday passes in a mood of general reflection of the events of the whole week and in preparation for the joy of Easter Sunday. On this Sunday church services re-tell the story of how Jesus rose from the dead. The hymns are lively and full of hope in the "Risen Lord', and the scripture readings are those similar to this one in the first letter of Peter:

> Although you have not seen him, you love him; and even though you do

not see him now, you believe in him and rejoice with an indescribable and glorious joy, for you are receiving the outcome of your faith, and salvation of your souls. (*1 Peter* 1:8–9)

The churches are filled with flowers, candles and perhaps banners of some kind, all which give a sign of the elation that Christians feel on this day. Easter Sunday is the one day in the year when Church members are instructed to make their Eucharist.

After the drama of Eastertide the ascension of Jesus Christ is one of the most important events in the *New Testament*. Luke records the final meeting with the disciples on the Mount of Olives outside Jerusalem, from where Jesus was "taken up" into heaven:

While he was blessing them, he withdrew from them and was carried up into heaven. And they worshipped him, and returned to Jerusalem with great joy. (*Luke* 24:51–52)

In these terms, then, the beliefs surrounding the circumstances of the birth, death, and resurrection and ascension of Jesus are at the centre of belief. The assent given to them allows for the Christian to see them as the perfect sacrifice, given once and for all time, and to ascribe to the actual person of Jesus the terms "fully human and fully divine'.

PAUL AND THE VERY EARLY CHURCH

The disciples   The earliest Christians were those whom Jesus had called on very early in his ministry "to follow him'. These were the twelve men called to be disciples, men who apparently left their families and friends and for the rest of their lives chose to engage with him: they were not without certain powers as Rowlands comments:

The disciples were regarded as the emissaries of Jesus with power similar to that which Jesus himself possessed (Luke 10:9). Indeed, Jesus explicitly links the task of the disciples with his own mission. (*Luke* 10:16f.; *John*: 20:21) [10]

Several weeks after the ascension they met in Jerusalem for the Jewish festival of Pentecost, when the people gave thanks to God for the gifts of the harvest, and whilst they prayed they became aware of the over-powering presence of God. This power and presence has become known as the "Holy Spirit" and those present were filled with the ability to go out and deliver the message of Jesus. Enthusiastically they began to teach the salvific nature of the reign of God, and of how it was present and at work in the world. All their fears about the future seemed to be gone for good. This experience of the empowering nature of the Holy Spirit is remembered by the Church today as Whit - Sunday.

Early converts   During the life of Jesus and for a short period after his death these people would have been active in the synagogues of the Jews, being seen as a kind of cult within Judaism. Many Jews were to become increasingly hostile to the Christian teachers and so worship began to take place in the houses of the baptized. These addresses needed to be kept secret from the authorities for fear of violence, but they were successful in providing places where groups of Christians could meet for worship when possible on the first day of the week, which was Sunday. These meetings would have taken the form of what was already familiar to them, psalms, readings, perhaps some singing and then teaching from the *Bible*. They would also often share a meal together during which they would solemnly break the bread and drink the wine as Jesus had done at the Last Supper.

The first Christian to be martyred, or killed for professing the faith, was Stephen, a deacon in the Church, someone who was involved in preaching, healing and charitable work. It is said that Stephen was stoned to death for his beliefs outside the city of Jerusalem, and someone who took an active part in that was Saul of Tarsus, later to become Paul – the one who was to take the teachings of Jesus to the Gentile world. This is acknowledged in "The Letter of Paul to the Galatians'. "The one who formerly was persecuting us is now proclaiming the faith he once tried to destroy" (*Galations* 1:23) Stephen was only the first among many to perish for their faith, and martyrdom has been a feature of the Church throughout its history. Most martyrs whose fate was known in history have been made saints, "those set apart by their holiness", and the Church recognizes their sacrifice by including in the Church calendar special days when particular notice is taken of their lives and deaths. Saint Stephen's day, for instance, is commemorated on the 26th day of December. All baptized Christians are believed to have received the potential to become saints of the Church.

Paul   From this point on it is Saul of Tarsus who takes the centre stage in Christianity. At the outset of his adult life he was an articulate and religious observer of Jewish Law, a Pharisee, and one who studied under the scholar Gamaliel. He was also a Roman citizen, a man who would have therefore received respect outside the confines of the area of Palestine. His ability to speak Aramaic and Greek would have been attributes that would have helped him enormously when he travelled extensively later in his life. He had actively engaged in the persecution of the Christians and even obtained permission to hunt them down in Damascus, where many had fled to escape death. However, on the way to Damascus he was converted to Christianity. He is said to have had a vision of Jesus and heard him call, and was struck with blindness for a short time. In this one instance Saul was to put all previous notions of persecution behind him and was to become the most zealous of missionaries, preaching to all about his new found faith in Jesus. He too was soon to find himself in difficulties with the Jewish authorities and only escaped from Damascus by being lowered over the sides of the city walls in a basket.

From this time he was to use the name Paul, and many Christians in history would see him as the greatest evangelist of them all. His three outstanding contributions to Christianity were in his missionary zeal, his ability to found new churches, and his passion for letter writing, giving to later generations of Christians insights into the complexities of what today is known as "Church planting". He was to undertake dangerous journeys throughout the then known world, to Antioch in Syria, to the island of Cyprus and through Asia Minor and on to Greece. He believed that God had given him the call to deliver the message of Christianity to the outside world and he converted many who were in the habit of worshipping pagan gods. He made many return journeys to the new groups and trained other men and women in the skills of evangelism. It is well argued by many Christians that had it not been for Paul, Christianity would have died from lack of exposure, being otherwise confined to the area around Palestine in the main.

Early theology   It is in the letters of Paul to the Christian churches which he founded that the beginnings of a Christian theology may be found: F. F. Bruce aptly comments that:

> Paul's letters are our primary source for his life and work; they are, indeed, a primary source for our knowledge of the beginnings of Christianity, for they are the earliest datable Christian documents.[11]

The beliefs of Christianity today are the result of the debates and controversies that surrounded the early centuries of the faith, and eminent thinkers within the Church at this time unpacked and analyzed the ideas and interpretations of the original teachings of Jesus. They became known in later centuries as "The Church Fathers", men who were given general approval in the Church for their doctrines, and to whom appeal was made in any dispute. The study of their work is known as "Patristic" theology. The study of Patristics has fallen from fashion in the twentieth century, but in a sense the Fathers grappled with many of the same thoughts that intrigue people today. Thus Frances Young comments:

> To see these questions debated in a quite different intellectual setting is important, for it enables us to step outside our own culturally-conditioned presuppositions and see the issues in a different way. [12]

**THE EARLY
CHURCH**

It was the very nature of the man Jesus that came under scrutiny, in terms of whether he might be described as human, divine, or both at the same time. The resulting theologies and beliefs arose after careful debate and much intellectualism, but many it seems were also adopted for political reasons.

Establishment of Christianity In the year 313 AD Christianity became the religion of the Roman Empire. This was due to the conversion of the then Emperor Constantine who believed that he had won a great battle due to the help of the Christian God. Close and Smith describe the way in which Christianity was helped to become entrenched in the West:

> Constantinople, dedicated in 325, was to be a new Rome but free from any taint of paganism. It was provided with splendid churches and the decoration of its public buildings and squares used Christian rather than pagan motifs. Its citizens were granted a status equal to that of Roman citizens and in the course of time it became the centre of religion in the east as Rome was in the west. [13]

The Church prospered by adapting to what was required of it, and became an institutionalized and prestigious organization. Some will say that it was during this period that it lost its way, becoming enmeshed in the grandeur and politics of the time. Constantine gave the Church land and fine buildings, he gave Roman soldiers Sundays off for worship, and the clergy began to wear fine vestments, identifying themselves as an important elite of Roman society. The Church was exempt from taxation on the revenues received from its large estates, and this led to greed on the part of some within the establishment of the Church, and to cause concern and annoyance in later centuries. State and Church interacted and today historians argue that this was the point in history when Christianity became a major religious force, through the benefits of positive discrimination.

With the establishment of an eastern capital, Constantinople, differences gradually developed in doctrine and practice between itself and Rome, helped, to some extent, by the differences in culture and civilization. These differences were discussed and debated at length, but it was authority which caused the greatest problems. Whilst Rome still held sway as the senior community, the Eastern Church found itself increasingly compromised by edicts from Rome. The bishops of the east saw their role as one of consultation with Rome, but not in any sense as having to agree on every aspect of doctrine and faith, and they frequently did not. Over the next few centuries several centres of Christianity emerged in the east, all with their own patriarchs or leaders. Great councils were held in an effort to give some semblance of harmony between Rome and the eastern Churches, but the results were less than convincing. Communication between east and west was difficult, with Greek being the language of the east, and Latin the language of the west. Eastern clergy could marry and wore beards, whilst western clergy were clean shaven and increasingly celibate. The rite of confirmation has always been undertaken by the bishops in the west, but in the east priests conduct the ceremony. Problems were inevitable in maintaining discipline and in the end two separate styles emerged, one following the Latin rite and the other taking its background from the Greek.

SCHISM

Divisions In 1054 the Pope, the supreme head of the Roman Catholic Church, agreed to provide military assistance to the then Emperor in exchange for ecclesiastical control of land under the jurisdiction of Constantinople. The Greek Church reacted by closing all the Latin rite churches in Constantinople, and when the Pope sent his emissaries to call on the Patriarch, head of the Eastern Church, to exercise obedience, they were obliged to excommunicate him when he would not comply. Many attempts in the preceding centuries were made to reconcile the differences, but with the Pope and the Roman Church concerned about establishing supremacy and the Eastern Churches seemingly unable to agree in full with all the statements made, complete separation was inevitable. The politics that had developed between the rival emperors of east and west were bound up in the decisions taken by the churches also, and it seems incredible that the Church continued to expand and develop in the midst of it. Close and Smith explain the shrewdness involved:

> Political factors were involved at every stage. There was rivalry between the emperors of west and east and the church was used by each side to proclaim power and influence. Sometimes popes and emperors bargained military support for ecclesiastical benefits.[14]

In recent years there has been a coming together of the eastern churches, known as the Orthodox Church, and the Latin western church (the Roman Catholic Church), and once again they are finding mutual ground on which they have begun discussions. However, the schism of 1054 has to be seen as the most serious in the history of Christianity.

THE
REFORMATION

Further divisions By the fifteenth century Europe was beginning to feel the pressures of the Reformation, and the Church prepared itself for further division. These divisions were many faceted, political and doctrinal, and the results were major for the Roman Catholic Church. Certain individuals began to protest at what they saw as corruption and immorality within the Church, and in Europe there had developed a new sense of individuality in the different countries. Robert D. Linder looks at the background:

The Reformation occurred against a vast back-drop of unrest and change in Europe. Politically the most salient feature of the era was the emergence of national states which challenged the old order, including traditional papal prerogatives and the medieval concept of higher loyalties.[15]

The constant outflow of money to Rome to finance wars and rebuilding efforts began to fuel discontent because there seemed nothing to be gained from it except for the further restrictions of a foreign power. The Roman Church appeared to grow richer and richer, combining the role of state and the role of religion. However, its authority was now questioned with the greater interest in new translations of the *Bible* which became available in the early sixteenth century. One important translation was that of the author Erasmus, who produced a version of the *New Testament* in Greek. Detailed study of all previous Christian theology was brought into focus.

The Reformers were to favour the theology of the *Bible,* which they took to be "revealed" theology. They accepted the authority of the earlier Councils and their creeds, but were to centre on the redemption aspect of Jesus in a more complete way. The main features concluded that those who respond to Christ in faith need no mediator, that the Church consists of a community of believers, that faith alone achieves salvation, and that God had spoken through the *Bible*. The decisive step was that taken by one Martin Luther, an Augustinian monk who had studied the *Bible* and church history at great length. Luther was a scholar who viewed the teachings of the *Bible* to be at variance with those of the Church. He understood the Church practice of selling indulgences, or pardons for misdeeds, as being totally against what Christianity stood for. To Luther, the grace of God was given freely to the individual. Hans Kung affirms the ideals of Luther as being biblically based:

> In his basic statements on the event of justification, with the "through grace alone", "through faith alone", the "at the same time righteous and a sinner", *Luther has the New Testament behind him*, and especially Paul, who is decisively involved in the doctrine of justification.[16]

Kung also recognizes the disappointments of the Reformation for Luther in later life, "First, the original Reformation enthusiasm soon ran out of steam".[17] "Secondly, the Reformation was coming up against *growing political resistance*."[18] In 1517, however, Luther posted his now famous ninety-five propositions on the door of the cathedral at Wittenburg as a challenge to the Church to account for itself. Their theme was "justification" by faith, the premise that by faith in Christ alone all are saved. There are no preconditions.

To take on the might of the Roman Curia or those who administered the doctrine of the faith meant that he was condemned immediately, and Luther is said to have defiantly stood on the principles he had laid down saying "Here I stand, I can do no other". Luther was excommunicated. Many people had already taken the thoughts of Luther on board, and it had developed to the stage where his ideas were not going to diminish. The Protestant Reform, a movement within the Church of those who believed the faith had been obscured by the innovations of medieval Catholicism, spread across Germany, Switzerland, the Netherlands and also into Britain, developing different characteristics as it went. Other names became associated with the movement, those of Zwingli and Calvin, European scholars of note.

Reform in Britain   Henry VIII of England, thought by many to be the instigator of the break with Rome by the church in Britain, was actually very much against Luther. He was to attack Luther's ideas and teachings vehemently and was awarded the title Defender of the Faith by the Pope for his efforts, and this title is still in use by the present British monarch. It is true that Henry wanted to be rid of his then wife Catherine of Aragon, but what was wanted was an annulment, or religious divorce which defines the marriage as never having existed in the true sense, an action of the Church which still applies in the Roman Catholic Church to this day. Annulments were by no means unusual in European royalty, but the Pope was pressured into refusing this one, by reasons political in nature. The situation at the time is acknowledged by William Havgaard:

> The Pope's canonical doubts about a possible annulment were strengthened by the presence in Rome of the soldiers of Catherine's nephew." [19]

The impatience of the King led to monies being with-held from Rome, and eventually to the "Act of Supremacy" being passed which allowed for the monarch to become head of both state and church. What has to be noted though is that had the wishes of the majority of the British people not been with the King it would probably never have got onto the statute books.

The other point is that it appears Henry had no notion of inviting the Protestant movement in. It seems that he always thought of the Church as Catholic, but reformed, and allied to England rather than Rome: Stephen Neill confirms this:

> But Mass continued to be said, as it always had been; and the official religion of England continued to be "Catholicism" without the Pope. [20]

Further legislation was passed giving Henry control of the wealth of the church, and this generated further resentment on the part of Rome.

Henry's daughter Mary succeeded to the throne eventually, and as an ardent Catholic she reversed all the Church legislation taken through by her father and pursued a policy of persecution of those who opposed her ideals. She was enthusiastic in her executions, and it is said that many more were put to death by hanging and burning at the stake during her short reign of five years, than in the combined reigns of Henry and Elizabeth. It was during the time of Elizabeth I as queen (1558–1603) that a compromise was reached between the reformers and the Church, and she was to assent to what are known as the *Thirty Nine Articles of Faith* in 1571. The *Articles* were the official summary of the Church's view of theology and points of doctrine in England, and are still a part of the Anglican Church today.

One other name that was influential during the Reformation in Britain is that of Thomas Cranmer who became Archbishop of Canterbury. His reformed principles were included in the *Book of Common Prayer* in 1549, and again in the one of 1552. He was burned to death for heresy when the Roman Catholic Sovereign, Mary, came to the throne.

Protestant groups   Several groups were to emerge with more fundamental Protestant ideas. The Anabaptists were one such group, who would only baptize those who would profess a personal faith, thus excluding infant baptism, believing it to be the correct teaching of the *New Testament*. Another substantial group within the Elizabethan Church, who adopted much more stringent attitudes to piety, were the Puritans. They opposed all signs of grandeur, including clergy robes, any form of dress code that might be considered frivolous, any activity on the Sabbath other than attendance at church, the signing of the cross on the body, and any practice that could not be defined as biblically correct. The Puritans eventually sailed for America in the seventeenth century and settled many churches in the then New World.

Roman Catholic Reforms   It could be said that the Protestant reformers were the initiators of a new positive outlook on the part of the Roman Catholic Church. New ways of working and conducting itself were instigated during the sixteenth and seventeenth centuries, and new religious orders were brought into being, such as the Theatines and the Capuchins. A Spaniard, Ignatius Loyola, founded a movement known as the Jesuits who made prayer and self-discipline their aim. They became a powerful missionary organization and spread Roman Catholicism around the world. Their missions to South America established schools, roads, work and hospitals for people who had none, and later in Europe they became involved in trying to save the continent for the Roman Catholic Church. By the end of the sixteenth century both Catholic and Protestant leaders were producing

COUNTER
REFORMATION

documents of faith, and the end result was to define more thoroughly the divisions that existed. Close and Smith note the negative side of what occurred:

> Denominations were defined by distinctions, and statements of belief tended to disregard common ground. As a result there was often a narrowing of horizons and impoverishment in religious faith.[21]

The Council of Trent (1545–63) was to restate a whole range of beliefs and practices in the Roman Catholic Church. It was convened by Pope Paul III and met over three periods. Major tensions were considered, such as the relationship between scripture and tradition, the doctrine of original sin, justification by faith alone, and the place of sacraments within the Church. The Council was suspended for a period but was resumed under Pope Julius III and for yet a third period under Pope Pius IV. Decrees on the Eucharist, on the sacraments of penance and the anointing of the sick, those of ordination, matrimony and the nature and duration of purgatory, were given. A whole range of disciplines and reforms were investigated, and were to lay the foundations for all future Roman Catholic teaching and theology.

THE ENLIGHTENMENT

The Age of Reason The eighteenth century in Europe was the period of history that has become known as the Enlightenment. This was the age of reason and enlightened philosophy, with science becoming the vehicle by which scholars explained the universe. The scenario of science versus religion was born. The stories of miracles and revelation were refuted and the ideas of heaven and hell were discounted. The scholars of the Enlightenment attacked what they saw as superstition, including the processions, the pilgrimages, and the idea of healing by faith. Explaining the Enlightenment simply, Wayne Detzler makes use of this interpretation: "Have the courage to make use of your own understanding, is therefore the watchword of the Enlightenment."[22] This was a time of huge discontent amongst the clergy and the laity, for never in history had these things been questioned. Everything became a matter for investigation, including biblical interpretation. All shades of Christianity felt threatened by the extent of it, and together with the secularism that had arisen in France due to the revolution, the authority of the Church was once again called into question.

Darwin's *Origin of the Species* was published in 1859, a book which explained his theory of evolution. The cry that went up at the time of course was: if humanity were descended from apes, what did that mean for the scriptures that told of humankind being made in God's image? The origin of humanity was brought into question, bringing an anxiety that had not been felt previously. The images of the *Old Testament* were thought to be primitive, and truth was no longer absolute, but relative, genetic and evolutionary. The search for reform became a breeding ground for all things radical. Marx, in his crusade to mobilize the masses, declared religion to be the opium of the people, the organized oppression of the upper classes, the manacles by which the poor and the destitute were kept in their place. For lack of clear thinking many lost their faith completely. They felt the historicity of Adam had been lost, and with it the doctrine of the Fall and the need for redemption. With hindsight it might be argued that it was this period of struggle between science and the Church that changed the British nation from a Christian one to the secular one it became.

Missionary faith   Remarkably, alongside all this radical investigation a more fervent reaction to all things orthodox emerged. This was the Evangelical Revival, a movement that was to reach a climax in the nineteenth century, a revival that was predominantly missionary in content, and one that found itself intellectually inferior to the scholars of the Enlightenment. Perry Butler regards those who participated as:

THE
EVANGELICAL
REVIVAL

> those "gospel" or "awakened" clergy who, between 1730 and 1760 underwent a conversion experience which drew them together in common cause to revitalize the Church and evangelize the nation. [23]

Expansion   This missionary activity was centered on land already colonized by the European powers, Africa, India, South America, all were given what at the time was deemed to be, the benefits of a superior civilization, a better attitude to work, education and religion. The indigenous peoples were taught to read and write, to be aware of the necessity for hygiene and clean water. They were shown how to make provision for their food and housing stocks, to cover themselves with clothes for the sake of decency, and all this of course in return for turning from their own forms of worship and embracing Christianity. There is no suggestion of course that the missionaries believed themselves to be doing anything other than good. They believed this was what God required of them and were only too happy to put themselves in all kinds of danger, bearing in mind that most were young women from the middle classes of Victorian Britain. Unfortunately the traders who followed the settlements to sell their wares were not so concerned for the native peoples' safety and brought with them all manner of disease and deviant behaviour.

In Britain   Evangelism was also continued at home, with ladies of a genteel persuasion giving time and money to show those engaged in drunken and loutish behaviour the error of their ways. The nineteenth century saw the intensification of family piety, with family prayers being the norm and grace being said before every meal. Self-examination and denial of pleasure were mixed with acceptance of one's role in life: one had a duty to refer to God, one's family and one's country. Organizations which are now part of the mainline Christian scene had their beginnings then. The Salvation Army, engaged then as it is now with those who find themselves in trouble, offered practical help where required. The Church Army, an arm of the Anglican Church, engaged in similar work, was out on the streets giving help where needed, and asking for repentance in return for salvation. Both organizations, as their names would imply, wear uniforms, and both are still engaged in the work of evangelizing and giving service to those who never go near a church building. Methodism was another church community which was to seek its independence from the main body of the church in Britain at this time. Its contribution to the education of adults and children alike was a major force in society at the time. Other groups over the years have emphasized different parts of the Christian faith, and gone on to form their own groups within the Church, and they are known as denominations. They adhere to their own kind of worship and practice, but all come under the broad umbrella that is Christianity.

ROMAN CATHOLICISM

Framework The Roman Catholic Church is the largest of the Christian denominations and is governed by its Pope, referred to as "The Holy Father', assisted by the Roman Curia, or those bishops who have become Cardinals. The Pope resides in the Vatican, a city which governs itself within the city of Rome, and from where all major statements of discipline are made. John F. Lahey explains the circumstances: "The Lateran Treaty with the Italian government recognized the independent sovereignty of the Vatican City State." [24] This Church considers itself to be the tradition that Peter the apostle founded when in Rome during the early years of the faith. Peter is deemed to have been its first bishop, and all his successors have been known as "The Pope", gaining this position of authority through what is called the Apostolic succession. This is the understanding that there is an unbroken continuation in the essential beliefs and practice of the Early Church, and this becomes visible in the way in which all bishops of the Church are appointed into their position by the laying on of hands by other bishops, thus ensuring union, each to the other throughout history. They all lead a diocese, or geographical area of the Church, conferring holy orders on those who are to be priested, administering confirmation to the laity, and blessing oils used in certain actions within the Church. Bishops in the Roman Catholic Church interpret teaching, and give pastoral and liturgical ministry.

There is a hierarchical structure, with the Pope being elected by those bishops who have become Cardinals, or figureheads in each country. When a Pope dies the Cardinals congregate in Rome, and by a series of voting procedures agree who will be appointed. The results of each vote are given to the outside world by means of smoke which rises from the Vatican chimneys. If no successor has been agreed black smoke rises, but if the smoke is white then a clear and convincing choice has been made. In 1870 the Vatican decreed that the position of Pope was "infallible", meaning that when the Pope speaks "*ex cathedra*" or from a seat of authority, then the content is true and binding on Roman Catholics.

There is a strict code of Canon or Church Law which is drawn up after consultation with the bishops, and is subject to change by them, which aims to express the teaching of the Church. Canon Law accords the Pope overall power, and the only way in which this may be rescinded is by death. The creeds form the code of beliefs and dogmas or decrees, and these are proclaimed as divinely revealed truths and are held to be binding on its people. They ratify the divinity of the Son, Jesus Christ, who is of the same substance as the Father, and directs that the Holy Spirit be worshipped and glorified. The theological principles engendered by these articles are the framework on which Roman Catholic thinking is based.

Sacraments   The sacraments, of which there are seven, are deemed to be those actions which reveal and communicate grace: "modern sacramental theology, . . . has emphasized that the Incarnation of Jesus Christ is the "first sacrament" [25] but the traditional sacraments are Baptism, when a child or adult may be admitted to the faith; Confirmation, usually around the age of eight years old; Ordination, by which priests are admitted to holy orders; Communion, which has the purpose of reliving the sacrifice of Jesus Christ on the cross; the service of Marriage; Penance, by which one receives pardon for past sins; and Unction when people or objects may be anointed with holy oil. The sacraments are deemed to be encounters with God through Christ, who has made the encounter possible. They are the visible signs of the invisible grace given.

The Mass   The Communion or Mass is central to the faithful, and celebrates the sacrifice of Christ as the full and final offering on behalf of humankind. In the same way that Christ shared the bread and wine at the Last Supper with the disciples, so the Church shares in this sacrament with all those who have been confirmed into the faith. The Mass is printed in a book called the *Missal* from which the congregation may read the form of words used, known as the *Liturgy*. The worship is divided into definite parts beginning with the penitential rite, when forgiveness is asked for, from both God and each other. Readings are taken from the *Old* and *New Testaments*, together with a passage from the Gospels, and this is known as the *Liturgy of the Word*. Then the priest consecrates the bread and the wine, a solemn act which allows for its setting aside for use by God. Roman Catholics believe that the substance of the bread and wine are changed at this point into the body and blood of Christ, and refer to this as transubstantiation. Before the bread and wine are distributed everyone says the Lord's Prayer, to confirm their belief, and then the priest asks the congregation to go forward to receive the Eucharist. Sometimes only the bread is given, constituting both kinds, but this is decided by local practice. It is received by communicants in their hands or straight to the mouth, and great care must be taken to ensure nothing falls to the ground because of its inferred status. For centuries the Mass was said in Latin but today is in the vernacular, although there are still those who feel something was lost when the Latin was dispensed with.

Mass is compulsory, and most Roman Catholics who practise will attend on Sundays and perhaps some other day as well, but will also partake when the marriage, funeral, or confirmation of one of their number is held. They may still only receive communion within the practice of their own denomination, and members of other denominations within the Christian Church are not allowed to receive in the Roman Catholic Church. This is due to the fact that the Roman Curia has never agreed that the Apostolic succession exists in any other group. Therefore all other priesthoods and ministry are seen as invalid, and so those Christians baptized and confirmed within other traditions are judged not to be of the Catholic faith and not eligible to receive communion with Roman Catholics. Whilst in most other aspects of worship there has been closer contact with the major denominations, the Eucharist remains a problem for those who wish to see greater ecumenism and causes great distress to those in mixed marriages, and to those who wish to see the Church united.

Baptism   The sacrament that receives a person into the Roman Catholic faith is that of Baptism, and may be given in childhood or adulthood. This initiation cleanses the person from the notion of original sin, a belief that all come into this world in a state of sinfulness. The child will have "godparents" or those who have agreed to make sure the child is brought up in the knowledge and experience of the Christian faith, preferably in the Roman Catholic tradition. In the case of an adult there will be "sponsors" present, friends who have come to give their support and advice to the initiate. During the service the person has the sign of the cross marked upon his/her forehead in water that the priest has blessed, and a lighted candle is presented. This symbolizes the light of Christ come into the world and that to always walk and talk in this light is the desire of the Church for the newly baptized.

Confirmation   Confirmation is a sacrament which compliments baptism, where the individual accepts responsibility for the living out of the faith. Children are "confirmed" at around eight years of age when they are deemed responsible enough to understand this commitment, and those who are not baptized until adulthood, would usually be confirmed at the same time. A bishop has to deliver Confirmation and this is done by the signing of the cross on the forehead with holy oil.

Ordination   Ordination provides for the entering into "holy orders" by the male members of the faith. Roman Catholicism has not yet allowed women to enter the priesthood, although there is a growing opinion amongst the laity for this to be done. However, given the male hierarchical nature of this denomination it is highly unlikely that this will proceed in the foreseeable future. The "sign" of priesthood is seen to be male, with the priest being the representation of Christ, who was male, at the altar. Together with the assertion that tradition and biblical writings only perceive him as calling men to be his disciples, this Church believes Christ to have instigated the male only priesthood. All those who enter the priesthood agree not to marry and to remain celibate for the rest of their lives, although this rule was only enforced in the Middle Ages. In recent years the office of deacon has been restored and this is open to married men but not to women.

Marriage   The sacrament of Marriage remains indissoluble, and so divorce is not an option for those who wish to remain fully within the faith. Where a divorce is instigated and concluded by a confirmed member, that member is unable to receive Communion thereafter, although he or she may still attend church. There is the option of annulment of the marriage by canon law, a long and technical procedure whereby statements are taken from those involved and canon lawyers will make a judgment. The judgment is reached as to whether a valid marriage in the eyes of the Church ever took place, and is dependent on whether those involved understood their total commitment to each other at the time of the marriage. Annulment gives the Roman Catholic the right to be married again in the church, divorce does not.

Unction and Penance   The remaining sacraments are those of Unction and Penance. Unction or anointing with holy oil is also given when a person is dying, as a preparation for death. It allows for the forgiveness of past sins and there is also the element of the provision of spiritual strength for the journey about to be undertaken. Masses may be said for the soul of the departed very soon after death, as an aid to its final destination, deemed to be with God. The sacrament of Penance is for the confession of sins. This takes place in a confessional "box", a number of which will be placed in the church. They are cubicles divided into two halves, one for the priest and one for the confessing member, where the priest is able to hear the confession through a grill section in the dividing wall. The priest will announce the forgiveness of the sin in the name of "the Father, Son, and Holy Spirit', and prescribe the penance to be made. This may involve the saying of a number of prayers with the help of a rosary, a string of beads used to count and identify prayers.

Buildings and practice   Places of worship, the church building, are those which have been consecrated, or set apart for this purpose. They are usually dedicated to a specific saint or idea, such as "Saint Mary" or perhaps "Our Lady of Sorrows', and every community of Christians, or parish, has its designated building. Every diocese, or group of parishes has a cathedral church, the seat of the bishop, which is normally the focus for large gatherings of members or for ordinations. Cathedrals may have schools attached to them, and will certainly have the benefit of large well-trained choirs and musicians to enhance the ritual taking place in them. Roman Catholic churches will vary in shape and construction but will contain those pieces of furniture which are to be found in many other denominations. These are the font, for baptism; the altar for the consecration of the Eucharist; a lectern for the delivery of the homily or period of teaching by the priest; and the confessional boxes already mentioned.

Other areas within the building are designated for the use of a Lady Chapel, used for private prayer, and the sacristy which houses the priest's robes and any other artefacts. There is always a special place, or tabernacle, reserved for the remains of consecrated bread and wine, and around the walls will be found statues of the saints and pictures or carvings of the stations of the cross, which depict Christ's actions on his last walk to his crucifixion. There is, of course, seating for the congregation and choir if there is one, and in the entrance to the church will always be found a niche in the wall, or perhaps a basin containing holy water with which each person will make the sign of the cross upon his or herself before entering the main body of the church. Roman Catholics always genuflect or bow the knee to the altar before taking their seat, and will also often light candles placed in areas within the church dedicated to saints or for personal dedications and prayer. In ritual, use is made of incense, the chanting of responses, and procession. Congregations make confessions of faith and of sins, sing hymns, say or chant psalms, and follow a particular form of words as laid out in the *Missal* during worship.

Teaching   Roman Catholic instruction on abortion and contraception are held to be sacrosanct, and therefore to participate in either is deemed absolutely wrong. "Catholic teaching continues to maintain the doctrine of the special creation of the human soul by God." [26] It teaches that life, and therefore the soul, begins as soon as the female's egg is fertilized by male sperm, and so to attempt to dispose of the result of that fertilization is tantamount to murder. It asserts that this position is unquestionable. Likewise with contraception, any attempt to prevent the fertilization of the female's egg is denying God's creation the ability to take place. Contraception, however, is widely used by Roman Catholic couples, and many within the Church hierarchy do not see it as a sin. Debates have arisen in the recent past as to whether contraception should be allowed, especially in African countries where the incidence of Aids is said to be epidemic. In these countries the Roman Catholic Church has many thousands of devotees led by very conservative bishops, who endorse the absolute doctrines of the faith.

For much of its history the Roman Catholic Church has kept itself separated from the rest of Christianity, due in the main to its exclusive understanding of its authority. It teaches authority over biblical interpretation, and priestly control over its sacramental life. However, it is far from unchanging, and as the twentieth century draws to a close there is a great diversity of opinion among its members, both ordained and lay. The Second Vatican Council of 1962–65, summoned by Pope John XXIII, did much to bring this about by promoting greater contact between the churches and with other faiths, and highlighting changes needed in its worship and practice. The present Pope, John Paul II, has been a reasonably popular figure travelling throughout the world, but caution and orthodoxy have been the traits of his leadership. Many of the changes that looked possible immediately after Vatican II were put to one side in preference for traditional teaching and this has caused much resentment and comment within the Church as a whole. It is impossible to forecast at this point the direction the Roman Catholic Church will take in the future.

Framework   The Anglican Church emerged from the period known as the Reformation explained earlier in this chapter. For political reasons Henry VIII gained the support of Parliament in rejecting the authority of Rome and making the English monarch "Supreme Head of the Church", a title modified by his daughter Elizabeth I to "Supreme Governor". It claims unbroken continuity with the original Catholic Church through its bishops, and consequently believes itself to be Catholic but Reformed. For this reason it holds together both extremes of Christianity within itself, having both those who would consider themselves fully Catholic and those who consider themselves fully Protestant.

THE ANGLICAN CHURCH

Some of its members will refer to themselves as Anglo-Catholic whilst others are known as Evangelicals, and between these two poles may be found many shades of both. This denomination then has been called the *The Via-Media* or Middle Way, a way of holding together in the face of dispute and disruption. Many see the genius behind this, as does James Atkinson:

The Elizabethan settlement produced an Anglicanism which was scriptural, traditional, and national, and which developed its own brilliant spiritual and cultural traditions.[27]

The present day sees this Church worldwide, an alliance of communities sharing a tradition and liturgy established in the sixteenth century, looking to a common titular head in the Archbishop of Canterbury, but being totally autonomous within its own region and boundaries.

Many of those people in Britain who have a tenuous relationship with the Church, if pressed would usually refer to themselves as C. of E. or Church of England, however even this tenuous relationship is misleading when in fact there are four Anglican communities in this country. They are the Church of England, the Church in Wales, the Church of Ireland and the Episcopal Church of Scotland, all having their own Bishops and governing bodies who decide on any issues within their own grouping. The Anglican Bishops throughout the world meet in London at Lambeth Palace, the official residence of the Archbishop of Canterbury, every ten years for talks on any of the major issues that affect the Church throughout the world, but none of the recommendations reached is bound to be endorsed by the different communities. Perhaps this is why it always appears to those outside the Anglican Church that it is always in dispute about what it actually believes, but this denomination maintains that exploration and interpretation are the keys to faith. Whilst the Anglican Church would base its practice on the *Bible*, its members have a freedom to explore and question the faith.

Church of England   The Church of England does have some aspects that are specific to itself, being the original seat of Anglicanism, and being the only Anglican province today that is still state established.

> The Anglican communion cannot be understood ecclesiastical and socially apart from a thorough comprehension of the Church of England, its mother [28]

The Crown, after consulting with the Church hierarchy, put forward the names of candidates to be appointed as bishops, who, when elected, also have seats in the House of Lords, a company made up of peers of the realm who sit in the upper chamber of Parliament. The bishops are subsequently elected by the chapters of the various cathedrals, but the church itself maintains the freedom to order itself through a body known as the General Synod, comprised of bishops, clergy and laity, although some of its decisions still have to be ratified by Parliament. England itself is divided into two provinces, those of Canterbury and York both having Archbishops, but with Canterbury still maintaining a superior status, and by tradition being the one who places the crown on the head of the monarch at a coronation. In recent years there has been much discussion as to whether the Church of England should remain the "established" church.

Local structures   The structure of all Anglican communions is basically the same. A Bishop presides over a diocese, which is subdivided into Rural Deaneries each with a Rural Dean, and these are made up of groups of parishes, each parish being administered by a Vicar or Rector. The Vicar or Rector is the priest responsible for pastoral and spiritual care to all those who reside within the parish boundaries, regardless of their religious affiliations, whereas the priests and ministers of other denominations only carry the responsibility to minister to their own members. Everyone who lives within the parish boundaries and wishes to be married in the parish church has that right, providing there are no legal complexities and that neither of the candidates has been married before. It can be seen then that the local Anglican priest may well have a heavier workload than the ministers of other denominations, especially today where there is such a shortage of priests that it is not unusual for them to be in charge of six or seven churches.

Each parish has a Parochial Church Council, or P. C. C. , which is made up of members of the church who are currently on the Electoral Roll, which is a list of communicants in the parish taken every Easter. It will also include the clergy of the parish and the church wardens, those who are elected to special office, plus members of the laity who have been elected by the parishioners. This group of people take responsibility for the practical and economic matters of running the local church, and they may also be asked to make known the feelings of the rest of the laity on spiritual or liturgical matters. Those who wish to put themselves forward for ordination must have the backing of the P. C. C. , and its support is crucial if there is to be a new incumbent priest, or the existing incumbent wishes to make any changes within the parish. Each committee includes the office of treasurer and secretary, and also includes sub-committees for such things as building work, social activities or the work of mission. There are elections every year for a new committee, but in practice it tends to be the same people over a period of years. Members are also chosen to represent the parish on other bodies within the diocese thus attempting to make church government democratic.

> There are lay readers, missionaries, lay pastoral assistants, laity on local ministry teams, in all, laity engaged in a vast variety of church work. [29]

Practice   There is much more diversity in terms of worship and practice than in most other denominations due to its representation of the "middle way". Those congregations which consider themselves to be

"Anglo-Catholic" have lots of ritual, candles, vestments and incense, whilst those of an Evangelical persuasion will have a much simpler service. In recent years many congregations have decided on a more liberal form of worship which uses modern language, music and dance, and there are those groups that have become "Charismatic", those who believe that through the gift of the Holy Spirit they may prophecy, perform healing and speak "in tongues". Singing, the saying of prayers and creeds, and *Bible* readings are common to all. What unites Anglicans throughout the world is the importance given to Holy Scripture, the Apostles' Creed, the Nicene Creed, the belief in the unbroken line of its Bishops, and the holding of two sacraments, those of Eucharist and Baptism. The use of Prayer Books for services is a common feature, and these include all the acts of public worship. This would be Morning Prayer, Evening Prayer, Baptism, Confirmation, Communion, Matrimony, and a set of prayers, psalms, and readings to be used on particular days throughout the year. The Doctrine and Beliefs of the Anglican Church will be set out here, and liturgical changes in the last twenty years means that they have been often revised or supplemented with pamphlets.

Baptism   The sacrament of Baptism is viewed in much the same way as in the Roman Catholic Church, in that water as a method of cleansing symbolizes the power of God in giving new life through the Church. Infant and adult baptisms take place, but in the case of adults there would have to be a commitment to confirmation in the near future. In the case of infants godparents are required and they take vows on behalf of the child, to ensure continuing involvement with the Church. A cross is signed on the forehead and a lighted candle and certificate of baptism is given, as in the Roman Catholic Church.

Eucharist   The other sacrament of Eucharist is similar in content too, except that Anglicans always receive it in both kinds, bread and wine, and not all would accept the transformation of it into the actual body and blood of Jesus Christ. Most would refer to it as a "memorial meal" understanding the content being received to be that of faith, and it is also termed as a celebration rather than the sacrifice that the Roman Catholic Church would have. In Anglican churches all baptized and confirmed members of other churches are invited to the Eucharist table, and many Anglican provinces are also in a wider Episcopal communion with other denominations which include the "Old Catholic Church" and parts of the Lutheran Church. Confirmation, ordination and marriage are seen as celebrations in the faith.

Confirmation   Confirmation is required before admission to Holy Communion and is usually undertaken about the age of fourteen, always after a period of instruction, always by the Bishop who lays hands on the candidate, and only to those who have already been baptized in the Church. Christians at this stage reaffirm the vows taken at baptism and make responses to questions from the Bishop regarding their repentance of sin.

Ordination   Ordination is for the laying on of hands by the bishop for those seeking to make their lives as priests and ministers of the Church. They will firstly be ordained as deacons and after further training will be ordained into the priesthood. Ordination is open in many provinces of Anglicanism to both men and women, although there are some who refuse to allow women ordination on the basis of tradition. Other offices are those of Lay Reader who may conduct Evening Prayer and preach at any service, and those in the congregation licensed to administer the chalice at Eucharist: both offices are open to men and women but are not part of ordained ministries.

Marriage   Marriage is seen as divinely ordained and therefore to be for life. Anglican priests are not allowed to marry those who are divorced and there is no concept of annulment as there is in Roman Catholicism. However, it is not unknown for some Anglican priests to preside at the weddings of divorced couples on the basis that it is not technically the Church that performs the marriage. The couple agree of their own free will to marry each other, and the priest is only there as a representative of the Church, to give a blessing, and to register the ceremony. There is a ceremony of Blessing that is freely available in churches after a civil ceremony has been performed.

Church buildings and religious garments   Most Anglican places of worship date from the Victorian period although there may be sections of the churches which date from much earlier periods, and are usually dedicated to saints. Most churches are in the shape of a cross, with the long central area being where the congregation sit (known as the nave), and the arms of the cross being known as the transepts. There may be an ornate screen which divides the congregation from the choir stalls, and this area is called the chancel; beyond that is the sanctuary where the altar is placed. The interior fittings are the same as those described for the Roman Catholic churches; the altar, being the table around which people gather to take Holy Communion; the font, placed at the entrance to the church to symbolize entry into the faith; the pulpit, for teaching; the lectern, usually in the form of the eagle symbolizing the Word of God being carried all over the world; and seating for congregation and choir. There may be statues, paintings and small chapels dedicated to certain saints or institutions, and there may be a confessional box, although this form of individual confession is something that takes place very rarely now. But all these will depend on the style of worship. Some places of worship will display a large suspended cross, which may or may not have the figure of Christ on it. Those crosses without Christ are to signify that Christ is not dead but risen, thus confirming the resurrection teaching. Some evangelical churches and those with a more liberal attitude to worship have reorganized the interior of their buildings, bringing the altar into the nave or body of the church, and in some cases closing off the chancel altogether. They may dispense with the use of the pulpit for the sermon, preferring to use a more modest lectern; and many of their priests now choose not to wear elaborate vestments but merely the stole around the neck, and the black cassock and white surplice. All still retain the clerical collar or "dog collar", which is a symbol for the halter of the slave. Bishops alone wear a mitre, a tall hat which symbolizes the flames of the Holy Spirit that descended at Pentecost.

Strengths   At its best the Anglican Church holds together all strands of the Church, those who wish to cling to the tradition of the past and those who seek to discover and interpret new ways of worship and investigation of theology. It may justifiably be called a "broad Church" for it is truly comprehensive, and it is this which gives impetus to its creativity. It has developed a particular concern for the unity of the Church as a whole, and in many cases shares buildings and services with other denominations and in some cases with other faiths, although it sometimes comes under criticism from some of its members for doing so. There has been a revival in religious communities in recent years, and this has led to greater spiritual awareness and the reintroduction of pilgrimages and retreats so prevalent in the early Middle Ages. There have been several meetings between the Archbishop of Canterbury and the Pope in recent years, and a closer association between Anglicans and Lutherans. All this contact and discussion is perfectly normal to the Anglican way of thinking, and whilst it may sometimes become uncomfortable for those who would prefer a more structured attitude to faith it is this which is the strength of Anglicanism.

THE METHODIST CHURCH

Framework   John Wesley and his brother Charles were the founders of Methodism, and this denomination, originating in the eighteenth century, now has worldwide membership of some twenty million worshipers. The Wesley brothers were born into a large family in Lincolnshire, sons of a Church of England clergyman, and were taught at home by a mother who was to influence their future thinking in relation to God and faith. They both studied at university in Oxford and became part of a group of students who met on a very regular basis to study the *Bible,* discuss theology, engage in prayer and the sacraments; They concerned themselves with social welfare. They lived and organized themselves to a method, earning for themselves the name Methodists. John and Charles both followed their father into the

Church of England, John becoming a noted preacher and Charles a celebrated writer of hymns. In 1735 they set sail for Georgia where they were to work for the Church, and it was during this time that they made contact with members of the Moravian Church, in whose company they experienced Reformation teaching as a simple faith in Jesus Christ.

On 24 of May 1738 John was to have a personal conversion experience, when he is reported to have felt his heart "strangely warmed", and from this moment on preached salvation by faith and individual experience. He was to organize groups of people in the pattern of the one he had been part of in Oxford, and they rapidly spread throughout the country, supplementing the local churches. The practical outcome of this type of fellowship could be seen in the care of the poor and the underprivileged, the provision of schools and clinics, the increased number of lay preachers, and the campaigns for better working conditions. John was so convinced that everyone needed to experience the saving grace of Jesus for themselves, that he was to travel many thousands of miles on horseback, preaching salvation and as to how this might be approached and received, and directing those who worked for the same cause. He was very successful, but brought much resentment and criticism upon himself from those who opposed this form of evangelism within the established religion. It seems throughout his life he always believed that this way of showing what faith was could be contained within Anglicanism, and it was never his intention to leave the Church of England. Yet steadily, after his death, these groups did break away and became the separate denomination we now know as Methodism. Charles remained active within the movement; he continued to write many hymns, some of which are still very well known today.

In 1744, John assembled in London all those clergy who were sympathetic, plus the increasing band of lay preachers who had joined, to formulate the organization and to establish doctrinal emphasis. The main belief was confirmed as salvation by grace alone. Salvation was achieved through faith, and faith in Christ could be seen at work through engaging in social care, thus giving witness to the work of the Holy Spirit. Everyone may be saved, Wesley declared, whatever their status, and no-matter how far they had fallen from God's grace. What was required was a personal relationship with God, which humankind was free to accept or reject, but one should not think that by good works alone an individual would enter into this relationship. The joy of receiving grace by the function of the Holy Spirit was to be conveyed to others, thus allowing for all to share in this gift, and through this way of networking there sprang up a familiarity between Methodists. They held meetings and regular house groups, would engage together in great joy to sing the hymns of Charles Wesley, and met many of the needs of society, which at that time was pulled apart by those who had too much and those who had too little. Methodism, then, was meeting the needs of local communities and the world, emphasizing freedom of worship and the priesthood of all believers.

Structures   The Methodist Church appears to be one of the best organized churches in the world. At the local level the church is governed by a Church Council which includes the minister, stewards and representatives of committees, who are elected by the members. Every Methodist church is part of a circuit, a group of churches sharing a team of ministers, and meeting twice a year chaired by a Superintendent. Circuits are grouped into districts, and meetings of districts are attended by representatives from the circuits. Each district has a chairperson who travels around visiting the churches and consulting ministers. Once a year the ruling body of Methodism meets in conference to decide policy and elect its President, a minister, and its vice-president, a lay person. A President's Council is appointed to govern throughout the year.

Buildings and practice   The Methodist Church accepts the Creeds and the principles of the Reformation, and so its worship follows the pattern of the non-conformist churches. The emphasis is on scripture, preaching, prayer and singing, and both men and women may become ministers, with services taking place in buildings which might look like just a large house from the outside. Inside the furnishing is kept very simple with a table from which to read the scriptures and to serve Communion, a pulpit to preach from, and a piano or organ to provide music. There may be a simple wooden cross stood on top of the table, and there are usually vases of flowers. In recent years some of their ministers have begun to wear vestments and stoles rather than the plain surplice and cassock of previous times. There are also local lay preachers who have received training in preaching and in leading services. The services include Family Services, a service of Holy Communion which is very similar to the Anglican one, apart from the use of individual glasses for the wine, and the probable use of bread broken from a loaf. There is usually a Junior Church or Sunday School for the children. Baptism of infants and adults is undertaken to receive them into the family of the church, and all may be confirmed into membership of the church at a service led by the Minister, Superintendent or Chairperson of the District. This denomination will marry divorced couples after discussing the responsibilities of marriage with them. They celebrate the usual Christian festivals plus some which are specifically Methodist, such as Wesley Day, held to commemorate the day John Wesley had his first experience of the Holy Spirit, and a Covenant Service once a year when Methodists, following John Wesley's practice, rededicate themselves to God's work.

Strengths Methodists play an important part in ecumenical discussions and projects, and in recent years have been involved in major discussions with the Anglican Church on matters of reconciliation. The talks did not succeed due to many on the Anglican side seeing reconciliation as a huge obstacle in any future dialogue they might have with the Roman Catholic Church. However, talks are ongoing and the long-term future may yield results. Within itself there have also been splits, with different groups being known as Wesleyan Methodists, Primitive Methodists and smaller individual groups. These divisions have healed over the years and the denomination in Britain is usually now referred to as "The Methodist Church of Great Britain and Ireland". Similarly in America it is called the "United Methodist Church".

Wesley, then, was concerned for the practice of Christian life. He made extensive use of lay people and this led to a more relaxed approach to Church structure, and to a greater awareness of social conscience. Methodism has seen a decline in its numbers in the last decade, but the memory of the evangelical revival of John Wesley and his brother Charles is still an integral part of the Christian faith, and may prove to be of invaluable help if there is ever another one. Methodists are in no doubt that biblical and theological unity are important in the Christian faith, and that there is one Church and one baptism only.

> In the twentieth century the Methodist Church has distinguished itself by continued emphasis on world mission, social reform, and ecumenism.[30]

THE BAPTISTS

Framework Baptists may be distinguished as a group by two main emphases, that of congregational government, and that of "believers" baptism. The first is made possible by the local community of believers being seen as both competent and able to interpret the teachings of Jesus Christ as written in the scriptures, the second by its members undergoing baptism as adults, being those persons who make an outward sign of an inward conversion. Most commentators view the early Baptists as indirectly coming under the influence of the Anabaptists of the Reformation, seeing them as developing out of the Puritan disturbances of Elizabethan England. Anabaptists were viewed as very radical in the sixteenth century, even, one might say, subversive, especially in denying the validity of infant baptism. Infant baptism was seen by them as an imposition, a way of enforcing religious conformity, and this was in direct conflict with the views of both Church and state, who saw the ritual as having a cohesive effect on society, and something to be desired. Consequently many Anabaptists were persecuted and many of their leaders executed.

The Baptist denomination itself may be said to have begun with an exiled group of English people in Amsterdam Holland in 1609. John Smyth had studied theology at Cambridge, and became a fellow of Christ's College, but was to go to Holland to escape persecution for his "extreme" views. He believed the Church needed to be seen as a company of believers, and saw the necessity of the outward sign of "believers" baptism. He baptized himself in 1608, and then proceeded to baptize others on confession of the truth in Jesus Christ. One of those he baptized was Thomas Helwys, who was to go on to form the first Baptist Church in England in 1612, known as "General Baptists". By the middle of the century another group emerged, and they were to be known as the "Particular Baptists", a group who were strongly Calvinistic in their theology. Whilst the "General Baptists" believed that Christ had died for all, and so salvation was applied to everyone by that single act, Calvinistic thought implied that Christ had only died for the elect, those who consciously repented and called Him Lord. John Spilsbury, a "Particular Baptist", was responsible for the establishment of seven churches in London by 1643, and by 1660 it is said there were twenty thousand converts in England and Wales. This appears confirmed by Ernest F. Clipsham: ". . . and by 1660 there were between 200 and 300 Baptist churches in England and Wales, most of them in London, the Midlands, and the South."[31] John Bunyan, the author of *A Pilgrim's Progress,* was a Baptist minister during that time.

American Baptists　One of the members of Spilsbury's group, Mark Lucar, settled in America where he introduced the new style of thinking to what remained of those Anabaptists that had sought refuge in New England. Baptist thought in America became more obvious when one Roger Williams, an immigrant, bought land from the indigenous Indians and started the settlement of Providence, which he founded on the principle of freedom of religious conviction. The eighteenth century brought many new converts in the wake of the new wave of evangelism, which became associated with the American Revolution and liberty of conviction. Many black Americans were to see something in the Baptist Church that raised issues that applied to them, and found the space within it to express their new freedom. By the end of the nineteenth century black Baptists had formed their own national organizations, and by the middle of the twentieth century two-thirds of all black Christians were Baptists. Baptists are now found in all parts of the world, being more visible in some continents than others. In Russia, for instance, they are opposed vigorously by the Russian Orthodox Church who see them as intruders, and are very conscious of the Baptist zeal in proselytism.

Authority of scripture　Very important in Baptist thought is the authority of scripture as the essence of faith and practice. *The New Testament* is seen as the principal means by which Christ has spoken to the Church, and as such, is the authoritative judgment for all credal statements, matters of faith and practice. Keith Clements sums it up:

> As the Declaration of Principle of the Baptist Union of Great Britain and Ireland states carefully: "Our Lord and Saviour Jesus Christ all matters relating to faith and practice, as revealed in the Holy Scriptures, i.e. the authority of scripture derives from the supreme authority and head of the church, who is directly accessible to believer and congregation, and to whom alone the conscience is ultimately responsible."[32]

The individual is said to have direct access to Christ through the Scriptures, and so the *Bible* is very visible during worship, and is studied in depth. Interpretation of scripture though tends to be conservative, and this can result in a rigid biblical theology which does not allow for any critique. The stress therefore is on prophetic rather than priestly aspects of religion and it may be said that they see dangers in any imposed uniformity, be that in worship, church government or definitive theology. The whole character of the denomination is that faith is voluntarily given and accepted, and this is a choice to be made by each one. Their faith is expressed in the responsibility they feel towards outreach. An effort has to be made to present the faith to those who have not perceived the revealed truth; their purpose is to win souls, to become missionaries of the Gospel. All this, however, takes place without the intrusion, as Baptists would see it, of any kind of synodical government.

Structures   Each local church has a minister who may be male or female, appointed and assisted by Deacons who share the role of leadership. Deacons are elected by church members and assist with the celebration of the Lord's Supper. Whilst each local church is independent, they do have connections with the international Baptist church through the Baptist World Alliance, founded in 1905. The Alliance was formed to indicate the cohesive nature of the unity found in Jesus Christ, and to promote cooperation amongst its members. Today it is a forum for discussion and inspiration amongst Baptist groups, with the World Congress being held every five years, as is a World Conference for Baptist Youth. However, there is no power to interfere at local level.

Buildings and practice   Worship can vary, from extreme informality to a quite formal and dignified choral extravaganza. What is common is that the worship has no liturgy, so requires no service book as such, and the emphasis is always on reading and preaching from the *Bible*, and prayers. The buildings usually look like large houses from the outside, and have fairly austere interiors. There is a pulpit, from where the minister will preach, normally wooden pews for the congregation to sit on, and always some form of accompaniment for congregational singing. A table is normally present on which may be a clean white cloth, flowers and a large edition of the *Bible*. No other furniture or decoration is expected. There is sometimes a Baptistry, a space down into which the person to be baptized descends. It will be filled with water when the event takes place, but at other times is kept empty and covered. Where there is no Baptistry the baptism may take place at some other public venue such as the local swimming baths, or certain rivers, and even the sea itself. "Believers" baptism is the baptism of those who acknowledge their own faith in Christ, and who are able to ask for forgiveness of past sin. It is usual to receive full immersion in water as a sign of the drowning of the past, and re-birth into new life. All baptized Christians are welcomed to take part in their services including the Lord's Supper or communion, and could be admitted to membership if they desired it.

THE EASTERN ORTHODOX CHURCH

As we have seen, it was in 1054 that a final schism occurred between the Eastern and Western Christian Churches. There were a number of disagreements which brought about this schism, but primarily it was because of the Eastern Church's objection to the West's addition of the word *Filioque*, which literally means "and the Son", to the Nicene Creed. This addition indicated that the Holy Spirit was believed by the Western Church to proceed from both God the Father and the Son, while the Eastern Church still maintained that God the Father was the unique source of both the Son and the Holy Spirit, and that the Holy Spirit proceeds from the Father, through the Son. Another difference that could not be reconciled was the fact that in the West the essential feature of Christian life is the individual's justification, whereas in the East it is his or her divinization. Justification means that God acquits man of the punishment due to his sins because of the sacrifice of Christ,[33] whereas divinization means that God became man in order that humankind might become divine like God. (This does not mean, however, that human beings are absorbed into the Godhead and lose their identification; indeed, the differentiation between humankind and God is still maintained.) Another cause of contention was the East's insistence on human beings' potential goodness, while the West emphasized humankind's original guilt or sin. In keeping with the West's emphasis on guilt is the idea of Christ as the victim, the sacrifice to God, which negates humankind's sin and thus leads to salvation, whereas in Eastern thought it is the concept of Christ the victor, triumphing on the cross over the powers of evil which is most strongly emphasized.

Another cause of disagreement was, and still is, that while Western theology tends towards a dualism, or distinction, between spirit and matter, Eastern theology conceives matter and spirit as two interdependent manifestations of the same ultimate reality. Then, too, for the

West it is of crucial importance that the right *dogmas* are held, while for the East it is believed that *worship* performed in the correct manner is of the utmost importance: indeed, the word "orthodox" literally means "right praise". Even more disagreements arose over the issues of celibacy for priests, and whether the bread used for the Eucharist should be leavened or unleavened. The final straw for the Eastern Church was the treatment it received at the hands of the Crusaders. As Ware says, "The pillage of Constantinople by the Crusaders is something that the Orthodox East has never forgiven or forgotten."[34] And so because of these differences, the Christian Church became divided into the Christian West and the Eastern Orthodox Church. The main Eastern Orthodox Churches are the Greek, Russian, Syrian, Armenian and Coptic Churches.

Holy Tradition   Eastern Orthodox Christianity has laid profound emphasis on tradition, and because of this has probably remained closer to the character of early Christianity than the Western Church. Tradition, therefore, is upheld in the scriptures, the Creed, the decrees of the seven Ecumenical Councils, the writings of the early Church Fathers, the liturgical service books, and in the use of icons. For the Orthodox Church, tradition means Holy Tradition, the divine revelations of God through his prophets, patriarchs and, ultimately, through the Incarnation itself. Ware comments:

> Tradition is the context in which scripture comes alive, the process whereby the truth of scripture is re-experienced by the Church in every generation.[35]

It is believed that Holy Tradition is the inspiration of the Holy Spirit itself, and, therefore, emanates from God. And if, it is argued, Holy Tradition is observed by the Church, then the Church itself becomes the truth of the Holy Spirit, and so cannot be wrong. Thus those who argue against Tradition and form new denominations or sects are deviating from divine revelation, from the truth. It is beliefs such as these which have allowed the Orthodox Church to maintain its purity of character. Holy Tradition is also maintained in practice because every aspect of worship, every object of ritual and every rite symbolizes some aspect of Christ's life and the Early Church.

Worship   One of the most important characteristics of Eastern Orthodoxy is its mystical dimension. Tradition emphasizes the mystery of Creation, the Incarnation, Redemption, the Resurrection, the Ascension and Pentecost, and it is this mystery, or mystical element, which the worshipper finds in the Orthodox Church. The bond between prayer and theology is a heavily emphasized one in Orthodoxy; theology is seen not merely as an academic pursuit, but is viewed as being pre-eminently liturgical and mystical because God, as a mystery beyond human understanding, cannot be described in words, but can only be conceived on a level beyond intellectual conception in a union of love.

Orthodox Church services are lengthy and the congregation often remains standing throughout. Much of the service is conducted from the eastern end of the church, behind the *iconostasis*, a tall screen covered with icons – pictures of Jesus, Mary and the saints. Again the *iconostasis* reinforces the idea of mystery because the laity is not permitted to go behind it to see what is taking place. Orthodox Christians frequently make the sign of the cross as a simple act of worship, and they may do so many times during the course of a day, for example, when entering a church, standing before an icon for a moment of prayer, passing a wayside shrine, or as a form of grace before a meal. Another simple act of worship which is widely used by Eastern Orthodox Christians is the "Jesus Prayer" which consists of the words "Jesus Christ, Son of God, have mercy upon me, a sinner". "The repetition of the name of Jesus brings purification of heart and singularity of desire. To call upon Jesus is to experience his presence in oneself and all things".[36] The prayer may be repeated over and over again while the individual reflects on the meaning of the words, and it may be said in rhythm with a person's breathing so that it becomes an unconscious act of prayer, performed while going about one's daily work. Another simple act of worship is the lighting of candles in front of icons.

Worship is intended to invoke Mary, the Mother of God, termed the *Theotokos*, as well as the saints. (Similarly to Roman Catholicism, Mary is placed above the saints, and her name is invoked both in public and private prayers.) The invocation of Mary and the saints is not seen as an optional extra, but as an essential element of Orthodox prayer, and thus occurs in every service. It is believed in Orthodoxy that those who have died still share in worship and complete the fullness of the Church. There is, then, in the Eastern Orthodox Church, an emphasis on the "other worldly" dimension: worship, whether solitary or congregational, is believed to be conducted in the company of unseen presences, and the participation of the unseen church in earthly worship is continually emphasized: "Now the powers of Heaven worship with us invisibly".[37]

Icons Icons, literally "images", play a very important part in Eastern Orthodox worship. Icons are stylized paintings or mosaics of Jesus, Mary, his mother, the saints and scenes from the *Old* and *New Testaments*, which occupy a prominent place in both private and public worship for members of the Orthodox Church. There is no attempt made at earthly realism in the icons because they are meant to be representative of the reality of the divine realm, and not the phenomenal one. They are venerated as windows to the eternal, as much a medium of revelation as the spoken or written word. The icon is not an idol to be worshipped, however, but is a symbol by means of which contact may be made with a more profound reality. The function of the icon is, as Baggley says, "to externalize the sacred tradition and to enable the beholder to enter into the unseen world of the spirit which transcends and yet interpenetrates the world of matter and the flesh".[38]

Many of the major icons are placed on the *iconostasis*, the screen that separates the congregation from the sanctuary at the eastern end of the church, where only the clergy may enter. On either side of the opening to the altar, which is a door in the *iconostasis*, are icons of Jesus symbolizing the Incarnation, the descent of God into earthly human life, and of Mary, the *Theotokos*, or God-bearer. Icons of God Incarnate, Jesus, together with icons of Mary and the saints, instil the idea that humankind is both the link and the cause of the separation between the two realms of the spirit and the flesh. Human beings were made in the likeness or image of God, therefore they are God's images or icons: thus Orthodoxy emphasizes that individuals may find God by searching within themselves.

Ceremonies   Eastern Orthodoxy, like Roman Catholicism, accepts seven sacraments, which are called "mysteries". These are Baptism, Confirmation, Divine Liturgy, Matrimony, Ordination, Penance and Unction. (After the Reformation, the Protestant Church came to accept only two sacraments: Baptism and Communion.) Baptism represents for the Orthodox Church the incorporation of a newly–born Christian into its community. At the baptism ceremony the naked new-born child is plunged into the font three times, and is totally immersed in the sanctified water, except in cases of emergency or sickness when it is deemed sufficient to pour water over the baby's forehead. Baptism represents the washing away of sin, and being born again as a child of God. Once dressed (in white), the priest anoints the child with oil, the chrism, which has been blessed by a patriarch or head of an autocephalus (self-headed) Church, making the sign of the cross on the forehead, eyelids, nostrils, lips, ears, chest, hands and feet. As he does so the priest chants the words, "The seal of the gift of the Holy Spirit." This last part of the ceremony, that is the anointing with oil etc., is called the Chrismation, and is the equivalent of the Confirmation ceremony in Western denominations. The child is now deemed to be a full member of the Church, and may participate in all forms of worship, including Divine Liturgy.

Divine Liturgy is the name Orthodoxy gives to the mystery or sacrament which is commonly called the Eucharist, Holy Communion or the Lord's Supper by the Western Church. Notwithstanding the different name the main parts of the service are similar to those of most

Western Christian denominations: readings from the *Bible*, prayers and the partaking of bread and wine which have been consecrated by the priest at the altar or "Throne" as it is called in Orthodox Christianity. Unlike the Western Church, however, the leavened bread is put into hot, red wine, and both are given to the communicant on a spoon, directly into the mouth. Divine Liturgy is seen as a feast for both body and soul, and the communicant does not kneel after the consecrated bread and wine have been consumed because his or her entire being has been sanctified and is in a state of divine grace. As at all Orthodox services, there is traditionally no instrumental accompaniment during Divine Liturgy.

It is believed by the Orthodox Church that the Holy Spirit comes upon the bread and wine, actually transforming them into the body and blood of Christ. Divine Liturgy, then, is seen as the revelation of the Divine Presence in the material world.[39] Because it is regarded as a mystery which should not be watched directly, much of the service takes place behind the closed door, known as the Beautiful or Royal Door, of the *iconostasis*. This is meant to convey the idea that God may not be seen directly, but can only be seen through those things in which God chooses to reveal himself. When the Royal Door is opened, it symbolizes the coming of Christ to the people, breaking through the barrier which separates them from God.

The mystery or sacrament of Matrimony or Marriage is known as "Crowning" in the Orthodox Church. Crowns of silver and gold are worn by the bride and groom respectively. Crowns are seen as signs of joy and victory, but also as crowns of martyrdom: there can be no true marriage without loving self-sacrifice on both sides. Rings are exchanged, but neither the bride nor the groom makes any promises during the service: all that is required is that they acknowledge that they are free to marry, and consent to do so. Ideally the marriage will last a lifetime, but the Orthodox Church nevertheless accepts that marriages do sometimes irretrievably break down and allows divorce and remarriage in certain circumstances. Although in the past contraception was forbidden, it is now widely tolerated, especially among Orthodox in the west. Abortion, however, is still regarded as a grave sin. Bishops have the authority to grant divorces, but these are usually only granted when someone has been deserted by his or her partner; when a partner is declared insane; when a partner is imprisoned for life; or when a partner is unfaithful. Second marriages, and occasionally even third marriages, may be celebrated in church, but a different ceremony from that of Crowning is followed, one which contains an element of penitence for failing to maintain the original marriage. But whether following the death of a partner or divorce, no more than three marriages are permitted. In some countries civil marriages only are considered legal and valid. In such cases couples may go to the church after the wedding for a blessing.

Ordination is the fifth mystery or sacrament – it is the ordination of priests into the priesthood. The Orthodox Church has continued the tradition of allowing only men to become priests or ministers. A man is usually over the age of thirty before he becomes ordained, and although he may marry, he must do so before his ordination. Married priests are permitted to work only in local churches, and may never rise to the position of bishop; indeed, bishops are required to take monastic vows and lead a life of celibacy. The training for married priests is consequently not as long and involved as it is for priests who choose to remain unmarried, and who can, it is believed, give greater commitment to the Church. If the wife of a parish priest dies, he may not marry again, even though he will never achieve higher office.

Penance or the sacrament of Confession is the penultimate mystery, and, as it is regarded as voluntary, it is left to the conscience of the individual how often he or she receives it. A person performing an act of penance is expected to have been reconciled first with any person that he or she may have hurt or offended. It is only after reconciliation has been effected that the penitent approaches the priest and makes his or her confession. The priest does not consider himself to be a judge, however, simply a fellow-member of the Church, whose aid and brotherly advice may facilitate the act of repentance.

Holy Unction is the final mystery, it is the sacrament of the Anointing of the Sick. It is not, and never has been, restricted to those in danger of death, and thus anyone may receive it. This sacrament is closely related to the sacrament of Confession: both transmit forgiveness for sins. As it is considered that human beings are a unity of body and soul, it is believed that the illnesses of both body and soul may, therefore, be healed together.

When an Orthodox Christian dies, that person is not treated as though he or she has lost all contact with the Church, but is remembered in the prayers of the living. The newly deceased is brought into the church building whenever possible and laid in an open coffin so that mourners may pay their last respects. A strip of cloth, containing images of Jesus, Mary and the saints, may sometimes be placed over the forehead of the deceased and, similar to the laurel wreath of an athlete, it symbolizes the idea that the earthly race has been won. During the funeral service, lighted candles, which are held by the mourners, become symbolic representations of Christ as the Light of the World, the giver of new life.

Festivals Pascha, or Easter, is the most important festival in Eastern Orthodoxy. (Christmas, the other major Orthodox festival, is very similar to the festival in the Western Church.) Pascha begins on Palm Sunday, which is the Sunday before Easter, with the bringing of palm branches into the church. This is done in remembrance of the time when Jesus rode into Jerusalem, and palm branches were laid before him as acknowledgment of his importance. The Lord's or Last Supper takes place on Great Thursday; and, following Jesus' example in washing the feet of his disciples, bishops wash the feet of some of their priests, as a gesture of humility and service on this day. On the following day, Great Friday as it is known in Orthodoxy, a cloth bearing the image of Christ is arranged on a stand in the middle of the church. This symbolizes the laying out of a body, and recalls the day of Jesus' death. People bearing candles stand around the cloth like mourners, and on Great Saturday the cloth is carried in a funeral procession around the church. Prayers are said for the dead during this time because the period after the Crucifixion is traditionally seen in Orthodoxy as the time when Jesus went to preach to the dead. Great Saturday is also the day when special food is brought into the church, food that will be consumed on the following day, Pascha. Often this food consists of elaborately decorated, coloured eggs which may be cracked together to symbolize the breaking open of Jesus' tomb.

As midnight on Great Saturday approaches, and the church stands empty and dark, worshippers, led by their priest, carrying a cross and an icon, walk slowly around it. At one minute past midnight, on Pascha, the doors of the church are flung wide open and the priest announces that Christ has risen, while light floods into the church symbolizing Jesus' Resurrection, the Light returning to the world. Liturgy follows. Pascha is celebrated at a different time in some Orthodox countries because while the churches of Jerusalem, Russia, Serbia and Poland continue to use the Julian Calendar, the remainder of Eastern Orthodox Churches use the Gregorian Calendar which was adopted by the Western Church in the sixteenth century.

The Trinity In Eastern Orthodoxy the teaching of the early Councils on God as trinity-in-unity, one essence in three persons, is accepted in its entirety. In other words, although it is agreed that all three persons of the Trinity are equal, co-eternal and truly personal, and that each is fully God, it is also accepted that the three are not completely separate from one another, and so do not form three Gods, only one. God is believed to be absolutely transcendent; far beyond humankind's knowledge and comprehension. So how, then, can humankind have any conception of God? Eastern Orthodoxy answers this question by distinguishing between the transcendent essence of God, which cannot be known, and the immanent, divine energies of God in which humankind can participate. As Basil of Caesara so aptly commented: "We know our God from his energies, but we do not claim that we can draw near to his essence. For his energies come down to us, but his essence remains unapproachable".[40] It is, therefore, these energies which make God personal to the Orthodox Christian. Jesus Christ, in Orthodox belief, is thought to be fully and completely divine and also to be fully and completely human, but this does not mean that he is two separate people, he is only one. And even though during the Incarnation Jesus had a human body and soul, and human emotions, still he did not cease to be the true God. Similarly, the Holy Spirit is not simply regarded as a quality of God or an impersonal force, but as fully personal, the third member of the Trinity, equal to both the Father and the Son, even though the Father is deemed to be the unique source of both the Son and the Holy Spirit.[41] As noted earlier, it was the differences in interpretations of the Trinity that finally led to the schism between Eastern and Western Christianity.

To illustrate the very diversity of Christianity, it is necessary at this point to examine some non-conformist Christian denominations or sects; and the four that have been chosen for this purpose are the Religious Society of Friends, the Church of Jesus Christ of Latter-Day Saints, Jehovah's Witnesses, and the Church of Christ, Scientist. A sect is, by definition, exclusive: that is, it claims that it alone has the authority of Christ; on the other hand, the term "denomination" is an inclusive, neutral term which suggests that the group referred to is simply one member of a much larger group to which other Protestant denominations belong.[42] The tolerance of one religious group towards others, then, appears to determine whether that group should be designated the title denomination or sect, and thus care should be taken when applying these terms.

We shall begin by examining the Religious Society of Friends. The choice of this particular movement for examination at this juncture is not an indiscriminate one; indeed, it has been chosen specifically because it follows the section on the Eastern Orthodox Church, and highlights the comparability of the two with regard to the belief of the divine within.

Founder George Fox, born in Fenny Drayton, Leicestershire in 1624, was the original founder of the Religious Society of Friends, perhaps more commonly known as "Quakers". After the Reformation in 1660 there were all manner of separist and dissenter groups springing up, with all kinds of non-conformist political and religious ideas, each "seeking" the truth. And on to this scene came a very powerful personality. George Fox united many of the disparate groups of "seekers" – people who could not accept that the forms of Christianity they observed around them were in keeping with Jesus' teachings – to form the Quaker movement, what was then seen as a return to "Primitive Christianity". Fox taught, in his first sermon, something very radical for the time: that each individual has a direct relationship with God and immediate access to him because there is "that of God in everyone". In other words, God is not to be found outwardly, but can be found deep within oneself. Thus Quakers believed, and still believe, that they can have direct communion with God, without the mediation of the Church and of clergy, because they

THE RELIGIOUS SOCIETY OF FRIENDS (QUAKERS)

rely, not on the outward authority of the Church and tradition, but on the inward authority of the spirit. However, Fox's teaching was considered by the religious establishment of the time to be heretical and blasphemous, and so early Quakers were persecuted for their beliefs. Following the restoration of Charles II, mass arrests were made: "Out of fifty thousand Friends, five hundred died in jail".[43] Fortunately, William Penn, the founder of Pennsylvania, USA, who was himself disowned by his family for becoming a Quaker, and others like him, advocated freedom of worship for non-conformist groups, and this eventually led to the Toleration Act of 1689.

In 1650, in court on a charge of blasphemy, Fox told the Judge that he should "Quake at the word of the Lord";[44] from this statement, and also because some members of the society "quaked" during services, the movement was given the derogatory nickname of "Quakers" by some of its critics. Over three hundred years later, it is no longer considered derogatory and it is by this name that the Society is now best known. Individual members are known either as "Friends" or "Quakers", and these names are used interchangeably, although members usually refer to each other as "Friend".

Organization The organization of the Society is kept as simple as possible; it is democratic, and both men and women take an equal share in it. There are no paid priests or ministers to lead the meetings for worship, although there are "elders" – Friends specially appointed to be responsible for the spiritual life of meetings and for the general well-running of the Church. These appointments last for a term of three years, although they may be renewed, and do not confer any particular status on the holder because Friends firmly believe in the equality of all worshippers. The Overseer is another office: Overseers are responsible for the more practical aspects of life in the Quaker community, for pastoral care and, in particular, care for those who are dying, ill, poor or in need for any other reason. The Registering Officer is a Friend appointed by members at a Monthly Meeting, who is recognized by the Home Office as being responsible for the organization of Quaker weddings; it is his or her responsibility to ensure that marriage regulations, both the legal requirements and the requirements of the Society itself, are met.

Beliefs The Religious Society of Friends has no set dogmas or creeds, so Friends have always found it relatively easy to tolerate a very wide range of views. There are, however, some commonly held views which unite them. The most important of these is the view that there is "that of God in everyone"; that God's real presence can be found amongst humankind, and that the Divine Will can be made known to anyone who seeks it. This, we might suggest, is reminiscent of the Eastern Orthodox concept of God in that, although transcendent, humankind may still participate in God's immanent, divine energies. Quakers believe that everyone is equally one of God's children whatever race, creed, sex or sexual persuasion one is; and that religion is a way of life, not something to be followed only one day a week.

Members of the Society have never been forced to conform to any particular concept of Christ, holding that the only true test of a Christian is whether a person lives in the spirit of Christ-like love, and not what a person says he or she believes. There are no set beliefs with regard to such concepts as the Trinity, the Incarnation or the Resurrection of Christ. There is also no set belief in an afterlife for Quakers: there are, on the one hand, Friends who are convinced that there is an afterlife, while there are, on the other hand, those who are equally persuaded that there is not. There is, however, no concept of an afterlife which is a reward for virtue, nor one which is a compensation for suffering. It is deemed more important to enjoy the present life, and to seek to improve conditions in this world rather than to waste time idly speculating about the next.

One reason why Quakers distrust credal statements is because of their awareness of the limitations of words to express the deepest human experiences. Nevertheless, the absence of creeds does not mean that what a person believes is unimportant; indeed, it is recognized that personal belief strongly affects a person's behaviour, the way in which a person lives his or her life. Thus Quakerism is a group of attitudes, insights and practices which together form a way of life rather than a dogma or creed: secular and religious life, consequently, for the Quaker, are inseparable.

Worship As a specially consecrated place is not required for the purpose of worship, Quaker meetings may be held practically anywhere. And, in the early years of the Society, Quaker meetings were often held in farmhouses, kitchens, barns or even in the open air. Nowadays, however, most meetings are held in Meeting Houses owned by the Society. There is one fundamental need for a Quaker meeting, and this is an adequately sized room where people can gather together comfortably. The room will be very simply furnished, with benches or chairs, depending on whether it is an old or new Meeting House, and the seating will be arranged to form either a circle or a square, so that Friends and Attenders (people who worship regularly with Friends, but who have not yet become members), can face each other. There are no trappings familiar in other Christian places of worship, such as an altar, pulpit, font, lectern or organ, and no ornaments or religious symbols, although there will probably be a table supporting a copy of the *Bible*. There might also be a copy of the Quaker publication *Christian Faith and Practice in the Experience of the Religious Society of Friends,* which is updated every thirty years or so. The meeting will usually be held on a Sunday morning, but this is purely for convenience as no day is considered more holy than any other day. Congregations may vary in size, from very large to very small ones.

Meeting for worship is the core of the Society's life. The service itself is very simple: there is no set procedure – no prescribed prayers, hymns or readings. There is no Eucharist or Holy Communion service to symbolize the presence of God by the use of bread and wine because Friends are aware of his presence within. No priests or ministers are required either because the responsibility for the meeting belongs to each and every member present. The meeting, which usually lasts for an hour, begins when the first person arrives and sits down in silence and stillness. Gradually others arrive, and so meetings assemble. The first thing that a newcomer will notice is that the meetings are held in silence, which is a unique feature of Quaker worship.

Although people come as individuals to the meetings, their aim is to achieve a sense of profound communion with others present. Quakerism is a religion which seeks to transcend ordinary consciousness in order to gain experience of God within. This is not an individual experience of God within, however, but a group one in which everyone shares, and it can be a somewhat mystical experience. Sometimes meetings are held entirely in silence, but more often there is some spoken contribution, and this is known as "vocal ministry". Anyone may speak; the only stipulation is that what is said must be spontaneous and in response to the spirit of the meeting: it must not, therefore, be prepared beforehand because this would deflect from the true atmosphere of the meeting. The spoken contribution might be in the form of a thought or an experience which the contributor wishes to share with the remainder of the congregation, something that he or she feels might help someone to a similar awareness. Alternatively, it might be a reading from the *Bible,* a poem, or perhaps something from the Society's own literature, or even from a science book, because Quakers believe that God did not finish teaching humankind when the *Bible* was completed – there is something of God in other teaching too. Vocal ministry might also be in the form of a prayer, but this is less common now than in former times.[45]

Children are accepted as an integral part of the community: it is felt that they have a role to play in upholding the life and worship of the Society. Provision is made for the children during meetings, where possible, in rooms on the premises. A wide range of activities are available, depending on age, ranging from painting and playing with plasticine for the youngest children to work projects, discussion groups and play-acting for the older ones. The children are given an introduction to the Quaker understanding of Christianity, but this is done objectively, without any hint of indoctrination, which would be abhorrent to Friends, and it is accepted that it is the responsibility of the parents to educate their own children in all matters of religion, which, as we shall see, is a view shared with Jehovah's Witnesses. Children take an active part in meetings, spending ten or fifteen minutes among the congregation, either at the beginning or towards the end, so that they can gain first-hand experience of silent worship.

Quaker marriage   Marriage has always been seen by Quakers as a religious commitment rather than simply a legal contract. George Fox, in 1669, described the Quaker view:

> The right joining in marriage is the work of the Lord only, and not the priest's or magistrate's; for it is God's ordinance and not man's . . . we marry none; it is the Lord's work, and we are but witnesses.[46]

Quaker marriages are solemnized in Meeting Houses during a meeting for worship appointed specially for the purpose, and the validity of the marriages is recognized in law. The wedding itself, as might be expected, is a very simple and informal one, compared with weddings from most other religious traditions. There is no priest or minister to lead the couple as they make their promises to each other and take each other equally as life-long partners. The start of the meeting begins, as usual, in silence; then, after ten or fifteen minutes, the bride and groom stand. Holding each other by the hand, they take it in turns to make their promises. The groom usually makes his promises first, but as Quakers believe in the total equality of the sexes, this is purely a matter of personal preference. The promises are the same for both:

> Friends, I take this my Friend (full name of partner), to be my husband/wife, promising through divine assistance to be unto him/her a loving and faithful wife/husband, so long as we both on earth shall live.[47]

The declaration must be made in English, except where Welsh is commonly spoken, then a Welsh version of the declaration is acceptable. The wedding certificate, which records the promises, is signed by the couple and two witnesses. The Registering Officer then reads it aloud in its entirety. Every person present is responsible for the witnessing and upholding of the marriage, even the youngest child, so everyone present is required to sign the certificate. As this might take some time, it is usual to defer the signing until after the meeting, which usually continues for a further half an hour, during which time anyone who feels moved to make a vocal contribution may do so.

After the conclusion of the meeting (which occurs when two elders shake hands), the couple, the Registering Officer and the two witnesses sign the civil register in a separate room. Quaker women may choose to keep their maiden surname as a testament to the equality of the sexes, or they may adopt the surname of their husbands. Traditionally wedding-rings were not exchanged as they do not play an official part in Quaker marriage; recently, however, the exchanging of rings has become more popular.

Non–Friends may also be married in Quaker Meeting Houses, if it is deemed appropriate and acceptable by the congregation. Divorced couples, too, may be granted permission to marry again in a Meeting House, but this is solely at the discretion of the particular members of a congregation. Although there is some diversity of thought concerning divorce, Quakers generally accept that marriages do sometimes irretrievably break down, and when this happens in a community there is a sense of failure for all the members, who will question whether they have been partially at fault in not offering enough love and support to the couple. When a breakdown does occur, Friends attempt to help couples separate as amicably as possible, so that there remains an attitude of care and respect for each other and any children involved.

Quaker funerals The current popularity of cremation has brought about a change in the style of Quaker funerals. Originally the coffin of the deceased would be carried into the Meeting House where a brief meeting for worship, giving thanks for the life of the deceased person, would be held before internment in the burial ground surrounding the Meeting House. Now it is more likely that the family and some Friends will participate in a meeting for worship at the crematorium. Sometimes a memorial meeting for worship is held at a later date in honour of the deceased Friend. In such circumstances and in keeping with Quaker tradition, the occasion will be a simple one, with no extravagant expenditure on wreaths and floral tributes or elaborate mourning clothes.

Absence of baptism There is no formal baptism ceremony for either adults or children in Quakerism because the use of outward ritual sacraments does not form part of Quaker worship, as we have noted. Friends tend to seek to experience the sacraments in an inward manner without symbols, feeling that the ritual can often become more important than the meaning it is intended to convey. When a child is brought to a meeting for worship for the first time, however, its arrival may be marked with a simple welcome at the end of the meeting. Whether or not children should be accepted as members has caused some discussion within the Society, and while some parents wish their young children to be accepted as members, others prefer to allow their children to wait until they are of an age to make the commitment to join the Society themselves.

Peace Since the beginning of Quakerism, Friends have been opposed to war, following the teachings of Jesus who emphasized the desirability of loving relationships and attitudes towards others: "Blessed are the peacemakers, for they shall be called Sons of God." (*Matthew 5:9*) In 1661, which was a time of great civil unrest in Britain, the peaceable intentions of the Quakers were called into question. In response, a declaration to Charles the Second from the Society of Friends was made which stated:

> We utterly deny all outward wars and strife and fightings with outward weapons for any end, or under any pretence whatever; this is our testimony to the whole world.[48]

And this has remained the Quaker attitude to war to the present day: as Barbour so aptly comments: "Outward violence they saw as only the devil's distraction, injuring God's good physical creation".[49]

In the nineteenth and twentieth centuries, most British Quakers have opposed all wars including the Crimean, Boer and other colonial wars, as well as the two World Wars, and the more recent Falklands/Malvinas conflict and the Gulf War. This attitude has meant imprisonment for many Quaker Conscientious Objectors who have refused point blank to participate in any active service which might assist a war effort. However, although Quakers will not accept active service, some have accepted non-combative service with the armed forces, and have served in the Friends Ambulance Unit, relieving the sufferings of civilian war victims, and helping with rehabilitation work, both during the time of hostilities and after. Many Quakers willingly put themselves at risk because of their love for humanity, for their belief of "that of God in everyone", and their desire to help those either rejected or neglected by society. This is why, since the time of Elizabeth Fry, they have taken, and are still taking, an active part in prison reform, and the rehabilitation of released prisoners, working with the mentally ill, and seeking to improve race relations, to name but a few.

Close relationships   Quakers are not unaware of changing social attitudes, and recognize that there can be loving, non-exploitative relationships outside marriage. Friends accept that it is the quality and nature of a relationship that matters, and that relationships should not be judged by their outer appearance but by their inner worth. Thus homosexual and heterosexual relationships outside marriage are accepted by most Quakers. Having said that, however, Quakers do not intend to alter their own views on the importance of marriage, still seeing it as "God's work" to quote George Fox. As for extra-marital sex, Quakers being the tolerant people that they are, recognize that people do sometimes fail, but still try themselves to remember the promises made during the Quaker wedding service when each partner promises to be "a loving and faithful wife/husband".

Contraception There is no official statement or view concerning contraception in Quakerism. The final decision is left to the individuals involved, so while many Quaker couples use contraception, preferring to limit the size of their family, other couples choose not to do so, allowing nature to take its course. All methods of contraception are acceptable: the contraceptive pill, inter-uterine devices (IUD), spermicides, condoms, avoiding sex at times of optimum fertility, or surgery to prevent contraception, whether for males or females. There is also no official view on abortion, each case being determined on its own merits or as a matter of personal choice or conscience. Quakers accept that there might be a variety of reasons why a couple might prefer a small family, or even no family at all: perhaps because the couple cannot financially afford more than one or two children; or because they are concerned that the woman may need to be free to play a full role in society; or because the couple are troubled about the ever increasing size of the world's population and its dwindling resources, which is a major concern for Friends. Since the advent of Aids some Quaker groups have considered whether to install condom vending machines in Meeting Houses which may be used by public groups other than themselves: "to provide the idea of safer sex",[50] not that Quakers wish to encourage promiscuity; rather, they wish to foster a sense of responsibility. Whatever their opinions, however, Quakers would never attempt to inflict their views on others as that would be an infringement of another person's rights, and this would be unacceptable to them.

THE CHURCH OF JESUS CHRIST OF LATTER-DAY SAINTS (MORMONS)

Founder Joseph Smith, the founder of this minority sect, was born in Sharon, Vermont, on 23 December 1805. As a young man Smith was disturbed by the differences in doctrine of contemporary Christian movements, and this made him uncertain which path he should follow. However, on 21 September 1823, while praying, Smith had a vision: a messenger from God, the angel Moroni, appeared before him and told him the whereabouts of a book written on gold plates which contained the Gospel as delivered by Christ to the ancient inhabitants of America. Nevertheless, it was not until four years later, on 22 September 1827, that the plates finally came into Smith's possession, and he was able to translate them.

The translated book became known as *The Book of Mormon*, because it had originally been written by Mormon, Moroni's father, fourteen centuries earlier (hence the more popular name of the sect: Mormons). Its style is not unlike that of the Authorized Version of the *Bible*. Smith originally translated the first section of the book to a wealthy neighbour, Martin Harris; unfortunately, Harris took the translation home with him and never returned it. And, to this day, the book lacks the initial 116 pages. The remainder was dictated to Oliver Cowdery, a faithful and trustworthy follower.

The Book of Mormon comprises 14 books, and covers the period from about 2200 BC to 421 AD. It purports to relate the history of the migration of two separate groups, both of Hebrew origin, to America. The Jaredites, the first group, have their story told in the *Old Testament Book of Esther*, while the next wave of immigrants who came from Jerusalem around 600 BC, Lehi and his family, who eventually become known as the Nephite and Lamanite tribes, have their story told in *Books 1 & 2 Nephi* of *The Book of Mormon*. In the *Third and Fourth Books of Nephi* the coming of Christ to America, after the Resurrection, is described, when the true Church was established among both the Lamanite and Nephite tribes. And, fourteen centuries later, directed by God, the book was revealed to Joseph Smith by the angel Moroni. Thus the Church of Jesus Christ of Latter-Day Saints came into being, and was officially founded on 6 April 1830. *The Book of Mormon* is so important to the Church that it is accepted as scripture, and put on an equal footing with the *Bible*.

Although at first *The Book of Mormon* was ridiculed, this soon gave way to interest because the book has a very optimistic, spiritual message that is very practical. It promises a reward not only in heaven, but also on earth, which was a very radical idea for the nineteenth century. Smith taught that God had chosen him as a latter-day prophet or saint who would revive the Old Church, and prepare people for the imminent Second Coming of Christ and his rule of one thousand years of holiness and light, known as the Millennium. The Mormons, Smith taught, were God's chosen people, the true sons and daughters of Israel. All members of Smith's Church, therefore, become known as Saints, all others, gentiles.

A variety of locations were tried for the Church: it was first based in Kirkland, Ohio, where an existing religious community that had converted to Mormonism was located. But when the Church ran into financial difficulties and problems with its neighbours, it moved on to Nauvoo, a place meaning "beautiful plantation", Illinois, leaving in its wake its newly completed temple. Because of some of the more contentious aspects of their doctrines such as polygamy, or plural marriage as Mormons themselves prefer to call it, they suffered much persecution. Smith was imprisoned several times, and in 1844 he and his brother Hyrum were both killed when a hostile crowd attacked the jail in which they were being held.

The previous year Joseph Smith had publicly announced his desire that his twelve-year–old son, also named Joseph, should succeed him in the event of his death. But, while a number of members acknowledged the prophet's wish and formed what later became known as the Reorganized Church of Latter-Day Saints of Jesus Christ, the majority elected to follow Brigham Young, a charismatic man, who had only converted to the religion in 1842.[51] It was Brigham Young who, in February 1846, led the Mormons into the uncharted desert areas of the west to find their promised land. On 24 July 1847 they arrived at the Great Salt Lake, Utah, and set about building a city there, and this is where Mormon headquarters have been located ever since.

Beliefs: the concept of God   The Mormon concept of God is a very anthropomorphic one, and it is believed that God is a tangible, material being. The belief is based on the *Genesis* statement that man is made in God's image (*Genesis* 1:26): if God is like human beings, it is reasoned, then he must have a physical body of flesh and bones. It is accepted, however, that God is superior to humankind. Another idea which is an integral part of Mormon theology is the concept of an ever-evolving God, who was once similar to human beings, but who has evolved to the state he is now. Mormons also teach that humankind, through its efforts in this life may aspire to literal godliness in the next. And so it follows logically that Saints believe in a plurality of gods: in the words of Joseph Smith:

> The weakest child of God, which now exists upon earth, will possess more dominion, more property, more subjects, and more power and glory, than is possessed by Jesus Christ or by his Father, while at the same time, Jesus Christ and his Father will have their dominion, kingdom and subjects increased in proportion.[52]

There is, then, Mormons maintain, a council of gods over whom the Supreme Spirit presides. The council includes Elijah, Abraham, Paul, Joseph Smith, Brigham Young as well as Jesus Christ.

Jesus Christ   The Mormon view of Jesus is that although he is superior to humankind, Christ is inferior to God, and so too is the Holy Spirit. The three are completely separate, independent entities: the Trinity, then, in Mormonism is not accepted in the way that it is in orthodox, mainstream Christianity. The Mormon doctrine of the pre-existence of all spirits (see below) holds that all spirits were "begotten by Heavenly Parents even as Jesus was".[53] This suggests one of two things: either that Christ is a being like human beings, that is to say Christ was simply a man, or that humankind is part of the Godhead like Christ which is a pantheistic or panentheistic viewpoint. In either case the uniqueness of Christ as put forward in the *Bible* disappears completely.

The Holy Spirit   As previously noted, in Mormon belief the Holy Spirit is believed to be inferior to God, but is, nevertheless, acknowledged as the third personage of the Godhead, after the Father and the Son. The Holy Spirit is further described as a personage who may manifest himself in the form of a man:

I spake unto him as a man speaketh; for I beheld that he was in the form of a man; yet nevertheless, I knew that it was the Spirit of the Lord; and he spake unto me as a man speaketh with another.[54]

In his actual person, it is believed, the Holy Spirit has a located existence and is therefore confined to a limited space: in other words he is not, and cannot be, omnipresent, like God.

Spirit Beings The belief in Spirit Beings, or Spirit Children, is derived from passages in the *New Testament* which suggest that Jesus existed before the creation of the world: "He was in the beginning with God" (*John* 1:2; cf. *Romans* 8:29; *Colossians* 1:15; *Hebrews* 12:23). Mormons consider that because Jesus existed in pre-mortal form, then humankind, too, must exist in a spirit form before being born on earth. Every person, it is believed, exists with God in a spirit form which is not unlike the form the resurrected Jesus took, that is, not an invisible, ghost–like form, but a physical spirit form. Coupled with this concept of premortal existence is the teaching of Jesus that God is not only *his* father, but is also *our* father: this suggests to Mormons that every being has lived with his or her Heavenly Father before coming to earth in mortal form. For this reason, Saints refer to God as "Our Heavenly Father". It follows, consequently, that all human beings are descendants of God and are, ultimately, God-like: they are literally the children of God, and life on earth is seen merely as one episode in a continuing spiritual life. This belief in Spirit Beings means that abortion is totally out of the question for Mormons: to destroy a fetus would be to destroy a Spirit Being.

The three heavens The traditional Christian concepts of heaven and hell are rejected by Mormons. It is believed that humankind has been given free will and so may choose to do good or evil, thus the concept of original sin is not accepted here – people are punished for their own sins, not for those of Adam. And because there are many different degrees of righteousness and wickedness on earth, this must also be reflected in the afterlife. From this line of reasoning, Joseph Smith concluded that there are three heavens: this is based on St. Paul's second letter to the Corinthians: "I know a man in Christ who . . . was caught up to the third heaven" (2 *Corinthians* 12:2). The first heaven, the lowest, is called "Telestial Glory", and though it is designed for those who have led sinful lives on earth, it is not a disagreeable place. An opportunity of rising to a higher level will be given to those who find themselves here.

"Terrestrial Glory" is the name of the second heaven. On this plane may be found righteous men and women, ordinary non-Mormon Christians, and those Mormons who have not reached the highest standards. The third and highest heaven, "Celestial Glory", where

God himself dwells, is reserved for those members of the Melchizedek priesthood and their wives who have accomplished all the necessary good works. Unmarried priests are disqualified from this state of bliss, such is the importance of family life to Mormons. Those who reach this elevated state need not remain, but may evolve further until they become gods in their own right. The belief in salvation through faith in Christ alone is thus not accepted.

The Millennium   Mormons believe that in a very short time Christ will return, set up his kingdom on the American continent, and from there rule the world for one thousand years (a belief also held by Jehovah's Witnesses), a period known as the Millennium. During the Millennium, Mormons will spend their time engaged in a threefold task – preaching, building temples and baptizing the dead. The preaching will be aimed at those non-Mormons who have been considered righteous enough to remain on earth during this period. The evil, although physically dead, will survive spiritually and will be afforded another opportunity to repent and cleanse themselves through suffering. At the end of the Millennium, Satan will assert his power for a short time, but his final doom will follow swiftly. Roundhill says:

> Those few (Mormons believe that there are not many) who are incorrigibly wicked and sinful will accompany him to everlasting punishment.[55]

Organization   The Mormon Church organization is hierarchical: at the top is the Prophet-President, who is reputed to be both the administrative head and a prophet through whom divine revelation may come. Next in importance are the Prophet-President's two counsellors; the Quorum of Twelve; the First Quorum of Seventy; and the Presiding Bishopric, all of whom are located in Salt Lake City, Utah.[56]

Areas are divided geographically into states and wards. Each state, which is presided over by a State President, is made up of between two thousand and four thousand members; states are further divided into wards, which usually consist of between two hundred and five hundred Mormons, and are governed by bishops. The bishop who is responsible for appointing local church officers and is concerned with both the spiritual and material needs of his members, is aided by two councillors. All members of the Mormon clergy are male and unpaid.

Congregations are divided into hierarchical grades: boys from the age of twelve may be ordained into the Aaronic priesthood. Aaronic priests are then subdivided into three groups: Deacons from the age of twelve to fourteen; Teachers aged fifteen to seventeen; and Priests aged eighteen and nineteen. Males above the age of nineteen are admitted to the Melchizedek Priesthood, which is also sub-divided: Elders, Seventies and High Priests. At the age of twenty-one, members of the Melchizedek Priesthood are eligible for any office in the Church.

Women, however, are not permitted into any of the priesthoods, and "are admonished to remain at home to raise children, while partaking of the priesthood only through the male heads of families".[57] The sole institutional role given to women by the Church is in the Relief Society which is devoted to charitable and educational work, and the only way that a woman might reach the highest heaven is through marriage to a Melchizedek Priest. Women, however, are not the only people to have been discriminated against in the past by the Mormon Church: it was not until 1978 that Prophet-President Spencer W. Kimball's revelation extended the priesthood to Mormon negroes.

Worship   Mormon worship is a very simple affair. The main service, held in the local Meeting House or chapel, is the Sunday evening "Sacrament Service" which lasts approximately an hour and a half, although Mormons spend most of the remainder of Sundays at the Meeting House, socializing with other Mormons. The service consists of hymns, an opening and closing prayer, and talks given by members of the congregation. Because of the system of tithing, there is no collection. Tithing provides all the finance necessary for the maintenance of the Church, but it is not compulsory: no one is excommunicated if tithing is failed to be paid! However, people are expected to attend church regularly, and the degree to which one is considered a "good" Mormon is assessed largely by such attendance. In addition to Meeting Houses there are Mormon Temples: magnificent churches built only in cities. Not everyone is allowed to enter a Temple, however:

> Only those Mormons who observe their religion's strict rules of conduct are allowed to enter the temple and participate in these ordinances and rituals.[58]

Baptism   Infant baptism is not practised by Mormons, who feel that the decision to become a member of their church should be a conscious and deliberate one. Baptism, then, takes place after the age of eight, when a child is deemed old enough to take responsibility for his or her own actions, and it is done through total immersion in water. Mormons do not smoke, drink alcohol or take drugs. Even "hot drinks" such as tea and coffee are forbidden because it is believed they might pollute the body which has been purified by baptism, and even during the Communion Sacrament, water is used in place of wine.[59]

Mormons believe that only those who have been baptized into their church may enter the highest heaven, as we have previously noted. In view of this, Mormons feel a compelling duty to arrange baptism for their dead ancestors in order that they, too, may enjoy the full benefits of heaven, even if the ancestors themselves were not Mormons. Thus Mormons have become active genealogists, tracing their forebears back centuries. Once a Mormon has sufficient evidence, he or she may go to one of the Temples and have the ancestor baptized by proxy. The genealogical evidence is then microfilmed and stored in enormous weatherproof and bombproof vaults which are located beneath the mountains of Salt Lake City.

Marriage   There are two classes of Mormon marriage: first and second class. The first class marriage is called "Celestial Marriage", which has to be performed in a Temple;[60] it may even be performed if one of the partners is no longer living. Joseph Smith taught his followers that while ordinary marriage, of the second class, was a covenant that ended when one of the partners died, Celestial Marriage, a marriage "sealed" for eternity, would survive the separation of death, and the couple would be reunited as husband and wife, together with their whole family, after resurrection.[61] It is believed that the highest grade of salvation, entry into the third heaven, may only be achieved if a couple has undergone Celestial Marriage.

Another of Smith's claims concerning marriage was that in 1843 God had commanded him to practise polygamy, or plural marriage as Mormons prefer to call it, and he enjoined his followers to do likewise. Both of the early founders of the religion practised polygamy: Joseph Smith had an indeterminate number of young wives and children, while Brigham Young died in 1877 having married twenty-seven women, and having fathered at least fifty-four children. The practice of polygamy was nevertheless officially discontinued on 25 September 1890, during the presidency of the fourth Mormon leader, Wilford Woodruff, when he issued a document known to Mormons as *The Manifesto*. Since 1890, any Mormons who participate in plural marriages are excommunicated.[62] (Nevertheless, there are still many polygamous Mormon groups).

The communion sacrament   An important sacrament in Mormonism is the Communion Sacrament or the Lord's Supper Sacrament. Wine is not used during the Sacrament, but it is replaced by water. Partaking of the bread and water reminds Mormons of the Resurrection of Jesus. The bread and water represent the body and blood of Christ, although they are not thought to be actually transformed into his flesh and blood. By partaking of the sacrament, Mormons are symbolically making a new covenant with God, promising to "walk before him" as Abraham did; in other words, promising to keep God's commandments and to live life according to his laws.

Family life   The Mormons place great emphasis on family life, which, as we have seen, they believe may be continued after death. Indeed, after faith, the family is perhaps the most important aspect of the purpose of life for the Mormon. Every Sunday the family, led by the father who is the divinely appointed head of the household, goes to worship in the local Meeting House. Family prayers are customarily said together, morning and evening, and Monday evenings are set aside for the "Family Home Evening". During these family home evenings, families may study the *Bible* and *The Book of Mormon* together, praying and singing hymns, then time might be spent playing games or discussing ways of improving the home environment, planning holidays and such – participating in activities designed to bind the family together in a stable unit. The family is also united by the Mormon missionary purpose. As soon as a child is born, money is set aside for the time when the child, as an adult, begins his or her two–year evangelical work as a missionary, spreading the Mormon gospel. Originally only males became missionaries, but exceptional females are also now accepted for this important work.

Education is of great importance for the Mormon family, because it is believed that whatever intelligence is acquired in the present life will be taken into the next, and learning continues in the world to come. Joseph Smith believed in the importance of education as an essential aspect for salvation: this belief has produced many Mormon schools, seminaries, colleges, religious institutions and, most famous of all, the Brigham Young University.

Another reason that the family is of such importance is because of the concept of Spirit Beings or Spirit Children, which was discussed above. Mormon couples have an obligation to produce as many children as possible, in order to provide earthly life for the Spirit Children waiting in heaven. Thus contraception is unacceptable in Mormonism whether it be through use of the contraceptive pill, condoms, surgery to prevent contraception, avoiding sex at times of optimum fertility, or abortion. This last would be an abomination – the destruction of a Spirit Child, preventing its return to its Heavenly Father.

JEHOVAH'S WITNESSES

The founder The original founder of this minority sect was Charles Taze Russell, born on 15 February 1852 in Pittsburgh, USA. Dissatisfied with the Presbyterian Church, the religion with which he had grown up, Russell first joined the Congregationalists, and then the Adventists from whom he absorbed some of his teachings concerning the Second Coming of Christ, the *Parousia*. Nevertheless, neither of these movements totally satisfied him, and so he set about forming his own religious sect.

In 1872 Russell published a pamphlet which predicted the Second Coming of Christ in 1874, and the end of the world in 1914. When Christ did not appear in 1874, as foretold, Russell accounted for this by assuring his critics that Jesus had returned, but the event was an invisible, secret one. In 1879 Russell began publication of *Zion's Watch Tower*, a magazine he personally edited for thirty-seven years until his death in 1916, which survives to this day under the title *The Watchtower*, and which is sold door-to-door by Jehovah's Witnesses in countries all over the world. Because of Russell's magnetic personality, his gift for oratory and his indefatigable work, he quickly built up a worldwide organization of over three million members, that has its headquarters today in Brooklyn, USA. When Russell died unexpectedly in 1916 there was, for a time, some confusion as to whom would be the most suitable person to succeed him. Finally, Joseph Franklin Rutherford, known as "Judge" Rutherford because he had previously been legal advisor to the sect, took over the presidency. It was Rutherford who, in 1931, gave the movement its name, Jehovah's Witnesses; it had previously been known either as "Bible Students" or, more popularly, "Russellites", after its founder. Rutherford remained President of the society until his death in 1942. The Presidency of the Jehovah's Witnesses is, in fact, a lifetime appointment.

Beliefs: Armageddon One of the major beliefs of Jehovah's Witnesses is their belief in Armageddon, the end of the world as we know it. This belief is based on *Revelation* 16:14;16 which states:

> for they are demonic spirits, performing signs, who go abroad to the kings of the whole world, to assemble them for battle on the great day of God the Almighty . . . (*Revelation* 16:14).
> And they assembled them at the place which is called in Hebrew Armageddon. (*Revelation* 16:16).

The word "Armageddon" comes from the Hebrew *Har Megiddo*, "Mountain of Megiddo", or the plain of Megiddo where, according to the *Book of Revelation*, the final battle between the forces of good and evil, God's armies, led by Jesus, and Satan's armies, will take place. The year 1914 was predicted by Jehovah's Witnesses as the time of Armageddon initially because, it was believed, this was the time indicated by Jesus in *Matthew* 24:7:

> For nation will rise against nation, and kingdom against kingdom, and there will be famines and earthquakes in various places. (*Matthew* 24:7)

The fact that in 1914 World War I broke out adds credence, Jehovah's Witnesses believe, to their claim that the beginning of the end of the known world has come. However, this would be no ordinary war: Roundhill comments:

> This battle will not be fought by earthly armies (it is not, for example, a Third World War) but is to be a conflict between good and evil on the spiritual plane.[63]

But despite its spiritual character, physical destruction and death will follow in its wake. After Armageddon, in which Jesus will achieve a resounding victory over Satan and his forces, everyone who is not a member of the Society of Jehovah's Witnesses, that is the "Gentiles", will die. The survivors will then obliterate all remnants of the old world, which will take seven years to complete. Satan, originally an angel who rebelled against God, will be chained up, unable to cause further harm, for one thousand years, and this period is what is known as "the Millennium". Paradoxically perhaps, although Jehovah's Witnesses believe in Satan, there is no concept of a fiery hell to which humankind will be condemned for eternity, only a state of permanent unconsciousness for the unworthy,[64] because it is believed that a loving God could never tolerate an everlasting torment for anyone, however evil.

The Kingdom of God   The concept of paradise, interchangeably known as the Kingdom of God, the Millennium or the New World, is rather more complicated than the concept of Armageddon. It is believed that 144,000 of the most righteous individuals, who are all Jehovah's Witnesses, given the name "Little Flock," will govern in Heaven with Jesus Christ. As the full complement was reached by 1935, anyone born after that date will not gain admission to the Little Flock.

The number 144,000 is arrived at from the teaching in *Revelation* 7:4–5:

> And I heard the number of sealed, a hundred and forty-four thousand sealed, out of every tribe of the sons of Israel, twelve thousand sealed out of the tribe of Judah, twelve thousand of the tribe of Reuben, twelve thousand of the tribe of Gad . . . (*Revelation* 7: 4–5) [65]

From this it would appear that every single person comprising the 144,000 must be of Jewish extraction; however, Jehovah's Witnesses argue that this interpretation is not meant to be taken literally. Notwithstanding, there is no distinct, formalized concept of Heaven; all that is understood is that the 144,000 are much to be envied.

The remainder of Jehovah's Witnesses, the "Great Crowd",[66] an indeterminate number, will remain on earth, but a transformed earth – a new world – a paradise where there will be no suffering or evil, no hunger or poverty, no crime, no trades unions, no employers' organizations: a place where each man will labour for the benefit of his own family alone.

Members of the Society, the faithful, who died before Armageddon will be resurrected to enjoy their just reward; and everyone will be blessed with health and youth:

> Wrinkles of care and age will be smoothed away, grey hair will have its

youthful colour restored and a surge of perfect health will invigorate the flesh with supernal youth.[67]

Human reproduction will continue until a satisfactory population size has been reached, and will then cease. However, this idyllic state will not last forever: after one thousand years Satan and his minions will once again be free to cause devastation and destruction.

Jesus Christ Another major belief which diverges from orthodox Christianity is that of the nature of Christ. Traditionally, Christianity accepts that Jesus is on the same plane of being as God; in other words Jesus is God: "In the beginning was the Word [Jesus], and the Word was with God, and the Word was God" (*John* 1:1). Jehovah's Witnesses, nevertheless, do not accept Christ's divinity, that he is God: for them Christ is merely a secondary or demi-God, whom they identify with Michael, the Archangel.[68] Another concept that Jehovah's Witnesses reject about the nature of Jesus is his eternity. When Jehovah, or God, began to create, his first creation was his son, Jesus; it follows, consequently, that Jesus could not be eternal if he did not exist prior to that time. The biblical evidence that is cited in support of this belief is *Colossians* 1:15 and *Proverbs* 8:22 ff respectively: "He is the image of the invisible God, the first born of all creation" and "The Lord created me at the beginning of his work, the first of his acts of old". And if Jesus was created by God, *ipso facto*, he must be inferior to God.

Yet another concept which is repudiated by Jehovah's Witnesses is the incarnation of Jesus as understood by orthodox Christians: Witnesses maintain that the life-force of the pre-existent son was transformed by God to the womb of the Virgin Mary, with the result that Jesus was born as a mere mortal man.[69] It appears, consequently, that Jehovah's Witnesses divide Christ's existence into what amounts to three separate, unconnected chronological stages: the first, as a Spirit Being after his creation by God; the second, his existence on earth as a human being; and the third, after his resurrection, when Christ was exalted once more to become a divine spirit, to sit at the right hand of God, his father. We may note here interestingly the comparison between Jehovah's Witnesses' belief in Christ as a Spirit Being and the Mormon's concept of Spirit Beings.

Salvation, for orthodox Christianity, is achieved through Christ who died for humanity and thus paid the penalty for sin. Salvation, therefore, is not something Christians earn, but is God's gracious gift, which is appropriated through faith in Christ. For Jehovah's Witnesses, however, Christ's death does not guarantee eternal life for anyone. It simply gives those who believe in Christ a second opportunity to earn eternal life for themselves after they have been resurrected from the dead. Put another way, everlasting life is not a gift from God for those who have faith in Christ, but is a reward earned through personal merit, what Burrell and Stafford-Wright describe as a "do-it-yourself" enterprise.[70]

The Holy Spirit   The concept of the Holy Spirit as accepted by mainstream Christianity is also denied. Jehovah's Witnesses regard the Holy Spirit as simply an impersonal force, and not the Third Person of the Trinity who dwells within every baptized Christian. In *Make Sure of All Things*, a booklet published by the Watchtower Society in 1953, the Holy Spirit is defined as "Jehovah's invisible energizing force (greater than atomic energy) that produces visible results in many manifestations experienced by men".[71] In other words, the Holy Spirit is simply God's invisible active force[72] through which he carries out his will. It follows, consequently, that the orthodox Christian doctrine of the Trinity is repudiated by Jehovah's Witnesses, and, indeed, there is no actual mention of the Trinity in the *New Testament*. It was in fact not until the Council of Constantinople in 381 AD that the concept of the Trinity first came into being.

Blood   Perhaps the most contentious belief of Jehovah's Witnesses is their objection to the receiving of blood transfusions and the giving of blood donations, even though such may save life. Jehovah's Witnesses base their objections on their interpretation of scriptural evidence such as *Leviticus* 17:10–14; *Genesis* 9:4–6; *Acts* 15,19, 20, 28 & 29. And, indeed, as Thompson says:

> The Old Testament forbids the eating of blood in meat, and Witnesses argue that, if it is wrong to take blood into the body through the mouth, it must also be wrong to take it directly into the veins.[73]

In *Old Testament* times it was considered that blood was the life-force of the body, and as such belonged to God; the transfer of that life-force without God's sanction, would not, therefore, have been acceptable then, and is still not acceptable to Jehovah's Witnesses today.

The *Bible*   The *Bible*, of which Jehovah's Witnesses have their own translation (entitled the *New World Translation of the Holy Scriptures*), is relied on very heavily, and members probably have a better working knowledge of it than members of most major Christian denominations. Their knowledge is used in conjunction with their own literature, *Watchtower* and *Awake!*, which are their own commentaries on the *Bible*. Any religious rites, theology, beliefs, teachings or customs which are not sanctioned by the *Bible* itself are totally rejected, as we have seen with regard to the Trinity and blood transfusions. The authority for this is based on *Acts* 17:11:

> Now these Jews were more noble than those in Thessalonica, for they received the word with all eagerness, examining the scriptures daily to see if these things were so. (*Acts* 17:11)

For this reason, Jehovah's Witnesses do not celebrate Christmas, which they believe is a festival of pagan origin, probably derived from the Roman festival of Saturnalia; and, in any case, Witnesses believe that the actual date of Christ's birth was 1 October 2 BC. (Christmas was not, in fact, an official festival in Christianity until the fourth century AD.) Similarly, Easter is rejected because it is not mentioned in the *Bible*, and because it was originally a spring festival in honour of the goddess of light, Oestre or Eastre. Birthdays, too, are not celebrated as there is no scriptural evidence in support of them: the only birthdays mentioned in the *Bible* are those of an Egyptian Pharaoh (*Genesis* 40:20) and Herod Antipas (*Matthew* 14:6, *Mark* 6:22) both of whom were pagans. Interestingly birthdays were not celebrated by early Christians either.

One of the fundamental claims of Jehovah's Witnesses is that the true meaning of the *Bible* was not revealed to humankind until the nineteenth century, when Jehovah revealed its inner meaning to Charles Taze Russell, the founder of their society:

> After the death of the apostles (they say) the Bible was treasured and read, but until Jehovah God began to reveal its meaning to Pastor Russell in the nineteenth century, it was as obscure as is a book in an unknown tongue.[74]

Thus it is believed that the Witnesses' interpretation of the *Bible*, one which often differs greatly from other Christian denominations, is the only true interpretation. The *Old Testament* is known to Jehovah's Witnesses as the Hebrew Scriptures, and the *New Testament* as the Christian Greek Scriptures.

Worship   Ritual for a Jehovah's Witness is minimal. Baptism, which is by total immersion in water and symbolizes dedication, is rarely performed in any purpose-built pool: often a swimming pool is specially hired for the occasion, and an invalid may even be baptized in a bath. Baptism is usually carried out at one of the circuit or district assemblies. Marriage is another accepted rite. As previously noted, there are no festivals since these are not supported by scriptural evidence; however; there are national, district and circuit assemblies which it is expected that members attend. Congregational gatherings, which take place at the Kingdom Hall, usually on Sunday afternoons, are important, "Kingdom Hall" being the name Jehovah's Witnesses give to their equivalent of other denominations' places of worship. Members are expected to prepare for these by reading the current

Watchtower magazine, verifying biblical references and answering the questions raised in advance. The same teaching is being promulgated through the *Watchtower* at the same time by Jehovah's Witnesses' congregations all over the world, which engenders a strong sense of unity.

Each member of the congregation is called a "publisher" because it is his or her duty to publish the "good news", the Witnesses' gospel, so that others might be saved when the Kingdom of God finally arrives. There is no paid clergy, and there are no ministers: every publisher is a minister. However, "elders" – mature, responsible men – have begun to emerge from the congregation as office-bearers: the Bible Study Servant; the Congregation Servant; the Assistant Congregation Servant; the Theocratic Ministry School Servant.

At public meetings, which are open to the public and have an outgoing, friendly atmosphere, an address is given which is constructed mainly from an outline forwarded from the society's head-quarters. This is followed by *Bible* study and discussion of the main article of the current *Watchtower*, which has been prepared for before-hand. Everyone is encouraged to speak, even children, and this helps in preparing for door-to-door evangelism which is a very important feature of the society:

> One of the most striking aspects of the whole Witness organization [is that] perfectly normal tongue-tied people, often uneducated and inartic-ulate are taught to project themselves both on the doorstep and also in speaking *ex tempore* at meetings.[75]

Little time is actually spent in prayer, however.

The one thing that Jesus commanded be done in commemoration of his death was remembrance of the Last Supper which he shared with his disciples. While most Christian denominations celebrate this at least once a week through Holy Communion or the Eucharist, Jehovah's Witnesses celebrate it annually at Passover time, through the Memorial Meal. They do so because the Last Supper was a Passover meal, and so would have been celebrated only once a year. Unleavened bread and wine are passed around the congregation, but only those who believe themselves to be part of the Little Flock, one of the 144,000, will partake of them. As the total number of the 144,000 was reached by 1935, the amount of people partaking of the bread and wine is obviously diminishing annually.

Family life   Jehovah's Witnesses see the family as the cornerstone of theocratic society, and they have a very strict moral code in support of it. Premarital and extramarital sex, for example, are considered immoral, an offence against Jehovah, as is homosexuality. So too is overindulgence in the consumption of alcohol. While the use of addictive and habit forming drugs such as tobacco, marijuana, cocaine and so on are not permitted, some members even ban the use of tea and coffee because they are stimulants. Gambling is also forbidden. Children are encouraged to remain separate from other children, to avoid unwholesome influences, and, indeed, most Jehovah's Witnesses remain separate from non-Witnesses, basing their reason for this on *New Testament* statements such as "They are not of this world" (*John* 17:16).

At home, families are encouraged to study the *Bible* together on a regular basis in order to foster fellowship between members. The emphasis on education, however, is not great – with Armageddon just around the corner there seems little point in spending too much time on education! On the other hand, the ability to read and write in order to study the *Bible* so that members can become proficient publishers is essential. The nature of the family, like that of the society itself, is paternalistic, and it appears that a woman's commitment to male supremacy is paramount: female Jehovah's Witnesses must submit to the dictates of their non-Witness husbands, even if those dictates prevent them from observing the duties of the society. Children are especially well thought of, are never talked down to, and are encouraged to take an active part in the society. The patriarchal family, which is an incredibly stable one, is seen as the antidote to almost every social evil ranging from women's liberation to juvenile delinquency or communism!

If a marriage does break down, however, divorce is acceptable although Jehovah's Witnesses would contend that fellowship in the family helps prevent the kind of serious marital problems that lead to divorce. The Society's magazine, *Awake!*, frequently gives advice on family problems, and even on family planning since all kinds of contraceptive methods are acceptable and some couples have made the conscious decision to delay starting a family until after the start of the Millennium. Abortion, however, is totally unacceptable because it is believed that life begins at conception.

Religion and school As we have already noted, young Jehovah's Witnesses remain separate from other children, both in school and out; and, in particular, they withdraw from communal assemblies, interfaith services, and Religious Education lessons at school. The reason for this is twofold: first, Jehovah's Witnesses believe it is the parents' God-given responsibility to instruct their children in all matters appertaining to religion; and secondly, in many schools, prayers such as The Lord's Prayer (*Matthew* 6:9–13) are repeated communally on a regular basis, and Witnesses, while accepting the importance of the prayers themselves, do not believe in the value of ritualistic repetition.[76] The authority for this is based on *Matthew* 6:7–8:

And in praying do not heap up empty phrases as the Gentiles do; for they think that they will be heard for their many words. Do not be like them for your Father knows what you need before you ask him. (*Matthew* 6: 7–8).

Notwithstanding, Jehovah's Witnesses are not averse to joining in objective classroom studies of the *Bible*, or of studies of other religions, as long as these are not attempts at proselytism, but are impartial, informative lessons.

The founder The Church of Christ, Scientist, perhaps more commonly known as Christian Science, was founded by Mary Baker Eddy (1821–1910) in 1879 in Boston, Massachusetts, USA. Mary was born the youngest of six daughters of a staunch Calvinist, New Hampshire farming family, the Bakers. From birth Mary suffered ill-health, and throughout her life she searched for answers to her problems in religion:

THE CHURCH OF CHRIST, SCIENTIST

> From my very childhood, I was impelled, by a hunger and thirst after divine things – a desire for something higher and better than matter, and apart from it – to seek diligently for the knowledge of God as the one great and ever-present relief from human woe.[77]

Nevertheless, Mary was unable to reconcile her deepest religious feelings with the theology of a then decadent Calvinism. Following a serious fall on ice on 1 February 1866, Mary's whole outlook on religion changed forever. So severe were Mary's injuries, it was feared that she would never walk again. Notwithstanding, three days later, on Sunday 4 February, while reading some of the healing miracles of Jesus in the *Bible*, Mary was instantaneously and miraculously cured not only of her most recent injuries, but also of all the other illnesses and afflictions which had plagued her from birth. Mary was convinced that she had found the truth – which for her was the realization that the quest for the divine, for God, and for health were synonymous, and that there was really only one path – Jesus' command to heal the sick was seen as the way to salvation. Gottschalk sums up the religion well, he says: "Christian Science is a religious movement emphasizing Christian healing as proof of the supremacy of spiritual over physical power".[78] In support of this, Mary Baker Eddy published a textbook for religious practice entitled *Science and Health with Key to the Scriptures*, and this text, together with the *Bible*, forms the basis of the Christian Science religion. It was not, however, Mary's original intention to found a separate movement; this came about following the realization that other Christian churches were not prepared to accept her teachings.

Science and Health with Key to the Scriptures   Mrs Eddy denied authorship of the book herself, but claimed that *Science and Health* had been dictated by God: she was merely its scribe:

> It was not myself, but the divine power of Truth and Love infinitely above me which dictated *Science and Health* . . . I should blush to write of the book as I have were it of human origin, and were I, apart from God, its author.[79]

As such, the book is accepted as scripture and revered by Christian Scientists as being second only in importance to the *Bible*. This is an interesting parallel with both Mormonism, which also relies on literature other than the *Bible*, and with the Jehovah's Witnesses, who believe that God revealed the true interpretation of the *Bible* to their founder, Charles Taze Russell. The first draft of *Science and Health* was published in 1875. In 1907 the text was standardized, and from that date all editions have had identical pagination. Also to ensure absolute uniformity, Mary Eddy secured by law a statute which stated that passages from *Science and Health* might only be read in Christian Science churches without any additional preaching or exposition by priests, ministers or other clergy, which has eliminated the possibility of deviations from her original ideas or personal interpretations of the text.[80] This was, perhaps, a sensible precaution because the book is rather mystical in places and might easily be misinterpreted. There are three major aims of *Science and Health*, and these are, first, to offer the correct interpretation of the *Bible*; secondly, to explain the science of healing as Mary understood it; and, thirdly, to counteract competing schools of thought.

Beliefs: Mortal Mind   Mary Eddy came to believe, after her miraculous cure, that matter is unreal, that it does not exist and is simply an illusion – the product of what she considered to be the "Mortal Mind". In *Science and Health*, Mortal Mind is described as:

> Nothing claiming to be something, for Mind is immortal . . . the opposite of spirit and therefore the opposite of God, or good; the belief that life has a beginning and therefore an end . . . the subjective states of error; material senses; that which neither exists in science nor can be recognized by the spiritual senses; sin, sickness, death.[81]

Fundamentally, then, for Mrs Eddy, illness, pain, evil, sin and death were all simply products of the Mortal Mind which have no basis in reality. The only true reality is God, who is wholly spiritual. Humankind, made in God's image, is also pure spirit;[82] thus it follows that suffering, evil, sin and death are simply products of the Mortal Mind, an illusion, and do not, in fact, exist at all (which, it might be suggested, is a concept reminiscent of Eastern religions such as Hinduism and Jainism). Discovery of this truth, and the steadfast practice of Christian Science, the science of healing, it is believed, will eradicate all pain and suffering, and lead to salvation. Similarly, the traditional Christian concepts of heaven and hell have been rejected:

> Heaven and hell are not believed to be places to which the good and wicked will be sent after death, but are states of mind that a person can experience. A person who does wrong will create his or her own hell, and the person who does good finds heaven.[83]

Thus those who acknowledge the truth are believed to find heaven in their transformed spiritual states, while those who remain in ignorance suffer in a hell of their own making.

Because of these beliefs, Christian Scientists do not normally accept the ministrations of orthodox doctors on the grounds that their attitude to disease – that is to say that it is real – is misguided and misinformed, and generally rely on their own Christian Science practitioners. So, Mary denied the reality of the material world and also the reality of sin. And the incarnation of God in the human form of Jesus is another orthodox Christian precept that has been rejected by Christian Scientists: how, they ask, could God have suffered hunger and thirst and pain on the cross if he had no material body?

God   Perhaps the most radical of all Mary Baker Eddy's concepts is her concept of God. For her, God was not, as he was for most Christians of her time, a stern, masculine God but a "Father–Mother God" – a God who has the maternalistic qualities of love and forgiveness coupled with the paternalistic qualities of strength and justice. God, too, is not an arbitrary being who predetermines a person's fate, and thus for Christian Scientists each and every person is capable of achieving salvation through his or her own efforts. The terms "Principle", "Mind", "Soul", "Love", "Spirit", "Life", "Truth", "All-Substance" and "Intelligence" are used synonymously and interchangeably to refer to God. Burrell and Stafford-Wright suggest that Mrs Eddy's ideas about God come very close to pantheism and to the Hindu concept of all separate existence as illusion.[84] (Pantheism is the concept that God is everything and everything is God.) The Trinity for Mrs Eddy and for Christian Scientists can be summarized as follows: God the Father–Mother; Christ, the Spiritual Idea of Sonship; Divine Science or the Holy Comforter (in other words, Christian Science).

Jesus Christ   The concept of Jesus Christ is rather more difficult. Christian Science accepts Jesus Christ as two separate and distinct entities: the first, Jesus, they believe was simply a human being, nothing more nor less. It is God who is seen to be the Universal Principle behind the life and healing power of Jesus. The second entity is the divine Christ or Christ Spirit. Although it is accepted that, like God, Christ is omnipresent and eternal, it is believed that Christ is, nonetheless, not God. It follows, therefore, that both the traditional Christian precepts of the Incarnation and the Resurrection are rejected by Christian Scientists. Jesus Christ's Resurrection is not seen as the rising again of a transformed, material body from its death on the cross, but at the Ascension:

> the human, material concept, or Jesus, disappeared, while the spiritual self, or Christ, continues to exist in the eternal order of divine Science.[85]

Jesus, therefore, is not deified by Christian Scientists, nor is salvation believed to be gained directly through faith in him: "Salvation . . . requires prayer, self-renunciation, and radical, unremitting warfare against the evils of the mortal condition."[86] It also includes obedience to Jesus' command to heal the sick.

Organization and Worship There are almost three thousand Christian Science churches in existence today, with over half a million members, three-quarters of which are located in the USA. Christian Science churches are governed according to *The Manual of the Mother Church* first published in 1895 by Mary Baker Eddy and developed until her death, the provisions of which are administered by a Board of five directors who are located in Boston, Massachusetts. It is these directors who handle the financial and publishing affairs of the Church. (The publishing side of Christian Science is a very lucrative one: its daily newspaper, *The Christian Science Monitor*, is read by many non-Christian Scientists and is respected throughout the world for its unbiased presentation of the news.) Lesson-sermons, which are read in Christian Science churches all over the world on Sundays, are also prepared by these same directors. There is no hierarchy in the churches; indeed, there is not even any ordained clergy, and local Christian Science churches are governed democratically by their members. The only professional members of the Church are Christian Science "Practitioners" – specially trained members who practise healing, like Mary Eddy herself, and who, like traditional doctors and homeopaths, receive fees for their services. The vast majority of these practitioners are women, perhaps because being a practitioner has always been a full-time occupation, but not a very lucrative one, and women have traditionally been prepared to work for smaller financial rewards. The healing aspect of the religion is very important because a substantial proportion of the members are converts from other denominations who have joined the Church because of their own personal experiences of healing. Unfortunately, however, membership appears to be declining because, unlike Mormonism or the Jehovah's

Witnesses, the Christian Science religion is rarely passed from one generation to another, and as there are no missionaries or evangelists travelling the world, promulgating the message of the Church, as there are with the Jehovah's Witnesses or Mormons, a larger membership is not forthcoming. Another reason why its membership may be declining is that with the advent of an increasingly medically orientated society, Christian Science's healing practices have encountered many new challenges.[87]

There is no "typical" Christian Science church building, although all are characterized by their simplicity; there are no icons, images or pictures within the buildings. There are, however, two separate lecterns. One holds a copy of the *Bible* and the other holds a copy of *Science and Health with Key to the Scriptures*. Like Mormonism, then, as we have already noted, Christian Science looks to another written source in addition to the *Bible*. The services, which take place on Sundays and Wednesday evenings, are very simple affairs devoted to the reading of selected passages from *Science and Health* and the *Bible*, the singing of hymns, and testimonies of healing. Silent prayer is also considered to be an extremely important feature of worship. No ritualistic sacraments such as the Eucharist or Baptism are observed, nor any marriage ceremonies or funeral services: the services of ordained ministers from other religions are required for Christian Science weddings and funerals. And no formal baptism ceremonies are performed either since it is believed that members are spiritually baptized when the truth is recognized. Christian Science worship, then, is almost Quaker-like in its simplicity. Members are expected to bring about their own salvation through prayer, study of the *Bible* in conjunction with *Science and Health*, and attendance at the twice-weekly services. To abstain from the use of all drugs, alcohol and tobacco is also expected of Christian Science followers, and some go as far as to refrain from the consumption of tea and coffee, too.

On such issues as euthanasia, abortion, contraception, blood transfusions or divorce there is no official stance: members are permitted freedom of choice. And, indeed, Mrs Eddy herself divorced her second husband, Dr Daniel Patterson, a dentist, in 1873. However, with regard to the rejection of traditional medical practices, Christian Scientists are given clear guidelines as regards the law and what medical practices they may perform in the particular countries they inhabit, for their own protection.[88] In Britain, for example, the removal of stitches, the extraction of teeth, and the delivery of babies all fall outside the Christian Science practitioner's frame of reference, and so outside help must be sought for these medical conditions.

3

Islam

David Norcliffe

To God belong the East and the West;
withersoever you turn, there is the Face of God;
God is All-embracing, All-knowing.

Qur'an

WHAT IS ISLAM?

Islam is, at one and the same time, the easiest to understand and the least understood of all world faiths. It is the easiest to understand because it involves a straightforward belief in one God, whose will was revealed to a man called Muhammad in a series of revelations which were written down into one book: the Holy *Qur'an*. It is the least understood because the very name is associated in the West with terrorism and intolerance, and it is often, therefore, dismissed with little thought or discussion.

The word Islam is based on the semitic tri-literal root *slm* which in Arabic means "to be in peace". Thus we have *salam* – peace (cf. the Hebrew *shalom*), *Islam* – peace through surrender or submission to God, and *Muslim* – one who is at peace through submission to God. Adam and Eve in the Garden of Eden are seen as the first Muslims, they lived, initially, in submission to God and were thus at peace. It is this aspect of absolute submission to the will of God which is central to Islam; indeed the word Islam can be translated as submission.

Any discussion of Islam should note from the outset that Islam:

> is what in Arabic is called a *deen*: a total frame of reference, a complete
> system and way of life which embraces the entirety of a man's existence.[1]

It is in fact an ideology. There is no divide in Islam between action which is commonly seen to be religious, such as acts of worship, and that which appears to be secular. Every action the Muslim performs should be effected with the express intention of pleasing God and such actions are therefore seen as worship. The social, political, legal, administrative and economic affairs of Muslim society are just as much a part of Islam as praying in the mosque or caring for one's relations. For the Muslim all of a person's life is for God and any division of life into secular and religious aspects has no warrant. As Salem Azzam remarks:

> Islam does not divide life into domains of the spiritual and the secular. It spiritualizes the entire existence of man and produces a social movement to reconstruct human life in the light of principles revealed by God.[2]

Thus, in Islam there is no notion of church and state, *Islam din wa diwla* – Islam is both religion and state. The same God-given laws govern every aspect of life: there is no "religious aspect" or "secular aspect" of life, each with different standards to be judged differently using different criteria. Islam is above all, a view of the total reality – humanity's relationship with God, the human being's purpose and function in the world, and the relationship between this life and the hereafter. Islam is a total system, an ideology, which guides the Muslim through every aspect of life, both as an individual and collectively.

The human being's position in the world is a dual one. He or she is both *abd* – slave; or more precisely, *abd-Allah* the slave of God. However, he or she is also, *khalifah* – vice-regent: a position which elevates the human being amongst creation. In the former role the human being should submit to the will of God, in the latter the human being should try to make sure, as far as he or she is able to do so, that the universe conforms to the will of God. Thus before beginning anything of importance Muslims will say *bis millah hirahman nir rahim* – In the name of God the beneficent, the merciful. Muslims make no promises without saying *inshallah* – God willing.

> And do not say, regarding anything, I am going to do that tomorrow, but only: "If God will".[3]

This ideology has been conveyed to Muslims via *hidayah* – revelation. Throughout history God has selected certain human beings to remind humanity who he is. According to Muslims all peoples have had a prophet, and Islam accepts all these revelations, known and unknown, but the *Qur'an* is seen as the final revelation, needed because previous revelations, through time, became mixed with human experience.

Islam is one of the three Abrahamic faiths. Along with Judaism and Christianity, it looks back to the patriarch Abraham as a source. According to Genesis, God called Abraham from Haran, promising him a land and his blessing (Genesis 12:1–3).[4] Sarah, Abraham's wife

THE ORIGINS OF ISLAM

was long past the age of child bearing, but because Abraham had obeyed God he was told that he would be rewarded with progeny. Sarah assumed that, since she was seventy-five years old, God must have meant Abraham to take another woman, and she offered her maidservant Hagar, as a concubine. Hagar became pregnant by Abraham and started to treat Sarah with contempt, so much so, that Sarah drove Hagar from the household.

After fleeing from Sarah, Hagar, we are told, was approached by an angel who told her to return and submit to Sarah. The angel also told Hagar that she would bear a son, and that his name would be Ishmael (God shall hear). Hagar returned as instructed and Abraham dutifully named the boy as the angel had requested. Some thirteen years later, with Sarah now in her ninetieth year, God informed an astonished Abraham that his wife would bear a son who would be called Isaac, but reassured Abraham that Ishmael would not be forgotten.

> I will bless him and make him fruitful and multiply him exceedingly; he shall be the father of twelve princes, and I will make him a great nation (Genesis 17:20).

Nevertheless, God's covenant would be established with Sarah's son, Isaac, not with Ishmael.

> Not one but two great nations were to look back to Abraham as their father – two great nations, that is, two guided powers, two instruments to work the will of Heaven . . . Abraham was thus the fountain-head of two spiritual streams, which must not flow together, but each in its own course . . . Two spiritual streams, two religions, two worlds for God; two circles, therefore two centres.[5]

The one centre was well known to Abraham already, for he had been an, albeit semi-nomadic, resident in the Promised Land for twenty-four years. The other centre was unknown to the patriarch, but it was here that Hagar and her child would eventually settle. Once Sarah had borne Abraham a son, she no longer wanted Hagar and Ishmael, a potential rival to Isaac, in her household, and so she drove them out.

Hagar and Ishmael fled southwards towards Mecca, but ran out of water. Hagar was becoming increasingly aware that the infant Ishmael was dying of thirst and in her efforts to find help ran back and forth between two hills, seven times in all (note the discrepancy here, Ishmael is, according to the account in *Genesis*, by now at least thirteen (Genesis 17:25), and thus an adult). The frantic Hagar, at her wit's end suddenly noticed the lad playing with the sand, with water gushing at his feet. The resulting well was called the *zamzam* well and soon became a drinking station for the great camel trains which brought their wares from South Arabia to the Mediterranean.

According to Muslim belief, God guided Abraham to his son in the valley of Mecca and they were instructed to build the *ka'aba*, a sanctuary, close to the *zamzam* well. *Ka'aba* is Arabic for "cube" and this was to be the shape of the new building, with its four corners aligned with the cardinal points of the compass. Its most holy part is a black stone which Abraham and Ishmael built into its eastern corner. Abraham was also instructed by God to institute the rite of pilgrimage to Mecca. This he did, but over time this practice was discontinued.

God's instructions, however, were sometimes painful, for Abraham was told by God to sacrifice his son, Ishmael, and Abraham prepared, albeit with a heavy heart, to do as God instructed. At the last minute, however, God substituted an animal which Abraham sacrificed instead. (The same story is also told in *Genesis*, with the exception that here it is Isaac who is prepared for sacrifice.) Abraham had been willing to obey God in all things and to submit to his will – according to Muslims the only possible response to God. He is therefore held by Muslims to be an exemplar. This action is commemorated in the pilgrimage to Mecca, which all Muslims try to make once in their lifetime, and by the sacrifice of an animal during this period. Hagar's frantic search for water is also commemorated with pilgrims passing seven times between the mounts Safa and Marwah.

THE LIFE OF MUHAMMAD

Over time Mecca came to be dominated by the tribe of Quraysh, and in 570 CE a woman of this tribe called Aminah, whose husband Abd Allah was already dead, gave birth to a son whom she named Muhammad. It was common practice at the time to send infants from the towns to wet nurses in the desert, and Muhammad's mother followed this tradition. During this period an extraordinary incident is said to have happened. Muhammad and his brother were with some lambs behind the tent when his brother came running back saying that two men had seized Muhammad. Some years later Muhammad was able to describe the incident in detail:

> There came unto me two men, clothed in white, with a gold basin full of snow. Then they lay hold upon me and, splitting open my breast they brought forth my heart. This likewise they split open and took from it a black clot which they cast away. Then they washed my heart and my breast with the snow.[6]

When his foster parents looked there was no sign of the men nor any wound, but nothing would make the boys shift from their story. Not long after this Muhammad returned to his mother in Mecca, but shortly after his mother died. Now an orphan, Muhammad was entrusted to the care of his grandfather, 'Abd al-Muttalib. Two years later he too died and Muhammad was brought up by his uncle Abu Talib.

Tradition sees Muhammad from youth as a thoughtful and questioning individual, with a growing reputation for prudence. Under his uncle's tutorship he learned to pursue a trading life, and tradition says that on one caravan journey into Syria his religious vocation was identified by a Christian monk, Bahira, who asked Abu Talib to take great care of the boy as he had already the signs of a great prophet.

The Meccan background   Mecca was at that time a very prosperous city, being the centre of trade routes connecting for example the port of Yemen with Egypt, Palestine and Syria, and also with Mesopotamia across the Arabian desert. Thus the Meccans were wealthy and powerful middlemen in the commerce of luxury merchandise. Muhammad was born into the tribe of Quraysh, the most influential tribe in Arabia, which until comparatively recently had been nomadic, but through conquest had transferred to a settled life in the valley of Mecca. This is noteworthy, for the moral standards and social behaviour of the recently settled Meccans underwent considerable change which Muhammad later questioned. Indeed Ruthven comments that:

> In the tribal society, poverty, like wealth, was shared . . . Now, in the emergent social order of Mecca, something approaching class divisions had begun to appear.[7]

Thus although there was some retention of the old nomadic organization and ethics, there was a considerable break with the strict ethical norms of Bedouin tribal existence. In the harsh and precarious tribal existence the pleasures of the moment were often taken where and when available. In settled society, however, such pleasures were readily available to some, but not all, and the resulting social tensions produced problems within Meccan society.

There was a great deal of rivalry between clans, and war was a part of everyday life. Even in their settled state, the people of Quraysh would still be vulnerable to rival attack. This situation tended to produce a stong clan solidarity and the obligation to protect the individual clan member; offence against an individual member provoked the offensive of the clan and tribe. This meant that if one belonged to a powerful clan, one had a certain degree of immunity from the results of one's deeds. In addition, raiding, even in mercantile settled days, was an occupation which many indulged in. Raids, in the old tribal days, tended to be cattle raids, but the trading caravans were a tempting target to these raiders, and were often attacked.

The increase in wealth brought about what to most moral codes would be called depravity, gambling, excessive wine drinking, treatment of women as goods and chattels, and slavery. Although there was strong moral code in the desert, it was also the case, as was previously stated, that pleasure was taken as it came, for it might not be there for long. There was also no real sense of universal religion or of purpose in life that might have underpinned a wider moral code. Certain deities were acknowledged such as the planets and stars, and spirits and demons, and also the concept of *dahr*, all-consuming "time", a blind, impersonal force which had simply to be accepted. There was, however, no strong religious force which could provide a focus for the people.

Muhammad seems to have been somewhat set apart from this milieu. He developed a reputation for high moral standards, he decried gambling and wine drinking, and refused to take part in idol worship. He was called by his friends, *al Amin* "The Trustworthy". He also seems to have felt the injustice of the concentration of wealth in private hands – the new merchant class.

During this early period of Muhammad's life a blood feud broke out between two clans, the Hawazin and the Kinanah. Quraysh were not directly involved but were to some extent drawn in on the side of the Kinanah. There were sporadic outbreaks of violence over a four-to five-year period. Muhammad was taken by his uncle to one of the battles but, though a good archer, did not take part. As a result of this war some of the leaders of Quraysh became disillusioned with the way disputes were settled. Many were widely travelled and had seen in the Roman Empire, Abyssinia, and Syria how justice could be achieved without so much violence. This problem became more urgent as a result of a dispute between two more of the tribes in Arabia. Quraysh split between those who wanted to support one of the tribes, and those who wanted the dispute settled on the basis of just principles rather than naked power. Some of the leaders from both sides came together and made a pact to support the poor and the weak within and beyond their society in the name of justice. It is said that Muhammad participated in this pact known as the *Hilf-al-Fudul*. He had realized the futility of such wars, and, being an orphan himself, recognized the weakness of those without powerful family and clan support. This resulted in a new direction in Arabian society underpinned by social justice.

Muhammad's reputation for prudence and honesty is evidenced in his meeting with his first wife. She was a very wealthy widow called Khadijah who, as a result of his trustworthiness, asked him to lead a caravan into Syria. She offered herself in marriage to Muhammad and in 595 CE, at the age of twenty-five, he married the forty-year-old widow. His three sons died in infancy but his four daughters survived. His marriage lasted until the death of Khadijah at the age of sixty-five.

The rebuilding of the *ka'aba* Ten years after Muhammad married Khadijah, Quraysh decided to rebuild the *ka'aba*. There had been a recent theft of treasures from a vault inside the edifice which was easy to get into, as the sanctuary was without a roof and the walls were little more than head height. The rebuilding was hindered, however, by a huge snake which lived in the vault and which emerged only in the heat of the day. One day an eagle appeared, carrying the snake off, and this was seen as an omen that building work should commence immediately. Quraysh razed the *ka'aba* to the ground and rebuilt its walls until it was time to reposition the Black Stone. At this point, however, a furious row broke out, for each of the clans involved in the rebuilding project thought that its leader should be the one to lay the Black Stone in place. The problem was referred to *al-Amin*, the Trustworthy. Muhammad spread a cloak on the ground, and placed the Black Stone in the middle he then instructed the leaders of the clans to grasp the border of the cloak, and lift it. It was carried in this fashion to the wall where Muhammad himself repositioned it.

Throughout the early years of his marriage, Muhammad developed a meditative, prayerful life, and for periods of time he became a meditative recluse. These periods climaxed in a momentous religious vision which set Muhammad on the path he was to follow for the rest of his life: the proclamation of the word of God.

The vision   According to tradition, the call came one night during the month of Ramadan (610 CE), when Muhammad was forty years old. As was his habit, he had withdrawn to the cave called Hira on the mount of Noor, to meditate and seek divine guidance. The revelation came in the form of a vision of gold lettering and a voice asking him to recite. Since Muhammad was illiterate these words meant little to him. The request was repeated three times, then he felt his throat, indeed his whole body, in a vice-like grip. To his astonishment he now found himself able to recite:

> Recite: In the name of thy Lord who created, created man of a blood-clot. Recite: And thy Lord is the Most Generous, Who taught by the Pen, taught man that he knew not.[8]

Muhammad, terrified, swiftly left and as he was running down the mountainside the angel Gabriel told him that he was a prophet of God. On his return to his home, he told Khadijah what had happened. She believed him and gave him her support and encouragement. There was obviously complete confidence and trust between them, and it is speculated that it was perhaps necessary for Muhammad to have an older and more mature wife whose trust and stability were able to sustain him through the early revelations.

Muhammad had been instructed to "proclaim" and he began to do so to friends and relatives, but maintained a level of secrecy about this. After his wife, the first person to accept his message was his ten-year old nephew 'Ali. He was followed by others, including Abu Bakr, a Meccan dignitary, whose influence helped to spread Islam. Most of

Muhammad's converts came from amongst the poor, the slaves, and the younger sons of the tribal elders. Eventually Muhammad came into the open. He asked 'Ali to prepare a meal, a leg of mutton and a glass of milk, and invited all his relatives. Most of the clan accepted and attended. They were fed in groups in a relay system and all were fed from the meal (cf. the feeding of the five thousand). The next day Muhammad asked 'Ali to do the same, but this time Muhammad spoke to them about the one God and his (Muhammad's) role as prophet. He was rejected.

The leaders of Quraysh were incensed by his teaching for a number of reasons. Muhammad's attack on immorality undermined Quraysh leadership and traditional authority, which were strong components of a tribal system rooted in ancestral patterns; genealogy was one of the main grounds of esteem in ancient traditions.

> The "virtue" of a tribe was conceived of as something inherited: a man
> would act nobly because of the noble blood which ran through his veins
> . . . The tribes' honour, and adherence to its norms, were imperatives to
> be followed at all times.[9]

The denial of their deities probably provoked little strong objection, what was objected to was the outrage against tradition. Moreover, Muhammad's teaching appeared as a threat to the Quraysh rulers, for if he was a prophet, he must be accepted as a leader. It also threatened the wealth of the rich, for they thrived on privilege, whereas Muhammad stressed the rights of the poor to share in this wealth.

After ten years preaching at Mecca, Muhammad had only a small following, mainly of the poor and slaves, who were persecuted heavily by Quraysh. So Muhammad advised his followers to migrate to the oasis of Yathrib, 200 miles north of Mecca at Medina. The Medinites themselves, having heard of Muhammad's preaching, were favourable to the migration of his followers. Negotiations continued over two years until later in the autumn of 622 CE. Muhammad himself fled Mecca for Medina. This is a very momentous event in Islamic tradition. It became known as the *hijrah* and is the date from which the Islamic calendar is reckoned.

Medina At Medina very different circumstances obtained than at Mecca. The community was agricultural and not mercantile, and it was a disturbed and divided community engaged in warfare between rival tribes. Muhammad's first task was to unify the people and create a community. In the oasis were several different tribal groups. Some of them, although Arabic speaking, were of Jewish religion. One of his first actions was to draw up the "Constitution of Medina", declaring all the people of Medina – Muslim and Jews – to be one community under his leadership, and laying down rights for each group. This was not easy and Muhammad had to struggle to establish himself fully at Medina: opposition was growing from those who feared his increasing power, and the hostility of Quraysh continued to increase. A rift occurred with the Jews, who refused to accept Muhammad as a genuine prophet. Tradition tells us that he was ridiculed as misguided and ignorant of Jewish prophecy. Muhammad had expected to be accepted as a prophet by both Jews and Christians. Over the course of time Muhammad dealt with these Jewish tribes: some Jews were expelled, others were sold into slavery or killed. Whilst establishing himself at Medina, Muhammad also extended his power through alliance with Bedouin tribes. The *ummah* (religious community) was divided into a federation of tribes which he trained as missionaries and warriors.

In 624 CE he was challenged by Meccan power. Greatly outnumbered, he defeated a large force of Meccans at the Battle of Badr. This served to confirm the Muslim sense of their divine mission. Further battles followed until, in 630 CE, Mecca was forced into submission after a supreme attack. The aim was to spill no blood and indeed very few were killed. The ancient *ka'aba* was reconstituted and the idols destroyed. In Mecca, Muhammad proclaimed the mercy and forgiveness of the one God and uttered prayer from the top of the mosque to which future pilgrimages were made from all places into which Islam penetrated.

In a subsequent pilgrimage to Mecca, Muhammad preached his last sermon, from the mountain of Arafat. On that day the last revelation was given: "Today I have perfected your religion".[10] In 632 CE, Muhammad died in Medina after a short illness. He was buried in the house which was later to be incorporated in the Mosque at Medina. For Islam, Muhammad was the last in line of the prophets of God. The *Qu'ran* makes clear that Muhammad was divinely chosen but in every sense a human being. Indeed, Muhammad on more than one occasion became extremely annoyed with Companions who wished to elevate him to being the greatest of the prophets.

Islam is not confined to one race or one nation. Anyone who accepts the message of Muhammad may become a Muslim. Simple and direct, Islam appeals to many people. By the end of Muhammad's life all of Arabia was under Muslim control. On his death Muhammad was succeeded by four of his closest Companions, each of whom bore the title *Khalifah* (caliph).

Abu Bakr 632–4 CE (11–13 AH)
'Umar 634–44 CE (13–23 AH)
'Uthman 644–56 CE (23–35 AH)
'Ali 656–61 CE (35–40 AH)

A number of the Muslims had felt that 'Ali, who was the son-in-law and nephew of Muhammad, should have been *Khalifah* earlier, but he was not accepted by all, and even after becoming *Khalifah* he experienced opposition and was eventually assassinated. The office of *Khalifah* then went to two powerful Quraysh dynasties:

The Umayyad Dynasty 661–750 CE (40–132 AH)
The Abassid Dynasty 750 –1517 CE (132–656 AH)

Then the rule passed to the Ottoman Turks until 1924, when the system of *Khalifah* rule was abolished by Turkey. The followers of 'Ali, the fourth *Khalifah*, continued to regard him and his descendants as the true leaders of the Muslim community. Called *Shi'as* or *Shi'ites,* a title derived from the *Shi'at Ali*, the followers of 'Ali, they are one of the two major sects of Islam. The *Sunnis,* the other major sect of Islam, who do not accept this view of 'Ali, constitute approximately 85 per cent of the world-wide Muslim population, the *Shi'ites* 15 per cent: the *Shi'ites* are the majority community in Iran.

The first revelation was given to Muhammad on the night which is known as the *Lailat ul Qadr* or "Night of Power". He was given the verses previously quoted. **THE *QUR'AN***

> Recite: In the Name of thy Lord who created, created Man of a blood-clot. Recite: And thy Lord is the Most Generous, who taught by the Pen, taught Man that he knew not.[11]

The revelation advised Muhammad that he was to be a prophet. There had been many prophets before, but none of their revelations had survived intact. Muhammad was urged to bring himself closer to God throughout his life and, though his message was nothing new, to deliver it to the people in no uncertain terms. "We sent forth among every nation a Messenger, saying: 'Serve you God, and eschew idols'."[12]

The word *Qur'an* comes from the verb *qara'a*, to read or to recite, and means literally recitation. Muhammad was given the command to recite, and this command, and the words given as recitation, were relayed directly from God. So the *Qur'an* "embodies the word of God – unchanged, unabridged, and uncompromised".[13] According to Muslims the recitations were learnt by Muhammad and his followers, and also written on various articles, skin, stones, leaves, bark etc., being brought together into one final collection at the latest during the reign of 'Uthman, the third *Khalifah*. Great care was taken to preserve not only the message, but the form in which it was given. This is an important point, and Nasr appropriately points out that:

> not only the content and meaning comes from God but also the container

and form which are thus an integral part of the revelation.[14]

It is still true for Muslims today that the actual words in the Arabic language are fundamental to the revelation:

> the formulae of the Qur'an read in prayers and acts of worship must be in the sacred language of Arabic which alone enables one to penetrate into the content and be transformed by the Divine presence and grace (barakah) of the Divine Book.[15]

This is why the *Qur'an* is still read in the original language in which it was given. It is seen not simply as a book to which one can go for information, but as a vehicle of inspiration and, indeed, as a means of transformation, the divine word penetrating and changing the believer:

> metaphysically, the Qur'an has an aspect of knowledge connected with its text as a book, and an aspect of being connected with its inner nature as the archetypal blue-print of the Universe.[16]

The *Qur'an* has three names in traditional Islam; *al-Qur'an*, a recitation; *al-Furqan*, a discernment or discrimination, in this case between truth and falsehood; and *Umm al-kitab*, the mother of all books or of all knowledge. The *Qur'an* is seen as containing the principles of all knowledge, though in a general rather than a particular sense.[17] It expounds the nature of reality and the human being's position within it, and contains a set of moral and juridical instructions, as well as a certain amount of history, and in addition, it contains a power separate from its content because it is the word of God. It is both *tadwini* – written or composed, and *takwini* – ontological in the sense that it pertains to cosmic existence.[18] The message of the *Qur'an* was unequivocal: believers had to put God before everything and everyone, and this included their own families as well as ancient customs. The *Qur'an* was to take precedence over everything and was to be believed with heart and mind. This was Islam (submission) and those who submitted were to be known as Muslims.

The revelations continued both in Mecca, and later in Medina. The voice Muhammad heard was on some occasions very clear like high-sounding bells, and accompanied by visions, on other occasions the bells were more muffled. Though he would always return to normal afterwards, he was profoundly influenced by each and every revelation. Those chapters of the *Qur'an* which were revealed before the *hijrah* are referred to as the Meccan *surahs*, those revealed after the *hijrah* as the Medinite *surahs*. The Meccan *surahs* offer terse advice about human emotions, God and his creation. They are full of hope for reward but they also contain dire warnings of punishment. The longer Medinite *surahs*, on the other hand, offer advice on ordering life in this world. The *hijrah* and subsequent settlement in Medina necessitated guidance on how to live an ordered life in accordance with the total life system of Islam: the Medinite *surahs* provided this guidance. Muslims do not, however, see a division between these two periods: the *Qur'an* is a whole, and whilst it covers different aspects, it is nevertheless a unity.

The *Qur'an* today is divided into 114 *surahs* or chapters. A single verse is known as an *ayah* (plural *ayat*). The 6616 *ayat* total 78,000 words making the *Qur'an* approximately the length of the *New Testament*. From the very beginning there grew up a practice of memorizing the *Qur'an*, which is still popular today. Memorizers are known as *huffaz*, a man who has memorized the *Qur'an* earns the honour of bearing the title *hafiz*, a woman *hafizah*.

The primacy of God   After the first chapter, the opening prayer, the *Qur'an* is arranged with the longest chapters first, reducing gradually in length until the short ones are reached. The short chapters were mostly uttered by Muhammad at Mecca. They are brief, forceful prophecies, telling of the oneness of God, calling human beings to serve him and abandon their idols, and warn of coming judgment. The chapters revealed at Medina are longer and many of them are concerned with the life of the Muslim community there, dealing with questions about property, marriage, work and war.

There is a clear statement near the beginning of the *Qur'an* that it "is the book, wherein is no doubt."[19] God is spoken of many times and his uniqueness is stressed. Nothing may be associated with God, placed alongside God, or even be seen to come close to God. This is the one truly unforgivable act: "God forgives not that aught should be with Him associated."[20] Since nothing may be associated with him, great emphasis is placed on the belief that God is "one", there is no multiplicity. The central concept in Islam is that of *tawhid* – oneness, unity. This is applied in general to the Muslim community in the belief in one world-wide Islamic *ummah* or community, and specifically it relates to God – God is one, an indivisible unity. This concept is central to any understanding of Islam. No one can begin to comprehend Islam without acknowledging the centrality of *tawhid*. As one Muslim scholar has remarked: "The entire Islamic system is, in fact, the consequence of its Doctrine of *Tawhid*".[21]

From this unity, from this essence, God has created all that exists. Nothing existed before God, therefore everything that exists must have come from God. Since God is one, and an indivisible unity, then everything must stem from that unity:

> He who created the heavens and earth, and sent down for you out of heaven water; and We caused to grow therewith gardens full of loveli-

ness whose trees you could never grow. Is there a god with God? Nay, but there are people who assign to Him equals. He who made the earth a fixed place and set amidst it rivers and appointed for it firm mountains and placed a partition between the two seas. Is there a god with God? Nay, but the most of them have no knowledge.[22]

Nor is God simply creator, he is also sustainer – he underpins all of reality, he "originates creation, then brings it back again".[23] In the Islamic framework God is not there just to watch over his creation to make sure everything is running smoothly, rather he is necessary for the universe's moment to moment existence. Were God to cease for one second from "bringing it back again", then the universe and everything in it would cease to exist.

This is much more than the idea that God is in heaven looking down on his creation with benevolence, it is a philosphical belief in a structure of reality, and God's relationship to it, which emphasizes above all else God's supreme omnipotent power:

Say: "O God, Master of the Kingdom, Thou givest the Kingdom to whom Thou wilt, and seizest the Kingdom from whom Thou wilt, Thou exaltest whom Thou wilt, and Thou abasest whom Thou wilt; in Thy hand is the good; Thou art powerful over everything."[24]

There is nothing in the universe which is not dependent on God, not simply for its creation, but for its continued existence. Without the will of God to support it nothing could remain in existence for a second. God does not simply underpin the universe as a whole, but by his will he sustains every particle of being within it. He has set up a structure within which every particle exists as a result of his divine will, and everywhere he supports it: "To God belong the East and the West; withersoever you turn, there is the face of God".[25]

God is also omniscient as well as omnipresent, for how else would he have the knowledge necessary to so underpin the life of the universe: "He knows what lies before them and what is after them, and they comprehend not anything of His knowledge".[26] His power, his knowledge, indeed his very being are beyond comprehension; yet, despite this, human beings can rely utterly on him – he is steadfast, never-changing, in fact, immutable. All of creation is subject to the laws of change and decay, but God is not part of creation, he is the force of creation which is not subject to its laws. He never changes, never alters; nothing in creation has the power to affect him, and there is nothing beyond creation except God himself.

Despite this, God is still seen as a personal God, one to whom Muslims can turn for help, guidance and support:

He who answers the constrained, when he calls upon Him, and removes

the evil . . . He who guides you in the shadows of the land and the sea
and loses the winds, bearing good tidings before his mercy.[27]

God's mercy and forgiveness are continually stressed throughout the
Qur'an. Human beings are urged to turn to him for forgiveness and
support: "do not despair of God's mercy; surely God forgives sins altogether".[28] He will not fail those who turn to him. He has created, he
provides and he will sustain. As Abdalati states: "the mercy of God
relieves the distressed, consoles the sick, strengthens the desperate, and
comforts the needy".[29] God urges justice on all people as a duty, they
are bound as Muslims to do right, for God himself is a God of justice
who will do what is right by his people. He becomes angry with those
who break his commandments, who mistreat the poor, or are unjust
to others, and he is pleased with those who perform actions in conformity with the justice he has laid down.

So God is seen by Muslims as one who is omnipotent, omniscient,
omnipresent and immutable. Yet he is also a personal God who is the
provider of justice, mercy and benevolence. There are many philosophical problems with this account, and great controversies arose
during the early centuries of Islam on these points. For instance,
personal relationships, by their very nature, change those involved in
them, but, according to Islam, God cannot change so it would be
impossible for him to enter into personal relationships. The answer for
Muslims is the doctrine of *mukhalafah* – absolute difference. God is
so absolutely different from human beings, that it is illegitimate to use
arguments stemming from human experience and apply them to God:
such comparisons are invalid. A further argument concerns the
"problem of evil". If God created everything, then by necessity, God
must have created evil, but why would he do this if he is merciful and
compassionate? The answer according to Muslims is beyond human
understanding: God did create evil, he hates it, and those who wish to
obey him must do the same. Such philosophical questions and
answers, briefly summarized here, can only highlight what were
extended and ferocious debates, and an in-depth study of them is
beyond the scope of this chapter.[30] The *Qur'an* itself is not primarily
concerned with metaphysical doctrines or even theological explana-
tions. It does not so much reveal God, rather it reveals the will (and
power) of God. Muslims wish to achieve a good relationship with
God, but feel that God is beyond comprehension. For Muslims, therefore, the best way to achieve such a relationship is to obey the
commands of God. Thus they need to know what it is that God
commands – they need divine guidance, they need the *Qur'an*.

The *Qur'an* is so important to Muslims that they often read parts
of it every day throughout their lives. It is the focal point of Islam and
the main source for the behaviour of the individual and society. It
speaks of God's power and his creativity, and discusses each human

being's relationship and responsibility to him. It speaks of the certainty of the Day of Judgment when all people will stand before God to receive their reward or punishment. It also tells the stories of some of the earlier prophets as examples of the correct approach to life. The dynamism of the *Qur'an* is well expressed by Ahmed when he says:

> The *Qur'an* is not a structured book or an academic set of arguments in recognizable sequence. It is like a vibrant powerful outpouring of divine messages. At one place it warns, at another it encourages, at another reflects. The messages cover all aspects of life.[31]

To Muslims the *Qur'an* is the most wonderful book. They handle it very carefully and hold it in a very high regard. It is never placed on the floor, neither is anything placed on it, and it has a special place in the home. A Muslim must be clean to hold or read the *Qur'an*, and if the book is too old to handle it must be burned. No pious Muslim would ever smoke, drink or make a noise while the *Qur'an* is being read aloud.

> And when the Koran is recited, give your ear to it and be silent.[32]

Hadith   There is a clear distinction in Islam between the divine word and the prophetic word. The former is the *Qur'an*, the literal word of God, whilst the latter is composed of the various messages from God to human beings given to the prophets who used their own words to explicate them. There is, therefore, a hierarchy in that the *Qur'an*, the divine word, is on a higher plane than the prophetic word, though both are sacred word. The sayings of Muhammad (the prophetic word), known as *hadith*, run into many thousands. A whole science has grown around the *hadith*, and Muslims are very rigorous in subjecting any particular *hadith* to close examination before admitting it to the corpus. Admittance is on the basis of *isnad* – support. Each *hadith* must have a reliable chain of transmitters going back to Muhammad.[33]

Some scholars, however, have argued that there were intermediary links between the divine word and the prophetic word. Within the *hadith nabawi* – the prophetic tradition – are found the *hadith qudsi*, also known as *hadith itahi* and *hadith rabbani*, or divine sayings. These are a variety of sayings ascribed to God which are not in the *Qur'an*. One scholar has suggested that in early Islam there was not such a firm distinction between divine and prophetic word as exists today.[34] Another scholar, Richard Bell, has even argued that *awha* and *wahy*, translated in Islamic theology as reveal and revelation, meant, in fact, suggest and suggestion.[35] The *Qur'an* itself states that Gabriel brought the message down to Muhammad's heart,[36] which could indicate inspiration rather than direct verbal revelation. There have, after all, been alterations made to the *Qur'an*: "And for whatever verse We abrogate or cast into oblivion, We bring a better or the like of it".[37]

This, and other sayings, have resulted in *an-nasikh wa-l-mansukh* – the doctrine of abrogation. This maintains that certain commands in the *Qur'an* only had temporary application and when circumstances changed they were abrogated or replaced. If, however, the word of God can be abrogated, then can a clear distinction be maintained between the divine word and the prophetic word? Muslims argue that there is a very important linguistic distinction between *hadith* and *Qur'an*, a distinction which is considered to be proof that the words of the *Qur'an* cannot be those of Muhammad:

> The *hadith* are in the ordinary spoken Arabic of Muhammad's time; the sayings in the *Qur'an* are in a unique and special style that is different from any other book or writing. Muslims believe the *Qur'an* was the word of Allah, exactly as Muhammad received it. Muhammad was simply the transmitter, the mouth-piece through which the words were revealed to people.[38]

If Muhammad had simply been inspired to write the *Qur'an*, then there would not be this clear difference. Indeed Muslims argue that the poetry of the *Qur'an* is such that no human being could have produced it.

There are, however, distinctions between the various prophets. Prophecy, although deriving from God, is given in a different form, or rather in different forms, for in Islam there are three levels of prophecy: (1) the *nabi*, the prophet, a person chosen to speak God's message, but this is not necessarily a universal message; (2) the *rasul*, the apostle, who does carry a universal message to be given to all people; and (3) the *ulu'l 'azm*, the possessor of firmness and determination, one who will found a new religion. Muhammad was all three of these, and he also marked the end of the prophetic cycle – he was the "seal of the prophets".

Prophethood is seen as:

> a state bestowed upon men whom God has chosen because of certain perfections in them by virtue of which they become the instrument through whom God reveals His message to the world.[39]

According to Islam there have been many prophets, in many places, in many times, bringing revelation and a "book". The knowledge the prophet brings comes directly from God, "his [the prophet] knowledge marks a direct intervention of the Divine in the human order":[40] God intervenes in the world. These prophets are all seen as part of Islam and some are even referred to by name – such as Adam, Abraham, Moses, David and Jesus. Although these prophets are mentioned and their memory is respected, it is to Muhammad, the seal of the prophets, that Muslims turn for their example. He was the unlettered prophet and, being illiterate and unread, there was nothing to disrupt the flow of the divine word: he was, in a sense, a *tabula rasa* upon which God could write with ease.

Muhammad's position is a special one *vis-á-vis* humanity for, although the *Qur'an* tells him to say to the people that, "I am only a mortal, like you are"[41] it also declares, "O believers, obey God and his Messenger,"[42] and states that, "You have had a good example in God's messenger".[43] So Muslims try to follow the example of Muhammad in the way they live their lives. Because of these words in the *Qur'an* there developed the belief that the prophets, at least after they became prophets, were sinless, protected from error. If Muhammad were thus sinless then all human beings should follow the way, the *sunnah*, of the prophet.

This example is essential for human beings, for, although we have in the *Qur'an* the perfect book, without the *sunnah*:

> men would in most cases read their own limitations in the Holy Book and the whole homogeneity of Muslim society and the harmony existing between the Qur'an and the religious life of Islam would be disrupted.[44]

Thus Muslims depend on the personal inspiration of Muhammad to interpret the word of the *Qur'an*. As W. Graham states:

> all succeeding generations would look back upon the time of the prophet as the paradigmatic age, the era hallowed by the divinely ordained mission of Muhammad and the divine revelation communicated through him.[45]

This indeed has been the case for, as Graham continues:

> when revealing ended and prophecy ceased, the revelations and prophetic guidance already given became the only fixed standards upon which life could be patterned.[46]

For Muslims Muhammad provides the means, in both his words and deeds, by which the timeless truths of the *Qur'an* can be interpreted in the everchanging situations which are encountered in the world. The *Qur'an* provides guidance, "a guidance to the godfearing", [47] "a guidance to the people".[48] Muhammad stands as one who was guided.

THE SHARI'AH

The *shari'ah* is often spoken of as the Islamic legal system, which indeed it is: but many non-Muslims regard it, therefore, as akin to the Roman or Napoleonic legal codes, which it is not. In the words of Murad:

[it] is the fulfilment of the total man – inner and outer, individual and corporate – as he seeks to live by the will of his one and only God.[49]

Shari'ah means literally "way to water", or "the way to a watering place". It is the "clear path" to God the fountainhead of life and sustenance, hence the image of an oasis so familiar and so essential to the Arabs on the Arabian peninsula. It is a way of living one's life; in many ways it is Islam, the heart of the faith. "Law is, therefore, in Islam an integral aspect of revelation and not an alien element".[50]

The *shari'ah* is comprised of four elements. First, and without equal, is the *Qur'an*, in which there are approximately 500 verses of legal instructions. Second is the *sunnah* – Muhammad is seen not simply as prophet but also as exemplar. He lived his life in accordance with God's will, and thus Muslims who also seek to live their lives in accordance with the will of God see him as the best example to follow. So, for example, the *Qur'an* urges Muslims to "keep up prayer", but it was Muhammad himself who, by his own actions, gave the details of the service. "Pay alms" is frequently repeated in the *Qur'an*, but it was Muhammad who gave the rules and regulations for its payment and collection.

In addition, Muhammad is also seen as the best human interpreter of the *Qur'an*. There is a saying that the *Qur'an* is the best interpreter of the *Qur'an*, meaning that if one is unsure of the meaning of a passage in the *Qur'an*, then one should look elsewhere in the book to see if there is a clearer statement on the issue. It is a tenet of Muslim belief that the *Qur'an* cannot contradict itself. If, however, it is still unclear, or the *Qur'an* does not cover the specific issue, then the sayings and deeds of Muhammad, the *hadith*, are consulted. Muhammad's word and example are binding on Muslims. Clearly, however, even the *Qur'an* and the *sunnah* combined did not cover every problem and eventuality, and there arose the need for further interpretation. This is provided by the third and fourth elements of the *shari'ah* – *ijma'* or consensus, and *ijtihad* or reason, the latter being sometimes referred to as *qiyas* or analogical deduction.

Consensus is achieved by means of *shura* or consultation, a process sanctioned by the fact that it was employed by Muhammad himself as well as his immediate successors. The Muslims would come together to discuss a particular problem or debate a particular issue, and hopefully a consensus would be arrived at, though the final decision was one for the leader to take. Clearly, it is not now possible, and has not been since the early days of Islam, for all Muslims to come together to discuss a particular issue. It is left, therefore, to the theologians and scholars of the Islamic world to discuss any problem to see if consensus can be obtained. This is acceptable to most Muslims because any discussion must be based on the interpretation of the *Qur'an* and the *hadith*. No consensus is acceptable which deviates from these. Those who have studied them in depth are thus the best placed to interpret them.

The same is true of *ijtihad* or reason: reason must not be contrary to the *Qur'an* or *hadith*, but rather reasoning must draw out the true meaning of these things. Despite the prominence of scholars and theologians in this process it is incumbent on all Muslims to try to work out their own path through life. Muslims will often consult scholars about problems they may have, indeed most mosques will have at least one *Imam* or religious leader and teacher, but simply following the word of another is unacceptable: *taqlid* or blind imitation, is strongly condemned in Islam:

> if a man takes the findings of any person or institution which are not substantiated by the revelations, as final and accepts them as gospel truths he is committing the grave offence of associating other gods with Allah.[51]

In the end it is the individual person who is alone responsible for the decisions he or she makes and the actions he or she carries out. Human beings have been given the capacity to reason and it is God's wish and their destiny to use it. Ahmed comments that:

> It is to fulfil this destiny that *ilm*, knowledge, is so emphasized; *ilm* is the second most used word in the Qur'an after the name of God. Human beings are told to use their mind and think in at least 300 places.[52]

Shi'ite Islam has a different emphasis on these points. The *Qur'an* and the *sunnah* have the same role and function as within Sunni Islam, but the Shi'ites give far greater weight to the religious leaders. The *Imams* are the leaders and teachers within the Muslim communities and, within Shi'ite Islam, are seen as the heirs to 'Ali, and the true authority on any point of debate. In 874 CE there occurred the Occulation of Muhammad Mahdi, the last Shi'ite *Imam*. This last *Imam* did not, according to Shi'ite doctrine, die; rather he was hidden from human sight and remains so to this day. There was then a period of specific agency in which the Hidden *Imam* was represented by deputies. After the death of the fourth and last of these deputies came the era of *velayat-e-ammah* or general agency in which the *Ulama*, the Shi'ite clergy, acted, as they still do today, as representatives of the Hidden *Imam*, and thus as interpreters of the *Qur'an* and the *sunnah*.

A code to live by   The *shari'ah* is the path through life of the Muslim, governing all actions in this world. It is derived from the word of God and the example of his prophet, and is not simply a list of do's and dont's, but a way of being in the world. Clearly, however, there are specific prescriptions. There is a distinction in Islam between *halal* which means permitted, and *haram* which means forbidden. *Halal* refers to those things which it is acceptable for Muslims to take or to do. So, for example, any meat which a Muslim eats must be *halal* meat, that is meat which has been slaughtered according to Muslim regulations. Within the province of *halal* there are further distinctions between that which is *wajib* (compulsory); that which is *mandub* (recommended); that which comes under the heading of *mubah* (i.e. no opinion has been expressed and it is thus permitted through silence – most things fall into this category); and that which is *makruh* (disliked). Smoking would be placed under this last heading by many Muslim authorities, but an example of the way that the *Shi'ites* can deviate from the Muslim norm is given by the banning of smoking in Iran. The Ayatollah Khomeini banned smoking in Iran, and it was generally recognized that he had both the right and the power to do so.

A further concept to be noted within *shari'ah* law is *istihsan* or the idea of the public good. Although some things may be prescribed, the law may be overruled in cases where it is felt to be in the public good. Thus a woman is forbidden to show certain parts of her body to any man other than her husband, but this law may be put aside if it is necessary for her to be examined by a doctor, and the only doctor available is male.

Western attitudes to the *shari'ah*   The *shari'ah* is often looked on in the West as a barbaric remnant from a past age, and many Westeners are bemused as to why Muslims should wish to see it implemented today. The preceding comments may give some idea as to why Muslims regard the *shari'ah* as so important: it is the way they can live their faith. There are also points where many people in the West would agree with Islamic ideas. For instance, the principle of *qisas* or retribution is fundamental to the Islamic idea of justice: "the recompense of evil is evil the like of it",[53] a life for a life. The idea is that those to whom injury has been done will feel that justice has been served if the guilty party is punished in a way that reflects the crime, an idea which would be acceptable to many, though not all, in the West. However, if the guilty person repents, the wronged party or parties can choose to accept this (or not), or they can accept payment in recompense, referred to as blood-money, which would be seen as less acceptable in the West.

There are also points on which there would be a direct clash. For instance, *zina* is unlawful sex, and within this overall classification there are various punishments prescribed. Premarital sex merits a hundred lashes be the person male or female: "The fornicatress and the fornicator – scourge each one of them a hundred stripes",[54] whilst adultery merits stoning to death. The *Khalifah* 'Umar's second son was given a hundred lashes for *zina* and died from them, thus emphasizing the equality of all Muslims before the law. For Muslims the family is the bedrock of the Muslim *ummah*, and its maintenance essential to the good ordering of society. Anything which would seem to undermine the family, such as *zina*, falls, therefore, within the criminal law.

The punishment for theft is amputation, for drinking or taking intoxicants it is flogging, for apostasy it is death. This last point was part of the case against Salman Rushdie, the author of *Satanic Verses*, who had been brought up in a Muslim household and, in the eyes of many Muslims, had turned and attacked Islam. Faith underpins not only society, but the very soul of all human beings: to attack this, therefore, is, for Muslims, to commit the greatest of crimes. Many people in the West are, for historical reasons, reluctant to allow theology to wield a veto over what may be thought and said, and many Western theologians would concur with this reluctance. Disagreements on this point within a multi-faith society are, therefore, inevitable.

Some Muslims have attempted to argue that although these punishments are prescribed, the circumstances in which they could be given are so ringed round with qualifications that they would hardly ever be employed. Most Muslims take the view that the *Qur'an* would not be likely to lay down punishments which could not be used, and would therefore see them as integral to the *shari'ah*. The arguments of this latter group of Muslims (the majority), in favour of these aspects of *shari'ah*, are first that they are given in the *Qur'an*, which is the word of God; hence they feel there is no need to apologize for them. The gifts of God to human beings are said to be the Book (the *Qur'an*), the Balance (justice), and Iron (punishment). Punishment is referred to as *hadd* (plural *hudud*), which means literally "boundaries": the guilty person has crossed the boundaries laid down by God, and is thus rightly punished in a way laid down by God. They have also argued that flogging, for instance, is preferable to imprisonment, the taking away of a person's liberty, which is not only terrible for that person, but may punish innocent parties such as the prisoner's wife and children, who will be deprived of both his presence and his earnings. They would also argue that crime in Muslim countries is much less because of the presence of these punishments, and thus that there is actually less need to use them. The further point is made that the Western obsession, as Muslims see it, with these aspects of the *shari'ah*, which, in fact, comprise such a small part of the *shari'ah*, is another example of the West's bias against Islam and its distortion of the message of Islam.

These arguments, however, have not convinced most people in the West, and it seems likely that, whilst punishments such as amputation for theft, flogging for premarital sex and death for apostasy are supported by Muslims, areas of strong disagreement will remain.

The Five Pillars of Islam are the five obligatory acts which all Muslims are expected to carry out, these are,

1. The declaration of faith
2. Prayer
3. Almsgiving
4. Fasting (throughout the month of Ramadan).
5. Pilgrimage to Mecca.

These acts are obligatory for all Muslims.

The First Pillar: the declaration of faith (*shahadah*)   *La ilaha 'illa 'llah muhammadun rasulu 'ikih*. This means "I bear witness that there is no god but God and Muhammad is his Messenger." Although not found in complete form in the *Qur'an*, but in two separate halves, this is the basic expression of faith for the Muslim. The expression and declaration of belief in one creator and sustainer, is the central belief of Islam. This all-powerful God has the right to demand complete submission, complete obedience from his worshipper. As previously stated it is obedience and not understanding which is required. Jornier points out that:

> The use of a negative phrase (there is no god but God) in the *shahada* formula gives the expression a manifest clarity. It does away with that which is not God, but it preserves the question of the mystery of God in himself, a mystery which it does not penetrate, and which the believers keep themselves from touching on by virtue of a characteristic attitude of Islam.[55]

This declaration must not simply be a verbal statement, rather it must come from the heart of the Muslim. It really signifies the total orientation of all the human being's goals and interests towards what God wills. The *shahadah* must always be spoken in Arabic, the language of the *Qur'an*. God spoke these exact words to Muhammad and, in repeating them, the Muslim reinforces the special nature of the declaration.

The second part of the declaration of belief, that Muhammad is the prophet (messenger) of God, implies the acceptance of his teachings in the *Qur'an* as the revealed scripture. This belief accepts that Muhammad was the last of a line of prophets stretching from Adam, and therefore the culminating definitive word on religious and moral truth. Inherent in the declaration, then, is not only belief, but acceptance that God's word as revealed in the *Qur'an* should be followed. Muhammad has often been called the "seal of the prophets", because his word is final. The message of former prophets who had also brought the word of God, had sometimes been misunderstood or indeed deliberately tampered with, until Muhammad delivered the message.

The declaration of belief in Muhammad as messenger of God, then, is tantamount to belief in his revelations. Other revelations accepted by Muslims include the biblical *Pentateuch,* revealed through the prophet Moses, and called *Taurat,* the psalms *(Zabur),* revealed through the prophet David, and the New Testament *(Injil)* revealed through Jesus. Only the *Qur'an*, revealed through Muhammad, is believed to be in its original form.

The Second Pillar: prayer (*salat*)   An old tradition says: "Prayer is like a stream of sweet water which flows past the door of each of you. A Muslim plunges into it five times a day." Of the five pillars in Islam, prayer takes second place only after the declaration of faith:

> The institution of prayer helps to remove weaknesses in individual character and strengthen the wall of the Islamic community with the cement of discipline, obedience and love.[56]

There are two types of prayer. There is *du'ah*, which means petition, supplication or invocation, implying that human beings in this world are weak and helpless without God's mercy. These prayers may be performed at any time, in any place and are most often done in the worshipper's own language. The other type of prayer is *salat*, which is the name given to the formal prayers and their essential ritual movements which have to be performed five times a day at set times, though these times comprise a period rather than a fixed moment. These prayers are compulsory and follow a precise pattern. The times of day when they must be performed are dawn (the *fajr*), after midday *(zuhr)*, mid-afternoon *(asr)*, sunset *(maghrib)*, and night *(isha)*.

In Britain some of these prayers can be very close together. In winter, *zuhr, asr,* and *maghrib* do not have many hours separating them, even given the periods of time allowed for each. Thus *zuhr* can be performed in winter, between 1.00 and 2.00 p.m., *asr* between 2.30 and 3.30 p.m., and *maghrib* between 4.00 and 5.00 p.m. In summer, the times for *zuhr* are more relaxed, between 1.00 and 4.00 p.m., so there can be a greater period of time between this prayer and *asr*, but *maghrib* (sunset), *isha* (night) and *fajr* (dawn) are very close together, and sleep is broken as a result. It requires a firm commitment, therefore, to keep up prayer.

Before prayers Muslims must wash themselves in a set of procedures known as *wudhu* or ablution. This procedure involves the repetition of the phrase "In the name of God the Beneficent, the Merciful", while washing the hands up to the wrists three times, then the elbows three times, followed by the washing of the mouth three times, with water then being inhaled into the nostrils. Then the head is washed, the ears and neck and lastly the right and left foot to the ankle are washed three times. This removes physical impurity and is also symbolic of an inner cleansing. During this process the Muslim turns his or her mind to concentrate on God, and so it involves mental as well as physical preparation. In order to stand before God they must wash to be pure, to be fresh, and to be alert for this very important and significant act. The Muslim should also perform *ghusl*, bathing from head to toe, at least once a week.

After performing the ablutions Muslims take off their shoes, stand on clean ground, or a prayer mat, and face in the direction of Mecca. The direction of Mecca is frequently indicated by arrows in cities, especially at railway stations, to encourage the traveller to pray, and often prayer mats are seen outside roadside cafes for the use of travellers. Then they call for prayer, saying:

> God is the greatest (four times). I bear witness that there is no god but God (twice). I bear witness that Muhammad is the messenger of God (twice) Come to Prayer (twice). Come to Security (twice). There is no god but God.

This, and the prayer itself, are always said in Arabic, for not only is this the sacred language, but "prayer through the bond of a common language serves as a great unifying force among the Muslims".[57]

When praying at the mosque, Muslims are summoned by a call to prayer, the *adhan*. Before the beginning of each set of daily prayers a man called the *muezzin* goes up into one of the towers of the mosque, called a *minaret*, and chants a set prayer. It is as above: "God is the Greatest" and for the first prayer call of the morning he adds the line: "Prayer is better than sleep." Inside the mosque the congregation faces Mecca, with the prayers being led by the senior male present, often the *Imam*. If no male is present, as may happen for instance within the home, the senior female may perform this role. Each person decides on the number of *rak'ahs* he or she is going to make. A *rak'ah* is literally "bending", it is the movements of prayer which accompany the spoken words. "The postures of bowing, kneeling and prostration are specifically designed to evoke humility and reverence in the worshipper".[58] A Muslim begins by lifting the hands to the ears and saying, *Allahu akbar* "God is the Greatest". The right hand is then lowered and placed on top of the left just above the navel; he or she recites the opening verses of the *Qur'an* and any other short chapter or verses. Then the words "God is the Greatest" are said and the worshipper bows with hands on knees and legs straight, repeating three times, "All glory to God the Greatest". Into the upright position next and the words "God has listened to him who has praised Him our God: Praise be to thee" are said. Then on the knees, placing hands on the ground and nose and forehead on the ground between them.

This position fully symbolizes the spirit of Islam in submission to God. In this position the worshipper says "All Glory to God the Highest". Then he or she sits back on the heels and says, "O God, forgive me and have mercy upon me", prostrates again and repeats, "All Glory to God the Highest".

This is the end of the first *rak'ah*. Once the designated number of *rak'ahs* is finished *du'ah* are said and the ceremony is completed by saying, "Peace be upon you and the mercy of God", with head turned to look once over the right and once over the left shoulder. It is said that the purpose of this is to say *as-salamul-'alaikum* (peace and blessings of God be upon you) to the two angels who sit on either shoulder. The one on the left records the person's bad deeds, the one on the right records the good deeds. The gestures involved in the whole ritual symbolize the humble submission of the believer before God. Rahman well illustrates the deep meaning behind the ritual when he states that:

> The physical postures and the movements in prayer also play a very significant role in revitalizing and reigniting the potential and latent sources of power in man to enable him to open a channel between himself and the Creator.[59]

The purpose of *salat* for Muslims is that first God has instructed them to pray. Second, they pray in order to praise and glorify God: it is their duty. In addition, those who faithfully keep God in mind throughout their lives in this world can expect reward in Paradise and, also, prosperity in this world. Note that God does not need the prayers of Muslims for he is entirely self-sufficient; rather Muslims need to pray to God in order to infuse themselves with *taqwa* – God-consciousness.

The private devotions *(du'ah)* come most naturally at the end of the *salat*. The worshippers raise their hands, palms upwards to about chin-level and petition God on their own behalf and for others. Muslims may also use a kind of rosary called a *subha;* it comes from words meaning "praise" as the *subha* is an instrument for counting the names of God. A *subha* consists of three groups of beads, each group being separated by two larger beads set transversely. There are 33 beads in each group, making a total of 99. The number represents the 99 beautiful names of God: names such as "merciful", "benificent". It acts as an aid to concentration so that the believer comes to be more aware of the presence and inner reality of God. A *subha* is also used in the counting of prayers by the individual worshipper.

On Friday the midday prayer is replaced by a congregational service at noon *(jumah)*, when the *Imam* delivers a sermon. Attendance at the mosque for prayers is always encouraged, but on Friday it is as even more important that all attend. This communal prayer brings the Muslims together as a community in worship before God. In the mosque the worshippers stand in straight rows, shoulder to shoulder expressing the solidarity and order of the Muslim community. As stated, the actions involved in prayer are expressions of submission and adoration, and the whole ritual of *salat* demands self discipline. *Salat* is a continual reminder of a direct relationship with the Creator: it is thus a constant reminder of the ultimate reality.

Men try to pray in groups, again emphasizing the sense of community which lies at the heart of the religion. This is particularly true during special festivals and on Fridays. Women do not attend the mosques as regularly as men, and when they do, they usually worship in a different room from the men. Sometimes they even use different entrances and worship in a separate gallery. In Britain, however, there are mosques where women worship in the same room as the men, in which case they will stand behind them. Women normally say prayers at home, together or alone.

Muslim worship, then, revolves very much around prayer. Although the emphasis within the second pillar is on devotional prayer, any action which follows the will of God is also seen as an act of worship: "eating, drinking, sleeping and the other wordly acts to satisfy one's physical needs become acts of worship if they are performed with true religious motives".[60] A Muslim will attempt to act with true religious motives, and, after doing his or her best, learns to accept what happens in life because it is God's will. The vagaries of fortune are accepted because devout Muslims believe that God knows what is best for all human beings. Islam is truly a religion of submission and this is manifested in the bowings, prostrations and devotional words of the formal prayer, *salat*.

The Third Pillar: almsgiving (*zakat*)   The *Qur'an* speaks of: "the believers who perform the prayer and pay the alms, and bow them down".[61] Literally translated, *zakat* means purification: in this context it means purification of wealth. This is the prescribed "poor due" of Islam, and in this, the Muslim expresses his or her love for God through the care of other human beings. "Love of Allah should be the motive behind all acts of charity".[62] *Zakat* is not a tax on necessary possessions, but on income. The tax is approximately 2.5 per cent and is assessed yearly for each individual who qualifies.

Zakat is a further example of belief in action, in proclaiming practically what the Muslim believes. Everything a Muslim has, including life itself, he or she owes to God. In returning something of this bounty to the poor and needy, converts to Islam who experience material hardship, travellers, debtors, those in prison, the *zakat* actualizes the prescription of the *Qur'an* to give to the poor and to visit those in prison. Abdalati declares that: "*Zakah* is a vivid manifestation of the spiritual and humanitarian spirit of responsive interactions between the individual and society".[63] The Muslim, in giving to other human beings, returns something to God of what has been given to him or her in trust. Thus "by paying poor due, the rich are not doing any favour to the poor or society but are doing their normal moral as well as legal duty".[64] This purifies or sanctions the individual's possession of the remainder of his or her property. *Zakat* also has a community function in strengthening the *ummah* by alleviating any jealousy or bitterness. Muhammad had always held that material excess in the midst of poverty was unjust. The tax is a move towards greater social equality without attempting to create a situation of total egalitarianism, something which Muslims feel would be an impossibility since we are all created differently.

Apart from specific *zakat*, charity as a voluntary response to human need is expected of the Muslim. This is called *sadaqah* and it is different to *zakat* in that it can be given by any Muslim from what is surplus to their needs and can be given to anyone, Muslim or non-Muslim. The *Qur'an* states: "They will question thee [Muhammad] concerning what they should expend. Say: "The abundance".[65] As one scholar has remarked:

> The spirit of Muhammad's Message is manifest in the fact that by rendering the poor tax, the Muslim does not absolve himself from further claims to his possessions; as long as there is need for the exercise of beneficence and charity, this need must be met.[66]

In the early days, *zakat* was collected by the authorities and distributed. Today it is often paid to the mosque commitee.

The Fourth Pillar: fasting (*sawm*)

> O believers prescribed for you is the Fast.[67]

Muslims are instructed to fast for the whole of the month of Ramadan. This is the month when, according to Muslim belief, Muhammad received his first revelation. The Muslim calendar is designed on a lunar pattern, each month being 28 or 29 days long. Ramadan is the ninth month. *Sawm* in Arabic means abstention from food, drink and sexual intercourse. So a Muslim is required throughout the day time to abstain completely from these until the fast ends at sunset. The command to fast was received during the period at Medina, when it was the practice of Muhammad to recite the *Qur'an* within the space of the month, and many present-day Muslims follow this aspect of the *sunnah*, "the Prophet's Practice". Fasting would not have been new to Muslims. Most religions, in ancient and modern times, include a period of fasting often at special times of the year. Jews and Christians at the time of Muhammad would have fasted at certain times and probably other peoples also.

Because of the lunar calendar, Ramadan does not always fall in the same season of the year: it falls eleven days earlier each year. Thus it sanctifies the whole year as it passes through it. In summer, when hours of daylight are longer and the temperature is higher, abstinence from food and drink is more difficult. However, even after sunset Muslims are not encouraged to eat or drink to excess. This would deny the spirit of the fast: "the stomach is emptied so spirit may be filled with piety and righteousness".[68]

Some categories of people are exempt from the fast – the old, the sick, young children, women who are pregnant, and travellers (travelling could be a very tiring occupation). The aim of the fast is to bring one's self closer to God, but not to the point of imposing an intolerable burden. Those unable to fast are urged to do so at a later period. Children are also exempt from the fast, though the age at which they would be expected to commence their participation differs between various Muslim communities, and indeed between different families. Many children, however, seeing their parents and older siblings fasting, will voluntarily elect to participate, at least in some days of the fast. Children as young as seven will do this.

The last ten days of Ramadan are the climax of the month. Muslims try to spend more time in the mosque praying and reading the *Qur'an* during this period. They seek to bring themselves closer to God and also closer to their fellow Muslims who are united with them in the fast. The *Night of Power* is celebrated during Ramadan, in remembrance of the time when Muhammad received the first vision and revelation. No one knows on which day it was, but by long established custom it is celebrated on the 27th of Ramadan. *Surah* 97:2 in the *Qur'an* states: "Behold, We sent it [the *Qur'an*] down on the Night of Power". Since it is impossible to eat or drink throughout the daylight hours it is necessary for the Muslim to get up before sunrise to eat a meal called *suhoor*. This has to be completed twenty minutes before sunrise. Then, throughout the day Muslims are not expected to chew or swallow anything external, neither are they permitted to take medicine via the mouth or nose (though not if its exclusion would be life-threatening). They can, however, use external medications such as skin creams or ointments or even perfume, and they are also permitted to clean their teeth. The breaking of the fast takes place after sunset and is called *iftar*. Muslims will usually have a very light meal for *iftar*, perhaps consisting of just a few dates. Before they eat they will say:

> O God, I have fasted for you, and I have believed in You, and with your food I break the fast. In the name of God, the Merciful.

Then follows the *maghrib*, the sunset prayer after which a full meal will be eaten. If the fast is broken a penalty has to be paid unless there is some extenuating circumstance. The transgressor may be asked to feed sixty people, or to give its equivalent in money to charity. He or she may even be asked to considerably extend the fast.

At the end of this ten-day period comes, *Eid-ul-Fitr*, the "festival of breaking the fast". Since *Eid-ul-Fitr* is one of the high points of the Muslims' year, it is also a religious obligation to keep this festival. Muhammad left instructions for the two main festivals of the year, one being *Eid-ul-Fitr* (*Eid* = Arabic for Festival or time of happiness). This takes place on the first day of the month of Shawwal. It originates from the time when the Prophet went to Medina and found a divided city where pagan gods were worshipped. He abolished all the pagan festivals and established the two main festivals instead. Before Ramadan ends, Muslim families give generously to charity – "*Zakat ul-Fitr*". The offering must be food or money and it is another of the duties of all Muslims. After this comes the festival prayer, when all go to the mosque, and then families and friends come together in their homes. New clothes are worn, presents are given and sweets are a major treat. Cards are sent to each other, bearing the greeting *Eid mubarak* (Blessed and happy festival), homes are decorated and parties held. In India and Pakistan there are wrestling matches, fairs and horse races. It is a time also for reconciliation when old quarrels are forgotten.

The meaning behind Ramadan   The discipline of fasting is believed in Islam, as in many other religious traditions, to increase moral and spiritual wholeness by concentrating the mind on the inner spiritual life: "fasting develops a very strong sense of nearness and closeness to God and of His Presence everywhere".[69] This teaches restraint and self-knowledge, strength of purpose, character and self-discipline. The deprivation involved creates an awareness of those things normally taken for granted; Muslims realize and appreciate the good things of life which are given by God. Like fasting in all religions, it is intended to heighten the spiritual experience of the human being by making him or her less dependent on material benefits. Over indulgence in food, drink and marital relations often make people slaves to their desires. Ramadan is a means of overcoming this dependence on desires. The ascetic implications of such a fast have been highlighted by Ruthven:

> In general it can be said that the fast confers on the community many of the benefits of asceticism, such as self-discipline and mental control over bodily needs, without falling into the excesses of the eastern churches, where "spiritual athleticism", by separating the ascetics from the ordinary lay believers, tended to undermine group cohesion.[70]

Ramadan is most particularly the month in which the Muslim must obey the ethical prescriptions of Islam, particularly the act of charity. The fast should produce empathy in the Muslim for those who are habitually deprived and poor. This awareness is then channelled into positive practical contributions to charity: Ramadan makes the rich feel what the poor feel. In addition, as with so many Muslim customs, it has a communal meaning and spirit which are important because they reinforce the sense of belonging to the community of Islam, which is felt by all Muslims:

> It originates in man the real Spirit of Social Belonging, of Unity and Brotherhood, of Equality before God as well as before the Law.[71]

Thus, to the Muslim, Ramadan provides the greatest opportunity for the development of his or her relationship with God; it is a time, as with many aspects of Islam, when belief is put into action. Many Muslims report a sense of real well-being during Ramadan because of the increase in self-awareness and spirituality. There is a requirement on the Muslim to be devout, and this is not easy; but Muslims believe through the practice of their faith that God is guiding them to the life which begins after death, and they can feel confident and happy about this. Submission to the laws of Islam brings security and peace of mind.

The Fifth Pillar: pilgrimage (hajj) *Surah* 3 v. 90ff of the *Qur'an* states that:

> The first House established for the people was that at Bekka [Mecca] ... It is the duty of all men towards God, to come to the house a pilgrim, if he is able to make his way there.

The *hajj*, the pilgrimage to Mecca in Saudi Arabia, is the fifth Islamic obligatory act of worship. It is a once-in-a-lifetime requirement for those who can afford it. This latter point is usually strictly interpreted. It must be financed from one's own money, one must be free of debt, one must be supporting one's parents where this is necessary, and no money must be diverted from them to the *hajj*. Indeed if one's neighbours are starving one must first support them, and this would still be seen as a form of *hajj*. This is so because the *hajj* is symbolic of the human being's journey towards God and, by obeying the commands of God, in this case by an act of charity, the Muslim would be making just such a journey.

In the *hajj*, the Muslim (male or female) assumes the status of the pilgrim, the servant of God. There is a traditional belief amongst Muslims that:

> in performing the Hajj they are literally re-enacting the birth of the primordial Islam of Ibrahim (Abraham), the "first monotheist", his bondswoman, Hagar, and his son Isma'il (Ishmael), ancestor of the Arabs.[72]

During this pilgrimage the Muslim foregoes luxury, comfort and worldly status: the Arabic word *hajj* means "to set out for a definite purpose". *Hajj* takes place in the first days of the lunar month of *Dhul-Hijjah*, the twelfth month of the Islamic year, reaching its most important point on the ninth day.

Before the age of modern transport the pilgrimage could take a long time, in some cases many years. Today things are somewhat easier, pilgrims will usually travel by airplane to the seaport of Jiddha/Jeddah and take the remainder of the journey to Mecca in the real fashion of pilgrimage. The pilgrims become consecrated as *ihram:* men undertake ritual bathing, the shaving of the head and the removal of normal dress, and all signs of worldly status. They put on two white unsewn and seamless sheets, also called *ihram*, and expose only the head and hands. There is, however, no prescribed dress for women, though they would normally wear white. In this state of *Ihram* the pilgrim must refrain from abuse, quarrelling, harming any living thing (e.g. hunting), from sexual intercourse, the use of jewellery or perfume, from cutting hair or nails, and for men, from covering the head.

While making the journey to Mecca the pilgrims chant the words *Lab baika Al Lahumma Labbaik*. "Here we come in answer to your call, O Lord". The area around Mecca is sacred. It is called the *haram* and no non-Muslim may enter it. The first act of a pilgrim on arrival at Mecca is to worship at the *ka'aba*, The *ka'aba,* as it stands today, is a rectangular structure 45 feet high, 33 feet wide and 50 feet long, and is contained within the sacred mosque in the centre of Mecca. The black stone – the stone of celestial origin according to tradition and known to be part of the original *ka'aba* – is set in a corner. The *ka'aba* is highly revered and is ceremonially draped in a black cloth. Embroidered on it with gold thread are some of the verses of the *Qur'an*. This cloth is replaced annually with a new draping. The *ka'aba* is the focal point of Muslim worship throughout the world. When they pray, Muslims should face it. The term *qiblah* is used for the direction of the *ka'aba* from any one point on the earth's surface. Thus continually, through day and night, there is throughout the world an unending focus of prayer on the *ka'aba*.

On entering the mosque, the pilgrims make a humble petition and offer a *salat* of greeting. They then approach the *ka'aba* and perform the rite of *tawaf* (circumambulation). With a vast number of other pilgrims they begin the procession in the vast courtyard of the mosque and make seven circuits of the *ka'aba*, moving in an anti-clockwise directon. During the seven circumambulations of the *ka'aba* the pilgrim kisses, touches, or raises his or her hand towards the black stone. In this vast crowd, all here to do the bidding of God, the Muslims feel their own smallness compared to the will and purpose of the Creator. After a final *salat* the pilgrims are directed to the *zamzam* well.

According to Muslim tradition this was the spring which God gave to Hagar, the concubine of Abraham when she and her son Ishmael were abandoned in the desolate valley of Mecca. The rite performed in this part of the *hajj* is called *sa'i* meaning literally "hastening". The pilgrim runs between two small mounds of lava rock, Safa and Marwah, along a marble-lined corridor adjacent to the courtyard of the mosque. This commemorates Hagar's search for water in the desert. According to Islamic tradition, she ran back and forth seven times between the hills but found none and returned to Ishmael. Then God revealed the spring of *zamzam* flowing from the feet of Ishmael. This water had attracted the settlement at Mecca. The "hastening" is also symbolic of the quest of the human soul for divine sustenance. Pilgrims will then take water from this well.

The *hajj* reaches its most important point on the ninth day of *Dhul-Hijjah*, on the day of Arafat. At this time, the vast crowd of pilgrims journey to Arafat, a vast barren plain, some 12 miles east of Mecca, where there is held a day of devotion. In the centre of the plain is the mountain of Arafat, the "mountain of mercy", from which Muhammad delivered his last sermon. Gathering there is the greatest experience of the *hajj*:

> There is no higher religious experience for the individual Muslim nor any greater expression of brotherhood for the Muslim community than the Hajj.[73]

The pilgrims leave Arafat at sunset for a resting place called Muzdalifah, a wasteland of lava rock. Here they perform sunset and night prayers and gather stones for the rite of *mina*, that is, the stoning of three columns (*jamras*) on three consecutive days in the village of Mina. It is said that the devil tried to tempt Ishmael three times when Abraham was leading him to the place of sacrifice. But Ishmael would not rebel against his father and stoned the devil on three occasions. After *mina* many of the requirements of *ihram* are lifted. After the stoning of the first pillar comes the sacrifice of a sheep, goat or camel which is eaten in commemoration of Abraham's sacrifice of the sheep (instead of Ishmael). This occurs on 10th of *Dhul Hijjah* and is called *Eid-ul-Adha*, the Festival of Sacrifice. This does not only take place on the *hajj*, all over the world such sacrifices will be made by Muslims. In Western countries Muslim butchers will prepare the sacrifices for people, at the time of *Eid-ul-Adha*. On the third day of *mina*, before sunset, the pilgrimage is ended and the pilgrim shaves or cuts off a few strands of hair to signify the end of *ihram*. The pilgims then leave; they may return to Mecca to perform *tawaf* again, and often travel to Medina to pay their respects to the prophet Muhammad at his tomb.

In all this complex rite of *hajj*, Muslims experience an intense feeling of community. This is a unity which transcends national, racial and class differences. In this act, they are first and foremost a Muslim before God, and therefore equal to other Muslims. This is well expressed by Rahman when he says:

> People of all colours, all nationalities, all races, and of all ranks, from all the four corners of the world come here and meet and live together. They have all come before their Lord in extreme humility, wearing two white sheets, as members of the Universal Muslim Brotherhood.[74]

There is also in the pilgrimage a sense of spiritual unity, and for many Muslims an awesome feeling of the greatness of God. It is so important that if a Muslim dies before undertaking the *hajj* he or she may appoint one of his or her descendants to undertake the *hajj* for them. Similarly, a sick person can choose someone to go in his or her place. When someone undertakes *hajj* for another he or she performs everything twice, once for his or her self and once for the sick or deceased person. Those who have performed the *hajj* are known as *Hajjis* and are highly respected in their communities.

The five pillars of Islam are designed to reinforce *taqwa* – God-consciousness for the Muslim and to bring him or her into direct awareness of God. They strengthen the faith both at an individual and communal level. As a result of the former they discipline the believer so that an approach to the ideal of the Islamic way of life becomes a greater possibility. As a result of the latter they consolidate in the believer a sense of the unity of Muslims, reinforcing the ideal of community – the *ummah;* and they make demands on the whole person spiritually, mentally and physically.

THE MOSQUE

After leaving Mecca Muhammad stayed for a few days at Quba', an oasis just outside Medina, and here laid the foundations for the first mosque. Since then, many thousands of other mosques have been built all over the world. Some of them have been very small, plain buildings, others magnificent feats of architecture; all of them have been influenced by the types of buildings already existing in Muslim countries. However, the basic essentials of any mosque are very simple. The mosque usually has two main sections – the inner part, or the sanctuary, and the outer part, or courtyard. The inner part is the main part of the structure and is built to face Mecca. There must be a place for Muslims to wash themselves before they pray; in hot countries this is often outside (but in Britain this would not be very practical). There must also be somewhere for worshippers to leave their shoes. The washing facilities may take many different forms from separate building with ladies' and gentlemen's cloakrooms to simply some jars of water.

Inside the mosque is almost bare, and non-Muslim visitors are often disappointed because there is, in the majority of mosques, nothing to actually see (though some of the older mosques do contain beautiful tiling). There are no seats because space must be left for worshippers to go through the various positions of prayer which include sitting on the ground (Muslims worship in bare feet so the floor is usually carpeted). Islam operates a strict prohibition against graven images, to avoid any danger of idolatry. There is, however, a structure known as a *minbar* from which the Friday sermon is preached. It consists of at least three steps. Muhammad used to preach from the third step, and, in acknowledgement of his status, some *Imams* only mount to the second step. In large mosques, however, there may be a wooden plat-form which is much higher so that the speaker can be seen and heard clearly. The men and women are usually separated, or the women will stand behind the men so that the men are not distracted. There is a small alcove called a *mihrab* in the centre of one wall, the purpose of which is to point the Muslims in the direction of Mecca when they are praying. It is also the place where the *Imam* stands to lead the prayers.

Kursi-al Qur'an (lecterns) were introduced into the mosque at a time when the *Qur'an* was written in the form of a book which, in those days, was too heavy to be held in both hands. Most mosques are square or rectangular, often with a domed roof, both to symbolize the universe and to magnify the voice of the *imam*. There are towers, often in each corner, from the top of which the *muezzin* calls the faithful to prayer. One of Muhammad's companions had a dream in which he heard a call to prayer, so Muhammad ordered Bilal, an Ethiopian and an ex-slave, to go upon the roof and call the faithful to prayer: he was the first *muezzin*. In the early days, the *muezzin* went on to the roof of the mosque and called the *adhan*. Later, in the seventh century, minarets were built.

The functions of the mosque The early mosques, as well as being places of prayer, were also administrative centres – places where foreign delegates were received and housed, treasuries, command headquarters for the army, and many other things. In Muhammad's time it used to be the centre of administration, where he had his head-quarters and where decisions of government were made. Today one of the most important functions of the mosque is that of acting as a school for Muslims. Everywhere in the Muslim world there are *Qur'anic* schools for teaching the *Qur'an* and the tradition of Muhammad. Muhammad himself used to teach and train Muslims. One of the most important schools is at the Al Azhar Mosque in Cairo from where many of the world's Muslim teachers of theology grad-uate.

The mosque is the heart of the Muslim community where people meet and discuss their problems. One of the most important functions of the mosque, however, is still a peaceful, quiet place of worship. The mosque in Islam is called *masjid* (a place of prostration) or *jami'a* (a gatherer). The mosque in Britain is often a building with many rooms, which, beside being a place of prayer and education, as mentioned above, may also be used as a community centre. Weddings may be celebrated there and part of the building may be used by the leader (*Imam*) as a home for himself and his family. The *Imam*'s function is as a teacher and prayer leader in the mosque. He has no divine authority but, as a man of knowledge, the Muslims seek his advice on everyday matters.

FAMILY LIFE

The family, according to Muslims, came into existence with creation, with Adam and Eve: "the human race is a product of this institution and not the other way around".[75] This is not to say that Islam concentrates on the community at the expense of the individual, for each person has a direct, personal relationship with God. Rather Islam looks for a balance in family relationships between the individual and the community. Individuals have been given freedom and responsibility by God, and God will judge them on how they make use of this freedom. Therefore no one has the right to take away this God-given freedom from another. There are, however, two forces at work on human beings, the divine and the satanic, affecting the different elements in our nature. So structures are provided to help the individual in choosing the right path. The main structure for this purpose is the family.

For Muslims, the family is, and always has been, of vital importance and all Muslims are urged to marry. Indeed, Ahmed goes as far as to say that: "The position is not that marriage is only permitted or tolerated as unavoidable. It has been positively enjoined."[76] Marriages are not just bonds between two individuals, but between two families, and they thus increase overall harmony within the Muslim community. Above all the family is seen as acting as the premier conditioning agent within society, ensuring social, ideological and cultural stability:

> it is the basic unit of society integrating its members within and enabling them to play their ideological and cultural role in the world . . . If this institution is weakened or destroyed, the future of the entire culture and civilisation will be threatened.[77]

The whole of Muslim society is seen as an interrelating nexus with the families as the basic units which refer constantly back to society as a whole. According to Elkholy:

> the general underlying factor of this highly complex Muslim community is the spiritual identification of each cell within the system as the historical manifestation of the universal community.[78]

The importance of marriage can be seen in the fact that approximately one-third of the legal injunctions of the *Qur'an* relate to it, the family, and the proper regulations for both. Marriage for Muslims necessarily implies a family since deliberately childless marriages would not be approved of. Despite the value placed on it, marriage is not seen as sacramental in the sense of being an unbreakable covenant with God, nor is it seen as purely a civil afffair, since for Islam no aspect of life is divorced from the religious.

> The ethical principles of the husband-wife relationship are believed to derive from a conscientious commitment by both sides to the divine designation of marital union as an abode of peace and serenity, a link of mutual love and compassion – all being God's sign for those who reflect.[79]

This last point is a reference to the *Qur'anic* statement:

> He created for you, of yourselves, spouses, that you might repose in them, and He has set between you love and mercy. Surely in that are signs for a people who consider.[80]

So not only are marriage and the family designated by God, but they also act as a sign that God exists, for they are part of the harmony of God's creation.

Since this is so, family relations should follow the pattern laid down by God in the *Qur'an* and the *sunnah*. In his analysis of family structure in Islam al Ati emphasizes the particular interrelation of family and society:

> Family rights and obligations are not private family affairs of no concern to the rest of society . . . if the situation becomes unmanageable, religion commands society . . . to take whatever action is necessary to implement the law.[81]

It might be objected that this would be gross violation of individual freedom, but in Islam "public morality and the individual's own integrity take priority over personal freedom when they come into conflict".[82] If creation is a harmony designed by God, then the disruption of that harmony affects not only the individual disrupter, but the society in which such disruption takes place. Muslims would also argue that within these clear boundaries there is a great deal of individual freedom:

> Islam, which is not a religion of oppression, allows to man a very wide margin in his personal and social existence, so that the various qualities, temperaments and psychological inclinations of different individuals should find their way to positive development according to their indi-

vidual predisposition. Thus a man may be an ascetic, or he may enjoy the full measure of his sensual possibilities within the lawful limits; he may be a nomad roaming through the deserts, without food for tomorrow, or a rich merchant surrounded by his goods. As long as he sincerely and consciously submits to the laws decreed by God, he is free to shape his personal life to whatever form his nature directs him. His duty is to make the best of himself so that he might honour the life-gift which his Creator has bestowed upon him; and to help his fellow-beings, by means of his own development, in their spiritual, social and material endeavours.[83]

Clearly such choices as are made depend not just on the individual, but on the society in which he or she is living. Although Muslims place great emphasis on the unity of the *ummah*, the community, there are, nevertheless, wide cultural divergences between different Muslim countries. These divergences are welcomed by most Muslims, who would, however, argue that within this diversity there is a central core of Islamic virtues. Islam attempts to use a good upbringing in a stable family to instil these Islamic virtues. The two most important of these virtues are spiritual unity and material solidarity. The love and feeling of belonging that exist in all good families should extend to the rest of society. This should result in acts: "those who have given refuge and help – those in truth are the believers".[84] So material protection and help become part of the Islamic mores. Thus:

> every citizen of an Islamic state, whether he is a Muslim or a non-Muslim, has the right to live decently, to ample food, decent clothes, a suitable dwelling and opportunities for education.[85]

Islam attempts to extend the love and support found in all good families to the whole of society, and to use the family as an example for, and the underpinning of, that society.

Thus Muslims are clear in their view of the roles of the individual, the family and society:

> These three elements are inseparable and interdependent . . . according to Islam there is no contradiction between the interests of the individual, the welfare of the family and the interests of society.[86]

The individual is part of the family's inter-relationships, and the family is part of society's inter-relationships. The family is thus the central pivot for the individual and the community. The aim of the family is to pass on the Islamic principles by providing spiritual and material sustenance both within itself, and outside itself in the community. Saud puts this well when he says: "man is a nucleus, the family is his plasma and society is his organismic tissue".[87] Many of these aims would, of course, be shared by other communities, but Islam clearly and specifically lays out the terms of the human being's religious responsibilities in this regard.

Many people in the West have pointed to the gap between the ideal put forward here, and the reality of oppression and discrimination which exists in some Muslim countries. Many Muslims would agree, to an extent, with this point. They would, however, make a distinction between Muslim countries, those countries which have a majority Muslim population, and Islamic countries, those countries which make a serious attempt to introduce an Islamic structure. For many Muslims there are at present no Islamic countries, though some would make a case for considering Iran to be one. The ideal, therefore, stands as both the acme of Muslim aspiration, and the standard by which present Muslim countries can be judged.

Marriage in practice   In Islam, marriage is looked on as a bond of love and mercy. Marriage customs vary in Muslim communities and marriages are often partially arranged, that is to say the parents of the young man or woman find a suitable partner, and if both the man and woman are compatible and they agree to the partnership, wedding arrangements are made. In some Muslim communities, providing a man can treat them equally and the first wife agrees, four wives are permitted. "Marry such women as seem good to you, two, three, four; but if you fear you will not be equitable, then only one."[88]

This custom would be illegal in most Western countries. Some women now insist that their husbands sign a clause in their marriage contracts to the effect that they will never take a second wife. Since it would be impossible to treat two, three or four wives equally emotionally and spiritually, some suggest that the *Qur'an* does not really endorse polygamy. It is pointed out that this particular passage was revealed during the struggle with Quraysh after the battle of Uhud where, despite a Muslim victory, over 10 per cent of the Muslim army had been killed. This left the problem of widows and a surplus of single women, and polygamy was a solution to this situation, but could be seen as unnecessary now. As with the debate surrounding the punishments laid down under the *shari'ah*, however, this view is strongly opposed by the orthodox. The *Qur'an* permits this practice, therefore the vast majority of Muslims would not question it. However, in practice most Muslims marriages are monogamous

A Muslim female is not permitted to marry a non-Muslim male. In Islam the man is designated as the head of the household, and it would be unacceptable to Muslims for a Muslim female to be under the authority of a non-Muslim within the home. It is felt that it could not provide the right environment either for her or for her children, and she might indeed feel pressurized to compromise, or even abandon her faith. The male, being the head of the household, can marry outside his religion. Though when this occurs, if the female is not a Jew or

Christian, she has to convert to Islam. Thus the man can take:

> believing women in wedlock, and in wedlock believing women of those
> who were given the Book before you [i.e. Jews and Christians],[89]

but is told that he may not "marry idolatresses, until they believe".[90]

In many Muslim countries marriage was undertaken at an early age. This does not specifically relate to Islam but rather to peasant-based, agricultural economies. In the twentieth century, modernization of many Muslim countries and the increased freedom of women has meant the modification of many traditional practices. Children can, now, voice agreement or disagreement concerning their marriage (in theory they always could – "The widow shall not be married until she is consulted, and the virgin shall not be married until her consent is obtained",[91] said Muhammad), and child marriages are less common. In Egypt, for example, the minimum legal marrying age is 18 for a boy, 17 for a girl, though many special dispensations for girls to marry at 15 can be obtained. It is also the case that marriages of those even younger are often allowed despite being theoretically illegal.

The marriage ceremony can take place at the mosque or at the house of the bridegroom or bride. There are no priests or ministers in Islam, but it is customary to invite the local *Imam* from the mosque to conduct the ceremony. Celebrations can be elaborate and most Muslim countries have their own traditions of dress and ceremony. It is a time of great happiness for all the relatives and friends who have been invited and preparations will have been made long before the day of the wedding.

In Muslim countries, when the contract is signed, the girl is usually taken from her parents' house direct to her new one. Then the man is paraded through the town to announce the new marriage. Sometimes there are fireworks as well as music and refreshments. The extent of the celebrations depends on the wealth of the families concerned. In Britain, couples often have a traditional British wedding reception. Wedding presents, however, are given on a smaller scale than Western custom. The dowry, the bride-gift – *mahr* – is far more important; it is negotiated by the families beforehand, being dependent on the wealth of the man's family, and is part of the marriage contract. It can be given in the form of money or property and is a payment from the man to his future wife, though the wife can, if she wishes, defer payment. In this case it would normally only be paid if the marriage is broken by divorce. It is then given by the husband to his wife to help her arrange her affairs until she goes back to her family or finds another husband, and would certainly help to deter divorce.

Divorce   Divorce is acceptable in Islam. Although it would seem to be easy for Muslims to divorce, in fact, it is not encouraged. Muslims believe that divorce is hateful to God: "Of all lawful things, the one which God dislikes most is divorce".[92] God has nevertheless permitted divorce in cases where there has been a breakdown of the marriage. If the wife wishes to divorce her husband she must sue for divorce in the courts, a procedure which can be difficult. The husband, however, can obtain a divorce by pronouncing: "I divorce thee" three times. In the past, the only consolation a repudiated wife had was the dowry. In many Muslim countries she had no recourse in law against the neglect or cruelty of her husband, no rights over marital property or over her children, and no rights to maintenance. Enlightened Muslim opinion is not satisfied with this state of affairs, and many Muslim societies have given women some rights in law. Of these, the laws of Egypt are probably the most humane, allowing the woman to sue for divorce in the case of cruelty, neglect or desertion and giving her rights of custody over her children. Certain criteria should be met before divorce is allowed. Both parties must try to solve the problem, and if unsuccessful, two relatives or close friends, one for each side, must be appointed to try to settle the difficulties. A four-month period must pass before the marriage is finally ended: even after this there is a waiting period before re-marriage is possible, in case of pregnancy. However, it must be said that the position of a divorced Muslim woman in a Muslim country, or even in Britain, is a miserable one. She is not likely to find another husband, is disgraced, humiliated and isolated, and fear of divorce can still be a nightmare for many Muslim women in the world.

Women   The position of women in Islam has been a source of friction between Muslims and the West, and there are many misconceptions as to the place of women within Muslim society. In pre-Islamic Arabia women were subservient to men. Some women by dint of personality, or more likely via connections, could achieve wealth and a degree of power in society (cf. Muhammad's first wife), but in terms of their legal status women were chattels. Indeed it seems it was the practice for unwanted baby daughters to be buried alive.

The position of women in Islam was different. They held spiritual equality with men. Eve is not blamed for the first sin. Adam and Eve both sinned, both repented and both were forgiven. Muhammad, referring to a man's mother, declared: "paradise is beneath her two feet".[93] Nor was the equality of women confined to simply spiritual matters. Education has usually been seen as very important in Islam, and education was for both sexes. Muhammad said: "It is the duty of every Muslim male and female to seek knowledge".[94] There have been a number of women scholars in Islam, as well as teachers, writers and poets.

There is also Western misunderstanding on other issues. Muslim women are exempt from prayer and from fasting during menstruation and pregnancy. This is not because women are regarded as unclean during these times (though the actual menstrual blood is), rather it is to spare them such obligations during these times. Also women do not have to cover their faces, but are expected to cover their heads. They should also wear loose fitting clothing that does not emphasize their figures, and which covers them apart from their hands and feet. This is so that they do not display their sexuality to men, who are not expected to look on women, apart from their wives, as sexual beings.

Women were instructed in the *Qur'an* to "draw their veils close to them".[95] Interpretation of this point has varied according to the time and country. For many centuries, the practice of veiling among women was common, but the veil is less common these days, especially in large cities and small villages, and is less common among the wealthy, the young and the educated. There is, however, general agreement amongst Muslims that modesty, decency and morality, as defined by Muslims, entails that a woman's legs and arms should be covered. Often loose-fitting trousers gathered at the ankles and waist called *shalwar* and a tunic called a *kameez* is worn by both girls and women. Women's heads should also be kept covered. Women are required not to be extravagant in the use of silks and gold but encouraged to keep their femininity. On occasions, however, these restrictions have been interpreted as sanctioning the practice of *purdah*, whereby once a woman was married she remained shut up in her husband's compound. If she was allowed to go out at all, she went veiled from head to foot, including her face.

The image in the West as regards the position of women in Islam has often been that they are oppressed and submissive. In some Muslim societies this is the reality, but many Muslims would argue that this is a product of culture and not religion, and that within Islam women have guaranteed rights and freedoms. Many in the West point to what they see as a restrictive dress code, and some Muslim women have rejected the imposition of the veil and the *hijab* (the traditional covering). But others welcome it, arguing that it forces men to view them not as objects of sexual desire, but as human beings whose minds, intellects and personalities are the first things encountered. Indeed there is a small but growing Muslim feminist movement, and the women involved believe that it is through Islam that they will be able to gain the rights and freedoms they desire.

Men are less restricted in matters of dress, but they too have been instructed to dress modestly. This, however, has been much more loosely interpreted than is the case with women. They should be covered from the navel to the knee, and should also avoid tight fitting clothes. They are also encouraged to retain their masculinity and not dress like women in any way; they are forbidden, for instance, from wearing gold and silk.

As far as wealth and property are concerned, Muslim women have a number of legal entitlements. When the couple marry the husband must give the woman *mahr* – a bride-gift (though the woman can defer it) – which the woman retains. Indeed she retains all her property and wealth as her own, and any money she receives in income (for example from rent), is hers to do with as she wishes. She can of course contribute this to the household, but is not legally obliged to. (We should not forget that it was not until 1870 that British married women gained legal rights to their own property.) Women also have rights of inheritance: a daughter is entitled to half the amount inherited by a son. This may appear inequitable, but it should be remembered that when the woman marries, she can keep this money for her own uses; the husband, on the other hand, is responsible for providing for the family, for the home, food, clothing, transport, education and medical care.

Women retain their individuality in marriage; the two partners do not merge, and the woman retains her own name, though the children take their father's. There is, however, a clear role-differentiation in Islam. The home is the responsibility of the wife, whilst the man has responsibility for relations between the family and the outside world. Ahmed reasons that:

> This is a functional distribution of roles and activities and is regarded as essential for the proper functioning of the different institutions of society, and for its moral and social health and well-being.[96]

This also has the effect that men and women do not generally mix socially outside the home, which is regarded by most Muslims as correct as it lessens the likelihood of sexual liaisons outside of marriage. Pre-marital sex is totally forbidden since it falls under the category of *zina*. This applies to both sexes, but as in many other societies, the emphasis usually falls on the female. Indeed a girl who did consent to pre-marital sex would bring total shame on her whole family. Some Muslim parents have their daughters circumcised before puberty to avoid the problems which puberty might present. This practice, though supported by some Muslim authorities, is not Islamic. It is not found in the *Qur'an*, and Muhammad did not in any way authorize it, so it is not part of the *sunnah*.

Many Muslims have argued that the clear role differentiation prescribed for the sexes does not imply inequality but simply acknowledges the different strengths of each. The *Qur'an*, however, states that the man is head of the household: "Women have such honourable rights as obligations, but their men have a degree above them".[97] On any decision women can expect to be consulted, but the man's word is final and it is her duty to obey him. "And those who you fear may be rebellious admonish; banish them to their couches, and beat them".[98] This is not a license for men to beat women, Muhammad said: "The most perfect believers are the best in conduct and the best of you are those who are best to their wives".[99] Nevertheless the above quotation from the *Qur'an* is not a passage which recommends itself to many Western women.

This clear role-differentiation is justified by Muslims on the grounds of the different pyschological and physical attributes of men and women. Men are not only stronger, but are seen as more rational, whereas women are seen as more emotional, more likely, therefore, to make rash judgements. Again, Ahmed comments on this point:

> The rules for married life in Islam are clear and in harmony with upright human nature. In consideration of the physiological and psychological make-up of man and woman, both have equal rights and claims on one another, except for one responsibility, that of leadership. This is a matter which is natural in any collective life and which is consistent with the nature of man.[100]

A Western woman who has converted to Islam has stated that the previous quotation from the *Quran* – "Women have such honourable rights as obligations, but their men have a degree above them",[101] – provides all she needs for her happiness:

> it grants me the right to depend on my husband, be it in matters of my livelihood or in regard to any important decisions that have to be taken for the benefit of the family. On the husband, however, rests the great responsiblity of caring for his family and finding by consulting his wife and making use of his wisdom, the best possible solutions. Does it not lie in the very nature of a woman that she wants a powerful, just, wise and considerate husband who is capable of making these decisions? [102]

Children   Children are considered to be gifts of God and joys of life. Islam makes it the responsibility of the parents to look after their children and give them a good chance in life, providing them with a sound education and good manners. Children are encouraged to show *ihsan* – kindness, compassion, reverence, conscientiousness and sound performance – towards their parents. Indeed *ihsan* should be the basis of all family relationships, so that balance and harmony become the characteristics of the Muslim family – a reflection of the harmony that God has built into creation. The father is responsible for his children all their lives. When a daughter marries, she does not take her husband's name, but uses her father's name and he will still be responsible for her. Children are expected to obey their parents in everything, even when grown up. If a serious injury is done to one member of the family, especially a woman, it is considered to be a reflection on the family's honour. Sometimes the family may deal with the offender themselves.

Education

Education has always been very important, and traditionally was focused on the *Qur'an*. Elementary education consisted of memorizing long sections of the *Qur'an* and acquiring the rudiments of literacy and numeracy. Schools operating on these lines still exist, and some of them have expanded the curriculum to include modern subjects so as to prepare young Muslims for the world today. Traditionally, higher education was also focused on the *Qur'an*, which became the basis for studies of the Arabic language and Islamic law. Western-style education was introduced into many Muslim countries, on a limited scale, by Western colonial powers, such as Britain and France. Independence has led to the spread of mass education, but in some countries this is uneven and not always available for the poor, and it was a desire for their children to be educated which led many Muslims to move their families to Western countries.

The values and beliefs of these Muslims, however, are often in opposition to Western schools' values. Most Muslim parents would prefer single-sex education. Some object to their children receiving non-Islamic religious education. Others dislike their children having to participate in art, physical education, music, dancing and, in particular, sex education. Sometimes, school uniform, particularly in the case of girls being forced to wear skirts, and diet present a problem. Some of these problems have led to the setting up of supplementary schools by mosques and Muslim educational organizations. Classes are held in the evenings or at week-ends. The emphasis is on teaching the *Qur'an* and the Arabic language.

Diet   Everything a Muslim eats must have been lawfully obtained. Some foods are completely forbidden – pig meat (pork, bacon, ham); foods prepared with pig fat (e.g. some ice cream); meat from the domestic ass; all carnivorous animals and birds. As with the Jews, there is a strong prohibition against blood: "Forbidden to you are carrion, blood, the flesh of swine, what has been hallowed to other than God".[103] The slaughter of animals for consumption has to be carried out in a specified manner. It must be done by a Muslim, and the windpipe, jugular vein and oesophagus must be cut. A blessing must be said to acknowledge that, whilst it is an animal, it is also one of God's creatures and must not be killed thoughtlessly. Meat slaughtered in this way is *halal*. Animals which die of other causes or are killed in the name of any other deity than God are not *halal* but *haram*, though Jewish *kosher* meat is acceptable.

To the devout Muslim, food is something to be eaten in moderation and not to be wasted. It is also something to be shared, and sharing a meal with a Muslim is a mark of friendship. Eating is done with the right hand. Indeed Eastern custom in general regards the right hand as that which does what is pleasant while the left does what is

173

unpleasant. Also forbidden are alcoholic drinks and food which has alcohol in its preparation. "O believers, wine and arrow-shuffling [games of chance] . . . are an abomination, some of Satan's work; so avoid it".[104] Muslims believe that alcohol leads to addiction and it diminishes a person's control over his or her mind, and damages the ability to relate to God.

Death

> Every soul shall taste of death; then unto Us you shall be returned.[105]

When a Muslim dies, there are many rites to be observed which are not found in the *Qur'an* but in the lawbooks. The latter sometimes disagree about ritual and there are also differences in rites for Muslims in different countries. In Britain there are variations because mosques differ in the provisions they make for Muslim burials, as do local authorities. Muslims prefer to have their own burial plots in order to have a specific alignment of graves, one body to a grave, and the grave raised a little above the ground to prevent anyone walking on it. British Muslims, however, have to put more than one body in a grave because of a shortage of land, and not many local authorities provide Muslims with a separate burial plot in their cemeteries, though the number is increasing. Muslims like to prepare a fellow Muslim's body prior to going to an undertaker. The body is placed with the head in the direction of the *qibla*. Major ritual washing follows, using soap and sweet-smelling substances. The body is then wrapped in a shroud (*kafan*), placed in a coffin and given to the undertaker. British law requires coffins to be used for burial, but Muslims in Pakistan and India place the body in the ground protected by planks of wood which are then covered over with earth.

For the funeral, a *salat* is performed either in the house of the dead person or in the mosque. This is like an ordinary *salat* except that it includes prayers for the dead. Burial should take place as soon as possible after death. British Muslims try to make this the day after death, but this is not always possible, nor is it compulsory within Islam. Some Muslims prefer their dead to be flown back to their home countries, such as Pakistan or India, to be buried. Muslims believe that the body should be buried with the face to the north and facing Mecca: a grave in Britain should therefore run north-east to south-west, with the head at the south-west end, facing right.

MUSLIMS IN THE WORLD TODAY

More than one thousand million Muslims account for one-fifth of the world population. In over 120 countries Muslims turn five times a day to face Mecca. Although often perceived as a religion of the Middle East and Central Asia, Islam has spread to many parts of the world. The largest Muslim population is in fact in Indonesia, where almost

90 per cent of the population is Muslim. Large indigenous Muslim communities are present in Eastern Europe, including Albania, Macedonia and what was formerly southern Yugoslavia, as well as in the southern states of the former USSR. There are also between five and six million Muslims living in Western Europe, with large Muslim communities to be found living in Italy, Germany, Britain and the Netherlands. Five per cent of the French population is Muslim: originally immigrant in origin, these communities now comprise first-second- and even third-generation European Muslims. Islam is also a expanding in the United States where there are between four and five million Muslims:

> The arrival of millions of Muslims in Europe during the last four decades represents the biggest change in the religious map since the Reformation. Initially, Imperial links with Africa, the Middle East and Asia led to hundreds of thousands of Muslims moving to Europe. In Britain Muslims came from Pakistan, India and Africa, in the Netherlands from Indonesia, and in France and Italy from North Africa. This has been followed in the past twenty years by the arrival of migrant workers to meet Europe's industrial demands, such as Turkish workers in Germany and Moroccans in France and the Low Countries.[106]

Although Muslims form the largest religious minority in Britain – there are now almost two million Muslims in Britain – the public at large has little knowledge of Islam and even less personal contact with Muslims living in the United Kingdom. Most regard Muslims as devout people with strong beliefs, although those with negative tendencies towards Islam have associated Muslims with fanaticism and extremism. Prior to the Second World War few Muslims were to be found living in Britain, and these were settled largely in the dock areas of London, Glasgow, Cardiff and other large ports. A Mosque was built at Woking in 1889, and, after the First World War, another was constructed at Aldgate in East London. After the Second World War, there was an acute labour shortage in Britain, and recruitment offices were set up by a number of British companies in the former colonies, including India and Pakistan:

> the British authorities drew on the Commonwealth for the people they needed. The result was a sudden on-rush of male Pakistanis, Indians and Bengalis. The pre-partition killings in the Punjab and Bengal also led many people to come to Britain and, in 1971, there was another rush of immigrants from East Pakistan (now Bangladesh), because of the civil war there. In 1961, the British Government allowed all Commonwealth people to opt for British nationality.[107]

The original intention of these new arrivals to Britain's shores was to earn enough money to return home and live comfortably with their families. A few years after the menfolk arrived, however, permission was granted for their families to join them. This changed the ethos considerably, especially since this meant that their children could receive a standard of education which was not available to them in their home countries. Gradually the Muslim families began to regard Britain as their new, permanent, homeland: this was particularly true of second- and third-generation Muslims who were not only born and bred in Britain, but were bilingual, having learnt English through being educated in Britain's schools. Commonly termed "Asian" (together with peoples of other religious persuasions) the British Muslim community is in fact quite diverse, consisting of people from countries such as Pakistan, Bangladesh, India, Iran, Somalia and from many Arab states.

Although there is an immense sense of *ummah* (community) amongst Muslims worldwide (particularly when they feel a common cause) each country of origin has its own customs and traditions to which Muslims adhere. The *Qu'ran*, it is true, is always read in Arabic, but this is not the *lingua franca* of all Muslims: a disparity of tongues cements the cultural differences. Unlike some other ethnic minorities settled in Britain, Muslims have never been assimilated into British society nor integrated fully into British culture. Indeed there has been a conscious effort on their part to resist assimilation. This has caused resentment in some quarters with the common complaint: "If they choose to live in our country they should speak our language and fit in with all our ways – otherwise they should go back home." This seems a curious complaint when viewed in the light of the behaviour of British settlers overseas. For centuries, people native to these shores have emigrated to far-flung reaches of the globe, yet seldom have they endeared themselves to the indigenous peoples by adopting their cultures and life-styles.

For the Muslim, Islam is a total life-style which at many points is at variance with the dominant Western culture. These areas of conflict are a source of great anxiety to Muslims, not least because of the fear that some of their children may forsake Islam (and their parents in old age) and marry non-Muslim spouses. Western society, with the accent on individual liberty can appear a threat and embarrassment to all that Muslims hold dear. This is particularly true in the area of sexuality, where television programmes, magazines, advertising hoardings, and other forms of media, are quite explicit in their use of sexual images. Sex-education lessons in British schools teach "safe sex" and instruct the children on various methods of contraception. Most Muslims are opposed to this. As one parent at a conference stated: "It is in the nature of men and women to know what to do when the right time is blessed by marriage".[108]

Privacy and modesty are two values dear to Muslims which they feel are under threat in school. Communal changing rooms, where children of the same sex appear naked before their peers, are unacceptable to Muslims. Girls are expressly forbidden the wearing of shorts, short skirts, or swimming costumes, and compulsory physical education in schools is a great area of conflict: many Muslim girls have never had a swimming lesson. Muslims consider that school uniform should include the option of trousers for girls, who should be permitted to do physical education in track suits, and that as soon as the sexual urge arises in children, boys and girls should be educated separately.

As tax payers, Muslims feel strongly that *halal* meat (where the animal has been slaughtered according to Islamic law) should be readily available in schools and hospitals, yet seldom is this the case. Indeed many Westerners feel a strong repulsion to the ritual slaughter of animals and regard it as an unnecessary cruelty – a charge vigorously denied by Muslims.

Muslims consider a dog to be a polluting animal, contact with which brings ritual defilement. For the Muslim who prays five times a day, any dog which wishes to befriend them and nuzzle them is a real nuisance since this act, albeit friendly, necessitates a change of clothing and repeating *wudhu* (ritual washing). Sniffer dogs are equally unwelcome:

> Airports now send Alsatian dogs on board to sniff out drugs and explosives. This presents a problem when the plane is bound for the Middle East, especially planes for Hajj, since on any long journey many Muslims will want to pray at the correct times. Officials might suspect any fuss made to be due to terrorists fearing detection, when really it is only that the plane was prepared for prayer, and was then made unclean again.[109]

Then there is the question of employment. Not all employers are sympathetic to Muslim employees who wish to pray during working hours, and who require time off at Friday midday to visit the mosque: few employers provide ritual washing facilities. Friday mosque visits are also required of Muslim youths, who may have to miss lessons at school. Whereas Muslim employers and teachers sympathize fully with human weakness which accompanies the onset of fasting and expect only a reduced workload during Ramadan, non-Muslims do not often understand this disinclination to work.

CONCLUSION

Islam is one of the world's great religions: it is a faith practised around the globe with a long and proud history. Today, however, it seems it is more likely to inspire distrust amongst non-Muslims than respect. The reasons for this are many, some historical, some political. There is often a scepticism towards absolute truth claims, a scepticism stretching back to the Enlightenment. The Inquisition, the religious wars, the witch burnings all conspired to produce, with the Enlightenment, a feeling that religious belief must never be allowed to dominate the political agenda. So when people see the acts of oppression and violence done in the name of Islam – the random car-bombings in Algeria, the excesses of the *taliban* in Afghanistan – their feelings are one of revulsion for those who carry out such acts and for the religion which inspires them.

Fear and mistrust of Islam is, however, not a modern phenomenon. As early as the Crusades, Islam was being portrayed in the West as a heathen faith whose adherents indulged in unspeakable and disgraceful practices. The truth is that, at the time, Islam was a far more civilized and tolerant faith than Christianity. It utilized Greek philosophy and science, and indeed a great deal of Greek knowledge came to the West via Islam. Jewish and other scholars were welcomed and allowed a degree of religious freedom denied them in the West.

Muslims are not instructed by their faith to show hostility towards other faiths. Indeed Jews and Christians are described as "People of the Book", that is, those who have their own revelation, given by God, albeit one which has, according to Muslims, become somewhat distorted over time. Muslims are urged to show tolerance to such people, and to live in peace with them.

> Dispute not with the People of the Book [Christians and Jews] save in the fairer manner . . . and say, "We believe in what has been sent down to us, and what has been sent down to you; our God and your God is One, and to Him we have surrendered." [110]

Yet as Gumly and Redhead aptly remark:

> Even today, the heart of Islam – the message which he [Muhammad] preached – is caricatured by the exesses, not by the excellence, of its followers. The Hezbollah in the Lebanon no more encapsulate the teachings of Muhammad than the paramilitary forces in Northern Ireland represent the way of Christ.[111]

Terrorist groups are often referred to as "Islamic", but such actions go against the teachings of the *Qur'an* itself.

From the Crusades onwards, the Western view of Islam has been a negative one. Colonialism and the theories used to justify it such as, "civilizing the heathen", added to this general feeling. The media reporting on Muslim affairs today is heavily weighted towards the negative. There are always members of any faith who are poor advertisements for their religion; unfortunately, it is this small minority within Islam which is given a prominent place in the reporting of the Western media.

Some Muslims, however, argue that their faith is widely misrepresented, not due to some accident of history, but because theirs is the one ideology left in the world which still presents an alternative to

Western, free-market capitalism. They argue that the ideal of Islam is far superior to anything the West can offer. The open discussion in the Western media of such social phenomena as child-abuse, prostitution and alcoholism is viewed with horror, and some Muslims look on this as proof of what they see as the degeneration of the West. They compare the ideal aspired to by Muslims with the day-to-day reality of Western life, and unreservedly condemn all things Western. Yet as Malvise Ruthven states:

> This attitude of moral superiority towards everything Western compensates psychologically for the experience of powerlessness: but it also reinforces Muslim isolation, the sense of being a people apart in a hostile world.[112]

There are some on both sides of this argument who seem determined on confrontation. Understanding is the key to avoiding confrontation. This does not mean that understanding can of itself eliminate disagreement, it cannot and will not: there are a number of issues on which Muslims and many in the West will differ. Understanding will, however, enable each side to see that the positions adopted by the others are not simply arbitrary, not endorsed as a means of attacking them, but genuinely held, and underpinned by rational choice based on a particular world-view.

> The Western media must look at Islam objectively, even with some empathy, and not respond to events in Muslim areas with constant aggression and hostility. It is also crucial that they should not impose their own intellectual frame on Islam . . . more conferences and seminars for the general public need to be organised to explain Islam in the West. There is a great demand but not enough is done in this field. Similarly an exercise in the opposite direction is necessary to explain the West to Muslim societies. Too often in the rhetoric there is the implication that because the Muslim ideal is such a fine and noble one everything else is to be sneered at and rejected.[113]

Most Muslims have a genuine desire to live in peace with their neighbours, and this is true of all the other faiths in this book. The promotion of understanding is the key to tolerance.

4

Hinduism

Jeaneane Fowler

To love is to know Me,
My innermost nature,
The Truth that I am.
Bhagavad Gita

WHAT IS HINDUISM?

Hinduism is something of a complex phenomenon because it is so diverse, sufficiently so to include in its character such variant aspects as profound metaphysical speculation, simple animism and even atheism. But it is this very diversity which makes it such a fascinating religion to study; and while it is diverse, it is also about depth – exploration into vast chasms which the mind can barely glimpse. Indeed, this is what Hinduism is meant to be, for each person is believed to be on a personal path of spirituality and how far into the chasms an individual can see will depend on the level of consciousness of that individual. For those who reach the ultimate point of the spiritual path, all the diversity will vanish, but until that point is realized there will always be countless paths to explore on the journey, and each path is necessarily different for each person. It could almost be said, then, that Hinduism is as diverse as the countless people who are said to practise it, for no two Hindus can really be identical in their beliefs. While mainly the religion of India, Hinduism is also to be found in Asia, Africa, the West Indies, Indonesia, and in many countries to which Hindus have migrated and this, too, has increased its diverse nature.

The overriding factor which has contributed to the diversity of Hinduism is its ability to accommodate varying beliefs over the centuries. Nothing ever seems to be lost from its traditions and whereas we might expect to see some sort of evolutionary development in the history of Hinduism, there is, in fact, little of this. Many beliefs and practices stand the test of time and have remained as important as newer ones in the Hinduism of today, while major immigrations such as those of the Aryans in the second century BCE only served to add religious ideas rather than overthrow any. It is such accommodation which enables Hindu temples to contain pictures of Guru Nanak of Sikhism, Jesus of Nazareth, or the Buddha, alongside the images and pictures of traditional Hindu deities. This has leant to Hinduism a considerable tolerance of the beliefs of others and a recognition that each has his or her own path to pursue, a path which may differ considerably from that of the next person. Additionally, India is geographically vast, and local customs become more important than national ones. Such is the vastness of India that different dialects often make it impossible for one Hindu to understand another if each comes from very different areas. Religious custom – particularly the worship of minor deities – is usually dictated by locale.

Because of the diversity of Hinduism there is no one belief system peculiar to it. Thus, there is much theistic belief and practice in Hinduism – belief in one or more personal gods or goddesses – but there is also belief in a totally transcendent Absolute with which it is impossible to have a personal relationship but which is identical to the deepest part of the self. Many consider Hinduism to be a polytheistic religion because of the possibility of belief in so many gods and goddesses, and this kind of belief system may be pertinent for some, but there are many Hindus who are monotheists, believing in one personal god or goddess. This is an important point, and we shall need to return to it below. Such different belief systems have resulted in very diverse religious practice ranging from dancing and singing to the divine in devotional theistic Hinduism to the transcending of the world in meditative introspection to realize the deepest self within in yogic practices.

This diversity is sometimes problematic for the Western mind which generally wishes to compartmentalize material into neat packages. Hinduism can rarely oblige by conforming to such rigidity: even the word *history* is foreign to its thinking. History is an alien concept because it suggests linear development and Hinduism is far too accommodating to a multitude of ideas to accept their neat ordering into old and new, past and present. Indeed, just as the past lives in the present in terms of the slowness of village life and the relatively little changes which have taken place there over the centuries, so the past literature is as valued in the present as eternally vibrant and meaningful. Hinduism would not dream of seeing its oldest scriptures of the *Vedas* as inferior to much later, classical literature.

This lack of a linear dimension to Hinduism is therefore sometimes difficult for the Western mind to grasp. The Hindu concept of time is cyclical not linear, and its focus is generally cosmic not anthropocentric. All life is believed to be caught up in a repetitive cycle of birth and death, from the plants and trees, the life of an individual, the seasons, and the paths of the planets, to the vast cosmic macrocosm itself. There is a distinct interconnection between the microscosm of the earth and the macrocosm of the universe, not only in the mirroring of its cycles of life and death, but in the ways in which the two are believed to mutually influence each other as dualities in an ultimate unity. This, too, is an important point to which I shall need to return below. The cosmic perspective of Hinduism enables its philosophical thought in particular to reach through the barriers of time to a more cosmic dimension of eternity. In this sense, history is of little importance when cyclical aeons of time are stretched behind and before us to eternity. Such a philosophical perspective translates into daily existence to account for a general slowness in Indian life, an unconcernedness about time, and a certain passivity of nature.

So what we have today in what is called *Hinduism* is a diverse number of beliefs and practices which have accumulated over a period of about five thousand years and a distinct lack of any particular founder, core beliefs, standard ritual and practice, or basic creed. Indeed, the term *Hinduism* is something of a foreign one, as is the term *Hindu*. The former was the name given by nineteenth century English people to the multiplicity of beliefs and practices which they encountered amongst the "Hindus", and the latter was originally a geographical term for those who lived beyond the river (S)indu. And while these terms were alien to Hindus in the past, the word *religion* is equally so. Words like *bhakti* "devotion", or *dharma* "what is right", *yoga* "discipline", *varnasramadharma* "class and stage of life *dharma*" are much more meaningful words to the Hindu to express what their "religion" is about. Moreover, the Western world has come to separate religion and culture to a considerable extent, but this is hardly so in Hindu traditions where the two are really synonymous: the enactment of stories from Hindu scriptures for example, on stage or screen, are a key form of entertainment in a culture which combines its social and religious dimensions of life to a point that they cannot be differentiated. A perfect example of this is the socio-religious nature of the class and caste system. This suggests that there is some kind of unity underlying all the diversity, and indeed this is so. To understand this we need to examine the concept of deity in Hinduism.

THE CONCEPT OF THE DIVINE

Most Hindus accept a belief in an Ultimate Reality which is the Source and Ground of all being but which is beyond all human comprehension. It is an *Absolute*, absolute because there is nothing which could be added to it or subtracted from it; it is all things and no things. Not only is this Ultimate Reality absolute but it is also a totally transcendent Absolute – so transcendent that it cannot be described, indeed to do so would be to limit its absolute nature. And if this is so, then this totally transcendent Absolute cannot be either male or female, therefore the word *God*, which is distinctly masculine, would be inappropriate. Hindus therefore use the neuter *It* to refer to this Ultimate Reality, but it is the term *Brahman* by which this totally transcendent Absolute is known, a Sanskrit term from a root *brh* "to burst forth", or "to grow, increase", suggesting the unlimited nature of Brahman[1], or a meaning "to be strong".[2] The former two meanings depict rather well the nature of Brahman as the Ground of all being for it is from Brahman that everything in the cosmos is believed to come forth. Brahman is thus the Source of all from inanimate matter to human beings and the vastness of the cosmos itself. Nothing, from the tiniest atom to the largest planet, sun or star, can exist independently of Brahman.

Brahman is indescribable because It is formless or *nirakara*, and without qualities, or *nirguna*. This last term is particularly important for when anything has qualities then it can be compared and contrasted with other things. The qualities of darkness, for example, can be compared with those of light, day with night, male with female, tall with short and so on. In fact, we make sense of the world in which we live by all the various dualities which compose it. Brahman, however, is beyond all dualities; it is the point at which all dualities meet so it is neither this nor that or, to use the Sanskrit expression, it is *neti neti*, "not this, not this". And because no qualities as such can be given to Brahman, It is usually depicted in negative terms, for it is easier to say what it is not than what it is. The Hindu scripture, the *Bhagavad Gita*, in particular, uses a number of such terms, for example *acyuta* "Immortal", "Immovable",[3] *aksara* "Imperishable",[4] and *avyakta* "Unmanifest".[5]

But while Brahman is Unmanifest and *nirguna*, without qualities, it is at the same time able to be *manifest*. That is to say that since Brahman is the Source of everything in the cosmos, then everything in the cosmos is a *manifestation* of Brahman, for everything emanates from It. Such manifest aspects of Brahman *can* be described: they are the myriads of entities which make up the cosmos: so in contrast to *nirguna* Brahman, the universe is *saguna* Brahman – the aspects of Brahman which are emanated to form the cosmos. A good analogy to help the understanding of this concept is that of the sun and its rays. The sun is like Brahman, something beyond our experience, but the *rays* of the sun can be experienced as the manifested aspects of the sun on earth. Sun and rays, just as Brahman and universe are, however, just different aspects of the same thing.

Unlike the *nirguna* aspects of Brahman, which are unknowable in the normal sense of the word, the *saguna* aspects are characterized by the very dualities to which we can relate. Indeed, nothing which is manifest can exist without its opposite: even "nothing" is the opposite of "something"! The *saguna* aspects of Brahman are manifold but, importantly, they extend to all life and to a multiplicity of divine forms. In relation to the former, the deepest part of the self is equated partly or wholly with Brahman. It is called the *atman* and in view of its identity with Brahman, the term *Atman* is also a synonym for

Brahman. It is the *atman* which is the only part of the self which transcends the dualities of life and can become *nirguna,* losing all differentiation between opposites. This *atman* is the essence of Brahman in all things in the cosmos and, for the human being, the means by which Brahman can be known – not in the sense of intellectually knowing, or knowing *about*, but in the deeply intuitive sense of knowing something within the depth of one's being. But to gain this kind of knowledge, an individual has to allow the mind to go beyond the dualities which are normal to existence.

There is thus an intimate link between Brahman and each individual human being or each life form, whether that form is insect, reptile, animal, bird or human. Indeed, non-human forms are a pronounced feature of the religious mythology of Hinduism, for once it is accepted that Brahman is the Source of all then all creatures are divine as, indeed, is the cosmos. Moreover, the presence of Brahman in all things not only intimately links the human and the divine but also the microcosm and the macrocosm: thus, the individual is to some extent a mirror of the universe and can have his or her effect on it. There is not in Hinduism the divorce between the human and the earth, the human and the environment and the human and the universe which there is in much Western thought: the interconnectedness of all things is ensured by the same Ground of all being. Brahman is rather like the string which holds together the beads of a necklace, forming them into a whole. And while the beads may be different, they are nevertheless united by the same thread: all is a unity because of Brahman.

But the degree to which beings and things are identifiable with Brahman varies in Hinduism. For some the relationship is essentially dualistic and each individual *atman*, while identical to all others, is only a part of Brahman. This system of belief is *pantheism* and it equates Brahman with the totality of the manifested cosmos. Other dualistic beliefs accept that the *atman* is part of Brahman but that Brahman is ultimately *greater than* the totality of manifested existence. This *panentheistic* belief system is perhaps the most prevalent and characterizes much of the literature of classical and devotional Hinduism with the dualism of a personal, theistic relationship with the divine. But for some, there is no relationship between the *atman* and Brahman, for they are identical. The *atman is* Brahman. This is well expressed in much of the philosophical thought of the Hindu scriptures known as the *Upanisads*. These many writings, while they do not present a coherent philosophy and were compiled from about 800–400 BCE, have a tendency towards *monism*, the identity of all things as one and as Brahman. The classic statement of the identity between the *atman* and Brahman is in the words *Tat tvam asi*, "That art thou", in the *Chandogya Upanisad*. The words *Tat tvam asi* equate *Tat* as Brahman with the true inner self, the "sphere of space in the chasm of the heart"[6] and depict Brahman as the essence of all, like the imperceptible salt in water. *You are Brahman*, then, is the message of many *Upanisads*.

While most Hindus accept Brahman as the Ultimate Reality and Absolute of Hinduism it would be a mistake to think that all do so. Hinduism is far too diverse for this to be the case. There were schools of thought such as *Samkhya* which maintained a strictly atheistic philosophy and a pluralistic idea of the separation of each individual *atman* from all others. Here, there is no linking thread to unite our beads, just individual beads, for there was no concept of Brahman in classical *Samkhya*. But even this school of thought accepted that there was a difference between the *nirguna* aspect of the *atman*, or *purusa* as they called it, that is to say its pure, true, permanent and real state, and the self which is bound up in the phenomenal world which is impermanent, transient and ultimately unreal. This distinction between the real and the unreal is an important one, for it is the search for the *Real* – for the Ultimate Reality which is permanent and unchanging – which is the final goal of Hinduism, a goal which unites many of its different philosophies. For most Hindus, this Ultimate Reality is Brahman, the realization of which provides the answers to all questions about life, death and the purpose of humankind. The search for such answers is beautifully depicted in the words of the *Brhadaranyaka Upanisad*:

> From the unreal lead me to the real, from darkness lead me to light, from death lead me to immortality.[7]

Divine manifestations   While Brahman is the Source and essence of all in the cosmos and is the *atman* of each living being, It is also manifest in a multiplicity of divine forms, indeed there can be no end to the potential forms which Brahman can take and to the many which already exist in Hinduism are added new expressions of the divine, especially in the village context. To the Hindu mind it would be illogical to see such divine manifestations as purely male. Indeed, the very fact that the manifest world itself is composed of all the multiplicity of dualities which make up life, along with the interrelatedness of microcosm and macrocosm, suggests that the particular duality of male and female must be evident at the divine level as much as the human one.

Religious traditions which derive from nomadic stock tend to view the divine in masculine terms. Religions like Judaism, Christianity and Islam stem from these kind of patriarchal cultures where the male head of a clan or tribe is responsible for the welfare of his entire family. Nomadic existence is precarious and the search for new pastures for flocks exigent. Not being long enough in one place to till the soil and settle, the fruits of the earth and the importance of fertility of the soil are absent, and the female in life is subordinate to the decision-making male. Quite the opposite is true of peoples who, from the very earliest of times were dependent on the land. Fertility was of immense importance and the whole concept of reproductivity of human and soil elevated the idea of the female to the level of the divine. Hinduism has these kind of roots, as we shall shortly see, so it would seem strange to have male deities without their female counterparts or to have supreme male Gods such as Visnu and Siva without a parallel concept of a supreme Mother Goddess. And because each person's conception of the divine is different, some will orientate towards belief in a male God, others preferring to focus on Brahman in female form. Since Brahman is all things, it is inconceivable that It could only be manifest at the divine level in masculine forms.

Again, such multiplicity of possible manifestations on the divine level of existence results in immense diversity in belief and practice. Western criticisms of polytheistic systems (if such Hinduism is) are largely without understanding and without justification. To be "God", in the ultimate sense of the word, is to be beyond what the entirety of humankind can know. And were it possible to combine all perceptions of "God" from all human beings, they would not add up to a fraction of what God really is – the picture could not be *absolute*. So each person's conception of the divine *contributes* to the overall knowledge of the divine, and a multiplicity of deities allows for this, each deity expressing and symbolizing some particular aspect of divine presence or power relevant to the character, life-situation and level of consciousness of the individual. Polytheism as a belief system, therefore, does not restrict the concept of the divine, but recognizes its vastness and true immeasurability, at the same time allowing for the diversity of human nature to approach the divine in whatever way is best for the individual.

Yet, in practice, despite the multiplicity of choice which a polytheistic system offers, most Hindus regard themselves as monotheists. This is for two reasons: first, it is practically impossible to devote oneself equally and *entirely* to a number of deities, so for many Hindus there would be a favourite deity which would be the main focus of worship. For some, this may be simply the major village deity whom it is prudent to worship alongside the other inhabitants of the village simply for the protection of family and village. For others, a major deity like Ram or Krisna may be the major focus of worship. This is not to say that other deities are rejected; indeed, five deities – Ganesh, Surya, Siva, Devi and Narayan, together termed *pancayatana* – are invoked in Hindu worship as a prelude to worship of an individual's chosen deity. But there is a second reason why most Hindus would regard themselves as monotheists and not polytheists and that is the fact that all deities are ultimately one – Brahman. The link between any particular deity and Brahman may, as in the case of village deities, become obscured and less obvious than in the case of the great Gods and Goddesses of Hinduism but, ultimately the unity of the divine is fundamental.

Avatars   The degree to which the multiplicity of deities in Hinduism are involved in the daily life and worship of humankind will vary, but one deity in particular, Visnu, is believed to incarnate on earth at times when the balance of good and evil is disturbed in favour of the latter so that divine manifestation in a much more explicit way is necessary to restore the correct balance between the two. While some Hindus accept that there are other deities who incarnate in the same way, strictly speaking it is only Visnu and his female counterparts who manifest themselves in earthly form. Such incarnations are termed *avatars*, literally "descents" of Visnu, and there have been nine in all (though later texts extend the number) with one, the *Kalkin* yet to come. While some of these *avatars* of Visnu have been in animal or part animal form, two human forms stand out as pre-eminent in Hinduism in general, and these are the *avatar* of Ram and that of Krisna. Both, partcularly the latter, are the focus of much devotional belief and practice.

The diversity of the divine   From what has been said about the nature of the divine it should now be clear why religious belief in Hinduism is so diverse. At one end of the scale we have the indescribable Brahman, and there are some Hindus whose religion focuses on the realization of Brahman in the self, the *atman*. Here, a particular *relationship* with the divine may be deemed impossible and for many such Hindus a non-theistic path to eventual identity with Brahman is characteristic. But for other Hindus, the great deities which form the focus of much of the religious literature of the classical period will be the focus of belief – deities such as Visnu, Siva or the Mother Goddess, Kali or Durga. Worship of these manifestations of Brahman varies enormously from the mysticism of the worship of such an inscrutable deity as Siva to the esoteric *Tantric* practices associated with some forms of worship of the Mother Goddess. Such worship may take the form of non-ritualistic asceticism as with the worship of Siva, or ritu-alistic practices which may involve animal sacrifice as with worship of the Goddess Kali. Even in the case of worship of one deity, belief and practice is considerably diverse. But one of the most popular forms of worship is the highly theistic devotional worship of the *avatars* of Visnu, Krisna and Ram. Indeed, when the deity is deemed to have lived on earth this is the epitome of closeness between divine and human resulting in a highly anthropomorphized concept of the divine, and a very popular one for it provides the most readily understandable expression of divinity to which all can relate. Then, too, there are the village deities or local urban deities who are worshipped for many immediate means in life – health, food, life, safety – most locales having their own particular deity which may or may not be known elsewhere or may be known elsewhere by different names. And there are also deities from the distant past, such as Agni, who are involved in ritual worship and life-cycle rites. Thus, Hinduism caters for different views of divinity with a multiplicity of deities: some of these now need individual examination.

Indus valley deities   Until the early part of the twentieth century scholars believed that the Aryan invaders of northern India from about 2000 BCE were the first to bring civilization to the Indian continent. Though these invaders were illiterate they brought with them an oral religious tradition which, when committed to written form, depicted the indigenous people whom they had met on their arrival in India as considerably barbaric and even ugly. But in the 1920s major archeological excavations in the Indus valley uncovered what has proved to be a remarkably advanced urban civilization on a par with those of ancient Babylon and Egypt, with cities scattered over many hundreds of miles. Finds at what seem to have been the two major cities of Mohenjo-daro and Harappa have revealed a Bronze Age culture which is dated fairly consistently to about 2500–1800 or 1500 BCE, or even earlier. While the script of this urban people has not been deciphered sufficiently to allow us insight into the culture of the people, the many archeological finds present something of a fuller picture.

The Indus valley people were great traders and made use of small seals, mostly made of steatite, though also of ivory and pottery. It is these seals which reveal a great deal about the kinds of deities which the Indus valley people worshipped, and some actually portray ritualistic scenes. Clearly, animals were of importance in religious ritual and in one scene, people are prostrated before a buffalo – an animal which probably figured prominently in the religion. Of particular importance are three seals on which a kind of divine being is identically seated with knees outspread and heels brought together, rather similar, though certainly not identical, to the well-known lotus position so basic to Eastern meditation and yogic practice. The body of the figure is naked except for bangle-clad arms reaching out so that the hands rest on the knees. The figure is reminiscent of the later deity Siva with the still, ascetic and meditative pose, the nakedness, and the possibly ithyphallic portrayal on two of the seals, suggestive of the same principles of fertility and reproductivity in nature which are associated with Siva. Then, too, on one of the seals, the figure is surrounded by wild animals perhaps comparable to Siva who is sometimes portrayed as Pasupati "Lord of Creatures", though in Siva's case the association is with domestic animals.[8] Importantly, however, the figures on the seals are *not* identical, and this suggests that to identify them as a "proto-Siva", an early form of the later great God of Hinduism, could well be erroneous. Indeed, one of the figures is animal-faced, possibly a buffalo, and this would accord well with many of the half human, half animal figurines which have been found in excavations. One figure may even be female.[9] Yet it is clear that this figure was a deity of some sort, and it was a deity which seems to have been associated with ascetic control, power, and animal associations.

Other seals suggest worship of tree spirits,[10] of trees such as the pipal tree, of half-human half-animal beings, and of both male and female divine beings. This last point is significant for it illustrates that the roots of Hinduism in the distant past allowed for worship of both male and female divine forms, a fact also supported by the many figurines which have been discovered. An abundance of terracotta female figurines have been found, many of which probably represented a female deity. Enough have been found to suggest that worship of the divine in female form was a feature of every home, and, where a continuous sequence of cultural change has been possible to determine as at Mehrgarh, it seems that worship of female divinities stretched back well before the Indus valley civilization to the sixth or fifth millennia. Worship of a Mother Goddess thus seems probable, though to suggest the unity of all female finds into one principle of divinity might be stretching the evidence too far. When the Aryans invaded India they brought with them a very male-orientated religion, but it is likely that worship of the divine in female form continued at village level. For a variety of reasons, the Indus valley declined and all but disappeared well before the arrival of the Aryans [11] but the diversity of its beliefs and religious practices was probably maintained in a variety of ways in the village culture into which the Indian people slipped when their great urban civilization had disappeared.

Vedic deities   The Aryans who migrated into northern India came from the plains of Central Asia east of the Caspian Sea and were just one of many migratory groups who filtered out from this area from about 2000 BCE. These people who entered India called themselves *Arya*, a term meaning "noble" and which served to set them apart from the indigenous people of the land they entered. Their religion was patriarchally orientated unlike the Indus valley religion which had catered for the forces of fertility and reproductivity symbolized by female divinities. Their religion was for a long time preserved orally in the four *Vedas* – *Rg*, *Sama*, *Yajur* and *Atharva*. While the Aryans brought many of the hymns of the *Vedas* with them in their migrations, they continually added to the collection: accordingly the dating of the *Vedas* is as wide as 1500–900 BCE. *Veda* means "knowledge" and it is the *Rg Veda* or "Royal Knowledge" which is the most important of the four, giving a very full, though sometimes obscure, picture of Vedic religion.

The religion of the Aryans was somewhat propitiatory, the gods (there were few goddesses) were felt to bestow the essentials of life –

health, wealth, longevity, success in battle, the milk-giving cow and reward in heaven. Their deities were mainly male, reflecting the patriarchal character of nomadic and herd-rearing people in general. While there were some female deities like the goddess of dawn, Usas, to quote Heesterman, they "remain diffuse, lacking in profile and to a high degree interchangebale with one another"[12] and none rose to the status of an independent goddess, even in the *Atharva Veda* where they are more prolific. Vedic gods, known as *devas* or "shining ones", symbolized the natural elements with which the Aryan human being was involved and symbolized the fundamental powers which controlled existence like rain, the rising of the sun, fire, thunder, wind, storm. Some, like Indra, were highly anthropomorphized, while others, like Soma, were more esoteric and mysterious. Some, like Rudra, represented the darker elements of life while a deity like Varuna seemed more like the omnipotent, omniscient character which is normally associated with a "high" God. Some of the Vedic deities are still important in the Hinduism of today: Agni, the Vedic god of fire was central to the sacrificial ritual of Aryan religious practice, for it was fire which transformed the sacrificial offering into a form accessible to the gods. It was thus the medium by which the world of humankind and the world of the divine could coalesce. And still today, Agni is central to much religious ritual; the bride and groom at a Hindu wedding, for example, circumambulate the sacred fire to seal their marriage, and it is Agni who consumes the material body at death in order to release the soul for transmigration. Kindling the sacred fire is important in much temple ritual also: every time it is lit, Agni is evoked.

It would be easy to accept Vedic deities at a rather simplistic level – this-wordly deities who merely serve to comply to the appropriate requests of human beings who can correctly communicate with them. But Vedic deities, like most aspects of later Hinduism, can only be understood according to one's level of consciousness. Thus Agni can be seen in a variety of ways – as the simple physical transformer of matter to smoke and ashes, or the means by which what is gross is turned into what is dynamically subtle, like the incredible process of combustion in the body by which gross food is transformed into subtle energy. Soma is another deity of this type, at one level a hallucinogenic, potent plant, but on the other the means by which the physical is transcended and the subtle worlds of the divine are penetrated.

But one deity who *was* somewhat this-wordly and who was highly anthropomorphized, was Indra. He was sufficiently prominent in the *Vedas* to survive in later Hindu mythology and to feature even in Buddhism. Indra was the supreme *soma* drinker and the ideal Aryan warrior:

He was a paradigm of the human qualities the Aryan most admired:

vigor, enthusiasm, strength, courage, success in battle, gluttony, and
drunkenness.[13]

Indra was thus a rather human deity who bestowed fertility on the
land. But at the same time he could be aligned with Agni when he
represented the fire aspect in space in the forms of lightning and
thunder. However, as the Vedic period progressed and something of
a more metaphysical ethos entered Vedic religion, the popularity of
Indra declined; indeed, he became more dignified in line with the
changing thought of the Vedic period as a whole.

Another important god was Varuna, the universal monarch and the
deity who safeguarded the cosmic order throughout the universe, *rta*.
It was this cosmic order which enabled the sun to rise each day, the
depths of the sea to occur, the stars to shine and the earth to have life.
Varuna was the epitome of morality and while a deity like Indra could
be viewed as this-wordly, Varuna was essentially cosmic, omniscient
and omnipresent. He could punish sins, and no-one could escape from
the consequences of his or her sin because Varuna's cosmic dimension
made no corner of the universe unknown to him. No amount of propi-
tiation could win the favour of Varuna for it would only be moral
purity which could be rewarded by him. He was in some ways feared
for the sins an individual *might* unknowingly have committed as for
the conscious ones which were perpetrated:

> O Varuna, whatever the offence may be which we as men commit
> against the heavenly host,
> When through our want of thought we violate thy laws, punish us not,
> O God, for that iniquity.[14]

Vedic deities were thus a means to bring cosmic forces in the
universe within the realms of understanding of Aryan people. Hindus
themselves regard this early period in the formation of what we know
today as Hinduism as critically important, the *Vedas* being regarded
today as the most sacred of scriptures with meanings that are lost to
all but those who are prepared to study them. A *Brahmin* friend, for
example spends several hours a day in pursuit of the wisdom he can
glean from them. Some of the Vedic deities were destined to become
a major feature of later Hinduism and the Hinduism of today. Rudra,
for example – something of a terrifying Vedic divinity – became the
Siva of present day Hinduism, and retained much of the inscrutable
nature of his Vedic image and, notably, the dualities of personality
with fierce characteristics on the one hand and gentle ones on the
other. Visnu, a minor deity in the *Vedas* was also destined to become
one of the great Hindu deities in later times.

The deities of classical Hinduism   Classical Hinduism is the

Hinduism of the later scriptures, like the well-known *Ramayan*, the *Mahabharat* and the *Bhagavad-Gita*. The major deities of classical Hinduism are Visnu, Siva and the Mother Goddess, though the three basic elements of life – light and evolution, inertia and dissolution and energy – are usually represented by the deities Visnu, Siva and Brahma repectively. These last three deities are often referred to as the *Triad* or the *Trimurti* and are sometimes depicted as one God with three heads. Of the three, Visnu and Siva are the most important, Brahma being rarely worshipped independently: his position as the third member of the triad is somewhat usurped by the female divine force, *sakti*. Both Visnu and Siva have many different names depending on the myths associated with them and on the local customs and traditions. Visnu, for example is sometimes worshipped as Narayan or is known as Govinda, Kesava or Madhava, while Siva has a multiplicity of names such as Mahadeva, Bhava, Nataraja, Mahayogi, Bhairava, Pasupati and Visvanat.

Visnu "The Pervader"   Followers of Visnu are known as Vaisnavites. Visnu symbolizes the preserving and pervading energies of life, the centripetal forces which bind atoms together to make life, light, matter and evolution possible. The image of Visnu is always easy to recognize because of its dark blue colour, and his *avatars* can be similarly recognized. This dark blue colour is important. At the deeper levels it reminds the thoughtful Hindu of all the dualities which make up existence and that nothing can exist in manifest existence without its opposite. Visnu, then, as a manifest form of the Unmanifest Brahman, has the same dualities, and, while he is associated with creation and preservation in the cosmos, his dark blue colour – darkness being associated more with death than life – is a reminder that the opposite of death is also inevitable for anything which he creates, for what is born must inevitably die. This kind of symbolism is associated with all the Hindu deities and many, like Visnu, have four or more arms. In Visnu this symbolizes the power to extend himself as "The Pervader" into all directions of the universe. Like other Hindu deities, Visnu is a symbol of Ultimate Reality – Brahman – pointing beyond himself to what is ultimate. In his four hands he carries a conch which symbolizes evolution and eternity, the shape of the shell emerging from a point to ever-widening spheres, and the sound of the conch shell being that from which creation was said to emerge. In another hand he carries a discus which represents the universality of all existence with all its myriads of forms, the hub of it being the Absolute, Brahman. In another he carries a lotus the symbol of enlightenment and the ability to raise consciousness in order to return to the ultimate Source which is again Brahman. The mace which he carries symbolizes his omniscience, and every aspect of his clothing and body acts as a symbol to stretch the mind and consciousness to its limits.[15]

Visnu's role as the creative mind behind the universe is expressed in a myth about the origins of the cosmos. In the myth he lies sleeping on a huge couch formed by a thousand-headed cobra called Sisa. Out of Visnu's navel a lotus blossom springs and from the centre of this, Brahma, the agent of creation is born. From the material of a vast primordial egg, Brahma shapes the universe and so begins a *kalpa*, a cycle of the universe. Throughout the *kalpa* everything is sustained and preserved by Visnu. During this time, life unfolds, and the whole of manifest existence comes into being – all sustained and preserved by Visnu. The whole of this *kalpa* is represented as a day in the life of Brahma – some 42,000 million earth years. And at night, when Brahma sleeps, the universe once again becomes non-existent and unmanifest until Brahma awakens to begin a new cosmic day and a new *kalpa* of the universe. Thus, the whole cosmos evolves and devolves, is born and dies, in endless cycles throughout eternity. As we shall see below in the context of the nature of the self, humankind, too, reflects this endless cycle of life and death.

Each time the universe is created it passes through four stages called *yugas*. These are termed *Satya*, *Treta*, *Dvapara* and *Kali*. The *Satya* or *Krta yuga* is a "golden age", a time when life is harmonious, and right actions, thought and speech characterize the interaction of all people. But just as the human being begins to wane soon after the first twenty years of existence, so, too, the ages succeeding the golden age of *Krta* show a gradual waning of observance of what is right until the final age, the *Kali yuga* is reached. And it is this age – the age in which evil predominates – in which we are now living. But while this cycle of existence is unavoidable, just as the night of Brahma is in the myth, there are believed to be times when the normal balance of what is right and wrong, of *dharma* and *adharma* to use the Sanskrit terms, is considerably upset and imbalanced. It is at times such as these that Visnu "descends" to earth in order to restore the balance. And it is two of these *avatars* of Visnu which are the focus of much devotional practice in the Hinduism of today. There have been nine *avatars* altogether, although some texts suggest as many as twenty-four. The first was a fish, followed by a tortoise, a boar, a half-lion and half-man, a dwarf, and a *Brahmin* priest. It is the next two, Ram and Krisna which have become major deities in devotional Hinduism: the Buddha is also accepted as an *avatar*. There is still one *avatar* to come, the *Kalkin*, and this will be Visnu as a warrior riding a white steed, with the role of overthrowing the final evils of the *Kali yuga* and establishing the age of gold, the *Krta yuga*.

The *avatar* Krisna As is the case with all his *avatars* Visnu "descends" to restore the balance of what is right (*dharma*) in the world. This, as the *avatar* Krisna, he tells to the hero of the *Gita*:

> Whenever there is a decline of *dharma*, Bharata, and a rise of
> *adharma*, then I manifest myself.
> For the protection of the good, for the destruction of the wicked, for
> the firm establishment of *dharma* I am born in every age.[16]

The attractiveness of Krisna as a deity is partly due to his diversity of character – from the attractive, naughty, chubby little baby in the scriptures known as the *Puranas*, to the majestic power of his personality in the *Bhagavad Gita*. And Krisna can be worshipped in any of his characteristics. His role on earth was to overcome evil, and this he did in many ways, from his slaying of evil demons and restoring good at the great battle of Kuruksetra on the more physical levels, to the more metaphysical level of presenting a path to conquer the evils of the inner self which prevent personal evolution.

Krisna, indeed, was born into an evil environment. The demon king Kamsa had been told that the eighth child of Prince Vasudeva and Princess Devaki would bring about his death, and to prevent this event he imprisoned them ensuring that any children they bore would be immediately killed. But the seventh and eighth children, Krisna and his brother, were transferred to safety in the village of Gokula "Cow-village", and were raised by foster parents. Krisna's name, which means "black", was given to him because of the dark colour of his skin, like that of Visnu. The stories of Krisna as a young baby are immensely attractive but we are never allowed to forget the fact that this baby is the supreme Visnu, and, ultimately Brahman, as when Yasoda, Krisna's foster mother looked inside his mouth in order to get some earth out of it. Inside, she saw the whole universe! Nor could Yasoda tie him up one day when he was naughty for, as the story shows, no-one can bind God unless he himself wishes to be bound.

The childhood and youth of Krisna portray a very happy, carefree, smiling, positive, laughing and playful deity. It is a beautiful picture of what the divine can be – a source of ultimate joy and bliss portrayed in earthly manifestation. Krisna is never sad and his aim is to attract the soul of the worshipper in real joy and happiness if that worshipper can surrender to him. This is devotionalism epitomized through love, love of a baby, a child or a lover – in fact it is the love which any human can experience transferred to the divine because the divine can be viewed in whatever human form one best knows how to love. Many people, therefore, worship Krisna as a baby, for the love that is felt for a baby by its parents, particularly the mother, is the kind of love which is readily understandable and to which so many can relate. And as a baby, child and boy, Krisna is portrayed as unconditioned and natural *fun*; he loved to play pranks, was naughty, stole butter from the villagers (though the cows always yielded more milk when he did) and was fond of singing. So full of fun and joy, Krisna showed that life is to be enjoyed and that laughter and spontaneous fun are a legitimate way to God. Worshipping him as a baby and a child requires the devotee to relate to him as a parent would – naturally, without formality and without thought of personal interest and selfishness.

Others worship Krisna as a youth – a handsome youth, irresistibly beautiful and characterized by the same carefree, joyful and happy youth as in his childhood. Again there is an appeal to the emotional love which human beings can experience, this time, the emotions of the love between lovers. While all the *gopis*, the cowherdesses, loved Krisna, it was the intense ecstatic love between one of the *gopis*, Radha, and Krisna which epitomizes the surrender of the self in loving-devotion or *bhakti* to the one who is loved. Since everything in manifest existence is composed of dualities and all deities have both a masculine aspect and a feminine one, Visnu, too, will have his female counterpart: this is the Goddess Laksmi. And when Visnu descends to earth, then the female aspect of him does so also: so we find Sita as the *avatar* of Laksmi accompanying Ram in the *Ramayan*, and Radha as the *avatar* of Laksmi as the consort of Krisna. Thus Krisna says to Radha on one occasion:

> You are dearer to me than my life, beautiful Radha. As I am, so are you; there is no difference between us. As there is whiteness in milk, heat in fire, and fragrance in earth, so I am in you always. A potter cannot make a pot without clay and a goldsmith cannot make an earring without gold. Likewise, I cannot create without you, for you are the soil of creation and I am the seed.[17]

The intense ecstacy of the love between Krisna and Radha symbolizes the love between God and the soul, expressing the divine relationship with humankind in terms of an emotion which all can understand – the emotions of the lover. Love of God is therefore understood in the same way in which sexual union is experienced on the human level – union, a oneness, a sense of participating in something beyond ordinary reality, an emotion transcending the normal. In the twelfth century a beautiful love song, the *Gitagovida* was composed by Jayadeva[18] and was entirely devoted to depicting the love between Radha and Krisna. But not only does it depict the earthly relationship between the two, it also emphasizes the cosmic relationship – the macrocosmic relationship between Visnu and Laksmi as two aspects of the same reality.

For those, then, who understand the deepest kind of love as the love of a lover, it is possible to relate to God in this way also, a very human and natural way. Thus Krisna became the means by which experience of earthly love could be transformed into love of the divine and experience of divine love: he is the very embodiment of love and joy, a deity who is a sheer delight to all people and who is devoted to his worshippers even though he may be hidden and separated from them. This is a handsome and winning God, one whom the devotee, the *bhakta*, would want to remember, return to, be devoted to, be forever with, desire, and, most importantly, love with the whole of his or her being.

But the worshippers of Krisna do not only worship him in the form of a baby or a handsome lover. For the mature Krisna is the supreme Lord in a scripture such as the *Bhagavad Gita*. Here, we see none of the youthful fun which characterized the earlier Krisna and what emerges instead is the omniscient manifestation of the unknowable, unthinkable immortal and imperishable Brahman, the deity who, while still calling to his devotees to focus their entire being on him, speaks also of the effort to lose all egoistic desire in order to become one with Brahman.

The *avatar* Ram   Ram is the hero of the epic scripture the *Ramayan*, though throughout this beautiful tale of devotion, duty, right relationships and the working out of the cause and effect principle of life, Ram is not portrayed as divine in the same way as Krisna. This is because Ram himself seems to be unaware of his divine status, even though his ability to conform to what is right, to *dharma*, is exceptional. But this is the attraction of Ram as an *avatar* for he is very human, bearing all the emotions and vicissitudes of a human being: this is the very aspect which allows Hindus to become close to this manifestation of Visnu – and ultimately Brahman – in human form. We meet Ram in the *Ramayan* as a mature man who has clear characteristics of honesty and uprightness. And Sita, again the consort or female energy of Visnu incarnated with him, is the embodiment of kindness, obedience and chastity. These are characteristics which make the ideal hero and heroine to the Hindu mind. There are many versions of the epic, the *Ramayan*, and in Tulsi Das' version Ram's extreme sorrow in exile is portrayed by relating how he has to sleep on the ground, find roots and fruit to eat, and how he cries when he hears his father has died. When his distraught mother tries to see him before he leaves for exile he is so overcome by emotion that he has to leave before she reaches him.

In contrast, then, to the deity Krisna, here we have an even more human portrayal of divinity, and Ram has become the focus of worship for many Hindus. When Mahatma Gandhi was shot, the last words which he spoke, "Ram, Ram!", epitomized the way in which a Hindu can feel intimately close to the *avatar* who is the main focus of devotion. It is likely that in the early, original version of the *Ramayan*, written by the poet Valmiki, Ram was thoroughly human and only later acquired the status of a part, and then full, *avatar* of Visnu.

Siva "The Auspicious"   Siva is a very ancient Hindu deity. Some have seen his origins in the figure of the horned deity of the Indus valley seals, the so-called Proto-Siva, because of the ascetic pose, the meditative stilllness associated with this often naked deity. In the Vedic period he was Rudra, the fierce and terrible deity who is both the destroyer of cattle and of human beings, and the bringer of disease, destruction and death, often arbitrarily. He could even be portrayed as a cheat, a murderer and a deceiver – characteristics which seem inappropriate in the context of a deity. Yet Rudra symbolized the darker aspects of life, the arbitrariness of disease and death and the unpredictable nature of life and the forces of darkness which pervade the world. But there was an opposite side to this fierce portrayal of Rudra in the *Vedas* for he had also a kindlier aspect and could appear as the protector of cattle and as one who could heal and restore.

The later character of Siva lost none of this paradoxical nature, for he has remained a God of opposites, one who maintains in his own being the dualities apparent in all existence, and yet unifying them into one. Thus life and death, time and eternity, passivity and activity, creation and destuction, and so on, are reconciled in this complex deity. Whereas Visnu is associated with the centripetal, binding forces of life, Siva is associated with the centrifugal, dissolving aspects of life, the pulling apart of atoms so that things no longer exist. And yet, the image of Siva is always depicted as white as camphor, the whiteness being a symbol of the life and rebirth which is contained in death. So while Siva is the source of death and dissolution, his whiteness symbolizes the concept that death is but a passage from one life to the next and therefore is the source of new life. The dualities present in this deity are clearly portrayed in what is called the *Nataraja*, the representation of Siva as "Lord of the Dance". Here he dances the creation of the universe. The drum in his right hand represents the primordial sound which caused the universe to become manifest, while fire in his left hand signifies the annihilation and dissolution which characterizes all life at both the microcosmic level of humankind and the macrocosmic level of the universe itself. His two other hands represent the granting of benevolence and prosperity, and the giving of refuge. He dances in a ring of fire which symbolizes the life process of the universe and he dances on a demon, symbolic of the ignorance which has to be overcome in order to achieve the final goal in life – liberation from reincarnation. The rhythm of his swaying limbs signifies time and change, while his calm face symbolizes eternity.

It is easy to see from just the *Nataraja* of Siva how much the images of deities serve to take the mind beyond the concepts of everyday life to abstract concepts which are of far deeper dimensions, always pointing the individual forward. Pictorialized, Siva will be portrayed with his hair piled high on the top of his head and in it will be the moon. From his hair tumbles the river Ganges, the most sacred river in Hinduism. Tradition states that the powerful river Ganges falls to earth from Siva's hair to save the destruction it would have caused had nothing broken its fall. His throat is blue because at one time, when the ocean was being churned by the gods and demons, a deadly poison came to the surface. Only a God as great as Siva and to whom life and death are equal, could swallow this poison without harm, and this Siva does. The story thus tells us that he is beyond all the opposites of life, even death itself. Though not always portrayed as such, Siva has three eyes, an extra one in the middle of his forehead which depicts his omniscient, all-knowing, nature. Around his neck is a coiled serpent representing *kundalini*, the spiritual energy within life. Such symbolism is an important aspect of the iconography of Hindu deities. There are considerable variations in what a particular aspect is said to symbolize but the complexity of them is sufficient to warn anyone about taking Hindu deities at their face value.

Hindus themselves often recognize the complex nature of Siva by putting his shrine in the temple separate from those of other deities. In order to convey the mystery and transcendence of Siva it is more usual to find his symbol rather than his image in temples. This symbol is the *linga*, which is a phallic symbol, but one should not make the mistake of seeing this as a mere sexual image. In Hinduism symbols on a phenomenal level point to some profound truth on the cosmic level and this is what the *linga* does. It represents the energies necessary for life on both the microcosmic level – the world in which we live – and on the macrocosmic level, the level of the cosmos, the level at which Brahman becomes manifest in the whole of the universe. In a Saivite temple, the *linga* would be placed right in the centre, underneath the spire, where it symbolizes the centre, the navel of the earth.

Because he brings life through death, his name Siva means "Bright One", "Happy One", or "Auspicious One". He is often depicted riding a bull called Nandi, and in Saivite temples Nandi, decked in garlands and chains, can usually be found just outside the shrine of Siva facing the *linga*, like a doorkeeper. Siva is often portrayed as the supreme ascetic, very still, passive and utterly calm, but because he is a God of opposites he always has within him the potential for quite the opposite, a ferocious and terrible aspect. It is this aspect of Siva which is noticeable in the earlier periods of Hinduism. Although a very complicated deity to understand, Siva is one of the most fascinating. To Saivites, his devotees, he is seen as Brahman, the Absolute, and it is not difficult to see why because just as all opposites are united in the unmanifest Absolute so also are they united in the manifest Siva.

Ganesh A lesser God, but a very important one, is Ganesh, one of the sons of Siva. His name means "Lord" (*isha*) "of attendants" (*ganas*). He is easily recognized because he has the head of an elephant. There are various stories which suggest how he acquired his head. Perhaps the main one tells of a time when Siva was away for many years and returned to find a youth guarding his wife Parvati's room. When the youth refused to allow Siva to enter her room, Siva cut off his head, only to find that he had killled his own son. To calm Parvati's obvious distress, he ordered the head of the first thing to be found to be placed on his son's body but in obeying this command to the letter, his attendant returned with the head of an elephant! Parvati was not very pleased with the result! To offset this it was decreed that Ganesh would be the bringer of good fortune to many worshippers; he should be worshipped before all other gods could be worshipped, except Siva; and he would be the medium for overcoming all obstacles. So anyone beginning a business, writing an examination paper, getting married and so on, would always worship Ganesh first. He is thus *very* popular all over India and is even found in remote cave shrines in Indonesia.

The Mother Goddess Perhaps the one word which is helpful in understanding the many complexities of most Eastern religions is *equilibrium*. In a state of equilibrium, one is neither this nor that, one simply *is*. But manifest existence is not in a state of equilibrium; it is full of dualities, called *dvandva* in Sanskrit. So we have good and evil, light and dark, peace and war and so on, and we also have male and female. Whatever is manifest in life is subject to these dualities and this is so on the macrocosmic level too. So Hindus would find it very strange to conceive of divinity as only *one* side of the duality of male and female: Brahman is the *equilibrium* between all opposites and is Unmanifest, but once Brahman is manifest in divine beings, it would not be logical for manifestation to be just male. Indeed, if there is any differentiation in importance between male and female deities on the macrocosmic level, or between male and female on the microcosmic level – the world of humankind – it is more the result of cultural practice than of metaphysical reasoning.

It is because of this idea of equilibrium that each manifestation of Brahman in divine form must be both male and female. The female side of each of the male deities is called the *sakti* force. It is usually the active energy of the God, while the male side is the more passive form. Sometimes the male or female aspect of the deity will be worshipped separately depending on which is the more important to the individual worshipper. We should always remember that in Hinduism there is a multiplicity of paths to God, like different fingers pointing to the same moon.

Worship of a Mother Goddess has been part of Indian tradition since its earliest times and it was only when the Aryan invaders brought a more patriarchal religion that the balance between male and female deities seems to have been upset. But life in Indian villages is very slow to change and has hardly changed at all in some, so that although the Sanskrit scriptures may well show a favouritism for worshipping male deities and often depict female goddesses as inferior, in the life of the villages and many urban areas, the goddess often remains paramount. While the word for goddess is *devi*, the more popular name for the goddess is *mata* or *amma*, both meaning "mother", and the names of many female deities are compounded with these or other forms to indicate a concept of the divine as Mother. Devi is also the name given to the Supreme Mother Goddess who is present in all female deities. Moreover, as this supreme Goddess it is Devi who is responsible for activating – and therefore making possible – all existence, for she is the active essence of all things, of all life. As Coburn so aptly states, "One might go as far as to say that whatever *is* is Devi."[19] It is she who unites all female divinity into one power, and every male deity is empowered by a form of Devi as his active energy.

Laksmi   Each of the major Gods of the *Trimurti*, then, has his female counterpart. The counterpart of Visnu is the Goddess Laksmi who is sometimes called Sri, though originally these were two different goddesses. Laksmi is the symbol of good fortune and prosperity in life, and like her consort Visnu she is an omnipresent and eternal being. Like Visnu she has four arms, in one of which she carries a lotus blossom, the symbol of the enlightened soul of each human being. In another of her hands she carries coins which are often depicted as falling from her hand, showing that she bestows blessings and wealth. According to one myth, gods and demons combined together to churn the ocean to obtain a nectar of immortality, and during the churning process, Laksmi rose from it in order to take care of the welfare of the earth. At that time, Visnu became present on earth in the form of a huge tortoise. Whenever Visnu comes to earth as an *avatar*, Laksmi accompanies him. Thus she, too, becomes an *avatar*: she is Sita, the wife of Ram in the *Ramayan* and she is Radha, the favourite *gopi* of Krisna.

Laksmi is the *active* energy of Visnu, so while Visnu is creator, Laksmi *is* creation. While Visnu supports and sustains the earth, Laksmi *is* the earth and identifiable with all females on it in the same way that Visnu is identifiable with all males. Visnu is speech, while Laksmi is meaning; Visnu is understanding while Laksmi is intellect; Laksmi is the creeping vine, Visnu the tree to which it clings; Visnu is love, and Laksmi is pleasure. There is a profound interaction between the two, it is as if Visnu is the thought behind the universe and Laksmi is the one who puts the thought into action. This is how the *sakti* force operates in all the male deities. Because of their inseparability, Laksmi and Visnu are known as Laksmi-Narayan, a name which designates them as a personal manifestation of Brahman: in whatever state Visnu appears, divine or mortal, Laksmi will always be with him.

Laksmi is one of the most popular Goddesses in India and is very widely worshipped by people of all castes. She is closely associated with right conduct, truth, generosity and social order, and she likes personal and environmental cleanliness. Those wishing to attract her benevolence at certain festivals, therefore, have to make sure their homes are scrupulously clean. Just as she was a model wife as Sita in the *Ramayan*, so she is a model consort to, and complement of, Visnu.

The *sakti* aspects of Siva: Parvati   As might be expected in view of the complicated nature of the God Siva, his *sakti* energies are very complex indeed. He has many consorts, and these rather suit the opposite natures of his own personality, mild and gentle on the one side and ferocious and terrible on the other, offering life on the one hand and death on the other and so on. If we look first at the gentler aspects, these are personified in Parvati and Uma. Parvati means "Daughter of the Mountain" which reflects her birth from the Himalayan mountain range. It is in the form of Parvati that the Goddess is the constant companion of her consort Siva; accounts of her in independent exploits, apart from the intimate relation between the two, are sparse. The role of Parvati as the consort of Siva is to balance his ascetic, passive and reclusive nature by making him more involved in the world, so most of the stories about Parvati are concerned with luring him into marriage or of recounting how helpless he is without his *sakti* energy. So Parvati is really an ideal domesticated wife, the perfect wife and mother. She is not worshipped as an independent Goddess.

Uma   Uma is really the original consort of Siva. Because he is sometimes called Mahadeva, "Great God", she is sometimes called Devi and at other times Sati. She was the daughter of Brahma, who opposed her marriage to the great ascetic God Siva. When Brahma refused to attend a great sacrificial celebration arranged by her husband, Uma flung herself in the sacrificial fires and died. It is because of her self immolation here, showing her utter devotion to her husband, that the practice of *sati*, the voluntary burning of a widow on her husband's funeral pyre, became common in India and is still practised occasionally today. But Sati could not be separated from her consort and was eventually born in earthly form and reunited with her husband as Parvati.

Durga   The name Durga means "Inaccessible" and immediately we see here the very active side of this *sakti* energy of the God Siva. Durga is usually portrayed riding a lion or tiger and killing a buffalo-demon. Being composed of the angry energies of all the male gods, there is nothing gentle about this image, for she is a ferocious protector of the good and faithful. She carries weapons, held in her many arms – a trident, a sword, a bow, and a discus. Despite her fierce nature, she is immensely popular in India because of her impressive role in destroying evil. She probably has links with the early goddess worship associated with fertility, for her main festival occurs at the time of the harvest and she is associated with crops and plants. Animal sacrifice, often associated with fertility rites, is still offered to her. Durga can take many forms but the most well known is probably that of Kali.

Kali   Kali is the most terrifying of the *sakti* forces of Siva. The name means "Black" and, indeed, she is associated with the darker sides of life. In her worst form she is portrayed as dancing in cremation grounds and as drinking blood, and thousands of goats are still sacrificed to her at the Kalighat temple in Calcutta as well as in smaller temples and shrines elsewhere. But despite her cruel image, her devotees worship her as the divine Mother, for it is Kali who releases humankind from reincarnation: indeed, this is why she is associated with cremation grounds, for it is only through accepting death that we can hope to be reborn, and only by letting go of this world and losing the ego, the personality self, that we can overcome such perpetual reincarnation. Kali, indeed, is depicted as overcoming the kind of enemies which would daunt even the bravest of gods. Once, in attempting to slay a giant, she found that every drop of blood which came from the giant produced another thousand of them. Her only recourse was to drink its blood as she slew him. This is why Kali is usually shown with her tongue hanging out and blood dripping from it. Like many of the Gods she has four arms, and in one she carries a sword and in the other the head of the giant. Her earrings are two dead bodies, her necklace is made of skulls and she is dressed only in a girdle of dead men's hands. She has red eyes and a body smeared with blood – no wonder her devotees feel protected! As an essentially active deity Kali personifies the dynamism of life, what one author has termed "growth, decay, death, and rebirth completely unrefined" – everything which is "lush and teeming" in life.[20]

Space limitations allow only a few of the major female deities to be outlined here but there are countless others, particularly in the southern parts of India where worship of the female divinities is far more popular than the male ones. Village goddesses are a particularly fascinating study, for the function of these goddesses is to protect the village – to guard the inhabitants from smallpox, for example (though this disease has now declined in India). These local, village and urban goddesses have little cosmic function but more of a local, existential one. In fact, in an Indian village these local deities would be far more important than the great deities of Hinduism.

Because of this it is not impossible for new goddesses to emerge: Santosi Ma "Mother of Satisfaction" is a case in point; she is rapidly becoming a goddess of such importance that she may be incorporated in the major pantheon of deities in time.[21] The cult of Santosi Ma has gained currency in the last forty years or so, especially in northern India, and while the origins of the goddess are obscure she has been declared to be an offspring of the deity Ganesh, of the genealogical line of Siva. In 1975 a film was made about her as a result of which Santosi Ma has become immensely popular. She is a good example of a modern goddess, one who serves the immediate needs of the people, who *satisfies* their needs and who is readily accessible to her devotees. Brand comments rather appropriately:

> Perhaps one reason behind Santosi Mata's astonishing rise to fame is that it was simply felt inappropriate to ask an ancient goddess for such modern appliances as radios and refrigerators.[22]

Certainly, worship of the female goddess is an important aspect of Hindu religion and in some cases all the female deities are absorbed into one great Mother Goddess, Mahadevi, "Great Goddess", who is worshipped as the ultimate manifestation of Brahman. But at the local level, village and localized urban goddesses are felt to be more appropriate to the needs of everyday life.

So at one end of the scale we have the great Gods and Goddesses who symbolize the cosmic energies of the universe and at the other, the *gramadevatas* or village deities so important in the daily life of the village Hindu, who relate much more pertinently to the life of the individual, family and caste. What is important is that the individual is able to relate to the divine in the form which best suits his or her level of consciousness and individual circumstances.

The paths to the divine are endless because the divine itself is considered to be so. The absolute nature of what divinity is conceived to be in Hinduism means that it contains all that ever was, is, or could be. While ultimately one, its manifested forms are infinite and it is this which underlies the great diversity which characterizes what is called Hinduism.

Aum Hinduism is replete with symbols and many examples of these in the context of the deities have already been given. They serve the purpose of projecting the mind beyond the immediate to what is less expressible, very often an abstract, metaphysical concept. From the opposite perspective, symbols make abstract concepts more understandable and tangible by providing visual focus for the mind. The symbol most sacred to Hindus is *Aum* or *Om*, which represents Brahman, the vastness of the cosmos and its oneness. It is made up of three Sanskrit letters, *aa*, *au* and *ma* which, when combined together, make the sound *Aum*.

SYMBOLS

The symbol represents both the unmanifest (*nirguna*) and manifest (*saguna*) aspects of Brahman and so is, in itself, a *saguna* means of knowing the Unmanifest Brahman:

> Aum is the one eternal syllable of which all that exists is but the development. The past, the present, and the future are all included in this one sound, and all that exists beyond the three forms of time is also implied in it.[23]

Aum is thus believed to be the basic sound of the world and to contain all other sounds. But while it symbolizes the most profound concepts of Hindu belief, it is written daily, at the head of letters, for example, as well as at the beginning of examination papers. At a deeper level it is also used as a *mantra* when, if repeated with the correct intonation, it can resonate throughout the body so that the sound penetrates to the centre of one's being. Then, since *Aum*, Brahman, is the very essence of the self, the *atman* is able to be experienced. All possibilities and potentialities exist in *Aum*; it is everything that was, is, or can yet be.

Even though it is *everything*, as ultimately it is the nature of Brahman, it cannot be defined in any way. Since *Aum* expresses so much and symbolizes what is spiritually perfect, the symbol is worn as a pendant by many Hindus and will be found on posters or in some form on family shrines, as well as in temples.

The *svastika*

The *svastika* is in the shape of a cross with "crooked" branches facing in a clockwise direction. This most auspicious and ancient of signs is ubiquitous throughout Hinduism. It is particularly a feature of the festival of *Divali* when red *svastikas* are found among the many decorations of the home for this colourful festival. The crooked arms of the *svastika* point away from the centre, symbolizing the fact that the human mind is incapable of understanding Brahman by any direct means for Brahman is beyond the logic of humankind. The *svastika* also points in all directions, suggesting the presence of the Absolute, Brahman, in all manifest existence. It also has no beginning and no end and is continually rotating, symbolizing the eternal nature of Brahman.

The lotus

The lotus is an exquisitely beautiful flower which grows in the East in the muddiest of waters. It has become a symbol of the human being living in the muddied waters of the world and yet whose soul can rise and blossom, like the lotus flower, to the point of enlightenment. The flower is symbolic of the true soul of each individual. The well-known meditation position, the lotus posture, is based on the flower. The flat green leaves of the plant are like the outspread knees when the feet are pulled up onto the opposite thighs, and the straight back is like the lotus flower itself. The lotus is also a symbol of creation. Brahma, the creator God in one of the creation myths of Hinduism, is said to come forth from a lotus which blooms from the navel of Visnu.[24]

Atman and *jivatman*   We have seen that Brahman as the Ground of all being is manifest in each aspect of the universe as the *atman*. Thus, each human being is in reality equated with Brahman; some Hindus believe identically and others only partially, depending on the monistic or dualistic perceptions which were noted in the context of the concept of the divine, above. The part of the self which is the *atman* is regarded as the enlightened, true Self, the Self which is devoid of all dualities, the Self which is at the point of equilibrium between all opposites. This is the Self which is, like Brahman, *nirguna*, without qualities; it is neither this nor that – and to become such is the goal of Hinduism. The norm for almost the whole of the Hindu religion is the identification of the deepest levels of the self, of woman, man, youth, maiden, old and young, with the one Ground of all being, the Reality and Source behind all manifest existence. There are many religions in which the concept of the self is of little import, but it is central to Hinduism for it is one which provides the answers to so many of the existential problems of life. The realization of the *atman* within the deepest elements of the self means union with the divine – union with Brahman – and this is to say that, like Brahman, he or she who realizes the *atman* within becomes immortal, permanent, unchanging and imperishable. This would be in total contrast to the transient, impermanent and finite self which is the general character of all human beings. To aim for realization of the *atman*, then, is to aim for Ultimate

THE HINDU CONCEPT OF THE SELF

Reality or Truth, for a Pure Consciousness beyond that of ordinary existence, and for bliss.

The opposite to this is the normal world of the personality self, a self involved with all the dualities of existence – this as opposed to that. The Hindu view of the self is traditionally threefold. First there is the physical body, often referred to as the *bhutatman*. Then there is the personality self consisting of the mind, the intellect, the ego – in short, the whole personality – which is the *jivatman*, or simply *jiva*. And then there is the *atman* itself. The self that we know is mainly involved with the world around it and is highly subject to responses to all the sense stimuli which continually bombard the mind. Through the environmental, dispositional, familial, social and societal and cultural influences we build up the so-called personality or psychological self which responds to the world beyond it in a highly egocentric way. This is a very unreal self in comparison to the *atman* because it is subject to constant change, it can never be, but must always be in a process of becoming and always influenced by the dualities of existence, the choices between this and that, desiring one thing and having an aversion for another. It is this personality self which obscures the *atman*, the true self, and the more an individual becomes focused on the dualities of the phenomenal world, the further he or she becomes from the *real* Self within, the *atman* which is Brahman. Senses are important to the *jivatman* and it finds itself bound up in the joys and sorrows of life. Only by looking beyond the world of the senses can the *real* Self, the *atman*, be known, not in the sense of knowing about something intellectually, but in the sense of knowing something deeply and intuitively, experiencing it as a fundamental pulse of one's being.

This search for the Self beyond the self is the goal of most Hinduism but while many are aware of the ultimate goal, most are enslaved by their egoistic selves and see the *jivatman* incorrectly as the real self. I sometimes ask my students if they would wish to have perfect health, perfect mental stability, perfect calm, bliss, peace of mind – in short, enlightenment – if I could wave a magic wand and make it so. All usually agree that this would certainly be a wish to be granted. But if I then add that at the same time they would be very old – with the hairlessness, toothlessness, and certainly the wrinkles of old age – there are very few who would then trade in life as they have it for enlightenment. Such is the enslavement of the *jivatman* to the phenomenal world! It is difficult to give up attachments to the world, to all the choices and dualities which it presents, and to youth (however old we are!), and yet, as the ancient Law Books of Hinduism, the *Laws of Manu*, state "He who has in this manner gradually given up all attachments and is freed from all the pairs of opposites, reposes in Brahman alone".[25] But unless egoistic involvement in the world is abandoned, the law of *karma* will ensure that reincarnation must ensue.

Karma   Karma (*karman*) literally means "action", "act" or "activity" but the word also means the law of cause and effect which governs existence. This is to say that, just as when we drop a pebble in a pond ripples occur, so, any action undertaken must have its effects: causes and their appropriate effects are inextricably bound to each other. The law of *karma* is thus action and *reaction*. Put simply, as far as human beings are concerned, this law states that whatever action a person does either bodily, mentally or vocally, a result must ensue, and that the personality or *jivatman* which created that action, that cause, is what must reap the effect. Thus, if a person acts negatively or thinks or speaks negatively, then negative *karma* will result for that person and, conversely, good *karma* will ensue as a result of positive actions. But just as when we throw a pebble in a pond some ripples are immediate and others are further away from the centre, so *karmic* effects may not be immediate. And given the Hindu conception of cyclical existence for all manifest phenomena, some effects will occur immediately, some later in life and others in the next or subsequent lives.

The complex network of *karmic* effects which are built up by any individual creates the pattern of the next life for that individual, so really each person is capable of shaping his or her next existence. And while one isolated action may have little *karmic* effect for the future, the deeper unconscious and subconscious drives of an individual, the general mental patterns of thought, are reaping *karma* almost every second. To be able to say at the end of life that our basic personalities have been sorted out, that all the things in our personalities we would like to correct have been corrected, is to suggest the impossible. Generally, we leave this world with the same faults and failings – even a few more, perhaps – that have characterized our lives. Thus, there are things about the self which still have to be worked on, still have to be sorted out. At death, the individual cannot be perfect and countless lives are needed before this can be so.

Since actions – physical, mental and vocal – appertain to all life, it would seem that there must be no end to future lives because there is no end to the actions an individual performs. Hinduism answers this point with the claim that it is only certain actions which bring results for an individual, and these are actions which are involved with the person's ego. It is not actions themselves which create fruitive *karma* but actions which are the result of desires and aversions of the personality, the egoistic self. It is because the individual is caught up in all the dualities of life, the choices between this and that, the liking of one thing and the dislike of another, and the myriad mental processes involved in daily existence in a world which presents such choices through multiple stimuli, that the ego is difficult to quell or to abandon. But it is an unreal world, a world which is always changing and which can never be permanent. So all the actions which take place from the level of the ego bind a person further to this unreal world. The *reality* of the world is Brahman, and the *atman* within, but the *jivatman* is generally ignorant of this and goes on making decisions and choices from egoistic involvement in the world. It is this which causes fruitive *karma*.

Samsara *Samsara* is the name given to the cycles of reincarnation for all things. All things, on both the microcosmic level of humankind and the macrocosm itself are subject to this cyclical nature of existence, so what is born must die and what dies must be reborn. However, on the human level it is the *jivatman* which is subject to reincarnation, because it is only the *jivatman* which reaps fruitive *karma*. The *atman*, on the other hand, is not subject to the dualities which help to create *karma*. Being beyond dualities it is neither this nor that, it is simply *there* as the presence of Brahman in the self and as the *real* part of the self. Importantly, reincarnation is not a fatalist principle. Combined with the law of cause and effect, *karma*, it ensures that each individual is responsible for his or her own life and for creating whatever befalls one in the next and even subsequent existences. Because actions *now* involve choices, at every moment an individual is capable of making the best possible ones to ensure a good life situation the next time round: the future of any individual depends entirely on the present existence or on previous existences if *karma* still has to be "worked out".

The *Brhadaranyaka Upanisad* describes this very well:

> An individual creates for himself his next life as a result of his desires, hopes aspirations, failures, disappointments, achievements and actions performed during this life of his. Just as a caterpillar, before it leaves one leaf, makes sure that his front feet have been firmly fixed on the next leaf of the branch of a tree, a *jivatman* creates its next life before it departs from the present one.[26]

Such a theory does much to answer the problems of suffering in any individual life for no one can really blame anyone else for the suffering he or she experiences in life. Nothing can be done to avoid such suffering – and it may be individual or collective – because past *karma* has created it, but in the present, much can be done to ensure a minimum of suffering in future lives. If, however, the positive choices are not made then it is possible for an individual to *devolve* and regress to the form of an animal or insect or the like, in order to reap the results of bad *karma* until it is used up sufficiently to allow reincarnation as a human being once more.

Dharma *Dharma* is what is right, what is right for the individual, for society, for class and caste, for one's stage in life and for the universe itself. It is like a *norm* to which each individual life is related, and it is the degree to which an individual can conform to such norms that dictates whether *karma* is good or bad. Thus, *dharma* is what Flood terms "an all-encompassing ideology which embraces both ritual and moral behaviour, whose neglect would have bad social and personal consequences".[27] At the individual level, a Hindu needs to conform primarily to his or her class and caste *dharma*, termed *varnadharma*, and this will be dealt with later as a separate issue. Here, however, it needs to be pointed out that it is the sum total of all an individual's past *karma* which places him or her in a particular class and caste in the present existence. Then, Hinduism divides life into four stages each with its own particular *dharma*, what is right for each stage; this is *asramadharma*. Some classes and many women do not need to observe such *dharma*, but it is an important aspect of what a Hindu would consider *dharma* to be. These four stages will also be dealt with in more detail later. Then there is the universal *dharma*, the *sanatanadharma*, the cosmic norm to which everything in life is subject. Its precursor lay in the concept of *rta* in the Vedic period with the Vedic deity Varuna being its safeguarder. In many ways all *dharmas* are subject to this cosmic norm of *sanatanadharma*.

For any individual it is *svadharma*, one's "own *dharma*" which is important in the context of *karma*, for it is the *karma* of an individual which will create a particular *dharmic* path for that individual in the next existence. This is to say that the *dharma* of a person in life is that best suited to his or her own evolution. It will be the path by which past *karma* can be worked out and the path by which a person can best evolve, but it is still very much created by each individual self. To go against this personal *dharma* is to be *adharmic* and this itself will ensure negative *karma* for the future. Thus following one's own *dharmic* path is essential. The *Gita* makes this clear:

> Better is one's own *dharma* devoid of merit, than the well-discharged *dharma* of another. Death in one's own *dharma* is better; the *dharma* of another is fraught with fear.[28]

This rigidity of maintaining the *status quo* in life because it is *dharma* has been much criticized in that poverty in India is allowed to exist unalleviated. Many Hindus claim, however, that service to others is a means for personal good *karma* and that *dharma* for the future is improved by the assistance one can give to others.

Moksa   But the ultimate goal of Hindus is not to achieve good *karma*, though this is certainly a proximate goal. The average Hindu knows full well that reincarnation for countless lives is the fate of each individual and that good *karma* is helpful on the hard journey from one life to the next. But the idea of reincarnating without end is an abhorrent one to most Hindus. The ultimate goal is to merge with Brahman, like the river merges into the sea. But to do this the *atman* within has to be realized. And since the *atman* is beyond dualities, it is beyond both good and bad *karma*. To be liberated from the *samsaric* cycle, then, one has to be devoid not only of bad *karma* but of good *karma* also, and to have no *karma* at all. This can only be done when the egoistic self is abandoned and there is no *jivatman* to reap the results of *karma*. While actions can take place, there is no "I" which does them, for the "I" ceases to be and actions are simply actions without anything to which results can accrue. This is the liberated Self of pure *atman* which is Brahman and it is this liberation or *moksa* which is the ultimate goal of Hinduism. To realize it, Hinduism has three main paths which assist the self on its evolutionary journey to loss of the egoistic self.

The paths to *moksa* There are traditionally four major paths to *moksa* but two of these, *raja* and *jnana* are quite similar so I shall deal only with the latter. The word for path is *marga* and the fact that Hinduism traditionally accepts more than one way or path to the divine suggests clearly its tolerance of different approaches. Indeed, within the definitions of each *marga* are a variety of expressions of both belief and practice.

Jnana marga The path of *jnana* is influenced considerably by the very introspective period which followed the Vedic period of formative Hinduism. Because of its highly philosophical nature this period at the end of the *Vedas* is generally termed the *Vedanta* (*anta* meaning "end of" the *Veda*). The scriptures of the Vedanta are known as *Upanisads* and it was *Upanisadic* thought which generally raised questions about the nature of the self and Brahman, and which particularly emphasized (though not consistently so) the identity between Brahman and the *atman*. It was this emphasis on the identity between the *atman* and Brahman which suggested that ritualistic worship of a personal god, goddess, or many deities was to some extent pointless. No personal relationship with the divine was possible, for the inner Self *is* the divine. And if the real Self is Brahman then it can only be experienced inwardly, mystically and meditatively, through intuitive knowledge called *jnana* or *vidya*. Like *raja marga* it is *yogic* meditation which brings the individual to the point where the senses are stilled and no longer responsive to the stimuli of the environment.

Jnana marga is a path to Brahman which tends to concentrate on the *nirguna*, the Unmanifest, aspect of Brahman rather than the *saguna* aspect of manifest deities (though not exclusively so). It is an individualistic path rather than a communal one, though it requires the guidance of a *guru* to raise the level of consciousness of an individual to the point where the ego is transcended through yogic concentration and meditation. However Mehta points out rather well the fact that the journey to realization of *atman* is essentially a solitary one. He depicts it as an:

> adventurous journey into the land of the Unknown where alone Wisdom can be discovered. This journey has to be unaided, for no teacher can lead a pupil into the realms of the Unknown. The journey to the Unknown is a flight of the alone to the Alone.[29]

For those who do not concentrate directly on the *nirguna* aspect of Brahman, Siva as the supreme *yogin* is the deity very much associated with the path of knowledge. Siva is also accepted as the supreme ascetic, able to remain in deep meditation with his senses withdrawn from the world – the goal of the *yogin*. Indeed, *yoga* is a word which stems from a Sanskrit root *yug* which is suggestive of "yoking" horses, that is to say, of controlling them in the same way that one on the path of knowledge needs to control the senses. And once the senses are controlled, all the dualities of life are transcended and everything is seen as one, as Brahman itself, and the impermanent and finite world is left behind for the reality of Brahman, because the true Self, the *atman* is experienced.

Karma marga *Karma marga* stresses action as its name suggests. So in contrast to the more reclusive path of intuitive knowledge, *karma marga* suggests the opposite of active involvement in the world. Yet it is involvement in action without the concomitant involvement of the ego. It is action taken for the sake of action, not for any desire for, or aversion to, the consequences of the action. Thus, it is egoless action which the path of *karma* advocates. Nevertheless, actions undertaken even without ego should never be contrary to the *dharma* of an individual, society, or the universe itself. A good example is that of the hero of the *Bhagavad Gita*, Arjun, whose *dharma* it is to be a warrior and to fight in a battle to destroy evil and restore the balance of good. But he is afraid to enter a fratricidal war and Krisna, as his charioteer, has to teach him about *dharma* and about egoless action. For it is only egoless action, as we have seen, which bears no fruitive *karma* for the future. Krisna therefore advises Arjun "Let not the fruits of action be the motive".[30] In other words it is attachment to the *effects* of what actions are done which will cause *karma*. Take away this attachment and there is no "I" to which future *karmic* results can be attached. And it is the egoless state which brings one to realization of the *atman*. Thus, the way of *karma* means that all actions are undertaken from the level of the real, enlightened Self, the *atman*, which is Brahman.

Bhakti marga *Bhakti* means "devotion", but this path for the self is not just ordinary devotion but *loving*-devotion and often ecstatic devotion, the kind of devotion I have dealt with earlier in the context of the deity Krisna, reflected in the love affair between him and Radha. Thus, *bhakti marga* focuses on the *saguna*, the manifest, aspects of the divine, those to which the devotee can relate to in a very personal way. It is this personal relationship with the deity which makes *bhakti* the most popular path to the divine in Hinduism particularly in the villages and urban areas, enough so to prompt Biardeau to say "For my part, I know of no so-called "local" cult which does not contain the general beliefs of bhakti".[31] Strictly speaking *bhakti* was really a very powerful movement of the sixth century, spread by wandering devotional poets who were both Vaisnavite and Saivite, but *bhakti* certainly features earlier, possibly in the second century,[32] and the *Bhagavad Gita* dated to the early centuries BCE certainly contains very powerful elements of it. The *Gita*, indeed, beautifully depicts not only the intense love that the devotee, the *bhakta*, should have for God, but also *God's reciprocal love* for his *bhakta*:

> Hear again my supreme and most secret word of all: I love you dearly, therefore I shall speak to you what is for your good.
> Fix your mind on me, be devoted to me, sacrifice to me, bow down to me, then I promise you in truth you will come to me, for you are dear to me.
> Having abandoned all *dharmas*, take refuge in me alone. I shall liberate you from all evils; grieve not.[33]

It is this kind of two-way personal and loving relationship between devotee and God which epitomizes what has aptly been called "full-blown theism"[34] in Hinduism.

Avatars of Visnu such as Krisna and Ram are very much the focus of devotional Hinduism but a deity such as Siva, too, while being on the one hand the epitome of the ascetic *yogin,* is also in some of his aspects the focus of devotional *bhakti,* as is also the Mother Goddess and many of the local deities in villages and towns. What is important about the path of *bhakti* is that it is class and casteless and is open to all. Women, in particular, can express their love for the divine in the ways best appropriate for them, and any visit to a Hindu temple at festival times would witness the powerful role which women play in devotional practice. The singing of hymns, dancing, playing musical instruments are all features of such devotional worship.

But what is important about this highly devotional approach to God is that it is a means of surrender of the self, termed *prapatti* in Sanskrit. Because the *bhakta* focuses all his or her attention on God, the ego is lost, and the self surrendered, bringing about what Biardeau describes as a "transfer of man's whole capacity for desire onto God".[35] It is this common denominator of an egoless self which unites the different *margas* by the same ultimate aim. The diversity in the concept of the divine in manifest form caters for a variety of paths and approaches to the ultimate goal. But the identical goal of the many paths is, for most aspects of Hinduism, pointing to the ultimate unity of all things. Whatever diversity we see in the phenomenal world or in the divine one will be transcended when the *atman* is experienced and exchanged for a vision of the unity of all existence – worldly and divine.

Sruti and *smrti* literature   There are two kinds of sacred writings in Hinduism, *sruti* and *smrti*. *Sruti* literature is the oldest and more sacred. For a long time it was handed down orally before being committed to writing. The spoken word in religious practice has always been important in Hinduism: priests may recite from memory, or occasionally read from the scriptures, but to *hear* scripture is itself an act of devotion. *Sruti* means "heard", "perceived", "understood", or "cognized" and refers to the habit of the ancient seers of early Hinduism going off to live in the forests alone, where they became so holy and so evolved in consciousness that they could "hear" or "cognize" the truths of the universe. The teachings they left for the Hindus who came after them through the centuries are believed to be universal laws, unchangeable and eternal. *Sruti* literature is divided into two main parts, the *Vedas* and the *Upanisads*. The word *veda* means "knowledge" while the word *upanisad* means "sitting down near to", probably referring to the disciples of the seers, who sat down in the forest at the feet of their teachers, or *gurus*, to learn about these truths of the universe. There are four *Vedas*: the *Rg Veda* or "Royal Knowledge", the *Sama Veda* "Knowledge of Chants", *Yajur Veda* "Knowledge of Sacrificial Ritual" and *Atharva Veda* "Knowledge of Incantations". There are many more *upanisads*, but scholars generally agree that about thirteen of these are the most important.

Smrti literature is not so sacred but is just as important. It is *smrti* literature which is popular with most Hindus today. *Smrti* means "memory", "remembered", and this literature is generally much easier to understand because it points to the truths of the universe through the medium of symbolism and mythology, and through some of the most beautiful and exciting stories in the history of religion. So popular is some of this *smrti* literature that in recent years when some of it has been made into serials for television, the entire inhabitants of a village, young, old, men and women, would gather round one television set to watch as many as 96 weekly episodes.

The *Mahabharat*   Though there are many writings within the *smrti* literature, three stand out as being very famous. These are the *Ramayan*, the *Mahabharat*, and the *Bhagavad Gita*. The *Mahabharat* is the world's longest poem and dates back to about the ninth century BCE. *Mahabharat* means "The great story of the Bharatas" and it tells the story of a tremendous struggle for power between two royal families, the Pandavas and the Kauravas. The King, Bharata (which is the old name for India), had two sons, Pandu and Dhritarasta. Pandu had five sons who were very noble and good, representing *dharma* in life, while Dhritarasta had a hundred sons who were generally evil and who represented *adharma* in life. The story of the power struggle between these two parties, the five Pandavas and the hundred Kauravas, forms the story of the *Mahabharat* and into this story are interwoven all kinds of episodes of love, war, intrigue, relationships and all the countless situations which make up life. Like much *smrti* literature, the stories can be told to children, to adults, to intellectuals or to the simple; it will depend on the individual level of consciousness as to what will be gleaned from the narrative. The attentive listener and reader, however, will discern much moral, social, political and religious teaching in these stories.

The *Bhagavad Gita* The *Bhagavad Gita*, "Song of the Adorable One", is perhaps the most well-known Hindu scripture. It is actually the sixth part of the *Mahabharat* but is usually referred to separately. It was probably written in about the second century BCE and contains some of the most brilliant theological teaching about the nature of God and of life ever written. The struggle between the Pandavas and the Kauravas has come to a head and a great battle is about to be fought. Arjun, one of the Pandavas is riding along the battle lines ready for war and he tells his chariot driver to stop in the centre of the battlefield. As he surveys the enemy he has to fight, he sees his family there, his great teachers and many whom he loves dearly and who also love him. He becomes filled with horror at the thought of the battle and drops his bow to his side, sits down in the chariot and tells his chariot driver that he cannot fight. However, Arjun's chariot driver is no ordinary mortal: he is Visnu, incarnated on earth in the form of Krisna in order to set right the balance of good and evil in the world. It is at this point that Krisna begins to teach Arjun about the nature of the self, about Brahman, about the paths to Brahman and about *dharma* and *moksa*.

As a result of this teaching, Arjun's consciousness is expanded to the point that he is able to act according to his *dharma*. He is able to fulfil his role in life as a warrior and become an instrument in the divine purpose of ensuring the triumph of good over evil.

The *Ramayan* The *Ramayan* is an epic loved by all Indians. Of all the Hindu literature which has emerged out of religious tradition the *Ramayan* has perhaps the greatest appeal to the everyday Hindu. Although overshadowed in literary dimensions by the other great epic, the *Mahabharat*:

as a poem delineating the softer emotions of our everyday life the

Ramayana sends its roots deeper into the hearts and minds of the million in India.[36]

There is a universality about the *Ramayan* which appeals to all races and nations. Gandhi regarded it as the greatest book in Hindu devotional literature and it seems to have a special appeal, notably because of its depiction of everyday domestic events and situations which appeal to rich and poor alike. As such, it became the focus of much of the devotional movement in Hinduism and was the theme taken up by generations of poets. The *Ramayan* spread to all parts of southern Asia and was represented in plays, poetry, song, art and sculpture and translated into many languages. For two thousand years the story has been celebrated in temple ritual, religious festivals, at home shrines, and at places of pilgrimage, in recognition of the noblest of ages and the noblest of characters in the hero and heroine, Ram and Sita. It is therefore not surprising that the last words which Gandhi spoke before he died were "Ram, Ram."

The story of the *Ramayan* is a beautiful tale of devotion, duty and right relationships, and of *karma*. Ram and Sita are the ideal royal couple, Ram is a brave, wise and good warrior, and Sita his devoted, faithful, kind and beautiful wife. The story is a tale of the workings of *karma* which destined Ram to be banished to the forests, accompanied by his faithful wife and brother. There they live the lives of hermits and are befriended by the holy men who live a life of meditative retreat in the seclusion of the forest. The central episode of the long narrative is the abduction of Sita by the demon Ravan, and Ram's pursuit and rescue of her aided by the brave monkey-general Hanuman. The story ends in Sita's rescue by Ram and their return to Ayodhya after fourteen years to be greeted by its citizens with the greatest possible joy.

Important in the *Ramayan* and in all scripture related to the *avatars* of Visnu, is the human nature of the *avatars*. It is this aspect which enables people to come close to them. The life of Ram, in particular, is a mixture of the divine and human, though his unawareness of his divinity throughout the narrative makes him all the more easy to relate to. And this human nature is further enhanced by his emotion. We meet Ram in the *Ramayan* as a mature man who has clear characteristics of honesty and uprightness, while Sita shows kindness, obedience and chastity, characteristics which make the ideal hero and heroine to the Hindu mind. Ram and Sita have to endure great hardships, but through this suffering and privation the qualities of right action come through thereby providing a model for the millions of Hindus today.

The *Ramayan* and the *Mahabharat* give us a thorough understanding of the concept of *dharma* – "what is right". Ram is the embodiment of *dharma*. So Ram and Sita are perfect examples of how man and woman should be, both individually and in their relationship with each other. The epics, then, bring the complex concept of *dharma* into real situations, in this way providing moral guidance in a very concrete form for the Hindu. "What is right" is learnt through the characters of Ram, Sita and Lakshman rather than through philosophical speculation. Not only, then, does such *smrti* literature bring people close to God, but it also shows what is required of them at their very best.

VARNADHARMA One aspect of Hinduism which everyone seems to have heard about is the caste system – the practice of differentiating people in society into different groups. Caste is an aspect of Hinduism which is often misunderstood. I intend, therefore, to highlight some of the misconceptions concerning it and to outline the nature of the system in India as well as the reasoning behind it. To begin with, the use of the term *caste* must be redefined. There are, in fact, two words which are used in Hindu society to refer to the various groupings of society, *varna* and *jati*. Unfortunately, some writers on Hinduism rarely differentiate between the two and simply translate both as "caste" referring to the "caste" system of India. This is incorrect for *varna* and *jati* refer to two *different* systems and it is necessary to examine each in turn to see why the term "caste" should be used with caution.

Varna The word *varna* means "colour" and it refers to a *religious* system of classification of people in Hinduism into four classes, dating back to the very earliest of times. In the second millennium BCE the *Aryans* invaded India and it was they who established the tradition of dividing society into four classes. Hindus consider this four-class system to be a religious one because in one of the *Aryan* scriptures, the *Rg Veda*, there is a hymn which tells of the sacrifice of a huge primeval man called *Purusa* from whom the four classes came:

> When they divided man
> Into how many parts did they divide him?
> What was his mouth? What his arms?
> What are his thighs called? What his feet?
>
> The Brahman was his mouth
> The arms were made the Prince
> His thighs the common people
> And from his feet the serf was born.[37]

Thus it can be seen clearly from this hymn that society was felt to be divided into four classes: the priestly class who were the *Brahmins*; the ruling, administrative and warrior class called the *Rajanyas*, or *Ksatriyas*; the artisans, merchants, tradesmen and farmers called the *Vaisyas*; and the labourers who were the *Sudras*. The hymn from the *Rg Veda* depicts the nature of these people in symbolic and mythological imagery and this is an important point in understanding the class system of Hinduism.

The *Brahmins* are the priests who spring from the mouth, and it is the mouth which one needs for chanting the sacred scriptures: so the myth of the sacrifice of this primeval man suggests that some people are born with the capabilities for leading others in important religious ritual. When the *Aryans* first arrived in India, their scriptures were not written down but memorized by the priests who were the only class of people capable of learning, memorizing and reciting them with precise correctness for the purpose of carrying out religious ritual and of being effective mediators between humankind and the divine. So by saying that the priestly class comes forth from the mouth of *Purusa*, the myth shows that it is the *dharma* of a *Brahmin* to be what he is. However, not all Hindu priests are *Brahmins* for there are many priests of the lower classes who carry out specific functions pertinent only to those classes. What distinguishes the former from the latter is the classical study of the *Vedas* and scholarship of the former, whereas the latter may not be very learned or educated at all. In fact, some priests are illiterate.

The myth also tells us that the arms formed the "Prince". This is the *Rajanya/Ksatriya* class, the people in society who are rulers like the *rajas*, the government administrators and, since rulership often involved protection of one's subjects and expansion of one's kingdom, warriors, in particular. It is the arms of *Purusa* which are needed for action, for an active way of life, so the myth shows us that it is the *dharma* of some people in life to be the protectors of others. This would be a function which a *Brahmin* could not perform because he would not have the right ingredients (of *Purusa*) in his personality to be a warrior.

The thighs of *Purusa* formed the common people, the *Vaisyas*, those in society who provide the necessary things for the rest of society to function. The thighs of the body are strong and supporting, so *Vaisyas* would have the temperament to work at more manual tasks, albeit sometimes skilled ones. But, not having the characteristics of the *Brahmin* or *Ksatriya*, they would not be able to carry out the particular responsibilities of those classes. Finally, the myth tells us, the serf is born from the feet of *Purusa* – the part of the body which supports all the other parts. So it is the *dharma* of the *Sudra*, the fourth class, to support the rest of society by acting as a servant.

What this myth is pointing out is that *religiously* people are destined to have different abilities and skills and that because the potentiality for other skills is not present, it would be useless for a *Sudra*, for example, to take on the functions of a *Brahmin*. Ideally, if society operated perfectly, each class would fulfil its own potential which would be seen as different from, but equal to, any of the other classes. The myth suggests that each class is necessary for the survival of the others and that, just as we do not despise the feet because they happen to be lower than any other part of the body, so we should not despise the *Sudra* for being the serving class in society. Ideally, we should treat all as equal but with different abilities. The early parts of the Hindu scripture, the *Ramayan*, depict very well this ideal interrelation of the four classes in the golden age of Hinduism. And while *religiously* such distinctions are made, economically it would be a mistake to believe that all *Brahmins* are priests and are wealthy or that all *Sudras* are servants and poor. *Religiously* it is only the top three classes which are *dvija*, "twice-born", and who are able to go through a ceremony to initiate them into the stages of Hindu religious life. *Sudras* and, indeed, women, are not generally deemed to have the required characteristics of personality to be *dvija*. But *Sudras* and women, can do, and have done, well economically. Nevertheless, the village scene tends towards a more rigorous economic classification by class and caste, as does much urban life.

Dalits   Beyond the class system, that is to say, too low to be even ranked in the four classes are those beyond its pale, the outcastes – a word not now legally accepted in India. The Government of India Act of 1935 called them "exterior castes" or "scheduled castes" but Gandhi termed them *Harijans*, "Children of God" though, rather unfortunately, the term can also mean "love-child" or "bastard". They prefer to refer to themselves in today's world as *Dalits* – "the oppressed" – and their sheer numbers means that they can wield considerable political power. Some rise to political fame and there have been a number of cabinet ministers and one prime minister from the *Dalit* class. But it would be true to say that, despite education to graduate and postgraduate levels, discrimination persists. Yet Killingley notes that, while some *Dalits* try to rise beyond their outcaste status, others try to claim *Dalit* status, because present government discrimination in favour of them can be a distinct advantage.[38]

From what has been described above, therefore, from a Hindu perspective the class system would be seen as a very logical way of viewing society. Added to this is another important perspective, the distribution of the *gunas*. Hinduism believes that everything in the cosmos is composed, in varying degrees, of three qualities called *gunas*. There are three of these *gunas* – *sattva*, *rajas*, and *tamas*. *Sattva* is light, truth, evolution, wisdom, intellect, the kind of quality which allows one to progress spiritually and to pursue what is right. Its opposite is *tamas*, which is dullness, inertia, the quality which tends to hold one back and which is averse to progress. *Rajas* is the active quality, the one which makes us go out and *do* things. Everything in life is felt to be a combination of these three *gunas* but while we have all of them in us and may experience one or another at certain times, Hindus believe that one of these *gunas* will be the dominating characteristic of each person's character, while there will be a less obvious secondary *guna*.[39]

If I turn back now to the four classes and apply the theory of the *gunas* to them it can be seen that each class is believed to have its own characteristics from the point of view of the *gunas*. Thus:

Brahmins	*sattva – rajas*
Ksatriyas	*rajas – sattva*
Vaisyas	*rajas – tamas*
Sudras	*tamas – rajas*

Thus, the Hindu would claim that the *Vaisyas* and the *Sudras*, for example, have no *sattvic guna* and would therefore not have the kind of qualites which could carry out the pursuit of religious practice typical of a *Brahmin* who is endowed with so much *sattva*. Similarly, it is only the *Ksatriya* who has sufficient active energies, combined with the necessary wisdom, to become involved in war or administration. A *Vaisya* would have the active energy but not the wisdom to be a warrior leader.

Hindus then see the class system as a very logical one and feel that they simply recognize the restrictive elements that are present in all societies. To go against your class, then, is to go against your own personality, it is to try to behave like someone else when you do not have the characteristics in your personality to do so. Hindu scriptures therefore often stress that it is always better to follow one's own *dharma* than to try to live that of another.

Jati When I refer to *class* in Hinduism I am really referring to the four religiously orientated and rather ancient classes highlighted above. When I refer to *caste* I am really speaking of *jati* which means "birth", and this is far more important for Hindus because it affects so many aspects of daily life. Whereas there are only four classes in Hinduism there are thousands of castes. Caste is not a religious institution, unlike *varna*, but is economic and geographical in origin, though it is impossible to say exactly why and how all the castes came about. While it is true to say that *jatis* are often subdivisions of *varna*, class, it would be overstating the case to say that this was the origin of the caste system as a whole. It is to *jati* that most Hindus today refer when they talk of caste and it is *jati* which really dictates the rules and regulations of life for the average Hindu. And caste is rigid. Flood aptly comments that "the caste of any individual is inalienable; it is a property of the body and cannot be removed (except according to some traditions by initiation").[40] Each *jati* has its own special caste regulations in terms of food, occupation, marriage, social interaction and the like, and from each caste will come a number of sub-castes making the whole system a highly complicated one which defies examination. Castes may often be occupational but this does not preclude a member of one caste working at the occupation of another, for example in agriculture; this results in a very complex system. What we can say is that there are many *Brahmin* castes, just as there would be many *Ksatriya* or *Dalit* castes, and just as the four *varnas* are hierarchically viewed, so also are the various castes within a particular *varna*.

The word caste was originally applied by the Portuguese in the sixteenth century, and since the Portuguese *casta* means "pure" or "chaste", it suggests very well the importance to the Hindu of maintaining the ritual and social purity of each *jati*. Important in Hindu society, too, is the idea that one does not marry outside one's *jati*; indeed, expulsion from the family and caste as a whole is likely to ensue should this happen, but it is not unusual for a whole section of a particular *jati* to separate off and adopt different dietary, ritual or occupational stances and thus become distinct.[41]

Underlying this whole concept of class and caste is the Hindu belief in *karma* and *samsara*. Because of the *karma* accumulated in past lives an individual is born into the kind of life which reflects the *karmic* balance of good or evil. So a *Brahmin* is such because of his past good *karma* from previous lives; others, whose past *karma* is sufficiently bad, may be born *outside* the caste or class system, as a member of the scheduled classes.

ASRAMA-
DHARMA

The *asramas* In Hindu scriptures the life of an individual is conceived of as being divided into four periods of unequal time called *asramas*. The observance of the four *varnas* and the four *asramas* were important foundations in Hindu social and spiritual life, but today in modern India fewer people observe the system. A third of the Hindu population is composed of *Sudras,* the lowest class, and it would be rare for a *Sudra* to observe the four *asramas*. And although some women may observe the custom, it does not, generally, apply to women for they are religiously excluded from the *asrama* system. The observing of the four *asramas* is based on the ideal that to renounce materialism and wordly pleasures should be an important aspect of the later stages of life, for it would assist a person to achieve *moksa*, liberation from reincarnation. But while this is the overall goal, it is also realized that there must be, at some time during one's life, a period when marriage, social status and material wealth are necessary. Such aspects are catered for in the four periods and are considered essential in the experience of an individual; indeed, without them, reincarnation is thought to be inevitable. The *asramas*, then, are four distinct periods of life, the first being a period from birth to anything from 12 to 25 years of age when a male studies the Vedic scriptures and remains celibate. The second *asrama* is the period of marriage and the life of a householder, *grhastha*, the third a period of retirement and retreat in celibacy, and the fourth, total renunciation of the world.

The ideal of renunciation of materialism and marriage, and a life of celibacy, was particularly evident in about the sixth century BCE and may have influenced the institution of the *asramas* in Hinduism for, by the fifth century, there is evidence of the system in Hindu society. However, in its beginnings, it seems that, after the first *asrama*, a young adult could choose which of the other *asramas* he would wish to pursue for the rest of his life. So, he could either remain a celibate student studying with his teacher or *guru* until he died, or he could marry, or go straight into the third or fourth *asrama*s. However, in many ways this went against the traditional teaching in Hinduism concerning the importance of marriage and procreation and it was not without its critics. So the system changed to one which advocated the passage of an individual through the four *asramas* in one lifetime. This passage represents the necessary stages of life, rather like rungs of a ladder, through which one travels to ultimate liberation. While it is not expected that every Hindu should go through the four *asramas*, indeed, many never advance beyond the second, once an individual has embarked on the next *asrama* it is virtually impossible to revert back, and indeed would result in turning oneself into a member of the scheduled castes.

The first *asrama*   This first period of life is a time of immaturity when the Hindu is undergoing a period of formal education. He is called a *brahmachari* and is taught by his elders and is prepared by them to become a useful and mature member of society. His education will not only fit him for a future profession, but will equip him also for family, social and religious life. However, many Hindus are not prepared to live such a disciplined life for a long period and some cannot afford such a formal education at all. So the first *asrama* has shrunk to between 12 and 15 years. This is even the case for many *Brahmins*.

The second *asrama*   This is the householder, *grhastha*, stage – the undertaking of marriage and the duties of raising and supporting a family. It is a measure of the importance of the family in Hinduism that the earlier idea of missing out this *asrama* in order to remain a celibate student, hermit in retreat, or wandering recluse, did not gain ground. Hindus always felt it important to raise a family and even today, despite immense poverty, a couple will continue to have many children, at least until a boy is born. During the householder stage it is expected that a man should work at a trade or profession to support his family, but also to contribute to the welfare of the community. Hinduism is perhaps unique in suggesting that the pursuit of wealth is a *necessary* goal in life at some stage. We could include here also the idea that pleasure (*kama*) is also a goal permissable at this stage of life. Though this always seems strange to the Westerner, we should remember that the Hindu is always subject to the laws of *karma* and *dharma* and that these two concepts ideally prevent the pursuit of the kind of pleasure which would be against social and cosmic norms. The vast majority of Hindus would be very reluctant to give up this householder stage and so it usually lasts a lifetime!

The third *asrama*   Traditionally, when a man becomes a grandfather, when his hair turns gray and his skin becomes wrinkled, when his children have grown up and are establishing lives of their own, then the duty of the man as a householder is at an end. In this third *asrama* the man is expected to retire from family and social life, give up his work, wealth and possessions and retreat to the forest as a forest hermit, a *vanaprastha*, to live a more spiritual life. Physical, social, material and sexual pleasures are renounced, although in some cases a wife could accompany her husband into retirement. Little contact, if any, would be maintained with other members of the family; the life would be that of the celibate recluse, though at times advice may be sought of the recluse from family and friends. In view of the denials which this kind of life brings, it is not difficult to see why the third *asrama* has become obsolete for all but a few.

The fourth *asrama*   The fourth *asrama* is when, in late life, a Hindu renounces the world, even his wife, his social duties and his religious obligations. All desires, hopes, fears and responsibilities are abandoned and his concentration is devoted to merging with God. This is the *sannyasin* who even today in India is treated with the greatest of respect, mingled with a certain degree of fear as well as skepticism. On taking up the life of the ascetic, such men will often burn an effigy of their bodies to show that they have died to the world.

Although these four *asramas* are now not widely practised they have remained an important ideal in Hindu religious tradition, comparable to the four *varnas*. In fact, they are so important that they rank as one of the two pillars of Hindu socio-religious tradition, the other being *varna*. The two are therefore often combined together as one *dharmic* basis of Hinduism – *varnasramadharma*. As we saw earlier, the term *Hinduism* is not really a very apposite one and is really one which has been assigned to Hindu religion from outside India. If we were to ask ordinary village Hindus to say what their understanding of Hinduism is they would more than likely reply *varnasramadharma*. This really sums up everyday life in Hinduism very well – doing what is right according to your class or caste and your particular role in life.

WORSHIP IN THE HOME AND TEMPLE   Worship of the divine in Hinduism, whether it be formal national or local festivals, at temple, outdoor shrine, or home shrine, is characterized by immense diversity. The very nature of Hinduism with its multiplicity of approaches to, and aspects of, the divine, facilitates this.

Worship in Hinduism is a *daily* event, whether performed at home or at a temple or outdoor shrine. It is *nitya*, "obligatory", for a practising Hindu. Such daily worship is called *puja*, a word which is not so easily translated since it has connotations of respect, honour, and veneration and therefore can be directed to parents, to one's teacher, one's *guru*, or to a holy man, as well as to a god or goddess. Ritual is important to the Hindu and much of it, while regional, is also ancient. This gives a certain stability to the diversity of Hindu ritual practice providing what Flood depicts as something "which anchors people in a sense of deeper identity and belonging."[42]

Images   Most people associate Hinduism with a multiplicity of deities which are represented in the form of images. The word *idols* is often used by Westerners in depicting such images, but there is a nuance of thought between the two words which makes "image" far more appropriate. Westerners use the term "idol" to suggest that it is the statue or idol itself which is worshipped, and nothing beyond it. "Image", on the other hand, suggests an image *of* something, and can therefore be representative of, or symbolic for, something beyond the visible form. This is an idea more appropriate to Hinduism, in which forms are but a manifestation of a formless Absolute. The term "idol", therefore, is partly incorrect, and in some Western senses could be said to be offensive. A Hindu would generally use the term *murti* to indicate the image of a deity and the way in which a *murti* is viewed by individuals would vary considerably. Many Hindus regard the *murtis* as representations of the deities, rather like a photograph represents a person. We can be very nostalgic about photographs, they can arouse emotive responses, but photographs project the mind to the reality *beyond* the print, no one identifies the photographic image as the *real* person. In the same way it could be said that a *murti* projects the mind of the worshipper to the greater essence of divinity beyond the immediate emotive representation. Thus, anthropomorphic representations of deities are by no means the norm in worship – a brass pot, a stone, or a *linga* of the deity Siva, will symbolize the power of the respective deity.

Having said this, a *murti* is often regarded as a manifestation of the presence of the *power* of a deity, something of the essence or spirit of the deity which is manifest in the world. It is in this sense that the *murti* is more directly representative of the deity itself, for the power or essence of the deity is believed to be *in* the *murti*, either temporarily, as for some festivals, or permanently, as in some temple images. But in containing a deity's power or essence, there is little suggestion that this *is* the deity in its entirety: more usually, the deity itself is conceived of as being beyond its manifestation of power in the *murti* and not confined by it. In many senses, all aspects of manifest existence are ultimately Brahman, so any image of a deity can be identified as such.

Either way, *murtis* are treated as if they are royalty and suggest the presence of the deity at the *puja* proceedings. Great care is therefore important in conducting *puja*, particularly the maintaining of purity and in terms of the regular, daily washing, dressing, and approaching of the deities. *Murtis* are specially consecrated in a ceremony called *pratistha* before they can be the focus of *puja* whether at home or in the temple, and an old or damaged *murti* is always thrown into the sea to dipose of it. Frequently, symbols serve the purpose of locating the deity, or the power of the deity. A *kalas* will often be seen. It is a small brass pot containing water, curds and ghee and has a coconut on top. This is a typical representation of a form of the goddess, some-times being placed beneath a picture of her. The great God Siva has both an anthropomorphic form and the powerful symbol of the *linga*, the phallic symbol which represents the potent energy which is mani-fest in the cosmos. It is also important to recognize that it is not the great Gods of Hinduism but the ordinary deities, especially village and localized urban deities, and what they symbolize, which are important to many Hindus, particularly those of lower castes.[43] The major deities such as Visnu and Siva are considered to be uninterested in the daily events of the ordinary man or woman.

Other objects of worship If the essence of Brahman is in all things, then all things in life have a basic sacredness. However, Hindus gener-ally single out certain species of animals and vegetation. The *pipal* and *banyan* trees are especially sacred and are often the objects of *puja*. The *tulsi* plant (basil) is a frequent object of *puja* in the home, for it is connected with the deity Visnu. Animals are also considered to be sacred, the cow being the most well known. While not actually worshipped, it is respected and venerated as a sacred animal and is allowed to roam unharmed. Many will touch its back as they pass it, but it has to be said that Gandhi became a vegetarian because he felt cows were ill-treated. Such is the respect for the cow that Indians offered to take in the millions of cows waiting for slaughter in Britain as a result of the recent crisis in beef production.[44] Snakes, while feared, are also venerated in India, and Hindu mythology features them widely. Monkeys are also venerated and may be allowed to roam free in some temples. Despite their sacred nature, they sometimes bite! At some festival occasions, even the tools of one's trade may be the object of *puja*, and what appears to be an ordinary stone is in fact a representation of a female divinity in many shrines. In many instances the object of veneration is a symbol or representation of the deity or divine power beyond it.

Significant aspects of *puja* The deity, represented by the *murti* or picture or other symbol, is considered to be an important guest, a royal guest, and is treated as such throughout *puja* with adoration, attention, care and entertainment. Purification is essential, and it would be usual to bathe in running water before performing *puja*. But in any case, a little water is sipped three times by the worshipper before performing *puja* in order to indicate purity. Washing the *murti* is essential, for a royal guest would need water to bathe after arriving from a long journey. Sometimes the washing is merely symbolic – a flower dipped gently in water is lightly touched on the face of the deity. It is the face, teeth and particularly the feet which are "washed", just as a guest would need after travelling through the dusty streets of India. Dressing the deity is also important and the clothes chosen are bright, beautiful and often embroidered with gold-coloured threads. Ornaments are also placed on the *murti* as well as flower garlands, perfumes and oils – again, the kind of gifts one would wish to convey to a royal guest. Since the deity remains at a temple, it is both woken up in the morning and its "needs" attended to, and put to rest at night with equal care.

Food is also important: cooked rice, fruit, ghee, sugar and betel leaf are the main types of food offered. Offering food is a very important way of honouring the deity. In Indonesia the Hindu women make elaborate pyramids of food (the wealthier they are, the higher the pyramid) which may be two or three metres high, and which are carried to the temple on the head as an offering to the deity. Such food is meticulously prepared and arranged. A cooked chicken may be splayed somewhere in the pyramid, surrounded by rice dishes and an abundance of fruit. The pyramid of food is left at the temple, to be collected later in the day. This is an important factor in all Hindu *puja*. The deity is believed to take the essence of the food, and the leftovers (*jutha*) are given back to the worshipper as what is known as *prasad*. This is a sign of grace from the deity to the worshipper. In Indonesia, the food (including the cooked chicken) is left exposed to the sun (and sometimes monsoon rains) for much of the day before being collected as *prasad*.

Fragrance and light are also offered the deity, fragrance in the form of incense sticks, and light in the form of a burning lamp usually made from a burning wick placed in ghee, which is waved before the deity. The deity is honoured in a number of ways: by applying a *tilak* to the spot between the eyebrows of the deity, the worshipper indicates awareness of the spiritual purity of the deity which, in turn, is passed to the worshipper. The worshipper may also entertain the deity with *bhajans/sabads*, hymns which offer praise and honour. This is a feature of temple *puja* in particular, as well as the home shrine, but it is possible to see groups of people singing hymns on the verandahs of the temples in the evenings, having come together specifically and informally for this purpose. This may occur once or twice a week, the company usually consisting of males, though occasionally women will join in but sit separately.

The standard way of showing respect to someone in India is by means of bowing (*pranama*) and, practically, the more respect one wishes to show, the lower the bow. In the case of a deity, or a royal person, total prostration is in order. *Anjali* consists of bringing the palms together and raising them to the forehead, and combined with the bow are the actions normally used in greeting in India. The words *Namaskar* (Sanskrit) or *Namaste* (Hindi) "I bow to you" are spoken as this is done, and these words, *anjali*, and the bow are indicative of recognition of the divine *atman* in the other person, the part of all individuals which is the same as oneself. Thus, there is a special link between the worshipper and the deity when this is done in *puja*. Since famous *gurus* are honoured in *puja*, people might touch their feet in respect, or remove the dust from a *guru's* feet before touching their own head, so indicating that the feet of the *guru* are purer than the head of the one paying respect.

Darsan   The point of *puja* in Hinduism is *darsan*, a word which means "audience", "viewing" or "sight of", the object here being the deity. This is rather like gaining audience to a royal personage, the result of which is the grace of that person being bestowed on the visitor. It is the requested audience with the deity which is represented by the ringing of a bell by the worshipper at a temple or, indeed, at a home shrine. The bell summons the deity as much as announcing the arrival of the worshipper. *Darsan* might involve sitting cross-legged on the floor (but not with the soles of the feet pointed towards the deity) or, preferably, circumambulation of the *murti*. This is always done in a clockwise direction so that the right hand faces the deity and not the left hand, the latter being associated with all the unpleasant tasks of life. While circumambulation is desired for *darsan* it is not obligatory; indeed, it would be impossible at shrines in most homes. *Darsan* is felt to be most auspicious first thing in the morning when the deities have only just been woken up.

Puja **in the home**   The home is the most popular place for *puja* for it is not obligatory for people to visit the temples. Women have a great deal of freedom in religious practice in the home and it is the head woman of a household who would normally conduct *puja*. *Puja* in the home is a daily occurrence and there will usually be a small shrine set aside somewhere. A Hindu friend utilizes the stairs in her flat which had once led to an upper floor, but, being converted into flats, the six or seven stairs lead to a blank wall. It is an ideal tiered setting to put the family deities, particularly Krisna, who is her favourite deity, and a picture of her deceased mother who had been instrumental in founding the local *mandal*, the Hindu temple, is nearby. Hindu home shrines are usually colourful, bright, and characterized by the small offerings of food, water, fragrance and light.

Sometimes, *murtis* or prints of deities are found in other parts of the home away from the main shrine, the only exception being the bathroom and toilet which are ritually unclean rooms. Westerners are often surprised to find the main shrine in the kitchen. Indeed, this is a very popular place for the family shrine, because it is always kept ritually clean. Preparation of food is very important in Hinduism and is responsible for much class/caste division. A person is felt to be impure if he or she comes into contact with impure food, so its preparation is meticulous. Shoes are never worn in the kitchen, so polluting leather, or the dust from the outside world is not allowed to enter its environs. To place a shrine in such a meticulously maintained room is common sense, so it may be that the family shrine will be located on the top of the washing machine. Sometimes the *murtis* are kept behind the closed doors of a cabinet, or closed curtains, which are opened for *puja*. Shrines will hold not only the household's chosen deities, but other deities also. There may be pictures of immediate ancestors, specially produced and highly colourful prints of deities, and pictures of modern *gurus* such as Sai Baba. It is possible that the particular deities chosen by a family may be caste specific.[45]

***Puja* in the temple**   Although the home has always been considered the focal point for most ceremonies, many Hindus call at their local temple, the *mandir*, whenever possible: the belief is that no image should be left unworshipped for a whole day. Gifts pour into the temples, and when costly food cannot be prepared for the deity, poor people could bring a grain of rice or a lump of sugar. Strictly speaking, because Hindus believe that Brahman is everywhere, It can be worshipped anywhere, so a river bank, forest grove, mountain top, or even a cowshed is a sacred place. But temples have been set up on special sites which are held to be auspiciously connected with a particular deity. However, temples are far more prolific in southern India than in the north.

The aspects which are most arresting in a Hindu temple are those which affect the senses – the colours, the sounds, the smells. The shrine or shrines within a temple house the *murtis*, the deities being dressed in brightly coloured clothes, sparkling jewellery and coloured garlands. Large temples are often highly decorated with tinsel, colourfully designed symbols and the whole atmoshpere is impressively bright. The sound of bells ringing, drums being beaten, *bhajans/sabads* being sung with the worshippers clapping their hands to the rhythm accompanied by small percussion musical instruments, all serve to make the temple very much alive with activity, while the smell of incense pervades the whole building. Temples can be any shape or size, some being not larger than a cupboard, though there are distinct patterns of temples in the northern parts of India which are different in the south. But all will have three features – a representation of the deity in the form of a *murti* or symbol of the deity, a canopy over the deity in order to honour it, and a priest who cares for the sacred image and who gives each worshipper *prasad*, a gift from the deity. There are likely to be several *murtis* in some temples, but the main deity will be housed in the womb of the temple, the *garbagriha*, literally "womb-house", over which is a tower or spire. The *garbagriha* is the inner sanctuary of the temple which is entered only by a priest. Interestingly, there is a difference between the deity in a temple and the *same* deity in the home, the former being the more powerful: the kind of restrictions which obtain in a temple, then, where only a priest can officiate, are not evident for the same deity in the home.

Although families sit together in some temples, men and women usually sit on either side of the shrine on the floor (there are no chairs). Worship can take place at any time, on any day. Usually a portable fire-altar is brought into the room and worshippers gather around it, facing the shrine. Some people will sing, some will chant, while others play musical instruments. The priest begins the temple *puja* by kindling the sacred fire in which are burned small pieces of wood, camphor and liquid butter, ghee. He chants verses from the *Vedas* and then prayers for purity are offered and priest and people take water into the left hand. Then, dipping the fingers of the *right* hand into the water, they touch their ears, nose, eyes, mouth, arms, body and legs. This symbolizes purification of the individual before he or she approaches his or her God. This entire ceremony is known as *havan*, the offering of fire.

Another ceremony is *arti*, worship involving light, and is a frequent act of worship, sometimes indicative of *puja* itself. *Arti* is an offering involving love and devotion to the deity. In this ceremony, symbols of the five elements of life are used, representing fire, air, earth, ether and water. A flat tray with five lights, called an *arti* tray, is waved before the images of the deities; the lights are also held in front of revered personages from other religions, perhaps Guru Nanak of Sikhism and Jesus of Christianity. At other times, *arti* is performed with a single flame of burning camphor.[46] A spot of red paste is put onto the foreheads of everyone present, including the images and portraits of the deities. The mark, known as a *tilak* or *chandlo,* is made from red powder, yellow tumeric powder or sandlewood paste. The *arti* tray is taken round by the priest, and everyone present holds their hands over the flames and then passes them over the forehead and hair. This symbolizes the receiving of divine blessing, protective grace and power. Each person then receives *prasad*, sometimes a mixture of dried fruit, nuts and sugar crystals. This represents the gift given by the deity to the worshippers, a symbol of the deity's love for them. Fuller suggests that this in some way divinises the recipient,[47] though since *prasad* is believed to be the leftovers of the deity it could be claimed that the subordination to, and dependency of, the recipient on the deity is the central concept: *prasad* as food leftovers (*jutha*) thus indicates subordination, not identity.

Temples need not be elaborate, nor are they necessary for worship for, as we have seen, worship is something which can take place anywhere and is particularly a home-focused practice. But temples are visited daily, albeit by different people. While the priests who tend the temples of the great Gods and Goddesses need to be of the *Brahmin* class, there are, as we have seen, a variety of castes within the *Brahmin* structure. Not all *Brahmins* would be practising priests and there are many priests who are not *Brahmins* at all, who would officiate at local shrines.

Of the different priests, *pujaris* are those concerned with temple or shrine ritual and they may well be illiterate, a *panda* is a temple priest at a site of pilgrimage, while a *purohit* is a family priest or *guru*. The emphasis in *puja* is on purity, love and devotion. Purity is of the utmost importance. Shoes, for example are never worn in a temple because leather is a highly polluting material, as is the street dust which is attached to them. Menstruating women are also considered to be highly polluting and would not be allowed into the temple. And while Gandhi fought hard for the rights of *Dalits* to enter all temples, they are still only allowed in the outer areas of some of the bigger temples. But, in any case, temples in India are often caste orientated; *Dalits* are likely to worship in a particular local temple, even frequented by certain *Dalit* castes and not others and with their own *Dalit* priest to officiate. Purity is also reflected in the products used in ritual. Cow products such as milk, dung and ghee are specifically purifying as well as water from a sacred river such as the Ganges. Turmeric and sandalwood are also considered to be purifying agents while water itself absorbs pollution and takes it away.[48]

Love and devotion are the main characteristics of *puja* whether at home or at the temple. And that devotion can take the form of singing, dancing, and offerings to the deity. Offerings need not be elaborate; in the *Gita* it states:

> Whoever offers to me with devotion, a leaf, a flower, fruit, water, that I accept when offered with devotion by the pure-minded. Whatever you do, whatever you eat, whatever you offer in sacrifice, whatever you give, whatever austerity you practise, . . . do that as an offering to me.[49]

Devotion is also *attention* and *care* of the deities and at a basic level they are felt to be both pleased and appeased by the attention, and therefore afford protection to their devotees. But no deity *needs* such care. Fuller aptly states:

> Gods and goddesses do not actually need offerings and services, because

they never are dirty, ugly, hungry, or unable to see in the dark. Hence the purpose of worship is not to satisfy nonexistent divine needs, but to honor the deities and show devotion by serving them as if they had such needs. By this method alone can human beings adopt a truly respectful attitude toward the deities. Such an explanation of how puja pleases deities is logically consistent with a relatively emphatic distinction between a deity and its image, the container of divine power, because then the deity itself is not directly touched by the offerings and services made to the image.[50]

This suggests that *puja* in the form of care and attention lavished on the images of the deities provides the kind of anthropomorphic theism necessary for the worshippers themselves but, at a deeper level, the more devotion and care that is lavished on a deity, the more an individual is able to transcend his or her own ego, and transcending the ego, is a means to the *atman* within.

Puja at shrines   Apart from the shrines in the home and the temples, there are also numerous open-air shrines in India and other eastern Hindu cultures. These may be quite elaborate affairs and some may be tended by a priest who can often be found seated at the entrance in white robes, or, they may be simply a small heap of stones. They may be quite shabby in appearance, and indeed many temples often convey this kind of image. Shrines occur generally at auspicious places. Practically every crossroads on some Indonesian islands have shrines which are decorated daily by the women of the locality. Anyone who has driven in the chaos of traffic in parts of Indonesia where there is no "Highway Code" at all will understand the rationale of placing shrines at crossroads where accidents most frequently occur and deities need to be propitiated to help prevent them. Some shrines are deep in caves and the symbolism here is very often connected with entering the womb of the Mother Goddess.[51] It is in the very depths of such caves that the usually untended shrine is to be found.

LIFE-CYCLE RITES IN THE HINDU FAMILY

The family   The family is of considerable importance in Hinduism. While the life of the *sannyasin* is respected, the second of the *asramas*, the householder stage of life, endorses the idea that it is one's *dharma* to marry, raise a family and provide for that family in whatever way is necessary. Family life, in this case, becomes a religious obligation. Unlike the nuclear family we are accustomed to in the West, the Hindu family is normally an extended one, though there are exceptions to this these days, in view of urban settlement. The extended family includes grandparents, parents, married brothers and their whole families, so that, if accommodation is large enough, a considerable number of people can live together in the same home. This has several advantages in terms of the welfare of the old and the young. There are no state pensions for the elderly in India and the aged therefore look to their sons for support, both physically and economically, when they themselves are no longer able to contribute to the home. Having said this, the senior male of the family continues to lead it, even in advanced old age, and the senior woman holds sway, likewise, over the female members of the family. This means that respect for the elderly in a family is the normal pattern. Then, too, children have an abundance of aunts to care for them, and a large number of cousins with whom they can grow up, being close enough to them during their lives to regard them as brothers and sisters. Women share household tasks, and men share economic responsibility for the family.

Roles are fairly well defined between the sexes in the Hindu family, the men being the providers and workers, the women responsible for the running of the home. The average woman is not expected or considered able to shoulder public or social responsibility, though they do have considerable freedom in the conducting of religious practices in the home. Like Sita in the *Ramayan*, wives are expected to be loving, faithful and loyal, and willing to share even the misfortunes of their husbands; they are expected to be perfect and to treat their husbands like gods. This is not to say that they are unable to achieve status beyond the home and the family. Indira Gandhi, for example, was twice prime minister of India before her assassination in 1984. But for the average Hindu woman, particularly in rural areas, life revolves around the family, although it is the women of the family who are mainly involved in the ceremonies which mark the rites of passage in life.

Samskaras In Hinduism there are sixteen life-cycle rites or *samskaras*, and eleven of these are concerned with the baby and young child, marking specific stages in their development. To raise children is an important aspect of the second *asrama*, the stage of the householder, and, traditionally, the birth of a boy is more important than the birth of a girl. Indeed, prestige often comes with a large number of sons, and until a Hindu male has had at least one boy born to him, he cannot progress to the next stage of life. Moreover, he will have no son to perform the important death rites which will ensure his safe passage to a better reincarnation. Boys, too, are an economic advantage in the home, whereas girls leave the home at marriage to live with their husbands' families. The *samskaras* involved with boys, therefore, tend to be more elaborate and, while not all families follow all eleven for the young child, more rites usually occur for boys than girls. But, in any case, only *Brahmin* males are likely to undergo all of them.

Birth, like death, is seen as a time of considerable pollution and danger, when the unborn child, and particularly the newly-born child, is very vulnerable to evil forces. So the first three *samskaras* are devoted to the safety and welfare of the unborn child, while the fourth ceremony takes place at birth. At this time, the child is ritually washed and has sacred sounds whispered in its ear, while the sacred syllable *Aum* is written on its tongue with honey. Probably the most popular of the early *samskaras*, however, is the naming ceremony, *namkaran*, which is held on the twelfth day after birth by the twice-born classes of Hindus only. This ceremony is important enough to be officiated by a *Brahmin*, though priests are not, generally, essential for ritual, especially amongst the lower castes. Wealthy Hindus make much of this naming ceremony and it is important in that it brings to an end the period of pollution associated with childbirth. Sometimes, the baby may have its ears pierced at this ceremony, though strictly speaking ear-piercing is a separate *samskara*. The naming event is accompanied by much singing, especially of songs in which the baby's new name can be inserted. The baby's horoscope is also prepared at this time and will be very important later at the time of betrothal and marriage.

Because of the belief in the vulnerability of a young baby to evil forces, it is not usually taken out of doors until the third or fourth month, and this occasion itself is a *samskara*, but so that the baby does not attract the evil eye it is dressed in dark clothing for the occasion and lamp black is put on its forehead to hide its beauty. When, at about six months old, the baby is given its first solid food – a little boiled rice mixed with ghee and honey – this is the occasion for another *samskara*, as is the cutting of the child's hair for the first time, a ceremony made much of by *Brahmin* boys. For some, it is this ceremony of hair cutting which marks the end of any remaining pollution connected with the birth process.

Upanayama: the sacred thread ceremony   Of the eleven rites, the sacred thread ceremony is the most important. It is practised only by members of the three highest classes – *Brahmins*, *Ksatriyas* and *Vaisyas* – but today it is mainly *Brahmins* and wealthy Hindus who carry out the ceremony. Killingley, however, notes that *advija* castes have adopted their own sacred thread ceremonies.[52] A *Brahmin* boy would be given the sacred thread at the age of six, eight or ten, a *Ksatriya* up to the age of twelve, and a *Vaisya* up to the age of four-teen. He is expected to wear it for the rest of his life and although it is changed at special times, the new one is put on before the old one is removed, so he is never without it. The thread, consisting of three strands of cotton yarn, reminds the Hindu that he is indebted to God, to his parents and to his teacher, his *guru*. But the three strands may also represent the *Trimurti* or remind the wearer of the need for disci-plined mind, speech and body. The ceremony is preceded by singing, dancing and feasting during the few days before the sacred thread is placed on the boy by his *guru*; it is placed over his left shoulder and under his right arm. He is then twice born (*dvija*), born again, and has come of age. The ceremony marks the beginning of his formal education.

Betrothal and marriage   The twelfth rite is that of betrothal, prior to the thirteenth which is marriage. There is considerable variety in marriage customs, even in the same caste. Unlike birth and death, marriage is a time of great purity in contrast to pollution; the bride and groom are considered to be like deities, like Ram and Sita, Visnu and Laksmi, and are treated accordingly. Hindu weddings may last as long as six days before the wedding night, and may continue for the same length of time afterwards. These days would be taken up with singing, dancing, feasting and various religious and social rites. The wedding ceremony, itself, however, only lasts for two to four hours. Traditionally, it should take place at night, because marriage vows are unchangeable and as final as the pole star, which is only seen at night.

In India, when the child reaches marriageable age, the family searches for a suitable partner. The marriage is arranged by mutual agreement of the families and involves the satisfaction of precise practical criteria, which would take into consideration caste, horoscope, education, financial and social backgrounds. An example of an advertisement in the matrimonial column of a newspaper is the following:

> Wanted, Vadama Non-Bharadwaja (caste) bridegroom for girl 28 Servai Thosham, Secondary Grade trained, well versed in domestic duties. Also bride for her brother, 31, employed in State Bank Madurai, drawing RS 450. Mutual alliance alone considered. Reply with horoscope and full particulars Box No. 6731 c/o *The Hindu*.

Traditionally, the girl's parents search for a husband, though in low castes it is the other way round. Financial arrangements are still important, even though the dowry system is now illegal in India. Among high caste Hindus, a dowry would be expected from the girl, but in low castes, the bride is paid for.[53] There are still cases of girls being ill-treated by their new in-laws if their dowry turns out to be insufficient, or even dowry-deaths, where new brides are killed. The poorer the family, the heavier the dowry, but an educated girl, who could actually earn a living, would only need a small dowry. In many families today, expensive presents have replaced the dowry, the presents being given to an entire family by the bride's parents; the closer the relative, the more expensive the present.

Such arranged marriages are difficult for those of the Western tradition to understand, but different sociological factors need to be recognized. The woman will be brought into the male's family, often a large extended one, and will have responsibility as a mother. It is argued that this necessitates the same caste and similar cultural and religious backgrounds: a new bride will be unable to adapt to her new home if she is from a different caste. Yet there has been much debate over this aspect of arranged marriages in Hindu life. There is a certain clash of cultures for some Hindu children living, for example, in Britain. Having been born in this country, they question the old tradition. The reasons for such marriages which are applicable to the extended family are not always relevant to the situation of the nuclear family. Thus in the West, the Hindu's situation has been slightly modified in terms of arranged marriages, for boys and girls have the ability to intermix at school more freely and sometimes socially before marriage, whereas in India they have no such opportunity. Hindu parents in such circumstances today will sometimes accept their children's wishes provided they see that the marriages are suitable according to the criteria of educational and social background. In this case the marriage may be said to be semi-arranged. Child marriages are now forbidden by Indian law though they still occasionally occur. Such a practice used to be a means of ensuring that illicit sexual relations – and hence mixed-caste relationships – could never take place. The practice, though virtually obsolete, highlights the importance of caste purity in India.

Vivah: the marriage ceremony   Marriage is the domestic obligation of the twice-born or high classes in Hinduism. It is regarded as a religious duty for the production of sons and the stability of family and societal life. The marriage ceremony as a religious rite is very important. It is solemn, profound, and complex in form, stressing the mutual co-operation of bride and groom and, in many ways, is the combining of two *families* as much as two individuals.

Before the wedding takes place there are traditional customs to be observed which vary enormously. Anointing the prospective bride and groom with oil and turmeric usually takes place several times on the days running up to the actual ceremony. In particular, the family deities would be invoked, and Ganesh, the deity of Good Fortune, who removes all obstacles, would be a prominent focus of *puja*. The wedding ceremony is conducted within a specially erected canopy, called a *mandap* or *mandva*, which is decorated with coloured lights and tinsel. It is set up at the home of the bride, for it is the bride's family who will pay for the wedding. Before the wedding ceremony, the bride is ritually bathed, and the hands and soles of the feet are decorated with henna dye, making very attractive, intricate and long-lasting *mehndi* patterns. For the wedding, the bride generally wears a red *sari* threaded with gold and an immense amount of traditional jewellery, particularly on the head and face. It is traditional too for the bride to look particularly sad at her wedding and she is usually helped by her sisters as she walks to take her place under the canopy with her husband to be.

The bride's parents welcome the bridegroom's family ceremonially and both sets of relatives attend the ceremony performed by the priest. The father of the bride welcomes the bridegroom in a reverential, worshipful manner in view of the Hindu belief of Brahman within all and on this day the groom is treated as a god, the bride as a goddess. The father uses the same gestures as in *puja* before a deity; the groom's feet are washed and he is given the best of offerings. Traditionally, the groom should travel to the bride's home on a horse, with much ceremony and parading, so in India, he may have travelled at least some of the way in this manner before being greeted at the bride's home.

During the ceremony, the genealogies of the bride and groom are recited. A sacred fire is lit and offerings are made while *mantras* from the *Vedas* are recited. The ceremony is a few hours long but the most important part is the circumambulation of the sacred fire: it is this action, called *phera* or *bhavar*, which seals the marriage. On the last circumambulation, the bride, who has been seated on the right of the platform with her family, now sits on the left, with her new in-laws; she has effectively passed from one family into another. While customs vary, there is usually some form of binding the couple together symbolically. A white cord may be strung between the shoulders of the couple, representing the indissolubility of their new bond in marriage, or, threads are tied round each others' wrists. Another important feature is the sacred ceremony of seven steps, *saptapadi*, in which the couple take seven steps, each one symbolizing a different aspect of, and wish for, the couple's future life together – food, strength, increasing wealth, good fortune, children, long life and eternal friendship. These seven steps are the blessings hoped for in the marriage. At the close of each round, the bride touches a stone symbolic of the rock-like stability given to herself, to her husband, and to his family, and the ability to overcome obstacles throughout married life.

There is much emphasis on the unity of the two and the wish for a happy and long life for them both. The groom promises to be moderate in *dharma*, *artha*, and *kama* (what is right, material wealth, and pleasure), to care for his wife, allow her financial management of the home and to be faithful and affectionate to her. The bride promises support to her husband, to be faithful, non-extravagant, and to render her wifely duties without expecting anything in return. She promises to respect her husband's family and friends – an important consideration in view of her taking up home with her new in-laws – and to perform her domestic chores well. The ceremony concludes with prayers for good fortune and peace. It is generally followed by great celebration, often of lavish expense, the result of years of saving by the family.[54] The ceremony usually takes place in the home, but it may be followed by a visit to the temple. According to tradition the couple are to be continent for the first three days; this is an indication of the importance of the *contract* in the marriage. A ceremony known as *gauna* marks the departure of the bride to the home of the groom, but in the case of child marriages which, though illegal, still occur in India, the girl will stay at her parents' home until puberty.

Life in the home   It is the women of the family who are responsible for the running of the home and the raising of children. Motherhood is regarded as very important and a woman is considered to be a failure if she is without children, especially if she has no son. Death in childbirth is particularly appalling to the Hindu mind. It is the women, especially the head woman of the family who perform *puja* in the home, but no menstruating woman is allowed near the deities of the home shrine because, during menses, a woman is highly polluted, and purity in *puja* and *darsan* is, of course, essential. Additionally, a menstruating woman will not be able to enter the kitchen or come into contact in any way with food preparation. Neither can she enter a temple or shrine outside the home. Only after ritual bathing at the end of menses can a woman then resume normal domestic and religious life in the home. High caste women tend to be subject to more seclusion than lower caste women during menstruation. The status of wifehood and motherhood is ideal in the Indian mind and a married woman is considered "auspicious" because of her status.[55] While controlled by their husbands, married women generally support the idea of this auspicious but subordinate status.

Despite the emphasis on motherhood, abortion, which is legal in India, is very frequent. The amniocentesis test is now used widely to ascertain the sex of a child, and if the outcome suggests that the foetus is a girl, it may be aborted. Abortion, then, has become a means of birth control for many Hindu women. Particularly amongst the poor, it is better to abort in the case of a girl than to support another child, and in any case, the dowry price is so high for a low caste girl that it is cheaper to abort.[56] While contraception is praised and encouraged by the Indian government the importance of having sons to provide economic support, particularly in old age, and the need for sons to perform death rites, means that contraception is unlikely to be used until sufficient sons have been born. The Indian government has been sufficiently concerned about the misuse of the amniocentesis test to restrict its use to determine sex in 1994.

Whatever life in the home may be like, divorce for a woman is difficult, and practically impossible for women of the higher castes, despite the fact that the Hindu Marriage Act of 1955 made divorce legal for women. While Babb suggests that divorce is quite common among the lower castes[57] as is also the remarriage of widows, there is still a general feeling in village life that a wife is to blame if her husband dies. The divorced woman is regarded as "inauspicious" without her husband, and like the widow she can become something of an outcaste. However, particularly in urban areas, women do have more status these days than hitherto and can now own land, have their own salaries and open bank accounts. Yet a woman's self esteem still has much to do with devotion and loyalty to her husband. Customarily, without a husband, a woman is too inauspicious to attend weddings, to wear jewellery or coloured *saris*, and should cut her hair as a mark of her inauspicious nature. It is something of a sin if a woman survives her husband. And while such harsh ideas are in decline, they have by no means disappeared, particularly among the higher castes.

Death   Death is the last *samskara* and there is far more emphasis in death rites on the deceased joining his or her ancestors than the more philosophical ideas of *samsara* and *moksa*. Like birth, death is considered to be a highly polluting time, so polluting in fact that the deities of the home are often removed entirely, and no one would partake of food from the home of the deceased. Contact with the dead cuts a person off from the normal routine of life. It is the sons of a person who become so important in the rites of passage concerning death. Their role is to send the spirit of the deceased to the realm of the ancestors through correct ritual. Immediately afer death, the deceased becomes a *preta*, a "ghost" and, if not sent on its way correctly, will disturb the living by remaining with them and causing them harm. The death rites are designed to change the *preta* into a *pitri*, an "ancestral spirit": this takes twelve days in all and when this is done, the spirit of the deceased leaves the family for the abode of his or her ancestors. On the twelfth day, four balls of rice, called *pinda*, are prepared to symbolize the union of the deceased with his or her forebears: one rice ball is for the newly deceased, three for the preceding three generations. The special ceremonies which are performed during the twelve days following the cremation are known as *sraddha* ceremonies. Death rites are important not only for the future of the dead but also for the continued welfare of the living and, since only a male can effectuate them, the importance of sons to ensure the safety of the deceased spirit is emphasized.

Cremation has always been the traditional Indian means of disposing of human remains. The reduction of the body to ashes by fire is not only an extremely hygienic way of disposing of the dead in the heat of India (fire being an efficient purifier) but cremation is commensurate with the Hindu belief that the soul is immortal but the body not so. The deceased is washed, and the corpse is wrapped in a cloth, white for men and red for women, and carried to the cremation ground in a procession led by the eldest son, who also lights the funeral pyre. The dead body will be placed on the funeral pyre with the feet facing south towards the home of Yama, ruler of the dead. It is covered with wood, and then ghee, and funeral rites are enacted by a priest. After cremation the youngest member of the family leads the procession home. The bones of the cremated body are thrown into water, an important process because immersing something in water has a cooling and purifying effect and, in this case, is deemed to purify and release the spirit from this world. The cremation grounds are to be found on the banks of a river for the purpose of immersing the bones in such a way.

A Hindu funeral is an inauspicious occasion: refreshment will not be partaken of by the mourners since the life-giving process should have no association with death and any food would carry pollution.

While cremation is the desired method of disposal of the dead, burial is not uncommon. The lower castes in particular practise burial because it is cheaper, and children who die are buried rather than cremated, especially babies who die before the naming ceremony. A *sannyasin* will also often not undergo cremation. Cremation frees the soul from the body, but because it is believed that a *sannyasin's* soul is already at one with Brahman, the body is dropped into the river and weighted with stones. As it sinks, disciples chant hymns and blow conch shells to celebrate the union of the soul with God. Some, however, are buried, for they have abandoned their families and sons and have given up all identity to make death rites pertinent to them as individuals. *Gurus* may also be buried, often seated in the lotus position. A monument called a *samadhi* is used to mark such a place of burial.

In the towns of India, cremation by gas or electricity is the norm as it is in Britain. In Britain the custom is slightly different because of legal requirements. The body will be washed and dressed in new clothes, placed in a coffin and surrounded by flowers. Cremation has to take place after a few days because of the necessary legal arrangements. At the crematorium the priest will talk about the life of the person and after returning to the house, prayers are said for the departed soul in front of the sacred fire. The ashes of the deceased would preferably be sent to a relative in India to be scattered in the Ganges or, failing this, cast into a fast-flowing river in Britain.

When the period of death rites is over, the close, male relatives cut or shave their hair in order to remove the pollution of death. The house has to be thoroughly cleaned and a washerman is given all the linen to wash, the washerman being traditionally low caste, because polluted materials are continually handled. Only when the house has been thoroughly cleansed can the household deities be returned.

FOOD AND DRESS

Vegetarianism Although Hinduism has few dietary laws, eating habits are influenced by religious belief, by caste regulations, and particularly by concepts of purity and pollution. On a more general level, since all life is sacred, it is considered wrong to kill animals for food, though many Hindus are not vegetarians. The cow, however, is sacred to Hinduism, and few Hindus would partake of beef or veal. While cows are not exactly worshipped, they are well-loved and would not be slaughtered for meat. They can be seen roaming through the towns in India, grazing on grass verges or munching vegetables discarded by street sellers and, often, vegetables which are for sale! Bahree points out, rather well, that the cow is sometimes believed to be a symbol of the earth because it gives yet asks nothing in return.[58] Apart from being afforded protection on religious grounds, it makes good economic sense to protect the cow. Meat is difficult to preserve in the heat of India, and few people having the economic standing to afford refridgeration. It is also expensive, so even those Hindus who are not really vegetarians cannot afford to buy meat on a regular basis. Many Hindus, however, eat meat at the weekends. Generally, too, meat is not considered to be very healthy to eat, whereas the by-products of the milk of the cow are considered to be very important for good health.

From a religious point of view, meat is a polluting material and considering that many homes have their shrines in the kitchen, the purest place in the house, bringing meat into the proximity of the deities would be sacrilegious, polluting the deities themselves. Some Hindus will not allow meat anywhere near the kitchen. On the other hand, people flock to the temples or shrines for the ritual slaughter of animals, the goat in particular, as an offering to the female deities. Since such sacrifice to the Mother Goddess, especially Kali, is such an important aspect of ritual, it is difficult to conclude that a principle such as *ahimsa*, non-violence to any living creature, is adhered to entirely. The sacrificial goat is offfered to the deity, its *essence* extracted by the deity, and it is then returned to the owner as *prasad*, for cooking and consumption. *Brahmin* priests are rarely involved in such sacrifice which is officiated over by lower caste priests mainly in the smaller village shrines and temples. Deities, however, could never be wholly offered animal sacrifices without other forms of *puja* offerings. Hindus have come to regard those who accept animal sacrifice as belonging to inferior castes, and their deities as inferior recipients.[59]

There are a significant number of Hindus who are vegetarians and most of these would avoid eating eggs also. Since India is so vast, there are considerable regional variations in diet and cooking, but there are a number of common elements. High protein foods are particularly important in a vegetarian diet, and *dal*, a lentil dish, is popular throughout India. Rice dishes are a particular feature of southern India, and the flat bread known as *chapatti* or *paratha* is preferred in many parts of India. Vegetables cooked in spices are also popular.

Caste regulations   A major area of influence on eating habits is that of caste. Traditionally, a Hindu should not accept food, especially cooked food, from someone of a lower caste, since the food would be polluted: any food which another person touches or smells, is really polluted, but cooked food is particularly vulnerable to the *essence* of the person cooking it. The danger of pollution is, therefore, far greater from cooked than uncooked food. Though the custom is now dying out, it used to be common sense to employ only *Brahmin* cooks and waiters in a restaurant, because anyone can eat the food prepared by a *Brahmin*.

Pukka and *katcha* foods   Certain foods are preferred because they are *pukka*. These would be foods which are deep-fried in ghee. In contrast, leftovers which are re-heated, or left to be eaten later or the next day, are considered as stale food, *katcha*. Food cooked in water is especially *katcha*. From a religious point of view foods which are *sattvic* in quality are superior. The *Bhagavad-Gita* tells us that such foods are "savoury, fatty and substantial"[60] by which is probably meant milk, butter and cheese. Also included would be rice, pulses, sugar and wheat. *Rajasic* food, the *Gita* says is "bitter, sour, saline, excessively hot, pungent, dry and burning"[61] and these are foods which are likely to make the eyes water and the stomach burn – something which could be said for the strong curries often associated with Indian food! Garlic and onions fit into this category, being harmful *rajasic* foods which militate against the more desirable *sattvic* qualities in life. *Tamasic* foods are stale, tasteless, rotten foods which have lost their goodness through staleness and over cooking. Rotten food is really something left over from one day to the next.[62] Meat would certainly be considered as a *tamasic* food. The particular balance between hot and cold foods and heating and cooling in cooking is believed to be very important for bodily and spiritual health.[63]

The role of women   It is the women of the home who are responsible for the diet, being in charge of all food preparation and even of the keeping of fasts in the family. They ensure that the kitchen is kept thoroughly pure and that no impurities such as leather are worn. Visitors would not normally be allowed in a Hindu kitchen because of such purity rules. Normally women bathe before preparing food, and it is the senior woman who organizes its preparation. Since the left hand is associated with unclean aspects of life such as use of the toilet, it is only the right hand which is used in eating food. But while women maintain the strict codes of purity in the preparation of food, they themselves eat only the leftovers from the males of the family. The *Laws of Manu*, an ancient religious code which lays down all sorts of regulations for class, caste, and kingly rule, had much to say about the role of women but emphasized especially that a woman should treat her husband as a god. And since food was offered to the deities and the "leftovers" were received back by the worshipper, the women were to treat their husbands as gods and eat their leftovers as *prasad*, a custom which is still maintained in India today, though not so frequently in Western Hindu cultures.

Dress There is no particular type of religious dress required in Hinduism and local and regional styles differ considerably. The traditional dress for women is the *sari*, a piece of material five or six metres long which is wrapped and pleated around the waist and then drawn round over the shoulder so that the free end is left loose and flowing. In different parts of India, the *sari* is wrapped in different ways. In company, in the temple or when attending *puja*, women will normally cover their hair with the loose end of their *saris*, or they may use a separate long piece of material called a *dupatta*: this is light in weight and matches the sari. Covering the head is a sign of respect to God as well as to other people. Underneath the *sari*, an ankle length skirt is worn and a bolero-type blouse called a *choli*. In northern India, especially in the Punjab, women prefer to wear light, baggy trousers called *salvar*, and a long loose-fitting tunic called a *kameeze*.

Indian women in general love jewellery and are particularly fond of bracelets and anklets. Bangles, rings, necklaces, earrings, toe rings and nose rings are also popular, as well as a jewel in the nose, something which has become popular amongst Western young people today. Long earlobes have always indicated nobility in Indian tradition and were a sign of respectability. Sometimes heavy earrings are used to stretch the earlobes slightly. A married woman can be recognized by the *bindi* in the centre of the forehead, between the eyebrows. This may be applied with a spot of red paste, or it may be a circle of adhesive felt which can more easily be put on. Felt *bindis* have the advantage of being decorated with sequins and can be different shapes. In some parts of India it is fashionable for young girls also to wear a *bindi*. Dress is designed to cover the legs, but Hindu women can have their arms and midriff bare.

Hindu men very often wear Western clothing, but many will wear a *kurta-pyjama*, a loose-fitting shirt and trousers. Typical Indian village dress for men has customarily been the *dhoti*, a garment immortalized by Mahatma Gandhi. This single piece of usually white cloth is worn wrapped around the waist and tucked up between the legs. In the south of India, a *lungi* is worn by men, a piece of usually brightly coloured cloth which is also wrapped round the waist but which reaches almost down to the ankles. The wearing of a turban is usually associated with Sikh men, but in India some Hindu men will also wear turbans though they are tied in a very different way to Sikh styles.

HINDU FESTIVALS

Hindu religion is rich in life, colour and emotion. Its festivals, in particular, are characterized by happiness, music, perfumed fires, countless candles, gaily decked elephants, and so on. Life is to be enjoyed, for the world is the joyous creation of God. Festivals are connected with the moon in Hinduism because the religion follows a lunar calendar. In some ways they are also suited to the seasons; the hot dry seasons will be characterized by certain types of festivals, while the rainy season, which brings out poisonous snakes, scorpions and disease, when the people feel insecure, will be reflected in different types of festivals. *Raksa Bandhan* is a good example of this.[64] Additionally, the rainy season begins about mid-June and is a time when the deities are believed to be asleep and demons and evil forces can become active. Hindus are very fond of their festivals for they are a time of great enjoyment. Most families have a festival day each week, depending on the particular God they worship. Monday, for example is in honour of the God Siva, or the Moon, Tuesday Hanuman (also Saturday), Wednesday Ganesh, Thursday Sarasvati, Friday the minor goddesses, and Sunday the Mother Goddess. Saturday is a very inauspicious day, a "dark" day, governed by the planet Saturn. Some festivals are celebrated every fortnight, others every year.

On a festival day a purification bath would be taken (in India, if possible, in a holy river or lake) and new, or at least clean, clothes put on. There would be longer *puja* than usual, singing, dancing, fasting, feasting and visits to the temple. Festivals can be national, regional or local celebrating also births and deaths of famous local or national people. The government even allows each citizen to have occasional days' holiday for celebration of festivals on those days when public holidays do not occur.

The Festival of *Divali* (Oct./Nov.)   *Divali*, a five-day festival, means "cluster of lights", the name being a contraction of *Dipavali*. The festival is so called because homes, cowsheds, temples, offices, etc., are decorated with coloured electric lights or clay *Divali* lamps (*divas*) containing a wick floating in oil. Lots of stories are associated with the festival. It is said that the Goddess Kali was born at this time, and that the Goddess Laksmi, the wife of the God Visnu, visits each house which is clean and brightly lit and will bring gifts and prosperity during the coming year. Another story concerns the God Visnu in his incarnation as Krisna. Krisna defeated a demon called Naraka but when Naraka was dying he asked a boon of Krisna. Naraka asked that his death should be mourned on its anniversary but in a happy way, with new clothes, fireworks, greetings sent to family and friends and lights to brighten the night. Krisna granted his request with the festival of *Divali*. However, the most well-known story connected with the festival is that of the *Ramayan*. In the holy city of Benares, the *Ramayan* is acted out over a period of thirty days for the festival. When Ram eventually found his wife Sita, with the help of Hanuman the monkey, they eventually returned to Ayodhya, from which place they had been banished fourteen years previously. They were met with joyous celebration and rows and rows of coloured lights to mark the triumph of light over darkness, good over evil.

At *Divali*, families will try to meet together, and a man will take his wife home to her parents. Boys are often given a party by their sisters and cousins, new clothes are worn, and each house is cleaned and decorated. It is a time for whitewashing the houses and buildings and making everything look as clean and attractive as possible. Girls make intricate designs called *rangoli* patterns in coloured chalk in front of their houses. Animals are washed, groomed and decorated and will have bells put around their necks and special food to eat. The festival marks the beginning of the new business year so accounts are settled so that no one is in debt and everyone, particularly children, tries to turn over a new leaf. In Britain there would not be so much emphasis on outdoor activities, but a lot of dancing, speeches and parties. In India, dancing groups tour the towns and cities performing for money. Presents will be exchanged and *Divali* cards sent to friends and relatives at home and abroad.

Divali also has a personal touch, since each girl makes a *Divali* lamp of her own and in India if she lives near a river, she will set her light afloat on the river on a small raft. This is done in darkness, and if the lamp stays alight for as long as she can see it, she will have good luck during the coming year. The festival also chases off demons, and peals of bells are often heard to ensure this. In essence, *Divali* is representative of the triumph of light over darkness, of good over evil and the rows of *divas*, the little lamps outside the homes, are symbols of this light and goodness.

Holi (**March/April**) *Divali* has traditionally been associated with the *Vaisya* class although every Hindu celebrates it. Similarly, *Holi* is a festival associated with the *Sudras*, the fourth class, and is celebrated in northern and central India. While not strictly a New Year festival, since the New Year begins two weeks later, many of its festivities are linked with the destruction in flames of the old and the bringing in of the new. It occurs at the time of the spring harvest and is associated with riotous merriment. Because it welcomes spring, it is an outdoor festival, although in the West it is often celebrated in February. In Indian villages, bonfires are lit and mothers often carry their babies five times in a clockwise direction around the fire, so that Agni the god of Fire will bless the babies with a successful life. People throw coloured powder dyes over everyone they meet or use such things as bicycle pumps to squirt this coloured water over anyone they can.

Holi possibly derives its name from Holika. Holika was the daughter of the mythical King Hiranyakasipu who commanded everyone to worship him. His little son Prahlada refused to do so and even learnt his alphabet with the names of the Gods – V = Visnu, S = Siva, etc. His father ordered Holika to kill him and she, possessing the ability to walk through fire unharmed, picked up the child and walked into a fire with him. Prahlada, however, chanted the names of God and was saved. Holika perished because she did not know that her powers were only effective if she entered the fire alone. The practice of hurling cowdung into the fire and shouting obscenities at it, as if at Holika, suggests a strong association of the festival with this particular story. But others celebrate *Holi* in memory of Krisna. In the legends about Krisna as a youth he is depicted as getting up to all sorts of pranks with the *gopis* or cowgirls. One prank was to throw coloured powder all over them, so at *Holi* images of Krisna and his consort Radha are often carried through the streets. *Holi* occurs at the hottest time of the year and is characterized by "heated" behaviour. At this festival practices are allowed which could not obtain at other times. It is obviously easy to victimize someone with whom an old score has to be settled, and there is much obscene behaviour connected with phallic themes. There is a relaxation of normal caste rules, though not to the extent that *Brahmins* and *Dalits* would engage in any kind of contact, and servants do not take advantage of their masters. Yet some sources suggest that *Dalits* will chase *Brahmins*, and labourers' wives have been known to beat the shins of their rich, high-caste farmers.[65] Women, especially, enjoy the freedom of relaxed rules and sometimes join in the merriment rather aggressively. It is a time too when meat can be eaten by vegetarians, a time when pollution is not important, a time for license and obscenity in place of the usual caste and societal restrictions. Coming at the hottest time of the year, it is a means for people themselves to release heat, to let off steam!

Raksa Bandhan (July/Aug.)   This festival has always been associated with the *Brahmin* class. It takes place when the rainy season has begun and has ideas of protection and security built into it. It is a time when members of the twice-born classes replace their sacred threads with new ones. In addition male Hindus may be given a bracelet of string or tinsel which they wear on their right wrist. This has its significance in another Indian myth in which the wife of the god Indra tied a magic string around the wrist of the demon Bali, adopting him as her brother so that he would not kill her husband. Sisters tie such *rakhis* on their brothers' wrists and girls on the wrists of men who are their protectors. The males are expected to reward the girls with a present, and protect them wherever they may be. The increasingly popular Goddess Santosi Ma is said to have been born at this time and her image is to be found on many of the *rakhis*.[66]

Krisna Janamastami (July/Aug.)   This celebrates the birthday of Krisna who was born at midnight. The baby Krisna is greeted with singing and dancing all night long. In the temple, sweet foods are eaten by everyone. Fasting follows in the daytime and a feast in the evening, while stories about Krisna are told, sung and danced.

Ugadi (March/April)   *Divali* forms the New Year Festival for some Hindus but the real New Year Festival is *Ugadi*. *Ugadi* is the real time for turning over a new leaf, and renewal and change are the hallmarks of the festival. People get up much earlier on the day of the festival in order to clean the house thoroughly and decorate it with patterns of flour or rice which is hoped will bring good luck and happiness. Then a purifying bathe is taken and sweet-scented oils are rubbed onto the body. New clothes are worn and the rich will often buy new clothes for the poor at this time. The sacred thread of the three twice-born classes is also renewed. Many Hindus consult astrologers to discover what will happen in the year ahead.

Ram Navami (**March/April**)   This is the birthday of Ram, the *avatar* of Visnu. The day is a fast day when certain usual foods cannot be eaten, but unusual delicacies are eaten instead. The reading of the *Ramayan* is particularly important at this festival.

Navaratri (or *Durga Puja*) (**Sept./Oct.**)   This is a nine-day festival, devoted to the goddess Durga. *Navaratri* means "nine nights" and so celebrations take place in the evenings. People dance around shrines of Durga and many fast, having one meal of fruit and sweet foods made with milk each day. The festival remembers the time when Ram turned to Durga for help when his wife Sita had been stolen by the demon king Ravan. The festival may once have been a harvest festival since sticks, perhaps representing sickles, are a prominent feature of the dances. Since Durga is the divine Mother, married daughters return home to their mothers. The festival is associated with the Spring and Autumnal equinoxes but the major festival has always been the Autumn event, the Spring festival being a minor occasion.

Dussehra (**Sept./Oct.**)   This festival occurs at the end of *Durga Puja* and means "the tenth". It celebrates the defeat of the demon King Ravan in the story of the *Ramayan*, and the death of Ravan along with his brother and son. Huge images are often carried through the streets and then burnt. It is a festival to celebrate the triumph of good over evil, like many Hindu festivals. Also at this festival, the power of the deity departs from the statue of Durga and the *murti* is immersed in the river taking with it all unhappiness and misfortune. The friendship involved in the rescue of Sita from the hands of Ravan is also embodied in this festival and Hindus try to make up any quarrels and renew loyalties. It reminds them of the importance of God's love and protection. The festival is a special time for *puja* in the home and temple and for wives to worship their husbands, as Sita did with Ram. So in some parts of India wives wash their husbands' feet, put a *tilak* on their foreheads, put garlands around their necks, give them offerings, and bow down to them. In the north of India the festival actually overlaps with that of Ram Lila, "Ram's Play", suggesting a possible convergence of festivals for both Durga and Ram.[67]

Mahasivatri (Feb./March)   Each lunar month is divided into two parts, the light part when the moon is waxing and the dark part when the moon is waning. *Mahasivatri* is celebrated on the thirteenth day of the dark part of every month. This day is sacred to Siva, the creator/destroyer God, and is thus called "The great Night of Siva". On this day there is a fast until 4.00 p.m. and then *puja* is offered to Siva. Afterwards no cereals or curries are eaten but sweet potatoes and cucumbers are a favourite substitute. Since the festival celebrates Siva's marriage to Parvati, married women worship Siva with requests for the welfare of their husbands and, traditionally, unmarried girls who keep vigil throughout the night hope that a suitable husband will be found for them by Siva. The following day is one of feasting. The festival is sometimes called *Chaturdasi*, "the fourteenth", after this feast day on the fourteenth.

Ganesh Chaturthi (Sept.)   At this festival the elephant-headed God Ganesh, God of Good Fortune is worshipped. Model images of the God made in clay are carried through the streets and then dropped in the sea or lake, taking misfortune with them.

Days of remembrance also occur for more contemporary Hindus such as Swami Vivekananda, a modern preacher and leader who introduced the Rama-Krishna movement in America. The birthday of Sri Ramakrishna, the nineteenth-century saint and reformer, is also celebrated in March.

YATRA: PILGRIMAGE

The importance of pilgrimage   Pilgrimages are rituals which are *kamya*, that is to say, they are desirable but not obligatory. Because Brahman is believed to be manifest in everything, It is everywhere and so every place is sacred – rivers, mountains, coasts, groves, etc. But there are many sites where the divine has in some way become more explicitly manifest on earth and such places are subsequently felt to be the best and most auspicious sites for contact with the divine. *Yatra* to such sites is considered very auspicious and *karmically* rewarding. Consequently, everyone seems to be on the move in India. Many pilgrimages are undertaken to acquire good *karma*, to perform certain rituals for deceased ancestors (something often considered obligatory) or because of a festival. Some people make the journey through an organized tour, some by public transport and some on foot. The emphasis is very much on showing devotion to the divine, and men and women of all castes travel on the same roads to a centre of pilgrimage. Whatever caste a Hindu belongs to, visiting a sacred place is believed to purify the inner self and so bring the individual closer to God. Thus in some cases pilgrimages offset the usual caste barriers, but in others, such divisions persist, especially where commensality is concerned.

There are hundreds of places of pilgrimage all over India but twenty-four temples have become the most important. Most Hindus hope to visit the four famous shrines of the Jagannath temple at Puri on the Bay of Bengal in East India, the temple of Ramesvaram in the South of India, Dvarkadheesh on the Western coast, and Badrinath in the north, 10,400 feet up in the Himalayas. Some Hindus spend their life's savings visiting these shrines, and will often undergo severe hardships on these journeys. At a deeper level pilgrimage, and its often arduous accomplishment, is like a journey within one's own self, a journey to the divine. The individual has to overcome both mental and physical challenges as well as plain discomfort, uncomfortable surroundings, theft, inadequate sanitation, shortage of food and so on. Such problems have to be transcended rather like the *sannyasin* transcends the world: it is a taste of the life of the renouncer. This again is an expression of devotion to God and to spiritual matters rather than material ones. Essentially, the *whole journey* becomes an act of devotion and is as important as the final destination. Pilgrims can often be heard singing *bhajans* on their way as they travel by walking or by coach. The journey itself serves to help people transcend normal ties and routines in life. Pilgrimage also helps the Hindu to be tolerant and aware of other Hindus in the vastness of India, since India has Hindus of different ethnic origins. On a pilgrimage Hindus will meet other Hindus who have differences in language and dialect and who eat different food. While undertaking a pilgrimage of a considerable distance from their homes they will encounter cultural differences as much in their own country of India as people elsewhere travelling to new and different countries: India is vast enough for this to be the case. So wherever one is in India one sees Indians from all backgrounds and areas. In many ways, then, pilgrimage epitomizes the Hindu religion, a point well expressed in the following words:

> The Hindu places of pilgrimage are the symbols of the religious beliefs
> of Hinduism; they reflect its vitality, resilience, and syncretism. They
> broadly define and continually reemphasize the Hindu sacred space.
> They have knitted the linguistically diverse Hindu population socially,
> culturally, and spatially at different integrative levels. Their significance
> is to be measured in their capacity to generate and maintain a massive
> system of religious circulation.[68]

Benares (Varanasi)   Benares is the most famous centre of pilgrimage. It is situated on the left bank of the Ganges, at the point near where the tributary of the Ganges, the Yamuna or Varuna, joins it. Confluences of rivers are considered to be particularly auspicious sites for temples and have traditionally been associated with *asrams*, the homes of famous Hindu sages. Benares is especially associated with the God Siva who is believed to have lived there as an ascetic. Also at

Benares, the thirty-day enactment of the *Ramayan* takes place each year at the *Dussehra* festival. Benares is associated with Vedic and Sanskrit scholarship so Indian scholars travel there. The place is considered to be so sacred that if one dies there and has one's ashes thrown into the Ganges, purification and release from *samsara* is achieved. The same is believed of the river at Hardwar in northern India.

Puri   At Puri in eastern India, there is a very famous temple dedicated to Jagannath, the Lord of the Universe. Jagganath is the manifestation of the God Visnu as Master of the Universe, and pilgrims and the people of Puri pull a huge cart around the town on which a statue of Krisna is placed (this is the origin of the English word "juggernaut").

Vrindaban and Ramesvaram   Two places in particular are associated with *avatars* of Visnu. Vrindaban on the river Yamuna is said to be the birthplace of Krisna. The area is associated with stories about the childhood and youth of Krisna and, in addition, pilgrims can visit Dvarka on the west coast, which is the place where Krisna had his palace. Also associated with the God Siva, Ramesvaram, on the southern-most tip of India, opposite Sri Lanka, is a famous place of pilgrimage associated with Ram. When Ram succeeded in rescuing his wife from the demon king Ravan he landed at this city and built a shrine to Siva in order to purify himself and his wife Sita after the killing of Ravan's soldiers.

Kumbha Mela   Every twelve years at Allahabad, and in turn at other highly sacred places, a huge religious fair is held called *Kumbha Mela*. Fifteen million people attended the last one there in January 1989. *Kumbha* means "Aquarius" and the gatherings take place when the sun passes the sign of Aquarius and so are called *Kumbha Melas*. Literally millions of people attend these huge fairs. Such fairs, *melas*, are common and have all the characteristics of fairs with the carnival atmosphere, side shows, numerous stalls, acrobats and so on, but the *Kumbha Mela* is a spectacular event, attended by people from all over India.

Rivers   Pilgrimages are called *tirthayatras*, a term which means "journeys to the sacred fords", even though many pilgrimages today have nothing to do with rivers. But the term highlights well the importance which rivers have always held in Hindu pilgrimage and most pilgrimages today are associated in some way with water.[69] Offerings of flowers, fruits or money are still thrown into the Ganges as an act of worship. Rivers are thus a prominent feature of pilgrimage. Water means life, and rivers represent the life-giving nature of God. Water not only washes outwardly but is symbolic of inner spiritual cleansing.

The banks of rivers have been the favourite dwelling places of the Gods, the Hindu *gurus* and sages, and have been the scene in which many Hindu scriptures have been composed. The Ganges is the most sacred river, a gift from heaven, and to ritually bathe in it (*Ganga snam*), or drink from it, is highly purifying and meritorious. So all Hindus hope to bathe in the Ganges once in their lifetime and hope that their ashes will be cast into it. The *ghats* along the river are the huge steps from which the bathers descend into the Ganges and the fires of the cremation *ghats* along the river are perpetually kept burning. Those cremated here are believed to be released from *samsara* as a result of a boon from Visnu. The Yamuna, or Varuna, is the second most sacred river and Krisna is said to have lived on its banks during his early years. Other sacred rivers are the Godavari, Narmada, Sindhu (or Indus) and Kaveri.

Hinduism is thus a complexity of widely different practices, beliefs, customs and traditions. Its classic accommodation of ideas, rather than the discarding of the old or the assimilation of the new, has served to make it a religion of colourful and profound variety, rich in myth and containing the kind of breadth in its dimensions to cater for all levels of consciousness. Yet, despite such openness to the infinite paths to God, societal life, as we have seen, remains largely class and caste bound, so it would be true to say that while the paths to the divine are infinite, the *karmic* and *dharmic* placements of birth dictate to a considerable extent which of the multitude of paths an individual must take. This typifies the complexities of the religion rather well, illustrating the dualities and opposites which manifest existence necessarily contains – yet all are ultimately united in the Absolute, Brahman.

5

Buddhism

Jeaneane Fowler

> This shall ye think of
> all this fleeting world;
> a star at dawn;
> a bubble in a stream;
> a flash of lightning in a summer cloud;
> a flickering lamp;
> a phantom of a dream.
>
> *Diamond Sutra*

WHAT IS BUDDHISM?

Although we cannot avoid using the designation, there is not really a single, identifiable phenomenon which could be called "Buddhism". While it is certainly true to say that there was, in the middle of the first millennium BCE, a mortal who seemed to have found answers to the existential suffering of life, and who became known as *the Buddha*, the kaleidoscopic strands which emerged from the life and teaching of that one man are as innumerable as the leaves of a giant oak tree emerging from one acorn. To define Buddhism is impossible and it has been aptly said that Buddhism is "whatever Buddhist men and women have said, done, and held dear".[1] And Buddhist men and women have said very different things about what it is to be Buddhist, have adopted widely different practices associated with being Buddhist and have adapted traditions to their own specific cultural and pre-Buddhist heritages.

So Buddhism is something of an "umbrella" term used to depict a variety of different beliefs and practices of those who call themselves "Buddhists". In some of the branches of Buddhism there is still evident much of the earlier, original thought, but in others there have been developments which have made the resultant beliefs and practices very different from the Buddhism of the time of its founder. We therefore need to be very careful about using the term "Buddhism" in a generalized sense since what may be relevant to one area of Buddhism may not be for another. In particular there are two major extant strands of Buddhism, *Theravada* and *Mahayana*, and although there are similarities between some aspects of the two, Mahayana Buddhism, being the later strand, is much more varied. And it is Mahayana Buddhism which has had the remarkable tendency to adapt readily to the environment in which it finds itself thus effecting the present diversity of Buddhism. Theravada Buddhism, however, being the more conservative of the two strands, is less diverse in character, and its historically conservative nature allows some generalism concerning beliefs.

Particularly in association with the Theravadin school, it could be suggested that Buddhism is more of a philosophy than a religion. This is because in Theravada Buddhism there is no concept of any kind of omnipotent, creator God who is responsible for the world, either an indescribable Absolute, or theistic or anthropomorphic God. Though there are gods these are nothing more than fellow travellers in the cycle of many lives of any individual. Theravada Buddhism has twenty-six different levels of such gods but they are all subject to *kamma* – the law of cause and effect – and to its related process of rebirth: though the gods of these realms are sometimes used as the focus of prayers for earthly matters, they are of no use on the spiritual quest. In Mahayana Buddhism, we would have less of a problem for there are a number of elements which accept some sort of Absolute or Ultimate Reality, though the theory is a contentious one.[2] But the term "philosophy" is not really a suitable one for many strands of Buddhism, since it suggests a system of belief which involves a great deal of theorizing and this is something which Buddhism, in general, does not agree with. Buddhism is very much an *active* religion, not one which you philosophize about but one which you actually *do*. The Buddha, Siddhatta Gotama (Sanskrit Siddhartha Gautama), did not really advocate wasting time in endless debate about whether beliefs were true, or would work. To use an analogy of his, if a person is shot with a poisoned arrow, what would be the point of not removing the arrow until he or she had discovered who had shot it, for what reason, from which position, and what was the nature of the poison on the tip! If we get on with things, we shall soon find out whether they work or not. Much of Buddhism is thus a way of *action* and it matters not to most whether there is an Ultimate Reality or not: it is making Buddhism a living way of life which is important. Trevor Ling stressed this practical, existential nature of Buddhism when he depicted it as a "theory of existence", a theory which diagnoses the existential condition of humankind and prescribes its active cure.[3]

THE LIFE OF THE BUDDHA

The word buddha means "enlightened one", "one who has intellect/ knowledge", or "awakened one" and it is a title given to Siddhatta Gotama because he became "enlightened" The idea of becoming enlightened or, in particular, awakening, is important, for to many, though not all, Buddhists, it suggests an awakening to what has previously been hidden or unknown, an enlightenment to the true nature of things, a waking up to what is already there. The word *buddha*, some Buddhists point out, is a common noun, thus indicating that anyone can "wake up" to the reality of what life is. But it is specifically used to refer to Siddhatta Gotama as the one who "awakened" in this aeon and who left his teachings, his *Dhamma*.[4] If we wanted to maintain a strictly accurate historical analysis of the life of the Buddha, very little of his life story would emerge. Indeed it is well nigh impossible to extract from the religious tradition, the more secular historical facts about his life. In any case, to do so would be to extinguish the flame of the beginnings of Buddhism and rob it of its whole essence and meaning in the lives of its adherents: indeed, such a model would present a distorted picture of what *living* Buddhism really is.

So any analysis of the life of the Buddha is beset by innumerable difficulties. To the early Buddhists it was not the life of the Buddha which was important but his *teaching*, the *Dhamma*. It was almost half a millennium later that the *life* of the Buddha was felt to be sufficiently significant to be recorded in minute detail, but by this time records were dependent mainly on oral traditions which had survived in a variety of schools and early canonical writings which did not focus on his life. The later the writing the more legendary the account, producing what has been described as "a fabric of myth and literary invention"[5] In presenting an account of the life of the Buddha, therefore, I do not intend to be pedantic about the historical facts but to portray instead something of the story of the Buddha in a way that would be acceptable to many Buddhists themselves: and this means to include the textual embellishments and hagiographical content which has become essential to many Buddhist traditions.

While being a Hindu by birth (though "Hinduism" was scarcely developed at the time), the Buddha was probably heir to less Hindu tradition than most, for the Sakya tribe to which he belonged was renowned for its independent spirit and for its rejection of the brahmanical teachings of the Hinduism of the time. Indeed, Siddhatta may have been a *samanna* (Sanskrit *sramana*), one who searched for the Truth independently of orthodox religion. He was born into a high class, prestigious and wealthy, Hindu family in Nepal about 560 years BCE[6] in the Lumbini garden at Kapilavatthu. The family was high class *Ksatriya* and would probably have been influenced in some ways by the Vedic traditions of early Hinduism. According to many texts, his father was a *raja*, a ruler of the area, though it is possible that his father, Suddhodana, was a leading citizen of Kapilavastu rather than a *raja*.[7] He may well have been head of a council of household leaders in the Sakya tribe of the particular clan of Gotama.[8] Many traditions, even early ones, record portentous and miraculous events associated with Siddhatta's conception and birth. His father, like all Indian fathers, would have been proud to have a son, and like so many fathers he would have expected his son to follow in his own footsteps, one day becoming a ruler or head official himself. However, when Siddhatta was still young, a *Brahmin* sage prophesied that he could become an enlightened being who would help others to overcome their suffering in life and eight *Brahmins* were soon to confirm this of the baby. Since the life of a sage meant the life of a mendicant, a wandering beggar, dressed in only a loin cloth and destined to wander from place to place with no permanent home and no connections with any family, this seemed far removed from the kind of life which Suddhodana had in mind for his son.

Anxious that Siddhatta should not leave his wealthy home, Suddhodana did everything in his power to ensure that his son was surrounded by all which was pleasant and that he would never know anything of suffering in the world: without knowing that there was suffering, how could one do anything about it? So Siddhatta was brought up in a life of luxury. His wealthy father probably owned three residences, one for each of the seasons – rainy, winter and summer: this would have been the custom for wealthy people at the time[9] and Siddhatta grew up in this kind of environment in which he had everything he could wish for.

Eventually, Siddhatta married and it seemed that he had everything good which life could offer and he had grown to manhood without any experiences of unpleasantness. But this was an extreme of indulgence and opulence, and life being what it is never allows such a perpetual and permanent imbalance. The earlier texts suggest that within himself Siddhatta began to turn away from carefree luxury as a result of gradual reflectiveness about the nature and meaning of life. The later texts, however, present a more dramatic picture of a Siddhatta who was curious about existence beyond the confines of his immediate environment. He was aware that there was a world beyond the palace about which he knew nothing and so he begged his father to allow him to travel outside. His father reluctantly agreed, but before Siddhatta could venture forth, he made sure that any unpleasant sights were removed; and of these, there must have been many in the India of his day.

At last, Siddhatta rode out with his chariot driver into the world beyond his wealthy home for the very first time. The later texts present the journey as a very physical one, the earlier texts being more suggestive of a journey into the self. Either way, the result was the same in that Siddhatta came to know in the very core of his being the existential fragility and impermanence of all life. To the later texts this experience took the form of three signs, and a further fourth one that transformed his experiences in a way which would redirect Siddhatta's life. On his first journey, whether in a vision or whether in reality, both Siddhatta and his chariot driver saw a very old man. Old age was something of which Siddhatta had no experience and when his chariot driver explained what it was and that everyone, including Siddhatta has to get old, he was shocked to the very roots of his being. Few human beings can cope with the concept of their personal degeneration into old age and it is a concept which dwells more in the subconscious and unconscious aspects of the self for most of the time. But here was Siddhatta experiencing it for the first time in all its stark reality. It was not something he could subtly push into his subconscious, it was something which he had to face with full consciousness at that very moment. The effect on him was immeasurable and he returned home aware, for the first time, of the suffering which the very fact of getting old can bring.

Whether Siddhatta experienced the first three signs in just one journey as some suggest[10] or on consecutive days[11] is debatable, but a second sign emerged in the form of a very sick person. The sight of such was something very terrible to one who never knew that any human being could become ill and suffer. Again, when his chariot driver explained that sickness is the fate of all humanity, Siddhatta was faced for the first time with the reality of the concept that he, too, would become ill at some time in his own life. And once again, his psyche had not been cushioned against the starkness of the reality of physical suffering in all life. However, it was the third sign which caused the greatest reaction – a dead man being carried to the burning *ghat*. And in answer to Siddhatta's incredulous inquiries, the chariot driver pointed out the inevitable fate of all humankind, including Siddhatta himself. We cannot overestimate the enormity of such an experience on one who has no conception of death. This, the greatest fear of humankind, was exposed to Siddhatta in the space of a few moments: its effect was devastating. Siddhatta gazed at all around him and realized that there was suffering in all life even though people laughed and tried to turn their backs on the facts of old age, sickness and death, which are the common denominators of life itself. He remembered the weary oxen pulling the ploughs, the farmers toiling in the hot sun and the tiny insects turned over at the foot of the plough, and he was filled with the view of the suffering of all life. When Siddhatta returned home, he was a different person.

Siddhatta had yet another excursion from his home. On this occasion he met a mendicant, a wandering beggar, one who had withdrawn from life to set himself on the path to Ultimate Reality. This was the ascetic path, and the mendicant explained that by giving up all possessions and wordly comforts in the search for enlightenment it would be possible to overcome the problems of old age, sickness and death. It was this final experience on his ventures to the world outside which caused Siddhatta to leave his home and family entirely, and to search for release through the path of the ascetic; he, too, would become a homeless wanderer. So, according to some traditions, one night when all was quiet, Siddhatta left his home for the last time, to embark on a totally new life.

For many years, Siddhatta lived the life of an ascetic, probably as a *samanna*, searching for Truth but not attached to any specific ascetic tradition. Just as he had had an abundance of pleasure in his former life now he experienced the complete opposite and was the very best of ascetics. Over the years, he became so emaciated that he could hardly move, and when he did so, the hair fell from his body. Such were his efforts that he was greatly admired by five fellow ascetics. But despite all his efforts to renounce any physical comfort he found that he was no nearer to any kind of release from the existential problems of the suffering involved in old age, sickness and death. He had not found any answers in the pleasures of life or in extreme asceticism. While he did not give up his search for the means to overcome suffering he realized that a healthy body was partly necessary in such a cause and so he nourished his body with milky rice after many years of starvation and was abandoned by his disdainful and shocked ascetic associates. Yet, still resolved to find an answer, that night he sat down under one of the many, old *assattha* trees and vowed not to move until his goal was realized. And there he stayed in deep meditation, reaching the point where he was doing neither this nor that, totally still, quiet, without any kind of striving, just *being*.

And it was here, in this quiet and serene state, that Siddhatta found his answer: he achieved enlightenment, something which Buddhists call *nibbana* (Sanskrit *nirvana*). At this point he was free from the suffering of fears of old age, sickness or death and he knew that these could not touch him. In the stillness, he had lost his ego: there was no longer an "I" which thought in terms of desires and aversions, of distinguishing between this and that. Without an ego, an "I", there was nothing to which *kamma* (Sanskrit *karma*) could be attached to cause his rebirth; he had reached the end of *samsara*, the cycle of births and deaths for any individual. Everything was such as it was, and he saw himself as being at one with all in the universe. He became a *buddha*, an "enlightened, awakened one". It is from this point on that we are able to call Siddhatta *the Buddha*. As the dawn broke sources tell us that the blind could see, the deaf hear, and the lame could walk; there was beauty and peace in all the world:

> the heavens shone out with the moon like a maiden with a smile, and a sweet-smelling shower of flowers fell down wet with dew. . . . the different regions of the sky grew clear, the moon shone forth . . .[12]

At that moment according to tradition "no one anywhere was angry, ill or sad; no one did evil, none was proud; the world became quite quiet, as though it had reached full perfection".[13]

The Buddha had discovered that neither extreme pleasure nor extreme asceticism could aid one on the path to *nibbana*. What was needed was a *middle* way, the middle path between pleasure and asceticism: indeed, many aspects of Buddhism can be understood as a middle way, as the equilibrium between all opposites, the point between this and that, rather like the centre balancing point of a see-saw. And having discovered these answers to the problems of life, tradition states that after remaining several weeks under the tree of enlightenment, the *bodhi* (or *Bo*) tree, the Buddha began to teach others about the kind of balance and harmony which they could bring to their own lives through practising the "middle way". Importantly, no supramundane deity of any kind had assisted Siddhatta in his enlightenment; it was his own awakening, and not the fusion in any way with some deity or abstract Absolute. Likewise his teaching remained independent of reference to any divine entity in the cosmos other than the early Hindu Vedic deities like Brahma who were conceived of as part of the cosmic backdrop and inferior to the fully enlightened one which Siddhatta had become.

THE TEACHING OF THE BUDDHA

His experiences of the first three signs and his enlightenment taught Siddhatta that existence is bound up in suffering, a suffering which could be overcome with the right kind of beliefs and practices. Compassion was elemental to his moral teaching and, indeed, to his teaching in general. It was the compassion of a human being who understood fully the very nature of humankind and the full extent of its suffering and disharmony. And it was the compassion of a human being who set out prescribed methods which would cure such suffering and disharmony. These were part of the Buddha's *Dhamma*, his teaching, which eclipsed entirely in importance the man himself and the life he lived, and is the "Buddhism" of many Buddhists. His first real teaching occurred at the Deer Park at Benares to the five ascetics he had known during his years of physical self-deprivation.

The *Four Noble Truths*   The basis of the Buddha's teaching is set out in what are called the *Four Noble Truths*, which have been appropriately called "the structural framework for all higher teaching".[14] They represent a diagnosis of the suffering of humanity, the cause of that state, the solution to the problem, and the treatment – much the same as medical procedure of the day. These *Four Noble Truths* are as follows:

1 All life is suffering
The word "suffering" may seem rather strong here to the Western mind, for we tend to equate suffering with pain, and, indeed, this is what the Pali word for suffering, *dukkha* (Sanskrit *duhkha*) means. But the Buddha meant something wider than mere physical pain, when he used the word. He saw so clearly the *disharmony* and *dis-ease* in life in terms of mental, physical, psychological, emotional, social, economic suffering, and the like – in short, the disharmony which

stops us feeling the kind of equilibrium so much needed for a sense of well-being in life. But the problem which he saw so clearly in his experiences of old age, sickness and death for the first time, was the ability of human beings to pretend that none of these common denominators of all life existed! A modern analogy to this is given by Clive Sherlock:

> we tend not to appreciate, nor realise when we suffer because we turn away from it. We blame something or someone else for how we feel. We look for an escape route: for example, if we are feeling bored, what do we do? We reach for the television, the radio, the video or, if they are not available, we pick up a magazine, a book, something to distract us from our unpleasant sensations and feelings. And if we have none of these means of distraction there are always two in-house means of escape: we go, in our own thoughts, to the past, the future or to an abstraction and most importantly, we are not aware of doing this at the time.[15]

Thus, part of the teaching of the Buddha is involved with getting people to *understand* life as it is, to recognize the anxiety and unsatisfactoriness which it involves. This is not to suggest that the Buddha meant humankind to be pessimistic about life; indeed, happiness is not wrong as the Buddhist text, the *Dhammapada*, positively asserts:

> Let us live in joy, never hating those who hate us. Let us live in
> freedom, without hatred even among those who hate.
> Let us live in joy, never falling sick like those who are sick. Let us live
> in freedom, without disease even among those who are ill.
> Let us live in joy, never attached among those who are selfishly
> attached. Let us live in freedom even among those who are bound by
> selfish attachments.
> Let us live in joy, never hoarding things among those who hoard. Let
> us live in glowing joy like the bright gods.[16]

This emphasizes the Buddha's view of true happiness as something which lies in the more certain equilibrium which is beyond the transient happiness of daily existence. But while the Buddha certainly saw the more subtle aspects of the suffering and general unsatisfactoriness of life he specifically referred to birth, decay, death, sorrow, lamentation, pain, grief and despair. In particular, the fact that all life is impermanent gives to it a certain depth of unsatisfactoriness, as does clinging to the egoistic self. These last two points are sufficiently important to be given separate consideration below.

2 The cause of suffering is craving
If we cast our minds back to the image of the see-saw, whenever we are not at the point of equilibrium, the middle point, then the see-saw is tilted one way or the other, depending on either negative or positive attitudes. It is these negative and positive reactions to life which cause

craving, *tanha*. It is our aversions to many things, like death for example, which make us crave life and immortality, or our aversions to suffering which make us crave happiness. Since all life is, in any case, impermanent, such craving is bound, ultimately, to end in frustration and unhappiness. It is when we have these desires and aversions in life that we create personal *kamma* which will bring about the kinds of results in present or future lives which cause suffering.

3 Cessation of suffering will occur with release from craving
The only thing which can cause suffering is personal *kamma,* and if personal *kamma* is caused by positive and negative thoughts and actions – desires and aversions which promote craving – then getting rid of the desires and aversions will prevent the chain of reaction which leads to suffering. The Buddha was roughly contemporary with early Hindu *Upanisadic* thought which had developed the ideas of *karma* (Pali *kamma*) the belief that positive and negative actions resulted in similarly positive and negative fruits for each individual. The concomitant belief in *samsara*, the endless cycle of reincarnation, "that which turns around forever", as Robinson and Johnson graphically describe it,[17] is intimately linked with the cause-effect, action-reaction concept of the doctrine of *karma*. The Buddha accepted both concepts but it would be incorrect to use the term "reincarnation" in the context of Buddhism, though there are arguably strong cases which could be put forward for it in some areas of Buddhism.[18] The better term is *rebirth* and this is a rebirth of the *kammic* residues, not of a complete personality. This is in contrast to the Hindu idea of reincarnation which suggests a much stronger link between a personality in one life and the next. But for both Hindu and Buddhist concepts *samsara* ceases when there is no fruitive *karma* to be reaped in the next existence. And cessation of craving was considered by the Buddha to be the means of preventing such *kamma*: indeed, the word for cessation, *nirodha*, is synonymous with *nibbana* (Sanskrit *nirvana*), the end of the cycle of *samsara*. But *kamma*, too, differed somewhat from the conventional Hindu concept of *karma* for the Buddha infused into the concept the nuance of *intention* behind words, deeds and thoughts which reaped corresponding negative or positive results in the future.[19] This places responsibility for actions firmly on the shoulders of the individual.

The *Noble Eightfold Path* The fourth and last of the *Four Noble Truths* states that the cure – the release from suffering – comes from following the *Noble Eightfold Path*. The *Noble Eightfold Path* is the second major teaching of the Buddha. It is a path for life, a guide or teaching, part of the *Dhamma* in Buddhism. There are eight parts to this teaching but, although it is called a "path", suggesting that it should be undertaken one step at a time, this is not so, for its eight aspects are to be practised *at the same time*. The Buddha taught this part of his *Dhamma* by drawing a wheel on the ground and putting eight spokes on the wheel, each representing one aspect of the *Eightfold Path*. So just as a wheel does not function properly without all its spokes, so success on the *Eightfold Path* will not come about unless all aspects are practised at once. The *Noble Eightfold Path* is a guide for living which covers all aspects of life in eight areas, dealing with what one thinks as well as what one does and incorporating wisdom, understanding, conduct, morality, and aspects of inner concentration of the mind. These are categorized into three important areas, *sila* which is morality, *samadhi* which is concentration, and *panna* (Sanskrit *prajna*) which is wisdom.[20] However, by following the eight strands of the *Path* suffering is not so much annihilated any more than happiness is; it is the differentiation between them that is transcended. The elements of the *Path* are the following:

Right understanding/view   This suggests that one needs to have a certain understanding about life and humankind. Three basic doctrines are important here. First, is the acceptance of life as suffering and disharmony and the way in which *kamma* creates the kind of result which will cause suffering in future lives. Secondly, understanding of the nature of the self is important. *Upanisadic* Hinduism taught what was to become a major concept of Hinduism – that within the deepest essence of everything is the permanent, unchanging *atman*, the part of everything which is the Absolute, Brahman. The Buddha disagreed with this theory and said that there was no permanent self at all: this is the doctrine of *anatta* (Sanskrit *anatman*). If we take away our sense experiences there is nothing left, nothing which we could call our "self". This is what Gombrich aptly terms "essence-lessness".[21] Trying to create a real "self", when this is impossible, causes suffering. The Buddha taught that a person is made up of five aggregates called *khandas* (Sanskrit *skandhas*), physical form, perception, mental constructions and ideas, volition and consciousness – and these are all changing, transient, impermanent factors. To see the Buddha's point it is necessary to ask what self remains if we take away *all* our senses and our consciousness: what then remains which we could call the "self"? A second century BCE monk named Nagasena illustrated the point well with the example of a chariot. A chariot, he said, cannot exist separately from the components which constitute it. Once you dissemble the parts, you no longer have a chariot. Similarly with the self; take away the five aggregates and you no longer have a self, an "I".

The third basic doctrine which the Buddha taught is that everything in life is impermanent and dependent on all sorts of conditions for its existence. This is the important doctrine of *anicca* (Sanskrit *anitya*). Nothing ever *is*, but is always in a state of becoming. When we try to give permanence to things in life then we are doomed to suffer. Because we have erroneous conceptions of permanence, we cling to things, desire and pursue things – whether concrete material ones, or abstract goals of life. This subjects an individual to what the Buddha termed *paticcasamppada*, "dependent origination", twelve causal links in a chain of incessant birth and death. These, each dependent on the previous one, are lack of right understanding which is ignorance; the build-up of volitional impulses; consciousness; differentiation of forms; the senses; contact of senses and objects; the possession of feelings; craving; grasping; becoming; rebirth; death. Breaking this endless cycle can only occur when the cycle itself is understood as promoting life after life. Right view and understanding of life, then, suggest a radical alteration in the way life is viewed and, in particular, one's view of one's own self. Because everything is impermanent and changes from one moment to the next the aggregates which combine to form what we know as a person are also different from moment to moment. So while there is a certain continuity between one moment and the next – the self in one moment and the self in the next – there is never the *identity* of moments to create a permanent self.

Right thought   This suggests that there must be a certain willingness in an individual to *want* to change, to want to alter the degree of disharmony in life by promoting the kind of harmony suggested by the Buddha's teachings. But in particular, thoughts should be devoid of desire, aversion, anger, covetousness and foolishness – all *kammic* producing states of mind.

Right speech   Having dealt with aspects of the mind, the Buddha went on to aspects of conduct, the putting into practice of the teachings. Thus, right speech is important in life; indeed, the tongue is one of the most difficult aspects of the self to control! But if thoughts are right, words often follow in character.

Right action   Because actions, like thoughts and words, produce *kammic* affects, they must always be the right kind of actions so that they do not result in suffering. Ideally actions should be performed without any hint of ego, but this is very difficult to achieve, so at least the action should be good, so that it produces good *kamma*. The Buddha said: "That action only is 'well done' which brings no suffering in its train".

Right livelihood   If our profession or daily work involves aspects which are contrary to the other parts of the *Noble Eightfold Path* then we are spending most of our lives engaged in doing the exact opposite of what we believe in. This, too, will result in the kind of *kamma* which will involve suffering. So the sale of weapons, alcohol or poisons and engaging in slavery, soldiery, fishing, fortune-telling or butchery are not the kinds of occupations which are conducive to the Buddhist way of life. A modern Buddhist might want to consider whether working in some aspect of an occupation which is involved with vivisection or testing of substances on animals is against this particular dimension of the *Eightfold Path*.

Right effort   This advocates self-discipline: without this aspect – the effort involved in pursuing the whole path – there can be little hope for change. Effort has to be made to prevent evil arising, to abandon it once it has arisen, and to produce and increase the good in life.

Right mindfulness and right concentration   The last two aspects of the *Noble Eightfold Path* are concerned with the kind of concentration and mindfulness which are part of the processes of meditation in Buddhism, the techniques which help the individual to lose the sense of ego and yet to operate in the world from the point of equilibrium, the middle of the see-saw. While such meditative and contemplative aspects are important dimensions for many Buddhists in many different schools, they are especially relevant to the more orthodox lives of monks. In many ways, the stages of meditation accepted by the Buddha were those of traditional Indian teaching.

The *pancha sila*   In addition to these basic teachings, early Buddhism added a number of other precepts. Of particular importance are the following five, known in Buddhism as the *Pancha Sila*, "the Five Moral Precepts". They are:

1 Not to harm living things
This is much wider than the rule "you shall not kill" for it extends to all living things. Many Buddhists believe strongly in the doctrine of *ahimsa*, non-violence, and extend their respect for life to all animals and creatures as well as humankind. Creatures are part of the *samsaric* cycle and they, too, will evolve into human form. Many Buddhists, therefore, are vegetarians, object to blood sports, and are pacifists, though many are not. Because such Buddhists wish to abstain from taking life, they need to chose their livelihoods carefully so this particular precept is very much linked to the right livelihood aspect of the *Eightfold Path*. In practical terms many Buddhists are meat or fish eaters because their cultures rely on these foods for protein. Japanese Buddhists, for example, rely on fish for their diet, as do Sri Lankan Buddhists, who also eat meat. Some Buddhists do not mind eating meat as long as they do not have to slaughter the animals themselves – a service which supermarkets and Muslims conveniently provide.

2 Not to take what is not given
Again, this is wider than a prohibition on stealing and in early

Buddhism kept the monks dependent on the generosity of lay people for their existence which is still the case for most monks today. Traditionally a Theravadin monk cannot ask for something but must be offered it; lay people are, however, only too eager to give to the monks in order to acquire good *kamma*.[22]

3 Not to misuse the senses
This was a prohibition against sexual misconduct.

4 Not to speak wrongly
This covered aspects of the third of the *Noble Eightfold Path*. Notably it can highlight not only unedifying speech but the kinds of body language which are harmful to another. We can, for example, portray a good deal with a facial expression, an appropriately timed "Well!" or just raised eyebrows! These kinds of actions are also dimensions of wrong speech.

5 Not to use drugs or alcohol
This moral precept suggests that the use of drugs clouds the mind so that it would be difficult to make the right kinds of choices, thoughts and actions.

To these five precepts were added a further three, so making the *Eight Precepts* mainly applicable to the early monks. These extra three were: to abstain from eating at the wrong times (which came to be considered as after midday); abstaining from dancing, singing, attending performances, wearing cosmetics and ornamentation; abstaining from using high seats or high beds (something always associated with the wealthier person). These eight precepts can also be divided so that they form nine, and with the addition of a further precept not to accept silver or gold, are known as the *Ten Precepts*.[23] A great number of other rules were added specifically for the monks of early Buddhism. Many Buddhists, particularly Theravadin Buddhists, still follow all the earlier precepts while other Buddhists may have adapted the earlier rules or will be guided by different precepts.

The death of the Buddha   For many years the Buddha taught about the nature of life, about *kamma*, selfishness, morality, the nature of the self, *nibbana* and all the many aspects which constitute his *Dhamma*. But it was not only through direct teaching and discourse that he promulgated the *Dhamma* it was also by active example in the daily life he led. At the age of eighty the Buddha died, at a very insignificant little place called Kusinara, in 486 BCE according to the Southern tradition, a hundred years later in the Northern tradition. Though his mind was clear and unruffled by egoistic thought, he was physically very weak. His last days and final death are recounted in the *Mahaparinibbanasutta*, the "Account of the Great Final Extinction". In this account it is recorded that he said to his faithful disciple Ananda:

> Ananda, I am now old, worn out, venerable, one who has traversed life's path, I have reached the term of life, which is eighty. Just as an old cart is made to go by being held together by straps, so the Tathagata's body is kept going by being strapped up. It is only when the Tathagata withdraws his attention from outward signs, and by the cessation of certain feelings, enters into the signless concentration of the mind, that his body knows comfort.[24]

It is clear that the Buddha was considered to have suffered physically but throughout the *Mahaparinibbanasutta* it is also clear that his mental energies were exceedingly alert and that his mind was always calm. His last words to his disciples were: "Now, monks, I declare to you: all conditioned things are of a nature to decay – strive on untiringly."[25] He had taught that the way to end the problems of old age, sickness and death – indeed all suffering in life – lay in the efforts of each individual alone. Through self-reflection, self-discipline, self-effort, self-control, self-knowledge and self-enlightenment, the self would, in fact, cease to exist at all, and there would be no self remaining to reap *kammic* results in the future: the cessation of *samsara* would have been gained entirely by one's own efforts.

Following the Buddha's death there were numerous disciples who embraced the *Dhamma*, the teaching of the Buddha, and who taught it to others. In his lifetime he had taught many people and right from the time of his enlightenment followers had gathered around him in what became the *Sangha*, the Buddhist corporate body of monks. To be a disciple of the Buddha it was necessary to undergo the simple ordination which marked the acceptance of the *Dhamma* – not only in theory, but also in the sense that the disciple had reached the egoless state in the process of its acceptance. Such perfected, enlightened individuals were called *arahats* (Sanskrit *arhat*): they were not enlightened in the same sense as the Buddha and so were not *buddhas* according to the more orthodox strands of Buddhism, for it was believed that there could only be one Buddha for each aeon and thus, Siddhatta Gotama was unique to this age. At their ordination the *arahats* shaved their heads and beards, squatted down in front of the assembled local *Sangha*, and recited three times what has become known as the *Three Jewels* or *Three Refuges* of Buddhism:

BUDDHIST TRADITIONS: THE HINAYANA AND MAHAYANA

I go to the Buddha for refuge

> I go to the *Dhamma* for refuge
> I go to the *Sangha* for refuge

As the *Sangha* grew, the Buddha could no longer ordain new monks himself and the *arahats* were sent out to teach and ordain new monks themselves. They also had the function of gathering alms from the local communities: this they did before midday, and it became established practice to eat in the morning and to devote the remainder of the day to more spiritual matters. Because this early Buddhism appealed to people so widely it became easy for the monks to depend on lay support for their very basic necessities.

This dependence of the monks on the laity has remained a characteristic of the more conservative strand of Buddhism. In return for food and the few possessions allowed them, the monks taught the laity the Buddha's *Dhamma*, and it became widely accepted by the laity that their individual support for the monks with food and gifts would bring good *kamma* – good merit for the immediate future and in future lives. Moreover, the monks became the selfless role models representing the ideal life, and while many could not enter the monastic life in this lifetime, they believed that with sufficient good merit they might do so in the next. The development of early Buddhism is thus characterized by mutual interdependence of *Sangha* and laity, an interdependence which has remained in Theravada Buddhism. Yet there was, and is, much to separate the monks and the laity: it is doubtful, for example, whether the laity were ever taught the same aspects of the *Dhamma* as the members of the *Sangha*.[26] Moreover, the pursuit of wisdom (*panna*) by the monks and the monastic emphasis on the practice of concentration and meditation, served to separate practice of the *Dhamma* into monastic and lay. And as more complex rules developed for the life of the monk, the lay person became more disposed towards acquiring good merit, content with admiring the monastic life but not participating in it other than perhaps a brief retreat during the rainy season. As the *Sangha* grew rapidly in size during the lifetime of the Buddha, and the simplicity of its rules developed a more sophisticated character, regular meetings at which the rules were recited became necessary.

The growth of the *Sangha* in the centuries following the Buddha's demise was not without its divisions. The Buddha had taught extensively but his *Dhamma* was not committed to writing for a long period of time. While a basic core of oral tradition was defined as authoritative at an important Council of the monks at Rajagaha (Sanskrit Rajagriha) in 483 BCE, and the monks were generally in agreement over the rules of discipline for the *Sangha* known as the *Pattimokkha*, other aspects of the Buddha's teaching were more open to interpretation, particularly the *Abhidhamma*, with its intensive philosophy and analysis of the Buddha's words. Thus, about a century after the

Buddha's death a group of monks calling themselves the *Mahasanghika*, "the great *Sangha* party", broke away from the mainstream *Sangha* and, while they were by no means the only dissidents, they may have been the origin of the major element of Buddhism known today as the *Mahayana*. Mahayana Buddhists gave the name *Hinayana* to their conservative and orthodox opponents, a name meaning "small vehicle" and therefore something of a derogatory term, in contrast to their own, *Mahayana*, meaning "great vehicle". While there were many schools encompassed by the term Hinayana, the only one to survive to the present day is that of the *Theravada*, "the way of the elders".

While Buddhism was eventually destined to decline in India, its birthplace, it spread far and wide in the centuries which followed. The acceptance of Buddhism by the Emperor Asoka (268–239 BCE) was an important factor in both the consolidation of Buddhism and its spread, for missionary activity took the Buddha's *Dhamma* well beyond the boundaries of India. In the mid third century BCE, Buddhism had spread south to Sri Lanka, and in the first millennium CE it was to be found in Kashmir, northern Pakistan, northern Afghanistan and Chinese Turkestan, and eventually it reached China, Japan, South East Asia and Indonesia. The countries which adopted Theravada Buddhism are Thailand, Burma, Sri Lanka (though here with a somewhat broken tradition), Laos and Cambodia, though political events in countries like the last two have seen the demise of Buddhist practice. It was the Mahayana schools of Buddhism which were adopted elsewhere, mainly in Central Asia includingTibet, Mongolia, Sikkim, Bhutan, and in China and Japan, Korea and Vietnam.

The way of the monks[27] With its fundamental pillar of the acquisition of *panna*, "wisdom", Theravada Buddhism is essentially involved with monastic life and considers that it is only by becoming a monk that *nibbana* can be realized. But while the corporate life of the monks, the *Sangha*, is important, each individual has to to work out his own salvation. And this last statement is not intended to be sexist, for there are no authentic nuns in Theravada Buddhism: since the rules for the monks state that nuns should be ordained by both ordained monks, and then again by ordained nuns, the fact that there is none of the latter has meant that there can be no *real* nuns in Theravada Buddhism. There are convents of lay nuns, but their status is inferior to ordained monks. But even in early Buddhism nuns were bound by extra rules and had to respect as their senior any male monk however young he may have been. Neither could they ever criticize or admonish a monk, and they were unable to observe many special ceremonies independently of the monks. In today's world, without legitimate ordination, they can only be classified as lay women, *upasikas*, and support is not as readily available for them from other lay people as it is for

THERAVADA
BUDHISM

the monks.[28] Theravada Buddhism is therefore concerned with the enlightenment of the male, and it is an elitist and disciplined path. Essentially, the individual monk has to obey the many rules of the *Vinaya*, the code of discipline, spend much time in meditation, and work out *his own* salvation, his own path to final release from the *samsaric* cycle. While the first ordained monks were expected to be enlightened *arahats*, today's monk knows that he has to work diligently in the pursuit of spiritual progress. And there is no concept of any kind of supramundane divinity to aid the monk on his path. As noted earlier, Theravada Buddhism does not accept the concept of any omnipotent creator deities who can assist human beings on their spiritual path. While gods such as the Vedic deities of Hinduism are accepted as having existence, they are seen as fellow wanderers in the *samsaric* cycle of existences just like ordinary mortals. The only difference is that their *kamma* is good enough to place them in a birth in a heavenly, and not earthly, realm. However, it must be said that such minor divine beings often supply the focus for propitiatory requests from lay Theravada Buddhists at auspicious times in life and at times of need or trouble, and fulfil a particularly anthropomorphic and perhaps theistic role in a religion devoid of an omnipotent creator God. The involvement of the laity with these deities often finds expression in colourful ceremony.

But the rejection of an overall concept of God or some kind of impersonal Absolute is critically important in Theravada Buddhism, setting it well apart from the religion of Hinduism and making possible the fundamental doctrine of *anatta*, no-self. Thus, *nibbana* is the freedom of an individual from fruitive *kamma* which prevents rebirth, but not that which allows the soul to become one with the Ground or Source of the universe. *Nibbana* is simply *nibbana* and has nothing to do with divinity or a divine being. So there is no one for the Theravadin monk to pray to, to praise, to worship: the Buddha was not divinized in any way by the Theravadin monastic tradition. When the Buddha passed into *parinibbana* at his death, he ceased to exist; it was only his *Dhamma* which remained and it is the *Dhamma* which is the central focus of the Theravadin monk. Theravada Buddhism is thus an atheistic system of belief which rejects the kind of Absolute of *brahmanical* Hinduism in favour of a fairly conservative teaching about the nature of existence which has changed little despite its spread outside India. Though it would be true to say that amongst the lay people there was, and is, a tendency to venerate the Buddha in a more overtly *religious* way, the orthodox monastic view is staunchly atheistic.

To the Mahayana Buddhist, the Theravadin monk was treading a selfish path, searching for his own enlightenment. He was primarily not to be concerned with society at large (though he did perform certain functions for the laity, such as funeral ceremonies), apart from teaching them aspects of the *Dhamma*. But the criticism is somewhat overstressed. Theravada doctrine is based on *panna*, which is wisdom (Sanskrit *prajna*), but basic to Theravada Buddhism are the *brahma-vihara*, four sublime states – the suffusing of the world with loving-kindness (*metta*), compassion (*karuna*), sympathetic joy (*mudita*), and equanimity (*upekkha*). A monk's concentration on spreading these four sublime states to the whole world "upwards, downwards, across, everywhere, . . . abundant, unbounded, without hate or ill-will",[29] suggests that the monk is not so divorced from concern for the welfare of all humanity.

The life of the monk is one of renunciation, though he is able to leave the monastery and return to lay life at any time without any sense of disgrace. The monastic rules, the *Vinaya*, allow him only a few possessions – three robes, one cloak, one undergarment and one outer garment, a fan, a belt, a razor to shave his head, eyebrows and beard, a staff, a toothpick, a strainer to strain liquid before he drinks to avoid swallowing (and therefore harming) living organisms, a needle for sewing rags together to make his clothes, and the traditional begging bowl. The traditional robe is usually yellow – considered to be the colour closest to old rags – but Sri Lankan monks wear orange robes and some Tibetan orders, dark burgundy. It is the laity which supplies these few possessions for the monk and it is by no means unusual for some lay people to get carried away in their enthusiasm to acquire good merit so that the monk may find himself in possession of a refridgerator or a car! As Gombrich rather amusingly points out, "It has often happened that a monk settles down to live in a forest cave, to find the cave rapidly equipped by admiring laity with 'all mod. con.'"![30] This rather highlights well the interdependence of monk and lay person, the monk not allowing the individual to forget his or her spiritual development and the individual not allowing the monk to become over ascetic and totally withdrawn – a neat working out of one dimension of the Buddha's "Middle Way"! Normally, the monk should eat only one meal a day and that before noon, having spent some time in the morning begging for his food amongst the lay community. The idea of the mendicant holy man to whom one gives food in order to acquire merit is commonplace in the East, but can be difficult for monasteries adopting the custom in the West, though these latter usually have attendant sympathizers who are prepared to provide the food for the monks. In some cultures the monks are allowed to have two meals a day, one very early in the morning and the other at the traditional time of before noon. In some places monks may be invited to the homes of lay people for their meals so the traditional morning begging is not by any means standard. Drinking at any time is not forbidden and neither is the chewing of betel leaf, or even smoking for monks in Thailand!

The monks live in a *vihara* either singly or collectively, so a *vihara* could be a simple hut or a cave housing one or a few monks or it may be large enough to be a wealthy monastery with considerable land appropriated to it. Strictly speaking the monks should not work, but we have to remember that they were teachers of the *Dhamma* to a largely illiterate laity from the days of the Buddha on. Teaching was therefore a natural occupation until the arrival of state provision of education. Some became scholars or became involved in social work and, given the amount of land attached to some of the larger monasteries, some became tillers of the soil, though somewhat against the disciplinary rules of the *Vinaya*, the part of the canonical scriptures dealing with regulations for the monks.

However, the life of the monk is devoted to following the disciplinary code of the *Vinaya*, which was important enough to be recited regularly and communally, and to meditation – the pronounced feature of the monk's life which separates his practice from that of lay people. Each monk has to work out his own path to *nibbana*; each is his own island, his own refuge and his time in daily meditative retreat is essential, as it is for those nuns who choose to adopt the life of a convent. Etienne Lamotte comments of the ideal of the monk:

> The ruling which imprisons the monk in a network of detailed prescriptions tends to make him a fully self-denying person: gentle and inoffensive, poor and humble, continent and perfectly trained.[31]

But while being required to spend long periods in meditation the monk also has periods of memorizing the scriptures, and of lively debate with the other monks generally as part of the daily routine; indeed, the word *thera*, while normally meaning "monk", can have the nuance of meaning "view" or "debate". It is in the rainy season that meditative practices are particularly emphasized and, when the roads and paths are waterlogged by the monsoon rains and it is difficult to travel any distance, the laity also will join the monks for some short or long period, accepting the traditional *Five Precepts* in entering the monastery. But when not engaged in the immediate monastic duty, the monk is not divorced from the world outside. In his morning begging for food he comes into contact with the laity on a regular basis and he may also embark on a pilgrimage. But the disciplinary rules of the *Dhamma* forbid him to be alone with a woman or to exchange more than a few words with her, and while he may use public transport, he will not sit next to a woman on the journey.

Puja While *puja* can mean "worship" it more generally means "honour, respect", and this is the sense in which it is used in Theravada Buddhism. The Buddha, therefore, is not worshipped but his teaching is respected and honoured at shrines and temples. And because such *puja* is a source of merit, of good *kamma* for the lay Buddhist, visits to temples and shrines are frequent, with traditional offerings of flowers, candles and incense. Flowers or flower petals are symbolic of the fragility, transience and impermanence of all life, while light from the candles represents the light of enlightenment and the dispelling of the darkness of ignorance. The fragrance of the incense symbolizes the spread of the Buddha's *Dhamma* to all corners of the world. Gratitude for the *Dhamma* of the Buddha is shown by bowing, kneeling and prostrating – the three often being combined together as if in one action. The palms of the hands are brought together during *puja* and may be raised to the forehead, then the mouth and back to the chest to symbolize that mind speech and body are combined in the action of honouring the *Dhamma*. Important would be the repetition three times of the *Three Refuges*. There is no prayer to, or focus on, a supra-mundane entity in such *puja*; it is fundamentally honour and gratitude which are expressed.

Meditation   Meditation is a very natural thing to do in the East, particularly in the heat of the day. It is a central practice of Theravada Buddhism and while it will be undertaken by many of the laity it is a daily requirement for the monk; indeed, the picture of the monk quietly seated in deep meditation is what springs to mind to most who recall something about Buddhism. It is through contemplation and meditation that the confines of ordinary thought and the sense stimuli which so attract our minds are transcended so that the mind becomes quite quiet and tranquil. Most of us spend our lives in busy thought and we rarely concentrate on a particular task in hand. Simple actions like cleaning one's teeth, peeling potatoes or driving the car become merely background occupations while the mind concerns itself about this and that. The mind easily becomes out of control and mindless rather than mindful, mindfulness denoting the ability to concentrate fully on the task in hand. And when we *do* concentrate on the task in hand movements become calmer, less rushed, and the mind and the body become correlated and harmonized. But even such simple practices of meditation are hard to accomplish without daily practice and perseverence. The meditative practices of the monks are highly developed, and help them on the path to enlightenment. Concentrating on a particular aspect of the *Brahma-vihara* such as *metta*, love, for example, promotes the kind of serenity of mind which is important for the monk, but it is also important to concentrate on the fragility of life, the emptiness of the self and the kinds of mind content which bring awareness of the finer teachings of the Buddha. Concentration and meditation are the two final components of the Buddha's *Noble Eightfold Path* and serve to wean the mind away from its usual ways of thinking, and from the mental habits which constitute personality. And once these mental habits are broken down then the world around can be seen as it really is, particularly because the egoistic self which views it all is lessened or lost.

The two fundamental types of meditation are *samatha* and *vipassana*. The former concentrates on mindfulness of body, feelings, mind and mental states and aims at detaching the mind from responses to sense stimuli through four stages until the level of pure consciousness of *samadhi* is achieved, then, beyond *samadhi* to four formless states where dualities cease to exist. *Vipassana* or "insight" meditation is more psycho-analytically based, analyzing the nature of the self in the context of the fundamental tenets of Buddhism.

The scriptures of Theravada Buddhism The teachings of early Buddhism were handed down orally and as they spread to many parts of India came to be preserved in local dialects. India is such a vast country that there are many different dialects which would not always be mutually understandable. Memorizing the *Dhamma*, and therefore preserving it, was an important role of the monks. They were required to recite much of the material, particularly the disciplinary code, but their task was often made easier by the repetitive nature of some of the material: nevertheless, it involved a considerable effort. An authorized Canon of this oral tradition was established at the First Buddhist Council shortly after the Buddha's death and was elaborated on at the Second Council about a century later. The first authoritative Canon was formulated by those monks who had memorized the Buddha's teaching. They prefaced their repetition of the material with the words "Thus have I heard. . . .", which is why these words appear in written accounts of the scriptures today. When eventually the oral Canon was committed to writing, the collection of texts was handed down in "Three Baskets", *Ti-pitaka* (Sanskrit *Tripitaka*). The Theravada school came to record the *Ti-pitaka* in the language of Pali and possessed the greatest amount of Indian Buddhist literature, the texts of many other schools of the Hinayana strand of Buddhism disappearing along with their schools into the mists of time. However, because there were many different schools of Hinayana Buddhism there were many Canons of scripture. The Pali texts of the Theravada school were written in southern India several centuries after the death of the Buddha.

The *Tipitaka* were accepted by both Hinayana and Mahayana monastic traditions particularly the material of two of the "Baskets", the *Vinaya* and the *Sutta*. It was the third "Basket", what became the Theravadin Pali *Abhidhamma*, and the Mahayana Sanskrit *Abhidharma*, over which differences occurred. The *Tipitaka*, then, constituted the Buddha's *Dhamma* in early Buddhism: their three categories are:

The *Vinaya Pitaka* The word *vinaya* means "discipline" and thus this *pitaka* contained the rules and regulations for the monks (*bhikkus*) and nuns (*bhikkunis*). Not only was a code of conduct established for the monks in the *Vinaya* – a conduct which covered all avenues of the monk's life – it also contained regulations for dealing with those monks who had committed offences, as well as regulations for the settling of disputes. Surprisingly the *Vinayas* which have survived are fairly diverse and are anything but uniform despite, as Lamotte observes, "exploiting a common basis".[32]

The *Sutta Pitaka*   This is by far the largest and most important of the *Tipitaka* and was recalled from the Buddha's teachings by his most faithful disciple Ananda. It is divided into five parts and collects together the Buddha's teachings in the form of dialogues each linked by a common "thread" (Pali *sutta*, Sanskrit *sutra*). The *Sutta Pitaka* consists of five sections of dialogues, long ones first, the *Digha Nikaya*, then medium-length discourses, the *Majjhima Nikaya*, the *Samyutta Nikaya* which are thematically grouped discourses, the *Anguttara Nikaya* or "Gradual Sayings", and the small texts of the *Khuddaka Nikaya*, which include the *Dhammapada* and the *Jatakas*. The *Dhammapada* is a well-known part of the *Sutta Pitaka*. *Pada* means "path" or "way" and elucidates the path of the *Dhamma*, the path to enlightenment. Its 423 verses give practical advice on how to live life, and exemplify well Buddhism as a way of action. So venerated is this teaching that even lay Buddhists would know much of it by heart and particular verses may be chanted in times of trouble, need, or for protection. Its contents epitomize the proximate goals – refraining from evil, learning to do what is good and purifying the mind – so important for lay participants in Buddhism, but the *Sutta Pitaka* as a whole is also important to the lay person because of its inclusion of practical advice for daily living such as care of the family, relationships in marriage, the choice of friends, relationships between teachers and pupils and between employers and employees. Even advice about money, gambling, idleness or roaming the streets late at night is to be found.[33] The *Jatakas*, literally "birth stories", are the past lives of the Buddha in which he was to be found in animal as much as human form (though never, it seems, in female form whether human or animal!). The legends are immensely attractive, the animal stories being reminiscent of Aesop's fables. The stories recount heroic deeds of the Buddha-to-be and acts of great self-sacrifice. While it is the moral of each story which is important, lay people in particular find the *Jatakas* immensely appealing. Embarrassing to the general doctrine of rebirth is the much stronger linkage between one life and the next which the *Jatakas* reflect, suggesting a more ready acceptance of Hindu concepts of reincarnation and a reincarnating self.

The *Abhidhamma Pitaka*   This is an analysis of the Buddha's teachings divided into seven sections, one of which is devoted to refuting the views of the other Buddhist schools. As its name suggests, this is the "higher *Dhamma*" and the material which comprises it is open to much interpretation, enough to have engendered the variety of schools within the Hinayana tradition in early Buddhism. If the *Sutta Pitaka* is suited to the lay person as much as the monk, then the *Abhidhamma* is definitely only for the scholarly monk.

MAHAYANA
BUDDHISM

Also called *Bodhisattvayana*, Etienne Lamotte says that Mahayana Buddhism is distinguished from Hinayana Buddhism "by a more ambitious religious ideal, a more complex Buddhology and, especially, more radical philosophical positions",[34] and indeed this is so. Such developments originate in the schisms which divided the early tradition and which had surfaced by the time of the Second Council in about 383 BCE, but the origins of Mahayana Buddhism are somewhat obscure. It may have been the Mahasanghika group in particular, "The Great *Sangha* Party" as they called themselves, which introduced more progressive and less exclusive ideas. To begin with they had a more relaxed attitude to the *Vinaya* and this may have meant that, without the strict emphasis on discipline, the laity could be more widely included in belief and practice. Indeed, it was the extension of the Buddhist *Sangha* to include the layman and woman which was a significant factor in the whole flowering of resulting Mahayana Buddhism. Mahayana Buddhism extended the *Sangha* to include householders, women and the less able as much as the gifted. With an emphasis on meditation rather than discipline, and a wider interpretation of buddhahood, it would no longer be necessary for an individual to enter a monastery to be a practising Buddhist: the *Sangha* would be extended to the home.

But the most "ambitious religious ideal", as Lamotte phrases it, emerged in the concept of *bodhisattvas*. This, too, was made possible through the developing conception of the Buddha for, unlike the Hinayana view that the Buddha had ceased to be, Mahayana Buddhism favoured the view that the *essence* of the Buddha was ongoing as much as was his *Dhamma*. This belief laid the foundations for many dimensions of Mahayana Buddhism today. Hinayana Buddhists, as the later Theravada Buddhist tradition, held that the Buddha was in no way divine. He had a special status as being the only Buddha for this aeon and respect was paid to his *Dhamma*, but he was not a divine being who could be worshipped in any way and he was not ongoing; he was not thought to be eternally present. Humankind, however, seems by nature to need some kind of ultimate essence or divinity to make sense of life's situations. In the history and evolution of many religions we find periods of philosophical and metaphysical thought which contain no elements of theistic or anthropomorphic belief; but this hardly suits the ordinary person in the village, street or town, for whom such intellectualism supplies little comfort. Mahayana Buddhism it could be said responded to such needs in a variety of ways. It was probably such needs of the ordinary person which began the process of change in ideas which provided the origins of Mahayana. After the Buddha died, people set up *stupas* or relic mounds, small or large buildings which housed something belonging to the Buddha's person, perhaps some of his hair or a piece of bone. The ordinary lay Buddhist gained a great deal from visiting such *stupas* and it was a short step from this kind of veneration of the Buddha's relics to veneration of the Buddha himself. And this is the major difference between the Theravada and Mahayana schools of thought. In most Mahayana strands of Buddhism the Buddha came to be regarded as being permanent in the cosmos, as being present before his birth on earth and continuing after it for all eternity. In developing such a concept of the Buddha, this opened the way for a variety of interpretations and different expressions of the Buddha's *Dhamma*, which resulted in Mahayana Buddhism.

Mahayana Buddhism refused to accept the exclusiveness of the enlightenment and buddhahood of Siddhartha Gautama and extended the potential for buddhahood to all. Since all people could become buddhas it was natural to assume that many had done so already and that many would do so in the future. There were, indeed, many great teachers and people who had followed the Buddha's *Dharma* who had realized *nirvana* too, and like the Buddha, Siddhartha Gautama, they too were felt to be continually present in the cosmos and in world systems other than the immediate one. Coupled with this idea is another very important one and this is the concept of *mahakaruna*. Theravada Buddhism believed, and continues to do so, that once a person reached *nibbana* he became an *arahat*, a perfected being, but not a Buddha – there could only be one Buddha in each aeon. Mahayana Buddhism saw no point to this, no point to someone realizing *nirvana* and then having no more involvement with those still struggling on the path to it. The Buddha, after all, helped countless people to find *nirvana* too by staying in the world to teach the *Dharma* and was a being noted for his considerable compassion for humanity. It is this idea of *compassion* which became so important in Mahayana Buddhism.

Bodhisattvas Compassion in Sanskrit is *karuna* and Mahayana Buddhism believes that when an individual achieves *nirvana* he or she stays in the world to help others to achieve *nirvana* too. Such people do this because of their great compassion for all suffering humanity and it is this concept of *mahakaruna*, "great compassion", which is one important pillar of Mahayana Buddhism, the other being *prajna*, wisdom. Mahayana Buddhists see no sense in the attainment of *nirvana*, or the achievement of buddhahood, unless it is of some value to the rest of humanity, so out of *mahakaruna* those who achieve *nirvana* do not pass on to *parinirvana*, supreme *nirvana*, but remain in the universe or become reborn in some form in order to help humankind. These beings, who have reached enlightenment but who are dedicated to helping all others to do the same, are called *bodhisattvas*. Their aim, enlightenment for all, is the "ambitious religious ideal" of which Lamotte writes, and it is this *aim* which is the important characteristic of *bodhisattvas*, the gradual achievement of which stores up vast amounts of *karmic* merit available to all beings. Thus the *bodhisattva* not only epitomizes wisdom, but the immense compassion he or she has for all beings.

It is with this concept of *bodhisattvas* that we are at the heart of Mahayana Buddhism. There are countless *bodhisattvas*, who have vowed to help all others to the ultimate goal of enlightenment. And it is because of this concept of many buddhas and *boddhisattvas* that there are so many different strands of Mahayana Buddhism, for some groups will favour one or more buddha or *bodhisattva*, while others will prefer another. This brings about the great diversity of Mahayana Buddhism, diversity which is sufficient sometimes to make one particular group fairly ignorant of the beliefs of another, yet all such groups would call themselves Buddhists.

Although there are many *bodhisattvas* they were originally all connected to the Buddha himself and on visiting Buddhist temples it would be usual to see the Buddha, Siddhartha Gautama, alongside other buddhas and *bodhisattvas*. Most Mahayana Buddhists refer to Siddhartha Gautama as *Sakyamuni Buddha*, the Buddha who was the Sakya sage, Sakya being the name of the tribe from which the Buddha came. In many ways, Sakyamuni Buddha remains the link between all buddhas and *boddhisattvas* even though, in some sects of Mahayana Buddhism, a different buddha may be predominant. Some Mahayana sects envisage many universes, each presided over by a buddha and accompanying *bodhisattvas*. *Bodhisattvas* practise six perfections – generosity, morality, patience, vigour, meditation and wisdom; these must be perfected for enlightenment to be achieved and traditionally there are ten stages on the path of a *bodhisattva* before he or she can become one with all the Buddhas. The merit incorporated by just one *bodhisattva* on such a path is immense.

In general Mahayana Buddhism denies that anything can have *svabhava* "own-being". This is to say that nothing at all can have any permanence and therefore can *really* exist: everything really is empty, *sunya*. So things can neither be nor not be, they are Void – a metaphysical analysis of the "Middle Way" between being and non-being. And because this Voidness or Emptiness (termed the doctrine of *sunyata* in Mahayana Buddhism) applies to *all* things, it applies to *bodhisattvas* as much as humans, and to *nirvana* as much as *samsara*. So there is no difference between a human being and a *bodhisattva* or between *nirvana* and *samsara*, they are ultimately the same, ultimately empty of *svabhava*, and are therefore unreal. But since we live in an "unreal" world, and continue to differentiate between this and that through our ignorance and ego-bound personalities, *bodhisattvas* provide an ideal at which to aim, a source of help, support, and transferable merit, and *nirvana* remains an ultimate goal in an ignorant *samsaric* world, in the realm of relative but not absolute reality. *Bodhisattvas*, though ultimately as unreal as a human being, are the means by which those on the Buddhist path can learn to pass from the unreality of life to the reality of enlightenment in *nirvana*. *Bodhisattvas* also fulfil the role of counteracting evil in the world and may be portrayed in ferocious forms like the Tantric deities of Hinduism. This is a feature paticularly of some Tibetan *bodhisattvas*.

Buddha-nature   One of the major developments of Mahayana Buddhist thought was the concept of *buddha-nature* which was to characterize the Buddhism of the Far East in particular. *Buddha-nature* came to be envisaged as the true nature of all things and the true nature of the individual. While the self is still accepted as completely changing and impermanent, once the egoistic self is lost what remains is *buddha-nature*, which is identical to the *Dharma* of the Buddha and, in some aspects of Buddhism, is identified with Sakyamuni as the Absolute.

The importance of this concept of *buddha-nature* in Mahayana Buddhism cannot be overestimated because if everything and everyone has *buddha-nature* within, and this *buddha-nature* is identical to the Absolute Buddha, then *everyone* contains buddhahood and *everyone* really is a buddha: the way to know this is to realize the *buddha-nature* within the self. It was this concept of *buddha-nature* and the concept of the potential buddhahood for all people which opened up Buddhism for ordinary people. The older Hinayana and subsequent Theravada Buddhism was the way of the monk, the *thera*. The only chance you could have of reaching *nirvana* and of ending the cycle of *samsara* would be by being ordained as a monk: lay people could never hope to achieve this. At best, by spending some time in a monastery with the ordained monks, they could hope to be born in their next existence in such a position that they, too, could enter a monastery as an ordained monk. But with this concept of *buddha-nature* came the logical conclusion that the potential for buddhahood was as much in the ordinary person as in the monk, in the foolish as much as the wise and in women as much as men. There was no need for the lay person to enter the monastery to strive for *nirvana*; it was as much obtainable in everyday life as it was in the monastery.

In recognizing the ongoing essence of the Buddha and the identical buddhahood in all beings it is possible to suggest some kind of permanent, indescribable, unchanging Absolute which exists in all things. Scholars vary in the degree to which they accept such a theory but the concepts of buddhahood and *buddha-nature* go far to support such a concept of an underlying Reality which, like the Tao of Taoism, is the common denominator of all, even if this common denominator is voidness or emptiness. Some Mahayana schools of thought term this the *Dharmakaya*, that which is manifest in the many buddhas and *boddhisattvas* in what is called *sambhogakaya* form, and in earthly manifestations such as Sakyamuni Buddha in *nirmanakaya* form, a doctrine known as the *Trikaya*, or "three bodies" of the Buddha. Far-eastern Buddhism especially tends to incorporate such ideas. While many scholars deny that there is such a thing as an "Absolute" in the sense of a totally transcendent unifying principle in Buddhism, there is much evidence to the contrary. One example can be found in the words of H. W. Schumann, who has stated:

> The Dharmakaya is the self-centred immanent as well as transcendent truth or reality of all beings and appearances: the indestructible, timeless Absolute, the one essence in and behind all that was, is, and will be. It is the bearer and the object of enlightenment or Buddhahood.[35]

The problem with this kind of statement of the existence of some kind of Absolute for Buddhism is that there are too many similarities with the Hindu concept of a Ground of all being, Brahman. Yet, even if this is so, there would be differences, for there is no conception in Buddhism of an absolute *Dharmakaya* as a principle and ground state from which all is manifested. And yet, should such a concept of a *Dharmakaya* be accepted, the characteristic of it as a unifying principle in the universe, suggesting overt monism, would have to be accepted. Again, Schumann makes this clear:

> The Dharmakaya is that one of the Three Bodies which all Buddhas have in common. Whereas there existed and exist innumerable Earthly Buddhas, there is only one Dharmakaya.[36]

This suggests that ultimate reality is a unity, and that a permanent, intransient Absolute, can be equated with *nirvana*. But while the *Dharmakaya* as an indescribable Absolute is beyond the conceptualization of humankind, the *sambhogakaya* manifestations of the *Dharmakaya* are not only describable but are also able to be related to in a more tangible way as the many buddhas and *bodhisattvas*.

With the presence of so many buddhas and *bodhisattvas* who had vowed to help the rest of the universe to reach enlightenment it came to be believed that they could be appealed to for help in times of need and that they would intercede for humankind if asked. It is here that we can see how many aspects of Mahayana Buddhism have adopted practices which are very similar, if not identical in many cases, to theistic practices involving belief in a personal God, Goddess or Gods and Goddesses. Again, we can see that humankind often prefers this kind of theistic approach to the divine and is content to approach a manifest aspect of divinity rather than try to comprehend something which is indescribable and beyond mortal conception. So not only is the *bodhisattva* an example of the kind of person one should want to be but he or she is also the medium for help and comfort or for praise and adoration. Thus, Kshitigarbha looks after the dead, Vajrapani conquers evil, Avalokitesvara bestows help and grace and Tara epitomizes motherly care. Images or *rupas* of the buddhas and *bodhisattvas* are extremely popular, even in Theravada Buddhism where they supply a focus for meditation and a reminder of the *Dhamma* of the Buddha for the Theravada Buddhist, and a means of assistance, a focus for worship, praise and prayer for the Mahayana Buddhist. In the *rupas* we have the anthropomorphic representation of the indescribable and this, again, seems to fulfil an inherent need of humankind.

Puja and meditation in the Mahayana traditions of Buddhism vary enormously, but, considering the proliferation of *bodhisattvas* it is easy to see how these would be approached, praised and propitiated in a somewhat theistic manner, even if there are those who deny that there can be any theism in Mahayana Buddhism at all. Perhaps this is the case in theory, but in practice it is difficult to see how such a theory can be maintained. *Puja* to the many *bodhisattvas* and buddhas is more elaborate in Mahayana Buddhism and the colourful shrines portray many *rupas*. Offerings are more numerous than the traditional three of flowers, light and incense, characteristic of the Theravadin tradition.

The scriptures of Mahayana Buddhism   The traditional Hinayana Buddhism and subsequent Theravada recognized only the scriptures of the *Ti-pitaka* as authentic. Mahayana Buddhism, on the other hand, has a much wider viewpoint and hence a large number of other scriptures which are considered to be important and authentic: a selection only can be outlined here. Hinayana and Theravada Buddhist scriptures are written in Pali, but because Mahayana Buddhism was less conservative it accepted many other writings in its canon of literature, which came to be recorded in Sanskrit. Although there are differences between the two languages it is often not too difficult to see the link between words in both. For example, the Pali for truth or teaching is *dhamma*, while the Sanskrit is *dharma*. When dealing with Theravada Buddhism, Pali terms have been used throughout this chapter, and Sanskrit terms have been used for Mahayana. The most complete collections of Mahayana Buddhist scriptures exist as translations in Tibetan and Chinese sources, probably all being originally Indian.

Wisdom sutras   In the early period of Mahayana Buddhism perfection of wisdom, that is to say having the kind of wisdom which led to a cessation of the ego self, of desires and aversions, and an understanding of the impermanence of life – in short, the *Dharma* of the Buddha – was the means to *nirvana*. So at this early time, there were a number of teachings or *sutras* on the "perfection of wisdom", *prajnaparamita* (*prajna* "wisdom" and *paramita* "perfection, supreme, highest") which originally came to be written down in the first century BCE, but were expanded and extracted from during the next century. The most important of such literature is the *Mahaprajnaparamita Sutra* "The Great Perfection of Wisdom Teaching". Many *prajnaparamita* texts are really extracts from this main one, two such examples being the *Diamond Sutra* and the *Heart Sutra*. They were both composed in the early centuries CE. A copy of the *Diamond Sutra*, dating to the ninth century is housed in the British Museum and this copy is said to be the oldest printed book in the world. The *Sutra* describes the stages in the life of a *bodhisattva*, that is to say, the processes by which *prajna*, wisdom, is achieved.

The wisdom which much of this literature elucidates is the principle of *sunyata*, the "emptiness" of all things as devoid of *svabhava*. The *Diamond Sutra* especially states this of a *bodhisattva*: "if a Bodhisattva has any notion of a being, a person, or a self, he could not be called a Bodhisattva. There is no actual person on the Bodhisattva path."[37] This is to say that the *bodhisattva* is not only devoid of a self but is ultimately unreal. The *Sutra* emphasizes that "all things are without self, without being, without soul, without personality"[38].

The *Prajnaparamita Sutras* thus stress that all life is unreal or *maya*. It has no reality because it is constantly changing and therefore impermanent. If I go back to the image of the see-saw used earlier, it is as if the see-saw is constantly moving because we are either one side of it or the other, we are this or that but we are never in the centre, never still. The point at the centre is the point of equilibrium, the point where this and that are not there: it is the point of *suchness* or *emptiness* in that it is empty of dualities; it is the point where all dualities meet. And because all life is impermanent and transient nothing can be said to have any permanent essence or "own-being", *svabhava*. Everything is Void, Emptiness, *sunyata*. This is the major teaching of the *Prajnaparamita Sutras*.

Other *sutras* are more devoted to the practice of meditation as a means to *nirvana* or to the teachings about *karma* and *samsara*, while some *sutras* concentrate on a particular buddha. An example of this last are the Pure Land *sutras*, which depict the heavenly realm or buddha-field of a particular Buddha, Amida, who is highly popular. Some of these *sutras* describe the exquisite land of Amida, the land to which those who have faith in him may go after death, while other *sutras* are directions for meditations on Amida.

One very influential *sutra* is the *Lotus Sutra*, the *Saddharmapundarika Sutra*, "The Lotus of the True Law". The *Lotus Sutra* is written as a kind of drama in which human beings, buddhas and *bodhisattvas* interact. It stresses the idea that all are potential buddhas and by faith in the Buddha and following his teachings the natural state for all humankind is buddhahood. In the *Lotus Sutra*, Sakyamuni Buddha is presented as the eternal, cosmic Buddha who came to earth in human form to save humankind and promote the enlightenment of countless beings. He was already enlightened before he came to earth for, being the cosmic Buddha, he was Absolute, but he went through the drama of being one on the path to enlightenment in order to help others on the same path. The *Sutra* also explains that there are many strands of teaching in the Buddha's *Dharma*: it would have been impossible for the Buddha to have taught the highest truths immediately for people would not have been ready for them, so he had to prepare the ground and build up his teachings over a period of time. But the *Lotus Sutra* is believed to unite all teachings of the Buddha into one, essential and supreme teaching.

The spread of Mahayana Buddhism   Because Mahayana Buddhism was more liberal in its outlook than the conservative Hinayana school, it was more conducive to spreading outside India. Strict adherence to the rules of the *Vinaya* of Hinayana Buddhism was not always necessary for Mahayana Buddhism was much more adaptable. For example, Japan relies on fish for its dietary protein and to this day, Japanese Buddhists still eat fish. The *Vinaya* would have forbidden this, but the more liberal Mahayana views were able to accommodate such divergences and therefore allowed the spread of Buddhism well outside India. Conze points out that the *Vinaya* prohibited monks being practitioners of medicine, but the experience of the Mahayanists on their missionary journeys showed them only too clearly that healing people in the physical sense was a much surer way to gain converts and so they cited the doctrine of *mahakaruna* and held that this was more important than any set of rules. It was this kind of adaptability which ensured the spread of Buddhism.[39]

It was Mahayana Buddhism which reached China somewhere in the first century BCE and although it was about five hundred years before Buddhism could be said to be a major force in China, it has remained highly influential in Chinese religion over the centuries. Here we see, too, the ability of Mahayana Buddhism to adapt to the host country and to allow the kind of syncretism which has produced the unique blend of three systems of belief – Taoism, Confucianism and Buddhism – which informs Chinese religion. Buddhism gave to Chinese religion, among other things, a belief in reincarnation and the concept of an inner essence of *buddha-nature*.

In India itself, Mahayana ideas spread northwards to Tibet and here there was an acceptance of ideas which are known as Tantric, often given the designation *Vajrayana* to distinguish it from Theravada or Mahayana Buddhism. While remaining under the umbrella term of

Mahayana Buddhism, Tibetan Buddhism was a much more esoteric type of Buddhism, suggesting that buddhahood could be obtained through passing through stages of training under a *guru*. Each Tantric school has its own secret initiations and teachings as a means to buddhahood and a wealth of divine forces and *bodhisattvas* to aid the process. Tantric Buddhism also gained ground in Nepal and Kashmir. Mahayana Buddhism also spread to Korea and from there to Japan, where it is prominent today. So although Hinayana Buddhism was not without some missionary success, it was the more adaptable and liberal Mahayana school of thought which made the greatest impact on Buddhism outside India.

SYMBOLS

Religious symbols are phenomena which express in word, sign and pictorial form some profound underlying concept, often pointing to concepts which are deeper than humankind can describe. Buddhism is particularly rich in symbols and images and the iconography of the Buddha is particularly expressive of symbolic meaning.

Immediately on looking at the Buddha it is possible to see the symbolic distinguishing marks of his buddhahood. To begin with, the head is not a normal shape but has a considerable bump on the top. This is called the *usnisa* and is symbolic of the special spirituality of the Buddha and the great mind which he had – all-knowing and enlightened. The *usnisa* will vary from one image to another, sometimes being more obvious, but on others appearing more in the form of a headdress, rather like flames from a fire. Between the Buddha's eyes is the *urna*, the third eye, which symbolizes his spiritual insight. To look at it it is no more than a small spot and looks nothing like an eye, but in Eastern thought, this place between the two eyes is often thought to be the seat of intuitive knowledge. The great *yogins* of Hinduism concentrate their thoughts on this spot in the head while in deep meditation, and at death, the *yogin* brings his focus on this point in order to contain his spiritual energy and keep it rooted in *atman*. The rings of hair on the Buddha's head are also symbolic of his super-human character. They are always coiled in a clockwise direction, though this may not be as evident on some images as others. Very characteristic of the images are the long ear lobes, which are a symbol of respectability and nobility. Indian women have always thought it essential to have long, noble, ear lobes and will often wear very weighty earrings in order to stretch their lobes a little. Thus the natural nobility of the Buddha is symbolized by his long ear lobes.

These characteristic symbols of the Buddha's person are usually clearly visible on the Buddha images but there are others which may not be quite so readily seen. Altogether, there are said to be thirty-two signs of his buddhahood, but most of these would not be visible on Buddha *rupas*. On some images, it is possible to see that the Buddha's fingers are all the same length as, also, are his toes. On the palms of his hands, or the soles of his feet, are the marks of the Wheel of the Law, itself an important symbol which will be examined separately below. Sometimes this Wheel of the Law can be found on other parts of the Buddha image. Often conspicuous, too, are some of the other signs of his spiritual buddhahood, in the wrinkles on his neck, his webbed fingers and the gold colour of his skin.

Not only are these distinguishing marks symbolic of the spirituality and omniscience of the Buddha but the whole image itself is also a symbol. To begin with the very posture of the Buddha has symbolic meaning as, also, his expression. In relation to the latter, the usual expression is one of serenity and calm, with the eyes half closed to symbolize meditation. Regarding the former, three particular postures are evident, sitting – in the traditional lotus posture of the meditator – standing, and reclining. The most frequent of these is the seated pose of the Buddha with the feet crossed over on top of the opposite thigh in the lotus position. The lotus itself is a very important symbol in Buddhism: it is a flower which grows in the filthiest of waters in the East. Its leaves are spread out flat on the surface of the muddy waters, just like the knees are spread flat when sitting in the lotus position. The muddy waters symbolize the world with all its suffering and tribulations and the leaves symbolize humankind. But from the heart of the green leaves outspread on the waters comes the most exquisite of flowers – the lotus flower – and this symbolizes the *buddha-nature* of the individual, rising in consciousness to the point of *nirvana*. Moreover, the lotus flower has the unusual phenomenon of bearing the flower and the fruit at the same time. This, for some Buddhists, symbolizes the idea of *karma* by which, any action produces at the same time the cause and the latent effect: once you act in mind or body you must have a result to follow, whether now or in the distant future: latent results are therefore present in all actions, just like the fruit of the lotus flower exists at the same time as the flower which causes it. Many images of the Buddha show him seated on a lotus and for some Mahayana Buddhists the lotus has the additional symbolism of each petal representing a whole world system.

When the Buddha is featured in this seated posture, the position of his hands is always highly symbolic. Some of these seated images show the Buddha with one hand touching the ground. This represents the time when he was in the process of becoming enlightened and was challenged by the enemy of enlightenment, called Mara. Mara is rather like the Christian concept of Satan and symbolizes the force which operates against the *Dhamma*. As Siddhatta was about to achieve enlightenment, Mara sent all sorts of temptations to discourage him and when these failed, then he sent all his hosts of evil forces. But as he did this, Siddhatta put his hand down to the ground and called the earth itself to witness that this moment was one he had risen to after a long process as a *bodhisattva*, and that enlightenment was therefore right for him. In response, the whole earth trembled with earthquakes and thunder and the hosts of Mara were defeated. So Buddha images which depict the Buddha with one hand pointing to the ground symbolize his "calling the earth to witness" at the time of his enlightenment.

The traditional meditative position of the hands in Buddhism is also to be seen on some Buddha images. Here, the hands are brought together in the lap with the fingers lined up with each other, back to back, and the thumbs gently touching on top of the fingers. This creates a kind of circuit and is the standard symbolic hand position for nearly all Buddhism, though the position of the fingers may vary. When in this position, the hands are showing the gesture of concentration and therefore symbolize the concentration needed in order to rid oneself of desire and ego, as the Buddha himself did. Another symbolic gesture of the hands is that of "turning the Wheel of the Law". I shall return to this particular symbol, the wheel, below but here, in the context of Buddhist iconography, it serves to represent the teaching, the *Dhamma* of the Buddha. To show this, the forefinger and thumb on each hand are brought together to form a circle or wheel and the two hands are brought together to touch just where the fingers and thumbs unite. These hand positions are called *mudras* and are a distinct feature of both Buddhism and Hinduism.

Apart from seated Buddha figures there are also standing figures and reclining ones. Standing postures very often show the Buddha's hands in the *mudra* of *namaskar*, the traditional Indian greeting which means "I honour you" or "I bow to you". Here, the palms of the hands are brought together, chest high. Other standing postures may have the right hand raised in blessing with the palm facing outward while the left hand is lower, palm upwards and fingers outward, as if giving. This is a *mudra,* which is particularly widespread in religious iconography. Apart from signifying the Law, or *Dhamma*, of the Buddha, this *mudra* is sometimes known as the gesture of fearlessness because of the Buddha's use of it in certain contexts. The Buddha had a cousin called Devadatta, who was quite the opposite of the Buddha in nature and something of a malevolent personality. On a number of occasions, he tried to have the Buddha killed and on one of these sent a stampeding elephant in the Buddha's direction. The Buddha, however, being in a state of equilibrium, could feel no fear and merely raised his hand to quieten and still the elephant. Similarly, those who follow the Buddha's *Dhamma* will also acquire the fearlessness which a state of equilibrium brings.

In addition to seated and standing images of the Buddha, are those which show him in a reclining position. The reclining figures show the Buddha lying on his right side with an expression of great serenity. This last point is important, for not only do the images themselves contain symbolism in terms of the *mudras* and distinguishing Buddha marks, but the very face of the Buddha epitomizes the calm serenity of the one who is beyond dualities, one who is free from craving, desires and aversions, and therefore from ego. His face has the expression of one who is released from suffering, indeed, of one who is *released*, and his eyes are half closed suggesting the deep contemplation of one in meditation who is withdrawn from the world and, at death, from *samsara*.

Theravada Buddhism, as we have seen, accepted only one Buddha in this aeon, Siddhatta Gotama, so here, there would only be found iconography associated with the Buddha. The fact that people felt it necessary to have images of the Buddha on which they could focus their attention, albeit in terms of honour and respect rather than worship, suggests that humankind needs this kind of visual representation in religion. In Mahayana Buddhism with its wealth of buddhas and *bodhisattvas*, such iconography abounds. Some of these images are exquisitely beautiful and, like that of the Buddha Sakyamuni, are often highly symbolic. The Buddha Avalokitesvara, for example, is often portrayed with eleven heads arranged in a pyramid above his shoulders to show that his compassion extends in all directions. Or he may appear with four, six, eight or more arms to show that he has the power to extend his help to all. Each hand will show a *mudra* symbolizing other aspects of this popular Buddha.

The Wheel of Life and the Wheel of the Law   When Sakyamuni Buddha became enlightened he immediately set about the task of teaching others about the *Dhamma*, the truths about the nature of existence which he had awakened to at his *nibbana*. He taught his first sermon at a deer park to a very small group of monks, those who had been with him during his years of asceticism. In order to explain his teachings, he drew a wheel on the ground. This idea of the wheel has become a symbol for many basic teachings in Buddhism. To begin with, the *Noble Eightfold Path* is often presented as a wheel with eight spokes. This reflects that the aspects of the *Eightfold Path* are something to be pursued simultaneously, not one by one, for the wheel symbolizes balance and an equal emphasis on all parts. If one of these aspects is neglected, then the approach to life is unbalanced, in the same way that imbalance is caused in a wheel which has a broken spoke.

The wheel in Buddhism is also associated with the Wheel of Life, the continued cycle of *samsara*, the never-ending cycle of life, death and rebirth. The Buddha also used the symbol of the wheel to explain why individuals are chained to the cycle of *samsara*. Clinging to the wheel, that is to say, to life, ensures that you stay on it, that you are reborn. This time, he divided the wheel into twelve conditions, or stages of life, each of which was dependent on the one before and affected the one after, rather like twelve links of a chain which are bound into a circle. This is the concept of "dependent origination" which was noted above in the context of the *Eightfold Path*. He showed how human beings could break the chain at certain points in order to overcome the *samsaric* cycle. The Wheel of Life also symbolizes the law of cause and effect, the law of *kamma* which is what keeps each individual bound to the Wheel of Life. By getting rid of the desires and aversions which cause *kamma*, the cycle of effects is ceased and so there is no need to be reborn to experience the results of the *kamma* one has accumulated: the wheel is effectively stopped. It is in this sense that the Wheel of Life is often referred to as the Wheel of the Law.

The Wheel of Life is particularly represented in Tibetan Buddhism as a complicated symbol with six spokes separating the six possible areas into which human beings may be born after death. The outer rim of the wheel is divided up into the twelve stages of life conditions which cause the cycles of life, and the inner hub of the wheel contains a cockerel, a snake and a pig. The cockerel symbolizes greed and passion, anger and loss of control. The snake symbolizes hatred, and the pig delusion and ignorance. The whole Wheel of Life is held in the mouth of Yama, the God of the Underworld.

Prayer wheels In Tibetan Buddhism it is believed that *mantras*, which are symbolic sounds and words, have a particularly vibrant effect on individuals and on the world at large. *Mantras* are an important aspect of meditation but Tibetan Buddhism has taken certain *mantras* and has caused their sounds to be more widely broadcast by the use of prayer wheels, sometimes called *mani* wheels. Prayer wheels will range from quite small hand ones to very large ones housed in public places. Inside them are usually *mantras* or *sutras* or parts of *sutras*, and on the outside of them a shorter *mantra* or decoration. These prayer wheels are not shaped like wheels but like cylinders and they are rotated in the hand or by passing the hand across them if they are large ones. Often there may be several in a row so that many may be set in motion at once. Not only does this vibrate the *mantra* into the environment so that it can spread to all the world, but it also symbolizes the spreading of the Buddha's *Dhamma* throughout humankind. The usual *mantra* to be found in these prayer wheels is *Om mani padme, hum*, "Hail to the jewel in the Lotus".

Mandalas Closely connected with the symbolism of the wheel in Buddhism are *mandalas*. The word *mandala* means "circle" and refers to a geometric design which revolves around a centre. Though particularly associated with both Hinduism and Buddhism, *mandalas* are really common to many religions, indeed, the psychoanalyst Jung believed that *mandala* patterns are common to the archetypal imagery of the subconscious of each human being. There is much that is mystical about the *mandala*; indeed, it is something of the ultimate in symbols for it projects the mind beyond the gross to the depths of the abstract. They are designed to represent the cosmos and are used for the purposes of meditation. The meditator uses them in a way which internalizes them in his or her own body, so that he or she becomes identified with the cosmos. The very centre of the *mandala* represents the ultimate reality, the goal of life, and enlightenment, and a *guru* is needed in order to help an individual through the labyrinth which the *mandala* presents. The journey through the *mandala* represents the journey of the mind from the microcosm to the macrocosm and ultimately to Reality at the centre. On some, there are representations of deities or *bodhisattvas*, while others are complex geometrical patterns. But always, the journey is from one of the four points of entry on the exterior, to the very centre of the *mandala*. Every single part of the *mandala* has symbolic meaning.

Mandalas are used in the more esoteric, tantric sects of Buddhism. Tibetan Buddhism, in particular, is associated with Tantrism, so it is here where we should expect to find *mandalas* being used considerably. The Japanese school of Buddhism known as Shingon, also, has two important *mandalas*, one of which contains 1,461 deities to be encountered on the way to the macrocosmic Ultimate.

Prayer beads   Prayer beads are called *malas* and contain the magical, mystical number of 108. They often consist of bone or wood, though they may be hand-made by their owners. They are used, as similar objects in other religions, to aid concentration or meditation and to indicate when prostrations should be done. Sometimes the 108 beads are reduced to 27 for easier use and beads 1, 7 and 21 are usually in a different colour or are larger than the others in order to remind the Buddhist of the *Three Jewels*, or *Three Refuges* – the Buddha, the *Dhamma* and the *Sangha*. As the Buddhists turn the circle of beads through their fingers, they are reminded of the Wheel of the Law, the *Dhamma* of the Buddha. Just like the prayer wheels were felt to spread the Buddha's *Dhamma*, so moving the beads through the fingers is felt to symbolize the spread of loving-kindness to all parts of the world. Monks have the larger number of beads (108) divided into two halves, representing the stages – said to be 54 – of becoming a *bodhisattva*. The large bead in the middle of the two halves represents the Buddha. When walking, the beads are held in the left hand but are wrapped around the hands to symbolize the holding of the hand of the Buddha.

Architecture and art   When the Buddha died his bones were distributed to some of the important cities, and mounds were built over them. These relic mounds increased with the number of relics found. The most famous relic is perhaps the sacred tooth of the Buddha, which is said to have been brought out of India secretly, hidden in the hair of a princess, but also famous is the great Shwe Dagon Pagoda in

Rangoon which, it is said, contains hairs of the Buddha, a sandal of the Buddha and robes of previous buddhas. What is important about these relics is that they symbolize the Buddha's *Dhamma* and in Mahayana Buddhism, the presence of the Buddha in the universe. Even cuttings from the original tree under which the Buddha sat when he sought enlightenment have been used to symbolize his eternal teaching.

The buildings themselves are called *stupas* in India and they are shaped like inverted bells, with the relic of the Buddha housed in a casket in the centre base. Elsewhere, they are called differently; in Sri Lanka, *dagobas*, which are also bell-shaped but *very* large (for example about 300 feet high); in Japan they are called *pagodas*, which are more elaborate in shape. These *pagodas*, in particular, symbolize the five elements of earth, water, fire, air and void or ether in their structure, earth being the base of the *pagoda*, water the next level of the building, and so on, until void or ether is represented at the top.

In art, too, there is much symbolism, particularly with colours which are thought to represent the different parts of the mind. Shape in art is also symbolic and in many aspects of Buddhism artistic expression is geared towards the utmost simplicity, with nothing but a few brush strokes producing a finished effect symbolic of the calmness and serenity of the mind which is still.

ZEN BUDDHISM

Far Eastern Buddhism is characterized by a number of different schools in the Mahayana tradition. Some of the most important of these are extant in the Japanese traditions of Zen, Pure Land Buddhism, Shingon Buddhism and Nichiren Shoshu Buddhism, and these are singled out here for further examination.

The origins of Zen   Buddhism first reached China in the first century CE but it was not until the sixth to ninth centuries that it really flowered. Chinese Buddhism is very much a syncretistic mixture of Buddhism, Taoism and Confucianism but, like Tibetan Buddhism, Chinese communism was to bring about its demise after the Cultural Revolution of the 1960s. But when Chinese Buddhism flourished, the influence of one particular branch, Ch'an, was destined to take root in Japan. In about 520 CE, a Buddhist from southern India called Bodhidharma arrived in China and founded the Ch'an school of Buddhism there. The word Ch'an means "meditation", synonymous with the Indian word *dhyana*, and this was the hallmark of the type of Buddhism which Bodhidharma taught, a kind of Buddhism which was in some ways different from the ideas within either Theravada or Mahayana Buddhism. Ch'an Buddhism stresses the same need for wisdom as other strands of Buddhism, but this wisdom is not something gradually achieved, it is something to be spontaneously realized outside normal tradition and scriptural foundation. Such wisdom brings experience of the non-dual nature of all and therefore the ultimate unity of all mind consciousness – once all the differentiation common to the ordinary mind has been annihilated. Ch'an Buddhism was simple, devoid of scriptural study and ritual, but tough and disciplined. In contrast to other monastic traditions which eschewed manual work through conformity to the old *Vinaya*, Ch'an Buddhism stressed its importance, and monasteries became self-sufficient through the efforts of the monks themselves. While there were about five different Ch'an sects, two – Lin chi and Ts'ao tung (Japanese Rinzai and Soto respectively) – were destined to have the most impact.

Although some ideas of Buddhism filtered through to Japan from China from an earlier period, it was eventually in the twelfth century that a Buddhist monk from China, called Eisai, undertook a missionary journey to Japan and established Ch'an Buddhism there. The Japanese word for Ch'an is Zen. Since Japanese Zen Buddhism originated in China, and Chinese religion is a blend of Buddhism, Confucianism and Taoism, we find many ideas within it which are influenced by Taoist thought, and perhaps also by Confucianism. Eisai took with him to Japan, not only Buddhist teachings but the habit of tea drinking, and the order and correctness of some of the tea-drinking ceremonies in Japan may reflect some of the Confucian sense of order.

The two major forms of Zen   Eisai belonged to the Lin chi school of Ch'an Buddhism and taught the Japanese the teachings of his Master Lin chi whose name in Japanese is Rinzai: this name is now that given to one school of Zen Buddhism. Rinzai Zen stresses intuitive knowledge as the means to enlightenment and teaches that only intuitive knowledge can be true knowledge. Knowledge *about* things is not knowledge of their essence, their reality. Deep intuitive realization of the true nature of things comes about, in this school of thought, as the result of sudden insight, sudden intuition, but to experience such insight it is necessary to break down all the usual barriers of the mind and the logical processes of thinking. This may be accomplished by such varied methods as rapid questioning and answering by the Zen Master and his pupil, or even by a sharp whack with a stick! Anything which breaks down the common patterns of thinking of the mind would be in order. The other school of Zen Buddhism is Soto Zen. It was introduced into Japan by a Japanese disciple of Eisai, called Dogen, and originated in the Ts'ao tung branch of Ch'an in China.

Rinzai Zen   Rinzai Zen believes that it is intuitive knowledge which leads to enlightenment; this enlightenment is experience of the *buddha-nature* within which is the essence of all things. Because of the emphasis on intuitive knowledge to achieve enlightenment, no-one else can achieve this for an individual, no one can produce such an intuitive insight for another. There is thus a considerable emphasis on *jiriki*, self-effort. These ideas of personal effort and intuitive knowledge combine in Rinzai Zen to form a kind of religion which is not dependent on the usual ceremonies, rituals, prescribed doctrines or even scriptures. Intuitive knowledge of the real essence of things will not come from reading massive numbers of books or from logical thinking: *buddha-nature* is beyond all this. Scriptures would be useful up to a point but would be better on a fire in a cold room (as would a wooden image of the Buddha) than being maintained as the only necessary path to enlightenment, while religious ceremonies and the like are nothing but symbols and cannot produce the insight necessary for the realization of *buddha-nature*.

Rinzai Zen not only eschews all the established ceremonies and rituals of religion but also conventional intellectualism. Zen Masters (Japanese *roshis*) try to break down all the traditional, conventional ways of thinking. This may be done in odd ways to a Westerner. A visitor to a Zen monastery, for example, may be kept waiting outside all day and all night! Such actions are designed to apply a blow to the mind and Zen teachers may also apply one to the body of a pupil from time to time! In Japan, this kind of teaching was thought to be thoroughly refreshing; conventional religions supported the idea that sense is acquired through the laws of thought and the result of reasoning and logic, but since *buddha-nature* is beyond this, Zen tries to go beyond sense too, to non-logical sense. In Zen Buddhism, the individual is taken to the limits of thought, but not through dogmas, codes of ethics, or other such formulae. All the objects of the senses and emotions, philosophies and *isms* of any sort are overthrown and cast aside, so that the individual cannot be trapped in set patterns or be a slave to the kind of knowledge which is knowledge *about*, factual knowledge. Thoughts must be pushed, as it were, to the borders of a precipice and then beyond. Conventional thought and adherance to orthodox concepts only serve to prevent the intuitive understanding of the *buddha-nature* within.

***Zazen*: meditation**   All Zen Buddhism is characterized by an emphasis on meditation as a means to intuitively discover the *buddha-nature* within. It is a means of causing an awakening to what is already there. When we think of the term meditation we usually associate it with passivity, at least of the physical self, but Rinzai Zen meditation is essentially dynamic and involves fiercely intense effort to reach the buddhahood within. So meditation may be on paradoxes called *koans*, some of which seem to be quite absurd but are designed to counteract intellectual reasoning and to produce the kind of sudden insight which reveals pure knowledge. Meditation is normally done in the lotus position and sometimes for long hours at a stretch. Yet even here, meditation is only a means. A traditional Zen story explains this well in the account of a Zen pupil who sat all day in the lotus position. His Zen teacher asked him what he was doing and the pupil replied that he was trying to become a buddha. The teacher picked up a stone and began polishing it until the pupil asked what *he* was doing. The teacher replied that he was polishing it until it became a mirror. The pupil pointed out that the teacher would never make a mirror out of a stone and the teacher retorted that the pupil would never become a buddha by sitting cross-legged.

But Zen is not all fierce meditation since the Taoist concept of *wu-wei* has found its way, via the Chinese origin of Zen, into Japanese Zen Buddhism. *Wu-wei* "inaction", in the sense of "going with" nature and life, is important in Rinzai Zen where there is an emphasis on naturalness of actions which stem from concentration on the action in hand. Zen Buddhists do not sit all day long in the lotus position doing nothing but meditating: most Zen Buddhists have to work in the fields and engage in the more physical aspects of daily life. Effort has to be put into these mundane tasks as much as into meditation in the temple, but it is a natural effort, not a conscious striving of the self to get rid of the self. *Wu-wei* in Rinzai Zen means the acquisition of the goal of enlightenment without really aiming for it. There would therefore be no distinction between ordinary, secular existence and a sacred life as a monk. *Satori*, "enlightenment", can be gained as much through practical activity as through intensive meditation on a *koan*.

Koans (**Chinese *kung an***) **and *Mondo*** *Koans*, are paradoxes, but the word really suggests an old story or document; *koans* are used to help intuitive knowledge of *buddha-nature*. They are short paradoxical riddles, or slightly longer stories, which often give a choice between two alternatives, and whichever choice is made, the outcome is still impossible. No amount of intellectual thought can solve a *koan*, for the *koan* is like life itself, which also cannot be solved intellectually for the solution to life will go beyond words and ordered conceptualizations. Since the answers to the deeper purposes of life can only be discovered intuitively through a flash of insight, *koans* are designed to break down logical thought in order to allow that insight. A typical *koan*, and the most frequently cited one, is "What is the sound of one hand clapping?" Another is: "If you meet someone along the road who has realized the truth, you may not walk past the person in silence, nor speaking. So how should you meet this person?" Then there are stories used as *koans*, like the man who kept a goose in a bottle which grew larger and larger until it couldn't get out of the bottle any more. Without breaking the bottle, or harming the goose, how did he get it out? Such *koans*, of which there are about seven hundred in Japanese Rinzai Zen, are not meant to have any meaning for the ordinary mind. Thinking about them pushes the mind beyond all logic and intellectualism, producing a tension which brings one to the limits of thought. All the riddles arose from the teachings of Zen Masters to their pupils and the records of interchanges between them were gathered and formulated into one collection. There is no one answer to the riddles, individual spontaneity is expected and non-verbal answers are encouraged.

The story or "case" of some *koans*, as well as other material, will be the subject of verbal interchange between Master and pupil in the form of rapid question and answer – the characteristic *mondo* of Rinzai Zen. Here, the speed of thought is normally expected to be so rapid that it is eventually transcended, and intuitive knowledge floods the mind. In other cases exchange need not always be rapid as long as instant intuitive knowledge is gained by the pupil. So, like other aspects of Rinzai Zen, the *mondo* is designed to change normal thinking and knowing in the empirical sense, to a direct experience of intuitive knowledge in the deepest possible sense, and in so doing, bring experience of the *buddha-nature* within.

Satori   Theoretically *satori* is enlightenment, the ultimate goal of Zen and the indescribable state that lies beyond the intellect and any conceptual thought. It is the point of equilibrium between all opposites, the point where everything comes to rest. It is something which is already there in each individual which just needs waking up to. It is Ultimate Reality and Truth, which is greater than the idea of it and the person who seeks it. Waking up through intuitive realization to the *buddha-nature* within is waking up to the fact that, as all Buddhism teaches, the "I", the egoistic self, is unreal. The state of enlightenment is one in which there is freedom from attachment to all things and all ideas, and in which there is an understanding that everything in the cosmos is *buddha-nature*. Yet in practical terms, *satori* is rather like the Indian *samadhi* which is achieved at the height of meditation and yet is not totally indicative of enlightenment. Some Zen Buddhists consider that they can have experience of *satori* but that full buddha-hood is beyond it.

The cultural influence of Rinzai Zen   It was from China that Japanese culture gained some of its now famous cultural and aesthetic artistic characteristics as in architecture, gardening, water-colour painting, literature and ceramics. The martial arts from China were attractive to the *Samurai* warriors of Japan, and Rinzai Zen taught that the warrior could engage in warfare and still participate in the spiritual life because the two were, in reality, one. The martial arts of judo, *kung fu*, *karate*, archery and fencing were engaged in from the point of view of *wu-wei*, action rooted in inaction, and from the point of intuitive knowledge, not simply the mastery of skills. In archery, for example there was no aim to hit the target, but to bring the deeper intuitive knowledge into the action, to let the self disappear, and to "go with" the action.[40] The Confucian orderliness and properness may be seen behind the famous Tea Ceremony, which is a religious and ritualistic ceremony used at group meditations. Here, everything is prepared and carried out with the utmost concentration, silence, gracefulness and serenity, an act of meditation just to watch.

One of the most beautiful expressions of Rinzai Zen is its Haiku poetry. Haiku poems, confined to a mere seventeen syllables, express the affinity of humankind with nature and have something of the Taoist touch about them in their utter simplicity and yet paradoxical depth. They express quietness and spontaneity, suchness of things and an element of mystery. Some examples follow:

In the dark forest
  A berry drops
    The sound of water[41]

The thief
  Left it behind
    The moon at the window[42]

A fallen flower
  Returning to the branch?
    It was a butterfly[43]

The great Japanese Master, Basho (1644–94), composed the following:[44]

Spring rain –
  under trees
    a crystal stream.

If I'd the knack
  I'd sing like
    cherry flakes falling.

Wake, butterfly –
  it's late, we've miles
    to go together.

Come, see real
  flowers
    of this painful world.

Spider, are you
  crying – or
    the autumn wind?

Soto Zen   Soto Zen was introduced into Japan by a disciple of Eisai named Dogen (1200–53). After visiting China he brought back the less volatile and simpler Buddhism of Ts'ao tung, which became Japanese Soto Zen. The practice of *zazen*, or meditation, is central to all forms of Zen, but in Soto Zen it is the single most important factor. There are no interchanges with Zen Masters or meditating on *koans*, for it is simply *sitting*, termed *shikan taza*, which is the sole practice. It is not even necessary to study the scriptures or to understand the teachings of the Buddha. The method of meditation is perhaps the most natural of all forms of meditation for there is no need to use *mantras* or to focus the attention on *mandalas*. The Soto Zen Buddhist simply sits on his or her chair or low stool or on the floor, with a straight back and facing a blank wall. The eyes remain open but focused down, following the line of the nose to a point on the wall a foot or so above the floor. When thoughts arrive in the mind, they are simply brushed aside and passed away without allowing them to develop. So as the sounds of the immediate environment filter into the mind, the mind does not react to them. Or, when the events of the day or previous day, or the concerns for the remainder of the day come into the mind, the mind does not react to them but softly brushes them aside. The mind, then, is not allowed to think; thoughts are not allowed to develop. In this case, the mind is able to become tranquil and the *buddha-nature*, which is beneath the ordinary levels of consciousness and mind processes, is allowed to surface. Soto Zen is a simple, quiet and natural form of Buddhism, even when walking meditation or *kin hin* is interspersed with "sitting". It accepts that the experience of buddhahood will gradually be awakened to, for buddhahood is already there in each being waiting to be experienced. None of the sudden and dramatic insight of Rinzai Zen is necessary here.

Zen belief   Generally Zen accepts the non-duality of all things and therefore their total monistic identity. *Nirvana* therefore is *samsara* and all beings possess buddhahood as the ultimate Reality and are equal to each other. This is beautifully illustrated when in Soto Zen initiation of lay people into the sect, the abbot bows to the lay person who is being initiated, symbolizing the inner equality between the two beings. Having buddhahood within means that one has to awaken to it – instantly in Rinzai Zen, gradually in Soto Zen – but both accept that each person is already a buddha, just as every animate and inanimate object down to a grain of dust. Buddhahood in all means ultimately the interconnectedness of all within the cosmos and that the cosmos itself is contained in each being and in every grain of dust.

Zen is not isolated from life, it is life; it is working, eating, cooking, gardening as much as meditating or engaging in spiritual activity, and working meditation is an important dimension of both Rinzai and Soto Zen. As a Soto Buddhist friend intimated concerning his being assigned to the working meditation of cleaning the temple during one of his stays at Throssel Hole Abbey in Northumbria, Britain:

> In cleaning the temple I came to realize that you are not cleaning the temple, the temple is cleaning you. And ultimately the temple is pure,

and so are you; neither needs cleaning, but I had to clean it to realize it. In such working meditation there is a formal cognitive commitment to the task after which comes an experience of the realization of things as they *really* are.[45]

Such words remind me of a story of someone raking the gravel of a very simple, scarcely ornamented, Zen garden. It took three months to get it right, but on the day that person got it right, there was no need to do it again; insight had occurred. Hubert Benoit cites a Zen dialogue between a Master and a monk which illustrates well the difference between the working world of the ordinary person and the working meditation of the monk:

A MONK: In order to work in the Tao is there a special way?
THE MASTER: Yes, there is one.
THE MONK: Which is it?
THE MASTER: When one is hungry, he eats; when one is tired he sleeps.
THE MONK: That is what everybody does; is their way then the same as yours?
THE MASTER: It is not the same.
THE MONK: Why not?
THE MASTER: When they eat they do not only eat, they weave all sorts of imaginings. When they sleep they do not only sleep they give free reign to a thousand idle thoughts. That is why their way is not my way.[46]

This kind of mindfulness is a hallmark of much Buddhist tradition, from the practices of Theravada to Soto Zen "sitting": underpinning it is the egoless mind and the need to still the mind from *karma*-producing desires, aversions, cravings and the differentiation of things in life which give a distorted picture of reality.

Britain has a significant Soto Zen organization based at Throssel Hole Abbey called the Order of Buddhist Contemplatives. Its Reverend Master, Jiyu Kennett, was the first woman to train in Japan for the title of Master. She set up Shasta Abbey in California in the United States. As a musician, she set the Buddhist *sutras* to music and the resultant effect of chanting in plainsong is quite exquisite to hear. In this order, cermonial bowings during group sessions are particularly prominent and possibly reflect something of the old Chinese order and grace of Confucianism in the distant beginnings of Zen.

PURE LAND BUDDHISM

One of the most popular strands of Mahayana Buddhism today is Pure Land Buddhism, which centres around one particular Buddha called in China by the Sanskrit Amitabha meaning "Infinite Light", and also Amityus, "Infinite Life". In Japan, he is called Amida, and it is this name, Amidism, which is sometimes given to this particular branch of Buddhism. Pure Land Buddhism, or Amidism, is not the name of one particular sect of Buddhism but is rather a collective term for a number of different sects, all of which focus their attention on Amitabha or Amida and believe in the existence of his Pure Land.

Buddhism, as indeed Hinduism, has a cosmic perspective of the universe and recognizes the existence of many planes and extra-terrestrial realms beyond the world in which we live. Some of these extra-terrestrial realms are the abodes of the buddhas, each buddha having his own particular region. Because of the incredible *karmic* merit of these great buddhas, which had been built up as *bodhisattvas*, the environment of their realms is exquisitely beautiful, blissful and paradisical. The realm of Amitabha is called Ching-t'u in China and Sukhavati, "Land of Bliss", in Japan and what is so special about Sukhavati is that Amitabha is believed to have made a vow that he would save all people and that anyone who believes in him and surrenders the self to him, will be born in Sukhavati and will remain there until they reach *nirvana*.

What we have here is the idea of Amitabha as a saviour, a former *bodhisattva* and now a Buddha who was, and is, dedicated to saving all sentient beings and whose grace is sufficient to reward all those who believe in him with an existence beyond death in paradise. There is much here which is similar to the Western concept of belief in Heaven and, indeed, Pure Land Buddhism is so far removed from the general Mahayana Buddhism of India that some scholars consider it to have originated from regions which were influenced by Zoroastrianism, a religion which teaches doctrines of good and evil and of Heaven and Hell.

Traditionally, Amitabha is believed to have existed many aeons ago as Dharmakara, a monk. Dharmakara took forty-eight vows, and said that he would not enter full buddhahood until these vows were fulfilled. Throughout his countless lives in successive aeons, Dharmakara accumulated the kind of *karmic* merit in fulfilling these vows, which enabled him to set up a buddha-world; indeed the establishment of such a world had been one of his forty-eight vows. It is this buddha-world which is the paradisical Pure Land of Amitabha. It is open to all people except the most evil, providing that people believe in Amitabha to the extent that they have *faith* in his saving ability. To those who have this faith, Amitabha will appear at death and carry the soul of the individual to Sukhavati. Once the soul arrives at Sukhavati, it will be reborn from the bud of a supernatural lotus into a new body and will experience spiritual bliss. In this paradise, the individual will hear the teachings of Amitabha and will eventually pass on to *nirvana*.

This tradition was current in written form in about the third century CE, and by the sixth century Pure Land Buddhism had become a distinct and important branch of Mahayana Buddhism. To those Buddhists who felt the impossibility of accumulating the kind of good *karma* which would place them in the position to lose all *karma* and thereby realize the ultimate goal of *nirvana*, this form of Buddhism came as light relief. Pure Land Buddhism replaced the idea of individual effort with the concept of faith, faith in a *bodhisattva* who had vowed to help each person by giving away his merit or grace to the devout believer.

Pure Land (*Ching-t'u*) Buddhism in China Devotion to Amitabha became popular in China in the seventh century. It was not difficult for the Chinese to accept this new religious teaching for there were aspects of Taoism which were rather similar. To begin with, Sukhavati was located in the far west and was not unlike the Taoist conception of the realms of the Immortals, also located in the west: Lao Tzu, the great Taoist philosopher, had disappeared into the mists of the west – imagery, to the Taoist, which suggested his demise to the realms of immortality. Additionally, worship of Amitabha requires concentration and meditation on the name of the *bodhisattva*, usually the repetition of his name hundreds of times, at the same time trying to visualize him in his paradisical land. These kinds of practices were not unfamiliar to Taoists and so were easily accepted in the religion of China. Yet it would also be true to say that Taoist and Chinese religion influenced Pure Land Buddhism by encouraging a host of elaborate practices and rituals much beloved by the Chinese. Since, too, Chinese religion is by nature syncretistic, Pure Land Buddhism in China tended to be mixed with Ch'an (Zen) Buddhism and Tantric Buddhism, so that the branches of Pure Land Buddhism in China were somewhat variable. Despite such variety, however, Chinese Pure Land Buddhism sees all other Buddhist practice and belief as inadequate.

The idea of Sukhavati was particularly popular with the ordinary person who no longer needed to think of countless lifetimes of accumulating good merit and attempting to lose the egoistic self in order to achieve salvation. Considering the amount of war in China, the poverty, natural disasters and the physical and mental weakness of people, it seemed that humankind could only be saved by some extrawordly, Buddha like Amitabha. This was a much easier path and, naturally, an attractive one, but we should not make the mistake of seeing it as a complete departure from earlier Mahayana ideas in Buddhism. There is certainly an emphasis on losing the self in surrender to Amitabha. And this would be done by prostrating oneself before Amitabha and by concentrating one's whole mind on being born into his Pure Land, his *Ching-t'u*; singing praises to Amitabha; making vows to be born into his Pure Land; visualizing Amitabha and his Pure Land, and vowing to be a *bodhisattva* oneself when enlightenment was reached. All these actions are physical and mental means of lessening the egoistic self. Recitation of the name of Amitabha remains the most prevalent practice but, at a more metaphysical level, there is little difference in the abstract ideas taught by Ch'an Masters and Pure Land philosophers; both accept the ultimate formlessness and non-duality common to most Buddhism. Pure Land Buddhism in China came to accept that spiritual practices are dependent on levels of consciousness, so whereas at the lowest level reciting the Buddha's name is the only recourse to rebirth in Amitabha's Pure Land, at the highest level, the equilibrium of non-duality is experienced. For the ordinary Buddhist in China, however, chanting the name of Amitabha remains the means to salvation and the popularity of such belief is echoed by the fact that it is this chant which would be heard in nearly all the Buddhist temples in China today.

Pure Land (*Jodo*) Buddhism in Japan   Amidism spread to both Korea and to Japan and was particularly popular in Japan by about the eleventh and twelfth centuries. Japanese Amidism arose from the ideas of two men. Honen (1133–1212) taught that there were two ways to reach enlightenment; one was the path of *jiriki*, "own effort", the path for those who were monks and who had the ability to spend long hours in meditation and spiritual pursuits; the other way is called *nembutsu*, which is reciting the name of Amida, along with *tariki*, which is relying on the strength of another (that is to say, on Amida). This latter way was the easier path for the ordinary person. Honen taught that, on the easy path, all that was necessary was to invoke the name of Amida and Amida himself would do the rest through his immeasurable merit, and that although it was the easier path, it was the superior one to *jiriki*. By reciting the name of Amida, *Namu Amida Butsu* (Adoration to Amida Buddha), the individual would come to have an insight into the nature of Amida's grace and would thus have the faith necessary to be born into his Pure Land.[47] Some even came to believe that *nembutsu* would only have to be undertaken *once* in order to ensure rebirth in the Pure Land.

The ideas of Honen were complemented by those of his disciple, Shinran (1173–1261), who taught that *nembutsu* was not enough, and that the individual had to surrender his or her self to Amida in total *faith*: neither *tariki* nor *jiriki* could suffice, only total surrender in faith. Whereas Honen taught that *nembutsu* would lead to faith in Amida, Shinran taught that faith in Amida was necessary first; *nembutsu* was simply the expression of this faith. But this faith, Shinran believed, was the result of the infinite grace of Amida, not the individual. Faith was not something the individual summoned in order to practise *nembutsu*, it was something which Amida himself granted. *Nembutsu* would not even bring good *karma*; it was simply, yet, profoundly, an abandoning of the self to Amida, to his grace – in faith which he himself had bestowed. What is particularly important about the teachings of Shinran is that he showed that Buddhism could be a household religion. He himself had realized this at a time when he was exiled and was compelled to live the life of a layman. He married, had a family, and came to realize that the religious life is just as possible in everyday, social activities as in the monastery: religious and secular life were to be seen as one. He also ate meat, something which other Buddhist sects in Japan refrained from. Modern-day Japan is still a meat-eating nation as a result of the massive influence of this sect. The Buddha, Siddhartha Gautama, had taught that there would come a time when his teachings would no longer be heard and when society would degenerate and become decadent. Japanese Buddhists call this period *mappo*. Shinran came to believe that any amount of practice of Buddhist precepts in the age of *mappo* in which he lived could not bring enlightenment; the times themselves militated against this. Something beyond humankind was needed, and Shinran believed that this was the Buddha Amida. Only through Amida's grace and his immeasurable amount of good *karma*, acquired by fulfilling the forty-eight vows he had taken aeons ago, could humankind hope to reach *nirvana*.

It is this idea of the grace of Amida which is the important key to the understanding of Jodo Shinshu Buddhism. Honen taught that the *individual* had to choose to have faith in Amida, whereas Shinran taught that it was *Amida himself* who chose to save humankind. All the individual really had to do was believe and accept this and the effects of *karma* would be wiped away by the grace and divine power of Amida. Hase Shoto comments on this point:

> what effectuates Amida's salvific power is the power of his Original Vow to save all beings as embodied in the Nembutsu. By participating in and allowing oneself to be permeated by this power, one transcends the world of causal necessity (*karman*).[48]

Important to note in these words is the concept of losing *karma* by being transparent to the grace of the Buddha. Thus, ego is lost in line with all Buddhist thought. But, as Shoto points out it was more than the vast accumulated merit of Amida as a former *bodhisattva* whch had salvific powers, it was also the *divine* power of the Buddha Amida which "transcends his individual personhood, breaking through the limited framework of time and space to embrace all living beings eternally and without limitation".[49]

It is easy to see why this form of Buddhism was so popular to the ordinary person. Today in Japan there are as many as ten different sects of Jodo Shinshu (True Pure Land Sect) Buddhism, making it the most popular form of Buddhism there, with some twenty million adherents. Jodoshu, the sect founded by Honen, also continues to thrive in Japan, though with less followers than Jodo Shinshu. "Shin" Buddhists tend to accept the Pure Land of Amida as the *final* goal, as *nirvana* and buddhahood itself and not just a stage prior to final *nirvana*. Other buddhas and *bodhisattvas* are generally disregarded in favour of total focus on Amida. Even Sakyamuni Buddha is seen as but an earthly manifestation of Amida.

Nembutsu *Nembutsu*, as noted, is the practice of reciting the name of Amida in Japanese Pure Land Buddhist sects. In China, the name Amitabha would be recited. However, it is important to recognize that it is not the recitation of the name of Amitabha or Amida itself which causes rebirth in the Pure Land of this Buddha; rather it is the *vows* of Amitabha/Amida which make this possible. It is the boundless merit and grace of this *bodhisattva* which can bring about salvation for the individual. Reciting the name, for example, *Namu Amida Butsu* in Japanese (*Namo-Amito-fo* in Chinese), "I bow to Amida Buddha", is a means of reaching out to the *bodhisattva* in a condition of faith: the faith is in Amitabha/Amida, rather than being faith in the words chanted, as if they were some kind of magical formula. Nevertheless, repeating the name of the Buddha Amitabha in China is thought to result in excellent merit, good *karma*, and at its less conscious level, some adherents may even keep a record of the number of times they have recited the name in order to assess the merit due to them. In Japan, recitation of the name of Amida is not linked at all to the acquisition of merit but is seen more as a means of access to the saving grace of Amida. *Nembutsu*, as any chanting, however, has a somewhat *mantric* effect which is likely to alter consciousness to some extent.

SHINGON
BUDDHISM

If Pure Land Buddhism can be seen as a somewhat straightforward path to salvation for the ordinary, everyday person, Shingon Buddhism is an example of the other end of the scale. It is what we would call *esoteric*, that is to say that it is beyond the understanding of the ordinary person and is understood only by a minority of initiates. It was founded in Japan by a monk called Kukai (774–835). Shingon Buddhism belongs to what we would call *Tantric* Buddhism, mystical Buddhism, the word *shingon* meaning "true word" and being a translation of the Sanskrit word *mantra*. Because it is a more mystical form of Buddhism, Shingon does not focus on the earthly Siddhartha Gautama but on the cosmic nature of the Buddha, on the totally transcendent absolute state of the Buddha which, although inexpressible, pervades the whole of the cosmos. This transcendent, cosmic Buddha is called Mahavairocana. Mahavairocana means "Great Luminous One" or "Great Illuminator", and has some connections with the concept of a solar deity. Just as the sun itself is the centre point of our universe and is the source of light, life and energy for the whole universe, so Mahavairocana is the Ultimate Reality, or *Dharmakaya*, the life and source of the whole cosmos. And just as the rays of the sun are manifest in the universe and shine on rich and poor alike, on old and young and good and evil, so the essence of Mahavairocana is within everything in the cosmos. However, although the essence of

Mahavairocana is in all things, Mahavairocana is *greater than* every-thing in the cosmos in a panentheistic sense. He is the creator and sustainer of the universe but is also its originator. All buddhas and *bodhisattvas* are merely expressions, or manifest aspects, of this great cosmic Buddha, and every individual is a microcosmic replica of Mahavairocana; every individual has within him or her part of the cosmic Buddha, the seed of enlightenment, *bodhicitta* or *buddha-nature*. So human consciousness is, in its *real* state, identical with the cosmic consciousness of Mahavairocana and the human body is iden-tified with the cosmic body of Mahavairocana.

Experience of Mahavairocana is brought about through ritualistic use of *mandalas* or "cosmograms", elaborate symbols of the cosmos. *Mandalas*, in some form or other, are perhaps common to all religions. The Tower of Babel in the Judeo-Christian religion, for example, was probably a *ziggurat*, a labyrinthine complex which, if reduced to an artist's plan from directly above, would appear just like a *mandala*. Early Buddhist *mandalas* were, in fact *stupas*, the relic mounds which were built to house the bones and other relics of the Buddha; when viewed from above, these were really three-dimensional *mandalas*. Right at the centre of the *stupa* would be the Buddha's relic or, later, the image of the Buddha in a temple. Just so, at the centre of a painted *mandala*, the ultimate Buddha would be placed.

There are two *mandalas* in Shingon Buddhism, the *Womb Mandala* and the *Diamond Mandala*. The *Womb Mandala* is divided into twelve courts, the very centre one containing the Buddha Mahavairocana with four buddhas and *bodhisattvas*, while many other buddhas and *bodhisattvas* (414 in all) are to be found in the other courts. All symbolize aspects of the cosmic Buddha in manifest form. The *Diamond Mandala* represents nine halls, eight of which are symbolic of a level of consciousness of the human mind, while the ninth symbolizes Mahavairocana. The two *mandalas* are like maps, maps of the truth and the means to the truth, but because of their complexities, realization of the *buddha-nature* within through contemplation on these *mandalas* can only be brought about by careful instruction. In addition, the Shingon Buddhist would consider *mudras* or body positions, *mantras* or symbolic sounds and phrases, and *yoga*, which is concentration or meditation, to be important aspects of daily practice in order to realize *buddha-nature* within. These three aspects of *mudras*, *mantras*, and *yoga* are considered to be the "Three Mysteries", and once they result in experience of *buddha-nature* or *bodhicitta*, then the Buddhist is capable of super-human powers.

Characteristic of Shingon Buddhism is an internalizing process of awakening to the *buddha-nature* within and an externalizing process by which one is involved in the world by showing compassion and morality and also strenuous effort. The integration of these two processes is an important concept, illustrating that the world itself and Ultimate Reality are not separate dualities but are one and the same. This will only be seen in a state of equilibrium, a state of *buddha-nature*. All life has this *buddha-nature*, so all life has to be honoured, for it is all an expression of the *Dharmakaya*, Mahavairocana. An added ingredient in Shingon Buddhism is the idea of faith, faith in the power of the "Three Mysteries", for example, to enable the individual to realize *buddha-nature*. This is the advocating of a kind of faith which results in loss of the ego by the lessening of the assertive, egoistic personality. Essentially, because *buddha-nature* is in all things and is the real essence of all things, Shingon Buddhism sees it as essential that activity in the world takes place. So although Shingon Buddhism is esoteric and mystical, it is also worldly. The whole of reality is the expression of the *Dharmakaya*, Mahavairocana, and therefore it is real, it is, in its essence, truth. By engaging in esoteric rituals, this truth can be experienced and then the individual will be a living expression of the *Dharmakaya*. When this happens the Buddha enters the self and the self enters the Buddha.

Tantric Buddhism, of which Shingon is the Japanese expression, is characterized by considerable magical practices. The idea of the use of spells is a very ancient one in India; the Hindu *Atharva Veda*, for example, contained incantations and spells for all kinds of situations. In Tantric Buddhism it came to be believed that the repetition of certain syllables or magical words could promote the experience of *buddha-nature* and, hence, enlightenment. Each deity, buddha or *bodhisattva* will have its own special magical *mantra* which, when repeated, will raise the consciousness of the adherent. So important are *mantras* in Tantric Buddhism that it is sometimes called *Mantrayana* instead of Mahayana Buddhism. A *mantra* is not so much a prayer as a means for the mind to come into contact with the Absolute Reality; and in the case of Shingon Buddhism, with Mahavairocana. The essence of the buddha or *bodhisattva* is believed to be actually present in the *mantra*.

When Shingon Buddhists use these magical formulae in conjunction with the *mandalas*, they have a means to raise their levels of consciousness to bring awareness of *buddha-nature* closer. When the Shingon Buddhist concentrates and meditates on the *mandala*, he or she focuses on a particular buddha or *bodhisattva* and tries to *become* that divine being. Despite its complexities, the *mandala* is a means to bring abstract, Ultimate Reality, the *Dharmakaya*, into accessible communication with humankind. So the *mandala* acts as a kind of bridge, as do the buddhas and *bodhisattvas* which are portrayed on it, between the wordly level and the level of an Absolute Reality. It unites the microcosm and the macrocosm, manifest divinity and unmanifest divinity: it is, in fact, the mid-point of the see-saw, the point at which all dualities and opposites become one.

Nichiren Shoshu Buddhism has its home in Japan and, alongside Pure Land Buddhism, is one of the most influential sects of Buddhism. It accepts that Sakyamuni Buddha was one who solved the four fundamental problems of birth and life, old age, sickness and death and that when he died he left his *Dharma*, the Law, as the teacher and leader of all Buddhists. It was to the truths of this Law which Sakyamuni awakened at the time of his enlightenment. He had realized what Kirimura depicts as "the Law of life which permeates the universe, nature, the human being, and all other phenomena".[50] Everything in the universe then is part of this Law: it was not something which Sakyamuni created but something which he experienced. In line with Buddhism in general Nichiren Shoshu Buddhism accepts that the psychological self is illusory, transitory and impermanent, but that there is a part of the self which is part of this fundamental and absolute cosmic Law. And because this Law always exists, then anyone can become a buddha by living their lives solely in relation to it; it is not a Law which is exclusive to one person. However, not many people have the level of consciousness to realize full buddhahood, but Nichiren Shoshu Buddhism accepts that this age witnessed one who was a Buddha – Nichiren Daishonin, who was born in 1222 in Japan.

Nichiren Daishonin   Nichiren Daishonin was born Zennichi-Maro, a name meaning "Splendid Sun". He was raised as a Buddhist and spent many years studying Buddhist scriptures. But he came to the conclusion that the most important of the Buddhist scriptures was the *Lotus Sutra* and that the title of the *Lotus Sutra* – *Myoho-renge-kyo* – contained in its essence all the teachings which Sakyamuni had given and, indeed, buddhahood itself. Prefacing the title with the honorific *Nam*, the chant *Nam-myoho-renge-kyo* became the central activity of Buddhist practice for the followers of Nichiren Daishonin. Outspokenly critical of all other sects of Buddhism, Nichiren Daishonin was for some time exiled on the bleak island of Sado where, supported by his followers, he survived the terrible winters. Successful predictions of future events in Japan eventually won him sufficient favour to ensure his return from exile. Before he died he wrote the title of the *Lotus Sutra* on a scroll in Chinese characters and this, called the *Dai Gohonzon*, and replicas of it, has become the focus of worship for all Nichiren Shoshu Buddhists.

The *Lotus Sutra* (*Saddharmapundarika Sutra*)   Crucial to the beliefs of Nichiren Shoshu Buddhism was the work of the sixth century Chinese Buddhist, T'ien-t'ai. Chinese T'ien-t'ai Buddhism represents an attempt to synthesize many of the different teachings of Buddhism into a unified system of belief. Classifying Sakyamuni Buddha's teachings into five periods and eight teachings, he demonstrated that the Buddha's teachings were evolutionary in nature: that is to say, his earlier teaching was of an easier nature reflecting the somewhat unevolved levels of consciousness of the people at the time. But as time proceeded, the Buddha's teachings according to T'ien-t'ai became more powerful, culminating in the ultimate teaching of the *Lotus Sutra* in the last of the five periods. The Chinese T'ien-t'ai school of Buddhism thus considers the *Lotus Sutra* to be the perfect teaching of Sakyamuni Buddha, transcending all other teachings and yet uniting them all. It is, indeed, one of the most popular of Mahayana *sutras*. Earlier teachings of Sakyamuni were simply considered to be *upaya kausalya* or "skilful means" to bring about greater awareness in people until they were ready to receive this supreme teaching. Even the birth, death and enlightenment of Sakyamuni Buddha are presented as *upaya kausalya* in the *Lotus Sutra*. But the *Lotus Sutra* particularly emphasizes the on-going nature of Sakyamuni Buddha and the potential for buddhahood in all people in that everyone possesses buddhahood – he or she just has to reveal it.

It was this elevation of the *Lotus Sutra* to pre-eminence by T'ien-t'ai Buddhism which was the most important factor influencing the subsequent founding of the Nichiren Shoshu sect. The chanting of part of chapter two (entitled *Hoben*) of the *Lotus Sutra* and the whole of the sixteenth (entitled *Juryo*) – a practice which takes about thirty minutes and which is called *gongyo* – forms the daily religious practice of Nichiren Shoshu Buddhists, along with the chanting of *Nam-myoho-renge-kyo*, which is called *daimoku*. For Nichiren sects of Buddhism the *Lotus Sutra* incorporates all teaching of the Buddha and yet surpasses it. Moreover, the *Lotus Sutra* is deemed to be not just a *sutra* to be understood and taken to heart, it is also one to be translated into *practical* living, and the action of *daimoku* ensures this. As the head of Nichiren Daishonin Buddhism and Soka Gakkai International, Daisaku Ikeda states:

> if one cannot apply the teachings of the text in one's daily life and translate them into practical and concrete terms in action, then one's understanding of the sutra is valueless.[51]

It is *daimoku* particularly which translates the power of the *Lotus Sutra* into the activity and dynamism of life.

Nam-myoho-renge-kyo   The title of the *Lotus Sutra* expresses all the philosophy of Nichiren Shoshu Buddhism and volumes could be written on each of its components. *Nam* is really an honorific title, suggesting that one respects and honours what follows. It is a Sanskrit word which is often prefixed to the names of deities or buddhas suggesting one's dedication to, and following of, the named divinity.[52] *Myoho* means "Mystic Law" which, according to Causton "expresses the relationship between the life inherent in the universe and the myriad different ways this life expresses itself".[53] *Myo* is the very essence of life and is beyond human understanding: it is the unmanifest subtlety which informs all life but which is beyond words or comprehension. It is *ho* which is the manifest aspect of *myo*, the aspect which can be experienced and explained because it is manifest in life. Causton explains the difference between the two as being that *myo* is the full potential of buddhahood while *ho* is where we are conceivably *at* at this moment: the former is unmanifest, while *ho* is manifest.[54] *Renge* refers to the law of cause and effect. Its literal meaning is "lotus flower". The lotus flower, as we have seen, is unusual in that it flowers and seeds at the same time, reminiscent of the Nichiren Shoshu belief about *karma* – that results inhere in their causes – something which we shall need to examine in more detail below. *Kyo* means *sutra*, a teaching of a buddha. And what the buddhas taught was that there is something deep within the cosmos to which it is possible to be awakened – the *myo* within. And since this inner mystical Law pervades all phenomena in life, *kyo* is the thread which links each phenomenon to it.

The *Gohonzon* *Daimoku* and *gongyo* are conducted before a *Gohonzon*, for those initiated into the Nichiren Shoshu sect of Buddhism, though both can be done without the presence of the *Gohonzon*. But what the *Gohonzon* does is to provide a focus in worship, not to something outside the self, but to something deep within:

> The most important object of the Nichiren movement is not a god, but rather an object which draws forth from the worshipper qualities of his Buddha nature: it is held to present what is already within the individual. Thus, it is often said that it is like a mirror, reflecting the buddhahood within.[55]

This suggests that the *Gohonzon* is more than just a focus of worship but, rather, is a *reflection* of the buddhahood within each individual adherent. The practice of *daimoku* is thus a very positive action, for it penetrates to the areas of the self which are closest to the *buddhanature* which is the inner essence of the individual. So by performing *daimoku* positive energies are created and, thus, positive *karma* must ensue: the individual begins to reap the results of positive action, thought and speech. Moreover, this positive *karma* is something which can be reaped in the immediate, present lifetime, as much as in future lifetimes. The interaction between the positive actions of *daimoku* and the immediacy of the life-situation is therefore an important issue. As Wilson and Dobbelaere point out, *daimoku* is believed "to affect both the subjective state of consciousness of the believer and the objective circumstances of the environment in which he lives".[56]

The Ten Worlds   Nichiren Shoshu Buddhism accepts that any individual has within him or her ten potential conditions. These are hell, hunger, animality, anger, tranquillity and rapture (termed the six lower worlds) and learning, realization (or absorption), *boddhisattva*, and buddhahood (the four higher worlds). The life of any one individual is spent mainly in the lower six worlds, from the hellish situation of perhaps being in a job, marriage or frustrating situation one really despises – conditions of considerable suffering – to the raptures experienced by one who has won the national or state lottery! Hunger represents desire, perhaps for recognition in life, for wealth, status, food, sex, pleasure – all the things which represent the *tanha* or craving, which Sakyamuni Buddha said were the cause of suffering. Animality is the instincts of an individual, the fight for survival which emerges so often in the characteristics of the realm of anger – selfishness, egocentricity, superiority and competitiveness. The worlds of tranquillity and rapture are more harmonious, though impermanent, and all these lower six worlds are sense orientated: they are the states one finds oneself in dependent on the immediate circumstances of the environment.

The four higher worlds are what are called the *noble paths* and are those which reflect the spiritual development of an individual. Learning and realization, or absorption, are similar realms in that they both involve the seeking and discovery of the truths about life, the self and the whole nature of existence. The highest two realms – those of *bodhisattva* and buddhahood – are the goal of the Nichiren Shoshu Buddhist. The world of *bodhisattva* is that in which the individual devotes his or her life in altruistic and compassionate service to others, though such service may not be entirely devoid of egocentric motivation. It is *buddhahood* which reveals the true condition of an individual, "the state of true, indestructible happiness, a condition of perfect and absolute freedom, characterized by boundless wisdom, courage, compassion and life force".[57]

Ichinen sanzen   T'ien-t'ai had also formulated the theory of *ichinen sanzen* and this has become an important basic doctrine of Nichiren Shoshu Buddhism. It is a principle which propounds that every moment of life contains "three thousand realms", a statement tantamount to expressing that each life moment of any individual is inseparably bound to the rest of the cosmos; indeed it contains the whole cosmos. The interplay, then, between any individual and the rest of the universe is taking place in every moment of life, only to change in the next moment, and the next, and the next – to infinity. Nichiren Shoshu Buddhism does not accept that there is a final *nirvana* which ends the cycle of rebirth when the egoistic self is finally lost. In many ways this is in line with the general concept of *bodhisattvas* who really will never reach that state of Buddha because there will always be beings in the world to encourage on the spiritual path: their vow to strive compassionately for the enlightenment of all cannot fully materialize, and so their lives – as those of any future *bodhisattvas* – must be infinite.

But the rationale for no end to the cycle of rebirth in Nichiren Shoshu Buddhism is somewhat different. Because each of the Ten Worlds contains the potentiality of the other worlds also, there can be no *tenth world* – buddhahood – without the lower worlds of hell, hunger, animality etc. This factor and the whole theory of *ichinen sanzen* ensures a permanent link of all moments in life to the cosmos – even though each life-moment is different from the next. There is thus both a fusion of all things in a unity and a mutual relation between all things. So even in the World of buddhahood, the potentiality for the other nine Worlds still exists, the only difference is that the lower conditions are filtered through the World of buddhahood. Thus, the condition of hunger is transformed through the condition of buddhahood into a hunger for peace in the world, for buddhahood to be experienced by all beings: anger is transformed by the condition of buddhahood to a passionate compassion for the liberation of all humanity into the freedom of the Tenth World. And, of course, even in the life-condition of hell, the potential for that of buddhahood is always present. In any event, life is eternal for the Nichiren Shoshu Buddhist and this is not meant pessimistically, as it would be in much Indian thought, but optimistically in that eternity offers the promise of buddhahood and the opportunity to use it for the benefit of all others. The eternal nature of life is reflected by the evergreen plants to be found on a Nichiren Shoshu shrine or *butsudan*, which houses the *Gohonzon*.

Cause and effect   The law of *karma* in Nichiren Shoshu Buddhism is distinctly one of cause – the physical, mental or verbal action – and *effect*, and the effect for this sect of Buddhism inheres in its cause. That is to say that, at the very moment an action is undertaken, the *latent effect* is sealed. Like the ripples which result when one throws a pebble in a pond, the principle of *ichinen sanzen* states that any action has its effect in the universe: actions cannot be separated from the cosmic moment in which they arose and the results which they accrue – be they negative or positive – are there, waiting for fruition. The effects of chanting the powerful words of *Nam-myoho-renge-kyo* – words which embody buddhahood, though which ultimately transcend it – create the kinds of positive actions from which only good fruitive *karma* can come; and that future good *karma* inheres in the very action of chanting itself. To a Nichiren Shoshu Buddhist, then, the act of chanting *must* bring its benefits in the life of any individual and, because of the principle of *ichinen sanzen*, benefit to the universe at large.

While Buddhism, particularly in its Theravadin form, taught that desire is wrong and must be overcome in order to reach an egoless state, Nichiren Shoshu Buddhism believes that desire is not wrong but *essential* in life, for without it there can be no drive towards spiritual fulfilment. There is then, no real emphasis on egoless action, the kind which cannot accrue any *karma*. Rather there is the opposite, a stress on the acquiring of good *karma* through positive action, and positive desires which seek to promote spiritual evolution. In the highest of the Ten Worlds the ability to change lower desires to desires which derive from wisdom is achieved, but there is no suggestion that desire is in itself wrong, or that *karma* must cease through a desireless state. Indeed, it is considered that the earlier teachings of Sakyamuni Buddha against desire were meant to be discarded in favour of the higher teaching.

Soka Gakkai International   There were many sects which emerged as a result of the teachings of Nichiren Daishonin. Most of these sects were priestly orientated, but outstanding in the present time is the lay organization called Soka Gakkai International (SGI). *Soka Gakkai* means "Value Creating Society", the name given to a movement which began with only a few members in the early twentieth century but which is now larger than all the other Nichiren sects put together with members in most countries throughout the world totalling in excess of twenty million. The President of SGI is now Daisaku Ikeda and it was he who founded SGI in January 1975, bringing together the lay men and women who practised Nichiren Shoshu Buddhism into one world-wide composite movement. One of the overriding aims of this lay movement is the establishing of world-wide peace and Mr Ikeda's efforts to this end secured him the United Nations Peace Award in 1983. Tensions between SGI and the priestly-orientated Nichiren Shoshu Buddhist sect in which it was placed have resulted in a recent schism by which SGI has now separated itself entirely from the priestly dominance which it so resented, and this powerful movement now prefers its independence to be reflected by the separate designation Nichiren Daishonin Buddhism.

Nichiren Daishonin Buddhism has become extremely popular. As a movement essentially for lay people it is easy to practise, requiring only the time to chant twice a day. Since all its philosophy is concentrated in the title of the *Lotus Sutra* no extensive study of scriptures is essential to its practice, though study groups are encouraged. Its goal is straightforward – the bringing out of the buddhahood within the self and the living of one's life in this state of buddhahood for the benefit of humanity and the harmonious existence of all individuals side by side. *Nirvana* is not some remote inner experience endless lifetimes in the future but is life on earth – the experience of living life in revealed buddhahood. But it is important to have *faith* in the *Gohonzon* to which one directs worship and in the *daimoku* of *Nam-myoho-renge-kyo* to effect positive changes in one's life and in the universe to which it is intimately connected.

Tibetans call their country the Land of Snow and, indeed, the picture one in the West has of Tibet is of magnificent, snow-covered mountain ranges and breath-taking scenery, the like of which is barely to be found elsewhere in the world. Tibet is also a land which seems mysterious, an abstract concept lent to the country perhaps because it is here that, for some people, something in the self is fulfilled in attempts to achieve what is almost impossible in the physical sense – the ascent of the highest mountains in the world, where so few have been. The proliferation of monasteries in the country has also suggested it as a place where one goes to witness the highest of spiritual attainment too. But today, Tibet is a land which has been swallowed up by China, its monasteries, once condemned, now tolerated under a watchful eye, though many were obliterated when China brought religion in Tibet to an end in 1959. Before 1959 Tibet had been mainly Buddhist, though not exclusively so. Tibetan Buddhism is also practised in Sikkim, Bhutan, north-west India and Nepal, and Tibetan Buddhism itself is kept alive by exiles.

TIBETAN BUDDHISM

Tibetan Buddhism is a fascinating phenomenon because, while fairly traditional in its composite beliefs, it is informed by not one but three traditional *yanas* or "vehicles" of Buddhism – Hinayana, Mahayana and Vajrayana. It was the Hinayana tradition which gave to Tibetan Buddhism its monastic tradition and it is worthwhile remembering that the tradition of monastic life is just as important in Tibet as in Theravada Buddhism, despite Tibetan Buddhism lying firmly in the Mahayana tradition which is generally not labelled as a religion of the monks. There are a number of different monastic orders that come under the general term Tibetan Buddhism but while there are traditional differences in ritual and practice, they do not differ from each other in fundamental issues. While the Hinayana influence is thus evident, the Mahayana belief in *bodhisattvas* and its emphasis on *mahakaruna* "great compassion" is sufficiently dominant for Tibetan Buddhism to be accepted as Mahayana rather than Theravada. Mahayana Buddhism also allowed for a more overt syncretism in Tibet, facilitating the absorption of pre-Buddhist religious belief and practice into what became Tibetan religion, giving it, at the same time, something very distinct and meaningful to lay person and monk alike. But it is the third *yana* which makes Tibetan Buddhism really distinct. The Vajrayana incorporates esoteric beliefs and practices which are part of the Tantric tradition of Buddhism – mystical, magical, supernatural and occultist.

Tibetan Buddhism, then, has many strands: while accepting Theravadin monasticism, the *Four Noble Truths* and three "marks" of existence, for example, it also accepts the Mahayana doctrines of the *Trikaya* and *sunyata* as well as specifically Tantric beliefs and practices and a belief in the potentiality for buddhahood in all people. We shall examine these influences on Tibetan Buddhism in some detail below, but before doing so it is important to recognize that Buddhism itself has been only one of three strands which compose what is known as Tibetan religion. Alongside Buddhism in Tibet is also a religion which is called Bon. This Bon religion pre-dates Tibetan Buddhism and, since its roots are deeper, it has remained embedded in the general religious culture of the people. In addition to these two strands are the beliefs and practices of village and town life which make up what can be called popular religion. Each of these three strands – Buddhism, Bon and "popular" religion – has a separate identity, yet there is much mutual interchange in practices and beliefs. Per Kvaerne highlights the level of syncretism which takes place between the three when he appropriately states that "beliefs that do not derive from Buddhism are shared by monks and laypeople alike".[58] indeed, it would be difficult in many cases to disentangle the three strands.

The origins of Buddhism in Tibet   Buddhism was to be found in Tibet in the seventh century but was not fully established there until the eighth century. At this time, Tibet was a powerful country and needed a state religion and it was Buddhism which it chose; by the eleventh century it had become the dominant religion. It was Indian Buddhism which won the day over Chinese Ch'an Buddhism, giving the characteristics of monasticism and Tantrism to Buddhism in Tibet. While Mahayana Buddhism is normally characterized by diversity, that which reached Tibet had been clearly formulated by only one Indian Buddhist tradition and this accounts for the considerable unity which characterizes the monastic orders of Tibetan Buddhism to this day.[59] The importance of monastic orders, in particular, has remained because of the practice of the leading monk or *lama* of a sect reincarnating after death to continue his leadership of his monks and followers. So important is the role of the *lama* in Tibetan Buddhism that the religion is sometimes called *Lamaism*, though it is not a term acceptable to Tibetan Buddhists themselves. Throughout the history of Buddhism in Tibet, the monks, in all the schools of thought, have been renowned for their learning and erudition; indeed, the path of a monk is not an easy one and involves a large part of one's life being devoted to study. Yet we should not gain a picture of the Tibetan monk being a recluse, pouring over endless texts without any vision of the outside world. Buddhist monks in monasteries throughout the world have always had a profound interaction with the laity, and this is particularly so in Tibetan Buddhism. Mutual support between the two has been one of the reasons for the success of Buddhism in the past but in Tibet the division between religious and secular, the monk associated with the former and the laity with the latter, has been considerably blurred over the centuries. The monastic orders took on political and economic roles in society, became wealthy landowners and powerful forces in the state. It was out of this kind of background that the concept of a combined religious and political ruler arose. This was not something new which developed with the introduction of Buddhism, for the concept of divine kingship had been a pre-Buddhist phenomenon.

Tibetan monks and *lamas* The religious leaders of the monastic traditions in Tibetan Buddhism are called *lamas*. There are four major sects. Two of these, the Nyingmapa sect and the Kargyupa sect, adopt many Tantric and magical practices. The Sakya school – formerly somewhat politically orientated – accepts in particular the idea that pursuing the Buddhist path *must* bring the fruit of buddhahood, since pursuit (the path) and buddhahood (the fruit) are identical. Then there is the Gelugpa school which emphasizes celibate monastic discipline and highly educated, scholastic monks. In this school, while buddhahood is accepted it is not something which everyone has and just has to reveal, but that which is to be realized only gradually through discipline. Tantras for this sect do not, therefore, bring instant insight to most, and are only for the most advanced scholars. This sect is distinguished by yellow, as opposed to red hats worn by other sects.[60]

The Dalai Lama is the spiritual leader of the Yellow Hats. The word *Dalai* means "ocean" symbolizing depth of knowledge, and *lama* comes from a Tibetan word *blama* meaning "religious teacher". In Tibet, the Dalai Lama was not only the religious ruler but, for over three hundred years, had also been the political ruler. The present Dalai Lama is the fourteenth in a line of reincarnations of the first Dalai Lama, though the actual idea of reincarnated *lamas* did not really gain ground until the fourteenth century. The concept of reincarnation is, of course, common to most Indian religious thought, but Tibetan Buddhism is unique in its idea of a spiritual leader being incarnated again and again as the leader of his monastic order: all the monastic schools of Tibet accept this doctrine and it is one which ensures a certain stability in the beliefs and practices of the individual order. So not only is the Dalai Lama himself believed to reincarnate again as the same leader, other leading *lamas*, too, are thought to do the same. This means that when the Dalai Lama dies, or any leading *lama*, a search has to be made for that person in his new form as a young baby or small child.

Naturally, searching for a reincarnated *lama* is a complex business. Usually, the *lama* who has died will give some indications of where or when his rebirth would take place. Some *lamas* would have visions of the new birth which would help in finding the old *lama*. But within nine months of the Dalai Lama's death, or the death of another leading *lama*, reports would come to light of a child who was sufficiently unusual to draw to it the attention of the monks. If they are satisfied that the child has the kind of qualities which suggest the possibility of its being a reincarnated *lama* then the child would be subjected to a number of tests. For example, recognizing some of his own personal objects from his past life in the midst of many others would be one method. The child would also be familiar with religious ritual or would be able to recognize and be at ease with the monks he had known before he died. Once the monks could satisfy themselves that the child was the reincarnation of their leader, he would be taken by them for a long period of training and teaching.

The present Dalai Lama was born in 1935 and although there were two other children who were also likely reincarnations of the predecessor, the present Dalai Lama passed all the necessary tests and was enthroned at Lhasa in 1940. When in the 1950s the Chinese invaded Tibet and enforced Communism, the young Dalai Lama had to flee. He was allowed to return for a while, but in 1959, the Tibetan people revolted against their Chinese oppressors in Lhasa and the Chinese government ended Tibetan rule entirely. The Dalai Lama fled to India, where he has remained in exile to this day.

The Dalai Lama and all those who preceded him are ultimately the same reincarnated person. However, additionally, the Dalai Lama is also the embodiment of the *bodhisattva* Avalokitesvara – incarnations in human form of this *bodhisattva* of compassion. Other leaders of monastic traditions are also considered to be incarnations on earth of *bodhisattvas* or buddhas. The Grand *Lama* of Bkra-sis-lhun-po, for example, is believed to be the incarnation of the Buddha Amitabha. As incarnations of important buddhas and *bodhisattvas* Tibetans accept their *lamas* as divine, and their right to political rule is commensurate with such divinity. It is this combination which has caused Westerners sometimes to refer to the Dalai Lama as the *God-King*, though it is not a term which is really acceptable to Buddhists.

While the Dalai Lama is an international figure, he can also be found at the smaller centres for Tibetan Buddhism. In May 1993 he was in Britain and as part of his itinerary visited the Buddhist Centre of Lam Rim at Raglan in Monmouthshire. Here, a new shrine had been built and the Dalai Lama undertook to dedicate and bless the shrine and to see his friend there, the Venerable Geshe Damcho Yonten. Geshe Damcho Yonten now lives permanently at Lam Rim with some British Buddhists. At the age of six he went to the University of Drepung in Tibet and studied there for twenty-three years. When the Chinese invaded Tibet he escaped and continued his studies in India and Ladakh, earning the title *Geshe*, as a measure of his learning. In 1976 he came to the West and set up the teaching centre at Raglan in 1978. Here, the only regulations required by the many visitors are the observance of the *Five Precepts*.

Buddhas and bodhisattvas Tibetan Buddhism accepts a variety of buddhas and *bodhisattvas*: these are the legacy of Mahayana Buddhism to Tibet. One of the most important is Avalokitesvara (referred to as Chenrezi in Tibetan Buddhism), the *bodhisattva* of compassion, important enough to be the national *bodhisattva* of Tibet, though he is also popular elsewhere. (In China, for, example, he is known as Kwan-yin and is often depicted in female form). His name is composed of two words, *avalokita* possibly meaning "what is seen", and *isvara*, a Sanskrit word meaning "Lord". His name thus means "Lord of what is seen", or "Lord who looks down", suggesting that he is both the surveyor of the whole of the world and the one whose compassion is such that he acts in relation to what he sees. He is often depicted with eleven heads, symbolic of his ability to see all, and a thousand arms, symbolic of his ability to help in any kind of difficulty and in any place in the universe. He is a *bodhisattva* who has unbounded compassion and he is prepared to be reborn in any situation and in any form in order to help all creatures and human beings to reach enlightenment, even if he has to suffer in one of the Buddhist Hells. The pre-Buddhist Bon concept of a divine ruler who had descended to earth from heaven is reflected in the reincarnation of Avalokitesvara as the Dalai Lama, illustrating the complementatry role of the head of a monastery as both spiritual and temporal ruler. In fact, in the rise of Buddhism in Tibet, considerable political and economic activity is characteristic of the various monastic orders. It was the fifth in succession of *Dalai Lamas* in Tibet who, as both a political and religious ruler, claimed also to be a reincarnation or a manifestation of Avalokitesvara. Since his time, all subsequent *Dalai Lamas* are also believed to be the embodiment of this *bodhisattva* and their role has become one of religious ruler and state ruler.

One of the characteristic features of Tantric Buddhism is its emphasis on the female aspects of the divine as much as the male. This is comparable to the *sakti* forces of the deities in Hinduism. One of the most important of the female *bodhisattvas* is Tara, the female counterpart of Avalokitesvara, and the *sakti* of the Buddha Amoghasiddhi. Tara is responsible for saving people in distress and is much beloved by the Tibetans also because she is the essence of loving-devotion, the deity who loves all of humankind regardless of their good or evil states. Meditation on Tara is always an important part of ritual *puja* in Tibetan Buddhism. There are twenty-one emanations of Tara but in pictorial form she often appears either as green, or as white; the green form symbolizes prosperity, while the white one symbolizes helpfulness, though she can appear in a number of forms. Although the relationship between the male and female aspects of the divine is usually depicted sexually in Tantric Buddhism, there is little of this in the relationship between Avalokitesvara and Tara, though there is a tradition that Avalokitesvara in the form of a monkey, and Tara in the form of a rock goddess produced monkey offspring who were the originators of the Tibetan people. Some forms of Tara resemble the Hindu ferocious *sakti* female Goddesses like Durga. Iconographically Tara often appears with four of the five major Tantric buddhas – Amoghasiddhi, Ratnasambhava, Amitabha and Aksobhya (though not with Vairocana).[61]

Another important *bodhisattva* is Manjusri, whose name means "Gentle Glory". He is not yet a Buddha and is something of a senior *bodhisattva*, being associated with teaching, learning and wisdom. He is a youthful, golden-complexioned, prince-like *bodhisattva* usually depicted with a five-peaked crown. He holds a sword in his right hand which symbolizes the kind of discrimination which cuts through ignorance to reveal the truth, while in his left hand he holds the *Prajnaparamita Sutra*, the Scripture of Supreme Wisdom. He is sometimes pictured sitting on a lion, the roar of the lion being symbolic of the sound of truth. He represents the purity of the truth and of Buddhist teaching. He can become manifest in any part of the universe, though he sits in perpetual meditation. He is believed to have been the founder of Nepal, having cut a huge opening in the mountains in order to drain a great lake so that Nepal could rise up in the valley of Katmandu.

Tantrism   It is the Tantric aspect of Tibetan Buddhism which gives it its definitive characteristic, enough so to warrant the separate term of *Vajrayana* Buddhism, alongside the Mahayana and Theravada traditions. *Tantra* means "loom", "doctrine" or "groundwork", meanings expanded by Guenther, for one, to suggest "living one's possibilities".[62] And indeed, this is a good extension of the meaning of Tantra for it suggests the infinite possibilities which can be opened up in the self by mystical and esoteric practices which serve to release the ego and sense-bound self to experience the more subtle possibilities of reality. Alex Wayman comments that Tibet "became an extraordinary center for Tantrism as well as the major storehouse of Tantric literature"[63] and it is easy to see from such a statement why Tibetan Buddhism is a distinct branch of Buddhism in its own right. Tantric beliefs and practices often reflect some of the oldest strands in religion, and in Tibet the magical and supernatural elements of pre-Buddhist religion provided a ready ethos in which Tantrism could develop. Each school of Tibetan Buddhism has its own practices and Tantric texts – all claimed to be the words of Sakyamuni Buddha, though they were not first evident until a thousand years after his death. Such texts were believed to have been hidden until the time was right for them to be revealed, especially since they were highly potent texts – far more so than the Sanskrit *sutras*. And it was the potency of the Tantric texts, their extraordinary power, which made buddhahood realizable in one lifetime for the initiated and dedicated. Unlike the Mahayana traditions, therefore, Tantrism offers a faster route to buddhahood.

Tantrism is a somewhat misunderstood phenomenon perhaps because the esoteric and mystical nature of the texts often deny access to the uninitiated and are easily open to misinterpretation. And while not generally the case, there are many aspects of Tantrism which incorporate seemingly unpleasant practices to the Western eye – ritual sex, demonic phenomena, horrific deities, to name a few. Tantrism emphasizes the feminine as the passive, wisdom principle in the universe, the male as the active, *skill in means*. The union of the two brings about the experience of wisdom and in ritual *puja*, sexual intercourse may be included in order to symbolize this acquisition of wisdom. Such Tantric expressions concentrate on the very aspects of Buddhism which are usually prohibited – sex, wine, meat-eating. To understand the philosophy behind such belief and practice we have to turn to the Buddha's teaching of the Middle Way and remember that enlightenment is devoid of dualities; it is the "empty" point between them. The tendency in Buddhism generally is to seek to quell craving and desires and perhaps to neglect the aversions. But of what use is it for a monk to quell his sexual energies only to develop an aversion for sex? He would be no nearer losing a sense of dualities. However, if he could treat sex as the same as no-sex, he will have transcended such dualities. After all, in the true Buddhist perspective, sex and no-sex are one and the same thing!

And what of the other aversions that we have? Many Buddhists will not eat meat; they develop an aversion to it, regarding it as abhorrent and one which is against the doctrine of *ahimsa* "non-violence". But this, again, gets rid of a desire by developing an aversion, a *reaction* to the stimulus of meat, when in fact it would be better to treat the meat as neither this nor that, as beyond dualities and therefore of no consequence if it is partaken or not! The same could be said for any other aversions which we have and some ascetic Tantric sects will mix (and eat) normal food with excrement and urine. And the more one finds this repugnant, the greater the presence of the egoistic self! If the Middle Way in its metaphysical sense is the point of non-existence of all dualities, then strawberry tart and excrement are one and the same thing!

But such Tantric practices are not the mainstay of Tibetan Buddhism and would be as repugnant to some orders as they are to Western readers. Suffice it to say that the *logic* behind the practices is sensible and, were it confined to meditative concentration instead of ritual practice, would be more indicative of balance. Far more important is the expression of the feminine in Tantrism, Tara being the most conspicuous element of this, as we have seen. The space for the feminine reflects perhaps the older Indian concept of worship of the mother goddess which has been characteristic of Indian tradition throughout time. The thought of a female as a buddha would have been anathema to the Buddha, as well as to his immediate Theravadin successors, but Tibetan Buddhism maintains a healthy balance between the male and female cosmic energies.

The distinctive characteristics of Tibetan Buddhism, then, render it often depicted as a third vehicle of Buddhism – *Vajrayana*. *Vajra* means "adamantine" or "unsplittable". Conze points out that, "In later Buddhist philosophy the word is used to denote a kind of super-natural substance which is hard as a diamond, as clear as empty space, as irresistible as a thunderbolt".[64] He sees *Vajra* as an Absolute Ultimate Reality equatable with the *diamond-nature* of all beings, indestructible ("unsplittable") and subtle. Importantly, however, the concept of *anatman* is maintained: *vajra* is not to be equated with a concept like the Hindu *atman*. As a vehicle to buddhahood a spiritual master would be essential in Vajrayana Buddhism and only the *lama* could fulfil this role. The goal is wisdom, the wisdom of enlighten-ment, and the stages into which the adherent is intitiated to reach this goal are carefully managed.

Mudras, mantras, **and** *mandalas*   The three dimensions of a human being – body, speech and mind – are expressed by three aspects of ritual, *mudras, mantras* and *mandalas* respectively. *Mudras* are the ritualistic body gestures, with the hands. Buddha *rupas*, the images of the Buddha were discussed earlier. *Mantras* depict the magical power of sound, the potency of the spoken word. Less obvious in today's cultures, at one time the spoken word in terms of blessings and curses was considered highly potent, and in Tibetan Buddhism the sound of certain ritualistic and meditative syllables is equitable with their forms. This link between sound and form is important in the visualization and summoning of the deities and *bodhisattvas* during meditation. *Mantras* are passed from teacher to disciple, appropriate to the stage of spiritual development of the disciple. Most are secret, but the most commonly known is that associated with Avalokitesvara, *Om mani padme hum*, "Hail to the jewel in the lotus" and this would have been found everywhere in Tibet, on buildings, rooftops, flagstones and on the many prayer wheels. It is also to be found printed on prayer flags, these flags being a feature of most Tibetan temples and shrines.

Mandalas are an important feature of Tantric Buddhism and they are designed to promote the journey of the mind to realization of enlightenment. They are highly symbolic and complex, and are used as meditation aids for the devotee. They originated from the medita-tive experiences of the great *lamas* of the past, who visualized them and put them into the figurative forms we see today so that they could help others on the path to enlightenment by meditating on them. They are usually associated with a particular buddha or *bodhisattva* or have different buddhas at different points. Such *mandalas* are prescriptively painted; every item must conform to the strictest traditions of colour and shape in order to maintain the spiritual symbolism. At a Tibetan shrine or temple, many of them would adorn the walls. There is an eternity of thought in a *mandala*: the word means "circle" (though some are square or triangular), and the mind is drawn into them through the concentric circles which they contain. They are what Powers calls "a sacred realm"[65] at the heart of which is a whole buddha-world and buddhahood.

Scriptures   The scriptures of Tibetan Buddhism are divided into two, the word of the Buddha which is known as *Kanjur* and includes the *Vinaya*, *Tantras* and a number of Mahayana *sutras* as well as non-Mahayana *sutras*, and philosophical and erudite commentaries known as *Tenjur*. Many of the Tantric texts, in particular, are difficult to understand. Designed to be obscure and mystical, they are actually "coded" and cannot be taken literally. They can only be understood through the interpretation and higher level of consciousness of a monk who has spent years in study. Many scriptures are considered to be what are called *termas* (*gter ma*), texts which had been hidden and discovered by trance mediums at propitious times when it was believed that the appropriate hidden meanings of their content would be of benefit. This characteristic of Tibetan Buddhism has lent it a richness and yet a complexity.

***Puja* in Tibetan Buddhism**   In visiting a Tibetan temple or shrine, it would be noticeable that there are a considerable number of buddha and *bodhisattva rupas* or images before which people will prostrate themselves three times, symbolic of the *Three Refuges*, before commencing *puja*. *Puja* varies considerably, but chanting is usual. The very deep base chant is traditional and lends something to the symbolism of the sounds. The chanting of *mantras* would be an important feature as a means to visualize the buddha or *bodhisattva*. Striking at Tibetan temples and shrines are the bright colours of the shrine room, which are highly symbolic. Offerings at a shrine represent sacrifice to the buddhas and *bodhisattvas* and, as in many aspects of Mahayana Buddhism, praise is chanted to particular ones. Visits to the temples, the giving of offerings of flowers, incense, water, food and white scarves for the images, prayer, and pilgrimage, are the important manifestations of lay practice. The monks in return offer education, protection from supernatural forces, and expert religious ritual. Community *puja* is accompanied by drums, gongs, bells and trumpets.

Today, of course, the presence of the Chinese in Tibet has made religious practice difficult, but exiled Tibetans who have moved to the Himalayas, still practise their religion there. There is much which is shamanistic about Tibetan religion, for Tibetans accept that there are spiritual forces which influence and animate all things in life. This element in the religion stems from pre-Buddhist times and is particularly maintained by the folk traditions. Yet shamanistic practices are also a part of the official cultic religious practices, expressed in the presence in the religion of priests responsible for oracles, visions, magic and healing. Shamanism is also evident in the prolific number of spirits connected with the land, the atmosphere and also the underworld, the Hells. Buddhism, however, accepts many different planes of existence, and these spirits, demons, gods, and the like, are simply other creatures living on other planes of existence but subject also to the *samsaric* cycle in the same way as humankind.

The shamanistic element is very evident at the New Year festival when a monk who is known as the oracle monk, and who is a medium, is dressed ceremoniously and is brought before the Dalai Lama in full view of the people. For this ceremony a butter and flour statue is built and the oracle monk, while in a state of trance, shoots an arrow at the heart of the statue, symbolically destroying all the evil forces of the previous year. After this the statue is burnt with great celebration. While in his trance the medium, as the mouthpiece of Avalokitesvara, blesses the people and the state.

The religious centre of Tibet in the past was Lhasa (now controlled by the Chinese) and it is here that a great palace existed, in honour of Avalokitesvara. It is called the Potala Palace and was built in the seventeenth century. Built as a great three-dimensional *mandala*, it was the seat of religious and political government in Tibet since the Dalai Lama became the religious and political ruler of Tibet until the Chinese invasion. This great palace, then, acts as a temple, a monastery and a palace and is at the same time a ritualistic *mandala*, at the very centre of which is considered to be the heaven on earth of the *bodhisattva* Avalokitesvara. So important is the Potala Palace that most Tibetan shrines would have a picture of it. Pilgrimage to this Palace as, indeed, to Lhasa itself, would be a means for the ordinary person to gain the kind of good *karma* which would promote a better birth in the next life. Pilgrims will circumambulate Lhasa itself, or the Palace, many times in order to increase this merit, and during their circumambulation they would repeatedly prostrate themselves. As they walk, they focus their minds on the *bodhisattva* Avalokitesvara in the very centre of the Palace, just as they would try to visualize the inner section of a *mandala*. This kind of visualization is a very important aspect of Tibetan, and indeed Tantric, Buddhism as a whole.

Traditionally, there are two paths to enlightenment in Tibetan Buddhism, wisdom and merit, but it is the latter which is more important to the lay person who does not have the time to study the complexities of some scriptures. Good-meriting actions, it is believed, will do much to override evil actions and their subsequent adverse *karma* in the present and future lives. Yet there is always a close interaction between the monastic element and the laity, and the support of the monks by the laity would be another means of accumulating good *karma*. Within the home, a Tibetan Buddhist would have guardian house deities. There would be a god of the hearth – an area of the home which has to be kept scrupulously clean in order not to offend the deity. There would be altars on the roof to the male and the female deities, both of whom are responsible for being in charge of their respective male or female personages in the home. There would also be a banner on the roof representing the enemy god who, despite his name, is responsible for the protection of the whole household.[66] Within the ground and the sea are the *klu*, spirits who, if annoyed by humankind or animals by disturbing the ground or the water, can cause all sorts of problems and diseases for people and animals. The many gods, goddesses and spirits of Tibetan Buddhism are, however, *karmic* beings, subject to the same wanderings through the cycle of *samsara* as humanity.

Apart from the multiplicity of gods in the immediate environment, two are particularly important in the body of each individual. These are a white god and a black demon, both of whom are responsible for recording the good and bad *karma* respectively. These deities will weigh the individual's appropriate scores in the scales of justice at death, white pebbles from the white god representing each item of good merit and black ones from the demon representing bad actions and thoughts. This dualistic idea of good and evil may have originated from Zoroastrian thought, or even from Taoist theories of *yin* and *yang*.

Deities are prolific as manifestations of the forces in life but ultimately they are believed to be empty of *svabhava*, "own-being" and, therefore, of reality. Yet they pervade all aspects of Tibetan life and religion. The monks themselves, as those dedicated to the spiritual path, use the deities, the buddhas or *bodhisattvas* as a means to enlightenment, as a focus for *yogic* meditation. They visualize and conceptualize these divine beings, aiming for full identification with them so that their essence becomes the meditators' whole being. Thus, by meditation on Avalokitesvara, for example, identity with his wisdom and great compassion is achieved. Ultimately, there is no difference between a deity and a mortal, so to concentrate in meditation on a deity is to become one. Usually, the practitioner will be assigned a particular divine being to suit his or her particular personality. For the monk, concentration and meditation are as important as in Theravada Buddhism. Their practice aims at the transcending of ordinary life and perception in order to experience perfection in the self and the universe through what are called "Highest Yoga Tantras". Those who can achieve this will have a certain control over their own reincarnation process.

Mediums are prolific in popular religion. They can be male or female and will serve the function of communicating religious ideas from the buddhas or *bodhisattvas* and even revealing new sacred literature. They may also be consulted by the lay people at times when help is needed or when decisions have to be made, or they may recite the exploits of a famous warrior from the past, or visit the Hells to tell people what will happen to them if they do not mend their ways. They provide a very colourful aspect of Tibetan religion, one which is thought to aid individual *karma* because of the countless spiritual forces which can be appealed to, and one which fulfils the deeper and older archetypal beliefs of this ancient people.

BUDDHIST CEREMONIES AND LIFE-CYCLE RITES

Ceremonies, especially those which mark important occasions such as birth, marriage and death, are an integral part of most religions and cultures. For many people they are occasions in which religious practice is shared collectively and are important enough to transcend the normal routine of daily life or religious practice. It would be impossible to portray the vast range of such events in the many Buddhist traditions for they vary enormously and have been, in many cases, influenced by pre-Budddhist traditions. But generally Buddhism is less concerned with the elaborate rites of passage which characterize many religions and when they occur they are secular rather than religious events. Nichiren Shoshu or Nichiren Daishonin Buddhism, for example, has very few ceremonial occasions, the main one being the celebration of the birth of Nichiren Daishonin, but no special rituals accompany this or any other celebration.[67] Yet even here Soka Gakkai members come together frequently for communal study meetings and for cultural events which include dance, music and poetry recital, for example. The annual general meeting has a festival atmosphere, but ritual is absent from the proceedings. Other Buddhist traditions by way of contrast enjoy very elaborate ceremonial and festivals, as in much Tibetan tradition.

Initiation   Initiation is an important feature of the monastic traditions such as Theravada and Tibetan Buddhism and if birth rites are minimal and secular, initiation and ordination make up for this in the life of the child. Initiation is into the Buddhist tradition, and into the monastic life for a few hours or days, with the hope that eventual rebirth will be into the kind of existence which would facilitate life as a monk. The age at which this takes place varies from about eight to twenty and is mainly confined to males. The most elaborate form of this ceremony involves the young boy – sometimes as young as four years old in Tibetan tradition – being dressed in clothes suitable for royalty and symbolizing the life lived by Siddhartha in his wealthy palaces. The child is then taken to the local monastery, sometimes on a small pony, and there his clothes are changed for the saffron robe of the monk. His head is shaved, and he is given a begging bowl. Then follows a short spell in the monastery – perhaps one night, several days or even longer. This is not usually any ordeal for the young boy since the monks are so involved with the laity that they would be well known to the local people and to the boy himself. His short time spent in the monastery would not be subject to many restrictions, and a game of football is quite permissable. The ceremony marks his coming of age, his passing from boyhood, and is important enough in some places like Burma to be pre-eminent amongst the ceremonies a male will undertake in life. Here, in Burma, there is much celebration over the event and gifts for the monks would be supplied. Some boys remain in the monastery for longer periods and would be educated there as a novice monk with a view to full ordination. June is the popular time for Thai boys to enter the monastery since it is just before the rainy season starts and they are able to stay then for about four months if they wish, taking more Buddhist precepts and so accumulating merit, self-discipline, and acquiring coming-of-age status.

Outside the monastic tradition sects like Nichiren Shoshu or Nichiren Daishonin Buddhism regard as very important the ceremony of *Gojukai* at which a *Gohonzon* – a replica of the *Dai Gohonzon* first inscribed by Nichiren Daishonin – is given to the member of the sect, and the initiate declares his or her rejection of other paths and dedication to the particular Nichiren movement. The replica of the original *Dai Gohonzon* inscribed by Nichiren Daishonin, which is given to the initiated lay member, is given great respect. If possible it is housed in a *butsudan* in the adherent's home. The *butsudan* is an altar which contains a cabinet specially designed for the *Gohonzon* so that when not chanting the doors of the cabinet can be respectfully closed on the *Gohonzon*. The main *butsudan* at Taplow Court in Berkshire, the centre of SGI UK, is a magnificent black-laquered Japanese *butsudan* with gold ornamentation, and looks spectacular when lit up on its raised platform.

Symbolic shaving of the head, when the abbot touches the head three times, is characteristic of initiation into the Soto Zen Order of Buddhist Contemplatives, for initiation is indicative of ordination for such lay Buddhists, though ordination as a lay minister or as a full monk is more elaborate. The lay Buddhist takes the *Ten Precepts* at initiation/ordination, having spent some time in retreat before the occasion. There is something very gracious and gentle about the bowings, the signal gongs and the ritual movements of Soto Zen, and a sense of order pervades the proceedings – an order meticulously set down in its liturgy.[68] The recognition of the buddhahood in all and therefore the total identity of, and equality between, one person and another, is beautifully portrayed in the circumambulation of the abbot around the altar on which the ordinands sit, in the place where the main Buddha image would normally be. The abbot then bows – not to the usual Buddha image, but to the buddhahood in the ordinand, expressing the words:

> Buddha recognises Buddha and Buddha bows to Buddha,
> Go around Mount Sumeru, go around the Buddha.[69]

The words and the action of the abbot express the non-duality of all things and the interconnectedness of all life.

Ordination In Theravada traditions it is at the age of twenty onwards that a man may decide to become fully ordained as a monk, but in Tibetan Buddhism it is possible for a boy of eleven to enter the monastery for life. But generally a monk's vows are not for life, and at any time he can return his vows, marry and undertake the life of a householder. However, while a monk he must remain celibate and divorce himself from family life, and certainly from any sexual craving. In the Theravadin tradition it is only a monk who can realize enlightenment, so it is important for all to spend at least some time in the monastery. This may be done at the initiation stage of one's life, but also at the rainy season, *Vassa*, when it is expedient to remain sedentary because of the monsoon rains. In Tibet, ordination is geared to the *bodhisattva* ideal – vowing to save all people, to end all delusions, to explore all the *Dharma* of the Buddha, and to attain enlightenment.

In the Theravadin tradition permission must be gained from parents, wife and employer before someone is fully ordained. A preliminary ordination as a novice, a *samanera* will precede full ordination as a *bhikkhu*. Ordination is an important occasion and the ritual for it contains basic elements but differs slightly from place to place. The ordinand, having bathed, with head shaved and dressed in white will proceed to the monastery accompanied by friends and relatives: music and dancing may sometimes be included as part of the celebrations. When the Buddha ordained new monks, the process was very simple, and, despite the extraneous celebrations, the rite itself retains such simplicity. Bowing to the monks and requesting ordination, the ordinand undergoes some careful questioning by them and there must be at least five monks present. He then changes into his yellow robe, recites the *Three Refuges* three times, takes the necessary vows of the *Vinaya*, gives gifts to his now fellow monks, and becomes fully ordained.

The Thai ordination ceremony is particulary elaborate and is extended over a number of days. The ordinand will be dressed in fine clothes, symbolizing Siddhartha's royal life before his enlightenment and the monks will come to the home to give him strength by chanting. The spirit or *khwan* of the ordinand, which is believed to accompany all living beings, is strengthened in a ceremony in which offerings are arranged in a tree-like conical structure, and the ordinand's wrists are tied together to bind the *khwan* to him. In Thailand dancing, feasting and singing will take place before the lively procession to the monastery on the following day. After ten years a monk is given the title of *thera*, "elder", and after twenty years the title *mahathera* "senior elder". Monks are usually well educated and have the opportunity to rise through a sound educational system.

In the Order of Buddhist Contemplatives of Soto Zen there is a lengthy period of training for any would-be monk. The final ordination ceremony is called "transmission" and it is at this special ceremony that the monk binds himself to his Master, accepting him or her as a manifestation of the Buddha. It is a ceremony not to be taken lightly. This is an Order which accepts the total equality of women with men – indeed, the founder of the Order as a woman suggests that it could not be otherwise, so women are ordained here with equal status.

Renewal of vows　Those who are not ordained but who are initiated into Buddhism sometimes wish to renew their initiation by spending some time in retreat, usually at *Vassa*. The normal *Panca Sila* or five vows of the Theravada tradition are extended while in retreat and the lay people meditate, study and share something of the ordained monk's routine of life. The end of *Vassa* is marked by a special festival involving the whole locality and it is a time, again, for bestowing on the monks all the necessary gifts which they are permitted to receive.

The Theravadin tradition, as noted at the outset, is largely male orientated; legitimate female orders no longer being possible. Girls more rarely undergo any kind of initiation ceremony in the monastic traditions of Buddhism, though rites similar to those of the boys are sometimes found. Where they choose to become ordained in the Theravadin tradition, they must necessarily attach themselves to a convent, which can never have the same status as a monastery.

Birth rites　Birth is not celebrated with the same emphasis as in many other cultures or religions. However, tradition and local custom, sometimes pre-Buddhist in origin, tend to mark the occasion in some way or other, but in the monastic traditions of Buddhism, monks would not participate, though they may be asked to give a blessing to the child, and sometimes to name the baby. Thus, ceremonies which celebrate birth sometimes have little to do with Buddhism itself. Such perhaps is the custom in Thailand where newly-born baby boys are placed in a cradle or basket with tools, pencils and books, while baby girls would be placed in one with needles and cottons. Burying the umbilical cord in an earthenware vessel is an important rite in Thai birth custom; it generally marks the settling down of someone, in this case, the new baby. Important, too, in Thai custom is the belief in an attendant spirit, a *khwan*, which dwells within the body and attends to its welfare: the baby's wrists are fastened with threads to welcome the *khwan*. To protect new babies from evil spirits the baby is not given its actual name until a few years after its birth, presumably when the good spirit, the *khwan*, is well established. A chubby, healthy-looking baby might be given an uncharacteristic name involving terms like "little" or "tiny" in order to deceive the evil spirits and it is not unusual for a person to have retained these names throughout life, or to retain his or her two names. While such customs are important at local level, it is generally the rite of initiation which is given precedence over physical birth in terms of religious significance.

Marriage Marriage in Buddhism is generally considered to be a secular occasion and therefore would not involve the monks. The idea of marriage as a sacred institution would generally be opposed to a monastic tradition in which it is possible for men to leave their families – as did the Buddha – for the life of a monk. Moreover, to suggest that marriage is a source of happiness, or that two people should be indissolubly bound to one another, is alien to the general impressions of Buddhism which advocate loss of the egoistic self and non-craving for happiness in a life which can only be impermanent and transient. To suggest that marriage can bring lasting happiness is therefore against traditional beliefs. Thus, wedding ceremonies are usually quite simple. For many Buddhists it would be important to ensure that the prospective couple had compatible horoscopes and that the marriage takes place at a favourable astrological time. The Indian tradition of binding the couple together symbolically often occurs as, for example, in the Burmese custom of tying the hands of the bride and groom together with a silk scarf, or the Sri Lankan custom of tying the thumbs together. Burmese rites also have the custom of holding the couple's hands together in a bowl of water, symbolizing that their union should be as indivisible as water.

The celebration of marriage in Nichiren Daishonin Buddhism begins with *Daimoku*, the chanting of *Nam-myoho-renge-kyo*, before the bride and groom enter in order to join the assembled guests for *gongyo*. This is followed by what is called *san san kudo*, a rite in which *sake* is given to the bride and groom who each takes three sips from three increasingly larger cups. This symbolizes the wish for the growing unity of the couple, their increasing commitment to each other, and the increasing effect of their own happiness on the environment around them. Thus the meaning of *san san kudo* is $3 \times 3 = 9$. Rings are exchanged and the marriage register is signed, followed by an address by the officiating Buddhist. In Tibet it sometimes happens that a number of brothers will marry one woman. Such polyandry may serve the purpose of keeping the population in check in areas where arable land is scarce.[70]

Death The acceptance of *samsara* means that death is but a passage from one life to the next in the same way that life consists of the passage from one moment to the next, each consecutive moment being brought about by similar, but not identical, factors. But the passage through death to a new life is dictated by the accumulated *karmas* of the individual. Buddhism accepts many world systems and thirty-one planes of existence ranging from a highly subtle, formless realm to those of tangible humans, animals, demons, hells and dead spirits. Dependent on the *karmas* which make up the first moments of the next life, an individual could find his or her self in any of these realms. Thus, while other rites of passage may be minimized, those concerned with death are considered to be very important. In monastic traditions the monks would attend the funeral and conduct part of the ceremony. The casket containing the deceased is often taken to the temple surrounded with gifts for the monks, and with flowers. The monks will chant appropriate parts of Buddhist scriptures, perhaps related to *karma*, to rebirth, and will emphasize the celebratory nature of a person passing from one life to the next. While it is recognized that comfort and consolation need to be given to the bereaved, Buddhist funerals are not the sad occasions which they are in some cultures. There may be festive music, children playing, and feasting to celebrate the passing through the door of death to a new life beyond it.

In both Theravada and Mahayana traditions – especially the latter – there is often an emphasis on ancestor worship. In such cases it would be important to comfort the spirit of the deceased so that it does not aggravate those who are still living. Indian religion has had a tendency to consider the acquisition and working off of *karma* to take place as much when one is deceased as when one is alive – the existence of heavens and hells being the usual mediums for this – but it is believed that the living can aid the dead by passing over as much spiritual merit as possible. So in monastic sects gifts to the monks would be particularly important at this time with the hope of effecting good *karma* for the living, and for helping to store up good *karma* for the deceased in order to promote a particularly favourable rebirth. This somewhat detracts from the fundamental teaching of the Buddha that each individual needs to work out his or her own salvation and that the *karma* one accrues is one's own and provides the continuity for the next life of any individual. Passing *karma* to the deceased, however, is as important in Theravada Buddhism as most schools of Mahayana.

The emphasis on the veneration of ancestors has led to the custom of burial in Mahayana Buddhism, while Theravada Buddhists generally cremate the body as the general Indian custom. Such is the importance of the role of ancestors in the former that there are festivals for the dead such as the Chinese "Festival of Hungry Ghosts" when offerings are made for the dead and lighted candles placed in paper boats in order to guide their spirits. At the Japanese festival of Higan, which occurs at the equinoxes, prayers and gifts for the dead are offered; while the Japanese Bon festival is a time when the spirits of the dead return to their homes and solicit help from their relatives.

Many Mahayana traditions have ceremonies that are held in memory of the deceased and these will vary in frequency from weekly events for those recently deceased to much longer periods as the death becomes more distant. Chinese and Japanese Pure Land sects accept that at death one is able to enter the paradisical realm of Amitabha/Amida if one has total faith in this Buddha. Here, liberation is by faith rather than loss of *karma* or the accumulation of excessively good *karma*.

In Tibetan Buddhism the body of the deceased is dismembered and exposed to the elements – practical measures in a country with little soil and little firewood in its mountainous land. Lamps are kept alight for seven weeks to light the spirit of the deceased to its new state in its next life. Most Buddhists view death positively. Nichiren Daishonin Buddhists try to express to families and friends at funeral ceremonies the on-going nature of life beyond death. Part of the address they give at ceremonies in the United Kingdom includes the following words:

> Buddhism teaches that life and death are but two constantly recurring phases of life. In other words, life is eternal and indestructible – forever existing. When we are in the "living" state we are actively contributing to the life of the whole universe – to our family and others. Death is but a state of latency – an interval like a night's sleep. Death is when we regenerate enough life force to take on a fresh new physical form so that we can continue to contribute to the well-being of the great universe, to our family and others.[71]

The funeral ceremony is simple, and positive, and includes the chanting of *daimoku* and *gongyo* either fully or in part.

Death rites in the Soto Zen Order of Buddhist Contemplatives are actually an ordination ceremony, ordaining the deceased person into the Buddhist Order as a lay person. This takes the form of symbolic shaving of the head, just as a monk would do before entry to the *Sangha*. In some cases the head may actually be physically shaved in the coffin. Such ordination of the deceased illustrates the belief that there is no birth or death, only continuity. If a funeral is held at a major temple of the Order, the body is laid in front of the altar (or on it if a senior monk). A strip of cloth is placed around the hands, possibly to keep the hands in the *gassho mudra*, the bowing position, and a rosary is placed around them. A deceased monk will have part of his robe – the *kesa* – placed round his neck, a lay person a *wagesa*, a black strip of cloth symbolic of the robe of the monk.

In general life-cycle rites, as in most cultures, reflect some of the very oldest folk customs and deeply ingrained traditions. In many respects, a good deal of syncretism has occurred between indigenous customs and Buddhist ideas as in the case of Japanese traditions, for example. Of the life-cycle rites, however, death is the most important one and the one which remains in touch with the tenets of the respective Buddhist tradition with an emphasis on rebirth as a positive step on the path of personal evolution.

Buddhism has been adapted to suit the cultures of different countries so each country is likely to have its own distinctive festivals. Even New Year celebrations occur at different times. Festivals provide an opportunity for the lay people to take an active part in their religion, and provide shared experiences and occasions for enjoyment as well as a profound change from the routine of life. They also reinforce the religion, giving tangible expression to its history and culture. The Buddhist year is based on the lunar calendar and many Buddhist festivals occur at the time of the full moon. While the time of the full moon is especially important, the other main phases of the moon are also times for religious activities, such as visits to the temples to offer gifts in honour of the *Dhamma* of the Buddha. But the full moon is most significant in that traditionally the Buddha became enlightened at such a time and wandering monks often met at the full moon to remind each other of *Sangha* rules. Nevertheless, there are differences between festival times of Theravada, Mahayana and Vajrayana (Tibetan) Buddhism.

BUDDHIST FESTIVALS

Theravada Festivals   Festivals in Theravada Buddhism are often a time for the laity and the monks to join together in a monastery or temple. In the lunar month, the first day and the fifteenth days are called *uposatta* days. *Uposatta* means "entering to stay" because on these days the laity is expected to join the monks in fasting, devotion and meditation at times when the moon is new and full. The weeks following the new and full moons are slightly less important *uposatta* times. While in the earlier phase of Buddhism such days were the occasion for monastic recitation of the *Vinaya*, they later became occasions in which the lay people could join in monastic life. Considering the emphasis on the acquisition of good merit for the lay person, and the desire to be born in the next life in such a position that entry into the monastery as a full monk would be possible, such periods when lay people can participate in monastic life are considered essential. Thus, apart from listening to the teachings of the monks, lay Buddhists would participate in chanting and meditation, and would reaffirm their acceptance of the *Five Precepts*, or even *Eight Precepts*.

***Vesak* or Buddha Day** [72]   This is an important three-day festival for Theravada Buddhists for it celebrates the Birth, Enlightenment and Death of the Buddha in one. *Vesak* is the name of the month which corresponds to our May/June and the festival coincides with the full moon. Images of the Buddha will be honoured with light, flowers and incense. In Sri Lanka *Vesak* is often called a festival of lights since so many are lit. This characteristic of light is an important one because it symbolizes the Enlightenment of the Buddha – arguably the most important aspect of the festival. Thus, temples and homes are brightly lit, "*bodhi*" trees are surrounded with lights and people make lanterns. *Vesak* cards are sent and these portray the Birth, Enlightenment or Death of the Buddha and are often decorated with a *bodhi* tree or lotus. Houses and streets are decorated for Vesak and gifts are given to the monks and the poor as an expression of generosity – an important Buddhist practice at all times, but especially at this festival. In Thailand, houses are cleaned and garlands of flowers hung up everywhere. The temple courtyard is spread with clean sand, Buddha statues in the temple are cleaned and polished and at night the largest of the statues is put on a platform outside and surrounded with lights. After throwing scented water on the statue, the people encircle the image with lighted lamps so that it is surrounded by moving lights. Thai Buddhists circumambulate the local monastery three times to symbolize the *Three Refuges*. It is a time particularly for practise of the doctrine of *ahimsa*, "non-violence" – even, as Erricker points out, to the extent of abstaining from agricultural work which might harm living things.[73] *Vesak* honours the memory and teachings of the Buddha and the flowers which are a feature of the festival remind the Buddhist of the destruction and shortness of all life.

Vassa   Called *Asala* in some Buddhist countries, *Vassa* is the rainy season from July onwards. At this time it is not easy to travel around, so monks spend time in study, meditation and stricter religious life. Special offerings are given to the monks at this time and no weddings or festivals take place. It was said to be the time when the Buddha rose to heaven, where he preached the *Dhamma* to the gods. His return to earth at the end of the rainy season marks the end of *Vassa* which is celebrated with many lights which symbolically illumine his path down to earth, as in the Burmese custom of placing lanterns throughout homes, on shrines and on trees. It is during this period that initiation, ordination and renewal of vows take place and many lay Buddhists spend time in the monastery until the end of the rainy season.

New Year festivals   As in most cultures, New Year celebrations are often times for more lively and less religious celebration. It is a time when families and friends can get together. In Sri Lanka and Thailand water is sprayed indiscriminately over friends and strangers. Cars and floats are decorated and Buddha images are washed. Apart from being a time of great merry-making it is also a time when basic activities such as cooking, eating, starting work and bathing are given religious significance. Emphasis on water is not only confined to sprinkling people and washing Buddha images. Bowls of cool water are offered to honoured Buddhists and this emphasis on water is probably connected with ideas of purification before the beginning of a new year. It is a three-day festival, and on the third day Buddhists take the *Three Refuges* and *Five Precepts*. It is thought, too, that merit is achieved by releasing captive animals, fish and birds. Kite flying is a special feature of the festival as also plays with shadow puppets, and traditional dancing. The more religious side of the New Year celebrations is shown in the respect paid to the Buddha images in both temple and home, and by placing robes on the images for the monks.

Kathina   This is a ceremony that takes place in October/November. People take gifts to the monks to thank them for keeping the religion alive, but especially gifts of new robes, for *kathina* means "cloth" (particularly the frame on which it is made). One special robe is a feature of the festival, about which Erricker comments:

> The robe is made according to ceremonial prescription, by sewing patches together in such a way as is said to imitate the patchwork of the paddy fields familiar to the early monks on their travels.[74]

The robe is sometimes made by the monks themselves and is given by them to the lay people for them to officially return it. In some places, however, the young girls of the neighbourhood make the robe. As Erricker points out, the bestowing of the finished cloth illustrates very well the continued interdependence of lay and monastic communities.[75] The monks bless the lay people and talk about *Kathina* as a time of kindness and generosity, which brings merit. A prerequisite of the festival is that it must have present five monks who have correctly observed *Vassa* and four of them must have done so in the same temple. In Bangkok, in Thailand, the King is rowed out to the Temple of Dawn (*Wat Arun*) to present the monks with a *Kathina* cloth.

Ksala perahera (Sri Lanka)   The Buddha's cremated remains were divided throughout the Buddhist world and housed in *stupas*. In Kandy in Sri Lanka, there is a small *stupa* in which is housed a tooth of the Buddha, said to have been brought from India in the fourth century. It was originally placed at Anuradhapura. In the month of Esala (July/August) there is the *Esala perahera* (*Esala* procession), which is a festival lasting for fifteen nights from the new moon to the full moon. In this festival, a reliquary is carried on a royal elephant which is finely decorated. The processions (*perahera*) are held at night and become more elaborate as the time proceeds. At the end of the festival a hundred elephants may be featured in the procession along with dancers, drummers, musicians, fireworks and important people. Whether the actual tooth is conveyed in the reliquary or retained in caskets in the temple remains uncertain. The festival also features four guardian spirits of Sri Lanka who are very akin to the old Hindu Gods.

Peraheras are a particular feature of Sri Lankan festivals and such processions, when relics are processed through towns to the accompaniment of much joyous celebration, occur at other times of the religious year, such as at *Poson*, which celebrates the time when Buddhism is thought to have arrived in Sri Lanka in the time of the Emperor Asoka.

Other festivals *Asalha Puja* is a Theravadin festival which celebrates the giving of the first sermon by the Buddha – and therefore the first turning of the Wheel of the Law – to the five ascetics in the Deer Park near Benares. It is known as *Chokhor* in Tibet. Processions carrying scriptures written on long wooden blocks were a particular feature of the festival: they symbolize the carrying and spread of the Buddha's *Dhamma* to all places. *Magha Puja* is a full moon festival which celebrates the selection of two chief disciples by the Buddha, the establishing of the *Vinaya* by which the monks should live, and the announcement by the Buddha that he would die in three months' time, before an audience of 1250 disciples. In some eastern temples 1250 candles are lit in memory of this last event. It is a festival of lights in some parts of Thailand, as it used to be in Laos.

Mahayana festivals: anniversaries of the Buddha's life Mahayana Buddhist festivals vary considerably and often incorporate traditional pre-Buddhist customs. Since ancestor veneration is a particular feature of many Mahayana Buddhist countries and has its roots in pre-Buddhist traditions, many festivals, especially in the Far East, combine Buddhist ritual with such belief. A comprehensive examination of the many festivals of Mahayana Buddhism is not possible here, but a number are highlighted from the Japanese and Tibetan strands of Mahayana Buddhism.

Japanese festivals Unlike the Theravadin tradition, the Birth, Death and Enlightenment of the Buddha are celebrated separately in Mahayana Buddhism. The Japanese celebrate the Birth of the Buddha in the festival of *Hana Matsuri* which occurs in April and, as its name suggests, is a flower festival. It is the most important of the many flower festivals in Japan. Models of flower gardens are made and placed in courtyards and temples to remind Buddhists of the Lumbini gardens where the Buddha was born. Tradition states that he was born from his mother's right side, and was so enlightened that he could stand upright immediately and took seven steps. The festival includes the use of delicately perfumed tea, reminding Buddhists that the gods provided perfumed water for the Buddha's first bath. The tea is poured over Buddha images in the temples. Since a white elephant was associated with the time when the Buddha was conceived, large papier-mâché white elephants are sometimes made to guard the model of the Lumbini flower garden. White elephants are symbols of royalty and when the Buddha's mother conceived, her dream of a white elephant heralded special birth.

Jodo-e is the Japanese festival which commemorates the Enlightenment of the Buddha and occurs in December. The Buddha sat beneath what came to be called the *bodhi* or *bo* tree until he achieved enlightenment and in Zen Buddhism this is commemorated with a period of intensive meditation called *rohatsu*. During this time Zen Buddhists meditate all day and night, and are not allowed to lie down, although food is brought to them. *Nahan-e* is the Japanese festival, held in February, which celebrates the death of Sakyamuni, his *parinirvana*. In Zen temples, lights are turned out while monks meditate and chant special scriptures before lights are turned on again. This is symbolic of the hope that the light which the Buddha brought into the world will continue for as long as Buddhists practise his teachings.

Other festivals reflect some of the older traditions of Japan, particularly ancestor worship. The festival of Obon is a good example. Tradition states that one of the Buddha's disciples had the ability to visit the heavens and hells (or other planes of existence) to find out what happened to people who had died. On seeing the suffering of his mother in hell, he asked the Buddha for her release. Through the Buddha's compassion this was done. So at Obon, everyone goes home much the same as people do for Mothering Sunday in the West. During the festival, offerings are made to Buddha images, and people pray that their ancestors will have good rebirths and realize *nirvana*. So the festival is a family reunion when people return to their native villages. Here there are fetes, side-shows, circular dancing and music. The festival lasts four days, beginning on 13 July. Graves are cleaned and decorated with flowers, incense lit and the spirits of ancestors are invited to return home. The people burn hemp reeds, which are thought to light the way of the spirits, guiding them home. At home, people decorate the family altar and prepare food for the spirits, sometimes actually talking to them, for the presence of the ancestors is felt to be very real. When the festival ends, lanterns, bearing the names of the deceased, are floated on rivers or lakes, taking the spirits away again. For this reason, the festival is often called the Festival of Lanterns or The Joyful Ceremony; it is also known as *Urabon*, or just *Bon*. The festival is a good example of the way in which Buddhism has been adapted to the customs – in this case ancestor worship – of a particular country.

Joya no Kane is the Japanese "Evening Bells Ceremony", which sees the old year out on 31 December. Temple bells are struck 108 times, this being a magic number of ancient tradition originating in India and is the number of beads on a Buddhist *mala* or rosary. *Higan* is the name given to the two festivals which celebrate the Spring and Autumn equinoxes (21 March and 23 September). At the heart of the festival is harmony, or "naturalness" expressed in the hope for the peace and tranquillity of *nirvana* in each person and in nature. At *Higan*, Buddhists visit the temples as well as the graves of their ancestors where they give merit to the deceased by pouring water over the tomb-stones from wooden ladles. The six traditional "perfections" of *bodhisattvas* – generosity, non-violence, patience, effort, meditation and wisdom – are remembered. These perfections are necessary so that enlightenment or "The Other Shore" can be reached. *Higan* also cele-brates the change in nature, the change in season, the harmony between one season and the next – like the harmony as one crosses spiritually from the world of *samsara* (this shore) to *nirvana* (the other shore). These festivals reflect a certain Chinese influence, the equinoxes being the time when *yin* and *yang* were in perfect balance before the assertion of one over the other for half of the year.

Setsubon is a festival which occurs in February when the Japanese spring begins. The head of each household puts a wooden rice measure containing beans on the family shrine. As it begins to get dark he scat-ters the beans at all the entrances to the house and in dark corners of the house, at the same time shouting "Devils out"! "Good luck in!" The festival, therefore, is one which drives out evil spirits and when they have been driven out, a little charm is put over each entrance so that they cannot sneak back in again!

Tibetan festivals: *Losar* Losar is the Tibetan New Year Festival and occurs in February. It is a critically important time when all the evil of the past year is dispelled, and extends into a number of different festi-vals and celebrations to this end. It is preceded by a festival called *Gutor* in which houses are thoroughly cleaned and whitewashed. A little of the dirt of the house is retained and later thrown away at places where spirits are thought to dwell, such as at crossroads. At *Gutor*, kitchens must be scrupulously clean and a special dish called *guthok* containing nine stuffed dumplings is prepared. Each dumpling is made with a different ingredient inside – a prophecy of the nature of the year ahead for whoever partakes of it. One has a piece of charcoal in it, indication a "black" heart for the person who eats it. Just before *Losar* begins the last day of the old year is one in which evil spirits must be chased away, often by monks in grotesque masks who take part in a ritual dance showing the victory of good over evil. Sometimes people go through their homes with lighted torches, fireworks and guns to chase away evil spirits. Signs drawn in flour may be found round the houses as good luck charms and houses are decorated with special decorations made of paper or cloth.

The first day of the New Year begins the festival of *Losar*. People get up early and wash at the nearest well or stream and put on new clothes. Special food is associated with *Losar*, such as *kapse* "cakes", and *chang*, an alcoholic drink which is warm and has extra ingredients added to it such as rice and sweet potatoes. Boxes of grain and barley flour are decorated with dried ears of corn and are placed inside houses. The festival is a happy one, family centred on the first day and neighbour centred on the following two days.

On the fourth day of *Losar* is the great prayer festival of *Monlam Chenmo* which celebrates the miracles performed by Sakyamuni Buddha, and was the traditional day for monks to sit their examinations for higher degrees, particularly for the highest award of *geshe*, in the days when Buddhism was the religion of Tibet. *Monlam Chenmo* means "Great Aspiration" and was one of the major festivals in Tibet with Lhasa being the centre of celebrations for Buddhists outside Tibet as well as Tibetan Buddhists themselves. It is an old festival originating from the fifteenth century and associated with the Gelukpa school.[76] *Monlam Chenmo* is probably the most important of all the Tibetan festivals because it is believed that not only does it focus on getting rid of evil but it also creates very powerful positive *karma* both for individuals and for the collective community.

On the fourteenth day of the New Year, the monks don elaborate costumes and masks and combine for a spectacular sacred dance which is also designed to exorcise all the evil forces of the previous year. When the religion flourished in Tibet, at the full moon, on the fifteenth day of the long festivities at the beginning of the Tibetan year, the well-known Butter Sculpture Festival occurred, when huge statues of butter and flour were made. This Butter Sculpture Festival involves elaborate preparations, the incredible sculptures taking many months to complete – only to be destroyed at the festival after just a few hours of public display. Powers aptly comments on this:

> This provided the audience with a graphic reminder of the Buddhist concept of impermanence, which teaches that all mundane human activities pass away, leaving nothing behind. Those who recognize the implications of this principle should understand the ultimate futility of worldly pursuits and devote themselves to religious activities, which bring lasting benefits.[77]

The whole emphasis of *Losar*, *Monlam Chenmo* and the festivals and celebrations which occur in the first month of the Tibetan New Year, is on the expelling of all the evil of the old year and this will be done with all sorts of customs in the home and in the community – the latter with much ritual, colour and ceremony. Circumambulation is a particular feature of Tibetan ritual – usually three times to represent the *Three Refuges*, and sometimes actually done entirely by prostrations. When Lhasa in Tibet thrived as a Buddhist city, many would circumambulate the city or the monastery in order to achieve good merit. Such circumambulation is also a special feature of the Tibetan celebration of the Birth, Enlightenment and Death of the Buddha in May, which is a more religious occasion, characterized by abstinence from meat eating, or even by fasting and long periods of silence.

Tibetan festivals are perhaps the most colourful and fascinating of the festivals of Mahayana Buddhism because of the many elements which inform their practices. Powers comments on this uniqueness and the particular blend of religion with secular festivity in the following rather apt statement about them:

> Tibetan festivals have a multifaceted character and exhibit a curious blend of the religious and the mundane, of serious Budhist rituals and humorous skits, sacred music and secular entertainments, all mixed together. These communal gatherings are important elements in the development of a sense of shared values and traditions: people gather together from a wide area to celebrate their religion and culture, to meet new people and old friends, and to drive out negative influences and ensure a brighter future.[78]

PILGRIMAGE

Although pilgrimage is not required in Buddhism, it is still a popular act of homage. Because Buddhism has a historical founder in the Buddha, places attached to his life history have become important sites of pilgrimage in India. Similarly in other countries, places containing important relics attract pilgrims. The Lumbini Grove is the place where the Buddha was born. It is situated near Kapilavastu in Nepal. In the third century BCE the Emperor Asoka placed a pillar there to mark the birth place. To visit the Grove, as other places of pilgrimage, brings merit to the pilgrim. Bodh Gaya is near Gaya in Bihar and is the most important Buddhist pilgrimage site since it is the place where the Buddha achieved enlightenment. A descendant of the *bodhi* tree (called *bo* tree for short) still stands marking the spot where the Buddha sat beneath the *bo* tree until he became enlightened. Thus it is believed to be a place of great spiritual significance and experience. Pilgrims circumambulate the tree in a clockwise direction, meditate beneath it and hang colourful flags on it. Beside the tree stands the Mahabodhi (great enlightenment) Temple, where offerings are made. Also featured at Bodh Gaya beneath the *bo* tree is a footprint, said to be that of the Buddha. For Tibetan Buddhists Bodh Gaya is the most sacred site of all and is considered to be the spiritual centre of the universe.

Sarnath, now a large city called Varanasi (Benares), and being easy to reach, is a popular place of pilgrimage. It was here at the Deer Park that the Buddha preached his first sermon to the five mendicant holy men. The Emperor Asoka built a large *stupa* there as a monument. The site of the Buddha's death at Kusinara is marked by a temple and monasteries of Buddhists from other countries.

At the top of a high mountain in Sri Lanka there is a footprint which is said to be the Buddha's. There is no evidence that the Buddha ever went to Sri Lanka but Sri Lankan Buddhists believe that the Buddha visited the country on three occasions, and on the third occasion the footprint was made. The Buddhist name for the mountain is *Sri Pada*, "honourable footprint"; but it is also called Adam's Peak because the Muslims associate the footprint with Adam, while the Hindus consider it to be the footprint of Siva, the great Hindu God. The more effort it takes to climb the mountain (2243 m) the more merit is obtained. Pilgrims often ascend the mountain at night and when the dawn breaks the beauty of the sunrise is thought to be symbolic of enlightenment.

Since cuttings from the *bodhi* tree have been planted all round the world, there are many venerated *bodhi* trees! Some *stupas* contain relics, such as a hair relic in the great Rangoon *stupa* called Shwe Dagon. On this *pagoda*, pilgrims place gold leaf to honour the Buddha and acquire merit. At Borobudur in Java is a massive fifteenth century *stupa* built in terraces. The lower terraces contain scenes depicting the life of the Buddha but as one climbs, and the more empty the terraces become, the more one is reminded of Buddhist teaching that the mind needs to be stilled and empty of the stimuli which attract it to the transient phenomenal world, and that all is ultimately empty. This is a *stupa* which reflects the spiritual evolution of any individual and each person will be attracted to the level of the *stupa* which suits his or her consciousness.

There are many *buddharupas*, statues of the Buddha, to be found in countries which embrace Buddhism. Some are huge, such as at sites in Sri Lanka. They provide a focus for pilgrimage and for quiet reflection on the calm and serene faces of the Buddha. But Buddhism is not, ultimately, an externalized journey. It is an inward journey which seeks to understand the nature of existence and of the self and, as a result of such understanding, to transcend phenomenal existence to that point of equanimity expressed in the faint smile portrayed by the Buddha's face – *nirvana*.

6

Sikhism

Merv Fowler

Why do you go to the forest in search of God?
He lives in all and is yet ever distinct;
He abides with you, too,
As fragrance dwells in a flower,
And reflection in a mirror;
So does God dwell inside everything;
Seek Him, therefore, in your heart.
Guru Granth Sahib

Sikhism is one of the world's youngest religions, for it was founded in the sixteenth century by a visionary called Nanak. "Sikh" means "disciple" in Sanskrit, that is a pupil or learner, an interpretation supported by its cognate in Punjabi which means "to learn". This suggests that a Sikh is a person who is learning, or a disciple of, *the Truth*.

The Punjab   Sikhs originate from the Punjab, meaning (land of the) "five rivers". It is an area which actually extends into both India and Pakistan, for in 1947 the British, on leaving India, divided the country into two. The dividing line cut straight through the Punjab, leaving some Sikhs in Pakistan and some in India. The Punjab refers to the whole area of the five rivers, but it is also the name given to a small state, the capital of which is Lahore, a province of Pakistan. The Punjab is generally flat and green and is less subject to the droughts that plague southern India, though when the monsoons fail it loses its fertile character. Normally, the fertile land can be used for the cultivation of wheat, corn crops and sugar cane.

Since the Punjab is the gateway to India, it has been subject to frequent incursions. Indeed, this is an important factor in examining Sikhism, for the development of a military character became essential for its survival, the Sikhs themselves becoming impressive soldiers in the British Army. Today, the Punjab is an area in which modernity combines with older traditions.

334

To define a Sikh precisely in today's world is a difficult task. Broadly speaking, we might say that a Sikh is one who follows the *Gurmat*, the spiritual teaching of the ten Gurus of early Sikhism, in the same way as we might say a Buddhist is a follower of the teachings of the Buddha, or a Christian of Jesus Christ. But traditionally Sikhs have more than a spiritual identity, for there have always been distinguishing marks of Sikh dress. While some insist that a true Sikh must conform to the traditional physical characteristics of Sikhism, such as the wearing of the Five Ks (see below) and the turban, others maintain that even when these are abandoned, a true Sikh need only follow the teachings of the Gurus. So not all Sikhs will wear a turban nor will all retain uncut hair (which is one of the Five Ks). Furthermore, the expectations of a new culture have often persuaded migrants from the Punjab to forsake their traditional distinguishing marks.

There are those Sikhs, too, who maintain some Hindu customs such as that of women wearing a *bindi* mark on the forehead. It is also possible at some Sikh places of worship to see some women covering their faces completely, in the custom of Muslim women. But the Sikh Gurus were intent on ensuring that Sikhism itself has a determinant character, a character which to some extent survives in the Sikh man and woman of today. Sikhism would not have survived had it not been for the strength of character of its adherents and today this is manifest in a determined, hard-working and proud people.

Sources   Virtually our only source for the life history of Guru Nanak is the Sikh writings, the *Janam Sakhis*, the "Birth Testimonies" *(janam* "birth", *sakhi* "testimony")*. As they appear in their present form, the *Janam Sakhis* were written about a century or later after Nanak's death. The gap between the death of Nanak and the first known devotional literature giving his life story, was filled by oral tradition. Early available manuscripts indicate that after many years of oral transmission the stories were first written down as isolated events. Only a vague attempt has been made to present this material chronologically, occasionally grouping together the stories according to stages of Nanak's life – birth, childhood, adulthood and death. A later stage of literary development ordered the material chronologically in a systematic way and grouped the various incidents in relation to his travels. Generally, the more recent the writing, the wider the bounds of Nanak's journeys, the narratives being interpolated with expositions of the writer. For Dr W. H. McLeod,[1] this would seem to question biographical accuracy, for there would appear to be inconsistencies between Nanak's teaching recorded in the Sikh scriptures, the *Guru Granth Sahib*, and religious assumptions implied in the *Sakhis*. For example, in the teachings of the *Guru Granth Sahib*, the Guru sees religion as transcending sectarian differences between Muslim and Hindu, whereas the *Sakhis* see Nanak as attempting a reconciliation between the two systems of belief. This perhaps reflects the writers' interpretations. Although the two ideas are not incompatible, they do seem to reflect different levels of religious understanding. The final stage of literary development was that in which expositions and discussions of the text were given alongside the narrative of Guru Nanak's life and teaching.

The *Janam Sakhis*, therefore, may be considered as *hagiographic* narratives with a central core of tradition. Many Sikhs today accept the *Sakhis* as biographically accurate and totally correct accounts, but equally so, many other Sikhs regard the *Janam Sakhis* as historical writings only. Thus, Dr Trilochan Singh, in a review of a book dedicated to refuting many of the aforementioned points raised by Dr McLeod, writes:

> Dr McLeod makes a misleading statement when he says that he is criticising the sacred records of the Sikhs when he is criticising the *Janam Sakhis*. There is nothing sacred about *Janam Sakhis* and no sanctity is attached to any historical works by the Sikhs.[2]

Dr Trilochan Singh adds that it is the *Guru Granth Sahib* and the *Dasam Granth*, a scripture written by the tenth Guru, which are *sacred* and therefore authentic. Thus we should not confuse hagiographical literature with the religious truths of the sacred literature. Nevertheless, the *Sakhis* are highly revered by the Sikhs and are read with great reverence in Sikh homes. They are also used for instruction in the *gurdwaras*, the Sikh places of worship. Therefore, as Cole and Sambhi point out, they:

> can too easily be dismissed as hagiographic accounts, but the theological statements which they make and the insights they give into Sikh belief in the seventeenth century to which, for the most part they belong, have been ignored as scholars question or defend their historical reliability.[3]

The life of Guru Nanak (1469–1539)   Nanak was born in the Punjab in 1469. The nature of the people of this area is said to be a product of the unique geographical situation. It is the meeting place of routes into India from the south west and east. The area is particularly vulnerable, having incurred successive invasions from the north-west through the Khyber Pass. It is, therefore, a land of cultural and ethnic variety. This is perhaps reflected in the independent attitude of the people, who frequently had the responsibility of defending their country.

Nanak was born at Talwandi, west of Lahore, at a time when the land was ruled by the Sultantate of Delhi. Talwandi is now called Nankana Sahib in honour of Nanak. Like the Buddha, Nanak was born into a *Ksatriya* family and was brought up as an orthodox Hindu. His father was a local official, working for the owner of the village of Talwandi who was a Muslim, so Nanak grew up conversant with both Hindu and Muslim traditions. The *Janam Sakhis* portray him as destined to become a great man, the village *pandit* foretelling his destined religious leadership. He is remembered as having been a very wise child, but not a very practical one in that his mind often wandered away from everyday tasks; instead, he focused on God. According to he accounts, he was religiously a very perceptive child, entering into discussion with teachers of both Hindu and Muslim belief; by his adolescence he had become critical of formal Hinduism. It seems he found little in either religion to satisfy his personal quest. However, he descriptions of his discussions with *Sant yogis* and wise men indicate the influence of the mystics on Nanak's thought and, like the *Sants,* Nanak came to believe that inner spirituality was more important than outward ritual.

At the age of sixteen, Nanak became employed as a government official and was introduced to the wider Muslim world, meeting mystics and intellectuals. However, he still pursued his own religious quest, not having found a satisfactory answer in either faith. Although still engaged in a devout life of prayer and meditation, he married at nineteen and had two sons. After his marriage he moved to Sultanpur for a while to stay with his sister's husband. There, Nanak and a group of people would gather together in the morning and evening for the purpose of singing hymns and meditating. It was at Sultanpur that he had some kind of mystical experience, one which became the foundation of the Sikh religion.

It was an experience of enlightenment. According to the *Janam Sakhi* narratives, it was his custom to bathe in the river before dawn. One morning, he failed to return for three days. When he reappeared, he remained silent until the following day, when he said:

> There is neither Hindu nor Musselman so whose path
> shall I follow? I shall follow God's path. God is neither
> Hindu nor Musselman, and the path which I follow is God's.

His enlightenment had been initiated by a journey to the court of God, where he was taken into the presence of the Divine. A cup was filled with nectar (*amrit*) and given to him. He was commanded to drink the nectar in adoration of God's name *(Nam)* and to become a Guru (religious teacher) for God. A hymn in the *Guru Granth Sahib* describes the vocation:

> I was a minstrel out of work,
> The Lord gave me employment.
> The Mighty One instructed me,
> 'Night and day sing my praise.'

The Lord summoned the minstrel to his High Court...
On me he bestowed nectar in a cup
The nectar of his true and holy name.
Those who at the Guru's bidding
Feast and take their fill of the Lord's holiness
Attain peace and joy.
Your minstrel spreads your glory by singing your word.[4]

From this point on Nanak became a spiritual leader and teacher, a Guru. Sikhs explain this word as the dispeller of ignorance and darkness *(gu)* and the proclaimer of enlightenment *(ru)*.

Missionary work Nanak, called to be a religious missionary to reveal God to men (the *Sakhis* refer to him as a Guru), left his official post and travelled as a missionary throughout India, the Himalayas, Tibet, Ceylon (Sri Lanka) and, according to tradition, west as far as Mecca. He thus visited the centres of Islam, Hinduism and Buddhism, preaching a religion freed from formalism, which taught that individual worth mattered more than status or caste. This last point is illustrated in the traditional episode concerning Lalo the carpenter. Nanak accepted the hospitality of a village carpenter, the poorest man in the village. He was reproved for this by a Hindu steward of a Muslim official. The Hindu invited Nanak to what he considered an appropriate gathering of Hindu *(sadhu)* and Muslim *(faqir)* wise men. Since the Guru did not come, he was fetched to the feast and asked why he preferred the food of Lalo, a low-caste carpenter. The Guru sent for Lalo's coarse bread and squeezed it in his hand until milk came from it. When he did this to his wealthy host's bread, drops of blood came from it, indicating that poverty through honest labour was preferable to wealth achieved by exploitation.

While on his travels, Nanak was accompanied by a Muslim musician called Mardana. When he taught, he did so by means of *sabads* hymns or poems which were easily memorized and are now contained in the Sikh scriptures, the *Guru Granth Sahib*. These *sabads* were now sung in Sanskrit like Hindu scriptures, or Arabic like Muslim scripture, but in the people's own language. They became the medium by which the Word of God was transmitted. Throughout his teaching he exhorted men to search for the truth within themselves, a more internalized spirituality, which focused on God as the *Sat Guru*, the True Guru.

The founding of the Sikh community The Sikh community was really founded during the next stage of Nanak's life when, in 1521, he settled with his family and established the entirely Sikh village of Kartarpur. During his travels he had adopted the garb and life of the mendicant *Sufi* mystic,[5] but now he resumed the status of a householder. The disciples who had gathered around him now became a community. Nanak spent his days in personal devotion and discussion. Devotion in the community was through meditation and the Guru's hymns. Of these, the *Sodar* and *Arati* were sung in the evening, and in the early morning the *Japji* was recited. By selecting his own hymns rather than the traditional sacred scriptures, the Guru was instituting a new source of religious understanding. Importantly, Nanak did not attract adoration towards himself, but directed attention to the *Gurbani*, the teaching or total expression of the Word of God. This, then, was the foundation of the Sikh community which later became a distinct religious group.

The succession of Gurus   Before his death, Nanak selected his successor. He considered his sons to be unsuitable, one being a pious ascetic who did not follow his father's teaching, and the other was not interested in religion. The tradition describes how, in September 1539, the Guru called an assembly and singled out one disciple, Lehna, to succeed him. It was felt that this disciple had the necessary character, being humble and obedient to the Word of God. Nine gurus followed Nanak:

Guru Angad	1504–1552
Guru Amar Das	1479–1574
Guru Ram Das	1534–1581
Guru Arjan	1563–1606
Guru Hargobind	1595–1646
Guru Har Rai	1630–1661
Guru Har Krishen	1656–1664
Guru Tegh Bahadur	1621–1675
Guru Gobind Singh	1666–1708

THE TRADITION OF THE GURU

Nanak had selected a spiritual successor, and established the central *Guru* tradition of Sikhism. The Gurus were felt to be one in spirit, entrusted with the sacred truth, and guides to the community. The nine successors of Guru Nanak extended and consolidated the Sikh community, and translated many of Nanak's teachings into practice. Although subsequent Gurus may have adopted practices which seem to depart from the original ideas of Guru Nanak, it is very important in the understanding of Sikhism to remember how the succession of Gurus is regarded; as McLeod puts it:

> It is interpreted as one person following himself. There were ten Nanaks or more precisely, ten manifestations in differing bodies of the one original Nanak commissioned by God and sent into the world for the salvation of mankind.[6]

Guru Angad (1539–1552)   The tradition tells us that Nanak called

Lehna to him, placed five coins and a coconut in front of him and bowed. He gave Lehna a woollen string called a *seli*, which *Sufis* wear around their caps, and which symbolizes renunciation, and possibly a book of his hymns. Nanak renamed Lehna *Angad*, claiming that Angad possessed the spirit of Nanak; the word *Angad* meaning "limb" or "part of me". This initiation has a number of symbolic significances. The coconut represents the created universe, and its hairs the vegetation. The five coins are the five elements, air, earth, fire, water and ether, and the coins are created by human hands. The offering, therefore, was made from nature and humanity, for the protection of Angad. The significance of the book of hymns (if, indeed, Nanak had recorded his hymns in written form) was to make him the guardian of the belief, the person who would be entrusted with the teaching of the community.

We should note the emphasis on Nanak and Lehna being one in spirit. Like torches with the same flame, or light blending with light, these two Gurus and all the Gurus who followed are one spirit – ten manifestations of one spirit. As Bhai Gurdas states in the *Guru Granth Sahib*:

> Before he died he (Guru Nanak) installed Lehna and set the Guru's canopy over his head. Merging his light in Guru Angad's light the Sat Guru changed his form. None could comprehend this, he revealed a wonder of wonders, changing his body he made Guru Angad's body his own.[7]

Indubhushan Bannerjee notes that this succession was extremely important:

> as it placed the movement under the guidance and control of a definite and indisputable leadership and gave it a distinctive turn at the very outset of its career.[8]

So Guru Nanak left his followers the foundations of a new religious faith to be carried forward in the religious community. His teachings are in the 947 hymns which are used for community worship and teaching; the singing of *kirtan*, devotional songs of Nanak, was (and still is) an important part of their early worship. The community is based on family life, since Nanak taught that one can love God and fulfil family obligations.

As Nanak's successor, Angad left Kartarpur and went to his home village of Khadur. Sikhism had spread to a number of places, and tradition states that Angad saw the need to write down the hymns of Nanak. However, there was no need for a written language in daily life, so the only written language available would have been used by tax collectors and in commerce. It was from this, tradition has it, that

Angad worked, and eventually perfected the *Mahajni* or written Punjabi script. This was the *Gurmukhi* (mouth of the Guru) in which Nanak's hymns were written. The *pothi* or collection of Guru Nanak's hymns has not survived, but we do have one hymn of Guru Nanak's which takes the form of an acrostic, thus suggesting that the thirty-five letter *Gurmukhi* alphabet existed before Angad's supposed invention of the *Gurmukhi* script. What Angad probably did was to perfect the original script. It is highly likely that Nanak gave his successor a written collection of his hymns at his investiture. This makes it even more unlikely that Guru Angad originated the script. However, the work of Angad meant that Sikhs could read the Guru's teachings themselves. This was not the case for Hindus, who could not read Sanskrit, or Muslims, who could not read Arabic. However, few Sikhs could read at that time, so Angad built up provision for the education of children in Sikh communities. Guru Angad composed sixty-two or sixty-three hymns of his own and this relatively small contribution is to be found in the *Adi Granth*. But, as Cole and Sambhi affirm:

> His importance is not that of a poet but of a consolidator. For thirteen years he held the community together and maintained its spread and growth.[9]

Amar Das (1552–1574)   Amar Das was a Hindu Vaisnavite and a great pilgrim. Tradition states that one day he heard Angad's daughter singing Guru Nanak's *Japji* and was so enchanted by it that he became Angad's utterly devoted disciple. The beginning of Guru Amar Das' guruship was not easy, for Guru Nanak's elder son, Sri Chand, who was the rather pious, ascetic, claimed that he had the right to become the present Guru. However, as Cole and Sambhi state:

> It is a sign of the character of Guru Amar Das that he was able to hold the community together in the early years of his leadership and leave behind him a growing and well-organised faith when he died.[10]

From 1556 to 1605, India was ruled by the Muslim Emperor Akbar. He was a tolerant emperor, who allowed Hindus and Sikhs to live in peace and freedom throughout India. Amar Das was a close friend, and was allowed to continue the work of Nanak. Indeed, Amar Das' association with the Mughal Emperor was such that he was able to persuade the Mughal government to repeal a tax on pilgrims visiting Hardwar, and grant remission of taxes in the Lahore district after food had become scarce owing to Akbar's campaigns there.

Nanak had set up a "temple of bread" to which corn and fuel were brought and where people worked together. Here the poor could find work and food. This free kitchen was continued by Amar Das, and termed *langar*. It was Amar Das who made *langar* a permanent Sikh institution, so in all Sikh temples a room is set aside as a kitchen where guests can be fed and housed if necessary. In order to illustrate equality, Gurus themselves served *langar* and ate their meals there, insisting that visitors should do likewise. Hindus, Muslims and, tradition has it, the Emperor Akbar, were treated in the same way. The motto of Amar Das was said to be *pehle pangat piche pangat* – "First eat together then meet together". Traditionally, this commensality is seen as a disregarding of caste distinctions, but we should not see it as an attempt to abolish caste. Caste has always existed in Sikhism. We should note that *all* the Gurus came from *Khatri* families (a group synonymous with Hindu *Ksatriyas*). Two castes obtain predominantly in the history of Sikhism, *Khatris* (urban-based) and *Jats* (rural-based). It is the *Jats* who probably later infused into Sikhism its more military aspects. Despite retention of many aspects of caste, the *Jats* may have been attracted to Sikhism because of its more egalitarian views and the *theoretical* rejection of caste. Indeed, in later years they would rise to prominent positions in the Sikh community.

Guru Amar Das also appointed Sikh missionaries, and strengthened the faith by calling Sikhs to appear in his presence at his headquarters in Goindval on the days of the Hindu festivals of spring (*Baisakhi*) and autumn (*Divali*). Amar Das was also concerned for the rights of women. He decried the Hindu practice of *sati*, the burning of a widow on her husband's pyre, as well as the local Muslim custom of insisting that women should be veiled. Because of his attitude, women could now become teachers and religious missionaries.

In one respect, Amar Das seems to have departed from Nanak's advice, for in his town, Goindval, he built a large well, a *baoli*, approached by eighty-four steps to serve the function of a *tirath*, a centre of pilgrimage. He may have felt this was necessary because of the expansion of Sikhism, even though Nanak had considered the human soul to be the centre of pilgrimage, and had rejected physical centres. But we need to set Guru Amar Das' actions against a somewhat different scene to that of Nanak. A second generation of Sikhs was emerging with no direct personal knowledge of Nanak. Amar Das himself had never met the Guru and may well have felt a need to return to some of the more traditional Indian religious customs such as pilgrimage, festivals, rituals, and a collection of sacred writings in order to unite the Sikhs into a more cohesive community. Though Nanak had rejected these, Amar Das felt compelled to return to them.

It is perhaps to the time of Amar Das, too, that we can date the particularly distinctive ceremonies for birth, marriage and death. Again this would serve to unite the Sikh communities with their own customs for life-cycle rites. The Sikh community, too, was growing larger, and Guru Amar Das divided up the Punjab into twenty-two areas, each under the responsibility of a Sikh leader.

Guru Ram Das (1574–1581) (Slave of God)   Ram Das was the son-in-law of Amar Das. The first two Gurus were originally Hindus, and had accepted the teachings of Nanak in adulthood. The Sodhi family to which Guru Ram Das belonged may have already been converted to Sikhism, but in any event, from the days of Ram Das onwards the Sodhis became the family from which all future Gurus would be chosen. Indeed, by the time of Guru Tegh Bahadur, no other choice seems to have been possible.[11] Realizing that Sikhism was spreading and that it would be a permanent religion in the Punjab, Ram Das believed it necessary that Sikhism should have a religious centre. It may have been the Emperor Akbar who gave the wife of Ram Das a gift of land where a thriving community grew up. The place was called Guru Ka Chak by some, Chak Ram Das by others, and Ram Das Pura also, but the modern name is Amritsar "the pool of nectar" named after the lake which encircles the main temple (Golden Temple) of Sikhism, built by the son of Ram Das. The founding of Amritsar was another very important development in the history of Sikhism. On the festival days of *Divali* and *Baisakhi*, it was now at Amritsar that the Sikhs gathered. Ram Das instituted a system of collections from Sikhs for works of charity. Today, this is still a very firm Sikh practice, since Sikhs contribute a tenth of their income, the *Daswandth*. The practice of *sati* and the veiling of women were forbidden, and widows were allowed to remarry.

Guru Arjan (1581–1606)   Arjan's guruship was one of peace and harmony. Relations with the Mughal authorities were very good. Arjan, the son of Ram Das, was the first Guru to be *born* a Sikh. Arjan was also a missionary and it was during his guruship that the *Jats* were attracted into Sikhism. Guru Arjan was not the eldest son of Ram Das but the youngest, and tradition states that the eldest son contested the accession of Arjan. McLeod, however, suggests that the *Panth* (Sikh community) was split at this time and *both* sons assumed guruship.[12] There is good reason to accept this, for the eldest son's, Prithi Chand's, followers were strong enough to compose one of the *Janam Sakhis*. In this, the *Miharban Janam-sakhi*, they stress the need to stay close to Nanak's teachings and be less concerned with social issues. Now extinct, this line was considered heretical, though its writings do not perhaps entirely justify the claim. For our purpose, the incident is important, for it shows that the *Panth*, the Sikh community, was changing and was becoming more socially and economically conscious. Perhaps this had something to do with *Jat* influence, the small peasant landowners, who would possibly have been attracted by the socio-economic growth of the Sikh religion.

During Arjan's guruship, the *Harmandir* was constructed at

343

Amritsar. The *Panth* was now regularly taxed, which provided funds for water reservoirs and buildings. The *Harmandir*, "the Lord's Abode", was built in a blend of Hindu and Muslim architecture. Arjan may well have seen the way of Nanak as a bridge between Hindu and Muslim. The Temple was built with doors on each of its four sides, which showed symbolically that it was open to all of the four classes. This was quite different from a Hindu temple with its single entrance. To enter it, one did not go up steps but down. Symbolically this was to make certain that whoever entered, from whatever class or caste, had to humble himself or herself even lower, before meeting God, the *Sat Guru*. Arjan also enlarged the artificial lake which had been built by Ram Das and the place of worship was built in the centre.

Apart from the building of the Temple, Arjan also set up Amritsar as an economic centre, encouraging the Sikhs to take up business, trade and adopt lucrative professions, carpentry, masonry, horse-trading, banking and so on.[13] This economic policy resulted in Amritsar becoming an important marketing centre with thriving trade internally and externally. Guru Arjan controlled the city with supreme authority both religiously, and economically as its chief administrator. Amritsar, however, did not always remain the central place of pilgrimage. In 1634 Arjun's son and successor, Guru Hargobind, moved to the Sivalik Hills, and for a century Amritsar declined in importance. The last Guru, Gobind Singh, in fact, never visited it. It recovered its status in the eighteenth century. It was in fact only one of four towns built by the Guru, but during his guruship it was of primary importance.

Under Arjan, Sikhism became more and more an independent religion. Arjan produced an authoritative collection of hymns, those of Nanak and those of subsequent Gurus. Under the direction of the Guru, they were written down by Bhai Gurdas and the resulting work was known as the *Adi Granth* (First Collection) and placed in the *Harmandir*. Guru Arjan wrote many hymns of his own which are included in the *Adi Granth (AG)* – for example the following hymn, in which the distinctiveness of Sikhism is emphasized as the true and only path:

> I do not keep the Hindu fast or the Muslim Ramadan. I serve him alone who is my refuge. I serve the one master who is also Allah. I will not worship with the Hindu, nor like the Muslim go to Mecca, I shall serve him and no other. I will not pray to idols nor say the Muslim prayer. I shall put my heart at the feet of the One Supreme Being, for we are neither Hindus nor Muslims.[14]

When the *Granth* was completed, tradition states that enemies reported to the Emperor Akbar that it was anti-Muslim. Akbar, himself, is said to have journeyed to Amritsar, where he read passages of the *Adi Granth*, but was so impressed that he showed his approval with gifts and remission of taxes. So Sikhism flourished throughout the reign of the Emperor Akbar. Its strength was centred in the Punjab. Cole and Sambhi note:

> In 1605 Sikh fortunes were at their height. The 42-year-old Guru enjoyed the Emperor's confidence. The Panth was increasing and within it he was an important temporal as well as spiritual figure using the title Sacha Padshah, a Persian form used by the Mughal and meaning True Emperor. Sikhs were found to be in Central and Western Asia trading especially in horses . . . Under Guru Arjan a theocracy seemed to be emerging.[15]

In 1595 Guru Arjan's son was born, whom he named Hargobind, and a successor was thus ensured. When Akbar died, however, the succession of Jehangir to the Mughal throne brought a great change. Under instigation from opponents of the Guru he arrested Arjan. Sikhs see Arjan as the first Guru martyr, though there is considerable doubt as to how he died.[16] Some suggest that he was executed in the River Ravi, and later his son, Guru Hargobind, commemorated this by building a *gurdwara* in Lahore, the place of his father's entry into the river.

Guru Hargobind (1606–1644)   Before his death, Arjan elected his son, Hargobind, as his successor. Since the new Guru was only eleven years old, he was advised by Bhai Gurdas during his youth. He became reconciled to the Emperor through mutual friends such as the Sufi Mian Mir. Hargobind was much like an emperor himself, and claimed spiritual and temporal power. He sat on a throne which he named the *Akal Takht* (Immortal Throne) and as Madanjit Kaur says:

> Subsequently, Akal Takht became the highest seat of spiritual and secular power of the Sikhs. It was from this place that the affairs of the Sikh community began to be administered.[17]

His spiritual and temporal powers were symbolized in the two swords he wore in his belt. "My rosary shall be the sword belt", he is claimed to have said. He believed it necessary to develop the militant group of the Sikh Panth, which would be capable of its own defence. This militarizing principle is referred to in the Sikh tradition as *piri* and *miri* "the two-sword theory":

> He declared that one sword represented "Piri" (spirituality or Bhakti) and the other represented "Miri" (Temporality or Shakti). He told his followers that in the Guru's house spiritual and temporal powers would be combined.[18]

Pir is an Islamic term of Persian origin for a religious guide, a guru.

Miri is also an Islamic term, connected with the idea of a commander of the faithful *(Amir)*. This came to represent the militant resistance of evil and the defence of the faith. To build up his military strength Hargobind accepted gifts of arms and horses. He hunted, held a court, sat on a throne and had an armed retinue. However, although he wrote no hymns, he seems to have been faithful to Sikh religious observances. He was arrested and imprisoned for a year by the Emperor Jehangir, but amazingly survived the Emperor's reign. In the reign of Shah Jehan which followed, Sikhs and Mughals were at war, and Hargobind lived like a Sikh Robin Hood, carrying out ambushes and skirmishes against the enemy.

It would be too simplistic to view the guruship of Hargobind as unnecessarily militaristic. His father, Guru Arjan, had died in the custody of the Mughal authorities and was the first Sikh martyr. This incident suggests that the Mughal saw Arjan as a powerful religious leader and that they were anxious to put an end to the new religion. It is in the light of this background that we must view the military nature of the guruship of Hargobind: without this military nature, Sikhism could not have survived. As McLeod comments:

> Nothing basic had, however, changed. The religious teachings of Nanak were retained intact, the only difference being that those who practised them would now be prepared to defend by military means their right to do so.[19]

This military aspect of the Sikh *Panth* was also brought about by the increasing influence of the *Jats*. Originally, the *Jats* were rural and agrarian peasants and landlords. It is possible that while their economic status improved, the social stigma attached to them by virtue of their pastoral origins remained. They were attracted to the Sikh religion, which they believed could theoretically and often practically remove that stigma. The *Jats* were energetic, straightforward, military, sturdy, and they could insist on the right of vengeance. When they joined the Sikh *Panth* they would have done so already bearing arms, and thus we should possibly not see the military nature of Hargobind's guruship as his own innovation.

> The growth of militancy within the Panth must be traced primarily to the impact of Jat cultural patterns and to economic problems which prompted a militant response.[20]

We should note, however, the comment of Dr Trilochan Singh against McLeod's view:

> All the military commanders in the armies of the Guru Hargobind and Guru Gobind Singh, except two or three were non-jats. All those who

distinguished themselves in the battles and whose names have come
down to us in history were mostly non-jats.[21]

The military tendency may also have evolved through another influence, *Saktism*. Guru Hargobind, in the face of Mughal threats, moved to the low range of mountains which separates the Punjabi plains from the Himalayas. This low range was called the Sivalik Hills, and appropriately so, for the culture here was heavily influenced by *Sakti* Hinduism. It is in *Saktism* that we find worship of the Mother Goddess and tales of her mighty exploits. Hargobind and his four successors were to live most of their lives in these surroundings, and McLeod considers that by the time of Gobind Singh, God was, "personified by steel and worshipped in the form of the sword".[22] Guru Gobind Singh called God *sarab-loh*, the "All-Steel" and we find the two-edged sword featuring later in the ceremony of *amrit pahul*. McLeod, in particular, accepts *Jat* influence as the source of the military tradition of the Sikhs. However, we should note, with Cole and Sambhi, that Sikh tradition teaches otherwise:

> Sikh tradition would emphasise the initiative of the Gurus in converting many Jats, and leading them in the fight against Mughal tyranny.[23]

Sikh tradition suggests that Guru Arjan's last command to his son was, "let him sit fully armed on his throne and maintain an army to the best of his ability". Perhaps it was in accordance with this command that Guru Hargobind's reign had a military resistance to tyranny and oppression. Then, too, Amar Das and Arjan had involved themselves in political and social considerations when necessary. We have seen that Arjan intervened for the remission of taxes when necessary. We have also seen that Guru Arjan in some ways had the trappings of an emperor, and was called Sacha Padsha. Guru Angad had been keen on physical fitness and after morning service it seems each community centre engaged in competitive skills, wrestling and drill – the precursor perhaps of training soldier-disciples.[24] Perhaps, then, the character of Hargobind's reign was already becoming evident in those of his predecessors. Bhai Gurdas, Guru Hargobind's contemporary, however was critical:

> Formerly the Gurus used to sit in the dharmsala,
> The present Guru does not stay in any one place.
> Emperors called at the residence of former Gurus,
> The present Guru was imprisoned by an Emperor
> Formerly the disciples could not find room in the
>   ever-crowded congregation,
> The present Guru leads a roving life fearing no one.
> Former Gurus gave consolation sitting on a manji,
> The present Guru keeps dogs and hunts.

The former Gurus would compose hymns, listen to them
  and would sing.
The present Guru does not compose, listen or sing.
His companions are not Sikhs, He has wicked and
bad people as his guides.[25]

However, later in the same *var*, Bhai Gurdas writes:

Yet truth cannot be concealed,
The Sikhs are enamoured of his lotus feet like bees.
He supports an intolerable burden
But he does not complain of it.

The determination of the Mughals to eradicate Sikhsim brought enormous pressure to bear on Guru Hargobind, but clearly he was equal to the occasion. In later years, when Jehangir's rule was followed by Shah Jehan's, Guru Hargobind fought for the religious freedom of Sikhs and Hindus from his refuge at Kiratpur in the Sivalik Hills. Some of the customs we associate with Sikhism today originated with Guru Hargobind. He devised a pennant for his troops, the *nishan sahib*, the present-day Sikh flag; he said that there should be a kettledrum in each *gurdwara*. Indeed, the very name, *gurdwara*, is associated with Guru Hargobind.

Guru Har Rai (1644–1661)   None of Hargobind's sons was suitable to become a Guru, Ram Rai probably becoming his father's enemy. Another son, Tegh Bahadur *later* became the ninth Guru, but it was the fourteen-year-old grandson of Hargobind who was selected. Har Rai was a very gentle, peaceful man who held the guruship at a difficult time. Guru Har Rai was compelled to leave Kiratpur and live in a remote village in the hills. He hunted animals, but kept them in his garden, and he grew herbs for medicine. Despite this outward gentleness he was not afraid to be firm when it was necessary. When Shah Jehan was about to die, war broke out between his two sons and Guru Har Rai, with two thousand men, supported one of these sons. Unfortunately, it was the other son, Aurangzeb, who became Emperor. Sikh hopes for some stability and peace were not realized.

Guru Har Krishen (1661–1664)   Before his death, Har Rai nominated his younger son to succeed him. This new Guru was only five years old and died three years later of smallpox in Delhi. Before he died he is reported as saying that the next Guru would be found in Bakala. Since this was the village of his uncle Tegh Bahadur, he became the next Guru. The guruship was obviously now firmly settled in the Sodhi family.

Guru Tegh Bahadur (1664–1675)   Tegh Bahadur was reluctant to accept the position, wanting neither power nor leadership. He contributed 115 poems to the *Adi Granth*. One of these reads:

> He who is unaffected by praise or blame or honour or ignominy, with
> whom gold and iron are alike;
> Sayeth Nanak, listen O Mind, he is liberated.
> He who is not moved by joy or sorrow, and to whom friend and foe
> are alike;
> Sayeth Nanak, listen O Mind, he is liberated.
> He who inspireth no fear and who hath no fear of others;
> Listen O Mind, sayeth Nanak, he is possessed of divine knowledge.[26]

The Emperor Aurangzeb favoured Ram Rai as Guru of the Sikhs, and
some supported this against the new Guru. Tegh Bahadur was a soldier
who had been courageous in battles against the Mughals but was not
the man who could unite men against the Emperor. He preferred the
name Degh Bahadur for himself, "brave cooking pot", rather than
Tegh Bahadur, "brave sword"! He preferred to be known as a Guru
who fed the hungry. Not having the support of the Emperor, he could
not live in peace. Opposition was strong against him; even the doors
of the *Harmandir* were slammed in his face and he was almost assassinated by his nephew.

Eventually, he left the Punjab and went to Patna where his son
Gobind Rai was born. He visited Sikh communities in Bengal, and in
his absence his patience and humility were seen in their true light.
When Aurangzeb began to persecute the Sikhs, messengers were sent
to Tegh Bahadur to come to the assistance of his people. Aurangzeb
had been discouraging Hinduism and Sikhism and promoting Islam
by destroying temples and taxing pilgrims. The Guru encouraged
Hindus and Sikhs to resist such practices, defending to the death the
principle of religious liberty for all. In making the supreme sacrifice,
he fought as much for Hindu freedom as for Sikh, sacrificing his life
for the beliefs of a religion to which he did not subscribe. As his son,
Guru Gobind Singh, later wrote of him, he:

> performed a heroic deed and made the supreme sacrifice in the dark age
> for the protection of their (i.e. the Hindus') right to wear the sacred
> thread and the frontal caste-mark.[27]

He was arrested in 1675 on the charge of being a stumbling block to
the spread of Islam in India, and beheaded in broad daylight, in the
middle of a public square in Delhi.

Guru Gobind Singh (1675–1708)   Gobind Rai became Guru at the
age of eleven. During his guruship, he came to the conclusion that
when all other means had failed, it would be righteous to use the
sword.[28] According to tradition, in 1699, he summoned the Sikhs to
an assembly on *Baisakhi* at Anandpur, and exhorted them to strength

and loyalty. He asked the people for a volunteer who would be beheaded. Eventually a *Ksatriya* came forward and disappeared into Gobind's tent. Gobind emerged alone with a blood-stained sword. This was repeated four times, and a *Jat* and three members of the servant class offered their lives. The astonished crowd again waited for the Guru to emerge from the tent but when he did it was with the five men – alive! He emphasized that just as these men had been fearless and ready to give up their lives, so should all Sikhs be. Sikhs everywhere should join the brotherhood of saint-soldiers. The brave five men are known amongst Sikhs as the *Panj Pyare* "the Beloved Five". They were asked to drink *amrit* "nectar" made of water and sugar crystals, mixed with a two-edged sword in an iron bowl. The Guru himself participated in this ritual, followed by all the assembled Sikhs, even those of low castes, and untouchables.

Male members of this new Sikh brotherhood, the *Khalsa*, took the name *Singh* (lion) as did Gobind Rai, and female members *Kaur* (princess). The giving of a special name was important. Since the caste of an Indian was revealed by his or her name, Sikhs were now not known as members of a caste, unequal to another because of their birth, but as members of the brotherhood of Sikhs in which all were equal. Women, too, had a name not determined by caste parentage or marriage.

The *amrit* ceremony became the initiation rite through which Sikhs express allegiance to the *Panth* (community). This initiation rite provides entry into the *Khalsa* "Pure Ones" and expresses loyalty to the Guru and to Sikh teachings. Gobind Singh, in establishing the *Khalsa*, had fused together the religious and military aspects of Sikhism. Guru Gobind Singh then gave the people a code of discipline, dissuading them from drinking alcohol and strictly fobidding the smoking of tobacco. Nor were Sikhs allowed to eat meat slaughtered according to Muslim ritual, in which animals have their throats cut, or to engage in sexual misconduct with Muslim women. Gobind Singh also instituted the *external* symbols of the *Khalsa*, the distinguishing features of Sikhism today, known as the "Five Ks", which will be examined below.

McLeod considers that tradition has telescoped what was really a more evolutionary code of discipline. He cites the evidence of the *rahat-namas* (Codes of Discipline) of the eighteenth century which suggest that such aspects as the "Five Ks" were not entirely settled until the eighteenth century.[29] Cole and Sambhi seem to support this view; they note: "The two major religious acts of the Guru's reign have also been telescoped by tradition,"[30] and follow this statement with an account of the *Baisakhi* events of 1699 and the institution of the "Five Ks" and other rules. Other historical/political events have also been telescoped, but concerning the Guru's religious acts, "This should not be allowed to diminish their importance within the community".[31]

McLeod further states that the ban on *halal* meat and intercourse with Muslim women also suit an eighteenth-century climate rather than a 1699 setting. McLeod believes that the features of Sikhism that we associate with this *Baisakhi* event were recorded as the Guru's instructions in the *rahat-namas* and were only *then* instituted – that is, in the eighteenth century.

McLeod's setting aside of the Sikh traditions, including his attribution of the militant development of Sikhism to seventeenth-century pressures exerted by the *Jat* agrarian caste, rather than any conscious influence of the Gurus, has been severely criticized by the Sikhs themselves, so much so, that a book edited by Mr Justice Gurdev Singh, *Perspective on the Sikh Traditions*, has been devoted to refuting McLeod's arguments. In Dr Trilochan Singh's review of this book, he states: "Dr McLeod seems to be hell bent on not only wiping clean the slate of historical traditions, but he is hell bent on breaking the slate so that it cannot be reinscribed".[32] This reveals not only how contentious the issue is but, more importantly, the sensitivity with which Sikhs view their traditions.

Be this as it may, it is important to recognize that in Guru Gobind Singh we see the fulfilment of the teachings and beliefs of the previous Gurus. In the tenth and last Sikh Guru we witness not a change in the direction of Sikhism, but its crystallization:

> In Guru Gobind Singh's teaching is found Guru Nanak's fervent belief in the One God who, though beyond human comprehension, can be experienced through love and practice of Nam – the Name . . . . Angad's exhortation to seva – the service of mankind . . . Amar Das's emphasis on mental and physical health . . . Ram Das's creative ability . . . Arjan's gentleness, his love of the Hindu and the Mussalman, his literary genius and his spirit of martyrdom . . . Hargobind's spirit of valour. And in Guru Gobind Singh's writings there is his father Guru Tegh Bahadur . . . Guru Gobind Singh had all that his predecessor Gurus had and something more – the power to change mice into men, to mould those men into a nation and then fire that nation with an ideal, the ideal of the Khalsa Commonwealth.[33]

Above all, Guru Gobind Singh will be remembered for an act he undertook just before his death on 7th October 1708. He declared that he would be the last of the human Gurus, and that the *Granth Sahib* would now become the True Guru, which is why it is now known as the *Guru Granth Sahib*. He also identified the *sangat* with God, the *Sat Guru*, declaring: "There is no difference between the Guru and the sangat. The sangat and the True Guru are one and the same."[34]

The Five Ks   Gobind Singh was responsible for the military character of Sikhism which ensured its survival. Sikhs of the Punjab have always had to struggle to maintain their religion and identity. He instituted

SIKH
SYMBOLS

certain distinguishing signs of Sikhism. These are the so-called Five Ks, each sign being the name of an object beginning with a letter "K". These Five Ks are:

Kesh   This is the long, uncut hair and beard of the Sikh. It distinguishes the Sikh from all other Indians. Tying the hair up is not too much of a problem, but long thick beards are often more problematic to secure out of the way, and so a kind of glue is sometimes used to tie the beard in place. The long hair is considered to be a symbol of devotion to God. In India, holy men often grew their hair long as a sign that they had no worldly cares. Similarly, Sikhs show their humility and faithfulness to God by this sign.

Kanga   Unlike Indian holy men whose long hair was uncombed, the Sikh was instructed by Gobind Singh to use a *kanga* (comb) to keep his or her long hair in place. This emphasized cleanliness, purity and discipline, particularly self-discipline. Children sometimes cover the *jura*, which is the knot formed on top of the head, with a small scarf called a *rumal*. The *kanga* is usually made of wood or ivory, though it may be plastic.

Kachs   This is a pair of shorts which are worn as an undergarment by both men and women. Originally, Sikhs had worn *dhotis*, which were cumbersome in battle. Because Gobind Singh realized that Sikhs must fight to survive and fight for the freedom of their religion, he introduced the *kachs* as one of the Five Ks. They gave greater freedom of movement in battle and athletic activities, and in the Punjab were worn as an outer garment. They symbolize readiness for action on the practical level but also spiritual freedom and high moral character and goodness.

Kara   The *kara* is a steel bracelet, usually worn on the right wrist. The circle, in Indian thought, has always been an important symbol, and in Sikhism it symbolizes unity. Originally it may have been worn as a protection from the bow-string but now it reminds Sikhs of the oneness of God, and eternity, as well as the unity of Sikhs everywhere. *Kara* means "link" or "bondage", and since it is made of steel this symbolizes strength and endurance under stress. These are qualities it is felt that all Sikhs must have.

Kirpan   This is a short sword (not a dagger) which symbolizes the duty of the Sikh to defend the weak and fight for righteousness. Some *kangas* contain a piece of metal inlaid into the top, which represents the *kirpan*. This piece of metal would be sword-shaped, maintaining the tradition, but other Sikhs may wear a miniature sword. In the Punjab, the *kirpan* may take the form of a sabre, but a full-size *kirpan* is usually 15–20 centimetres long. British law permits the carrying of such weapons, but in Britain, many Sikhs carry only small brooch-size *kirpans*. The word *kirpan* is composed of two parts: *kirpa* "favour", "act of kindness", and *ann* "honour", "respect". The *kirpan* has become a symbol of authority, justice and freedom, as well as honour, dignity, bravery and self-sacrifice.

Problems of identity   Given the significance of the Five Ks, not to mention the wearing of the turban and the importance given to the issue of Sikh identity, the question of identifying a Sikh would appear to present few problems. However, this is far from the truth, as McLeod has shown:

> Sikh identity cannot be described with the ease or clarity which so commonly we assume. Paradoxically it is the increasingly clear definition of Sikh identity which produces an increasingly acute problem of identity.[35]

The problem of identity to which McLeod refers includes the reluctance of some employers (who may well have no racial prejudice) to offer employment to Sikhs who are *keshdari* (turbaned Sikhs who have uncut hair and beards). The problem is accentuated by second-generation Sikhs who do not wish to seem unlike their peers, and by the unsound initial advice given by earlier migrants. Other reasons were certainly racial:

> Some migrant Sikhs made the error of cutting their hair and abandoning the turban when they arrived from India, being assured by Sikhs already there that they would not find employment otherwise. In Canada the embarrassment of being called "ragheads", and even more physical attacks, led to the turban being discarded by some migrants. Mexican wives discouraged their husbands from keeping turban and beard.[36]

Other problems faced by the Sikh dispersion to North America and the United Kingdom are highlighted by Cole and Sambhi.[37]

The *khanda,* the Sikh emblem, combines three Sikh symbols:

the *khanda* – two-edged dagger representing freedom and justice
the *chakar* – circle, showing balance between the swords, and unity.

two *kirpans* – curved swords, one for religious, one for worldly matters.

The circle represents the oneness of God, one *kirpan* represents the spiritual power of the *Sat Guru*, the other the power of the *Sat Guru* as the ruler of the Sikhs. The emblem occurs on the Sikh flag (the *nishan sahib*); this flag is triangular and usually yellow/orange in colour. At the pointed end of the flag is a tassel. Often, Sikhs bow to the flag or touch the flagpoles with their foreheads on the way into the *gurdwara*.

Ek Onkar

This is the sacred word of the Sikh faith, *EK ONKAR*, meaning "God is One". It is written in Punjabi and is a symbol which may be seen outside many *gurdwaras*. It represents the opening words of the Sikh scriptures, the *Guru Granth Sahib*. A detailed exposition of the term is to be found in an article by Gopal Singh Puri, who summarizes his position succinctly: "Although scholars may have different views on the subject it seems sensible to me to stick to the concept of Mool Mantar and accept EK ONKAR as the only name of God for contemplation."[38]

SACRED BUILDINGS

The Golden Temple at Amritsar Amritsar, in north India, is the most important town of the Sikhs. The name Amritsar means "Pool of Nectar", for at Amritsar there is a sacred artificial lake which is fed by spring water. On all sides of the lake are black and white marble pavements on which there are small shrines depicting the sites where Sikh martyrs have died. Along the pavements are *banyan* trees, and leading down to the lake are steps, so that one may descend to drink the water or to put it on one's head. Along a causeway about two hundred feet long, in the middle of the lake, is the famous Golden Temple. The Sikhs call it *Sri Durbar Sahib*, meaning "Divine Court", as well as *Sri Hari Mandir* (or *Harmandir*) *Sahib*, "Temple of the Lord".[39]

The Golden Temple was built by Guru Arjan, the fifth Guru. His father, Guru Ram Das, had had the lake dug in 1577, when the site had been presented to his wife by the Emperor Akbar. The town, known as Ramdas Pur, grew up around the site and was built by Ram Das. It was his son Arjan, however, who was to build the Temple. As

I have noted,[40] the Temple differed from the usual Hindu temples. Instead of going up into the Temple, it was built so that one went down into it. This symbolized the humbling of oneself before God on entry. Hindu temples had only one entrance, whereas the Golden Temple has four, one on each side. These four entrances showed that the Temple was open to people of all castes. When the Temple was completed, the pool was filled, and the town Ramdas Pur became Amritsar. At the beginning of the nineteenth century, Maharajah Ranjit Singh had the Temple rebuilt in marble, also covered with gilded copper and inlaid with semi-precious stones. Hence it became known as the Golden Temple. Some of the verses of the *Adi Granth*, "First Collection", are inscribed on the copper surface.

At the gateway, which is silver, armed guards are posted and flags with the Sikh emblem fly above. Inside the Temple the decor is a black and white marble with birds, bees and flower representations on the walls, as well as pictures of Nanak with Hindu and Muslim disciples. In the inner sanctuary is a copy of the *Guru Granth Sahib* under a canopy, around which is a rail. Sometimes, on the occasion of festivals, the *Guru Granth Sahib* is read outside in open areas around the Temple. Each morning, the *Guru Granth Sahib* is brought out on a silver casket carried on the shoulders, and is taken along the causeway to the Temple where it is placed on a cushion under a canopy while its verses are chanted. At night it is taken back along the causeway to the treasury, where it is guarded until the following day.

Since the Temple is a sacred place, at the entrance all visitors must remove their shoes and socks and wash their feet in a tank provided for the purpose. No alcohol or tobacco are allowed to be taken inside. The Temple depicts many aspects of devotion in Sikhism: its four entrances showing the universality of Sikhism; its low entrances, humility; its blend of Muslim and Hindu architecture showing its transcendence over (or merging of) earlier religious differences. The building itself is graphically depicted by Douglas Davies as being:

> like a lotus plant growing from the murky water of life, yet producing a beautiful flower of devotion and good works, teaching man to reach above the evil of the world which would choke his higher desires.[41]

The gurdwara Gurdwara is a Punjabi word meaning "house or place of God", what we would call "temple". It is composed of two words, *guru* and *dwara* "place"; *guru* here refers to the *Sat Guru* or God. The first *gurdwara* was the Temple at Amritsar, the *Harmandir*, in which, in 1604 the fifth Guru, Arjan, placed the very first *Adi Granth*. When handwritten copies of the *Adi Granth* were sent round to other Sikh communities, the places where these were housed also became *gurdwaras*. If a building is to be a *gurdwara* it must have a copy of the *Adi Granth* and the *Adi Granth* must be housed according to all the regulations and respect which are traditionally obligatory for its instalment.

Since the *Guru Granth Sahib* contains the sacred Word of God, it is given the greatest respect and honour. Heads are covered in its presence and Sikhs would always take off their shoes. Before coming into the presence of the Book, Sikhs bathe, and to show their esteem for the Book they bow before it on arrival at the place of worship, or when reading the *Guru Granth Sahib* at home. It should be noted that Sikhs do not worship the Book. Rather, they honour it, for without it Sikh religion and the Sikh way of life could not exist. When referring to the Book it is customary to use a capital "B", again, to show respect. The *Guru Granth Sahib* is always handled with great care. When it is carried into a room, it is done so on the head. Out of deference for the Book no Sikh may touch it with unwashed hands.

Because the *Guru Granth Sahib* is so respected, no Sikh would own a personal copy unless he or she could be certain that the necessary requirements for housing it could be provided. According to tradition, it must have a room to itself which must not be one over which someone could walk, though of late, some Sikh families afford the Book a corner of a room. It would need to be read before dawn each morning after bathing and again at night, and its teachings meditated on. If a copy is brought into a home, the room in which it is placed becomes a *gurdwara*.

The *Guru Granth Sahib* is always the focal point of a *gurdwara* with all the attendant symbols of royalty – the throne and a canopy over it, the brightly coloured cloths, the *chauri* waved over it, the head-covered congregation who bow before it, the offering of food or money given to it – all suggest how privileged the Sikh is to have the treasure of the original words of the Gurus and the Word of God. Nothing has been altered in the *Adi Granth* since the time it was compiled.

Not all *gurdwaras* have been purpose built. In countries outside India, such as Britain, and North America, a suitable building may be converted into a *gurdwara*. Although the building may be of any size or shape it will always have one distinguishing feature, and this will be the Sikh flag flying from the roof or nearby flagpole. The flag, the *nishan sahib*, rises above the surrounding buildings to identify this particular building as a *gurdwara* belonging to the Sikh community. In April, at the Sikh New Year Festival of *Baisakhi*, a new flag replaces the old one. On the yellowish-orange flag is the black *khanda*, the emblem of Sikhism. Sometimes outside *gurdwaras* the *ek-onkar* symbol is found.

Although *gurdwaras* vary in size, there are usually many rooms. The largest room is usually the one used for worship and the kitchen will probably be the next largest. There may also be offices, a library, store-rooms, a room where the *granthi* lives, rest rooms where guests may stay, cloakroom, bathrooms and rooms in which children are taught Punjabi and learn about Sikhism.

The prayer room In any *gurdwara* the prayer room is the most important. It is the room which houses the *Guru Granth Sahib* and, therefore, the one in which worship is conducted. In *gurdwaras* in the West the carpeted floor is normally covered with white sheets, and down the centre is a narrow carpet leading to the *Adi Granth*. There are no seats, and men sit, usually cross-legged, on the floor on the one side and women on the other. Children tend to stay with their mothers. This reflects custom rather than inequality.

The most important part of the prayer room is the raised platform or *takht*. It is on this platform that the *Guru Granth Sahib* is placed and behind it sits the reader. The *Guru Granth Sahib* is put on a kind of small bed called a *manji sahib*, which is covered with a soft quilt and then two white cloths. Three small cushions are then placed on top and these help to support the large Book. A cloth covers the whole platform on which the *manji sahib* stands and other cloths, the *rumalas*, cover the *Guru Granth Sahib* in order to protect it from dust and dirt and as a token of respect. When the Book is being read, the reader, an attendant, or the next person, man or woman, to read, will wave a *chaur* (or *chauri*) over the *Guru Granth Sahib*. The *chaur* is made of yak or other hair held by a wooden (or other) handle. The focal point of the prayer room is thus the enthroned *Guru Granth Sahib*. The idea of a throne is further enhanced by the canopy, called a *palki*, which is a large, square piece of cloth with a frill or fringe at the sides. All the cloths used usually have these attractive trimmings at the edges. With the raised platform, and the congregation seated on the floor, we may note again the symbolic royalty of the *Guru Granth Sahib* and, at the same time, the equality of all who sit on the floor in its presence.

The *granthi* and *giani* The religious affairs of the *gurdwara* are looked after by a *granthi*. The *granthi* takes care of the *Guru Granth Sahib* and is also responsible for reciting from it and for leading the daily prayers. Occasionally, the *granthi* may also be a caretaker, though this aspect of *gurdwara* care may be undertaken by a separate person. A *giani* is not found in every *gurdwara* community, but when he or she is, they are regarded highly and given great respect. A *giani* is a scholar and is thoroughly conversant with the language and literature of the Punjab. Since the Sikh scriptures are written in poetic form they may be difficult to understand in parts, and the *giani* explains them.

One of the important functions of the *granthi* is to put the *Guru Granth Sahib* to rest. Before doing this, the *granthi* says the night prayer called the *Kirtan Sohilla*. Then the *rumala* and the two side

cloths of the *Guru Granth Sahib* are removed, the Book is closed and
wrapped in the two white cloths. It is then carried on the *granthi's*
head to the special room in which it is placed at night. It rests on a
manji sahib under a *rumala* until it is brought out again in the
morning, or when the community meets again.

Other functions of the *gurdwara* *Gurdwaras* have many functions.
Apart from the religious aspects of *gurdwara* community life there are
many social aspects. Some may have a senior citizens' club, where
elderly Sikhs can go during the day time to meet. They may learn
English or help with some of the chores at the *gurdwara*. Language
classes are nearly always a feature of *gurdwara* life. In Britain, English
is taught alongside Punjabi. This is important for many women, whose
opportunities to speak English may be limited. Women's groups may
also be a feature of the *gurdwara*, and in these groups all sorts of activities may be undertaken. Some *gurdwaras* would also have a youth
centre which would be open to non-Sikhs as well as Sikhs. Indoor
sports such as billiards, table tennis and badminton are popular, while
Sikhs excel at hockey and enjoy football. *Gurdwaras* usually have a
library which is open to non-Sikhs as well as Sikhs. In India the *gurdwara* was always a place where the traveller could find temporary
accommodation. This is known as *visran* and is a feature of all *gurdwaras* today. In India, weddings and funerals can be held in the open
air. Since this is not always possible in the climate of non-Indian countries, the *gurdwara* has become the place where these ceremonies are
now held. The traditional naming of a baby also takes place in the
gurdwara.

**SIKH
WORSHIP:
*DIWAN***

The *sangat* Guru Nanak is acclaimed to have said:

"My refuge is the Sat Guru, the *sangat* and *bani*".

The *Sat Guru* is God, the *sangat* is the Sikh community or congregation, and the *bani* is the "Word" or teaching which Nanak received
from God. The three are united in Sikh worship. The earliest forms of
Sikh worship were concentrated on the *sangat*, the first community
being set up by Nanak at Kartarpur. People came to join Nanak in
meditation, work and the singing of hymns when the day's work was
over. During this evening period, Nanak taught the Sikhs about the
nature of God. This congregational nature of worship is still a feature
of Sikhism today, and is unlike Hinduism and more in line with Islam
in this respect. Wherever the *sangat* gathers together for worship, the
Guru Granth Sahib is opened and read.

   In Sikhism, worship in a congregational sense is not confined to
particular days or times. Just as in the early days of Sikhism, people
visited Nanak at the beginning or end of the day and worship took

place at these meetings, so modern-day Sikhs visit the *gurdwara* any day, at any time for worship. There is no particular holy day, but Sunday tends to be popular in the West since, for many, it is not a working day. Worship, also, does not begin at any particular time, Sikhs come and go as they wish. The *Guru Granth Sahib* is brought from its special room to the prayer hall and placed on the *manji* from which its hymns are chanted. People will continually enter and leave as they wish, while the proceedings are going on.

The approach and procedure for *diwan* Corporate Sikh worship is known as *diwan*, a word formerly used to denote an audience with a Mughal emperor. Before entering a *gurdwara* it is important to bathe. (In fact, the Sikh begins each day in such a way, an act which also precedes every ritual.) Shoes are always removed because it would be disrespectful to bring dirt and dust into the cleanliness of the *gurdwara*, and into the presence of the *Guru Granth Sahib*. When entering the prayer room each person kneels and bows before the Book until the forehead touches the floor. A gift of vegetarian food for the kitchen, or money, is usually offered, and is placed on the platform. As it is disrespectful to turn one's back on the *Guru Granth Sahib*, it is customary to back away and sit cross-legged on either side of the long carpet leading to the Book – men on one side, women on the other.

Order of the *diwan* The opening of the *Guru Granth Sahib* commences the service. The congregation remains seated while the *granthi* removes the cloths covering the Book, and opens it at random. Many a visitor to a *gurdwara* has been puzzled as to why the service takes so long to begin, not realizing that it has already started! As important as the reading of the *Guru Granth Sahib* is, this takes very much a second place to the singing of the scriptures in that essential part of the service known as *Kirtan*:

> Guru Arjan says that the reading of the scriptures is like water from the well. The well can irrigate the nearby fields only. Listening to discourses on them (the Gurbani) is like the drizzling clouds. They irrigate the levelled and prepared ground only. Kirtan is a shower of rain which irrigates all the high, low, levelled, unlevelled and distant ground. Those who seed their fields at the right time and manure them properly shall reap a rich crop.[42]

Kirtan This is the main part of the service and consists of singing the hymns *(sabads)* from the *Guru Granth Sahib*, accompanied by musicians *(ragis)*. The importance of *Kirtan* cannot be overestimated, as J. Singh Sarna has shown:

> The significance of Kirtan can be gauged fom the fact that the entire Adi
> Granth is set to music and is structured on the basis of Indian classical
> ragas in which the portions are supposed to be sung . . . Guru Arjan Sahib
> the compiler of Guru Granth Sahib, arranged the sacred hymns on the
> basis of ragas and not on the basis of authorship or chronology.[43]

Devotional music has long been of paramount importance to Sikhism,
since the days of Guru Nanak. Nanak himself would sing while accompanied on a stringed instrument by his Muslim companion, Mardana.
At an early age, children learn to play the *tabla* (drums), the harmonium (*baja*) and the *sitar*. The musicians sit at the side of the canopy
and this part of the service lasts a few hours. During some parts, the
ragis sing alone, and in others the congregation joins in. Occasionally,
during *kirtan*, hymns are sung without any accompaniment. *Kirtan*
means far more to the Sikh than simply the singing of hymns in God's
praise, for it has a very strong mystical element, being the Word and
essence of God in the world, and the means to develop the spirituality
of both the individual and the *sangat*:

> Through the ears, kirtan enters the body. It reaches the innermost cells
> and illuminates the unconscious self. The devotees, too, start singing
> along with the singers, thus they enter a state of trance, ecstacy and inner
> bliss . . . Kirtan is the food of thought, heart and soul. Meditation on
> God's Holy Name is the part and parcel of congregational prayers. Those
> prayers, too, are sung in devotional music.[44]

Following the singing of the *sabads* there is a set pattern to the
worship which is called the *Anand*. Particular hymns will be sung such
as Amar Das' Hymn of Bliss, Guru Arjan's Hymn of Peace, called the
Sukhmani and, most important is the reciting of the *Mool Mantar* and
part of the *Japji* (sometimes led by the children of the congregation).
There will be a short sermon and announcements, and it is during the
Anand that the *karah parshad* is distributed to the congregation.
During the service the *karah parshad* is kept in a large metal bowl
covered with a cloth, and at the appropriate time in the service, it is
touched with a two-edged short sword, divided into smaller bowls,
and a little is then given to each person present. Again, sharing *parshad*
symbolizes equality, brotherhood and unity. It also welcomes the non-
Sikh in equality and brotherhood before God. The food is considered
to be sacred. It consists of flour, water, sugar and ghee (melted purified butter). To taste, it has a pudding-like consistency, is sweet, sticky
and warm. Only a small amount is given to each person and it is taken
with the two hands cupped together and is eaten immediately after
raising the hands in gratitude to God. Since it is sacred food, it is
prepared with scrupulous cleanliness: even shoes must be removed
outside the kitchen. While being prepared, hymns from the *Guru*

Granth Sahib are recited. When it is carried to the prayer hall, water is sprinkled over and before it to symbolize cleanliness, and it is placed on a table near the *Guru Granth Sahib*. Since it is sacred and a symbol of the common brotherhood of every human being, it should never be wasted.

The whole congregation, including the *granthi* faces the *Adi Granth* for the special Sikh congregational prayer called *Ardas*, which is best translated "To ask for what you desire".[45] It recalls the suffering of the Sikhs in the early years of Sikhism. *Ardas* is chanted by the *granthi*, the congregation joining in with the response *Waheguru* "Wonderful Lord". *Ardas* ends with the words *Waheguru ji ka khalsa*, to which the congregation responds *Waheguru ji ki fateh*. These words mean "The *Khalsa* is of God, the victory is to God". Following this an untranslatable war cry is called in a loud voice, *Jo bole so nihal!* to which the congregation shouts, *Sat sri akal!* "Truth is eternal!" At the end of the *Anand*, the *Guru Granth Sahib* is wrapped carefully in *rumalas* and is carried on the head to its place of rest, while the congregation sings

Sat Nam, Sat Nam, Sat Nam ji
Waheguru, Waheguru, Waheguru ji

When the Book is laid down, the call *Jo bole so nihal!* is repeated and the congregation replies with *Sat sri akal!*, touches foreheads to the floor, and *Ardas* is over.

Langar, the communal Indian vegetarian meal, completes the *gurdwara* service, and visitors are invited, indeed expected, to eat with their hosts. To decline this hospitality would be disrespectful. In some *gurdwaras* there will be separate dining rooms, but in many the white sheets covering the floor will be removed and rush mats will be put down on which food can be placed. People sit in long rows cross-legged for the meal which follows, but still the sexes do not mix.

At festival times, the Sikhs in India prepared food for everyone in the village, so outside India on special occasions passers by outside a *gurdwara* may be offered fruit. *Langar* is associated with equality and brotherhood in practical ways also in that both men and women cook, serve and clean up after the *langar*. Before eating *langar*, one takes off one's shoes before sitting down to eat in the dining hall. Sometimes a person will pay for the *langar*, providing food for many: this is regarded as a great act of charity as, also, cooking or serving *langar*. It is thus an opportunity to serve others. One may eat as much as one wishes, but, since the food is blessed before it is served, one should eat all that one takes. Other rules are also evident: food is always vegetarian; no beggars are allowed to partake of *langar*; no smoking or alcohol are allowed. Since large numbers of people eat daily at the *gurdwara*, a large and well equipped kitchen is essential. Food is prepared with meticulous attention to hygiene, and since catering for large numbers is essential, the kitchen is well stocked with very large utensils. *Langar* is prepared daily in prominent *gurdwaras,* though in the West some are open only a few times in the week.

Gurmukhi   When Sikh children visit their place of worship, the *gurd-wara,* they are taught to read and write the special script of the Punjabi language, called the *Gurmukhi.* Although the children may not speak Punjabi at home (a source of concern to many Sikh families), at the *gurdwara* they learn about the Sikh religion in (spoken) Punjabi, and (written) *Gurmukhi.* The *Gurmukhi* script is precisely that. It is *not* a language, nor is it the sole preserve of one language. It is, rather, the means of committing the spoken word to writing. The script is read from left to right and, like biblical Hebrew, always hangs from the line like washing, rather than resting on it.

Before the time of Guru Nanak, there was no written form of Punjabi. It is possible that Nanak used neighbouring scripts to compile a new written vocabulary and language, for his hymns were the first to be written in *Gurmukhi.* It has many similarities to the Sanskrit alphabet and is arranged in groups of letters classified according to their sounds, as in Sanskrit. Indeed, the shapes of some of the letters are identical or very similar. However, it is also possible that Guru Angad, the second Guru, introduced the language, much of which he gathered from the world of trade and economy, which was one sphere of life in which language in written form was essential. The *Gurmukhi* alphabet has thirty-five characters and these letters thus came "from the mouth of the Guru", which is the meaning of *Gurmukhi.* Services in Sikh places of worship are always read in this script, but although the *Gurmukhi* is so closely associated with the Sikh religion, its spoken form, Punjabi, is used by Hindus and Muslims in the Punjab area. Thus, the *Gurmukhi* refers to the written *script* and Punjabi refers to the spoken language, the language of the Punjab.

The *Guru Granth Sahib*   The Sikh scriptures are the focal point of Sikh worship; all aspects of Sikh life and worship focus on them. As we have seen, Guru Gobind Singh, the last of the Gurus, did not appoint anyone to succeed him. Instead, he stated that the Sikh scriptures should be the next, indeed the last, Guru. For this reason Sikhs called the *Adi Granth, Guru Granth Sahib – sahib* being a title of respect such as "sir" or "lord", normally given to a person.

It was Guru Nanak who compiled the first contributions to the Sikh scriptures: 974 of his hymns are included in the *Adi Granth.* At first, their transmission would have been oral, but later they were written down, possibly in Nanak's lifetime. It was the labour of the fifth Guru, Arjan, which produced an authoritative collection of the hymns of his predecessors which was housed in the *Harmandir* at Amritsar. On the last page of the book, Guru Arjan wrote:

In this platter are placed three things, truth, contentment and meditation. The nectar-bestowing name of the Lord, the support of all, has been put therein. If someone eats and relishes this food he is liberated (from rebirth). This should not be forsaken so keep it always enshrined in your mind.[46]

Arrangement   Guru Arjan arranged the hymns so that they formed a sequence in order of the Gurus. He also added the poems of men such as Kabir, Sheikh Farid, Namdev, Ravidas and others. These men were not all Sikhs, and the *Adi Granth* is one of the few sacred books which contains the writings of people from other faiths. Arjan arranged the work into thirty-one sections and assigned a different "tune" to each. Since Arjan wrote more hymns than any other Guru, his are to be found in nearly every section.

Printing   Because the *Adi Granth* is so sacred, for many years it was handwritten. This meant that copies were very expensive, and villages could not afford one, apart from the fact that they took so long to copy. Since, also, the *Adi Granth* was treated with great respect and reverence, it was felt that if it were too readily available it may be treated irreverently, but finally, towards the end of the nineteenth century, it was agreed that copies could be printed. Every copy is exactly the same length (1430 pages) so that each page is identical. Nowadays, translations in a variety of languages are available, though these cannot of course be of uniform length.

Use in Worship   Every aspect of Sikh life is determined by the *Guru Granth Sahib,* because its words contain divine revelation, which therefore should be at the centre of humankind's existence. Apart from being the focus of worship, Sikhs are so much a "People of the Book" that their life-cycle rites are governed by it. Birth, initiation, marriage and death are all ceremonies in which the *Guru Granth Sahib* is the focal point. When important decisions have to be made, the *Guru Granth Sahib* is opened at random and advice is accepted from this random reading. When moving house, the new premises are often blessed by an *akhand path*, which is a continuous reading of the Book from beginning to end for about forty-eight hours. This continuous reading may also take place when a person opens new business premises, as well as at the anniversaries of the births and deaths of the Gurus. Sometimes, if a family is suffering bereavement, they may arrange for the *Guru Granth Sahib* to be read in its entirety during the evenings, when the whole family gather together to listen. These readings are not continuous and therefore take about two weeks.

The *Dasam Granth*   Not as important as the *Adi Granth* is the *Dasam Granth,* "tenth collection," which was the work of Guru

Gobind Singh, the last of the Gurus. This collection of poems is 1428 pages long and was collated in 1734, nearly thirty years after the death of the Guru. Guru Gobind Singh did not allow any of his poems to be included in the *Adi Granth*, and although he wrote in the *Gurmukhi* script, the language varies from Persian to Sanskrit as well as Punjabi. This makes it difficult for Sikhs to read, so many Sikhs and even some *gurdwaras* do not own copies of the *Dasam Granth*. Thus, it is not given the same respect and honour as the *Adi Granth*. However, the poems have great quality and beauty.

The *Janam Sakhis*   Many stories about Guru Nanak's life have been written. These have been gathered together to form the collection called the *Janam Sakhis*, which were noted at the outset of this chapter. They recall all sorts of incidents from the life of Nanak, some of which recount miracles, and and legends associated with the Guru. Compiled between the seventeenth and nineteenth centuries, the *Janam Sakhis* are the traditional biographies of Guru Nanak.[47]

The *Gurbani*   The *script* of the *Guru Granth Sahib* is called the *Gurmukhi*; the *Word* of the Book is called the *Gurbani*, the "Word of God". Stated this simply, *Gurbani* translation would seem a straight-forward task indeed, but, as Harchand Singh points out, it is far from simple:

> Translation from one language to another is not an easy task. And when one has to deal with the material involving subtle spiritual verities the task of the translator becomes all the more difficult.[48]

It must be recognized that *Gurbani* features the Divine Name as a dynamic *continual revelation*, hence it *must* by its very nature, contain contradiction. Any study of *Gurbani* which seeks to avoid or ignore this contradiction is doomed to miss the entire point of the dynamism of "the word of the Gurus", subsequently reducing *Gurbani* to a one-dimensional ethic:

> The belief that it is possible to systematise the Gurus' thought in totality without contradiction and reduction or acknowledging one's motives and presuppositions, should be held with suspicion. However, the fact that the whole can never be communicated need not render the interpretative process without value or meaning. Indeed, without such attempts to define, interpret and comprehend Gurbani, no such thing as Sikhism could exist.[49]

THE TEACHINGS OF SIKHISM

Sikhism has a distinct belief in a formless Absolute and, strictly speaking, even to use the term "God" to refer to this Absolute is incorrect, because it takes no form and is always indivisible. However, Sikhs themselves retain the word "God" to refer to this Absolute, and I have done so throughout this chapter. But it is precisely because God is formless and indescribable, and can have no concrete manifestation in the universe that the Word, the *Sabad*, of God expressed in the *Gurbani* is so important, for it is the one essential way in which the impersonal Absolute can be known in the world. The Word of God, then, is the immanence or presence of God in the world, particularly in the depths of each individual. It is what Koller calls, "the revelation of God's own being, resounding in the deepest recesses of the human heart".[50]

The *Adi Granth* begins with the *Mool Mantar*, which are the words Guru Nanak used to describe God. The *Mool Mantar* begins each section. It is the Sikh creed and epitomizes the Sikh concept of God:

IK ONKAAR	There is one and only ONE GOD
SAT NAAM	TRUTH is HIS name
KARTA PURKH	He is the CREATOR
NIR BHAU	He is without fear
NIR VAIR	He is without hate
AKAAL MOORAT	IMMORTAL
AJOONI	He is beyond births and deaths
SAIBHANG	He is self illuminated (the Enlightner)
GUR PARSAAD	He is realised by the Kindness of the TRUE GURU.[51]

Thus, the opening words of the *Adi Granth,* like the symbol *Ek-onkar,* emphasize the unity of God as the Primal and Ultimate Reality, the *Sat Guru,* whose very Name is Truth. Sikhism, therefore, is an extremely monotheistic faith believing in one True God who is Creator of all and yet, importantly, is greater than all. But though a totally transcendent Absolute, the Sikh God is felt to be personally immanent in his creation through his Word *(Sabad),* his Name *(Nam),* his Grace *(Nadar),* and his Will *(Hukam).* The *Adi Granth* makes it clear that nothing in Creation can occur without the Divine *Hukam,* and many Sikhs believe that because of this all life is predestined; but such a theory remains questionable, for the law of *karma* still obtains in Sikhism.

Sikhism stresses a highly *personal* relationship with God through an inward, non-ritualistic response to the Divine. So because God is in the heart of each of us, each man or woman must find God for him or herself; no mediator in the form of a priest is necessary. Nanak asked people to look for the Truth which is behind religion and which lies in the essence of humankind. This is a Truth that pervades the entire universe and which is open for all to experience:

As He was in the beginning, the Truth
So throughout all ages

He has been the Truth
So even now He is the Truth immanent
So for ever and ever He shall be the Truth eternal.[52]

The *Adi Granth* teaches about the nature of God, about creation and about the nature of humankind and its place in the created universe. It teaches also how one is able to seek enlightenment and achieve salvation. Guru Angad wrote:

Were a thousand moons to arise
Were a thousand suns to be shining
All that external brightness
Would leave the world within, in darkness
Unless it had the benign Guru's light[53]

Importantly, the *Adi Granth* incorporates the idea of the equality of all people. Guru Amar Das shows this in the following hymn:

One God creates all men
All men were moulded out of the same clay
All men are mixed of the same five elements[54]

It is an equality which is extended also to non-Sikhs, for the *Adi Granth* contains the writings of those of other faiths who are believed to have experienced God and Truth in their own way. Thus, the following hymn was written by Sheikh Farid, a Muslim who lived in the thirteenth century:

Why leave your home, why roam the wild, why spike your feet on horns?
Why seek him in the jungle waste, the Lord who dwells within?
I thought that I alone had pain, yet what should meet my gaze,
When from my rooftop looking out I saw the world ablaze.[55]

Also included are poems by Hindus of all castes, even what were then Untouchables. God is one, and lives in all, so all people are equal whatever their income, faith or sex. Equality between the sexes was important to Nanak:

By woman we are conceived and from her we are born;
With her we are betrothed and with her married.
It is woman who is our friend and she who perpetuates the family.
When one woman dies, man seeks another
And with her he is established in society.
Out of woman comes woman herself; without her no other exists.
Why call woman evil when she gives birth to kings?[56]

Guru Nanak taught that one should always keep God's Name in one's heart; one's mind would then be on God, who would always be the centre of one's every thought and action. So Sikhs repeat the Name of God, morning and night. Nanak called God *Nam*, "Name", or *Sat*

Guru "True Guru". The *Nam* of God is another way in which God, as an impersonal, formless Absolute, is immanent in the word; the *Nam* is not just a name for God, but refers to the being or essence of God. The *Nam,* then, *is* the *Sat Guru,* God himself, and so meditating and focusing on the *Nam* means the Sikh is bringing the essence of God into the depths of the self in a very personal way.

Sikhism retains a belief in reincarnation, *samsara,* and in *karma.* It is meditation on God's *Nam,* as well as serving other people, which will bring about release from reincarnation. To the Sikh, heaven is this world! Good *karma* means rebirth as a human being; rebirth as an animal is felt to be the equivalent of hell, the consequence of bad *karma.* Yet in Sikhism there is no suggestion that loss of fruitive *karma,* or complete devotion, entirely guarantees liberation. So great is the Sikh Absolute, that it is only by his Grace, his *Nadar,* that any human being can be on the path to enlightenment, or can ever achieve it. To focus one's entire being on God, to be *Gurmukh* as Sikhs put it, is to put oneself in the position in which God's *Nadar* may bring about liberation.

Initiation into Sikhism involves three vows: *Nam japna,* meditation on the *Nam* of God, *kirt karna,* honest hard work, and *vand chakna,* almsgiving to all. This may be summed up as the Sikh motto for life, "devotion, labour and charity". Many Sikhs carry out *Nam japna* at all times, on the way to work, while working, when getting up in the morning or when retiring. They may repeat *Nam,* or they may say or sing quietly to themselves the Gurus' *sabads. Kirt karna* means that a Sikh finds it a *religious duty* to have some kind of honest occupation and support himself. At the same time he or she recognizes that some are not able to do this, so *vand chakna* makes it a religious obligation to give to those who cannot support themselves. Basically, Sikhs are expected to serve God and serve others. They are tolerant of all faiths believing that all, ultimately, worship the same God, but at the same time, Sikhism has been a missionary religion in the Punjab.

Birth   When a baby is born, it is customary for Sikhs to visit the baby's family and give gifts to the baby. In addition, gifts are given by the baby's parents to those who visit. These may vary from lengths of turban, *salwars* and *kameeze,* or *saris,* to boxes of chocolates. Gifts may also be given to others to thank God for the gift of a baby. The birth of a baby boy is celebrated with much rejoicing and exchanging of gifts though, at least in India, the birth of a girl is less welcomed. At birth, the *Mool Mantar* is whispered in the baby's ear and honey put on the baby's tongue.

SIKH CEREMONIES

Name-giving   As soon as possible after the birth, when the mother feels strong enough, the family goes to the *gurdwara* to bring the child into the presence of the *Guru Granth Sahib.* It is traditional to give a certain amount of money for the purpose of making *karah parshad*, though in Indian villages women often make it at home and take it to the *gurdwara* for the ceremony. A *rumala*, the covering for the *Guru Granth Sahib*, is also given by the family and one is also given to the baby.

Some parents ask that a complete reading of the *Guru Granth Sahib* should precede their visit, and some ask that their baby should be given *amrit*. If *amrit* is given, sugar crystals *(patashas)* are dissolved in water and stirred with a *khanda* (two-edged sword) whilst the first five verses of the *Japji* are recited. The *granthi*, who conducts the ceremony, puts the tip of the sword in the *amrit* and places a little of it on the baby's tongue. The mother drinks the remainder. Then, the *Guru Granth Sahib* is opened at random and the hymn in which the first word on the left occurs is read. From the first letter of this or the succeeding word, the child's name is normally chosen, though strictly speaking any of the letters contained in these words could begin the child's name. The name is then announced by the *granthi*. Traditional Sikh names do not distinguish the bearer's sex, and the same name could be given to a boy or a girl. However, if it is a boy, the name *Singh* would be added, if a girl, the name *Kaur*. The *granthi* then shouts, *Jo bole so nihal*, and the congretation responds with *Sat sri akal*. Parts of the *Anand* are then read and *Ardas* follows.

It was Guru Gobind Singh who gave all Sikh men the surname *Singh* "lion" and Sikh women the surname *Kaur*, "princess". This was significant in that at that time a person's name indicated his caste which automatically created inequality between one individual and another. With common surnames, people could be regarded as equal one with another. It also served to identify Sikhs as part of one brotherhood. Yet, as Cole and Sambhi observe:

> Nevertheless, surnames have not disappeared because they are useful, as any teacher with eight Singhs and five Kaurs in the class will know! They denote the sub-caste of the family, e.g. Grewal (Jat), Bansal or Kalsi (Ramgarhia), Jas, Chand or Rasila (Bhatra), or its home village (e.g. Gill, Mirpuri).[57]

Initiation: the *charn amrit* ceremony   The last Guru, Gobind Singh, was responsible for the introduction of many practices which have become lasting traditions of Sikhism, and we recall the initiation of the *Panj Pyare*, the "five beloved ones" into the *Khalsa* brotherhood. Today, initiation into the *Khalsa* is by the *charn amrit* ceremony. *Charn amrit* means "foot nectar". The rite of initiation is performed at any time of the year, though Baisakhi is a popular time. The Sikh to be initiated should wish to accept Sikh teachings and should possess the Five Ks. He should also be neatly dressed. The rite is carried out by five *Khalsa* members, who represent the original *Panj Pyare*.

At the beginning of the ceremony, the *Guru Granth Sahib* is opened and the Sikh teachings are explained to the initiate, and he or she is asked if they are accepted. Prayer is said before preparing the *amrit* and a sixth person reads from the scriptures. The five people then kneel around an iron bowl called a *batta*, which is placed on a pedestal (a *sonera)*. They place their right knee on the ground, and raise their left knee. In the bowl, water and sugar crystals are placed and the nectar *(amrit)* is made. The five keep their hands on the bowl but all five in turn stir the *amrit* with a *khanda*. During this rite they recite *sabads* from the *Adi Granth*. When the *amrit* is ready, a prayer is said and the initiates come forward one by one, kneeling as the five *Khalsa* members. They say the words:

> *Waheguru ji ka Khalsa, sri Waheguru ji ki fateh*
> The Khalsa is of God, the victory is to God.

Then the *amrit* is put into the cupped hands five times to drink and is sprinkled five times on their hair and their eyes. The initiates drink any *amrit* which is left. The *Mool Mantar* is said by the five and repeated by the initiates five times. The initiates are asked not to participate in any other religious beliefs or practices; to pray daily; pay tithes; and to observe certain rules amongst which are the Five Ks. They must not cut their hair, eat meat slaughtered in the Muslim way, commit adultery or use tobacco. Other, less important prohibitions are also added. Initiation closes with *Ardas* and a random reading from the *Guru Granth Sahib*. This is followed by sharing of *karah parshad* and non-Sikhs would be given a name from the *Guru Granth Sahib*, according to the traditional name-giving practice.

Gobind Singh's *amrit* ceremony, though probably much changed today was responsible for uniting the Sikhs into one distinct brotherhood, the *Khalsa*. Once the *Panj Pyare* and Gobind Singh were initiated, everyone present at Anandpur on that day was initiated into the *Khalsa*. So, the *Khalsa* began with Gobind Singh. It was this last Guru, also, who, on the same day, instituted the Five Ks, the turban, and the prohibitions noted above, according to accepted Sikh tradition.

Because of Gobind Singh, the Sikhs began to view themselves as a consolidated brotherhood and it was this which allowed Sikhism to survive, for the new community became powerful and strong. Every Sikh had status and equality in the *Khalsa*. Since initiation into the *Khalsa* is a serious step, no Sikh should undertake it until he or she is mature enough to understand and accept fully the Sikh way of life. "Strictly speaking the initiates should be over 14 years of age but there is ample evidence of young people being initiated in the Punjab."[58] Non-Sikhs have to undergo training for acceptance for initiation. Because of the seriousness of the occasion, only the five initiators representing the *Panj Pyare*, the *granthi* and the initiates are present at the ceremony.

Since the first initiation took place at the time of the festival of *Baisakhi*, this festival now commemorates the formation of the *Khalsa*. Just as at the first ceremony of initiation a Sikh had to declare publicly his acceptance of Sikhism so, today, through the same ceremony, the Sikh commits himself or herself to the faith, and by adopting the Five Ks is seen publicly to be a member of that faith.

Sikh marriage   Sikh family life is based on the extended family, and when a woman marries she enters the extended family of her new husband. It is, therefore, of paramount importance that not only the husband and wife, but also the two families get on well. For this reason, Sikh marriages are said to be "assisted marriages", that is to say the parents exercise considerable influence in helping their children to choose the right partner, or even choose for them. Cole and Sambhi state the position well:

> Through the couple two families become closely connected and into one family group comes a stranger, the wife. She has therefore to be compatible not only with her husband but with his parents, brothers, their wives and his unmarried sisters.[59]

Family life is thought to be something which God has ordained, and so few Sikhs remain unmarried.

The choice of partner would depend on character, age, possibly social status, economic status and caste. Cross-caste marriage is not impossible for Sikhs although, "A Jat is likely to marry a Jat, an Arora an Arora, a Ramgarhia a Ramgarhia, but there are many exceptions. It is most important that a Sikh marries a Sikh":[60] only in this union would children be raised as true Sikhs. When a couple are to be married they will have met socially a number of times, though not alone, will know each other fairly well, and will themselves have made the final decision to marry.

Sikh weddings are social and religious events which take place on any day, but must always take place in the presence of the *Guru Granth Sahib*. The groom sits in front of the Book and the bride takes her place on the left-hand side of the groom. She is usually looked after by a friend. When the service begins, the couple and their parents stand and a prayer is said for the blessing of the marriage, followed by the singing of a hymn. Sikh marriage believes in the union of two souls; though physically two, in reality the couple is one, just like, in Sikh belief, God and the individual is one. Advice to the couple is given in the form of appropriate hymns from the *Adi Granth*, such as the following:

The bride should know no other man except her husband so the Guru ordains. She alone is of a good family, she alone shines with light who is adorned with the love of her husband. There is only one way to the heart of the beloved, to be humble and true and to do his bidding. Only thus is true union attained. They are not man and wife who have physical contact only. Only they are truly wedded who have one spirit in two bodies.[61]

The couple agree to the marriage by bowing to the Book and then sit down. In the East, marriage is often solemnized by tying or joining the couple with a garland or scarf. A similar custom occurs in Sikhism. The bride's father puts garlands over the *Guru Granth Sahib*, his daughter and the groom. He ties the end of his daughter's *dupatta* to a muslin scarf hanging over the groom's shoulders. Then another hymn is sung:

> Praise and blame I forsake both. I seize the edge of your garment. All else I let pass. All relationships I have found false. I cling to thee, O my Lord.[62]

Guru Ram Das composed a hymn for the wedding of his own daughter (*AG* 773), and this is then sung. As the hymn proceeds, the couple walk slowly in a clockwise direction around the *Guru Granth Sahib*, the groom in front. Each verse of the hymn is spoken whilst the couple sit, and sung while they circumambulate the Book. This happens four times, and on the final one, flower petals are thrown over the couple. This hymn, written by Ram Das, is known as the *Lavan* (circling) hymn, and it has four verses corresponding to the four circumambulations of the Book. The hymn not only gives advice to the couple but stresses the importance of the union between God and man. The *Lavan* stresses the importance of the life of the householder. Family life is, therefore, an essential ingredient of Sikhism which does not accept the Hindu practice of separation of husband and wife later in life. The Sikh devotes himself or herself to God *within* the status of marriage. Since the essence of God pervades everything in the universe, one has only to concentrate one's whole attention on God for the love of God to fill the mind and hence the marriage. After the *Lavan*, the first five stanzas of the *Anand* are sung and then the last one, followed by *Ardas*. A random reading *(Vak)* of the *Guru Granth Sahib* is taken, *karah parshad* shared and the marriage party leaves for celebrations at the bride's home. Later, the couple leave to take up their new life in the husband's home.

The whole marriage rite has at its heart the message that the secret of happiness is devotion to God, and no marriage would be valid unless undertaken before the *Guru Granth Sahib*. Apart from being the joining together of two people, it is also the joining together of two families, and this is noticeable at the beginning of a wedding when the two families meet in a ceremony called *milni* during which both fathers of the couple embrace each other and exchange turbans. One seemingly odd gift given at weddings is a coconut. The groom may be seen with one tied in the end of the sash by which he leads the bride around the *Guru Granth Sahib* and others may be given to the groom during the celebrations. The coconut is a sign of good luck, like the horseshoe at a Western wedding.

Family life   Sikh family life is based on the extended family, the idea that cousins, aunts, uncles as well as brothers and sisters are all part of a close family unit, often living together in the same village and sometimes under the same roof. Special terms are used for the people in the family:

chachaji	for father's younger brothers, i.e. uncles
mamiji	for wives of one's paternal uncles, i.e. aunts
masiji	for the sister of one's mother, i.e. aunts
maserji	for the husband of one's mother's sister, i.e. uncles
taiyaji	for the father's older brothers, i.e. uncles
taiji	for the wives of father's older brothers, i.e. aunts
phraji	brother
phanujaji	brother-in-law

The ending *ji* is one denoting affection or repect, and has no English equivalent. The senior male presides over the *whole* extended family and often has the final word in family matters such as the arrangement of a marriage. After marriage, a girl normally goes to live in her husband's home, so before her marriage she is brought up to be a competent wife, able to cook and sew and fulfil household duties. In the Punjab, boys often follow the trade of their fathers and boys learn to help the adult men in the family work well before they themselves are ready for permanent employment.

Although, basically, Sikhism stresses equality between men and women, traditionally this tends to be thought of in terms of equality of status, and no clash is seen between differing roles for men and women which in Western ideas would possibly suggest inequality. Women tend to separate from men in other aspects of Sikh life also: for example, they sit apart from the men in the *gurdwara*. In addition, Sikh women are expected to obey their husbands and to follow them wherever they go, and Sikh girls are encouraged to remain in the home during the evenings, learning the home crafts essential for their future lives as married women. Today, however, education is often considered important for both sexes, and Sikh women will often achieve graduate and post-graduate status.

Because the senior male presides over the whole family, responsibility for one's family extends long after they have become adult.

Parents are loved, respected and obeyed even when a couple has a home and children of their own. With this emphasis on family commitment to other members of the family, Sikhs visit their relatives often and the home is traditionally a place of entertainment as well as being important in maintaining the traditions of the faith. Sikhism stresses the importance of family life. This is because Guru Nanak did not accept that asceticism practised by Hindus was a necessary path to God. He himself was a family man and he encouraged men to earn their living through honest toil – now a basic precept of Sikhism. God is to be found in the home in the life of the family.

Normally, all members of the family would know and recite the *Japji*, the opening hymn of the Sikh scriptures. Children learn it at a very early age and it is something which is recited by many Sikhs wherever they are, at work, at festivals and at any point during the routine of the day but particularly at the beginning and end of each day. To know it by heart is to be a member of the family of Sikhism.

Death rites in Sikhism   Cremation has been the traditional practice in Sikhism – understandable in view of the hot climate in India. The remains are sometimes buried, but more usually are thrown into the nearest river. The body is washed and clothed and dressed in the Five Ks and is carried in a procession by the family to the place where it will be cremated. As the procession moves along, hymns are sung and when the funeral pyre is eventually lit by a close relative, the evening hymn is sung by those present. Other prayers are then offered and the service is concluded with *Ardas*.

When the mourners return home, it is customary to wash the hands and faces, and a complete reading of the *Guru Granth Sahib* is undertaken, either continuously or in sections over about ten days. The mourners share *karah parshad* before leaving the family. This tends to emphasize the social nature of Sikhism, the community fellowship and "family" of the Sikhs, which is a comfort to those who have lost someone. No suggestion is made that the family must fast or perform any particular rituals. Normal life should be experienced as soon as possible. If a Sikh has lived a good life, his or her death will result in union with God – the ultimate goal of Sikhism. If he or she has lived a life which is not God-centred, then rebirth will result from the accrued *karma*. The *Adi Granth* states:

> You are departing having lost even the accumulation of good
> works which you have brought into the world.[63]

The *Sohilla*, the evening hymn, is a reminder that if one pursues God and has God in one's heart and mind, there is no need for grief at death for the deceased will not be reborn, but will be in union with God:

Know the real purpose of being here and gather up the treasure under the guidance of the Sat Guru. Make your mind God's home. If he abides with you undisturbed you will not be reborn.[64]

In Sikhism, therefore, death is a home-coming, not something to be feared or to occasion deep grief. Sometimes grief for a young person who has died is more consuming, since it is felt that to die young is to die too soon. With old people, however, there is thanksgiving and happiness that a full life has been lived. For this reason, in India a brass band may accompany the procession to the funeral pyre:

> There is a place called City-of-no-Sorrows
> There is no grieving, no man suffers there.
> There are no tax-gatherers. No one levies tribute.
> There is no worrying, or sin, or fear, or death.
> My friends, I have found myself a wonderful home town
> Where everything is good, everyone is happy![65]

SIKH FOOD

Vegetarianism   Nanak did not stress vegetarianism as necessary for a Sikh, but although some Sikhs do eat meat, many Sikhs are, in fact, vegetarian. In the *gurdwara* kitchen, the food prepared is always vegetarian, usually consisting of vegetable curries and *chapattis*. Popular, and now available in Western stores, are *samosas* which are pancakes filled with vegetables and fried in hot oil. Nanak stated that whatever went into a person's stomach could have no possible effect on his or her spiritual state, so to argue about whether or not one should eat meat was a waste of energy. What is important is the sharing of food, particularly in respect to *langar* and *karah parshad*, for it is on occasions such as these that the equality of Sikhs is expressed.

Food in the home   Sikh food is not as hot as that associated with the south of India, although spices are used considerably in cooking. Cooking to Indians is an art. Normally, a Sikh girl is taught by her mother to be an expert cook, one who is versatile enough never to need a cookery book! When meat is eaten, Sikhs have only one rule to consider and that is not to eat meat which has been slaughtered by Muslims (i.e. cutting the throat of the animal). This rule obtains because the method of Muslim slaughter is considered to be cruel, and because Hindus accused Sikhs at one time of being Muslims because they ate meat. Some Sikhs do not eat beef out of respect for the Hindu reverence of the cow. Typical Sikh dishes are *pakoras* or savoury fritters. They can be made by mixing gram flour (made from chick peas or lentils) with *garam masala* and chilli powder and adding water to make a thick batter. Then thin slices of potato, cauliflower, aubergines, onions, tomatoes or fish are dipped in the batter and fried in hot oil or ghee until brown. *Rotis* are also popular. These are wholemeal *chapattis*. A dough is made of wholemeal flour and water and is rolled into pancakes about 1–2 cms thick. Water or ghee is spread on one side and the *chapatti* is fried in warm oil, water side down, for a few minutes. They are then baked in the oven until firm and golden. Yoghurt containing herbs and spices is also popular with the main meal.

The turban   Apart from instituting the wearing of the Five Ks, Guru Gobind Singh also asked Sikhs to wear a turban, and it is this aspect of dress which is the most notable among Sikh men, though some Sikh women may also be turbaned if they have been officially initiated into Sikhism. However, Sikhs are not the only people to wear turbans, since other Indians may do so. A Hindu attending a wedding may well be attired in this manner, and it has been a feature of Muslim dress. A Sikh will always know whether another Indian is a Sikh by the way he ties his turban, and if he is, whether he comes from the Punjab or East Africa. It is not important *how* a Sikh wears a turban or what colour it is, but it *is* important that a Sikh wears one. All the Sikh Gurus are portrayed as wearing turbans themselves, so the turban has a number of important reasons for being worn:

SIKH DRESS

1. Since the Gurus wore turbans, when a Sikh copied the Gurus in style of dress, he was raised to a status of equality with them, not only imitating appearance, but faith and moral behaviour also. Thus the *Adi Granth* affirms, "The Guru and the Disciple are one."[66]
2. By wearing a turban, a Sikh is distinguished from other men. In the past, it served as a uniform on the battlefield; no Sikh could be cowardly and turn to fight for the other side since he was always recognizable. The turban also prevented persecution of innocent non-Sikhs.
3. By wearing a turban, a Sikh expresses to all that he lives by his faith and accepts it totally. Because he lives by the rules of the Sikh scriptures, he obeys them and therefore, as the *Adi Granth* requires, "must, comb his hair twice a day and tie his turban smartly".
4. The turban is not worn to keep the hair in place, its purpose is far more symbolic, showing faith in Sikh belief, identity with other Sikhs and unity of Sikh brotherhood. This is particularly evident at a Sikh wedding when turban lengths are exchanged. When a Sikh dies, relatives bring turban lengths to the successor of the deceased who ties his turban in public, symbolizing his authority and declaring his identity and status.

Tying a turban is not easy, and boys do not wear turbans until they can tie their own. Turbans are five metres long (16 feet) and are sometimes starched so that they keep their shape. The Punjabi word for turban is *pagri*, and the turban is replaced by a *putka* which is a small scarf-like covering used when men take part in sports. Boys who are too young to wear a turban cover their top-knots with a *rumal*, a small, handkerchief-sized scarf. The finished product shows the Sikh as a man of wisdom, dignity, smartness and grace.

The wearing of the turban is not without its problems. Sikhs have traditionally worn turbans in the British army, a right now recognized by the armed forces of the United States, but private clubs and institutions in both countries have proved less amenable. In recent decades the British Parliament has legislated in favour of exemption for the Sikh from wearing a motorcycle crash helmet (1976), a hard hat on certain building sites (1989), and a wig for a Sikh judge in the high court,[67] but the problem for the young Sikh so susceptible to peer pressure remains.

Many Sikhs now wear European clothes, suits or trousers and shirts (along with the turban). For religious occasions and visits to the *gurdwara*, men may wear Punjabi clothing. This consists of white trousers, a long white shirt and a turban. The *granthi* is often dressed in this way. Punjabi Sikhs also wear European dress, but in the countryside men wear the *kachs* (shorts) with a loose shirt or tunic called a *kurba*. The long, well-fitting, knee-length tunic worn by men is called an *achkan*, while the tight or loose trousers are called *churidar pyjamas*.

Female dress   Since Islam dominated northern India for two or three centuries, Indian women may well have adopted some forms of Islamic dress. A Muslim woman will usually cover her body from head to toe, and some women also cover their faces. Perhaps this is why Sikh women prefer to wear clothes with high necklines and to cover their legs. Similarly, in the presence of men, in the *gurdwara* and as brides, they will cover their hair, and in the Punjab some young women may well cover their faces before a stranger. The regional dress of the Punjab, and of women Sikhs in the West, is the *salwar* and *kameeze*. The *salwar* is a specially designed pair of trousers and is comfortable and functional. These trousers tend to be loose fitting and are made of silk, nylon or cotton. The *kameeze* is a tunic top usually knee length, and often hand-embroidered, since embroidery is practised at an early age by many Sikh women. The *kameeze* is straight, fastens up to the neck and has elbow length or long sleeves.

Around their shoulders, Sikh women wear a scarf, a *dupatta* or *chuni*, which can be placed over the head when entering the *gurdwara* or in the presence of men. The *dupatta* is two metres long and about one metre wide and is made of very light material. At home it is worn over the shoulders, but outside it is worn over the head. Sometimes it is worn on the head in the company of older people or in the company of someone to whom respect should be paid. The *dupatta* usually matches the *salwar-kameeze*. Since the *salwar-kameeze* is the traditional Sikh dress for women, it tends to be worn more than the *sari*, though the latter is becoming more popular. *Saris* are more particularly worn for special occasions and are often made of fine silk, and may be intricately embroidered. Underneath the *sari* is usually a full blouse which covers the midriff, unlike the similar garment worn by Hindu women: perhaps, again, this reflects Muslim thought. However, on this point we should note the rule in the Sikh scriptures which states the importance of not, "wearing clothes which cause pain to the body or breed lustful thoughts".[68]

The distinguishing aspects of Sikhism as we see them today do much **CASTE** to stress the concept of equality. This is seen in such aspects as *langar*, the common surnames, the inclusion of all castes in Sikhism, the four entrances of the *Harmandir* and so on. Both Guru Nanak and Guru Amar Das stressed the worthlessness of caste:

> Worthless is caste and worthless an exalted name.
> For all mankind there is but a singe refuge.[69]

> Observe the divine light in a man and ask not his caste
> For there is no caste in the hereafter.[70]

> When you die you do not carry your caste with you.
> It is your deeds (and not your caste) which will determine
> your fate.[71]

The concept of caste equality is a complex one in Sikhism. To begin, we find included in the *Adi Granth* the hymns of outcastes such as Ravidas, a leather worker, which suggests spiritual equality. Also, Guru Gobind Singh's *Panj Pyare*, the "Beloved Five", drank from a common bowl at the *amrit* ceremony, which indicates equality in commensality. Yet in 1920 it was necessary to resort to a random reading of the *Guru Granth Sahib* to settle a dispute concerning whether outcastes should be allowed to present *karah parshad* at the Golden Temple. Having been presented by outcastes, it would have been eaten by other higher castes from the common bowl in which such offerings were placed. Despite the random reading being in favour of the outcastes, the incident shows that caste was still very much evident.

The ten Gurus were all of the *Khatri* class, *Khatri* being cognate with Hindu *Ksatriya*. It was mainly a mercantile class and was certainly a high status class. McLeod sees this fact as "a great pity" and also notes that all the Gurus arranged marriages for their children "in strict accordance with traditional caste prescription".[72] McLeod has been severely criticized by Sikhs for this hitherto unpublished perspective. He does, however, go on to defend the Sikh position by saying that:

Caste can remain, but not the doctrine that one's access to salvation depends upon one's caste ranking. The way of salvation is open to all regardless of caste. Stripped of its religious content it can retain the status of a harmless social convention.[73]

McLeod adds that the Gurus probably intended the abolition of caste to go further than it did. He concludes that while opposed to *vertical* distinctions they maintained *horizontal* links, but this begs the question whether the maintainance of *horizontal* links is exactly what caste is all about. In defence of the custom of Gurus all belonging to the same class, we might add the observation that since Guruship was often hereditary or given to someone in the same family, we could hardly expect a change of class: it became traditional for the Guruship to remain in the Sodhi family.

FESTIVALS

There are two different kinds of Sikh festivals, *melas* and *gurpurbs*. Since Sikhism originated in India, it was natural for the religion to retain the Indian calendar, with its New Year in April. Many of the Hindu festivals were incorporated into Sikhism but given new interpretations and became important Sikh gatherings during the year. These festivals were called *melas*. However, those events which were important in Sikh history, such as the birth, death or martyrdom of the Sikh Gurus, were also commemorated on festival occasions and became known as *gurpurbs*. So *melas* are Hindu in origin while *gurpurbs* are Sikh in origin.

Gurpurbs　The word *gurpurb* comes from two words, *guru* and *pur* "holiday". Thus festivals which are *gurpurbs* are times when the Gurus are remembered and honoured. Three *gurpurbs* are particularly important, these being the birthdays of Guru Nanak and Gobind Singh, and the anniversary of the martyrdom of Guru Arjan. These three *gurpurbs* would be celebrated worldwide, whereas other *gurpurbs* tend to be local events. In India, *gurpurbs* are celebrated by the carrying of the *Guru Granth Sahib* through the town or village in a procession. The Book would be placed on a van or a float, and the whole would be covered in flowers. Five initiated Sikhs, probably wearing yellow turbans, blue sashes and carrying ceremonial swords, will head the procession, and represent the *panj pyare*. Many Sikhs contribute financially to pay for speakers who address the large gatherings, to pay for *langar*, and to pay for prizes given to winners of the competitions which are a feature of *gurpurbs*. Many of these *gurpurbs* are characterized by an *akhand path*, a continuous reading of the *Adi Granth* taking about forty-eight hours. The end of the reading is timed to coincide with the period before dawn on the day of the festival. During the *akhand path*, many people visit the *gurdwaras*, so extra amounts of *karah parshad* have to be made. As the reading comes to a close, all those who are able come for the reading of the last five pages. When the reading is complete, the usual prayers, readings and hymns follow, but are connected with the Guru who is being remembered and honoured. Sikhs follow a lunar calendar, therefore festivals do not occur on the same day each year, with the exception of Baisakhi. Some *gurpurbs* need a special mention.

The Birthday of Guru Nanak   This is a three-day festival, held each year in the month of *Katik* (Oct.–Nov.). It is the most holy of the Sikh festivals. Nanak was born in November 1469 and, according to Sikh tradition, the heavens rained flowers on earth, and musical instruments made music of their own accord at the time of his birth. In the West, when the procession does not take place, the *gurdwara* is the centre for the festival. Apart from being a religious occasion there are games, fêtes, fairs and stalls for foods and sweets.

The Birthday of Guru Gobind Singh   The birth, life and works of Guru Gobind Singh are celebrated each year in the month of *Magh* (Dec.–Jan.). The tenth, and last Guru, he was born in December 1666, and the celebration of his birth is the most important *gurpurb* with the exception of that celebrating Guru Nanak's birth. He was born at Patna where he lived for five years before moving to the Punjab. He is remembered particularly because he gathered the Sikhs together when he became Guru and established the Sikh brotherhood, the *Khalsa*, at the festival of *Baisakhi* in 1699. Because of Gobind Singh, Sikhs were able to defend their religion against the persecuting Mughal rulers. His four sons were martyred, two being buried alive because they would not convert to Islam (at the ages of five and eight) and two dying in battle aged fourteen and eighteen. Like Guru Nanak's birthday, Guru Gobind Singh's is celebrated by Sikhs all over the world.

Martyrdom of Guru Tegh Bahadur   Because he refused to convert to Islam, Tegh Bahadur was tortured and beheaded in 1675. The anniversary of his martyrdom occurs in the month of *Poh* (Nov.–Dec.). He was born at Amritsar in April 1621, at a time when the Mughal Emperor Aurangzeb ruled India and persecuted those who were not Muslims. When Tegh Bahadur became Guru this situation had worsened. Sikhs are proud of this Guru because he sacrificed his life for those of another faith. Hindus were being killed because they would not convert to Islam, and others were so terrified they accepted it. The Hindu priests turned to Tegh Bahadur for help and as a result Aurangzeb was told by the Hindus that if Tegh Bahadur accepted Islam, then so would all the Hindus. But Tegh Bahadur did not. He journeyed to Delhi with five disciples and although these five disciples were tortured to death before his eyes, he could not be converted. Eventually, after great suffering himself, the Guru was beheaded in

November 1675. His sacrifice showed Sikhs something new; that martyrdom and suffering could also be undertaken for others, as well as Sikhs. The festival centres mainly in Delhi, where a large temple called the *Gurdwara Sisganj* has been built. At this festival, when the *Guru Granth Sahib* is paraded along the streets, pictures of the Mughal atrocities line the route, as well as pictures of Hindus discussing their problems with the Guru.

Martyrdom of Guru Arjan   Guru Arjan, the fifth Guru, was the first Sikh martyr. He was tortured to death by the Mughal Emperor in May 1606. The anniversary of his death occurs in the month of *Jaith,* our May or June. It was Arjan who had built the *Harmandir* at Amritsar and who collected the hymns of the Gurus together to form the first Sikh scriptures, the *Adi Granth*. When he was tortured to death by the Emperor Jehangir, he was not allowed to drink anything. Therefore, on the anniversary of his death, in the hottest time of the year, Sikhs offer free drinks to passers-by in order to remind themselves of the sufferings of their Guru.

Significant among the "fairs" which are celebrated in Sikhism are the following festivals. Most are Hindu in origin and do not have their roots in Sikhism: hence they are not *gurpurbs,* but *melas.*

Baisakhi   The Punjabi New Year's Day occurs on 13 April; it is the only festival which occurs on the same day each year because it is the only one based on the solar calendar. Once every thirty-six years it is held on 14 April. Hindu *Baisakhi* was a time when the first fruits of the harvest were offered to Brahmin priests. In Sikhism it became a time when devotion was offered to God. It was at *Baisakhi* that Guru Gobind Singh instituted the *Khalsa*. In the eighteenth century, the Sikhs began to assemble at Amritsar for *Baisakhi,* and it was here in 1919 that the British fired on the harmless assembly of Sikhs, killing 337 men, 41 boys and a baby, and wounding over 2000. Today, when *Baisakhi* is celebrated at Amritsar, many pilgrims visit the *Harmandir*. There are political rallies, an animal market and it is a popular time for initiation into the *Khalsa*. Since it precedes the gathering of the harvest, it is a time of enjoyment before hard work. As at most New Year Festivals, new clothes are worn, and turbans are exchanged. *Baisakhi* is the name of the first of the calendar months and the festival falls on the first day. This New Year period is also the time when some important battles against the Mughals were fought. It is also a festival at which a new flag is flown outside *gurdwaras*. On the flag pole the *nishan sahib* is wrapped with saffron-yellow cloths which are changed once a year at *Baisakhi*. On the evening of *Baisakhi* there is singing and dancing. Two dances are the speciality of the night: the *bhangra,* danced by men, and the *giddha* danced by women. In Sikh eyes, *Baisakhi* celebrates the birthday of Sikhism as we know it today.

Diwali   To Hindus, *Diwali* is a festival of light, and this aspect has been taken over by Sikhs. The *gurdwaras* are lit up with coloured lights and lamps, and children are given presents. The story behind the Sikh festival is that involving the sixth Guru, Hargobind. Guru Hargobind was imprisoned because a fine imposed on his father had not been paid, and because he was suspected of raising an army against the Mughal rulers. The Emperor Jehangir looked into Hargobind's case and decided to free him. But Hargobind would not leave the prison unless fifty-two Hindu princes imprisoned with him were also set free. Jehangir stated that as many could be free as could hang on to the clothes of Hargobind, and pass through the narrow passage of the prison to freedom. Hargobind had a cloak sent to the prison with long tassels attached so that every prince was saved. At *Diwali* in Armritsar, the Golden Temple is lit up and fireworks are also a widespread feature. Like the Hindu festival of lights, Sikh *Diwali* celebrates the triumph of good over evil, but it is also said that when Hargobind returned from prison every Sikh home was lit with candles to welcome him.

Diwali occurs in October/November, at the end of the very hot season and the beginning of the winter. It is at this time that crops are sown. In a way, it is a New Year Festival beginning the winter half of the year. As at *Baisakhi,* people wear new clothes and celebrate with music and dancing. Popular at the festival is the exchanging of boxes of Indian sweets – *burfi, laddoo, gulab jaman, rasgoolas* – and other gifts. Sikh *Diwali* is a five-day festival, the third day being the proper festival day. The Hindu festival is associated with cleaning the houses, and the Sikhs do likewise. This is usually a practical consideration since people often sleep outside in the summer, and at *Diwali* insects and lizards are moved out of the house before the beds are moved in!

Hola Mohalla (February/March)   Hindus celebrate the festival of *Holi* dedicated to the God Visnu and his *avatar,* Krisna, and in 1700 Gobind Singh diverted Sikh attention from the Hindu festival by creating this Sikh festival and re-naming it *Hola Mohalla*. It is mainly observed in Anandpur. *Hola Mohalla* means "attack and place of attack" and when the Sikhs were gathered at this festival the *Khalsa* was trained in martial arts and military discipline. So, at *Hola Mohalla* mock battles took place under Gobind Singh, as well as archery, wrestling, music and poetry.

Cole and Sambhi have suggested that the original *Hola Mohalla* was first instituted in 1680, that is *before* the institution of the *Khalsa* in 1699: "The general emphasis was clearly military and the festival was a means of expressing the belief that every Sikh was a Kshatriya 19 years before the Khalsa was formed."[74] At Anandpur, the home town of Gobind Singh, many pilgrims gather and visit shrines and *gurdwaras*; there is also a fair, and a carnival procession led by the Sikh flags heralds the climax of the festival. The festival occurs in the Sikh month of *Phagan* and lasts for two or three days. It coincides with our February/March and is springtime in India, and therefore a time of colourful flowers and rich fields. *Hola Mohalla* is still a festival associated with sports and games of many kinds. Sometimes, as in the Hindu festival of *Holi,* coloured water called *gulal* is sprayed on people from sprinklers which are made specially for the festival.

Rakhi or Rakhsa Bandhan (August)   This, too is a Hindu festival in origin. It is a time when a sister ties a *rakhi,* a ribbon, on her brother's wrist and gives him a box of sweets. In return, the brother promises to defend his sister through life and gives her some money. These exchanges are tokens of love. *Rakhis* can be bought in Indian shops and are usually highly decorative with tinsel flowers and threads. They are placed on the boy or man's right wrist. The festival is not a religious one in Sikhism, but stresses the closeness of brother–sister family relationships.

Basant   *Basant* is a festival which takes place in the Indian spring, our January/February, and is observed by Hindus and Sikhs. Yellow is the colour which characterizes the festival, because yellow is a spring colour. People wear yellow *saris, salwar-kameez* and *chuniz* (scarf); yellow turbans are worn by the men; and people eat rice which is coloured yellow. It is a family occasion when the family is united, and in India kite flying is popular. *Basant* is like St. Valentine's Day for those who are in love and is thought to be a holy day for those who start school at the age of five.

Maghi (January)   *Maghi* is a festival associated with Guru Gobind Singh. When the Guru was besieged by the Mughals, forty close followers deserted him. When they arrived home their wives refused to let them in their homes and one of the women, Mai Bhago, told the men that they should be brave enough to die for their cause. Under her leadership the men returned to Gobind Singh but lost their lives in battle. The festival, held at Muktsar, commemorates this occasion. The Hindu festival of *Magha* is connected with the God Siva.

CONCLUSION   It is fitting that we close our study of Sikhism with a tribute to the bravery of Sikhs who, in the face of tremendous adversity, faced the challenge to their faith and, in the end, were willling to lay down their lives for their belief. This typifies the strength of the belief of a people who see the Word of God in their sacred scriptures, the *Guru Granth Sahib,* and who will dedicate and, indeed, sacrifice their lives for the *Sat Guru.* Truly such a people deserve to be called a *People of the Book.*

Conclusion

As we approach the third millennium we are living in a world of ever-widening experiences, a world in which our life-styles are changing rapidly and in which advanced technology is now evident as much in the home as in the world at large. Today people of different backgrounds travel more widely to many parts of the globe and are more acutely aware of the diversity of cultures which make up the world. The word *humankind* has thus come to have a more realistic meaning and through the medium of television even those who have travelled little can enjoy the visual experiences of places on other sides of the globe. Then, too, many people today live in multi-ethnic societies and are well aware of the changing and more cosmopolitan nature of society itself. But it is primarily in education that such wider experience and exploration is taking place, and this is no less the case with the whole spectrum of the concept of "religion".

The traditional "confessional" approach to the teaching of Religious Education in schools in the West sought to inculcate and nurture Christian values and knowledge in a way which confined the term "religion" to a very exclusive perspective. But religion is not something which obtains only in one particular culture, it is a dimension of existence, and to many it is a characteristic of what it is to be human. Religion, indeed, has informed social and cultural existence world wide from the advent of humankind through to the present day, and will continue to play a dynamic role in the lives of the majority of people on Earth. To be in the process of understanding religion from this wider perspective is what being educated in religion really means. Religious Education today, then, has a broader remit than it had years ago and has changed from *instruction* in a specific religion to a more reflective analysis of the broader dimensions of religion in a variety of cultures. Thus, the teacher of Religious Education today has become a co-explorer with pupils and students into the whole spectrum of religion. It is in the light of such changes in the educational approach to the teaching of Religious Education that this book was written.

The emphasis in this book has been on the *living* religion which makes world religions such an interesting discipline in the field of education. The broader dimensions of religion offer the opportunity to create greater awareness of cultures and life-styles which are different from one's own and which encourage reflective enquiry into the way others live their lives. Religion and culture are, for many people, one and the same thing, so to understand the religion is to understand a good deal about the daily life of people from other cultures – what they eat and what they wear, where and how they worship, and how their beliefs affect their general existence. Widening the dimension of religion in this way serves the purpose of breaking down the cultural barriers which, so often in the past (and, sadly, also in the present) have been the causes of friction and animosity. Greater awareness and greater understanding of other cultures should engender tolerance and empathy for those in cultures other than one's own who are trying in their own ways and in their own environments to make sense of the world in which we live.

We live in an age of reductionism in which the human being is reduced to his or her genetic, biological, chemical, physical, sociological, psychological and behavioural characteristics. But the one dimension of the human being which is less readily reduced to such basic components is the spiritual dimension. It is this dimension of the human being which causes him or her to reach far beyond the confines of the self in a search for greater harmony in life, and for answers to some of its more perplexing metaphysical questions. Religions have this search as their common denominator, and even if individual beliefs and practices can at times be more easily subjected to reductionist methods, this is by no means the case for the spiritual dimension *per se*. Religions, too, often bear witness to those individuals who have transcended the genetic, biological, sociological, behavioural and psychological characteristics and who have become the epitome of full human potential. And while the average human being may never reach this full potential, he or she is still capable of experiencing those few, but precious, moments in life when the world is transcended, the pulse of the universe is experienced. Religion is one response to life – and a varied and diverse one – and whether one would consider oneself religious or not, studying this response in others can only broaden one's understanding of humanity and, therefore, of life itself.

The concept of education is concerned with the development of a "whole" person, an autonomous person, and to be "whole" or "educated" is impossible unless we are aware of the ways in which religion offers interpretations for life. It is not necessary to be "religious" to explore this dimension of existence, it is only necessary to travel with an open mind, to explore, to develop awareness, and to share the lives and thoughts of other human beings.

This book is the result of the teaching experience of its contributors, a collective experience of the teaching of world religions to all ages from infants to post-graduate students. The authors would welcome the responses of teachers and students from both sides of the Atlantic on its contents and would be pleased to incorporate such advice in any future editions.

Notes

Introduction

1 W. Owen Cole is an Honorary Fellow at Chichester Institute of Higher Education, West Sussex, and an eminent scholar in Sikhism. He is also a prolific writer in the field of world religions and has made an outstanding contribution to Religious Education for schools and teacher training.

Chapter 1 Judaism

1 The question of Jewish identity is discussed at length in the beautifully illustrated *Atlas of the Jewish World* by Nicholas de Lange (Oxford: Equinox, 1984), pp. 78–9.
2 See E. B. Borowitz, "Judaism: an Overview", in M. Eliade, *The Encyclopedia of Religion* (hereafter *ER*) (New York: Macmillan, 1987), vol. 8, p. 137. This 16-volume work on multifarious aspects of many different religions is a mine of information on Judaism, as is the 16-volume *Encyclopaedia Judaica* (Jerusalem: Keter, 1972).
3 The *Sephardi* Diaspora from Spain in 1492 is illustrated in the *Atlas of the Jewish World*, pp. 46–7, and the *Ashkenazi* Diaspora on pp. 50–1.
4 L. Trepp, *A History of the Jewish Experience* (New York: Behrman House, 1973), p. 245.
5 S. J. Zipperstein, "Judaism in Northern and Eastern Europe since 1500", in *ER*, vol. 8, pp. 188–9.
6 Many important questions about Jewish life and practice are addressed in A. J. Kolatch, *The Jewish Book of Why* (New York: Jonathan David, 1981). See also *The Second Jewish Book of Why* by the same author.
7 L. Trepp, *The Complete Book of Jewish Observance* (New York: Behrman House, 1980), p. 36.
8 *Ibid.*, p. 37.
9 *Ibid.*, p. 38.
10 Illustrations are to be found in *Atlas of the Jewish World*, pp. 114–15
11 For interesting illustrations of some unusual wooden *yadim* from a synagogue in Prague, see S. Kalman et al., *Celebrating the Jewish Holidays* (New York: Crescent Books, 1992), p. 33.
12 See J. Goldin, "Midrash and Aggadah", in *ER*, vol. 9, pp. 509–15.
13 See D. Kraemer, "Tannaim" in *ER*, vol. 14, pp. 271–2.
14 L. Trepp, *The Complete Book of Jewish Observance*, p. 222.
15 *Ibid.*, p. 291.
16 The interested reader is again referred to *The Jewish Book of Why*, chapter 3, *passim*.
17 L. Trepp, *The Complete Book of Jewish Observance*, p. 24.
18 As noted, the first woman rabbi was ordained in 1972.
19 A. Unterman, *The Jews: Their Religious Beliefs and Practices* (Brighton: Sussex Academic Press, 1996), p. 147.
20 L. Trepp, *The Complete Book of Jewish Observance*, p. 56.
21 For a unique collection of three hundred traditional and modern recipes, see S. Lesberg, *At the Table of Israel* (London: Tom Stacey, 1973).
22 See S. Kalman et al., *Celebrating the Jewish Holidays* (New York: Crescent, 1992), pp. 74–6.
23 *Ibid.*, p. 80.
24 It is customary to refer to God's Chosen People as "Hebrews" prior to the settlement in Canaan, the Holy Land; "Israelites" up until the time of the Babylonian captivity; and "Jews" upon their return from Bablyon.
25 L. Trepp, *The Complete Book of Jewish Observance*, p. 6.
26 For the Sabbath service and especially the menus for the Sabbath meals, see S. Kalman et al., *Celebrating the Jewish Holidays*, chapter 1.
27 For detailed explanation see Unterman, *The Jews: Their Religious Beliefs and Practices*, p. 161.
28 Unterman, *ibid.*, p. 165, notes that secularist Jews in the State of Israel make a point of expressing their defiance of the hold Orthodoxy has by rejoicing in much publicised picnics on Yom Kippur!
29 H. Schauss, *The Jewish Festivals* (London: Jewish Chronicle Publications, 1986, first published 1938), p. 225, adds that the legend of the flask of oil was created in order to, "imbue the Chanukkoh lights with a religious aura, with a sacred tradition".
30 A detailed explanation of the dreidle game is given in D. H. Renberg, *The Complete Family Guide to Jewish Holidays* (New York: Adama, 1985), pp. 94–5.

31   Music and lyrics in D. H. Renberg, *ibid.*, p. 96.
32   In some ancient cities of Israel *Purim* is celebrated on the 15th.
33   L. Trepp, *A History of the Jewish Experience*, p. 45.

Chapter 2   Christianity

1   R. A. Kreig, "Christian" in R. P. McBrien (ed.) *Encyclopedia of Catholicism* (New York: HarperCollins, 1995), p. 309.
2   B. Nicholls, "We All Believe In Something" in D. English et al., *An Introduction to the Christian Faith* (Oxford : Blackwell 1994), p. 27.
3   A. E. McGrath, *Christian Theology* (Oxford: Blackwell 1994), p. 234.
4   *Ibid.*, p. 22.
5   *Ibid.*, p. 20
6   *Ibid.*, p. 177.
7   R. P. Martin, "Approaches to New Testament Exegesis" in H. Marshall (ed.) *New Testament Interpretations* (Carlisle: The Paternoster Press, 1992 reprint of 1985 revised edition first published 1977), p. 229.
8   Nicene Creed may be read in any Roman Catholic or Anglican Prayer Book.
9   Nicene Creed.
10   C. Rowlands, *Christian Origins* (London: SPCK, reprint of 1993, first published 1985), p. 152.
11   F. F. Bruce, *Paul Apostle of the Free Spirit* (Carlisle: The Paternoster Press, 1995 reprint of revised edition 1980, first published 1977), p. 16.
12   F. A. Young, "Patristics" in A. Richardsons and J. Bowden (eds) *A New Dictionary of Christian Theology* (London: SCM Press, 1993 reprint, first published 1983), p. 434.
13   B. E. Close, and M. Smith, *Christianity* (London : Hodder and Stoughton, 1992), p. 57.
14   Close and Smith, *Christianity*, p. 73.
15   R. D. Linder, "The Reformation" in J. D. Douglas (ed.) *The New International Dictionary of the Christian Church* (Michigan: Regency, Zondervan, 1994 reprint of 1978 edition), p. 830.
16   H. Kung, *Great Christian Thinkers* (London: SCM Press, 1994), p. 146.
17   *Ibid.*, p. 148.
18   *Ibid.*, p. 149
19   W. P. Havgaard, "From the Reformation to the Eighteenth Century" in S. Sykes and J. Booty, *The Study of Anglicanism* (London: SPCK, 1993 reprint, first published 1988), p. 6.
20   S. Neill, *Anglicanism* (London: Mowbray, 1993 reprint of 1977 edition, first published 1958), p. 61.
21   Close and Smith, *Christianity*, p. 93.
22   W. Detzler, "Enlightenment" in J. D. Douglas, *The New International Dictionary of the Christian Church*, p. 343.
23   P. Butler, "From Early Eighteenth Century to the Present day" in Sykes and Booty, *The Study of Anglicanism*, p. 32.
24   J. F. Lahey, "Vatican" *Encyclopedia of Catholicism*, p. 1295.
25   M. R. Francis, "Sacrament" *Encyclopedia of Catholicism*, p. 1147.
26   C. A. Taver, "Abortion" *Encyclopedia of Catholicism*, p. 5.
27   J. Atkinson, "The Reformation" An Introduction to the Christian Faith, p. 307.
28   W. S. Pickering, "Sociology of Anglicanism", *The Study of Anglicanism*, p. 370.
29   F. Harris Thopsett, "The Laity", *The Study of Anglicanism*, p. 257.
30   D. W. Dayton, "Methodist Churches America", *The New International Dictionary of the Christian Church*, p. 655.
31   E. F. Clipsham, "Baptists", *The New International Dictionary of the Christian Church*, p. 101
32   K. Clements, "Baptist Theology" *The New Dictionary of Christian Theology*, p. 63.
33   E. A. Livingston, *The Concise Dictionary of the Christian Church* (London: Omega Books, 1988 reprint of 1977 edition), p. 284.
34   K. Ware, "Eastern Christianity" in M. Eliade (ed.), *The Encyclopedia of Religion* (hereafter *ER*), vol. 4 (New York: Macmillan Free Press, 1987), p. 565.
35   *Ibid.*, p. 571.
36   M. P. Fisher and R. Luyster, *Living Religions* (New York: I. B. Tauris & Co. Ltd., 1990), p. 239.
37   Liturgy of the Presanctified Gifts.
38   J. Baggley, *Doors of Perception* (London and Oxford: Mowbray, 1987), p. 55.
39   N. Zernov, "Christianity" in R. C. Zaehner, *The Hutchinson Encyclopedia of Living Faiths* (Finland: Helicon, 1993 reprint of 1959 edition), p. 85.
40   Basil of Caesara cited in K Ware, "Eastern Christianity" in Eliade (*ER*), vol. 4, p. 571.
41   *Ibid.*
42   W. S. Hudson, "Denominationalism" in Eliade, *ER*, vol. 4, p. 292.
43   H. Barbour, "Quakers" in Eliade, *ER*, vol. 12, p. 130.

44 G. Fox cited in G.H. Gorman, *Introducing Quakers* (London: Quaker Home Service, 1981 reprint of 1974 edition), p. 8.

45 G. H. Gorman, *Introducing Quakers*, p. 36.

46 G. Fox cited in "Quaker Views – Close Relationships" (London: Quaker Home Service, August 1995).

47 "Quaker Views – Close Relationships".

48 G. H. Gorman, *Introducing Quakers*, p. 57.

49 H. Barbour, "Quakers" in Eliade, *ER*, vol. 12, p. 130.

50 "Quaker Views – Close Relationships".

51 J. Roundhill, *Meeting the Mormons* (London: Lutterworth Educational, 1974), p. 18.

52 J. Smith cited in Roundhill, *Meeting the Mormons*, p. 18.

53 M.C. Burrell and J. Stafford-Wright, *Some Modern Faiths* (Glasgow: Collins, 1983), p. 54.

54 *The Book of Nephi: 1 Nephi*: 11:11.

55 J. Roundhill, *Meeting the Mormons*, p. 32.

56 L. Beier, *Mormons, Christian Scientists, Jehovah's Witnesses* (Hong Kong: Ward Lock Educational, 1981), p. 20.

57 K. J. Hansen, "Mormonism" in Eliade, *ER*, vol. 10, p. 111.

58 *Ibid.*

59 J. and M. Thompson, *The Many Paths of Christianity* (London: Hodder and Stoughton, 1992), p. 78.

60 Burrell and Stafford-Wright, *Some Modern Faiths*, p. 52.

61 J. And M. Thompson, *The Many Paths of Christianity*, p. 78.

62 L. Beier, *Mormons, Christian Scientists, Jehovah's Witnesses*, p. 15.

63 J. Roundhill, *Meeting Jehovah's Witnesses* (London: Lutterworth Press, 1977), p. 13.

64 L. Beier, *Mormons, Christian Scientists, Jehovah's Witnesses*, p. 44.

65 As there are twelve tribes of Israel, the figure 144,000 is arrived at by multiplying the twelve tribes by the twelve thousand which are "sealed" or saved from every tribe.

66 J. And M. Thompson, *The Many Paths of Christianity*, p. 81.

67 J. Roundhill, *Meeting Jehovah's Witnesses*, p. 15.

68 *Ibid.*, p. 17.

69 Burrell and Stafford-Wright, *Some Modern Faiths*, p. 29.

70 *Ibid.*, p. 31.

71 *Make Sure of All Things* (USA: The Watchtower Tract Society, 1953), p. 360.

72 L. Beier, *Mormons, Christian Scientists, Jehovah's Witnesses*, p. 44.

73 J. And M. Thompson, *The Many Paths of Christianity*, p. 81.

74 J. Roundhill, *Meeting Jehovah's Witnesses*, p. 17.

75 R. Brandon cited in J. Roundhill, *Meeting Jehovah's Witnesses*, p. 23.

76 Watchtower Bible and Tract Society of Pennsylvania, *Schools and Jehovah's Witnessee* (Brooklyn, New York: Bible and Tract Society of New York, 1983), p. 27.

77 M. Baker Eddy cited by S. Gottschalk, "Christian Science" in Eliade, *ER*, vol. 3, p. 443.

78 *Ibid.*, vol 3, p. 442.

79 M. Baker Eddy cited in Burrell and Stafford-Wright, *Some Modern Faiths*, p. 83.

80 Burrell and Stafford-Wright, *Some Modern Faiths*, p. 83.

81 M. Baker Eddy, *Science and Health with Key to the Scriptures* (Boston: The First Church of Christ, Scientist, 1994 reprint of 1907 edition), pp. 591ff.

82 L. Beier, *Mormons, Christian Scientists, Jehovah's Witnesses*, p. 27.

83 J. And M. Thompson, *The Many Paths of Christianity*, p. 82.

84 Burrell and Stafford-Wright, *Some Modern Faiths*, p. 90.

85 M. Baker Eddy, *Science and Health*, p. 334.

86 Gottschalk, "Christian Science" in Eliade, *ER*, vol. 3, p. 444.

87 *Ibid.*, p. 455.

88 In the USA in 1990 the Twistles, a husband and wife who were both practising Christian Scientists, were prosecuted for murder, and found guilty, after their young son died. The boy had been suffering from a twisted bowel, but his parents refused to call in traditional medical help, fervently believing that the ministrations of their own Christian Science Practitioner and faith were all that were necessary to save him. Unfortunately, they were not.

Chapter 3 Islam

1 S. Haneef, *What Everyone Should Know About Islam and Muslims* (Kazi, 1979), p. viii.

2 S. Azzam in the foreword to K. Ahmad (ed.) *Islam – its meaning and message* (Leicester: The Islamic Foundation, 1983 reprint of 1975 edition).

3 Q. 18:24. All Qur'anic references from A. Arberry, *The Koran* (Oxford: Oxford University Press, 1985 reprint of 1983

edition).
4 All Biblical references are from the *Revised Standard Version*.
5 M. Lings, *Muhammad* (London: Unwin: 1986 reprint of 1983 edition), pp. 1–2.
6 From M. Ibn Sa'd, *Kitab at-Tabaqat al-Kabir* in M. Lings, *Muhammad*, p. 26.
7 M. Ruthven, *Islam in the World* (Middlesex: Penguin, 1991 reprint of 1984 edition), p. 54.
8 Q. 96: 1–5.
9 Ruthven, *Islam in the World*, p. 52.
10 Q. 5:5.
11 Q. 96:1–5.
12 Q. 16:37.
13 T. Irving, K. Ahmad and M. Ahsan, *The Qur'an: Basic Teachings* (Leicester: The Islamic Foundation, 1979), p. 29.
14 S. Nasr, *Ideals and Realities of Islam* (London: George, Allen and Unwin, 1985), p. 42.
15 *Ibid.*, p. 44.
16 *Ibid.*, p. 53.
17 *Ibid.*, p. 49–50.
18 *Ibid.*, p. 53.
19 Q. 2:1.
20 Q. 4:52.
21 A. Azzan, *The Eternal Message of Muhammad* (Cambridge: The Islamic Texts Society, 1993), p. 192.
22 Q. 27:61–3.
23 Q. 27:65.
24 Q. 3:25.
25 Q. 2:109.
26 Q. 2:257.
27 Q. 27:63–4.
28 Q. 39:54.
29 H. Abdalati, *Islam in Focus* (Islamic Teaching Centre, n.d.), p. 5.
30 For accounts of the debates see: D. MacDonald, *Development of Muslim Theology* (Beiruit: Khayats, 1965); M. Sharif, *A History of Muslim Philosophy*, vol. 1 (Wiesbaden: Otto Harrassowitz, 1963); W. Watt, *The Formative Period of Islamic Thought* (Edinburgh: Edinburgh University Press, 1973).
31 A. Ahmed, *Living Islam* (London: BBC Books, 1993), p. 36.
32 Q. 7:204.
33 There are a number of collections of *hadith* which have been accepted by Muslims. The "two sound collections", as they are known, are those of Muhammad al-Bukhari and Muslim b. al-Hajjaj. There are four others, those of Abu Dawud al-Sijistani, al-Tirmidhi, al-Nasa'i, and Ibn Maja

al-Qazwini which together with the first two make up the six canonical collections. There are also composite collections and, in addition there are a number of other collections of differing veracity.
34 W. Graham, *Divine Word and Prophetic Word in Early Islam* (The Hague: Mouton and Co. 1977), p. 14.
35 W. Watt, *Bell's Introduction to the Qur'an* (Edinburgh: Edinburgh University Press, 1970), p. 20.
36 Q. 2:92.
37 Q. 2:100.
38 R. Maqsood, *The Qur'an* (Oxford: Heinemann, 1993), p. 10.
39 Nasr, *Ideals and Realities of Islam*, p. 84.
40 *Ibid.*, p. 84.
41 Q. 41:5.
42 Q. 8:20.
43 Q. 33:21.
44 Nasr, *Ideals and Realities of Islam*, p. 82.
45 W. Graham, *Divine Word and Prophetic Word in Early Islam*, p. 9.
46 *Ibid.*, p. 11.
47 Q. 2:2.
48 Q. 2:181.
49 K. Murad, *Shari'ah The Way to God* (Leicester: The Islamic Foundation, 1981), p. 4.
50 Nasr, *Ideals and Realities in Islam*, p. 95.
51 A. Siddiqui, "What Islam Gave to Humanity" in A. Ahmed, *Islam – its meaning and message*, p. 202.
52 Ahmed, *Living Islam*, p. 37.
53 Q. 42:37.
54 Q. 24:2.
55 J. Jornier, *How to Understand Islam* (London: SCM, 1989), p. 54.
56 A. Rahman, *Islam* (London: Seerah Foundation, 1980), p. 77.
57 *Ibid.*, p. 110.
58 K. Brown and M. Palmer, *The Essential Teachings of Islam* (London: Arrow, 1990 reprint of 1987 edition), p. 95.
59 Rahman, *Islam*, p. 97.
60 *Ibid.*, p. 195.
61 Q. 5:60.
62 Brown and Palmer, *The Essential Teachings of Islam*, p. 111.
63 Abdalati, *Islam in Focus*, p. 96.
64 Rahman, *Islam*, p. 115.
65 Q. 2:217.
66 Azzan, *The Eternal Message of Muhammad*, p. 98.
67 Q. 2:179.
68 Brown and Palmer, *The Essential Teachings of Islam*, p. 116.

69 Rahman, *Islam*, p. 133.
70 Ruthven, *Islam in the World*, p. 84.
71 Abdalati, *Islam in Focus*, p. 88.
72 Ruthven, *Islam in the World*, p. 35.
73 Brown and Palmer, *The Essential Teaching of Islam*, p. 119.
74 Rahman, *Islam*, p. 142.
75 K. Ahmad, *Family Life in Islam* (Leicester: The Islamic Foundation, 1974), p. 14.
76 Ahmad, *Family Life in Islam*, p. 16.
77 *Ibid.*, p. 27.
78 A. Elkholy, "The Concept of Community in Islam" in K. Ahmad, Z. Ansari, *Islamic Perspectives* (Leicester: The Islamic Foundation, 1979), p. 179.
79 H. al Ati, *The Family Structure in Islam* (Indianapolis: American Trust Publications, 1977), p. 185.
80 Q. 30:21.
81 al Ati, *The Family Structure in Islam*, p. 21.
82 *Ibid.*, p. 80.
83 M. Asad, "The Spirit of Islam" in Ahmad *Islam – its meaning and message*, p. 51.
84 Q. 8:76.
85 M. Saud, *Concept of Islam* (Indianapolis: American Trust Publications, 1983), p. 131.
86 *Ibid.*, p. 114.
87 *Ibid.*, p. 117.
88 Q. 4:3.
89 Q. 5:7.
90 Q. 2:220.
91 B. 67:42 (from the collection of Muhammad al-Bukhari – see note 33).
92 MM 3280 (this quotation is from the composite collection of al-Tabrizi known as the *Mishkat al-masabih* – see note 33).
93 N. 25.6 (from the collection of al-Nasa'i – see note 33).
94 MM 218 (see note 92).
95 Q. 33:59.
96 Ahmad, *Family Life in Islam*, p. 17.
97 Q. 2:228.
98 Q. 4:38.
99 TR 10:11 (from the collection of al-Tirmidhi – see note 33).
100 Ahmad, *Family Life in Islam*, p. 138.
101 Q. 2:228.
102 Fatima Heeren and B. Lemu, *Women in Islam* (Leicester: The Islamic Foundation, 19780 p. 43.
103 Q. 5:3.
104 Q. 5:92.
105 Q. 29:56.
106 *IQRA Trust Information Sheet* (1991).
107 S. Ashraf, *Islam* (Cheltenham: Stanley Thornes, 1991), p. 125.
108 In M. McDermott and M. Ahsan, *The Muslim Guide* (Leicester: The Islamic Foundation, 1980), p. 47.
109 R. Kendrick, *Islam* (Oxford: Heinemann. 1981), p. 119.
110 Q. 29:45–6.
111 F. Gumley and B. Redhead, *The Pillars of Islam* (London: BBC Books, 1990), p. 8.
112 M. Ruthven, *A Satanic Affair* (London: The Hogarth Press, 1991), p. 72.
113 Ahmed, *Living Islam*, pp. 210–11.

Chapter 4   Hindusim

1 E. Gough, *The Philosophy of the Upanishads: Ancient Indian Metaphysics* (New Delhi: Cosmo, 1979), p. 38.
2 See J. C. Heesterman, "Brahman" in M. Eliade (ed.). *The Encyclopedia of Religion* (hereafter *ER*) vol. 2 (New York: Macmillan, 1987), p. 295.
3 1:21; 11:42; 18:73.
4 3:15; 8:3,4,11,21,28; etc.
5 2:25,28;   7:24;   8:18,20,21;   9:2,3,4; 12:,1,3,5; 13:5.
6 *Taittiriya Upanisad* 2:1:11.
7 1:3:28, translator S. Radhakrishnan, *The Principal Upanisads* (New Delhi: Indus, 1994 reprint of 1953 edition), p. 162.
8 See A. Hiltebeitel, "The Indus Valley 'Proto-Siva", Reexamined through Reflections on the Goddess, the Buffalo, and the Symbolism of *vahanas*" *Anthropos* 73 (1978), pp. 769, 770.
9 *Ibid.*, pp. 768–9.
10 See B. and R. Allchin, *The Rise of Civilization in India and Pakistan* (Cambridge: Cambridge University Press, 1982), p. 213.
11 See J. Fowler, *Hinduism: Beliefs and Practices* (Brighton: Sussex Academic Press, 1997), pp. 91–2.
12 J. C. Heesterman, "Vedism and Brahmanism" in Eliade, *ER*, vol. 15, p. 224.
13 T. W. Organ, *Hinduism: Its Historical Development* (Woodbury New York: Barron's Educational Series Inc., 1974), p. 64.
14 *Rg Veda* 7:89:5, translator R. T. H. Griffith, *The Hymns of the Rgveda* (Delhi: Motilal Banarsidass, 1991 reprint of 1973 new, revised edition).
15 The symbolism associated with the deities varies considerably amongst sources, but an excellent outline of the symbolism of the iconography of Visnu can be found in Alain Daniélou's work, *The Myths and Gods of India* (Rochester, Vermont: Inner Traditions

International, 1991, first published 1985), pp. 152–63. Similar full discussion of the images of Siva can also be found on pp. 213–21.

16 *Bhagavad Gita* 4:7–8.

17 *Brahmavaivarta* 4:16 cited in J. M. Koller, *The Indian Way* (New York: Macmillan, 1982), p. 226.

18 See L. Siegel, *Sacred and Profane Dimensions of Love in Indian Traditions as Exemplified in the Gitagovinda of Jayadeva* (Delhi: Oxford University Press, 1990 reprint of 1978 edition).

19 T. B. Coburn, "Devi The Great Goddess" in Hawley, J. S. and Wulff, D. M. (eds), *Devi: Goddesses of India* (Berkeley, Los Angeles, London: University of California Press), p. 35.

20 D. R. Kinsley, "Kali: Blood and Death Out of Place" in Hawley and Wulff, *Devi: Goddesses of India*, p. 82.

21 See the foreword by A. L. Basham in J. N. Tiwari, *Goddess Cults in Ancient India with Special Reference to the First Seven Centuries AD* (Delhi: Sundeep Prakasham).

22 M. Brand, "A New Hindu Goddess" *Hemisphere: An Asian Australian Magazine* 26, no. 6 (May/June 1982), p. 382.

23 *Mandukya Upanisad* 1:1:59 translator A. Daniélou, *The Myths and Gods of India*, p. 39.

24 See also A. Mookerji, *Kali: The Feminine Force* (London: Thames and Hudson, 1988), pp. 34–5 for a good description of the lotus in Tantric symbolism.

25 Translators and editors S. Radhakrishnan and C. A. Moore, *A Sourcebook in Indian Philosophy* (Princeton, New Jersey: Princeton University Press, 1989, first published 1973), p. 184.

26 Part 3, 10:13.

27 G. Flood, *An Introduction to Hinduism* (Cambridge: Cambridge University Press, 1996), p. 53.

28 *Bhagavad Gita* 3:35.

29 R. Mehta, *The Call of the Upanishads* (Delhi: Motilal Banarsidass, 1990 reprint of 1970 edition), p. 2.

30 *Bhagavad Gita* 2:47.

31 M. Biardeau, *Hinduism: The Anthropology of a Civilization* translated by Richard Nice (Delhi: Oxford University Press, 1992 impression of 1989 English translation), p. 91.

32 See J. B. Carmen, "Bhakti" in Eliade, *ER*, vol. 2, p. 130.

33 18:64–66.

34 F. W. Clothey, "Tamil Religions" in Eliade, *ER*, vol. 15, p. 262.

35 *The Anthropology of a Civilization*, p. 117.

36 R. Dutt, *The Ramayana and the Mahabharata* (New York: Dent, 1978 reprint of 1910 edition), p. 156.

37 *Rg Veda* 10:90.

38 D. Killingley et al., *Hindu Ritual and Society* (Newcastle upon Tyne: Grevatt and Grevatt, 1991), p. 5.

39 Each of the three *gunas* is associated with the *Trimurti*, the triad of deities, Visnu (*sattva*), Siva (*tamas*) and Brahma (*rajas*). Thus these three deities are believed to have their representative factors in all existence. This demonstrates very well the unity of all existence and the particular relationship between microcosm and macrocosm.

40 *An Introduction to Hinduism*, p. 59.

41 Killingley et al., *Hindu Ritual and Society*, p. 9.

42 *An Introduction to Hinduism*, p. 198.

43 See C. J. Fuller, *The Camphor Flame: Popular Hinduism and Society in India* (India: Viking, 1992), p. 51.

44 *Hinduism Today*, June (1996), vol. 18, no. 6, p. 26.

45 See Babb, *The Divine Hierarchy: Popular Hinduism in Central India* (New York: Columbia University Press, 1975), p. 106.

46 Fuller, *The Camphor Flame*, p. 73.

47 *Ibid.*, p. 74.

48 Babb, *The Divine Hierarchy*, pp. 48–9.

49 *Bhagavad Gita* 9:26, 27.

50 *The Camphor Flame*, p. 70.

51 See Mookerji, *Kali: The Feminine Force*, pp. 30ff.

52 See Killingley, *Hindu Ritual and Society*, p. 16 and Babb, *The Divine Hierarchy*, p. 79.

53 Babb, *The Divine Hierarchy*, p. 82.

54 See R. Lannoy, *The Speaking Tree* (Oxford: Oxford University Press, 1971), p. 300.

55 See Fuller, *The Camphor Flame*, p. 22.

56 See O. Cole and V. P. Kanitkar, *Teach Yourself World Faiths: Hinduism* (London: NTC Publishing Group Hodder and Stoughton, 1995), p. 53.

57 *The Divine Hierarchy*, p. 82.

58 P. Bahree, *Hinduism* (London: Batsford, 1984), p. 18.

59 Fuller, *The Camphor Flame*, p. 95.

60 *Bhagavad Gita* 17:8.

61 *Ibid.* verse 9.

62 *Ibid.*, verse 10.

63 B. Beck, "Colour and Heat in South Indian Ritual", in *Man (N.S.)*, (1969), vol. 4, pp. 553–72.

64 Babb, *The Divine Hierarchy*, p. 30.
65 M. Marriott, "The Feast of Love" in M. Singer (ed.), *Krishna: Myths, Rites and Attitudes* (Chicago: University of Chicago Press, 1968), pp. 210ff.
66 See J. S. Hawley, "Prologue: The Goddesses in India" in Hawley and Wulff, *Devi: Goddesses of India*.
67 Fuller, *The Camphor Flame*, p. 109.
68 S. M. Bhardwaj, *Hindu Places of Pilgrimage in India: A Study in Cultural Geography* (California: University of California Press, 1983), p. 228.
69 See R. Barber, *Pilgrimages* (Woodbridge: The Boydell Press, 1991), p. 87.

Chapter 5 Buddhism

1 F. E. Reynolds and C. Hallisey, "Buddhism" in M. Eliade (ed.) *The Encyclopedia of Religion* (hereafter *ER*) vol. 2 (New York: Macmillan, 1987), p. 335.
2 Cf. for example Paul Williams' view that the *dharmakaya* is equatable with the teaching of the Buddha, in *Mahayana Buddhism: The Doctrinal Foundations* (London: Routledge, 1989), p. 172, and Edward Conze's statement that "The Mahayana writings, and in particular the *Prajnaparamita* Sutras, are almost exclusively concerned with the problem of the Unconditioned, nothing but the Absolute over and over again." *Buddhist Thought in India: Three Phases of Buddhist Philosophy* (London: Allen & Unwin, 1983 reprint of 1962 edition), p. 202.
3 *The Buddha* (London: Temple Smith, 1973), p. 120.
4 This is the Pali term associated with the Theravadin school of thought which retains Pali terminology and scriptures. The term *dharma* is the Sanskrit equivalent and is associated with the Mahayana strands of Buddhism.
5 R. H. Robinson and W. L. Johnson, *The Buddhist Religion: A Historical Introduction* (Belmont, California: Wadsworth Publishing Company, 1982: first published 1970), p. 6.
6 The date is according to southern Buddhist tradition. Northern Buddhist tradition dates his birth to 460 BCE.
7 Ling, *The Buddha*, p. 89.
8 P. Harvey, *An Introduction to Buddhism* (Cambridge: Cambridge University Press, 1992 reprint of 1990 edition), p. 15.
9 See A. K. Warder, *Indian Buddhism* (Delhi: Motilal Banarsidass, 1980 second revised edition), p. 45.
10 For example Ling, *The Buddha*, p. 95. Siddhatta's son, Rahula, it seems, was born on this same day.
11 See for example Harvey, *An Introduction to Buddhism*, p. 18.
12 From the *Buddhacarita* 13: 72–3 translator E. Cowell, *The Buddha Carita or The Life of the Buddha* (Delhi: Cosmo, 1977), p. 147.
13 E. Conze, *Buddhist Scriptures* (Harmondsworth: Penguin, 1959), p. 51.
14 *Ibid., p.* 47.
15 "The Four Noble Truths", *The Middle Way*, vol. 71, 1996, p. 162.
16 197–200 translator E. Easwaran, *The Dhammapada* (London: Arkana, 1987 edition: first published 1986), p. 138.
17 *The Buddhist Reliigion*, p. 16: "it is the mortal realm into which karma-laden beings are reborn to experience endlessly transforming destinies determined totally by their prior choices and actions in this and previous lives".
18 For example in the *Jatakas* and in the reincarnation of Tibetan *lamas*.
19 R. Gombrich, *Theravada Buddhism: A Social History from Ancient Benares to Modern Colombo* (London: Routledge and Kegan Paul, 1988), p. 67.
20 For an excellent discussion of these three aspects see R. Gombrich, *How Buddhism Began: The Conditioned Genesis of the Early Teachings* (London: Athlone, 1996), pp. 110ff.
21 *Theravada Buddhism* p. 63.
22 This is a good example of areas of Buddhism which border on belief in reintion rather than rebirth, for good merit is sought after in order to procure a better birth in the next existence. It is thus the lay element of Theravada Buddhism which tends to retain the more general Hindu conceptions of *karma* and *samsara*.
23 For a full discussion and analysis of the precepts see H. Saddhatissa, *Buddhist Ethics: The Path to Nirvana* (London: Wisdom, 1987: first published 1970), chapter 4, pp. 73–98.
24 *Mahaparinibbana Sutta* 2:25, translator M. Walshe, *Thus Have I Heard: The Long Discourses of the Buddha* (London: Wisdom, 1987), p. 245.
25 *Ibid.*, 6:7 translator Walshe p. 270.
26 See Gombrich, *Theravada Buddhism*, p. 74.
27 For an excellent and detailed insight into the life of the Theravadin monk in Sri Lanka see M. Carrithers, *The Forest Monks of Sri*

Lanka (Delhi: Oxford University Press, second impression 1986, first published 1983) and for a more general and historically detailed view see S. Dutt, *Buddhist Monks and Monasteries of India: Their History and Their Contribution to Indian Culture* (Delhi: Motilal Banarsidass, 1988, first published by George Allen & Unwin Ltd., 1962).

28 At Bodh Gaya, the place where the Buddha attained enlightenment, there was a conference of Buddhist nuns in 1987 which led to the establishment of an organization called Sakyadhita "Daughters of the Buddha". The aim of the organization was the revival of the order of Buddhist nuns and to try to discover an unbroken line of *bhikkunis* somewhere in the world. There was some opposition from monastic male orders, particularly the Sri Lankans. Some of the members of Sakyadhita were officially ordained at Los Angeles in the United States and a group from Britain founded the Amaravati Buddhist Centre in Hertfordshire and a training monastery at Chithurst in Kent. At Chithurst the inferiority of the nuns to any visiting monks is clearly evident when the nuns bring their hands together before their faces in veneration before addressing any monk: the action is not reciprocated from monk to nun. And while monks kneel on a raised platform around a magnificent *rupa* of the Buddha during *puja*, the nuns occupy a lower area near the rear of the room with visitors and novices. (See Y. S. Chindoo-Roy, *Aspects of Theravada Buddhism*, unpublished dissertation, UWCN, 1990).

29 *Tevijja Sutta* 13.76ff translator Walshe, p. 194.

30 R. Gombrich, "Buddhism in Ancient India" in H. Bechert and R. Gombrich, *The World of Buddhism* (London: Thames and Hudson, 1984), p. 81.

31 "The Buddha" in *The World of Buddhism*, p. 57.

32 E. Lamotte, *History of Indian Buddhism: from the Origins to the Saka Era* (translated from the French by Sara Webb-Boin, Louvain-la-neuve: Université Catholique de Louvain, Institut Orientaliste, 1988, original French edition 1958), p. 165.

33 See *Digha Nikaya* 3:181 and 185–91.

34 "Mahayana Buddhism" in *The World of Buddhism* p. 90.

35 *Buddhism: An Outline of its Teachings and Schools* (London: Rider & Co. 1973), p. 102.

36 *Ibid.*

37 *The Diamond Sutra* (Leicester: Buddhist

Publishing Group, n.d.), p. 21.

38 *Ibid.*, p. 22.

39 See E. Conze, *A Short History of Buddhism* (London: Unwin, 1988), p. 61.

40 This point is very well illustrated in E. Herrigel, *Zen in the Art of Archery*, Routledge and Kegan Paul, 1982 reprint of 1953 edition).

41 Translator A.W. Watts, *The Way of Zen* (Harmondsworth: Penguin, 1957), pp. 204–8.

42 *Ibid.*

43 *Ibid.*

44 Basho, *Haiku* (translator Lucien Stryk, London: Penguin 1995), pp. 4, 9, 18, 31 and 42, respectively.

45 Brian Gay, a lay minister of the Order of Buddhist Contemplatives in a conversation with the author, April 1997.

46 H. Benoit, *The Supreme Doctrine* (Brighton: Sussex Academic Press, 1995) first published in English in 1955 by Routledge and Kegan Paul), p. 25.

47 See F. Jikai, "Jodoshu", in Eliade, *ER*, vol. 8, p. 105.

48 "Jodo Shinshu", in Eliade, *ER*, vol. 8, p. 101.

49 *Ibid.*, p. 102.

50 Y. Kirimura, *Outline of Buddhism* (Tokyo: Nichiren Shoshu International Center, 1982 reprint of 1981 edition), p. 15.

51 *Buddhism in the First Millennium* (translated by Burton Watson, New York: Kodansha International, 1977), p. 126.

52 R. Causton, *Nichiren Shoshu Buddhism: An Introduction* (London: Rider, 1991 reprint of 1988 edition), pp. 212–13.

53 *Ibid.*, p. 101.

54 *Ibid.*

55 B. Wilson and K. Dobbelaere, *A Time to Chant: The Soka Gakkai Buddhists in Britain* (Oxford: Clarendon Press, 1994), p. 6.

56 *Ibid.*, p. 22.

57 "The Art of Living: An Introduction to Nichiren Shoshu Buddhism", *UK Express* no. 180, June 1986 p. 24.

58 "Tibetan Religions" in Eliade, *ER*, vol. 14, p. 500.

59 D. Snellgrove, "Tibetan Buddhism", in Eliade, *ER*, vol. 2, p. 493.

60 For an excellent discussion of the four schools see J. Powers, *Introduction to Tibetan Buddhism* (New York: Snow Lion, 1995), pp. 313–430.

61 See L. S. Kawamura, "Tara", in Eliade, *ER*, vol. 14, p. 338.

62 H. Guenther, "Buddhism in Tibet", Eliade, *ER*, vol. 2, p. 406.

63 "Esoteric Buddhism", in Eliade, *ER*, vol. 2, p. 474.
64 E. Conze, *Buddhism: Its Essence and Development* (Cassiter, 1974), p.178.
65 J. Powers, *Introduction to Tibetan Buddhism*, p. 227.
66 See P. Kvaerne, "Tibetan Religions" in Eliade, *ER*, vol. 12, p. 501.
67 See Wilson and Dobbelaere, *A Time to Chant*, p. 19.
68 Jiyu Kennett, *The Liturgy of the Order of Buddhist Contemplatives for the Laity* (California: Shasta Abbey Press, 1990 revised edition).
69 *Ibid.*, p. 45.
70 See E. Turner and P. Freze, "Marriage", in Eliade, *ER*, vol. 9, p. 220.
71 From the Funeral Address given to the author at the SGI UK Headquarters at Taplow Court, Berkshire.
72 Also termed *Vaisakha* (Indian) or *Visakha* (Thai). *Vesak/Wesak* is the Sinhalese term.
73 C. Erricker, *Teach Yourself World Faiths: Buddhism* (Chicago: NTC Publishing Group, 1995), p. 144.
74 *Ibid.*, p. 148.
75 *Ibid.*
76 Powers, *Introduction to Tibetan Buddhism*, p. 191.
77 *Ibid.*, p. 196.
78 *Ibid.*, p. 201.

Chapter 6 Sikhism

1 W. H. McLeod, *The Evolution of the Sikh Community* (London: Oxford University Press), pp. 20–36.
2 *The Sikh Courier International*, vol. 28, no. 65 (London, 1988), p. 43 (hereafter, *SCI*).
3 W. O. Cole, P. S. Sambhi, *The Sikhs: Their Religious Beliefs and Practices* (London: Routledge, 1978), p. xvii. Cf. 2nd edition (Sussex Academic Press, 1995), p. 43.
4 *Guru Granth Sahib* 150 (hereafter, *AG*).
5 A *Sufi* was one who accepted the more mystical path to God in the Muslim faith. It is doubtful whether Nanak was directly influenced in any way by the *Sufis*, despite his early dress. Many *Sufis* had joined the movements of the *Sants*, mystical thinkers who searched for a more inward and non-ritualistic expression of spirituality. Though not characterized by formal beliefs, some of the *Sant* teachings are similar to those of Nanak. But this would be inevitable, given the mystical quest which itself has certain general characteristics. If Nanak gained anything from *Sufis* or *Sants*, he placed his own distinctive stamp on such beliefs.
6 W. H. McLeod, *The Evolution of the Sikh Community*, p. 39.
7 *Adi Granth* (*var* 1, *pauri* 45).
8 I. Bannerjee, "Guru Angad: The Foundation of the Sikh Panth", in *SCI*, vol. 27, no. 64, 1987, p. 1.
9 *The Sikhs*, 1995 edition, p.19.
10 *Ibid.*, p. 20.
11 See Cole and Sambhi, *The Sikhs*, 1995 edition, pp. 34, 97–8.
12 *The Evolution of the Sikh Community*, p. 44.
13 Madanjit Kaur, "Amritsar under Guru Arjan Dev and Guru Hargobind (1581–1634)", *SCI*, vol. 28, no. 65, 1988, p. 22.
14 *AG* 1136.
15 *The Sikhs*, 1995 edition, p. 27.
16 See "Guru Arjan Martyred: Shamanistic Law" (author not cited) *SCI*, vol. 31, no. 72, 1991, pp. 19–24.
17 *SCI*, vol. 28, no. 65, 1988, p. 25.
18 S. S. Kapoor, 'Guru Hargobind: the founder of "Miri" and "Piri"', *SCI*, vol. 31, no. 72, 1991, p. 3.
19 *The Evolution of the Sikh Community*, p. 4.
20 *Ibid.*, p.13.
21 *SCI*, vol. 28, no. 65, 1988, p. 45.
22 *The Evolution of the Sikh Community*, p. 13.
23 *The Sikhs*, 1995 edition, p. 25.
24 See Khushwant Singh, "Guru Angad: The Building of the Sikh Church", *SCI*, vol. 27, no. 64, 1987, p.12.
25 *AG*, *var* 26.
26 Lakhinder Singh, Satinder Singh, *The Supreme Sacrifice of Guru Tegh Bahadur* (Southall: The Sikh Missionary Society, 1985 reprint of 1975 edition), p. 28.
27 H. S. Shan "Guru Tegh Bahadur: A Unique Martyr", *SCI*, vol. 33, no. 75, 1993, p. 4
28 D. K. Varma, "Guru Gobind Singh's Relations with Emperor Aurangzeb", *SCI*, vol. 31, no. 72, 1991, pp. 12–14.
29 *The Evolution of the Sikh Community*, p. 51.
30 *The Sikhs*, 1995 edition, p. 36.
31 *Ibid.*
32 *SCI*, vol. 28, no. 65, 1988, p. 42.
33 K. Singh, "Guru Gobind Singh", *SCI*, vol. 31, no. 72, 1991, p. 9.
34 Cited in Cole and Sambhi, *The Sikhs*, 1995 edition, p. 38.
35 W. H. McLeod, *Who is a Sikh?* (Oxford: Clarendon Press, 1989), p. 4.

36 Cole and Sambhi, *The Sikhs*, 1995 edition, p. 194.
37 *Ibid.*, pp. 182–99.
38 "EK ONKAR, OM AND OANKAR", *SCI*, vol. 29, no. 67, 1989, p. 30.
39 See Sarap Singh Alag, "Varied sentiments for the Golden Temple", *SCI*, vol. 26, no. 62, 1986, pp. 36–7.
40 See S.S. Bhatti, "The Golden Temple. A Spiritual Marvel of Architecture", *SCI*, vol. 32, no. 74, 1992, pp. 8–11.
41 D. Davies, "Religion of the Gurus: The Sikh Faith", R. P. Beaver et al. (eds) *The World's Religions* (Tring, Hertfordshire: Lion, 1982), p. 202.
42 R. S. Wahiwala, "Kirtan (Devotional Music)", *Sikh Bulletin* no. 6, 1989, p. 20, (hereafter *SB*).
43 J. Singh Sarna, "Importance of Kirtan in Gurmat", *SCI*, vol. 32, no. 74, 1992, p. 12.
44 R.S. Wahiwala, "Kirtan (Devotional Music)" *SB*, no. 6, 1989, p.18.
45 Shamsher Singh, "The Concept of Prayer in Sikhism", *SCI*, vol. 28, no. 66, 1988, p. 6.
46 *AG* 1429.
47 See Kirpal Singh, "An Historical Perspective of the Janam-Sakhis", *SCI*, vol. 34, no. 77, 1994, p.5.
48 "Translation of Gurbani: Our Difficulties", *SCI*, vol. 30, no. 70, 1990, p. 69. Cf. D. Singh, "A Welcome Concern about the translation of Gurbani", *SCI*, vol. 32, no. 73, 1992, pp. 12–13.
49 B. Bhogal, "Interpretative Ideals Concerning Sikhism and Gurbani", *SB*, no. 13, 1996, p. 11.
50 J. M. Koller, *The Indian Way* (New York: Macmillan, 1982), p. 340.
51 Gurinder Singh Sacha, *The Sikhs and their Way of Life* (Southall, Middlesex: The Sikh Missionary Society, 1982), p. 33.
52 *Japji.*
53 *AG* 463
54 *AG* 1128.
55 W. H. McLeod (ed.) *Textual Sources for the Study of Sikhism* (Manchester University Press, 1984), p. 54.
56 *AG* 473.
57 *The Sikhs*, 1995 edition, p. 119.
58 *Ibid.*, p. 131.
59 *Ibid.*, p. 120.
60 *Ibid.*
61 *AG* 788.
62 *AG* 963.
63 *AG* 1126
64 *AG* 13.
65 *AG* 345.
66 *AG* 444.
67 See Cole and Sambhi, *The Sikhs*, 1995 edition, pp. 194–6.
68 *AG* 16.
69 Guru Nanak, *AG* 83.
70 Guru Nanak, *AG* 349.
71 Guru Amar Das, *AG* 363.
72 *The Evolution of the Sikh Community*, p. 88.
73 *Ibid.*
74 *The Sikhs*, 1995 edition, p. 137.

Glossary

Judaism

Adonai literally "Lord", a term used by Jews to avoid using the name of God.

Amidah a Jewish prayer.

Ark the cupboard in which the *Torah* scrolls are kept in the *synagogue*, originally the chest in which the Israelites transported the two tablets of stone on which the Law was written.

Ashkenasi one of the two main cultural streams of Judaism which embraced Jews of northern and eastern Europe.

bar mitzvah "son of the commandment", the coming of age ceremony when a Jewish boy becomes thirteen years and one day.

bat mitzvah "daughter of the commandment", a ceremony held by Liberal and Reform Jews when their daughters attain the age of twelve, but unrecognized in Orthodox Judaism.

b'rit the covenant between God and the Children of Israel.

bimah a raised platform in the *synagogue* from which worship is conducted.

circumcision the physical sign of the covenant.

get the religious document of divorce which the husband hands to his wife.

hallah loaves baked for the Sabbath to remind the Jews of the *manna* they ate in the Wilderness.

Hanukah the Jewish Festival of light.

hanukkiyah a nine-branched candlestick used solely in the Festival of *Hanukah*.

Hasid literally "the pious one", a branch of Orthodox Judaism.

kappel see *kippah*

kashrut the dietary laws observed by Orthodox Jews.

kippah an embroidered silk skull cap.

kosher acceptable to God.

menorah the oldest symbol of Judaism, a seven or nine-branched candlestick.

mezuzah a small case found on the doorposts of Jewish homes containing passages from the *Torah*.

minyan a quorum of ten males necessary to conduct worship from the *Torah* scroll.

Mishnah the written record of what was originally the oral interpretation of the *Torah*, which provided a "fence" around the *Torah*.

mitzvah "commandment" (plural *mitzvot*).

mohel the Jew who performs the operation of circumcision.

Pesah the Festival of the Passover.

patul unacceptable to God.

Purim the Festival of Lots.

rabbi originally scribes or copyists who recorded the words of the *Torah*, their accumulated knowledge made them authorities or "teachers" of the Law, i.e. lawyers.

Rosh Hashanah literally "Head of the Year", the Jewish New Year's Day".

sabbat "rest", the Jewish Sabbath and the only day in the Jewish week which has a name. *Sabbat* begins at sunset on Friday and ends at sunset on Saturday.

Seder "order", a special meal on the first night of the Passover.

Sephardi one of the two main cultural streams of Judaism which included mainly Mediterranean Jews.

Shavuot the Festival of Weeks, also called Pentecost.

Shema The most well-known Jewish prayer, found in *Deuteronomy* 6:4–9.

shohet a professional slaughterer who ensures that the ensuing meat is *kosher*.

shofar the ram's horn trumpet.

sofer a trained scribe.

Sukkot the harvest festival also known as "Tabernacles" and "Booths".

synagogue "gathering"; a gathering of Jews for the purpose of worship, education or meeting; a Greek word for the Hebrew *Knesset*.

Talmud sometimes known as the *Babylonian Talmud*, this great work is a compilation of the *Mishnah* and the *Gemara*.

tallit a prayer shawl.

tefillin two leather boxes containing passages from the *Torah* bound by leather straps to the upper arm and forehead, and worn by Orthodox Jewish men at morning weekday prayer.

Torah the *Law* or *Instruction* given by God to his Chosen People, also the name given to the first five books of the *Bible*.

tzitzit the four white tassels, one on each corner of the *tallit*.

yad "hand", the pointer which indicates the words of the text to the reader of the *Torah*.

yarmulka (Yiddish) see *kippah*.

YHWH the tetragrammaton, Hebrew letters which indicate the name of God, and pronounced *Adonai* by Jews not wishing to profane God's name.

Yom Kippur the Day of Atonement.

Christianity

Anabaptists a group who were members of a radical wing of the Reformation.

Anglican a member of the Church of England, or one of the Churches derived from it, e.g. the Church of Australia.

anthropomorphic literally "with human qualities and attributes"; the use of the human image for God

apostle literally "one who is sent"; the name given to the twelve chief disciples of Christ.

Apostles' Creed a statement of faith used *c.* 390 CE, but linked by legend to the Apostles.

Ascension the withdrawal of Christ into heaven after the crucifixion.

Atonement the saving that was gained for humankind by the death and Resurrection of Christ.

baptism the sacrament by which candidates are admitted to the Christian Church, used since the beginning of the religion, and the name from whence the Baptist church takes its name.

Bible the writings known as the *Old Testament*, being the writings of the Jewish religion, plus those of the *New Testament* written by those who had close contact with the teachings of Christ, collected by the Early Church.

bishop the highest order of clergy in the Anglican, Roman Catholic and Orthodox Churches, regarded as the successors of the apostles.

Calvinists those who were influenced by the Protestant reformer John Calvin.

charismatic a style of worship emphasized by the presence of the Holy Spirit.

Christology the interpretation of the human and divine natures of Christ.

Church (1) the collective term for the Christian community, local or universal; (2) a particular denomination, e.g. Church in Wales.

church the building in which Christians meet for worship.

clergy ordained ministers; spiritual leaders of the Church.

communicants those who participate in the sacrament of "Holy Communion", thereby entering into a "spiritual union" with Christ.

Creation the universe being brought about by God as an act of love, and the understanding that God is the Creator of all there is.

Creed the statement of Christian belief common to some Christians.

crucifixion death by the nailing and binding of the body to a cross of wood; a form of execution used extensively by the Romans during the time of Jesus.

denomination the different names by which the various groups within the orthodox Church are known.

disciples denotes those twelve men called by Christ at the outset of his ministry, who accompanied him throughout, and who continued to teach his ideology after his death.

divinization the tenet that God became man in order that humankind might become divine like God.

doctrine an approved teaching of the Church.

dogma principle, tenet or doctrinal system laid down by the authority of the Church.

ecumenical literally "one world"; a movement within the Church that seeks to unite all Christians to raise their belief above the problems of theology, ritual, dogma or politics, and become one.

Eucharist literally "thanksgiving"; a sacrament; the central act of Christian worship (other names: the Lord's or Last Supper, Holy Communion, Mass), conveying to the believer the Body and Blood of Christ through the partaking of bread and wine.

evangelical a description of those who place importance on the use of scripture and its use in the conversion of others.

Fall (the) how, through the disobedience of Adam and Eve in eating the "forbidden fruit" in the Garden of Eden, humankind entered into sin and evil, thereby altering God's original purpose for the world, and consequently share in their punishment.

gentiles a biblical term usually applied to non-Jews; also the name given by Mormons to non-Mormons.

gospel literally "good news"; the message of salvation through faith in Christ.

Gospel one of the four *New Testament* books (*Matthew, Mark, Luke* and *John*), in which the gospel is contained.

Grace a free gift of God that sanctifies human life.

Heaven a place where God, the saints and the "redeemed dead" are believed to reside.

holy the quality of religious feeling that permeates objects, buildings and people, and marks a sharp distinction with the profane.

Holy Spirit the third person of the Trinity, and the way in which God is perceived to be active in the world today.

icon an image, statue, painting, mosaic etc. of a sacred personage, usually Jesus, Mary, the apostles or the saints; a medium through which it is possible to worship God, although the *icon* itself is not worshipped.

iconostasis (Greek) the screen that separates the

congregation from the Sanctuary in Eastern Orthodox churches.

Incarnation the way in which God was revealed in the human form of Jesus.

Justification the doctrine that God acquits humankind of the punishment due to its sins because of the sacrifice of Christ.

Kingdom of God a teaching of Jesus, that Divine rule and God's purpose for the world will be evident at some final point in the future.

laity literally "people"; members of a denomination or sect who are not ordained.

Last Supper (also known as the Lord's Supper). The last meal Christ shared with his disciples, on the night of his arrest.

liturgy the written form of service contained in denominational prayer books.

martyr one persecuted, and prepared to die, for the faith.

Messiah literally "anointed"; the expected deliverer of the Jews, a descendant of the House of David.

missionary one who propagates the Christian faith.

Nicene Creed a statement of Christian belief, agreed at the Council of Nicea in 325 CE.

orthodox conventional belief; traditional doctrine.

Orthodox literally "right praise"; the term used to refer to the Christian Churches of the East.

Ordination the sacrament of priesthood and ministry, conferred by bishops, on those who wish to have authority to administer the other sacraments to members of the Church.

panentheism the doctrine that God is in all things, but is ultimately greater than everything.

pantheism the doctrine that the universe *is* God, or that all things are manifestations of God.

parable a short narrative with a hidden meaning, used by Christ to convey a deeper, spiritual significance.

Passover a Jewish festival celebrating the deliverance of the Jews from slavery in Egypt.

parish an area under the spiritual care and guidance of a priest or minister.

patriarch (1) one of the early leaders of Israel up to the time of Jacob; (2) a title dating from the sixth century for the bishops of Rome; (3) the title given to the heads of certain autocephalous (self-headed) Eastern Orthodox Churches, e.g. Russia and Bulgaria.

patristic refers to the theologians, writers and writings of the first period of the Church.

Penance a sacrament of the Roman Catholic and Orthodox Churches that puts emphasis on reconciliation to God and the Church.

piety refers to the need to be "holy" and act

with reverence in everyday life.

Pope literally "Father"; the title given to the Bishop of Rome, the Supreme Head of the Roman Catholic Church.

Protestant refers to those who protest at the practices and beliefs of the Roman Catholic Church; used from the sixteenth century.

Redemption the deliverance from sin, suffering and death given through belief in Jesus Christ.

Reformation the period of the sixteenth century when the influence of Roman Catholicism was resisted throughout Europe.

Resurrection the rising of Christ from the dead after his crucifixion.

sacrament a rite of the Church which is a sign of spiritual blessing or grace, believed to have been initiated by Christ himself; (applied by the Eastern, pre-Reformation Western and Roman Catholic Churches to the seven rites of Baptism, Confirmation, the Eucharist, Penance, Extreme Unction, Ordination and Matrimony; restricted by most Protestant Churches to two: Baptism and the Eucharist).

sacrosanct sacred and inviolable.

saints people who, through actions in their lifetime, were deemed to exhibit a "holiness" and conviction of faith in the teachings of Jesus Christ and the Church.

salvation the faith that God has "saved" humankind through the knowledge of life, death, resurrection and teachings of Jesus.

Schism the break in the unity of the Church, in 1054.

scriptures the collection of writings in the *Bible*, and the writings considered sacred to minority sects.

sect a religious group that claims that it alone has the authority of Christ, that is, salvation may only be achieved through adherence to its doctrines and practices.

spirituality practices and experiences achieved through prayer, meditation and reflection that sharpen the senses of all things "holy".

Theotokos (Greek) Mary, the Mother of God.

Transubstantiation the Roman Catholic doctrine of the mystical transformation of the bread and wine into the body and blood of Christ consumed at the Mass.

theology an intellectual investigation into religious beliefs which has many themes.

Trinity the doctrine that perceives of God as being in three parts but remaining one; that is, God the Father, God the Son and God the Holy Spirit.

Unction the process of anointing with oil, usually applied to the Sacrament of Anointing the Sick.

worship   thanksgiving and adoration of God.

Islam

adhan   the call to prayer issued by the *muezzin*.

ahadith   saying or tradition of the prophet Muhammad. Plural – *hadith*.

amin   Arabic form of Amen – "verily", "so be it".

asr   mid-afternoon prayer.

ayah   an individual verse of the *Qur'an*.

du'ah   private devotions.

Eid   a festival or time of happiness.

Eid-ul-Adha   festival of sacrifice which takes place at the end of the *hajj*.

Eid ul-Fitr   the second major festival of Islam which takes place at the end of   *Ramadan*.

fajr   dawn prayer.

hadith   sayings or traditions of Muhammad – plural of *ahadith*.

hafiz   a man who has memorized the *Qur'an*.

hafizah   a woman who has memorized the *Qur'an*.

hajj   the pilgrimage to Mecca which all Muslims should try to make once in their lifetimes. The fifth of the "five pillars of faith".

halal   that which the Muslim is allowed to take or to do.

haram   that which the Muslim is forbidden to take or to do.

hijrah   the flight of Muhammad and his followers from Mecca to Medina in the year 622 CE. This is the starting date of the Islamic calendar.

huffaz   those who have memorized the *Qur'an*.

ihram   the two white pieces of unsewn cloth which is the traditional dress of the male pilgrim on the *hajj*, and the spiritual state which this signifies.

ihsan   virtue and other qualities such as, kindness, compassion, reverence.

ijma'   consensus.

ijtihad   reason.

Imam   a Muslim religious leader.

iman   faith.

isha   night prayer.

jami'a   "a gatherer" – one of the names given to a mosque.

jumah   the noon congregational prayer performed on Friday.

ka'aba   the cube-shaped building which lies in the centre of the Grand Mosque   of Mecca.

Khalifah   Caliph   –   the   successors   to Muhammad as rulers of the Muslims.

Kursi-al Qur'an   lecterns.

Lailat-ul-Qadr   "the night of power" – the night the *Qur'an* was given to Muhamad, traditionally held to be the 27th of Ramadan.

maghrib   sunset prayer.

mahr   bride-gift – the goods or money given by the husband to his wife when they marry.

Mecca   the city where Muhamad was born and raised, and which is now the spiritual centre of Islam. Originally known as Bakkah.

Medina   the city to which Muhammad and his followers fled from the persecution in Mecca, and where Muhammad is buried.

mihrab   the alcove in a mosque which indicates the direction of Mecca.

Mina   a place approximately three miles from Mecca where Abraham is said to have sacrificed a ram. The place now plays an important role in the *hajj* in the rite of *mina*, the stoning of the three pillars which represent Satan.

masjid   "place of prostration" – one of the names given to a mosque.

minbar   pulpit.

minaret   tower of a mosque

mosque   the building where Muslims come together to worship.

muezzin   the person who issues the call to prayer, usually from the minaret.

Muhammad   a man through whom God revealed the *Qur'an*.

Qur'an   the Holy book of *Islam*.

qiblah   the direction of prayer.

rak'ah   literally "bending" – in this case in the ritual prayer movements.

Ramadan   the Islamic month during which the fast takes place.

salat   ritual prayer, the second of the "five pillars of faith".

sawm   fasting, the fourth of the "five pillars of faith".

shahadah   the traditional declaration of faith the first of the "five pillars of faith".

shari'ah   the Islamic system of law.

Shi'ite   the smallest of the two major sects of Islam.

shirk   literally "association". The act of associating anything else with God, e.g. idol-worship.

sunnah   the way of the prophet Muhammad.

Sunni   the largest of the two major sects of Islam.

surah   a chapter of the *Qur'an*.

tawaf   the ritual circumambulation of the *ka'aba*.

tawhid   unity.

ummah   community.

wudhu   ritual washing.

zakat   the poor-due, the third of the "five pillars of faith".

zakat-ul-fitr   non-obligatory alms, usually given at the end of Ramadan.

zamzam the well which sprouted at the feet of Ishmael when he and his mother Hagar were lost in the desert, and which now plays a role in the *hajj.*

zuhr midday prayer.

Hinduism

A guide to pronunciation of Sanskrit words
Sanskrit has a number of letters representing the English "s". Where the pronunciation of the "s" in the Sanskrit is as *sh*, as in English *she,* this will be indicated: where not indicated the pronunciation is an ordinary "s" as in English *sat.* Sanskrit also has a number of aspirated letters indicated with an "*h*" following the consonant. When these combinations of letters occur, the reader is advised to separate the two consonants in pronunciation to gain a more accurate sound: thus *artha* "wealth" is *art* (as in English *art*) plus *ha* (as in English *have*). The particular sound *th* as in English *that* or *theatre* should be avoided. Sanskrit consonants carry the vowel "*a*" with them, which is why translated Sanskrit words have so many "*a*"s in them, like *Mahabharata.* This "*a*" is normally more like the "*u*" in English word *but.* Where this is not so, diacritical marks are usually added in transliteration to indicate a change of sound. The text of this book does not contain these indicators but the reader will acquire a nearer pronunciation by using a "*u*" sound rather than the long "*a*" as in father. While these general ideas about pronunciation of words pertain specifically to the chapter on *Hinduism,* the tips are generally relevant also to the chapters *Buddhism* and *Sikhism.*

adharma contrary to what is right; evil. Cf. *dharma.*
Agni Vedic god of fire.
ahimsa non-violence.
Arjun one of the sons of Pandu and the main (human) character of the *Bhagavad-Gita.*
artha wealth and social status.
arti act of worship celebrating light.
Aryans migrant invaders of India from approximately 1500 BCE.
asram (pronounced *ashram*) place of quiet and solitude, often in a forest, where a Hindu sage lives alone or with his disciples.
asramas (pronounced *ashramas*) the four stages of life in Hinduism.
Atharva Veda "Knowledge of Incantations", one of the four *Vedas.*
atman the presence of Brahman as the deepest essence of the self in all entities; a synonym of Brahman.

Aum the sacred sound and symbol which represents Brahman in its unmanifest and manifest aspects.
avatars literally "descents", the incarnations of Visnu and his consort Laksmi.
avidya ignorance.
Bhagavad-Gita Hindu scripture dated to approximately the first two centuries BCE.
bhajans hymns in praise of a deity.
bhakta ardent devotee of a deity who expresses loving-devotion to the divine.
bhakti ecstatic loving-devotion to the divine.
bhakti marga the path of devotion.
bindi mark worn on the centre of the forehead to show that a woman is married.
Brahma Creator God.
brahmachari young boy at the first of the four stages of life, the stage of the student.
Brahman the impersonal Absolute of Hinduism which is the source of all manifest existence and which is present in all things as their deepest essence or *atman.*
Brahmin a priest and member of the most prestigious of the four classes of Hinduism.
chela disciple and student of a *guru.*
Dalit person outside the class system of Hinduism who was formerly termed an Untouchable.
darsan (pronounced *darshan*) literally "view" or "sight of" referring to audience with a deity.
deva male deity; literally "shining one".
devi female deity.
dharma what is right for the self, the class and caste, society and the universe.
Divali Hindu festival.
Durga Hindu Goddess, one of the energy forms of Siva.
Dussehra Hindu festival.
dvija twice-born, referring to those of the three classes of *Brahmins, Ksatriyas* and *Vaisyas* who undergo initiation into the Hindu religion at a sacred ceremony.
Ganesh Chaturhi Hindu festival.
garbagriha literally "womb-house", the central part of a temple where the main deity is enshrined.
gauna the ceremony marking the departure of a bride for the home of her new husband.
gopis cowherdesses.
gramadevatas village deities.
grhastha person at the second of the four stages of life, the stage of the householder.
gunas the three qualities or strands (like the strands of a rope), *sattva, rajas,* and *tamas,* which constitute all life.
guru enlightened spiritual teacher.
Hanuman monkey general who rescued Sita

from the demon Ravan in the *Ramayan*, now deified.

havan   an offering of fire in Hindu worship.

Holi   Hindu festival.

Indra   Vedic god of storm and thunder who was also king of the gods.

jati   birth and the caste system.

jivatman   the personality self.

jnana   intuitive knowledge.

jnana marga   the path of knowledge.

jutha   the "left-overs" of food offered to a deity, the deity having extracted the essence of the food.

kalas   (pronounced *kalash*) brass pot containing water, representative of a goddess.

Kali   Goddess characterized by ferocious appearance.

kama   pleasure, particularly sexual pleasure.

karma   literally "action" but also the theory of cause and effect i.e. action and reaction.

karma marga   the path of egoless action.

katcha   poor quality, impure food.

kirtan   hymn in praise of a deity.

Krisna   (pronounced Krishna) Hindu deity who is an incarnation of the great God Visnu.

Krisna-Janamastami   Hindu festival.

Ksatriya   (pronounced *Kshatriya*) person belonging to the second of the four Hindu classes of society, traditionally a warrior, ruler or administrator.

Laksman   (pronounced Lakshman) the brother of Ram in the *Ramayan*.

Laksmi   (pronounced Lakshmi) female Goddess of Fortune and consort of Visnu, sometimes called Sri.

linga   phallic symbol associated with the God Siva.

Mahabharat   Hindu epic scripture.

Mahadeva   "Great God", one of the names of the deity Siva.

Mahadevi   "Great Goddess", the Mother Goddess of Hinduism.

Mahasivatri   (pronounced *Mahashivatri*) Hindu festival.

mandal   Hindu temple which can also be used for socio-cultural purposes.

mandap/mandva   the canopy under which a wedding ceremony takes place.

mandir   a Hindu temple.

mantra   sacred syllables or sounds which contain in their essence divine cosmic power.

maya   illusion, particularly the illusion of the transient, impermanent, phenomenal world.

mehndi   long-lasting pattern made with henna dye on the hands of a woman at her wedding and sometimes at festival occasions.

moksa   liberation from the cycle of reincarnation, loss of the egoistic self, and union with Brahman.

monism   the theory that everything in the cosmos is a unity and is equated with the divine.

monotheism   belief in one personal god or goddess.

murti   the image and representation of a deity in a temple, shrine or in the home.

Namaskar/Namaste   "I bow to you", the greeting which acknowledges the *atman* in another person.

Navaratri   Hindu festival.

neti neti   literally "not this, not this", the expression used to denote that Brahman is beyond all dualities and human thought.

nirakara   "without form", referring to Brahman as Unmanifest.

nirguna   "without *gunas*", "without qualities" referring to Brahman as Unmanifest.

nitya   "obligatory", referring to aspects of religious practice.

panda   a temple priest at a pilgrimage site.

panentheism   the belief that the divine is in all things and unifies all things but is ultimately greater than all things.

pantheism   the belief that the divine is in all things and is equated with the totality of all.

Parvati   Goddess, the consort of the God Siva.

pinda   four balls of rice prepared on the twelfth day after someone has died to symbolize the union of the deceased with his or her forebears.

polytheism   belief in many personal gods and/or goddesses.

prasad   the grace of the deity given to the worshipper in the form of food after worship: see also *jutha*.

puja   honour, respect or worship of a deity or person.

pujari   temple or shrine priest who performs *puja*.

pukka   good quality food which is considered ritually pure.

purohit   a family priest or *guru*.

Purusa   (pronounced Purusha), literally "person": the original, primeval being the sacrifice of which was believed to create from its body the phenomenal world, in particular the four classes. Also a synonym of Brahman and therefore of *atman*.

Radha   a cowherdess who was the favourite of Krisna and an incarnation of the Goddess Laksmi, also a Goddess in her own right.

raja   a tribal chieftain, local ruler or monarch.

rajas   one of the three *gunas* or qualities in existence, associated with the creator God Brahma and representing the active energy in the universe.

rakhi   a band symbolizing protection which is tied round the wrists of males by girls at the estival of *Raksa Bandhan*.

Raksa Bandan (pronounced *Raksha Bandhan*) Hindu festival.

Ram An incarnation of the deity Visnu and hero of the epic the Ramayan.

Ramayan Hindu epic scripture.

Ram Navami Hindu festival.

Rg Veda "Royal knowledge", one of the four *Vedas*, the major Aryan scriptures.

sis Vedic seers, enlightened men who composed Vedic hymns and *upanisads*.

ta the Vedic cosmic norm which regulated all existence and to which all had to conform.

aguna manifest, referring to manifest aspects of Brahman.

Saivites (pronounced Shaivites) devotees of the deity Siva.

akara "with form", referring to the manifest aspects of Brahman.

akti (pronounced *shakti*) the female active energy in the universe.

Sama Veda "Knowledge of Chants", one of the four *Vedas*.

samsara reincarnation.

amskaras life-cycle rites.

sanatana dharma what is right for the universe.

sannyasin person at the last of the four stages of life, the stage of the wandering ascetic.

Santosi Ma (pronounced Santoshi Ma) a modern Hindu goddess.

saptapadi the seven steps taken by a couple during their marriage ceremony symbolizing seven different wishes for the future.

ari traditional dress for women consisting of a piece of material of five or six metres long which is draped around the body.

Sati consort of the God Siva, also called Uma.

sati voluntary burning of a widow on her husband's funeral pyre.

sattva one of the three *gunas* or qualities in existence, associated with the preserving God Visnu and representing light and spiritual evolution.

Savitr Vedic solar deity.

Sita the wife of Ram in the Hindu epic the *Ramayan* and an *avatar* of the Goddess Laksmi.

Siva (pronounced Shiva) one of the major deities of Hinduism.

smrti literally "memory" or "remembered": a category of sacred scriptures which contains much popular and devotional literature.

Soma Vedic deity equated also with a potent hallucinogenic drink.

sraddha ceremonies for the deceased in the twelve days following cremation.

srauta (pronounced *shrauta*) official sacrificial ritual of the Vedic period.

Sri (pronounced Shri) the Goddess Laksmi,

consort of Visnu.

sruti pronounced *shruti*) category of sacred scriptures which are "heard" or cognized by the ancient seers.

Sudra (pronounced *Shudra*) the fourth of the Hindu four classes, traditionally the servant class.

svadharma what is right for an individual.

tamas one of the three *gunas* or qualities in existence, associated with the dissolver God Siva and representing the inertia aspect in existence.

Tantras esoteric, mystical teachings.

tat tvam asi "That art thou", the equating of the *atman* and every being in total identity with *That*, which is Brahman.

theism belief in a personal god, goddess, gods or goddesses.

tilak the mark placed on the forehead of a devotee during ritual worship.

Trimurti literally "three-form", the Hindu trinity of three deities, Visnu, Siva and Brahma, representing the three qualities or *gunas* of all existence.

Ugadi Hindu festival.

Uma consort of the deity Siva.

upanayama ceremony of the sacred thread undertaken by the top three classes.

Upanisads (pronounced *Upanishad*) scriptures occuring at the end of the *Vedas* characterized by mystical and philosophical speculation on the nature of the self and Ultimate Reality.

Vaisnavites (pronounced Vaishnavites) devotees of the deity Visnu.

Vaisya (pronounced Vaishya) person belonging to the third of the four Hindu classes of society, traditionally an artisan or skilled labourer.

vanaprastha person at the third of the four stages of life, the stage of the forest dweller.

varna literally "colour", the word for the four-class system in Hinduism.

varnasramadharma what is right for class and stage of life.

Varuna Vedic deity of cosmic order.

Veda knowledge.

Vedangas rules on ritual, astronomy, morals, grammar and phonetics.

Vedas the four Vedic scriptures of *Rg*, *Sama*, *Yajur* and *Atharva*.

vidya knowledge.

Visnu (pronounced Vishnu) one of the major deities of Hinduism.

yajna sacrificial ritual.

Yajur Veda "Knowledge of Sacrificial Ritual", one of the four *Vedas*.

Yama ruler of the realm of the dead the "Land of the Fathers": he was the first man to die and therefore the welcomer of others to his realm.

yatra pilgrimage.

yoga discipline or "yoking" of the senses and the ego.

Buddhism

Abhidhamma Pali (Sanskrit *Abhidharma*): one of the "Three Baskets" of Buddhist scriptures containing discussion and commentary on the teaching of the Buddha; literally "higher knowledge".

ahimsa the doctrine of non-violence in relation to all things.

Aksobhya a *bodhisattva*.

Amida/Amitabha a buddha.

Amoghasiddhi a *bodhisattva*.

anatta Pali (Sanskrit *anatman*): the Buddhist doctrine of no-self.

anicca Pali (Sanskrit *anitya*): the Buddhist doctrine of impermanence – that nothing ever is but is always in a state of becoming.

arahat Pali (Sanskrit *arhat*): an enlightened person.

Asalha Puja Theravadin festival to celebrate the giving of the first sermon by the Buddha.

Avalokitesvara a buddha in Mahayana Buddhism.

bhikku (male) a Buddhist monk.

bhikkuni (female) a Buddhist nun.

Bodh Gaya the place where the Buddha became enlightened and an important pilgrimage site.

Bodhidharma the legendary founder of Ch'an Buddhism in China.

bodhisattva a buddha to be; a major concept of Mahayana Buddhism where it refers to one who vows to help all to attain buddhahood.

bodhi tree the name given to the tree under which the Buddha sat when he became enlightened.

brahma-vihara four sublime states: see *metta*, *karuna*, *mudita*, *upekkha*.

buddha one who is enlightened or awakened.

buddha-nature the buddhahood within all things.

butsudan a Japanese shrine.

Ch'an "meditation", the name given to a branch of Buddhism in China corresponding to, and being the foundation of, Japanese Zen.

Chokhor see *Asalha Puja*.

dagoba Sri Lankan monument housing relic(s) of the Buddha.

daimoku the chanting of the title, *Nam-myoho-renge-kyo* by Nichiren Shoshu and Nichiren Daishonin Buddhists.

Dalai Lama spiritual leader of one Tibetan monastic sect.

Dhamma Pali (Sanskrit *Dharma*): the teaching of the Buddha; Truth.

Dhammapada Important and popular Buddhist scripture.

Dharmakaya the "Truth body" of the Buddha, ultimate reality.

Dogen the founder of Japanese Zen Buddhism.

dukkha Pali (Sanskrit *duhkha*): pain, suffering, dis-ease, disharmony.

Eisei Founder of Zen Buddhism in Japan.

Gohonzon a scroll with the title of the *Lotus Sutra* inscribed on it, the focus of worship for Nichiren Shoshu and Nichiren Daishonin Buddhists.

gojukai ceremony at which a member of the Nichiren schools of Buddhism is presented with a *gohonzon*.

gongyo the chanting of parts of the *Lotus Sutra* by Nichiren Shoshu and Nichiren Daishonin Buddhists.

Hana Matsuri Japanese Mahayana Buddhist festival.

Higan Japanese Mahayana Buddhist festival held at the time of the equinoxes.

Hinayana "Small vehicle", the rather pejorative term given by Mahayana Buddhists to the conservative Buddhist schools of thought.

ichinen sanzen the theory of Nichiren sects of Buddhism which accepts the interconnectedness of all life through three thousand operative factors in any one given moment.

Jatakas stories relating the past lives of the Buddha.

jhana Pali (Sanskrit *dhyana*): meditation.

jiriki the path to enlightenment by "own effort".

Jodo-e a Japanese Mahayana Buddhist festival.

Joya no Kane a Japanese Mahayana Buddhist festival.

kamma Pali (Sanskrit *karma*): action and the fruits of acton.

karuna compassion, one of the four *brahma vihara*.

Kathina a Theravada Buddhist festival.

khandas Pali (Sanskrit *skandhas*) the five constituents which make up the self as we know it.

khwan the Thai belief in a spirit believed to accompany an individual throughout his or her life.

koan Rinzai Zen paradoxical riddle.

Ksala perahera a Theravada Buddhist festival.

Kusinara the site of the Buddha's death and an important pilgrimage site.

lama leader of a monastic sect in Tibetan Buddhism.

Losar the Tibetan New Year festival.

Lumbini Garden the place where the Buddha was born.

Magha Puja a Theravada Buddhist festival.

mahakaruna great compassion, one of the two pillars of Mahayana Buddhism.

Mahaparinibbana "Account of the Great Final Ninnana", the death of the Buddha.

Mahavairocana a buddha and the central buddha of Shingon Buddhism.

Mahayana "Great vehicle", the name given to the more progressive strands which emerged from early, conservative Buddhism.

mandalas geometric, symbolic designs used as aids in meditation.

mantra symbolic sounds and words.

Mara the Buddhist enemy of enlightenment.

metta loving-kindness, one of the four *brahma-vihara*.

mondo verbal interchange between Master and pupil in Rinzai Zen Buddhism.

Monlam Chenmo Tibetan Buddhist festival at the time of the New Year.

mudita sympathetic joy, one of the four *brahma-vihara*.

mudra symbolic hand positions.

Nahan-e Japanese Mahayana Buddhist festival.

Nam-myoho-renge-kyo the title of the *Lotus Sutra* chanted by Nichiren sects of Buddhism.

nembutsu the reciting of the name of the Buddha Amida/Amitabha as a means to enlightenment.

nibbana Pali (Sanskrit *nirvana*): enlightenment, total egolessness.

nirmanakaya "transformation body", a manifestation of a buddha in earthly form.

Obon a Japanese Mahayana Buddhist festival.

pagoda Japanese monument housing relics of the Buddha.

Pancha Sila the Five Moral Precepts basic to most Buddhism.

panna Pali (Sanskrit *prajna*): wisdom which brings enlightenment.

parinibbana Pali (Sanskrit *parinirvana*): the final extinction of the Buddha and the end of his rebirths.

paticcasamppada the Buddhist doctrine of dependent origination.

prajnaparamita highest wisdom; Mahayana scriptures.

puja honour, respect, gratitude.

Ratnasambhava a *bodhisattva*.

rupa image of a buddha or *bodhisattva*.

Sakyas (pronounced Shakya): tribe of people in northern India into which the Buddha was born.

Sakyamuni (pronounced Shakyamuni): "Wise one from the Sakyas", the name given to the Buddha by many Mahayana Buddhists.

samadhi concentration, the advanced state of meditation.

samanna Pali (Sanskrit *sramana*) one who rejected orthodox teachings and who searched for Truth independently.

samatha meditation.

sambhogakaya "glorious body" of a buddha.

samsara the process of rebirth.

Sangha the assembly of monks in Theravada Buddhism; the community of Buddhists in Mahayana Buddhism.

Sarnath Deer Park the place where the Buddha taught his first sermon, and a place of pilgrimage.

satori sudden, intuitive enlightenment in Rinzai Zen Buddhism.

Setsubon a Japanese Mahayana Buddhist festival.

Soka Gakkai Japanese Buddhist lay movement which accepts the teaching of the International Buddha Nichiren Daishonin.

stupa monument housing some relic(s) of the Buddha. See also *dagoba* and *pagoda*.

Sukhavati the paradisical realm of the Buddha Amida/Amitabha.

sunya (pronounced *shunya*): empty.

sunyata (pronounced *shunyata*): Emptiness, a major doctrine of Mahayana Buddhism that all things are empty of permanent essence.

sutta Pali (Sanskrit *sutra*) one of "Three Baskets"; a general term for a scripture.

svabhava own-being.

tanha craving, the cause of suffering and the second of the Buddha's *Four Noble Truths*.

Tantrism literally "loom"; the esoteric, mystical aspects of Buddhism.

Tara popular female *bodhisattva*.

Ten Worlds the theory of Nichiren sects of Buddhism that each individual at any moment has the potentiality for ten life conditions.

thera an elder, a monk.

Theravada "Way of the elders", the name given to the only surviving school of conservative Buddhism.

Three Jewels or *Three Refuges* The Buddha, the *Dhamma* and the *Sangha*.

Tipitaka Pali (Sanskrit *Tripitaka*): "Three Baskets", the scriptures of Theravada Buddhism and some Mahayana.

tulku *bodhisattvas* in Tibetan Buddhism who are born on earth many times for the purpose of asisting humankind.

upekkha equanimity, one of the four *brahma-vihara*.

urna the third eye of the Buddha.

usnisa the projection on the top of the Buddha's head which signifies his spirituality and great mind.

Vairocana a *bodhisattva*.

Vajrayana literally "diamond" or "adamantine

vehicle"; Tantric Buddhism, particularly as it is evident in Tibet.

Vassa the rainy season and a time for retreat to a monastery.

Vesak festival in Theravada Buddhism which celebrates the Birth, Enlightenment and Death of the Buddha.

Vinaya monastic rules, one of the "Three Baskets" which comprise orthodox Buddhist scriptures.

vipassana insight meditation.

wu-wei inaction; going with the flow of things.

yogin an adept at meditative practice.

zazen meditation and the name it is given in Japanese Zen Buddhism.

Sikhism

Adi Granth literally "First Collection." Another name for the Sikh scriptures, the *Guru Granth Sahib*.

akhand path a continuous reading of the *Guru Granth Sahib* which takes forty eight hours to complete.

Amar Das the third Guru. He called all the Sikhs together three times a year at the times of the three major Hindu festivals.

amrit the mixture of sugar crystals and water used as nectar in the Sikh initiation ceremony.

amrit pahul the Sikh initiation ceremony.

anand a set pattern to *diwan*, which follows the singing of *sabads*.

Angad "limb", the second Guru and successor of Nanak, formerly called Lehna. He collected the *sabads* of Nanak together and is acclaimed as having compiled a vernacular language in which they were written.

Ardas "To ask for what you desire", the special congregational prayer which ends *diwan*.

Arjan the fifth Guru, who completed Amritsar and collected all the hymns of his predecessors into the *Adi Granth*, the first version of the Sikh scriptures.

Baisakhi the Sikh spring festival, Hindu in origin, which always takes place on April 13.

Bani/Gurbani the Word of God, as found in the *Guru Granth Sahib*.

bindi the "mark" worn on the foreheads of Sikh (and Hindu) females, nowadays for cosmetic reasons.

charn amrit the Sikh initiation ceremony.

chauri the whisk of yak's hair waved over the *Guru Granth Sahib* in order to show it respect.

Dasam Granth a collection of writings by the tenth and last Guru, Gobind Singh.

Diwali an autumn festival, Hindu in origin

diwan the Sikh corporate act of worship.

Ek Onkar the Sikh symbol which indicates the oneness of God.

Five Ks: five distinguishing signs of Sikhism, each beginning with the letter K:

giani a person (usually a man) well versed in the Sikh teachings.

Gobind Singh the tenth, and last in the line of human Gurus, he appointed the Sikh Holy Book, the *Guru Granth Sahib* to be his successor.

granthi one who reads the *Guru Granth Sahib* during the service.

Gurbani the Word of God as a dynamic continual revelation as contained in the *Guru Granth Sahib*.

gurdwara the Sikh place of worship, which also functions as a place of education and a place of meeting.

Gurmat the teaching of the Sikh Gurus.

Gurmukhi the script in which Guru Nanak's hymns were written.

Gurpurb a festival, Sikh in origin, commemorating the birth or death of a Guru.

Guru "teacher", used in Sikhism as a religious title given to Nanak and the nine Gurus who succeeded him.

Guru Granth Sahib the Sikh Holy Book.

Hargobind the sixth Guru, who was the first Guru to give the Sikhs a military character.

Har Krishen the eighth Guru.

Harmandir the "Golden Temple" at Amritsar.

Har Rai the seventh Guru

Hola Mohalla a Sikh festival derived from the Hindu festival of *Holi*.

Hukam the Will of God.

Janam Sakhis (birth testimonies), Sikh writing which are the only source for the life history of Guru Nanak.

Japji an important hymn written by Guru Nanak, which opens the Sikh scriptures.

kachs a pair of shorts worn as an undergarment by Sikh men and women.

kameeze traditional Sikh dress in the form of a loose fitting, long sleeved tunic.

kanga a comb to keep the hair in place.

kara a steel bracelet usually worn on the right wrist, signifying the oneness of God and the unity of Sikhs everywhere.

Kaur "princess", the name borne by all Sikh females.

kesh the long uncut hair and beard of the Sikh

Khalsa the brotherhood of initiated Sikh men and women.

khanda the Sikh emblem, a two-edged sword.

kirpan a short sword symbolizing the duty of the Sikh to defend the weak and fight for righteousness.

kirtan the main part of the service consisting of

singing *sabads* from the *Guru Granth Sahib* accompanied by *ragis*.

langar the communal Indian vegetarian meal. It is also the name of the kitchen in the *gurdwara*.

Lavan the (circling) marriage hymn.

manji sahib a kind of small bed on which the *Guru Granth Sahib* rests.

mela a Sikh festival of Hindu origin.

Mool Mantra a short verse which begins each section of the *Guru Granth Sahib*. It embraces the heart of Sikh teaching.

Nadar the Grace of God.

Nam the name of God.

Nanak the founder of Sikhism.

nishan sahib the Sikh flag to be found outside every *gurdwara*.

Panj Pyares "five beloved ones", the original five initiates into Sikhism.

Panth the worldwide Sikh community.

Punjab (land of the) five rivers, the place of origin of the Sikh people

ragis musicians.

Ram Das the fourth Guru.

rumalas beautiful cloths which cover the *Guru Granth Sahib*.

sabads (pronounced "shabads") hymns or poems.

salwar (pronounced "shalwar") traditional Sikh dress in the form of loose fitting trousers.

sangat the local Sikh community/congregation in a *gurdwara*.

Sat Guru the True Guru, God.

Sat Sri Akal "Truth is Eternal", the usual Sikh greeting.

Sikh a pupil or learner.

Singh "lion", the name borne by all Sikh males.

Tegh Bahadur the ninth Guru.

vak a random reading from the *Guru Granth Sahib*, in order to seek advice from God.

var a ballad or song of praise.

Waheguru! "Wonderful Lord !"

Further Reading

Judaism

The 16-volume *Encyclopedia of Religion* edited by Mircea Eliade, published in 1987 (New York: Macmillan), is an excellent source for all aspects of Judaism, with over 200 entries under the rubric *Judaism*. In the general index of volume 16 many other entries are listed separately, with 18 further entries on *Passover* alone: each article has an apposite bibliography. The 16-volume (plus year books) *Encyclopaedia Judaica* (Jerusalem: Keter, 1972) remains the definitive reference work for Jews and Judaism. *The Jewish Religion: A Companion* (Oxford: Oxford University Press, 1995), by L. Jacobs is an erudite examination of all major aspects of Judaism.

Newcomers to the study of Judaism are recommended to read N. Solomon, *Judaism: A Very Short Introduction* (Oxford: Oxford University Press, 1996) and C. M. Pilkington, *Teach Yourself World Faiths: Judaism* (London: Hodder and Stoughton, 1995). Many of those perplexing questions as to why Jews do this or that, are addressed by A. J. Kolatch in his appropriately named work, *The Jewish Book of Why* (New York: Jonathan David, 1981). A standard, yet affordable, introduction is Jacob Neusner's *The Way of Torah: An Introduction to Judaism* (Belmont, California: Wadsworth, 4th edition 1988, first published in 1979).

Two books in particular by Alan Unterman are worth reading, *The Jews: Their Religious Beliefs and Practices* (Brighton: Sussex Academic Press, 2nd fully revised edition 1996), and *Dictionary of Jewish Lore and Legend* (London: Thames and Hudson, 1991). As the title suggests, the latter deals with Jewish customs and folklore. Modern Judaism's contribution to the world's environment is ably treated in *Judaism and Ecology*, edited by Aubrey Rose (London: Cassell, 1992). Modernity's challenges to Jewish tradition are met by the British Chief Rabbi, J. Sacks, in *Crisis and Covenant: Jewish Thought after the Holocaust* (Manchester University Press, 1992).

Jewish spirituality up until modern times is examined by Arthur Green (ed.) in *Jewish Spirituality: From the Sixteenth-Century Revival to the Present* (London: Routledge and Kegan Paul, 1987). The standard introduction to Jewish mysticism is G. Scholem, *Major Trends in Jewish Mysticism* (New York: Schocken, 1961).

As one would imagine, whole libraries have been written on Jewish Festivals, though Hayyim Schauss, *The Jewish Festivals* (London: Jewish Chronicle Publications, 1986, first published in 1938 by Union of American Hebrew Congregations), is both readable and informative. Two illustrated books on Jewish festivals which have craft and other activities for children are D. H. Renberg, *The Complete Family Guide to Jewish Holidays* (New York: Adama, 1985) and *Celebrating the Jewish Holidays* (New York: Crescent, 1992) by S. Kalman, D. Levinrad and A. Hirsch.

Christianity

An excellent source for all aspects of Christianity is the 16-volume *Encyclopedia of Religion* edited by Mircea Eliade, originally published in 1987 by Macmillan, New York. The General Index, in volume 16, includes a comprehensive list of all the articles relating to Christianity to be found throughout the *Encyclopedia*. Each article has its own bibliography, with suggestions for further reading.

Those students who are new to the study of Christianity could do no better than read a work by B. E. Close and M. Smith entitled *Christianity* (London: Hodder and Stoughton, 1992). It provides a simple yet thorough understanding of important historical figures within it. It also provides a valuable introduction to those who are just starting research.

As the student progresses, *An Introduction to the Christian Faith* (D. English, *et al.*, Oxford: Blackwell 1994), might be used. It has been compiled by a group of international academics from a variety of backgrounds. The themes in the book follow the order in which students normally engage in their studies, and so a more complete structure may be viewed. It provides a description of beliefs and doctrines essential to study, as well as biblical references and pertinent questions.

What all students need is a good one-volume reference work, and in the case of the Christian Church, the one to look at might be *The New International Dictionary of the Christian Church* (J. D. Douglas [ed.] Michigan, USA: Zandervan Company, 1990). With 4,8000 articles, and contributions from more than 180 scholars, it is an excellent aid to study. It gives a vast array of information in a convenient form with many useful cross-references.

For those who wish to discover more about non-conformist Christian denominations or sects, M. C. Burrell and J. Stafford-Wright's *Some*

Modern Faiths (Glasgow: Collins, 1983) is highly recommended. Those interested in The Religious Society of Friends should approach the Society direct for a comprehensive list of books and leaflets explaining the Friends' philosophy. The address is Quaker Home Service, Religious Society of Friends (Quakers), Friends' House, 173–177 Euston Road, London, NW1 2BT. The author found the Society extremely helpful and informative.

Islam

The 16-volume *Encyclopedia of Religion* edited by Mircea Eliade, published in 1987, New York, Macmillan is a very good source of information, in particular the section entitled *Islam* by F. Rahman. In addition there is an excellent reference work for Islam alone in the *Concise Encyclopedia of Islam* whose consultant editor was J. P. Hobson, and whose editors were N. Drake and E. Davis, published in 1989, London, Stacey International.

For those who are new to the study of Islam, and who require a basic text, G. Sarwar's book *Islam* (London: Muslim Educational Trust, 1994) provides a good introduction, as does M. Abu-Saud, *Concept of Islam* (Indianapolis: American Trust Publications, 1983). A very good book as an introduction, but one which also covers wider themes is C. Farah, *Islam* (New York: Barron's Educational Series, 1994, first published 1968). In this regard see also B. Lewis (ed.), *The World of Islam* (London: Thames and Hudson, 1994, first published 1976), which in addition to the text also contains some beautiful photographs and art work. For an introduction to Islam in the world today, which also includes some basic information, a commendable work is that of A. Ahmed, *Living Islam* (London: BBC Books, 1993).

Classic source books for the life of Muhammed include M. Lings, *Muhammad* (London: Unwin, 1986, first published 1983), and K. Armstrong, *Muhammad* (London: Victor Gollancz, 1991). For those who wish to see something of the great diversity that exists within Islam then an excellent introduction to this aspect is M. Kelly, *Islam: The Religious and Political Life of a World Community* (London: Praeger, 1984). In this context see also I. Lapidus, *A History of Islamic Societies* (Cambridge University Press, 1993 reprint of 1988 edition).

Hindusim

An excellent source for all aspects of Hinduism is the 16-volume Encyclopedia of Religion edited by Mircea Eliade, published in 1987, New York, Macmillan. Under the entry of Hinduism in the sixteenth volume, which is the index, is a list of all topics and articles to be found on the religion of Hinduism. The reader is particularly recommended to look at the overview of Hinduism to be found in volume 6, pp. 336–60.

For the reader who wishes to consolidate the material found in this chapter the works particularly recommended for their clarity at this level are O. Cole and V. P. Kanitkar, *Teach Yourself World Faiths: Hinduism* (London: NTC Publishing Group, Hodder and Stoughton, 1995), Stephen Cross, *The Elements of Hinduism* (Shaftesbury, Dorset: Element, 1994), and R. Jackson and D. Killingley, *World Religions in Education: Approaches to Hinduism* (London: John Murray, 1988).

For a more detailed analysis of Hinduism, particularly many of its conceptual ideas *An Introduction to Hinduism* by Gavin Flood (Cambridge: Cambridge University Press, 1996) is highly recommended, as also the treatment of Hinduism in John Koller's book, *The Indian Way* (New York: Macmillan, 1982), a book which also contains chapters on Buddhism and Sikhism. Those interested in the deities of Hinduism are directed to the work of Alain Daniélou, *The Myths and Gods of India* (Rochester USA: Inner Traditions International, 1991 reprint of 1985 edition), and an excellent source for information on the feminine aspect of the divine is to be found with D. Kinsley's work *Hindu Goddesses: Visions of the Divine Feminine in the Hindu Religious Tradition* (Delhi: Motilal Banarsidass, 1987).

Three books are invaluable for those interested in the anthropological aspects of Hinduism: these are L. Babb, *The Divine Hierarchy: Popular Hinduism in Central Asia* (New York: Columbia University Press, 1975), C. J. Fuller, *The Camphor Flame: Popular Hinduism and Society in India* (India: Viking, 1992), and M. Biardeau, *Hinduism: The Anthropology of a Civilization*, translated by Richard Nice (Delhi: Oxford University Press, 1989).

As an introduction to the richness of the primary source texts of Hinduism *A Sourcebook in Indian Philosophy* by S. Radhakrishnan and C. A. Moore (eds), Princeton, New Jersey: Princeton University Press, 1989 reprint of 1957 edition) is recommended.

Buddhism

The new *International Encyclopedia of Buddhism* (editor Nagendra Kr. Singh, 1997,

New Delhi: Anmol Publications Private Limited) now amounts to 36 volumes, with more to come. It is an excellent, detailed and well referenced source. Also recommended are the excellent articles to be found in the 16-volume *Encyclopedia of Religion* edited by Mircea Eliade, 1987, New York: Macmillan.

For those who are completely new to the study of Buddhism other good introductions to the religion are to be found in P. Harvey, *An Introduction to Buddhism: Teachings, History and Practices* (Cambridge: Cambridge University Press, 1992 reprint of 1990 edition), D. Keown, *Buddhism: A Very Short Introduction* (Oxford: Oxford University Press, 1996), D. Cush, *A Student's Approach to World Religions: Buddhism* (London: Hodder and Stoughton, 1993) and C. Erricker, *Teach Yourself World Faiths: Buddhism* (London: HodderHeadline, 1995).

At a more specialized level, students interested in studies of the Buddha and of Theravada and Mahayana Buddhism would find of interest Trevor Ling's work *The Buddha* (London: Temple Smith, 1985 edition), Richard Gombrich's work *Theravada Buddhism: A Social History from Ancient Benares to Modern Colombo* (London and New York: Routledge and Kegan Paul, 1988) and Paul Williams' *Mahayana Buddhism: The Doctrinal Foundations* (London: Routledge, 1989). An excellent comprehensive coverage of Buddhism is to be found in Heinz Bechert and Richard Gombrich's (eds) work, *The World of Buddhism* (Thames and Hudson, 1984).

A very readable and clear account of Tibetan Buddhism is to be found in John Powers' book *Introduction to Tibetan Buddhism* (New York: Snow Lion Publications, 1995) and for Nichiren Shoshu and Nichiren Daishonin Buddhism the late Richard Causton's work *Nichiren Shoshu Buddhism: An Introduction* (NSUK 1991, first published 1988) is recommended. The student interested in Zen Buddhism would find of interest Hubert Benoit's work *The Supreme Doctrine* (Brighton: Sussex Academic Press, 1995, first published in France in 1951 under the title of *La Doctrine Supreme*). As Aldous Huxley states in the Foreword: "This is a book that should be read by everyone who aspires to know who he is and what he can do to acquire such self-knowledge".

Excellent primary sources are to be found in Maurice Walshe's *Thus Have I Heard: The Long Discourses of the Buddha* (London: Wisdom, 1987), W. E. Soothill, *The Lotus of the Wonderful Law or the Lotus Gospel: Sadharma Pundarika Sutra* (London: Curzon Press, 1987),

The Dhammapada, by Eknath Easwaran (Arkana, 1987 edition, first published in 1986) and Edward Conze's *Buddhist Scriptures* (London: Penguin, 1959).

More advanced students might find the studies of Etienne Lamotte, *History of Indian Buddhism* (Louvain-la-neuve: Université Catholique de Louvain, 1988) and A. K. Warder's *Indian Buddhism* (Delhi: Motilal Banarsidass, 1980 second revised edition: first published 1970) of particular use. The more advanced student is also referred to David Snellgrove's eminent work *Indo-Tibetan Buddhism: Indian Buddhists and their Tibetan Successors* (London: Serindia Publications 1987).

Sikhism

The sixteen-volume *Encyclopedia of Religion* edited by Mircea Eliade (New York: Macmillan, 1987) is a mine of information on all aspects of Sikhism. The general index in volume 16 lists the articles to be found in the *Encyclopedia*. Each article has an apposite bibliography.

The Sikh Missionary Society in the United Kingdom, at 10 Featherstone Road, Southall, Middlesex, has published a veritable treasury of low-cost booklets, all erudite yet readable. The Society has produced another low-cost publication of primary source material in *Hymns from Bhai Gurdas's Compositions* (1988), translated and edited by Gobind Singh Mansukhani.

Newcomers to the study of Sikhism are referred to Owen Cole's *Teach Yourself World Faiths: Sikhism* (London: Hodder and Stoughton, 1994) one of a number of informative books and articles written by this author. Dr Cole often wrote with Piara Singh Sambhi, until the latter's death in 1992, and their publication, *The Sikhs: Their Religious Beliefs and Practices* (Sussex Academic Press, 1995, 2nd and fully revised edition) is the standard work, thoroughly researched, very readable and with an extensive glossary and bibliography.

Translations into English of primary source material are not plentiful, the most recent version of the *Adi Granth* being published in 1993 by Crescent Printing Works, Delhi, and translated by Pritam Singh Chahil and Manju Deshbir Singh. Nikky-Guninder Kaur Singh's translation of well-known hymns was published in 1995 by Harper: San Francisco under the title *The Name of My Beloved*. W. H. McLeod's anthology of scriptural passages entitled *Textual Sources for the Study of Sikhism* (Manchester University Press, 1984, reprinted Chicago, 1990) is a standard work and a must for the serious student.

Essential reading in the form of secondary sources include Khushwant Singh's two-volume work, *History of the Sikhs* (London: Oxford University Press, 1991), and *The Sikh Religion* by M. A. Macauliffe, reprinted in three volumes by Oxford University Press in 1985 (first published in 1909). The interested reader might like to compare J. S. Grewal's *The Sikhs of the Punjab* (Cambridge: Cambridge History of India, 1990) with W. H. McLeod's *The Evolution of the Sikh Community* (London: Oxford University Press, 1976). An excellent, if expensive, dictionary is W. H. McLeod's *Historical Dictionary of Sikhism* (Folkestone: Scarecrow, 1995).

Two journals worthy of subscription are *The Sikh Courier International,* obtainable from 88 Mollison Way, Edgware, London, and *The Sikh Bulletin* (Chichester Institute of Higher Education, College Lane, Chichester, PO19 4PE).

Bibliography

Judaism

Note: Eliade, M. (ed.) 1987: *The Encyclopedia of Religion*, New York: Macmillan, is referenced as *ER*.

Judaism

Borowitz, E. B. 1987: Judaism: an overview. In *ER*, vol. 8, pp. 127–49.

De Lange, N. 1984: *Atlas of the Jewish World*. Oxford: Equinox.

Goldenberg, R. 1987: Talmud. In *ER*, vol. 14, pp. 256–60.

Green, A. (ed.) 1987: *Jewish Spirituality: From the Sixteenth Century Revival to the Present.* London: Routledge and Kegan Paul.

Jacobs, L. 1987: Jewish Religious Year. In *ER*, vol. 8, pp. 41–5.

Kalman, S. *et al.* 1992: *Celebrating the Jewish Holidays.* New York: Crescent Books.

Knobel, P. 1987: Jewish rites (of Passage). In *ER*, vol. 12, pp. 392–8.

Kolatch, A. J. 1981: *The Jewish Book of Why.* New York: Jonathan David.

Lesberg, S. 1973: *At the Table of Israel.* London: Tom Stacey.

Lieberman, C. 1987: Orthodox Judaism. In *ER*, vol. 11, pp. 114–24.

Meyer, M. 1987: Reform Judaism. In *ER*, vol. 12, pp. 254–63.

Neusner, J. 1974: *The Life of Torah.* Belmont, California: Wadsworth.

Neusner, J. 1987: Mishnah and Tosefta. In *ER*, vol. 9, pp. 559–63.

Neusner, J. 4th edition 1988 (first published 1979): *The Way of Torah.* Belmont, California, Wadsworth.

Renberg, H. R. 1985: *The Complete Guide to Jewish Holidays.* New York: Adama.

Rosenblum, H. 1987: Conservative Judaism. In *ER*, vol. 4, pp. 62–9.

Sarna, N. M. 1987: Hebrew Scriptures. In *ER*, vol. 13, pp. 331–3.

Schauss, H. 1950: *The Lifetime of a Jew.* New York: Union of American Hebrew Congregations.

Schauss, H. first UK edition 1986: *The Jewish Festivals.* London: Jewish Chronicle Publications.

Trepp, L. 1973: *A History of the Jewish Experience.* New York: Behrman House.

Trepp, L. 1980: *The Complete Book of Jewish Observance.* New York: Behrman House.

Unterman, A. 1991: *Dictionary of Jewish Lore and Legend.* London: Thames and Hudson.

Unterman, A. 1996 (second edition): *The Jews: Their Religious Beliefs and Practices.* Brighton: Sussex Academic Press.

Urbach, E. E. 1987: Torah. In *ER*, vol. 14, pp. 556–65.

Christianity

Baggley, J. 1987: *Doors of Perception.* London and Oxford: Mowbray.

Baker, F. 1988: Methodist Churches. In *ER*, vol. 9, pp. 493–5.

Baker Eddy, M. 1994 (reprint of 1907 edition): *Science and Health with Key to the Scriptures.* Boston, Massachusetts: First Church of Christ Scientist.

Barbour, H. 1988: Quakers. In *ER*, vol. 12, pp. 129–32.

Beier, L. 1981: *Mormons, Christian Scientists, Jehovah's Witnesses.* Hong Kong: Ward Lock Educational.

Boojamra, J. L. 1988: Schism: Christian Schism. In *ER*, vol. 13, pp. 102–7.

Bruce, F. F. 1981: *Paul – Apostle of the Free Spirit.* Carlisle: Paternoster Press.

Burrell, M. C. and Stafford-Wright, J. 1983: *Some Modern Faiths.* Glasgow: Collins.

Butler, P. 1993 (first published 1988): From early eighteenth century to the present day. In Sykes, S. and Booty, J. (eds) *The Study of Anglicanism.* London: SPCK, pp. 28–47.

Close, B. E. and Smith, M. 1992: *A Student's Approach to World Religions: Christianity.* London: Hodder and Stoughton.

Davies, R. E. 1985 (reprint of 1963 edition): *Methodism.* London: Penguin Books.

Davies, R. E. 1988: *What Methodists Believe.* London: Epworth Press.

Douglas, J. D. (ed.) 1978: *The New International Dictionary of the Christian Church.* Michigan: Regency.

Edwards, D. L. 1994: *What is Catholicism?* London and Oxford: Mowbray.

English, D., Fackre, G., France, D., Gitari, D., Kirk, A., Nicholls, B., Packer, J., Padilla, R. (consultant eds) 1992: *An Introduction to the Christian Faith.* Oxford: Lynx.

Ferguson, S . B. and Wright, D. F. (eds) 1993: *A New Dictionary of Theology.* Leicester: Inter-Varsity Press.

Fisher, M. P. and Luyster, R. 1990: *Living*

Religions. New York: I.B. Tauris.

Gaffney, C. and Trenchard, J. 1980: *The Illustrated Catechism.* England: Redemptorist Publications.

Gaustad, E. S. 1988: Baptist Churches. In *ER*, vol. 2, pp. 63–6.

Gorman, G. H. 1981 (reprint of 1974 edition): *Introducing Quakers.* London: Quaker Home Service.

Gorman, G. H. 1973: *The Amazing Fact of Quaker Worship.* London: Quaker Home Service.

Gottschalk, S. 1988: Christian Science. In *ER*, vol. 3, pp. 442–16.

Hansen, K. J. 1988: Mormonism. In *ER*, vol. 10, pp. 108–12.

Harrison, S. W. and Shepherd, D. 1987 reprint of 1986 edition: *A Christian Family in Britain.* Oxford: Pergamon.

Harris Thompsett, F. 1993 (first published 1988): The Laity. In Sykes, S. and Booty, J. (eds) *The Study of Anglicanism.* London: SPCK, pp. 245–60.

Hastings, A. (ed.) 1991: *Modern Catholicism: Vatican II and After.* London: SPCK and New York: Oxford University Press.

Haugaard, W. P. 1993 (first published 1988): From the Reformation to the Eighteenth Century. In Sykes, S. and Booty, J. (eds) *The Study of Anglicanism.* London: SPCK, pp. 3–28.

Hillerbrand, H. J. 1988: Reformation. In *ER*. vol. 12, pp. 244–54.

Hudson, W. S. 1987: Denominationalism. In *ER*, vol. 4, pp. 292–8.

Jewett, R. 1988: Paul the Apostle. In *ER*, vol. 11, pp. 212–21.

Kung, H. 1994: *Great Christian Thinkers.* London: SCM Press.

Ling, T. 1992 (reprint of 1968 edition): *A History of Religion, East and West.* London: Macmillan.

Livingston, E. A. 1977: *The Concise Dictionary of the Christian Church.* London: Omega Books.

Macquarrie, J. 1990: *Jesus Christ in Modern Thought.* London: SCM and Philadelphia: Trinity Press International.

Martin, R. 1992 (reprint of 1985 edition): Approaches to New Testament Exegesis. In Marshall, I. H. (ed.) *New Testament Interpretation – Essays on Principals and Methods.* Carlisle: The Paternoster Press.

Marshall, I. H. 1985: *New Testament Interpretation – Essays on Principles and Methods.* Carlisle: The Paternoster Press.

McBrien, R. P. 1988: Roman Catholicism. In *ER*, vol. 12, pp. 429–45.

McBrien, R. P. (ed.) 1995: *Encyclopedia of Catholicism.* New York: HarperCollins.

McGrath, A. 1994: *Christian Theology.* Oxford: Blackwell.

McGrath, A. (ed.) 1985: *Modern Christian Thought.* Oxford: Blackwell Publishers.

McKenzie, P. 1988: *The Christians: Their Practices and Beliefs.* London: SPCK.

McManners, J. (ed.) 1992: *The Oxford Illustrated History of Christianity.* Oxford: Oxford University Press.

Neil, S. 1993: *Anglicanism.* London and Oxford: Mowbray.

Nicholls, B. 1994: We all believe in something. In English, D. et al. *An Introduction to the Christian Faith.* Oxford: Blackwell, pp. 23–7.

O'Collins, G., Farrugia, S. J. and Farrugia, E. G. 1991: *A Concise Dictionary of Theology.* London: HarperCollins.

Penney, S. 1987: *Discovering Religions, Christianity.* Oxford: Heinemann Educational.

Pickering, W. S. 1993 (first published 1988): Sociology of Anglicanism. In Sykes, S. and Booty, J. (eds) *The Study of Anglicanism.* London: SPCK, pp. 364–75.

Pollock, J. 1989: *John Wesley.* London: Hodder and Stoughton.

Punshon, J. 1991 (reprint of 1984 edition): *Portrait in Grey.* London: Quaker Home Service.

Richards, H. J. 1989: *Focus on the Bible.* Suffolk: Kevin Mayhew.

Richardson, A. and Bowden, J. (eds) 1983: *A New Dictionary of Christian Theology.* London: SCM Press.

Rogerson, A. 1969: *Millions Now Living Will Never Die: A Study of Jehovah's Witnesses.* London: Constable.

Roundhill, J. 1974: *Meeting the Mormons.* London: Lutterworth Press.

Roundhill, J. 1977: *Meeting Jehovah's Witnesses.* London: Lutterworth Educational.

Rowlands, C. 1985: *Christian Origins.* London: SPCK.

Shepherd, jnr. M. H. 1988: Anglicanism. In *ER*, vol. 1, pp. 286–91.

Smith, J. (translator) 1991: *The Book of Mormon.* Salt Lake City, Utah: The Church of Jesus Christ of Latter-day Saints.

Stroup, H. H. 1988: Jehovah's Witnesses. In *ER*, vol. 7, pp. 564–6.

Sykes, S. and Booty, J. (eds) 1984: *The Study of Anglicanism.* London: SPCK/Fortress Press.

The Holy Bible, Revised Standard Version 1973: London: Collins.

The New Revised Standard Version Bible, 1989:

New York: World Bible Publishers Incorporated.

The Religious Society of Friends, 1995: *Quaker Faith and Practice: The Book of Christian Discipline*. London: Religious Society of Friends.

The Religious Society of Friends, 1996: *Quakers*. London: The Religious Society of Friends.

The Religious Society of Friends, 1995: *Quaker Views: Close Relationships*. London: Quaker Home Service.

The Watchtower Bible and Tract Society, 1953: *Make Sure of All Things*. Pennsylvania: Watchtower Bible and Tract Society.

The Watchtower Bible and Tract Society of Pennsylvania, 1983: *Schools and Jehovah's Witnessses*. Pennsylvania: Watchtower Bible and Tract Society.

Thompson, J. and Thompson, M. 1992: *The Many Paths of Christianity*. London: Hodder and Stoughton.

Ware, K. 1988: Eastern Christianity. In *ER*, vol. 4, pp. 558–76.

Ware, T. 1963: *The Orthodox Church*. Harmondsworth: Penguin.

Islam

Abdalati, H. n.d: *Islam in Focus*. Islamic Teaching Centre.

Abu-Saud, M. 1983: *Concept of Islam*. Indianapolis: American Trust Publications.

Adams, C. 1987: Qur'an: The Text and Its History. In *ER*, vol. 12, pp. 156–76.

Afkhami, M. (ed.): *Faith and Freedom: Women's Human Rights in the Muslim World*. London: I.B. Taurus.

Ahmad, K. 1974: *Family Life in Islam*. Leicester: The Islamic Foundation.

Ahmad, K. and Ansari, Z. 1979: *Islamic Perspectives*. Leicester: The Islamic Foundation.

Ahmed, A. (ed.) 1983 (reprint of 1976 edition): *Islam – its meaning and message*. Leicester: The Islamic Foundation.

Ahmed, A. 1993: *Living Islam*. London: BBC Books.

Ahmed, A. 1995: *Discovering Islam*. London: Routledge and Kegan Paul.

Ashraf, S. 1991: *Islam*. Cheltenham: Stanley Thornes.

al Ati, H. 1977: *The Family Structure in Islam*. Indianapolis: American Trust Publications.

Ayoub, M. 1987: Qur'an: Its Role in Muslim Piety. In *ER*, vol. 12, pp. 176–9.

Azzan, A. 1993: *The Eternal Message of Muhammad*. Cambridge: The Islamic Texts Society.

Bashier, Z. 1990: *Sunshine at Medinah*. Leicester: The Islamic Foundation.

Bashier, Z. 1991 (revision of 1978 edition): *Makkan Crucible*. Leicester: The Islamic Foundation.

Brown, K. and Palmer, M. (1990 reprint of 1987 edition): *The Essential Teachings of Islam*. London: Arrow.

Cragg, K. and Speight, M. 1980: *Islam from Within*. Belmont: Wadsworth.

Cragg, K. 1986 (reprint of 1956 edition): *The Call of the Minaret*. London: Collins.

Esposito, J. 1992 (revision of 1988 edition): *Islam*. New York: Oxford University Press.

Goldziher, I. 1981: *Introduction to Islamic Theology and Law*. Princeton: Princeton University Press.

Graham, W. 1977: *Divine Word and Prophetic Word in Early Islam*. The Hague: Mouton and Co.

Gumley, F. and Redhead, B. 1990: *The Pillars of Islam*. London: BBC Books.

Heeren, F. and Lemu, B. 1978: *Women in Islam*. Leicester: The Islamic Foundation.

Hobson, J. P. (consultant ed.), Drake, N. and Davis, E. (eds) 1989: *The Concise Encyclopedia of Islam*. London: Stacey International.

Irving, T., Ahmad, K. and Ahsan, M. 1979: *The Qur'an: Basic Teachings*. Leicester: The Islamic Foundation.

Izutsu, T. 1980: *The Concept of Belief in Islamic Theology*. New York: Arno Press.

Jornier, J. 1989: *How to Understand Islam*. London: SCM.

Kendrick, R. 1981: *Islam*. Oxford: Heinemann.

Kamali, M. 1987: Islamic Law: Personal Law. In *ER*, vol. 7, pp. 446–53.

Lewis, B. 1994 (reprint of 1976 edition): *The World of Islam*. London: Thames and Hudson.

Lewis, B. 1995: *Islamic Britain: Religion, Politics and Identity among British Muslims*. London: I.B. Taurus.

Lings, M. 1986 (reprint of 1983 edition): *Muhammad*. London: Unwin.

McDermott, M, and Ahsan, M. 1980: *The Muslim Guide*. Leicester: The Islamic Foundation.

MacDonald, D. 1965: *Development of Muslim Theology*. Beirut: Khayats.

Maqsood, R. 1993: *The Qur'an*. Oxford: Heinemann.

Maudoodi, M. 1983: *The Laws of Marriage and Divorce in Islam*. Kuwait: Islamic Book Publishers.

Mayer, A. 1987: Islamic Law: Shari'ah. In *ER*,

vol. 7, pp. 431–46.

Mernissi, F. 1996: *Women's Rebellion and Islamic Memory*. London: Zed Books.

Murad, K. 1981: *Shari'ah The Way of Justice*. Leicester: The Islamic Foundation.

Murad, K. 1981: *Shari'ah The Way to God*. Leicester: The Islamic Foundation.

Naseef, A. 1988: *Today's Problems, Tomorrow's Solutions*. London: Mansell.

Nasr, S. 1985: *Ideals and Realities of Islam*. London: George, Allen and Unwin.

al-Qaradawi, Y. 1985: *The Lawful and the Prohibited in Islam*. London: Sharouk International.

Rahman, A. 1980: *Islam*. London: Seerah Foundation.

Rahman, F. 1987: Islam. In *ER*, vol. 7, pp. 303–22.

Rippin, A. 1990: *Muslims Their Religious Beliefs and Practices, vol. 1: The Formative Period*. London: Routledge.

Ruthven, M. 1991 (reprint of 1984 edition): *Islam in the World*. Harmondsworth: Penguin.

Ruthven, M. 1991: *A Satanic Affair*. London: Hogarth Press.

Sarwar, G. 1994: *Islam*. London: Muslim Educational Trust.

Sharif, M. 1963: *A History of Muslim Philosophy vol 1*. Wiesbaden: Otto Harrassowitz.

Stewart, P. 1995: *Unfolding Islam*. Reading: Garnet Publishing.

Taymuya, I. 1982: *Public Duties in Islam*. Leicester: The Islamic Foundation.

Waldman, M. 1987: Sunnah. In *ER*, vol. 14, pp. 149–53.

Watt, W. 1970: *Bell's Introduction to the Qur'an*. Edinburgh: Edinburgh University Press.

Watt, W. 1973: *The Formative Period of Islamic Thought*. Edinburgh: Edinburgh University Press.

Watt, W. 1987: Muhammad. In *ER*, vol. 10, pp. 137–46.

Zakaria, R. 1991: *Muhammad and the Quran*. Middlesex: Penguin.

Hinduism

Allchin, B. and Allchin, R. (1982): *The Rise of Civilization in India and Pakistan*. Cambridge: Cambridge University Press.

Altekar, A. S. 1995 (reprint of 1959 edition): *The Position of Women in Hindu Civilization*. Delhi: Motilal Banarsidass.

Aurobindo, Sri. 1986 (2nd impression of 1971 edition): *The Upanishads: Texts, Translations and Commentaries*. Pondicherry: Sri Aurobindo Ashram Trust.

Babb, L. 1975: *The Divine Hierarchy: Popular Hinduism in Central Asia*. New York: Columbia University Press.

Bahadur, K. P. 1989: *The Wisdom of the Upanishads*. New Delhi: Sterling Publishers Private Limited.

Baker, S. 1990: *Caste: At Home in Hindu India*. London: Jonathan Cape.

Barber, R. 1991: *Pilgrimages*. Woodbridge, Suffolk: The Boydell Press.

Basham, A. L. 1975: *A Cultural History of India*. Delhi: Oxford University Press.

Basham, A. L. 1982 (reprint of 1967 third, revised edition): *The Wonder That Was India*. London: Sidgwick and Jackson.

Basham, A. L. 1991 (reprint of 1959 edition): Hinduism. In Zaehner, R. C. *Hutchinson Encyclopedia of Living Faiths*. Glasgow: Hutchinson, pp. 217–54.

Beck, B. 1969: Colour and Heat in South Indian Ritual. *Man (N.S.)* 4.

Bhardwaj, S. M. 1973: *Hindu Places of Pilgrimage in India: A Study in Cultural Geography*. California: University of California Press.

Biardeau, M. 1992 (impression of 1989 English translation): *Hinduism: The Anthropology of a Civilization*, translated by Richard Nice. Delhi: Oxford University Press.

Brand, M. 1992: A New Hindu Goddess, *Hemisphere: An Asian Australian Magazine* 26, 6.

Buck, W. 1973: *Mahabharata*. New York: Mentor.

Buck, W. 1978: *Ramayana*. New York: Mentor.

Carmen, J. B. 1987: Bhakti. In *ER*, vol. 2, pp. 130–4.

Chakravarti, M. 1986: *The Concept of Rudra-Siva through the Ages*. Motilal Banarsidass.

Chaudhuri, N. C. 1979: *Hinduism*. Oxford: Oxford University Press.

Cole, O. and Kanitkar, V. P. 1995: *Teach Yourself World Faiths: Hinduism*. London: NTC Publishing Group Hodder and Stoughton.

Cole, W. O. 1984: *Six Religions in the Twentieth Century*. Amersham, Bucks: Hulton.

Coward, H. G., Lipner, J. J. and Young, K. K. 1989: *Hindu Ethics: Purity, Abortion, and Euthanasia*. Delhi: Sri Satguru Publications.

Cross, S. 1994: *The Elements of Hinduism*. Shaftesbury, Dorset: Element.

Daniélou, A. 1991 (reprint of 1985 edition): *The Myths and Gods of India*. Rochester, USA: Inner Traditions International.

Dowson, J. 1991 (impresssion of 1982 edition): *A Classical Dictionary of Hindu Mythology* and Religion: Geography, History and Literature. Calcutta: Rupa and Company.

Dumont, L. 1980 (first published in French 1966): Homo Hierarchicus: The Caste System and Its Implications. Chicago: University of Chicago Press.

Dutt, R. 1978 (reprint of 1910 edition): The Ramayana and the Mahabharata. New York: Dent.

Eastman, R. 1993 (reprint of 1975 edition): The Ways of Religion: An Introduction to the Major Traditions. Oxford: Oxford University Press, pp. 7–60.

Edgerton, F. 1994 (first published 1944): The Bhagavad Gita. Delhi: Motilal Banarsidass.

Embree, A. T. (ed.), 1988: Sources of Indian Tradition: Volume 1: From the Beginning to 1800. New York: Columbia University Press.

Embree, A. T. (ed.), 1972 (first published 1966): The Hindu Tradition: Readings in Oriental Thought. New York: Vintage.

Flood, G. 1996: An Introduction to Hinduism. Cambridge: Cambridge University Press.

Fuller, C. J. 1992: The Camphor Flame: Popular Hinduism and Society in India. India: Viking.

Griffith, R. T. H. 1991 (reprint of 1973 revised edition): The Hymns of the Rgveda. Delhi: Motilal Banarsidass.

Hammer, R. 1982: The Eternal Teaching: Hinduism. In The World's Religions. Tring: Lion, pp. 170–96.

Hardy, F. E. 1987: Krisnaism. In ER, vol. 8, pp. 387–92.

Hardy, F. 1990 (reprint of 1988 edition): The classical religions of India. In F. Hardy (ed.) The World's Religions: The Religions of Asia. London: Routledge, pp. 37–71.

Hawley, J. S. and Wulff, D. M. (eds) 1996: Devi: Goddesses of India. Berkeley and Los Angeles, California, and London: California University Press.

Heesterman, J. C. 1987: Brahman. In ER, vol. 2, pp. 294–6.

Herman, A. L. 1991: A Brief Introduction to Hinduism: Religion, Philosophy and Ways of Liberation. Boulder, Colorado: Westview Press.

Hiltebeitel, A. 1978: The Indus Valley "Proto-Siva" reexamined through reflections on the goddess, the buffalo, and the symbolism of vahanas, Anthropos 73, 767–97.

Hopkins, T. J. 1971: The Religious Life of Man: The Hindu Religious Tradition. California: Wadsworth Publishing Company.

Jackson, R. and Killingley, D. 1988: World Religions in Education: Approaches to Hinduism. London: John Murray.

Johnson, W. J. 1994: The Bhagavad Gita.

Oxford: Oxford University Press.

Killingley, D. et al. 1991: Hindu Ritual and Society. Newcastle upon Tyne: Grevatt and Grevatt.

Kinsley, D. R. 1993: (first published 1982): Hinduism: A Cultural Perspective. New Jersey: Prentice Hall.

Kinsley, D. 1987: Hindu Goddesses: Visions of the Divine Feminine in the Hindu Religious Tradition. Delhi: Motilal Banarsidass.

Kinsley, D. 1975: The Sword and the Flute: Dark Visions of the Terrible and the Sublime in Hindu Mythology. California: University of California Press.

Koller, J. M. 1982: The Indian Way. New York: Macmillan.

Kosambi, D. D. 1991 reprint: The Culture and Civilization of Ancient India in Historical Outline. Delhi: Vikas Publishing House Private Limited.

Lal, B. B. 1975: The Indus civilization. In Basham, A. L. (ed.) A Cultural History of India. Oxford: Oxford University Press.

Lannoy, R. 1971: The Speaking Tree. Oxford: Oxford University Press.

Ling, T. 1990 (reprint of 1968 edition) A History of Religion East and West. London: Macmillan.

Lorenzen, D. N. 1987: Saivism. In ER, vol. 13, pp. 6–11.

Mackenzie, D. A. (1993) Myths and Legends: India. London: Studio Editions.

Mahony, W. K. 1987: Upanisads. In ER, vol. 15, pp. 147–52.

Mascaró, J. 1962: The Bhagavad Gita. Harmondsworth: Penguin.

Mascaró, J. 1965: The Upanishads. London: Penguin.

Masih, Y. 1983: The Hindu Religious Thought 3000 B.C.–200 A.D. Delhi: Motilal Banarsidass.

Mehta, R. 1990 (reprint of 1970 edition): The Call of the Upanishads. Delhi: Motilal Banarsidass.

Mookerji, A. 1988: Kali: The Feminine Force. London: Thames and Hudson.

Mukerji, B. 1988: The Hindu Tradition: An Introduction to Hinduism and to Its Sacred Tradition. New York: Amity House.

Mukherji, P. 1988: Beyond the Four Varnas: The Untouchables in India. Delhi: Motilal Banarsidass.

Narayan, R. K. 1989 (reprint of 1987 edition): The Ramayana. Delhi: Vision Books.

Narayan, R. K. 1991 (reprint of 1987 edition first published 1964): Gods, Demons, and Others. Delhi: Vision Books.

Nigosian, S. A. 1994: World Faiths. New York:

St. Martin's Press.

O'Flaherty, W. D. 1981 (first published 1973): *Siva: The Erotic Ascetic*. Oxford: Oxford University Press.

O'Flaherty, W. D. 1975: *Hindu Myths*. Harmondsworth: Penguin.

O'Flaherty, W. D. 1988: *Textual Sources for the Study of Hinduism*. Manchester: Manchester University Press.

O'Flaherty, W. D. 1983 (reprint of 1988 edition): *The Rig Veda*: Harmondsworth: Penguin.

Olivelle, P. 1996: *Upanisads*. Oxford: Oxford University Press.

Organ, T. W. (1974): *Hinduism: Its Historical Development*. London: Barron's Educational.

Pandey, R. 1994 reprint of 1969 edition: *Hindu Samskaras: Socio-Religious Study of the Hindu Sacraments*. Delhi: Motilal Banarsidass.

Parrinder, G. 1996 (first published 1974): *The Bhagavad Gita: A Verse Translation*. Oxford: One World.

Radhakrishnan, S. 1994 (reprint of 1953 edition): *The Principal Upanisads*. New Delhi: Indus.

Radhakrishnan, S. and Moore, C. A. (eds), 1989 reprint of 1957 edition: *A Sourcebook in Indian Philosophy*. Princeton, New Jersey: Princeton University Press.

Ramanujan, A. K. (translator) 1973: *Speaking of Siva*. Harmondsworth: Penguin.

Shearer, A. and Russell, P. 1978: *The Upanishads*. New York: Harper and Row.

Siegel, L. 1990 reprint of 1978 edition: *Sacred and Profane Dimensions of Love in Indian Traditions as Exemplified in the* Gitagovinda *of Jayadeva*. Delhi: Oxford University Press.

Singer, M. (ed.), *Krishna: Myths Rites and Attitudes*. Chicago: University of Chicago Press.

Smart, N. 1971 (first published 1969): *The Religious Experience of Mankind*. Glasgow: Collins.

Smith, H. 1991: *The World's Religions*. San Fransisco: Harper.

Subramuniyaswami, S. S. 1993: *Dancing with Siva*. California: Himalayan Academy.

Swami, S. P. and Yeats, W. B. 1985 reprint of 1937 edition: *The Ten Principal Upanishads*. London: Faber and Faber.

Thapar, R. 1996: *A History of India, Vol 1*. London: Penguin.

Tripathi, R. S. 1985 (reprint of 1942 edition): *History of Ancient India*. Delhi: Motilal Banarsidass.

Weightman, S. 1988 (reprint of 1988 edition): Hinduism. In Hinnells, J. R. (ed.) *A Handbook of Living Religions*. Harmondsworth: Penguin, pp. 191–236.

Wilkins, W. J. 1992 (impression of 1975 edition): *Hindu Mythology: Vedic and Puranic*. Calcutta: Rupa and Company.

Yogananda, P. 1991 (first published 1950): *Autobiography of a Yogi*. London, Sydney, Auckland, Johannesburg: Rider.

Zaehner, R. C. 1982 (reprint of 1966 edition): *Hindu Scriptures*. London: Dent.

Zaehner, R. C. 1973 (first published 1969): *The Bhagavad-Gita*. Oxford: Oxford University Press.

Zaehner, R. C. 1984 (reprint of 1962 edition): *Hinduism*. Oxford: Oxford University Press.

Buddhism

Basho (translator Lucien Stryk), 1995: *Haiku*. London: Penguin.

Batchelor, S. 1987: *The Jewel in the Lotus: A Guide to the Buddhist Traditions of Tibet*. London: Wisdom Publications.

Bechert H. and Gombrich, R. 1984: *The World of Buddhism*. London: Thames and Hudson.

Benoit, H. 1995 (first published in English in 1955): *The Supreme Doctrine*. Brighton: Sussex Academic Press.

Carrithers, M. 1983: *The Buddha*. Oxford: Oxford University Press.

Carrithers, M. 1986 impression (first published 1983): *The Forest Monks of Sri Lanka*. Delhi: Oxford University Press.

Causton, R. 1991 (reprint of 1988 edition): *Nichiren Shoshu Buddhism: An Introduction*. London: Rider.

Conze, E. 1988: *A Short History of Buddhism*. London: Unwin.

Conze, E. 1974: *Buddhism: Its Essence and Development*. London: Cassiter.

Conze, E. 1959: *Buddhist Scriptures*. London: Penguin.

Conze, E. 1983 (reprint of 1962 edition): *Buddhist Thought in India: Three Phases of Buddhist Philosophy*. London: Allen and Unwin.

Conze, E. 1988 (first published 1958): *Buddhist Wisdom Books: The Diamond and the Heart Sutra*. London: Unwin Hyman.

Cowell, E. 1977: *The Buddha Carita or The Life of the Buddha*. Delhi: Cosmo.

Cush, D. 1995 (first published 1993): *A Student's Approach to World Religions: Buddhism*. London: Hodder and Stoughton.

Dutt, S. 1988 (first published 1962): *Buddhist Monks and Monasteries of India: Their History and Their Contribution to Indian Culture*. Delhi: Motilal Banarsidass.

Easwaran, E. 1987 (first published 1986): *The*

Dhammapada. London: Arkana.

Erricker, C. 1995: *Teach Yourself World Faiths: Buddhism*. London: Hodder Headline.

Gombrich, R. 1996: *How Buddhism Began: The Conditioned Genesis of the Early Teachings*. London: Athlone.

Gombrich, R. 1971: *Precept and Practice: Traditional Buddhism in the Rural Highlands of Ceylon*. Oxford: Clarendon.

Gombrich, R. 1988: *Theravada Buddhism: A Social History from Benares to Modern Colombo*. London: Routledge and Kegan Paul.

Guenther. H. 1987: Buddhism in Tibet. In *ER*, vol. 2, pp. 406–14.

Harvey, P. 1992 (reprint of 1990 edition): *An Introduction to Buddhism*. Cambridge: Cambridge University Press.

Hopkins, J. 1985 (reprint of 1984 edition): *The Tantric Distinction: An Introduction to Tibetan Buddhism*. London: Wisdom.

Hurvitz, L. 1976: *Scripture of the Lotus Blossom of the Fine Dharma*, translated from the Chinese of Kumarajiva. New York: Columbia University Press.

Ikeda, D. (translator Burton Watson) 1977: *Buddhism in the First Millennium*. New York: Kodansha International.

Ikeda, D. (translator Burton Watson) (1996 reprint of 1976 first English edition): *The Living Buddha*. New York: Weatherhill.

Ikeda, D. and Wilson, B. 1987 (first published 1984): *Human Values in a Changing World: A Dialogue on the Social Role of Religion*. Secaucus, New Jersey: Lyle Stuart.

Jikai, F. 1987: Jodoshu. In *ER*, vol. 8, pp. 104–7.

Kalupahana, D. J. 1976: *Buddhist Philosophy: A Historical Analysis*. Honolulu: University of Hawaii Press.

Kawamura, L. S. 1987: Tara. In *ER*, vol. 14, pp. 337–9.

Kennett, J. 1990 (revised edition): *The Liturgy of the Order of Buddhist Contemplatives for the Laity*. California: Shasta Abbey Press.

Kennett, J. 1976: *Zen is Eternal Life*. California: Shasta Abbey Press.

Keown, D. 1996: *Buddhism: A Very Short Introduction*. Oxford: Oxford University Press.

Kirimura, Y. 1982 (first published 1981): *Outline of Buddhism*. Tokyo: Nichiren Shoshu International Center.

Kirimura, Y. 1991 (first published 1980): *The Life of Nichiren Daishonin*. Tokyo: Nichiren Shoshu International Center.

Kvaerne, P. 1987: Tibetan Religions. In *ER*, vol. 14, pp. 497–504.

Lamotte, E. translated from the French by Sara

Webb-Boin 1988, original French edition 1958: *History of Indian Buddhism: from the Origins to the Saka Era*. Louvain-la-neuve: Université Catholique de Louvain, Institut Orientaliste.

Ling, T. 1973: *The Buddha*. London: Temple Smith.

Lopez, S. Jr. (ed.) 1997: *Religions of Tibet in Practice*. Princeton, New Jersey: Princeton University Press.

Mascaró, J. 1988 (reprint of 1973 edition): *The Dhammapada*. London: Penguin.

Mehta, P. 1988: *Buddhahood*. Dorset: Element Books Limited.

Mizuno, K. 1988 reprint of 1987 edition: *Basic Buddhist Concepts*. Tokyo: Kosei Publishing Company.

Mizuno, K. 1987 (reprint of 1980 English edition): *The Beginnings of Buddhism*. Tokyo: Kosei Publishing Company.

Powell, A. 1989: *Living Buddhism*. London: British Museum Publications Limited.

Powers, J. 1995: *Introduction to Tibetan Buddhism*. New York: Snow Lion.

Prebish, C. S. 1993: *Historical Dictionary of Buddhism*. Metuchen, New Jersey: The Scarecrow Press, Inc.

Pye, M. 1979: *The Buddha*. London: Duckworth.

Rahula, W. 1974 (second, enlarged edition of 1959 original): *What The Buddha Taught*. New York: Grove Press.

Reynolds, F. E. and Hallisey, C. 1987: Buddhism. In *ER*, vol. 2, pp. 334–51.

Rhie, M. and Thurman, R. A. F. 1991: *Wisdom and Compassion: The Sacred Art of Tibet*. London: Royal Academy of Arts; New York: Asian Art Museum of San Fransisco and Tibet House, in association with Harry N. Abrams, Inc., Publishers.

Robinson, R. H. and Johnson, W. L. 1982: first published 1970: *The Buddhist Religion: A Historical Introduction*. Belmont, California: Wadsworth Publishing Company.

Saddhatissa, H. 1987 (first published 1970): *Buddhist Ethics: The Path to Nirvana*. London: Wisdom.

Sangharakshita. 1987 (revised edition first published 1957): *A Survey of Buddhism: Its Doctrines and Methods through the Ages*. London: Tharpa.

Sangharakshita. 1985: *The Eternal Legacy: An Introduction to the Canonical Literature of Buddhism*. London: Tharpa.

Sangharakshita. 1991 (first published 1967): *The Three Jewels: An Introduction to Buddhism*. Glasgow: Windhorse.

Schumann, H. W. 1973: *Buddhism: An Outline*

of its Teachings and Schools. London: Rider and Company.

Shoto, H. 1987: Jodo Shinshu. In ER, vol. 8, pp. 100–4.

Snellgrove, D. 1995: A Cultural History of Tibet. Boston, Massachusetts:: Shambhala.

Snellgrove, D. 1987: Indo-Tibetan Buddhism: Indian Buddhists and their Tibetan Successors. London: Serindia Publications.

Snellgrove, D. 1987: Tibetan Buddhism. In ER, vol. 2, pp. 493–8.

Snelling, J. 1996 (reprint of 1991 edition): The Elements of Buddhism. Dorset: Element.

Snelling, J. 1987: The Buddhist Handbook: A Complete Guide to Buddhist Teaching and Practice. London: Rider.

Soothill, W. E. 1987: The Lotus of the Wonderful Law. London: Curzon Press.

Spiro, M. 1971: Buddhism and Society: A Great Tradition and its Burmese Vicissitudes. London: Allen and Unwin.

Suzuki, B. L. 1990 (first published 1938): Mahayana Buddhism. London: Mandala.

Suzuki, D. T. 1991 (reprint of 1949 edition): The Zen Doctrine of No Mind. London: Rider.

Turner, E. and Freze, P. 1987: Marriage. In ER, vol. 9, pp. 218–22.

Walshe, M. 1987: Thus Have I Heard: The Long Discourses of the Buddha. London: Wisdom.

Warder, A. K. 1980 (second revised edition): Indian Buddhism. Delhi: Motilal Banarsidass.

Watts, A. W. 1958: The Spirit of Zen. London: Mandala.

Watts, A. W. 1990 (first published 1957): London: Arkana.

Wayman, A. 1987: Esoteric Buddhism. In ER, vol. 2, pp. 472–82.

Williams, P. 1989: Mahayana Buddhism: The Doctrinal Foundations. London: Routledge.

Wilson, B. and Dobbelaere, K. 1994: A Time to Chant: The Soka Gakkai Buddhists in Britain. Oxford: Clarendon Press.

Yeshe, Lama, 1989 (reprint of 1987 edition): Introduction to Tantra: A Vision of Totality. Boston, USA: Wisdom Publications.

Sikhism

Alag, S. S. 1986: Varied Sentiments for the Golden Temple. In Singh Kapoor, S. (ed.), The Sikh Courier International, London: The Sikh Cultural Society of Great Britain, vol. 26, no. 62, pp. 36–7.

Bannerjee, I. 1987: Guru Angad: The Foundation of the Sikh Panth. In Singh Kapoor, S. (ed.), The Sikh Courier International, London: The Sikh Cultural Society of Great Britain, vol. 27,

no. 64, pp. 1–6.

Barrier, N. G. 1987: Nanak. In ER, vol. 10, pp. 307–9.

Bhatti, S. S. 1992: The Golden Temple. A Spiritual Marvel of Architecture. In Singh Kapoor, S. (ed.), The Sikh Courier International, London: The Sikh Cultural Society of Great Britain, vol. 32, no. 74, pp. 8–11.

Bhogal, B. 1996: Interpretative Ideals Concerning Sikhism and Gurbani. In Cole, W. O. and Nesbitt, E. (eds) Sikh Bulletin, Chichester Institute of Higher Education, no. 13, pp. 11–15.

Cole, W. O. and Sambhi, P. S. 1st edition 1978: The Sikhs: Their Religious Beliefs and Practices. London: Routledge.

Cole, W. O. and Sambhi, P. S. (second, revised edition 1995): The Sikhs: Their Religious Beliefs and Practices. Brighton: Sussex Academic Press.

Davies, D. 1982: Religion of the Gurus: The Sikh Faith. In Beaver, R. P. et al. (eds) The World's Religions. Tring, Hertfordshire: Lion, pp. 197–206.

Kapoor, S. S. 1991: Guru Hargobind: the founder of "Miri" and "Piri". In Singh Kapoor, S. (ed.) The Sikh Courier International, London: The Sikh Cultural Society of Great Britain, vol. 31, no. 72, pp. 3–4.

Kaur, M. 1988: Amritsar under Guru Arjan Dev and Guru Hargobind (1581–1634). In Singh Kapoor, S. (ed.) The Sikh Courier International, London: The Sikh Cultural Society of Great Britain, vol. 28, no. 65, pp. 21–8.

Kohli, S. S. 1987: Adi Granth. In Eliade, ER, vol. 1, pp. 28–9.

Kohli, S. S. 1987: Dasam Granth. In ER, vol. 4, pp. 241–2.

Koller, J. M. 1982: The Indian Way. New York: Macmillan.

McLeod, W. H. 1995: Historical Dictionary of Sikhism. Folkestone: Scarecrow.

McLeod, W. H. 1976: The Evolution of the Sikh Community. London: Oxford University Press.

McLeod, W. H. (ed.) 1984: Textual Sources for the Study of Sikhism. Manchester University Press.

McLeod, W. H. 1989: Who is a Sikh? Oxford: Clarendon Press.

Sarna, S. S. 1992: Importance of Kirtan in Gurmat. In Singh Kapoor, S. (ed.) The Sikh Courier International, London: The Sikh Cultural Society of Great Britain, vol. 32, no. 74, pp. 12–13.

Shan, H. S. 1993: Guru Tegh Bahadur: A Unique

Martyr. In Singh Kapoor, S. (ed.) *The Sikh Courier International*, London: The Sikh Cultural Society of Great Britain, vol. 33, no. 75, pp. 3–5.

Singh, D. 1992: A Welcome Concern about the translation of Gurbani. In Singh Kapoor, S. (ed.) *The Sikh Courier International*, London: The Sikh Cultural Society of Great Britain, vol. 32, no. 73, pp. 12–13.

Singh, H. 1990: Translation of Gurbani: Our Difficulties. In Singh Kapoor, S. (ed.) *The Sikh Courier International*, London: The Sikh Cultural Society of Great Britain, vol. 30, no. 70, pp. 69–73.

Singh, K. 1987: Sikhism. In *ER*, vol. 13, pp. 315–20.

Singh, K. 1987: Singh, Gobind. In *ER*, vol. 13, pp. 331–3.

Singh, K. 1987: Guru Angad: The Building of the Sikh Church. In Singh Kapoor, S. (ed.) *The Sikh Courier International*, London: The Sikh Cultural Society of Great Britain, vol. 27, no. 64, p. 12.

Singh, K. 1991: Guru Gobind Singh. In Singh Kapoor, S. (ed.) *The Sikh Courier International*, London: The Sikh Cultural Society of Great Britain, vol. 31, no. 72, pp. 9–11.

Singh, K. 1994: An Historical Perspective of the Janam-Sakhis. In Singh Kapoor, S. (ed.) *The Sikh Courier International*, London: The Sikh Cultural Society of Great Britain, vol. 34, no. 77, pp. 5–6.

Singh, L. and Singh, S. 1985(reprint of 1975 edition): *The Supreme Sacrifice of Guru Tegh Bahadur*. Southall: The Sikh Missionary Society.

Singh, S. 1988: The Concept of Prayer in Sikhism. In Singh Kapoor, S. (ed.) *The Sikh Courier International*, London: The Sikh Cultural Society of Great Britain, vol. 28, no. 66, pp. 6–11.

Varma, D. K. 1991: Guru Gobind Singh's Relations with Emperor Aurangzeb. In Singh Kapoor, S. (ed.) *The Sikh Courier International*, London: The Sikh Cultural Society of Great Britain, vol. 31, no. 72, pp. 12–14.

Wahiwala, R. S. 1989: Kirtan (Devotional Music). In Cole, W. O. and Nesbitt, E. (eds) *Sikh Bulletin*, Chichester Institute of Higher Education, no. 6, pp. 16–22.

Index

GAYLORD FG